CINEMA SEWER

THE ADULTS ONLY GUIDE TO HISTORY'S SICKEST AND SEXIEST MOVIES

EDITED BY
ROBIN BOUGIE

VOLUME

A
**FAB
PRESS**
PUBLICATION

CINEMA SEWER VOL. 5

THIS SECOND PRESSING PUBLISHED BY FAB PRESS, AUGUST 2020
FIRST EDITION PUBLISHED BY FAB PRESS, JULY 2015

FAB PRESS LTD
2 FARLEIGH
RAMSDEN ROAD
GODALMING
SURREY
GU7 1QE
ENGLAND, UK

www.FABPRESS.com

A CIP CATALOGUE RECORD FOR THIS BOOK IS AVAILABLE FROM THE BRITISH LIBRARY.

ISBN 9781903254837

COVER ART BY THE ALWAYS AMAZING VINCE RUARUS. VISIT HIM AT:

WWW.VENIVIDIVINCE.COM

THIS BOOK IS DEDICATED TO:

...RX COMICS AND PULP FICTION BOOKS HERE IN VANCOUVER, BC, CANADA. THESE TWO RETAIL STORES, LOCATED RIGHT NEXT TO EACH OTHER AT MAIN STREET AND 8TH AVENUE (A FEW SHORT BLOCKS AWAY FROM MY APARTMENT) HAVE BEEN THE MOST FAITHFUL SUPPORTERS OF CINEMA SEWER AND MY VARIOUS OTHER PRINT-RELATED PROJECTS OVER THE YEARS. THEIR OWNERS (AARON BIRKENHEAD AND CHRIS BRAYSHAW), HAVE NOT JUST BEEN PURVEYORS AND ENTHUSIASTIC DRUM-BEATERS FOR THE CINEMA SEWER BRAND, BUT GREAT PERSONAL FRIENDS OF MINE AS WELL. NOT ONLY HAVE I HELD MANY A CINEMA SEWER LAUNCH PARTY THERE, BUT VISITING AND SHOPPING IN THEIR TWO STORES IS SOMETHING I HAVE BEEN DOING ONCE OR TWICE A WEEK FOR OVER 15 YEARS NOW. I KNOW THAT IF EITHER WERE GONE MY OVERALL PERSPECTIVE ON MY LOCAL COMMUNITY WOULD SOUR TO A LARGE EXTENT-- SO LONG LIVE RX AND PULP FICTION!

VISIT:
WWW.CINEMASEWER.COM
AND MY DAILY ART BLOG:
BOUGIEMAN.LIVEJOURNAL.COM

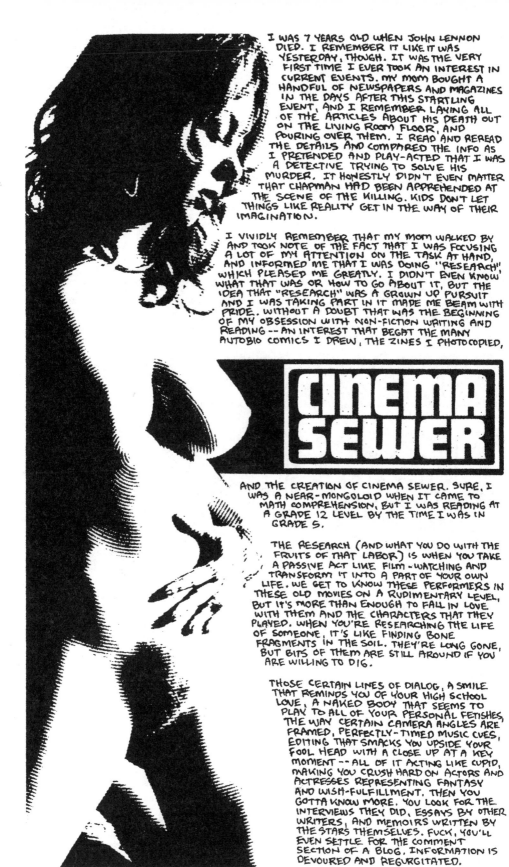

I WAS 7 YEARS OLD WHEN JOHN LENNON DIED. I REMEMBER IT LIKE IT WAS YESTERDAY, THOUGH. IT WAS THE VERY FIRST TIME I EVER TOOK AN INTEREST IN CURRENT EVENTS. MY MOM BOUGHT A HANDFUL OF NEWSPAPERS AND MAGAZINES IN THE DAYS AFTER THIS STARTLING EVENT, AND I REMEMBER LAYING ALL OF THE ARTICLES ABOUT HIS DEATH OUT ON THE LIVING ROOM FLOOR, AND POURING OVER THEM. I READ AND REREAD THE DETAILS AND COMPARED THE INFO AS I PRETENDED AND PLAY-ACTED THAT I WAS A DETECTIVE TRYING TO SOLVE HIS MURDER. IT HONESTLY DIDN'T EVEN MATTER THAT CHAPMAN HAD BEEN APPREHENDED AT THE SCENE OF THE KILLING. KIDS DON'T LET THINGS LIKE REALITY GET IN THE WAY OF THEIR IMAGINATION.

I VIVIDLY REMEMBER THAT MY MOM WALKED BY AND TOOK NOTE OF THE FACT THAT I WAS FOCUSING A LOT OF MY ATTENTION ON THE TASK AT HAND, AND INFORMED ME THAT I WAS DOING "RESEARCH" WHICH PLEASED ME GREATLY. I DIDN'T EVEN KNOW WHAT THAT WAS OR HOW TO GO ABOUT IT, BUT THE IDEA THAT "RESEARCH" WAS A GROWN UP PURSUIT AND I WAS TAKING PART IN IT MADE ME BEAM WITH PRIDE. WITHOUT A DOUBT THAT WAS THE BEGINNING OF MY OBSESSION WITH NON-FICTION WRITING AND READING -- AN INTEREST THAT BEGAT THE MANY AUTOBIO COMICS I DREW, THE ZINES I PHOTOCOPIED,

CINEMA SEWER

AND THE CREATION OF CINEMA SEWER. SURE, I WAS A NEAR-MONGOLOID WHEN IT CAME TO MATH COMPREHENSION, BUT I WAS READING AT A GRADE 12 LEVEL BY THE TIME I WAS IN GRADE 5.

THE RESEARCH (AND WHAT YOU DO WITH THE FRUITS OF THAT LABOR) IS WHEN YOU TAKE A PASSIVE ACT LIKE FILM-WATCHING AND TRANSFORM IT INTO A PART OF YOUR OWN LIFE. WE GET TO KNOW THESE PERFORMERS IN THESE OLD MOVIES ON A RUDIMENTARY LEVEL, BUT IT'S MORE THAN ENOUGH TO FALL IN LOVE WITH THEM AND THE CHARACTERS THAT THEY PLAYED. WHEN YOU'RE RESEARCHING THE LIFE OF SOMEONE, IT'S LIKE FINDING BONE FRAGMENTS IN THE SOIL. THEY'RE LONG GONE, BUT BITS OF THEM ARE STILL AROUND IF YOU ARE WILLING TO DIG.

THOSE CERTAIN LINES OF DIALOG, A SMILE THAT REMINDS YOU OF YOUR HIGH SCHOOL LOVE, A NAKED BODY THAT SEEMS TO PLAY TO ALL OF YOUR PERSONAL FETISHES, THE WAY CERTAIN CAMERA ANGLES ARE FRAMED, PERFECTLY-TIMED MUSIC CUES, EDITING THAT SMACKS YOU UPSIDE YOUR FOOL HEAD WITH A CLOSE UP AT A KEY MOMENT -- ALL OF IT ACTING LIKE CUPID, MAKING YOU CRUSH HARD ON ACTORS AND ACTRESSES REPRESENTING FANTASY AND WISH-FULFILLMENT. THEN YOU GOTTA KNOW MORE. YOU LOOK FOR THE INTERVIEWS THEY DID, ESSAYS BY OTHER WRITERS, AND MEMOIRS WRITTEN BY THE STARS THEMSELVES. FUCK, YOU'LL EVEN SETTLE FOR THE COMMENT SECTION OF A BLOG. INFORMATION IS DEVOURED AND REGURGITATED.

BUT WHAT YOU'RE FALLING IN LOVE WITH IS A GHOST. SOMEONE WHO IS GONE, EVEN IF THEY ARE STILL ALIVE AND TALKING TO YOU RIGHT THERE IN PERSON. SHE'S NOT THE PERSON SHE WAS WHEN SHE WAS 21 YEARS OLD. NONE OF US ARE. A LIFETIME HAS BEEN LIVED. SHE'S A MOM OR A GRANDMOTHER NOW, OR LONG DEAD. MAYBE THEY HAVE THEIR MEMORIES, BUT THE ONLY THING LEFT OF THOSE MEN AND WOMEN ON THE SCREEN THAT IS STILL CLEAR AND TANGIBLE IS WHAT YOU FELL IN LOVE WITH IN THE FIRST PLACE: THAT CELLULOID FOOTPRINT IN THE SAND. EVERYTHING ELSE IS ETHEREAL AND DISTORTED BY TIME. GROUND UP BY RUMOUR. BURIED BY OBLIVION.

THERE IS SOMETHING SO SAD AND YET BEAUTIFUL ABOUT THAT. UNREQUITED LOVE IS ROMANTIC AND PATHETIC ALL AT ONCE. GHOSTS CAN'T LOVE YOU BACK, BUT YOU ADORE WHAT THEY REPRESENT ALL THE SAME.

————————————————————————

WITH THAT SOMEWHAT MAUDLIN INTRODUCTION OUT OF THE WAY, ALLOW ME TO USHER YOU INTO THIS FIFTH VOLUME OF THE CINEMA SEWER BOOK SERIES! AS I SIT HERE AND LOOK OVER WHAT I'VE WRITTEN AND DRAWN OVER THE LAST YEAR OR SO, I'M PRETTY HAPPY WITH EVERYTHING. THE STACKS OF ORIGINAL PAGES ARE ALL OVER MY LIVING ROOM TABLE, IN SOMEWHAT OF A DISARRAY, AND YET IN PILES THAT SORT OF MAKE SENSE. I'M IN THE PROCESS OF TRYING TO FIGURE OUT WHICH PAGES SHOULD GO WHERE, AND IF ANYTHING NEEDS TO BE REDONE OR RETOOLED. IT'S SORT OF LIKE PUTTING TOGETHER A MIXTAPE FOR A FRIEND. THE ORDER IN WHICH YOU PUT THE SONGS MAY NOT BE READILY OBVIOUS, BUT THEY DO SEEM IMPORTANT WHILE YOU'RE DOING IT -- AT LEAST IN TERMS OF GENERATING MAXIMUM IMPACT FOR THE LISTENER, OR IN THIS CASE, READER.

THIS COLLECTION, LIKE THE PREVIOUS 4, IS MADE UP OF ROUGHLY 110 TO 115 PAGES OF REPRINTS FROM THE BEST OF CINEMA SEWER MAGAZINE, AND THEN TOPPED OFF WITH 75 TO 80 PAGES OF BRAND NEW MATERIAL THAT HAS NEVER BEEN SEEN BEFORE. IN THIS CASE, THE MATERIAL PREVIOUSLY PUBLISHED (IN ANNUAL PRINT RUNS OF 2000 COPIES EACH) CAME FROM CINEMA SEWER MAGAZINE ISSUES #24, #25, AND #26. IF YOU'RE LOOKING TO SNAG SOME OF THE MAGAZINES (OR THE DIRTY COMIC BOOKS THAT I DRAW AND SELF PUBLISH), FEEL FREE TO DROP BY MY ONLINE STORE WHICH IS LISTED BELOW, AND IF YOU'RE WANTING TO SAY 'HOWDEE DOO', FEEL FREE TO FRIEND ME ON FACEBOOK EITHER UNDER ROBIN BOUGIE, OR CINEMA SEWER. I'M AWFULLY FRIENDLY, ASSUMING YOU'RE NOT AN ANNOYING FUCKWIT.

ANYWAY, THANK YOU ALL FOR YOUR SUPPORT. AS PER USUAL, I'M HAVING A BLAST PUTTING THIS SERIES TOGETHER, AND IT FEELS FAR MORE LIKE PLAY THAN WORK, EVEN THOUGH SOME OF THE ARTICLES IN HERE LITERALLY TOOK YEARS TO RESEARCH. I WOULD ALSO LIKE TO OFFER SOME SERIOUS THANKS TO ALL OF THE OTHER CONTRIBUTORS AS WELL. IF YOU LOOK CLOSELY, YOU'LL SEE THAT I HAD A LOT OF HELP, AND I'VE BEEN CAREFUL TO CREDIT MY FELLOW SEWERPHILES ACCORDINGLY. YOU GUYS AND GALS ARE AMAZING, AND I APPRECIATE ALL OF THE HELP.

AND SO:

OK, NOW?

OK -- ENOUGH FIDDLE FADDLE! LET'S DO THIS THAAANG! YIPPIE!

RoBiN BouGie
WWW.CINEMASEWER.COM
·2015·

DROP BY AND ORDER MY STUFF

HELL YEAH!
FIRE IT UP, SWEETCHEEKS!
IT'S TIME TO ENJOY THE SICKEST AND SEXIEST MOVIES EVER MADE! (SOMEONE GET THE LIGHTS)

The XXX filmography of MISA -- 2001-2004

YOGA IS AN ANCIENT PRACTICE TO PHYSICALLY, MENTALLY, AND SPIRITUALLY TRANSFORM BODY AND MIND. ITS ROOTS DATE BACK TO PRE-VEDIC TRADITIONS OF INDIA, WITH A WHOLE VARIETY OF SCHOOLS, ELEMENTS AND GOALS DEPENDING ON WHAT RELIGIOUS SECT OR PART OF THE WORLD YOU WERE IN. IN RECENT DECADES, YOGA HAS FOUND ITSELF MAINSTREAMED, SECULARIZED, AND INTRODUCED TO THE WEST AS AN EVERYDAY RECREATIONAL ACTIVITY. THIS FORM OF YOGA IS KNOWN AS HATHA YOGA, AND IT IS PRACTICED BY PEOPLE FROM ALL WALKS OF LIFE.

BUT THERE ARE STILL MYSTERIOUS YOGA-BASED STUDIES, SCHOOLS AND SECTS THAT CAREFULLY GUARD THE ANCIENT SPIRITUAL SECRETS AND RELIGIOUS HERITAGE OF YOGA. ONE OF THEM IS A LARGE GROUP BASED IN EUROPE NAMED MISA (WHICH STANDS FOR "MOVEMENT FOR SPIRITUAL INTEGRATION IN ABSOLUTE"), AND IN RECENT YEARS THEY WERE EXPELLED FROM THE EUROPEAN YOGA COUNCIL FOR THEIR "ILLEGAL PRACTICES" AND "AN UNHEARD OF LACK OF MORAL INTEGRITY." WHY? WELL, THAT'S WHAT I WANTED TO KNOW, TOO. AND I'M GOING TO SHARE WITH YOU WHAT I'VE FOUND AFTER A FEW WEEKS OF RESEARCH.

I CALL MISA A CULT, BECAUSE IT'S HARD NOT TO WHEN ONE TAKES DIRECT ACCOUNT OF HOW MUCH IT HAS IN COMMON WITH SOME OF THE MOST NOTORIOUS AND DANGEROUS CULTS. NAMELY; AN AUTOCRATIC LEADER WHO MUST BE OBEYED AT ALL TIMES AND WHO IS SEEN AS HAVING DIVINE AND SUPERNATURAL POWERS. AS PER USUAL, SAID LEADER IS ELDERLY AND UNATTRACTIVE, YET FUCKS THE MUCH YOUNGER AND PRETTY FEMALE MEMBERS WHO TAKE PART IN A DOCTRINAL PHILOSOPHY THAT INCORPORATES THE IDEA OF SACRED YET OPEN SEXUALITY. MISA ARE MOSTLY UNHEARD OF IN NORTH AMERICA (ALTHOUGH THEY ARE WORKING TO BREAK NEW GROUND AS WE SPEAK) BUT THEY HAVE FORTY THOUSAND DEVOTED MEMBERS WORLDWIDE, AND ACCORDING TO THE TIMES OF INDIA, CURRENTLY OPERATE UNDER DIFFERENT NAMES IN DIFFERENT COUNTRIES. THE GROUP IS KNOWN AS NATHA IN ICELAND, DENMARK AND PORTUGAL, SATYA IN INDIA, AND TARA IN ENGLAND AND IRELAND.

THE CULT LEADER IN THIS CASE IS A BELOVED ROMANIAN GURU NAMED GREGORIAN (AKA GRIEG) BIVOLARU, AND FROM THE OUTSIDE EVERYTHING IN HIS TANTRIC CLUB SEEMS PRETTY HAPPY AND BENIGN, NO ONE HAS A BAD WORD TO SAY ABOUT HIM, AND ARE VERY ANTAGONISTIC AND CRITICAL OF ANYONE WHO DOES. BUT EX-MEMBERS HAVE REVEALED MUCH MORE. FOR INSTANCE, DANISH YOGA PRACTITIONER KIM SCHMOCK BOUGHT A FARM IN DENMARK IN THE LATE 1990S, AND ALONGSIDE HE AND HIS FEMALE PARTNER, SEVERAL MISA MEMBERS MOVED IN. BEFORE HE KNEW IT, THE PLACE WAS CONVERTED INTO AN ASHRAM, AND A FEW YEARS LATER HE BEGAN TO REALIZE HIS FARM WAS NO LONGER HIS PROPERTY. HE, LIKE MANY MEMBERS OF THIS CULT WHERE INDIVIDUALITY IS ENTIRELY FROWNED UPON, HAD GOTTEN IN TOO DEEP.

GREGORIAN BIVOLARU

THIS SCRAGGLY OLD YOGA CULT LEADER HAS BANGED MORE HOTTIES THAN HUGH HEFNER

"YOU GET INVOLVED MORE AND MORE", KIM SAID TO FINNISH REPORTER, RIIKKA KAIHOVAARA. "THEY ARE SUDDENLY CONTROLLING YOUR LIFE, YOU KNOW-- AND ALL THE EXPECTATIONS THEY HAVE: 'YOU HAVE TO DO THIS, YOU HAVE TO DO THAT', AND SUDDENLY YOU DON'T HAVE TIME TO YOUR FRIENDS, YOU DON'T HAVE TIME TO YOUR FAMILY. THEY WILL BE YOUR FAMILY — AND ACTUALLY, WHEN YOU REALIZE THIS, IT'S OFTEN TOO LATE."

"GRIEG BELIEVES THERE IS AN INTERNATIONAL CONSPIRACY AGAINST HIM", AN EX-MISA MEMBER TOLD KAIHOVAARA. SHE REFUSED TO ALLOW HER NAME TO BE USED FOR FEAR OF REPRISALS. "THEN THERE WERE THE UFO-STORIES: THAT SPACE BEINGS CALLED VRILLONS ARE BEING CONTACTED TELEPATHICALLY, AND STUFF LIKE THAT. I COULD NOT SEE THE CONNECTION TO YOGA ANYMORE. I SAID 'I CAN'T BELIEVE THIS'. BUT THEN I WAS TOLD I MUST BELIEVE, THAT WHEN THE GURU SAYS IT IS SO, THEN SO IT IS. IN A WAY YOU ARE FORCED TO MAKE A CHOICE: EITHER YOU ACCEPT THE GURU OR YOU DON'T. I THEN CHOSE NOT TO ACCEPT."

BIVOLARU'S GROUP HAS VARIOUS WAYS OF MAKING ITS MONEY. EACH OF THE THOUSANDS OF YOGINS HOSTED IN THE VARIOUS SQUALID ASHRAMS MUST RENOUNCE ALL OF THEIR WORLDLY GOODS, EXTRICATE THEMSELVES FROM THE EVILS AND DISTRACTIONS OF SOCIETY AND HAND OVER THEIR CASH BEFORE CARRYING OUT A COMPULSORY "TAPAS" (AKA SACRIFICE) OF "KARMA YOGA" (BENEVOLENT LABOUR).

"MAKE PROOF OF YOUR DEVOTION TOWARDS THE GURU, OFFERING HIM ANYTHING HE DESIRES", A PRIVATE MISA DOCUMENT FOR NEWCOMERS OBTAINED BY B1TV ROMANIA, READS. "(GIVE HIM) EVERYTHING YOU HAVE THAT IS MOST PRECIOUS, EVEN THE OBJECT WHICH YOU LOVE THE MOST. ANYTHING HE MAY ASK OF YOU, DO IT."

DESPITE MISA'S SECRECY, THE GROUP'S DIRE MOTIVES ARE THERE FOR ANY OUTSIDERS WHO CARE TO SEARCH FOR THEM, PLAINLY OUTLINED ON SOME OF THEIR WEBSITES IN DOCTRINES SUCH AS "THE TEN USELESS THINGS". IT'S A LIST MADE UP OF "USELESS" STUFF LIKE HAVING LOVED ONES ("SEEING THAT WHEN WE DIE WE MUST GO ON OUR WAY ALONE AND WITHOUT KINSFOLK OR FRIENDS, IT IS USELESS TO HAVE DEVOTED TIME TO THEIR HUMOURING AND OBLIGING, OR IN SHOWERING LOVING AFFECTION UPON THEM"), A HOME ("WHEN WE DIE WE MUST DEPART EMPTY-HANDED AND ON THE MORROW AFTER OUR DEATH OUR CORPSE IS EXPELLED FROM OUR OWN HOUSE, THEREFORE IT IS USELESS TO LABOUR AND TO SUFFER PRIVATIONS IN ORDER TO MAKE FOR ONESELF A HOME IN THIS WORLD") OR YOUR OWN PERSONAL INTERESTS OR EDUCATION OUTSIDE OF MISA ("IT IS USELESS TO HAVE DEVOTED ONESELF TO THE PROFITLESS DOINGS OF THIS WORLD RATHER THAN TO THE SEEKING OF DIVINE WISDOM").

ONCE IN THE CULT, MEDITATION TAKES UP MOST OF YOUR EXISTENCE, BUT THE TAPAS ARE DONE FOR A MINIMUM OF 6 HOURS PER DAY -- ALTHOUGH 20 HOUR WORK DAYS HAVE BEEN REPORTED. MANY OF THE MEN WORK IN THE PRINTING HOUSE AND ON CONSTRUCTION SITES, WHILE WORKING AT MISA'S VEGETARIAN BAKERY IN RAHOVA IS MAINLY A JOB FOR THE WOMEN. THEN THERE ARE VARIOUS PORN SITES AND LIVE CAM PORN ON THE INTERNET. THIS CONTENT -- WHICH CONSISTS OF THE GIRLS MASTURBATING FOR LIVE ONLINE AUDIENCES WHO GIVE THEM INSTRUCTIONS IN RETURN FOR MONEY -- IS MADE INSIDE ONE OF THE ASHRAMS OR IN THE WOMEN'S APARTMENTS, AND THEN MADE AVAILABLE THROUGH SITES SUCH AS THE NOW DEFUNCT CAMANIA.COM, CAM-HOT.COM AND INTERCLIMAX.COM. YOU EVER WONDER WHY SO MANY CAM GIRLS ARE ROMANIAN? NOW YOU KNOW.

ANOTHER MAJOR SOURCE OF FUNDING IS THE DELIVERY OF DANCERS TO NIGHTCLUBS AND STRIPPER BARS IN JAPAN, WHERE SLUTTY WHITE GIRLS ARE VERY POPULAR AMONGST WEALTHY JAPANESE SALARYMEN. THIS LUCRATIVE HUMAN TRAFFICKING SCHEME SENDS THE GIRLS OVER WHERE THEY MAKE AS MUCH AS THEY CAN DANCING AND WHORING, AND THEN AFTER SIX MONTHS, RETURN WITH THE MONEY TO THE MISA ASHRAMS IN ROMANIA.

FAR LESS MONEY HAS BEEN BROUGHT IN VIA PORN MOVIES, BUT HIGHER-UPS IN THE SECT REPORTEDLY SEE THEM AS A POWERFUL EDUCATIONAL AND PROPAGANDA TOOL -- A WAY TO NOT-SO-SUBTLY USHER THE MESSAGE TO THE PUBLIC WHILE THEY ARE SEXUALLY STIMULATED AND THEREFORE FAR MORE OPEN TO SUGGESTION -- A TACT KNOWN IN OTHER CULTS AS "FLIRTY FISHING". THE MOVIES ARE OFTEN CREDITED AS BEING DIRECTED BY BELLA MAESTRINA (WHICH TRANSLATES FROM ITALIAN AS "BEAUTIFUL YOUNG TEACHER"), BUT HER REAL NAME IS CARMEN ENACHE, AND FROM WHAT I'VE READ SHE WAS CLOSE TO BIVOLARU DURING THE 2000S.

IN THE DVDS THE FEMALE PERFORMERS ARE ALWAYS 100% FREE OF PUBIC HAIR (WHICH DOESN'T SEEM PARTICULARLY NEW-AGEY TO ME, BUT I HANG OUT WITH HAIRY CANADIAN WEST COAST GRANOLA HIPPIES) AND ARE SOMETIMES REFERRED TO AS THE "URINARI TANTRA GROUP", OR THE "ECSTASY GROUP". ONE OF THE COMPANIES MISA MEMBERS LAUNCHED TO RELEASE THESE MOVIES WAS KARESSA STUDIO (AKA KARESSA UNIVERSAL -- WHICH EXISTED FROM 2001 TO 2004), AND THERE HAVE BEEN OTHERS AS WELL, INCLUDING EROTIC ART, AND LOTUS ART PRODUCTIONS. SOME OF THE FILMS HAVE STORIES WITH CHARACTERS AND SCRIPTS, AND OTHERS ARE MORE GONZO-STYLE. HERE ARE SOME OF THE MORE NOTEWORTHY ONES:

MAGIC PASSAGE (2001)

MOSTLY SHOT IN GREECE, THIS IS MISA'S FIRST XXX RELEASE, AND IT STARS MIHAI STOIAN (AKA PAUL DIAMOND), CRISTINA GAINA, AND ADINA STOIAN (AKA ADINA SECARA), IT WAS PRODUCED BY THE COPENHAGEN-BASED PRODUCTION HOUSE SUBLIME EROTICA, WHICH MISA HAS CLOSE TIES WITH. MIHAI IS A SEXY GUY AND ONE OF THE HIGHEST RANKING SPIRITUAL LEADERS IN THE CULT. HE'S REPORTEDLY TREATED WITH REVERENCE

MISS ॐ SHAKTI

PARAGON OF FEMININITY

PRINCESS OF SHAKTI PEETHAS

BY MANY OF THE FEMALE MEMBERS IN PARTICULAR, AND THEY HANG ON HIS EVERY WORD WHEN HE'S TEACHING GROUPS AT SPECIAL CAMPS WHERE NEW MEMBERS ARE RECRUITED. MAGIC PASSAGE'S MOST INFAMOUS SCENE HAS ITS TWO STARS BANGING EACH OTHER UNDER THE WATCHFUL, GLOOMY GAZE OF A MATRON WHO IS SITTING IN AN ARMCHAIR RIGHT NEXT TO THEM.

SECRETS OF SEDUCTION (2001)

THE CREW PUTTING THIS ONE TOGETHER COVERTLY SHOT A SCENE IN THE ROMAN CATHOLIC CATHEDRAL OF CONSTANTA (BUILT IN 1885), SOMETHING THAT SCANDALIZED THE CATHOLIC CHURCH AND THE ROMANIAN MEDIA WHEN THEY DISCOVERED THE BLASPHEMY IN 2008. "THEY USED THE CHURCH ABUSIVELY. THE PEOPLE WHO MADE THIS MOVIE ARE IRRESPONSIBLE", PRIEST ENACHE DRAGUS COMPLAINED TO GARDIANUL, THE DAILY PAPER IN BUCHAREST.

THAT'S NOT THE ONLY SCANDAL TO BE ATTRIBUTED TO THIS PORNO, HOWEVER. NAKED, DEBAUCHED PHOTOS AND VIDEOS OF THE WOMAN WHO BECAME KNOWN AS THE "PORNO JUDGE", SIMONA LUNGU, WERE SENT IN NOVEMBER 2005 TO THE ROMANIAN MAGAZINE FORTUNE. INCLUDED WAS FOOTAGE FROM HER PARTICIPATION IN A 2002 ORGY TO CELEBRATE THE 50TH BIRTHDAY OF GURU BIVOLARU, AND AN APPEARANCE IN THIS 2001 XXX RELEASE. "SHE HAS NO EXCUSE," WROTE THE ROMANIAN WEBSITE, NEWSPAD. "HER IMAGE OF 'RADIANT ANGEL' IS IRRETRIEVABLY BROKEN."

WHAT LUNGU DID TO ANGER THE CULT REMAINS UNKNOWN TO THE PUBLIC, BUT SHE DIDN'T REMAIN A JUDGE FOR LONG. HER EXPLANATION THAT COMPUTER WIZARDRY HAD BEEN USED TO PUT HER FACE ON A PORN PERFORMER'S BODY WAS SOUNDLY DISMISSED BY THE FORENSIC INSTITUTE, A STATE CRIME LAB WHOM SHE HAD APPROACHED TO HELP HER CLEAR HER NAME.

MUCH OF THIS MOVIE (AND 3 OR 4 OF THE OTHER MISA VIDEOS I HAVEN'T REVIEWED IN THIS ARTICLE) WAS FILMED EITHER DURING MISA YOGA CAMPS OR AT THE MISS SHAKTI COMPETITION QUALIFICATIONS, AND RAW ELEMENTS OF IT WERE ALSO SHOWN MULTIPLE TIMES IN MISA SCHOOLS ON DIFFERENT OCCASIONS TO LARGE NUMBERS OF PEOPLE. MISS SHAKTI IS A "CELEBRATION OF FEMININITY", AND BASICALLY A BEAUTY PAGEANT FOR WHO IS THE BIGGEST ORGASM-HUNGRY TANTRIC SEX GODDESS OF THE CULT FOR THAT YEAR. ONE OF THE POTENTIAL MISS SHAKTIS SPOKE ABOUT THE EXPERIENCE SHE HAD THERE AS AN 18-YEAR-OLD ON HER DEVIANTART.COM PAGE IN AUGUST OF 2011. SHE GOES BY THE ONLINE NAME, "THEOTHERSARSHI".

"THERE ARE DIFFERENT CHALLENGES" SHE WROTE. "THERE WAS AN INTELLIGENCE CHALLENGE, WHERE A FEW TRICK QUESTIONS WOULD BE ASKED... THE 'SUBTLE PERCEPTIONS' CHALLENGE, WHERE THEY'D HAVE TO GUESS THREE STATES EXEMPLIFIED TELEPATHICALLY BY THE SPIRITUAL MASTER GRIEG (ALMOST EVERYBODY GOT THEM WRONG; EVEN MORE WRONG THAN STATISTICS WOULD SAY RANDOM RESPONSES WOULD HAVE A CHANCE OF BEING RIGHT. THE PROBLEM WAS THAT GRIEG ISN'T TELEPATHIC AND HE CAN'T TRANSMIT A STATE TO SAVE HIS LIFE)... A CHALLENGE IN WHICH WOMEN ARE MADE TO DRINK A LOT OF WATER (OR EAT WATERMELONS) AND THEN THEY'RE TAKEN TO SOME RANDOM LOCATION AND MADE TO MASTURBATE AS THEY PEE, SO THAT THE SPIRITUAL 'MASTER' WOULD JUDGE THEIR ABILITY TO HAVE A 'URINARY ORGASM'... A NIGHT HELD IN A MORE PRIVATE LOCATION WHERE WOMEN ARE ENTIRELY NAKED, ACTUALLY POLE DANCE, AND READ ALOUD ONE OF THEIR 'SECRET' SEXUAL FANTASIES."

"ONE OF THE LAST CHALLENGES IS THAT OF THE 'VIDEO'. THEY HAVE TO STAR IN EROTIC VIDEOS... IF YOU CAN GET PAST THE FACT THAT SUCH A CHALLENGE SHOULDN'T APPEAR IN A BEAUTY PAGEANT (BUT THEN THE 'URINARY ORGASM' ONE WAS WAY WORSE), THEN SOME OF THE VIDEOS ARE QUITE OK, REALLY. THEY CAN BE NICELY DONE AND HAVE A MINI-STORY. THEY'RE USUALLY PRETTY, WITH NICE, MORE OR LESS ELEGANT IMAGES. WELL, UNLESS YOU HAVE THE EXTREME BAD LUCK TO END UP WITH A DIRECTOR WHO IS DOING STUFF THE PORN WAY. THE BAD PART IS THAT WOMEN DON'T GET TO CHOOSE THE VIDEOS THEY'LL BE IN. THERE ARE A NUMBER OF STORIES AND THEY'RE RANDOMLY PAIRED WITH GIRLS.

BE EROTIC! DO IT!! C'MON!

C'MON!

SEXIER!

"BY THE END OF THE FIRST DAY I MET MY BOYFRIEND, WHO ASKED ME HOW IT WAS. 'MENTION THE WORD EROTIC OR ANY VARIATION THEREOF TO ME AND YOU DIE IN PAIN,' I ANSWERED. (I WAS) TIRED AND SICKENED, AS IF I'D EATEN TOO MUCH CHOCOLATE AND NEEDED TO THROW UP. FOR THE FIRST TIME IN MY LIFE, I HATED SEX, I HATED WOMEN, I HATED DANCING, I HATED THE CHOREOGRAPHY AND THE CHOREOGRAPHERS, THE COMPETITION, MISA, THE WORLD AND EVERYTHING BESIDES. AFTER HOURS UPON HOURS OF BEING SUCKED DRY OF MY ENTHUSIASTIC SPIRIT, OF HAVING TO PRACTICE DANCING, OF BEING TOLD TO 'BE MORE EROTIC' NON-STOP, I WAS SPITEFUL. I'D EXPECTED

SOMETHING ELSE. SOMETHING NICER. SOMETHING MORE UPLIFTING. NOT SOMETHING THAT MADE ME FEEL LIKE A TWO-DOLLAR SHOW IN A NIGHT CLUB."

"THE WINNER GETS APPLAUDED. SHE'S SEEN AS A VERY SPIRITUAL WOMAN, A PARAGON OF FEMININITY. HER STORY IS RECORDED. SHE IS THE WOMAN OF THE HOUR — CHOSEN BY GRIEG, OF COURSE. SHE GETS TO PARTICIPATE IN YOGA CLASSES FOR FREE FOR A YEAR, GETS SOME BOOKS AND I'M NOT SURE IF SHE GETS MONEY... AND SHE WILL SOONER OR LATER BE INVITED TO GRIEG'S BED, BY THE BY. IF SHE HASN'T BEEN THERE ALREADY."

ECSTASY WATER (2003)

THIS ONE IS AWESOME, AND IN ONE PART VARIOUS NAKED COUPLES MEET IN A CAVE, LAY DOWN ON SOME UNCOMFORTABLE LOOKING ROCKS AND FEED EACH OTHER MUSHROOMS WHILE A BEARDED YOGI (CLEARLY A STAND-IN FOR GRIEG) RINGS A BELL AND FREAKY MUSIC PLAYS. THEN SOME ROCKS FALL DOWN A CLIFF, SOME GEMS SHOOT OUT OF THE GROUND, AND BUFF DUDES START GRIND-HUMPING ROMANIAN PUSSY LIKE THEIR LIFE DEPENDED ON IT. EVERYONE IS COVERED IN SPARKLES, AND VARIOUS FREAKY SEX POSITIONS ARE EMPLOYED BEFORE EVERYONE STARTS PISSING ON EACH OTHER. "YOU ARE THE WATER", THE CULT LEADER SAYS, STONEFACED. "THE WATER TEACHES US. IT COMFORTS AND PURIFIES US." BITCHES DRINK PISS RIGHT FROM THE DONG LIKE IT WAS SUNNY DELIGHT, AND THEN WE SEE WAVES CRASH AGAINST SOME ROCKS ON THE BEACH.

NOW IT'S TIME TO FUCK AGAIN, AND THE MUSIC GETS REAL ROMANTIC AS A PIANO PLAYER TICKLES THE IVORIES. LOTS OF CROSS FADES AND SLO-MO WRITHING AS GIGGLY WOMEN MOAN AND THE GUYS TRY TO LOOK SERIOUS. SUDDENLY A TRAIL OF FIRE SHOOTS ACROSS THE GROUND AND BURNS A TREE UP. "YOU ARE THE FIRE" THE YOGI NARRATES. "THE FIRE MAKES THE LIGHT RISE IN US. MAKES US MASTERS OF THE WILD STALLION OF OUR SENSES". STALLIONS? THAT'S RIGHT, IT'S TIME FOR THE GIRLS TO RIDE THOSE BALONEY PONIES, SO THEY HOP ON THE DICKS AND BOUNCE AROUND.

SUDDENLY THE WORLD GOES SUPER NOVA AS ORANGE LIGHT SHOOTS FORTH, SO THE GUYS START PISSING IN THE GIRLS' FACES AGAIN. "YOU ARE THE AIR", MONK-MAN SAYS SOOTHINGLY. "THE AIR IS OUR HEART. IT MAKES OUR HEART BIGGER THAN A STAR". SOME NEW-AGE ELECTRONICA PLAYS THAT SOUNDS EXACTLY LIKE THAT 1990s FRENCH BAND ENIGMA, AND IT'S BACK TO MORE FUCKING. THIS TIME, EVERYONE ENJOYS DOGGY STYLE POSITION AS THEY ARE BATHED IN BRIGHT BLUE LIGHT. AS AN EXCLAMATION POINT, A CHICK PISSES ON A GUY'S FACE BACKWARDS FROM A WHEELBARROW POSITION, WHICH IS CERTAINLY A NIFTY LITTLE TRICK I HADN'T SEEN BEFORE. NO SIR.

PRETTY SOON EVERYONE COLLECTS IN A LIT CIRCLE, AND A COUPLE KNEEL IN THE CENTER WHILE EVERYONE PISSES ALL OVER THEM. A BEAM OF LIGHT SHOOTS UP INTO THE SKY, AND EVERYONE STARTS GLOWING LIKE ANGELS. PRETTY SOON THE SIMPLE LIT CIRCLE THEY'RE STANDING IN BECOMES A CIRCULAR SHAFT OF LIGHT THAT SHOOTS HUNDREDS OF FEET IN THE AIR THANKS TO SOME SWEET CGI ANIMATION. "ALL THE FEELINGS, ALL THE EXTRAORDINARY AND ECSTATIC STATES IN THIS MOVIE ARE OBTAINED ONLY THROUGH TANTRIC TECHNIQUES", THE CREDITS READ.

IN ANOTHER SCENE A HUNKY HIMBO WITH A PONY TAIL SHOWS A WOMAN HOW TO HAVE "URINARY ORGASMS". HE PERCHES HER ON A ROCK, AND PROMPTS HER TO PISS IN SHORT BURSTS, AS HE TRIES TO CATCH IT IN HIS MOUTH. HE CUPS HIS HANDS AND POURS SOME OF HER OWN PEE IN HER MOUTH WHILE TELLING HER WHAT IS WHAT. "DRINK IT. IT'S THE POWER OF LIFE", HE SAYS LIKE A DRUNK GUY TRYING TO PICK UP SOMEONE IN A EURO DANCE CLUB. "THIS IS NOT JUST SIMPLE WATER. IT ELEVATES YOU. FEEL IT'S POWER? OF COURSE YOU DO. IT TAKES YOU STRAIGHT TO HEAVEN IF YOU KNOW HOW TO DO IT." SHE GETS SO INTO IT THAT SHE IMAGINES HERSELF FUCKING HIM IN A FIELD OF SUN FLOWERS. IN HER FANTASY, THEY BOUND AROUND IN EACH OTHER'S PISS FOUNTAINS LIKE KIDS WITH A SPRINKLER ON A HOT DAY. SPENT, THEY REPLENISH THEIR WIZ RESERVES BY EATING WATERMELONS (WHICH THEY ALSO PISS ON) AND THEN IT'S RIGHT BACK TO THEIR SATISFIED-SOUNDING BLADDER-GULPING AS THEY GET TELEPORTED INTO A WEIRD PITCH-BLACK DIMENSION. HERE THEY STAND IN FRONT OF ONE ANOTHER NAKED AND (PREDICTABLY) PISS AS SOME WEIRD BLUE LASER LIGHT FLICKERS. WTF.

LATER, WHILE CHILLING IN HIS BREAKFAST NOOK EATING HIS CORN FLAKES, THE GUY ISN'T QUITE SURE IF HE'S GOING CRAZY OR NOT, SO HIS TEACHER (THE GURU FROM THE CAVE) SITS THERE AND CHILLS HIM THE FUCK OUT. "YOU ARE NOW SEEING LIFE AS IT REALLY IS", THE BEARDED YOGI INTONES. "I FEEL AT HOME IN ALL DIMENSIONS. EVERYTHING I WANT IS POSSIBLE." PONYTAIL DUDE SAYS, TO WHICH HIS MENTOR EXPLAINS, "WHEN YOU USE THE MAGICAL POWER OF URINE, YOU PRESERVE THE SEXUAL ENERGY."

THE MOVIE WON THE 2003 NINFA AWARD (SPANISH PORN AWARDS) FOR BEST COVER ART. MADALINA RAY, A SUCCESSFUL PORN ACTRESS FROM GERMANY PLAYS A MAJOR ROLE, AND IT'S WORTH NOTING THAT DIRECTOR CARMEN ENACHE DEDICATED THIS PRODUCTION TO THE ESCAPEE GURU, WHO WAS HERE PLAYED BY ACTOR IOAN POHARIU.

ECSTASY WATER 2 (2003)

THIS WAS RELEASED THE SAME YEAR AS PART ONE, AND THAT PITHY OLD GURU IS TEACHING HIS JUICY LESSONS AGAIN, THIS TIME TO A DIFFERENT STUDENT WHO DOES LOTS OF HARD STUDYING. NO, SERIOUSLY, THERE IS EVEN A MONTAGE OF HIM READING BOOKS, WRITING NOTES, AND TYPING ON HIS LAPTOP. WHEN THE CAMERA PANS OVER, WE CAN SEE THAT HE'S WRITTEN: "STILL NOTHING ABOUT URINCOR. I HAVE TO LOOK MORE. GREAT! I FINALLY FOUND WHAT I WAS LOOKING FOR! THIS IS IT! I FOUND IT AT LAST!" THEN HE RUBS HIS FINGERTIPS SLOWLY OVER SOME SACRED TEXTS, AND WE'RE OFF TO THE RACES. OH, AND IF THAT MONTAGE WASN'T ENOUGH, THEN WE GET A TRAINING MONTAGE WHERE HE TAKES A LEAK IN HIS OWN MOUTH, DOES A BUNCH OF FUNKY MASTURBATORY TECHNIQUES, DRINKS HIS OWN PISS A BUNCH OF TIMES, AND GENERALLY LOOKS STOIC WHILE DOING SO.

THE NARRATION IN THOSE DUSTY OLD TANTRIC PEE-DRINKING MANUALS IS READ IN THE GURU'S VOICE, AND WHAT HE DESCRIBES IS THEN ACTED OUT BY THE CULT'S USUAL CAST OF SMOKIN' HOT NEW-AGE BITCHES. "IN THIS RITUAL, THE TANTRIC PRIESTESSES RAISE THEIR INNER SERPENT POWER, AND EXPERIENCE OVERWHELMING STATES OF GROUP ECSTASY", THE VOICE SAYS

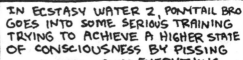

IN ECSTASY WATER 2, PONYTAIL BRO GOES INTO SOME SERIOUS TRAINING TRYING TO ACHIEVE A HIGHER STATE OF CONSCIOUSNESS BY PISSING ON EVERYTHING.

YEE!!!AHH!

SQZ!

FAP
FAP
FAP
FAP

BOUGIE · 2014

YO, IT'S A YOGA THANG

YOU WOULDN'T UNDERSTAND, DUDE

SOLEMNLY. "IN ORDER TO ASSIMILATE THE BENEFICIAL QUALITIES OF THE TWELVE CONSTELLATIONS, THE UNIFIED MUST DRINK THE URINE FROM A WOMAN FROM EACH OF THE ZODIAC SIGNS, WITHOUT DRINKING THE FIRST OR THE LAST BURST OF THE STREAM."

THEY DRINK ALL RIGHT. IF IT WAS POSSIBLE TO GET DRUNK ON URINE, EVERYONE IN THIS MOVIE WOULD HAVE ALCOHOL POISONING. LIKE PART ONE, WE'RE TRANSPORTED BACK IN THE HOLY CAVES OF GROIN-GRAVY, AND THERE ISN'T A DRY EYE (OR ANY OTHER BODY PART) IN THE PLACE. THE WOMEN SCRAMBLE AROUND ON THE ROCKS, FIND A GOOD PERCH ON WHICH TO RAIN THEIR GOLDEN RAIN DOWN UPON THE CAMERAMAN AND THE REST OF THE CAST, AND LET THEIR SPRAY FLY. SHIT GETS PROGRESSIVELY WILDER AND THEN THE WHOLE GODDAMN THING CULMINATES WITH TWO TIERS OF NAKED LOVELIES, 45 TO 50 WOMEN IN ALL, SQUATTING IN A BIG CIRCLE AND SHOOTING THE CONTENTS OF THEIR BLADDERS ALL AT THE SAME TIME ON AN OLD BEARDED MAN. IT'S JAW-DROPPINGLY WEIRD, AND ARGUABLY THE GREATEST SINGLE MOMENT IN THE ENTIRE MISA PISS PORN CULT FILMOGRAPHY. AMAZING.

KINGDOM OF GOLDEN PEE (2003)

THIS FEATURED THE 2003 MISS SHAKTI CONTEST, AND AS MENTIONED PART OF THAT WAS TO PISS AND HAVE YOURSELF AN ORGASM WHILE DOING IT. A TALL ORDER BUT THE LADIES INVOLVED GAVE IT THEIR BEST SHOT. AFTER THE FOOTAGE WAS SHOT AND THE WINNERS ANNOUNCED, THIS GROUP WAS SENT TO A LIVE STAGE SHOW IN BARCELONA, SPAIN, WHERE THEY FUCKED EACH OTHER WITH DILDOS, ATE WHIPPED CREAM OFF EACH OTHERS BUTTS, AND PISSED ALL OVER THE FIRST TWO ROWS OF AN APPRECIATIVE AUDIENCE. SOME OF THE

CONTESTANTS APPARENTLY KNEW THIS FOOTAGE WAS GOING BE SEEN BY THE PUBLIC, BUT ACCORDING TO VARIOUS SOURCES THERE WERE OTHERS THAT HAD <u>NO</u> IDEA.

"I BOUGHT THE DVDS WITH THE FILMS FROM MISA" AN ANONYMOUS WOMAN POSTED ON EXMISA.ORG, A MESSAGE BOARD SUPPORT GROUP FOR FORMER MEMBERS. "I WOULD SUE THEM, BUT I DON'T WANT TO WASTE YEARS IN COURT. IT IS INCREDIBLE WHAT THEY WERE ABLE TO DO... I THINK IT'S THE FIRST TIME IN MY LIFE WHEN I FELT SO MUCH REVOLT AND HUMILIATION."

"WE WERE FILMING FOR THE SECRET TEST", SHE CONTINUED. "(IT) WAS COMPULSORY AS PART OF THE ELIMINATIONS FOR THE MISS SHAKTI COMPETITION. THE TAPES WERE TO BE SEEN ONLY BY GRIEG AND THOSE FROM THE EDITING. IT NEVER OCCURRED TO ANY OF US THAT IN TIME SOMEONE IS GOING TO THINK ABOUT SELLING THEM. EVERYONE FILMED IN TRUST AND THIS CAN BE SEEN -- A CERTAIN INTIMATE ATMOSPHERE OF TRUST. SOME WERE EVEN MEDITATING, THEY WERE ROLLING THEIR EYES WHEN THEY WERE URINATING. THIS IS NORMAL STUFF FOR OUR SHAKTIS. YOGA CAMP BEHAVIOUR."

"IN ORDER TO PASS THE SECOND STAGE, IT WAS COMPULSORY TO TAKE THE TEST OF URINARY ORGASM... BUT NOW WHEN I THINK ABOUT IT, I FEEL LIKE LAUGHING. WHAT, CAN'T IT BE DONE OTHERWISE? IT CAN'T BE DONE WITHOUT BIVOLARU SEEING YOU ON TAPE, SEEING HOW YOU HAVE URINARY ORGASM AFTER YOU'VE EATEN THREE WATERMELONS? I KEPT HOPING THAT I WASN'T THERE. THE MORONS SHOWED <u>EVERYTHING.</u>"

INDEED THEY DID. THE WOMEN, OUT IN THE OPEN AIR WITH A RICH BLUE SKY BEHIND THEM AND THE SUN BEATING DOWN, RUB EACH OTHER'S EXCITED TWATS AND BLAST PISS LIKE RACE HORSES. THE NEW AGE MUSIC RISES TO A CRESCENDO AS THEY SAPPHICALLY SUCK FACE AND WORK HARD TO IMPRESS THE CAMERAS. ABOUT HALF OF IT IS KINDA BORING, BUT A FEW SCENES ARE GENUINELY HOT SHIT, AS SOME OF THE GIRLS MASTURBATE THEMSELVES TO LEGITIMATE ORGASMS. SEEING WOMEN CUM IN PORN ISN'T NEARLY AS COMMON AS IT NEEDS TO BE.

EXALTATION OF PEE (2003)
NEAR THE CENTER OF COSTINESTI, ROMANIA, GREGORIAN THE GURU BUILT A LAVISH ORGY-DEN FOR HIMSELF. THIS IS THE SO-CALLED SHAKTI-VILLA, AND IT IS SURROUNDED BY A HIGH FENCE AND A LOCKED GATE. HERE, MR. BIVOLARU INITIATED HUNDREDS OF YOUNG, BEAUTIFUL WOMEN. "HE NEVER USES PROTECTION," 13-YEAR MISA VETERAN AND FORMER MISA ASHRAM TEACHER MICHAELA FRINCU NOTED IN A CONCERNED LETTER TO THE ADVAITA STOIAN SPIRITUALITY GROUP. "THERE ARE MORE AND MORE WOMEN WHO REPORT HAVING BEEN INFECTED BY HIM WITH SEXUALLY TRANSMITTED DISEASES. ALTHOUGH HE HAS REPEATEDLY BEEN INFORMED ABOUT THIS SITUATION, HE CONTINUES TO DENY AND KEEPS SPREADING THE DISEASES."

NOT FAR AWAY FROM STD-CENTRAL, ON THE BEACH IN COSTINESTI, AN ABANDONED FREIGHT SHIP SITS. ITS RUSTED DECK SERVED AS THE LOCATION FOR THE MOSTLY WORDLESS PORNO RELEASE, ENTITLED EXALTATION OF PEE. 'EXALTATION' MEANS 'A FEELING OR STATE OF HAPPINESS', AND THE TITLE FITS. SHITTY EURO TECHNO MUSIC PLAYS AS ABOUT 20 NAKED WOMEN WATCH THE SUN SET ON THE BEACH. THEY WRITHE IN SLOW-MO, AND IN FACT, NEARLY THE ENTIRE MOVIE PLAYS IN SLOW MOTION. THIS WOULD WORK REALLY WELL IF IT WEREN'T SO OVERUSED, BUT THIS REALLY IS A BORING MOVIE IF YOU AREN'T TITILLATED BY THE SIGHT OF URINATING WOMEN STANDING WITH THEIR HEADS THROWN BACK IN HALF-SPEED PSEUDO-ORGASMIC BLISS. HONESTLY, THEY ACT AS IF TAKING A LEAK WERE THE SINGLE MOST EROTIC THING THAT HAD EVER HAPPENED TO ANYONE. NONE OF THE PERFORMERS ORGASM FOR REAL -- OR IF THEY DID THE CAMERAS CERTAINLY DIDN'T CATCH IT.

TO PEE OR NOT TO PEE FOR ECSTASY (2004)
THIS DVD RELEASE FEATURES CRISTINA PETREA (AKA HANNA) A FORMER MISS SHATKI, AS WELL AS COUNTLESS OTHER LOVELY NAKED MISA MEMBERS (100 IN ALL!) OUT IN THE WOODS DOING THEIR WET THING WHILE COVERED IN BODY GLITTER AND HENNA TATS. BUSINESS AS USUAL, ESPECIALLY IN TERMS OF THE STORY-FREE ASPECT. IT'S LIKE EXALTATION OF PEE IN THAT RESPECT -- REPETITIVE AND SORTA BORING -- JUST A BUNG-LOAD OF GALS PEEING IN SLOW MOTION FOR AN HOUR WHILE NEW AGE EUROTURD MUSIC TRIES ITS BEST TO ALIGN YOUR CHAKRAS. TO PEE OR NOT TO PEE? I THINK WE KNOW WHICH SIDE OF THAT QUESTION THIS GROUP IS STANDING ON, AND HOW BIG THE YELLOW PUDDLE IS.

DRINKING PISS FOR EROTIC AND SPIRITUAL BENEFITS ISN'T THE ONLY MANDATE THAT MISA HAS WHEN IT COMES TO URINE. THEY ALSO PUSH "URINOTHERAPY", A CONTROVERSIAL METHOD OF HEALING DISEASES VIA PEE-GULPING, THAT CAN BE OBVIOUSLY INCREDIBLY DANGEROUS WHEN USED IN PLACE OF COMMONPLACE MEDICINE, ESPECIALLY WHEN A DISEASE IS LIFE-THREATENING.

"FOR THE FIRST TIME IN THE HISTORY OF THE WORLD," THE OPENING NARRATION BREATHLESSLY EFFUSES, "A SECRET TANTRIC SOCIETY IS BREAKING THE SILENCE. 100 INITIATED WOMEN ARE DETERMINED TO PROVE THE FASCINATING RESULTS OF THE URINARY ORGASM. THEY DARE TO PRESENT A GIGANTIC FLOOD OF PEE; A UNIQUE OCEAN OF LUST. THESE 100 WOMEN SHOW YOU THEIR

PUSSY IS MAGIC!

WHICH TRANSLATED INTO ROMANIAN IS: VAGIN ESTE MAGIE

TRUE UNFAKED EXPERIENCES — THEIR SPONTANEOUS ECSTASY — A GROUP URINARY ORGASM WHICH CHANGES THE EROTIC MOOD OF THE PLANET."

MAN, AN OCEAN?! I GUESS NOTHING WILL DISTRACT THEM WHEN THESE EUROS ARE PEEIN! GET IT? EUROPEAN?! HAAAAH. OK, MOVING ON TO THE NEXT ONE.

BIG BOOB SUMMER BREAK (2004) THIS FEATURES FIVE LARGE-CHESTED ROMANIAN MISA GIRLS DRINKING BOOZE, LAUGHING, SLURPING AND SUCKING ON THEIR HUGE KNOCKERS, AND FUCKING THEIR OWN CUNTS AND BUTTS WITH DILDOS. CRISTINA STROE (AKA CRISA) IS ONE, A YOGA INSTRUCTOR FROM COSTANTA WHO USED TO BE ONE OF THE HORNY GURU'S LOVERS. IOANA BUTRUM (AKA JOANNA) IS ONE OF THE CULT'S CAM GIRLS, AND SHE AND HER MASSIVE SWEATER PUPPIES ARE IN THIS AS WELL. A SIXTH GIRL, KELLY KAY, IS A BRITISH PORN ACTRESS AND FROM WHAT I CAN TELL WAS SIMPLY A HIRED GUN TO HELP MARKET THE DVD. THE DRINKING OF ALCOHOL AND TOTAL LACK OF TANTRIC SEX EDUCATION OR PEEING IS A PRETTY BIG TIP-OFF THAT THIS ISN'T A MISA PRODUCTION AT ALL, AND WAS INSTEAD MADE BY MEMBERS THROUGH AN UNRELATED PRODUCTION COMPANY. I FIGURED IT WAS WORTH MENTIONING ANYWAY.

SO JUST WHO IS THE GUY BEHIND ALL OF THIS? GREGORIAN BIVOLARU WAS A ROMANIAN PLUMBER WHO STARTED TEACHING YOGA IN HIS SMALL CLASSROOM IN BUCHAREST BACK IN 1978, AND HE SAW HIS FAIR SHARE OF TROUBLE OVER THE YEARS. THE ROMANIAN GOVERNMENT WAS A COMMUNIST TOTALITARIAN DICTATORSHIP, AND OFFICIALLY ISSUED A LAW AGAINST ALL ORIENTAL PRACTICES OF MEDICINE AND TEACHING. THIS INCLUDED MARTIAL ARTS, TRANSCENDENTAL MEDITATION, ACUPUNCTURE, AND YOGA — AND THIS BIZARRE AND DRACONIAN LAW STAYED IN PLACE UNTIL THE REGIME WAS TOPPLED BY A VIOLENT REVOLUTION IN DECEMBER OF 1989.

GRIEG WAS BROUGHT UP ON CHARGES ON NUMEROUS OCCASIONS, AND SENTENCED TO PRISON AND MENTAL HOSPITALS MULTIPLE TIMES. BEING CHARGED WITH "PERFORMING BLACK MAGIC" AND DISTRIBUTING OBSCENE MATERIAL, AND THEN BEING LOCKED UP AND TORTURED FOR THOSE OFFENCES OBVIOUSLY DIDN'T SIT WELL WITH BIVOLARU, AND IT HELPED FOSTER HIS SEVERE DISTRUST OF AUTHORITY, BELIEF IN CONSPIRACIES, AND HIS ANTAGONISTIC STANCE TOWARDS THE WORLD RESIDING OUTSIDE HIS NEW AGE EASTERN RELIGION PHILOSOPHY. DESPITE THESE SETBACKS, HIS YOGA SECT'S POPULARITY AND HIS EGO GREW STEADILY THROUGH THE DECADES.

"MISA HAS TENS OF THOUSANDS OF MEMBERS IN THE COUNTRY AND THEIR NUMBER IS GROWING FAST", MIHAI RAPCEA, A LAWYER AND FORMER MEMBER OF MISA TOLD ROMANIA'S ZIUA NEWS IN MARCH 2012."OVER 80% OF THOSE WHO JOIN ARE INTELLECTUALS, SOME EVEN HAVING KEY POSITIONS IN THE STATE. PROSECUTORS, JUDGES, DOCTORS...IF THEY'RE NEEDED AND THEY DON'T DO WHAT THEY'RE SUPPOSED TO, OUT COMES THE FILM. DO YOU REMEMBER THE PORNO JUDGE SIMONA FLORINA LUNGU AND THE VIDEO SHOWN IN THE PRESS? WHO DO YOU THINK SENT IT?"

"I'VE LAST MET HIM ABOUT FOUR MONTHS AGO IN PARIS", RAPCEA CONTINUED. "HE LIVES IN THE SUBURBS, BUT IF YOU WANT TO MEET HIM, YOU MEET FOR COFFEE IN PLACE PIGALLE. IT'S A PLACE FULL OF SEX SHOPS AND HE ADORES GOING THERE. HE PICKS UP YOUNG, BEAUTIFUL WOMEN WHO SPEND THEIR TIME AROUND THERE. I TRIED TO EXPLAIN THAT I THINK HE'S WRONG IN DOING SO...BUT IT WAS FUTILE...HIS FOLLOWERS OCCASIONALLY SEND HIM NAKED PHOTOS OF YOUNG LADIES WHO HAVE JOINED MISA RECENTLY. HE CHOOSES ONE, TWO, MORE AND THEN CALLS THEM TO PARIS TO SPIRITUALIZE THEM THROUGH SEX. ONCE THEY 'LOSE THEIR INHIBITIONS' THEY ARE SENT TO JAPAN OR OTHER PLACES TO GET INVOLVED IN STRIPTEASE AND VIDEOCHAT... GURU HAS AN EXCEPTIONAL POWER OF CONVINCING PEOPLE, HE IS TRULY FASCINATING, AND THE YOUNG LADIES SOON COME TO THE CONCLUSION THAT THEY ARE DOING EVERYTHING FOR NOBLE PURPOSES, EVEN THOUGH THE SITUATION IS NOT LIKE THAT AT ALL.

AGNES MARQUES: 29 YEAR OLD POP SINGER AND VICTIM OF THE MISA CULT

A 29-YEAR-OLD PORTUGUESE MODEL AND POP SINGER BORN IN ROMANIA, AGNES ARABELA MARQUES, BECAME THE KEY WITNESS IN A ROMANIAN SUPREME COURT TRIAL IN 2013. MARGUES, ONE OF THE MISA LEADER'S FORMER LOVERS, CLAIMED THAT BIVOLARU USED HER, TRICKING HER INTO PROSTITUTING FOR HIM WHEN SHE WAS A 15-YEAR-OLD GIRL. SHE WAS THE KEY WITNESS FOR THE PROSECUTION IN THE

TRIAL OF THE SPIRITUAL LEADER.

"(HE) SAID THAT A GIRL'S SEXUAL CONTACT WITH HIM, AS A MASTER, ENSURED THAT THE GIRL WOULD BURN KARMA RAPIDLY", AGNES TOLD THE COURT. "WHICH MEANT THAT IN THIS WAY THE PERSON WOULD BE ABLE TO RID HERSELF OF ALL THE MISTAKES SHE'D DONE IN A PREVIOUS LIFE... I CONSIDERED THAT YOGI SPIRITUALITY WAS THE ONLY WAY TO LIVE AND BE HAPPIER, AND GREGORIAN BIVOLARU WAS LIKE A DIVINITY; I OFTEN PRAYED TO HIM HOPING THAT MY PRAYERS WOULD COME TRUE."

"HE TOOK MY VIRGINITY", SHE CONTINUED IN HER STATEMENT. "HE USED ME AT A YOUNG AGE FOR HIS SEXUAL SATISFACTION, TAKING ADVANTAGE OF THE FACT THAT HE WAS A YOGA TEACHER, BUT HE ALSO USED ME FOR MATERIAL PURPOSES, SINCE I WENT TO JAPAN FROM JANUARY TO JUNE 2003, UNDER THE TERMS THAT I SHOULD 'DONATE' ALL THE GOODS AND MONEY I RECEIVED THERE TO BIVOLARU. I UNDERSTOOD THE TRUE PURPOSE HE HAD IN MIND, NAMELY TO GET RICH.... HE GOT ME INTO SO MUCH TROUBLE HE MIGHT AS WELL HAVE PUT A BULLET THROUGH MY HEAD."

"BIVOLARU ALSO CLAIMED IN HIS TEACHINGS ABOUT YOGA THAT SEX WAS A PATH TOWARDS SPIRITUAL LIBERATION AND, MOREOVER, THAT IT ALLOWED THE YOUNG FEMALE YOGA PRACTITIONER TO ASCEND RAPIDLY TO A HIGH LEVEL OF TANTRIC SPIRITUALITY, WHICH GRIEG CALLED 'SAMADHI.' IN BUCHAREST I LIVED IN GREGORIAN BIVOLARU'S APARTMENT, ON CONSTANTIN MUAT STREET... NUMEROUS FEMALE YOGA STUDENTS WERE ALWAYS THERE. I KNOW THAT AT ONE POINT THERE WERE AS MANY AS 12 GIRLS WITH WHOM BIVOLARU HAD SEXUAL RELATIONS. THE GIRLS LIVING IN THAT APARTMENT STAYED THERE USUALLY FOR A FEW DAYS OR A FEW WEEKS, AFTER WHICH ANOTHER GIRL TOOK THEIR PLACE. BIVOLARU HIMSELF DECIDED WHO STAYED AND WHO WENT, BECAUSE HE WISHED TO ENSURE THE SO-CALLED 'STATE OF AVALANCHE'. THIS PHRASE, THE WAY BIVOLARU EXPLAINED IT, MEANT THAT IN ORDER TO KEEP SEXUAL DESIRE ALIVE IT WASN'T GOOD TO LIVE WITH YOUR PARTNER FOR TOO LONG."

"DURING THE COSTINETI YOGA CAMP IN 2002, A 12-YEAR-OLD GIRL, BLONDE, WITH LONG HAIR, RECEIVED ACCOMMODATION IN THE 'SCOICA' VILLA. I CAN'T REMEMBER THAT GIRL'S NAME AT THE MOMENT, BUT I CAN RECOGNIZE HER IF I SEE HER PHOTO. I THINK GRIEG HAD SEXUAL RELATIONS WITH HER, BECAUSE SHE STAYED OVERNIGHT IN THE SAME VILLA AS HIM, AND IT WAS NOTORIOUSLY KNOWN THAT HE ONLY ALLOWED THOSE GIRLS WHOM HE MADE LOVE TO, TO BE ROOMED IN THE VILLA."

THE JUDGE, MATEI IONUT, DELIBERATED ON THE CASE DESPITE RECEIVING A LETTER THAT TOLD HIM HE WOULD SOON "FEEL AND LIVE (PERSONALLY) THE DESERVED CONSEQUENCES" IF HE CONVICTED THE CULT LEADER. "AFTER YOU EXECUTE THE ORDER GIVEN (YOU KNOW BY WHOM!) TO THROW THE INNOCENT BIVOLARU BEHIND BARS, YOU WILL HAVE TO FACE THE OUTRAGED, FOR MANY YEARS TO COME AND ANSWER FOR YOUR ACTIONS", THE LETTER READ. MATEI GAVE THE LETTER TO THE POLICE AND MEDIA, AND THEN CONVICTED ANYHOW. BIVOLARU WAS FOUND GUILTY OF SEXUAL CONTACT WITH UNDERAGE WOMEN, SEXUAL PERVERSION, TRAFFICKING IN MINORS, AND OF ATTEMPTING AN ILLEGAL CROSSING OF ROMANIA'S BORDER. HE WAS SENTENCED TO 6 YEARS IN PRISON.

IN THE FIRST WEEK OF MAY 2014, THOUSANDS OF YOGINS GATHERED IN THE BEAUTIFUL ROMANIAN RESORT OF BAILE HERCULANE, SITUATED IN SOUTH WESTERN ROMANIA. THEY WERE GREGORIAN BIVOLARU'S FOLLOWERS AND WERE THERE FOR AN INTERNATIONAL YOGA SYMPOSIUM. CURRENTLY ON THE RUN FROM ROMANIAN AUTHORITIES AND REPORTEDLY RESIDING IN BOTH PARIS, FRANCE AND SWEDEN (WHERE HE'S BEEN ENJOYING POLITICAL ASYLUM SINCE 2005), BIVOLARU, NOW 62 YEARS OLD, MADE AN APPEARANCE FOR HIS DEVOTEES ALL THE SAME. IF THE PARTICIPANTS IN THE SYMPOSIUMS IN ROMANIA WANTED TO HANG OUT WITH HIM, THEY WERE TOLD THAT ALL THEY HAD TO DO WAS MEDITATE REALLY HARD, AND HE WOULD "TELEPATHICALLY CONNECT", IN LIEU OF ACTUALLY APPEARING IN PERSON.

SPECIAL THANKS TO MY NORWEGIAN PAL, VIDEO MIXTAPE CREATOR MIKKEL CHRISTENSEN, FOR THE IDEA TO DO THIS ARTICLE.

BOUGIE '14

Raw Force (1982. aka "Kung Fu Cannibals" Dir: Edward Murphy)

AS A DOCUMENTARY SUCH AS MACHETE MAIDENS UNLEASHED (2010) WILL ATTEST, THERE WERE A LOT OF VERY ENTERTAINING LOW-BUDGET AMERICAN MOVIES THAT UTILIZED THE PHILIPPINES AS A CHEAP WAY TO GET SOME EXPENSIVE-LOOKING EXOTIC ELEMENTS INTO THEIR DRIVE-IN FILMS IN THE 1970S. ONE OF THE LATER ONES (NOT APPEARING IN THEATERS UNTIL 1982) ALTHOUGH ONE OF MY FAVOURITES IF ONLY FOR ITS SHEER LUNACY, IS RAW FORCE.

THE MOVIE IS ALL ABOUT WARRIOR'S ISLAND, A DESOLATE HAUNTED PLOT OF EARTH FLOATING IN THE PACIFIC OCEAN THAT IS ENCIRCLED BY SCHOOLS OF FLESH EATING PIRANHA AND HOME TO BOTH FEMALE SLAVE TRAFFICKING, A DRUG RING HEADED BY A GUY WHO LOOKS LIKE HITLER, A GROUP OF GIGGLY CANNIBALISTIC MONKS IN ROBES (LED BY FILIPINO EXPLOITATION LEGEND VIC DIAZ), AND BLUE-SKINNED ZOMBIE MARTIAL ARTISTS. WITH THAT UP FOR GRABS, OF COURSE THE BURBANK KARATE CLUB WANT TO VACATION THERE, AND HOP A LITTLE CRUISE SHIP CAPTAINED BY CAMERON MITCHELL AND HIS REAL LIFE

GIRLFRIEND, HOPE HOLIDAY, WHO IS A FRAZZLED COMBINATION OF PHILLIS DILLER AND CLORIS LEACHMAN. THAT'S RIGHT, THIS INHOSPITABLE HELLISH ISLAND OF THE UNDEAD HAS A TRAVEL BROCHURE REPRESENTING IT! WHO PRINTED THOSE UP AND HOW DID THE HIMBOS IN THE BURBANK KARATE CLUB GET ONE?!

THIS MOVIE IS MIND-NUMBINGLY STUPID AND FUCKING HILARIOUS — NOT SO MUCH BECAUSE IT IS INEPT, BUT BECAUSE IT'S AGGRESSIVELY ILLOGICAL AND STUPID IN A CONFOUNDINGLY EARNEST WAY. IT'S TRYING SO HARD, YOU CAN'T HELP BUT LOVE IT. IT ALSO HELPS THAT IT IS RARELY DULL, AND SOMETHING INTERESTING IS HAPPENING AT ALL TIMES. EVEN DURING THE OH-SO PREDICTABLE DOWNTIME BETWEEN ACTION SCENES, NAKED SLAVE GIRLS, AND ZOMBIES, THE FILM STILL MANAGES TO BE TOTALLY ENTERTAINING — IF ONLY FOR THE WEIRD CHARACTERIZATIONS AND ODD DIALOG IT LOBS AT THE AUDIENCE LIKE TURD GRENADES. IF YOU LOVED SHOWS IN THE 1980S LIKE TALES OF THE GOLD MONKEY OR BRING 'EM BACK ALIVE (WHICH WERE BASICALLY LOW-BUDGET, HAM-FISTED TV VERSIONS OF RAIDERS OF THE LOST ARK), BUT WISHED THEY HAD MORE STRIP CLUBS, BAR FIGHTS, FULL FRONTAL NUDITY, KUNG FU, AND GORE, THIS NON-STOP BARRAGE OF TRASH BRILLIANCE WAS MADE FOR YOU. PARTAKE IN IT, POSTHASTE!

How far should a Teacher go to protect her students?

CROWN INTERNATIONAL PICTURES PRESENTS

They forced her to commit the ultimate sacrifice!

R

COLOR

TRIP with the TEACHER

TRIP WITH THE TEACHER (1975) DIR: EARL BARTON

FEATURING SCUMMY BIKERS, UNSEEMLY RAPE, A TASTE OF TAWDRY NUDITY, LUDICROUS DIALOGUE, AND A HEAD RUN OVER BY A MOTORCYCLE, TRIP WITH THE TEACHER IS ONE OF THE CLASSIC EXPLOITATION FILMS OF ITS ERA. NO, IT IS NOT AS SICK AS SOME (THE RAPE HAPPENS OFF SCREEN, FOR INSTANCE) BUT THERE IS A CRUEL EDGE TO THIS MOVIE THAT MIGHT SHAKE A FEW JADED FILMGOERS, EVEN.

WHEN A PRETTY TEACHER FERRYING A SCHOOL BUSLOAD OF GIGGLING TEENAGE SEXPOTS HAVE ENGINE PROBLEMS IN THE DESERT, A BUNCH OF SLEAZY RIDERS HEADED BY ZALMAN KING (WHO WOULD LATER GO ON TO DIRECT 9 1/2 WEEKS) SHOW UP AND TOW THE BUS WITH THEIR BIKES (WHAT?) TO AN OLD DILAPIDATED SHACK.

A SHACK IN THE MIDDLE OF THE DESERT WHERE A GANG HAVE NOTHING BUT A FEW KIDNAPPED TEENAGE VIRGINS TO KEEP THEM ENTERTAINED? OH, YOU KNOW WHAT GOES ON, AND THERE IS AN UNCOMFORTABLE AND POLITICALLY INCORRECT BRUTALITY IN THE WAY THE INNOCENCE CRUSHING IS DEPICTED.

KING IS MELODRAMATIC AS HE CHEWS SCENERY IN HIS WRAPAROUND SUNGLASSES THAT LEAD HIM TO RESEMBLE AN EVIL HOUSEFLY. HIS APPEARANCE HERE STANDS AS ONE OF THE BETTER PSYCHOPATH PERFORMANCES OF AMERICAN '70S DRIVE-IN CINEMA. HE'S THE KIND OF DIRT BAG THAT GROWLS CLASSY SHIT LIKE "YOU'LL BE SURPRISED WHAT A PIECE OF ASS WILL DO FOR MY DISPOSITION" TO A TEACHER WHILE GIVING HER SHUDDERING STUDENTS THE HAIRY EYEBALL.

—BOUGIE · 2010 ·

TANYA (1976. DIR: NATE RODGERS)

EVER SINCE VIEWING THE 2004 DOCUMENTARY GUERRILLA: THE TAKING OF PATTY HEARST, I'VE BEEN OBSESSED WITH THE STORY OF THE DAUGHTER OF A MILLIONAIRE INDUSTRIALIST WHO WAS KIDNAPPED AND BRAINWASHED INTO BECOMING A RADICAL POLITICAL TERRORIST. I'VE ALSO TRACKED DOWN MOST OF THE EXPLOITATION/SEXPLOITATION FILMS THAT USED THE STORY (WHILE IT WAS STILL IN THE HEADLINES) AS A SPRINGBOARD FOR TASTELESS GRINDHOUSE ENTERTAINMENT.

ONE SUCH TURD IS TANYA, AND DESPITE IT BEING MOSTLY UNLIKED BY OTHER GENRE FILM REVIEWERS, I REALLY ENJOYED IT. TRUE, THE CAST ARE DOWNRIGHT UNATTRACTIVE, AND THE RUNTIME IS A LITTLE TOO INUNDATED WITH SEX SEQUENCES FOR A SOFTCORE (BUT NEARLY HARDCORE) MOVIE, BUT DAMMIT, I ADORE THE CONCEPT OF THE LITTLE RICH WHITE GIRL (MARIA ARNOLD) KIDNAPPED BY THE BIG VIOLENT BLACK GUY (B.B. HINDS) IN AN OAKLAND GHETTO; A PRISONER OF WAR IN THE FIGHT AGAINST THE "CAPITALIST PIGS".

AFTER SOME STRIDENT TRAINING, OUR HORNY LIL' HONKY IS REBORN AS "TANYA", ALTHOUGH IT ISN'T THE POLITICAL STRUGGLE THAT HAS SWAYED HER, IT'S THE LIBIDINOUS AND GRAPHICALLY DEPICTED SEXUAL FREEDOM HER CAPTORS ENJOY. FREE TO LOSE HER SEXUAL HANG-UPS, SHE HAPPILY DOES SO WITH ANYONE AND EVERYONE WHO WILL BEND HER OVER AND THROW A SWEATY FUCK INTO HER GREASY MEATFLAPS. GO TANYA, GO! STICK IT TO THE MAN! YOU SHOW OL' TRICKY DICK NIXON WHO'S BOSS, BITCH.

TANYA IS ODDLY PLAYED FOR LAUGHS, AND WEIRDER STILL WRITER CHARLES TOWNSEND SEEMS QUITE SYMPATHETIC TO THE SLA CAUSE. I GUESS IN THE INSANE "ANYTHING GOES" WORLD OF '70S GRINDHOUSE MOVIEMAKING, NOTHING SHOULD BE SURPRISING.

—BOUGIE · 2010 ·

HARRY NOVAK presents

TANYA

EVERY SOLDIER NEEDS HIS PIECE!

SHE'LL MAKE YOU JOIN THE SEXUAL LIBERATION ARMY!

A BOXOFFICE INTERNATIONAL PICTURES RELEASE • COLOR ADMISSION RESTRICTED

BREAKNECK THRILLS:
INCREDIBLE DAREDEVIL DOCUMENTARIES!!

◆◇◆◇◆◇◆◇◆◇◆◇◆◇◆◇◆◇◆◇◆◇◆◇

Y'KNOW, I WAS JUST LOOKING AT MY COLLECTION OF DOCUMENTARIES TODAY, AND REALISED THAT I HAVE A LOT MORE FILMS ABOUT STUNTMEN THAN I THOUGHT I DID. I DON'T MEAN THE KIND OF STUNTMEN WHO SUBSTITUTE FOR ACTORS WHEN THERE IS A DANGEROUS SITUATION TO BE FILMED ON A SET, I MEAN THE EVEL KNIEVEL-ESQUE DAREDEVILS THAT CAPTURED THE IMAGINATION OF THE ENTIRE WORLD IN THE '70s. THESE WERE GLORYHOUNDS, AND I SUPPOSE THEIR MODERN DAY EQUIVALENT WOULD BE THOSE GUYS FROM **JACKASS**.

> ANOTHER R. BOUGIE ARTICLE FOR YOUR PLEASURE

THERE HAVE BEEN A HANDFUL OF CONTEMPORARY DOCUMENTARIES CATALOGUING THE EXPLOITS OF SUCH FEAR-FREE INDIVIDUALS. MOVIES LIKE **MAN ON WIRE** (2008), AND JULIE COHEN'S **THE WALL CRAWLER** FROM 1998. BUT I WANT TO FOCUS ON THE CLASSICS. THE STINK OF GASOLINE IN THE AIR AND THE SOUND -- NO -- THE FURIOUS <u>SCREAM</u> OF METAL-ON-METAL THAT REMINDS ME OF CHILDHOOD VISITS TO THE TRACTOR PULL AND THE SMASH-UP DERBY. THE SALT-OF-THE-EARTH FUNNY CARNAGE OF HAIRY MEN IN LEATHER WHO MADE VERY LITTLE COIN EVERY TIME THEY NEARLY GAUKED THEMSELVES -- BUT DID IT ANYWAY -- SIMPLY FOR THE SHOWMANSHIP OF IT ALL.

THE DEVIL AT YOUR HEELS (1981)

THIS ONE IS JUST ASTOUNDING, AND ONE OF MY FAVE DOCUMENTARIES OF ALL TIME, BAR NONE. SIMPLY PUT, THIS IS A CHARACTER SKETCH OF A MONTREAL-BORN STUNT MAN NAMED KEN CARTER. AS MENTIONED, THESE DAREDEVILS WERE GODDAMN <u>MENTAL CASES</u> -- AND KEN IN PARTICULAR MIGHT HAVE BEEN THE MOST INSANE OF THEM ALL. LISTEN, THIS CAT WANTED TO SHOOT OFF A GIANT TAKEOFF RAMP, FLY A CAR A FUCKING MILE ACROSS THE ST. LAWRENCE SEAWAY, AND LAND WHAT WAS LEFT IN SOME FLOWER BUSHES IN A COW PASTURE. HAHA!! GIVE THIS A WATCH AND SEE HOW THAT TURNED OUT! EVEN THE GREAT EVEL KNIEVEL SHOWS UP FOR A SCENE, AND ADVISES KEN TO GIVE HIS IMPOSSIBLE DREAM UP -- BUT NOTHING WOULD STOP HIM, AND NOTHING PREPARES YOU FOR THE SHOCKER ENDING.

> ☆ KEN CARTER ☆
> 1938 TO 1983

THE MOVIE WAS NARRATED BY CANADIAN ICON GORDON PINSENT, DIRECTED BY ROBERT FORTIER, AND PRODUCED BY THE NFB. IT CHRONICLED THE 5 YEARS OF SETBACKS (HOW SCARY IS AN EXPLODING FUEL TANK?) AND FUNDING MISHAPS (A MILLION DOLLARS WAS A <u>LOT</u> OF MONEY IN THE LATE '70s) TO BUILD A JET CAR, TEN STOREY RAMP, SEVERAL BLOCKS OF PAVEMENT IN A FARMER'S FIELD -- AND FINALLY THE JUMP ITSELF.

> KEN WAS JUST A GOOD OLD BOY... NEVER MEANIN' NO HARM...

15

◆◇◆◇◆◇◆◇◆◇◆◇◆◇◆◇◆◇◆◇◆◇◆◇◆◇◆◇◆◇◆◇◆◇

DEATH RIDERS (1976)

DOWN GO THE LIGHTS AND UP ROCKS THE DEATH RIDERS THEME SONG BY ROCKABILLY BAR STAR DORSEY BURNETTE. "DEATH RIDER... I DIDN'T NEED TO LEARN HOW" HE WARBLES IN A SOUTHERN DRAWL AS FLAMING BODIES FLY AND METAL CARNAGE ON WHEELS ROCKETS LOOSE IN A DANGEROUS DEMONSTRATION OF DESTRUCTION. MAMAS, DON'T LET YOUR BABIES GROW UP TO BE STUNTMEN.

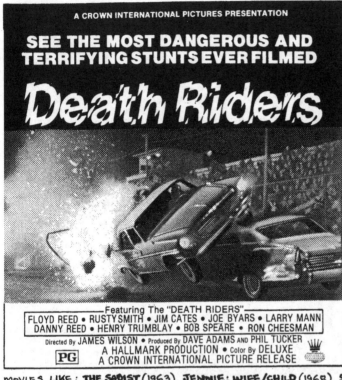

A CROWN INTERNATIONAL PICTURES PRESENTATION

SEE THE MOST DANGEROUS AND TERRIFYING STUNTS EVER FILMED

Death Riders

Featuring The "DEATH RIDERS"
FLOYD REED • RUSTY SMITH • JIM CATES • JOE BYARS • LARRY MANN
DANNY REED • HENRY TRUMBLAY • BOB SPEARE • RON CHEESMAN
Directed By JAMES WILSON • Produced By DAVE ADAMS and PHIL TUCKER
A HALLMARK PRODUCTION • Color By DELUXE
[PG] A CROWN INTERNATIONAL PICTURE RELEASE

MAYBE THE MOST UNDERRATED OF THIS SUBGENRE OF DOCUMEN-TARY, IT IS ONE THAT I KEEP COMING BACK TO. I FOUND THE AWESOME ORIGINAL CROWN INTERNATIONAL PRESSBOOK ON EBAY, AND IT IS ONE OF THE PRIZES OF MY COLLECTION. I REALLY LOVE THE LITTLE ILLUSTRATIONS DEPICTING EACH ONE OF THE DEATH DEFYING "SHATTERING CRASHES" THAT THE HIGHLIGHTED TRAVELLING GROUP PERFORMS FOR SMALL TOWN AUDIENCES WHO COME OUT TO SEE THEM AT STATE FAIRS AND WHATNOT.

VISUALLY, THIS MOVIE CRUSHES PUSS. THERE IS ALWAYS SOMETHING INTERESTING HAPPENING ON SCREEN, AND IT IS DOWNRIGHT EXCELLENT CINEMATOGRAPHY BY OSCAR WINNER, VILMOS ZSIGMOND. PRIOR TO HIS WORK HERE, HE'D BEEN DIRECTOR OF PHOTOGRAPHY FOR SOME OF MY OTHER GO-TO MOVIES OF THE SIXTIES AND SEVENTIES.

MOVIES LIKE: **THE SADIST** (1963), **JENNIE: WIFE/CHILD** (1968), **SATAN'S SADISTS** (1969), **DELIVERANCE** (1972), **THE SUGARLAND EXPRESS** (1974), AND BRIAN DEPALMA'S **OBSESSION** (1976). DESPITE VERY FEW DOCUMENTARIES IN HIS FILMOGRAPHY, THE RESULTS HERE TELL ME HE'S SUITED TO A CINEMA VERITE STYLE.

THE FILM DILIGENTLY FOLLOWS THE DEATH RIDERS MOTORCYCLE THRILL SHOW AS THEY

YOU WILL SEE THESE SHATTERING CRASHES... AND MORE!

Dive Bomber   **The People Jump**   **The Human Bomb**   **Tunnel Of Fire**

TOUR ACROSS AMERICA -- CIRCA 1974. ORIGINATING FROM DANVILLE, ILLINOIS, THE THRILL SHOW CONSISTED OF A GROUP OF 17 AND 18-YEAR-OLD KIDS WHO DIDN'T SEEM TO KNOW FEAR, AND ADVERTISED THAT THEY DID THEIR STUNTS WITH "NO TRICKY GIMMICKS, NO REHERSALS, AND NO SPECIAL SAFETY PRECAUTIONS!". OF COURSE AS A TEENAGE BOY, THE BEST PART OF YOUR SHOW IS THE END IF YOU'VE REMAINED ALIVE TO MEET-N-GREET WITH ALL THE RUTTING TEENAGE GIRLS THAT SURROUND YOU -- THEIR BOUNCING SNOOPIES STRAINING AGAINST TIGHT T-SHIRTS DECORATED WITH MUSCLECAR IRON-ONS. YES, DESPITE THE CARNAGE, THE HEAD-ON COLLISIONS, AND ALL THE BREATHLESS ACTION, THESE SHORT REVEALING SCENES ARE THE MOST CANDID ON DISPLAY IN DEATH RIDERS -- A MOVIE TRULY FROM A DIFFERENT ERA. FIND IT!

WARNING: THESE STUNTS ARE PERFORMED BY PROFESSIONALS, AND ARE EXTREMELY DIFFICULT AND DANGEROUS. PLEASE DO NOT ATTEMPT THEM YOURSELF!

◆◇◆◇◆◇◆◇◆◇◆◇◆◇◆◇◆◇◆◇

THE LAST OF THE GLADIATORS (1988)

THOSE "WIDE WORLD OF SPORTS" EPISODES FEATURING THE TESTICLE-TWISTING MOTORCYCLE LEAPS OF MR. EVEL KNIEVEL WERE BREAD N' BUTTER STAPLES OF THE SEVENTIES, AND HAD KIDS ALL UP AND DOWN MY BLOCK RECREATING WHAT THEY'D SEEN WITH THEIR OWN MINIATURE FEATS OF DARING ON LITTLE BANANA SEAT BIKES. CAN YOU IMAGINE PARENTS TODAY DEALING WITH THAT? SHIT, THEY DON'T EVEN LET THEIR KIDS TRICK OR TREAT ALONE THESE DAYS -- MUCH LESS LAUNCH THEMSELVES OFF RAMPS.

IN 1988 A DOCUMENTARY COLLECTED THE EYE-POPPIN' HIGHLIGHTS OF EVEL'S '70s HEYDAY, AND IT REMAINS THE BEST VISUAL DOCUMENT ABOUT THE MAN I'VE BEEN ABLE TO FIND. THIS ISN'T THE KIND OF BOUNCING AROUND THAT HIS SON, ROBBIE, DOES TODAY ON LIGHT MOTOCROSS BIKES. DUDES, EVEL WAS POWER-JUMPING 300+ POUND XR-750 HARLEYS -- THE KIND OF BIKES THAT WERE NOT DESIGNED TO LEAVE THE GROUND. HIS RECORD WAS A FOURTEEN GREYHOUND BUS LEAP (133 FEET) AT KING'S ISLAND, OHIO IN 1976 -- A RECORD THAT WOULD STAND FOR 25 YEARS.

HIS TRIUMPHS WERE WIGGIDY-WILD, BUT HIS DEFEATS WERE JUST AS ENTERTAINING. WHEN EVEL ATE SHIT AT WEMBLEY STADIUM IN LONDON WHILE ATTEMPTING TO CLEAR 13 DOUBLE DECKER BUSES, THE WORLD'S MOUTH HUNG AGAPE AS WE ALL WITNESSED A MAN'S PELVIS BEING COMPLETELY SHATTERED. OR HOW ABOUT WHEN KNIEVEL SOARED HIGH OVER THE FOUNTAIN THAT FRONTED CEASAR'S PALACE IN LAS VEGAS, AND THEN SLAMMED UNCEREMONIOUSLY INTO THE PAVEMENT, BREAKING HIS BACK?

"IT WAS A HORRIBLE JUMP", EVEL WOULD RECOUNT. "I JUST WASN'T GOING FAST ENOUGH, AND I WAS UNCONSCIOUS FOR 29 DAYS. MY WIFE WAS THERE WHEN I CAME OUT OF IT. SHE WAS SITTING THERE ALONGSIDE OF ME, SHE'D BEEN THERE WITH ME THE WHOLE TIME."

ANOTHER MAJOR EVEL EVENT THAT IS MOSTLY FORGOTTEN TODAY (PROBABLY BECAUSE THE FOOTAGE IS SADLY MISSING FROM LAST OF THE GLADIATORS) IS THE 1977 "JAWS" JUMP IN CHICAGO WHEN EVEL TRIED TO SOAR OVER A TANK OF LIVE SHARKS. HE DIDN'T END UP SWIMMING WITH THE BLOODTHIRSTY MAN-EATERS, BUT THERE WAS A WICKED WIPE OUT, ANOTHER SERIOUS INJURY, AND

THE EXCITING ADVENTURES OF

EVEL KNIEVEL AND HIS STUNT CYCLE

EVEL KNIEVEL™ SCRAMBLE VAN™ COMPLETE WITH RAMP, TRAILER, LIVING QUARTERS AND WORKSHOP WITH SCALE TOOLS!

SHIT, YEAH!

REMOVABLE HELMET

SPELLBINDING HANDSTANDS FROM ONE ROOM TO ANOTHER!

ADD MORE EXCITEMENT WITH 2 STUNT RIDERS!

REMOVABLE SWAGGER STICK

WTF?!

JUMPS YOUR SET OF ENCYCLOPEDIAS VOLUMES A THROUGH W!

SHOCK-ABSORBING FRONT WHEEL

FUCKING SWEET!!

A CAMERAMAN WHO LOST AN EYE TO A FLYING METAL SHARD.

ALSO IN 1977, A BIOGRAPHY (EVEL KNIEVEL ON TOUR) WRITTEN BY HIS FORMER PUBLICIST, SHELLY SALTMAN, CATAPULTED EVEL INTO A REDNECK RAGE CULMINATING IN A SEVERE BEATING FOR SHELLY ON THE 20TH CENTURY FOX STUDIO LOT. A BASEBALL BAT WIELDED BY KNIEVEL BROKE MULTIPLE BONES IN THE ARMS OF THE "JACK OFF" WRITER, AND WHEN THE NEWS OF THE ASSAULT WAS BROADCAST ON TV, SALTMAN'S MOTHER WITNESSED IT AND HAD A HEART ATTACK. SHE PASSED AWAY 3 MONTHS LATER.

A CIVIL COURT JUDGE CALLED KNIEVEL'S ACTS "COWARDLY" AND AWARDED SALTMAN NEARLY $13 MILLION IN DAMAGES. ON TOP OF THAT, EVEL WOULD END UP IN PRISON AFTER A CONVICTION FOR THE VIOLENT CRIME, DOING A STRETCH OF FIVE MONTHS AND 22 DAYS. AT ONE POINT HE FOUND HIMSELF SHARING THE CELEBRITY TIER WITH CHARLES MANSON.

"THEY BROUGHT HIM IN AND PUT HIM NEXT TO ME." EVEL TOLD POPSMEAR MAGAZINE IN OCTOBER OF 1998. "HE WAS THERE FOR A PSYCHIATRIC EVALUATION FROM THE PRISON HE WAS IN. THERE WERE ONLY SIX CELLS IN THERE. YOU COULDN'T EVEN SEE YOUR HAND IN FRONT OF YOUR FACE WHEN THEY LOCKED THE DOOR."

WHAT WORDS WERE SHARED BETWEEN THE TWO ICONIC MEN WERE NEVER MADE PUBLIC BY EITHER, AND AFTER KNIEVEL'S DEATH IN LATE 2007, SALTMAN ANNOUNCED HE WOULD BE SUING THE ESTATE FOR THE UNPAID MONEY, WHICH HE CLAIMS NOW TOTALS OVER A HUNDRED MILLION BUCKS WITH INTEREST.

THE STUNTMEN (1973)
MUCHO THANKS GO TO CODE RED DVD FOR INCLUDING THIS FEATURE LENGTH RARITY AS A BONUS FEATURE ON THEIR RELEASE OF THE SPECIAL EDITION OF OZPLOITATION MAESTRO BRIAN TRENCHARD-SMITH'S **STUNT ROCK** (1978) -- WHICH NOT SO COINCIDENTALLY WAS MY FAVOURITE DVD RELEASE OF 2009. TRENCHARD-SMITH'S DOCUMENTARY ABOUT THE MAN WHO MADE STUNT ROCK POSSIBLE, AUSSIE STUNT-KING, GRANT PAGE, IS SO MUCH MORE THAN A DVD EXTRA FEATURE. THE MOVIE PAYS TRIBUTE TO THE GREATEST AUSTRALIAN STUNTMEN OF THE DAY, SHOWING VARIOUS TYPES OF STUNTS (BURNS, FALLS, CRASHES, EXPLOSIONS), THEN BREAKING THEM DOWN AND SHOWING HOW THEY'RE ACHIEVED.

– BOUGIE '12

CINEMA SEWER HALL OF FAME:

ROBERTA PEDON

ROBERTA PEDON STARTED MODELLING HER GORGEOUS 48-24-34 FRAME IN JUNE OF 1973 FOR HOLLYWOOD'S AMERICAN ART ENTERPRISES, A COMPANY THAT SUPPLIED A LOT OF PORN PRODUCT (BOTH SMUT MAGAZINES AND PAPERBACK PULP) TO THE NEWSTANDS OF THE DAY. HER MODELLING CAREER LASTED A SHORT TWO AND HALF YEARS, AND SHE ONLY MADE ONE SINGLE MOVIE -- THE 1975 DRIVE-IN CLASSIC **DELINQUENT SCHOOLGIRLS**. DESPITE THIS MEAGRE RESUME, WE NONETHELESS DEEM ROBERTA MORE THAN WORTHY OF CS HALL OF FAME STATUS. IN FACT, IT WOULD BE HARD TO ARGUE THAT SHE DID NOT END UP AS ONE OF THE MOST POPULAR NUDE MODELS OF THE 1970S.

THIS GORGEOUS GREEN-EYED GIRL WITH ENORMOUS HOOTERS AND A KNOCKOUT CURVY FIGURE WAS REPORTEDLY BADGERED BY HER OVERBEARING MOTHER TO LOSE WEIGHT AS A 15-YEAR-OLD, A MOM THAT TOLD HER OFTEN THAT HER BODY WAS "FREAKISH". INTRODUCED TO SEX AT THE AGE OF TWELVE, SHE ONCE REVEALED THAT HER CONSIDERABLE COCKSUCKING SKILL WAS A BY-PRODUCT OF FREQUENT PREGNANCY AVOIDANCE IN HER TEENS. INDEED, OVER THE NEXT FEW YEARS ROBERTA DELVED INTO A LIFESTYLE OF NEARLY NON-STOP FUCKING AND DRUGS, A SAD AND EXTENDED GRASP FOR LOVE AND ACCEPTANCE FROM THE MEN WHO CONSISTENTLY USED AND REJECTED HER.

. CONTINUED ON THE NEXT PAGE .

YOUNGBLOOD

LAWRENCE
HILTON
JACOBS
IN
"YOUNGBLOOD"

I'M ON A LAWRENCE HILTON-JACOBS KICK AT THE MOMENT. HE'S BEST KNOWN FOR HIS ROLE ON **WELCOME BACK KOTTER**, BUT THIS DUDE COULD REALLY ACT, AND IF NOT FOR THE FACT THAT IT WAS HARDER BACK IN THE DAY FOR BLACK FOLK TO GET GOOD ROLES, HE WOULD PROBABLY HAVE DONE MUCH BETTER FOR HIMSELF AND HIS CAREER.

SEEING HIM IN **COOLEY HIGH** (1975) WAS WHAT STARTED ME ON HIM. WHAT A GREAT LITTLE MOVIE. IN FACT, L.H.J WAS SO GOOD, IT WAS THIS PERFORMANCE THAT GOT HIM NOTICED BY THE KOTTER CASTING DEPT. HIS OTHER CAREER STANDOUT WAS PLAYING JOE JACKSON IN THE TV MOVIE **THE JACKSONS: AN AMERICAN DREAM** (1992).

TONIGHT I GOT TO SEE A RARITY FROM 1978 CALLED **YOUNGBLOOD** AND I REALLY ENJOYED IT. IT'S A DECENT LITTLE GANG MOVIE, WITH LAWRENCE STEALING THE SHOW AS THE LEADER OF A GROUP CALLED THE KINGSMEN. A KID NAMED YOUNGBLOOD (BRYAN O'DELL) JOINS UP, AND THE GANG DOES WHAT IT CAN TO RID THE HOOD OF DRUG DEALING SCUMBAGS. PICTURE A BLAXPLOITATION THE OUTSIDERS, AND YOU'LL BE IN THE RIGHT BALL PARK. ANYWAY, IT'S GOOD, BUT UNFORTUNATELY YOU DON'T HAVE MUCH ELSE TO CHOOSE FROM IF YOU WANNA SEE MORE L.H.J STARRING ROLES FOR ANOTHER DECADE AFTER YOUNGBLOOD. HIS NEXT "BIG" MOVIE (IF YOU CAN CALL IT THAT) IS THE LOW-BUDGET TRILOGY OF **L.A. HEAT** (1989) WITH JIM BROWN, **L.A. VICE** (1989) WITH WILLIAM SMITH, AND **ANGELS OF THE CITY** (1989), ABOUT A BUNCH OF PIMPS WHO KIDNAP SOME SORORITY GIRLS. ALL THREE FILMS FEATURE LAWRENCE AS DETECTIVE JON CHANCE. A FOURTH MOVIE SIMPLY CALLED **CHANCE** WAS ALSO SHAT OUT IN 1990.

WHAT HAPPENED TO HIM FOR 10 YEARS? I MEAN, ASIDE FROM DATING LATOYA JACKSON AND RELEASING THREE LPS. (HE SANG GOOD TOO!) THE MAN WAS IN HIS PRIME AND HEADLINING MOVIES BASED ON HIS 1975-79 KOTTER FAME, AND THEN POOF. HE SHOULDA BEEN A STAR.

· CONTINUED FROM PREVIOUS PAGE ·

THE EMBODIMENT OF THE QUINTESSENTIAL FANTASY HIPPIE CHICK, PEDON MADE HER HOME IN VENICE, CALIFORNIA, WORKED AS A STRIPPER AT THE 'CLASSIC CAT' IN HOLLYWOOD WHEN SHE WASN'T MODELLING FOR STROKE MAGS, AND FILLED THE REST OF HER DAYS WHORING IN ORDER TO FEED HER VORACIOUS DRUG HABIT. DURING THIS TIME SHE DATED ACTOR BOB CRANE AND AMERICAN ART EDITOR GUS HASFORD, WHO IS BETTER KNOWN TODAY AS THE AUTHOR OF "THE SHORT TIMERS" -- THE STORY STANLEY KUBRICK WOULD ADAPT AS **FULL METAL JACKET**. YES, EVEN AS A JUNKIE HOOKER ROBERTA MANAGED TO BREAK HEARTS WITH HER WINSOME SMILE AND GIANT BOUNCING RACK.

THINGS WOULD SOON GET FAR WORSE THOUGH. SHORTLY AFTER BEING ARRESTED IN SEPT. 1975 FOR PROSTITUTION, A.A.E TOLD HER TO GET LOST, AND SHE SPENT THE REST OF THE DECADE IN A DRUGGY HAZE AMONGST VARIOUS CHARACTERS OF ILL-REPUTE. THE LAST PERSON TO REPORT SEEING HER WAS A FORMER LOVER WHO TOLD PEDON MEGAFAN CHARLES L. SMITH THAT IN DECEMBER OF 1979 HE DROVE ROBERTA TO A HARDCORE SHOOT IN PACIFIC PALISADES, SOUTH OF LA. BY THIS POINT SHE WAS HOMELESS, AND HER FAMOUS FULL FIGURE HAD WITHERED AWAY TO A MERE 90 POUNDS SOAKING WET.

DETAILS GET VERY VERY SKETCHY IN THE EARLY '80S (I LIKE THE CRAZY BANK ROBBERY RUMOUR), BUT THE MOST LIKELY SCENARIO FINDS ROBERTA STREETWALKING IN SAN FRANCISCO BEFORE SHE FINALLY EITHER CLEANED UP HER ACT OR PASSED AWAY.

NOTE: VARIOUS ONLINE SITES CLAIM THAT OUR GAL DIED OF LIVER DISEASE ON THE 30th OF JULY 1982 IN THE ALAMEDA COUNTY HOSPITAL -- BUT THIS INFORMATION IS BASED ON THE ASSUMPTION THAT HER BIRTH NAME WAS ROSMA GRANTOVISKIS, A FACT THAT STILL REMAINS TOTALLY UNPROVEN.

— BOUGIE '12

HAUSU (JAPAN. 1977)

"MY DAUGHTER CHIGUMI WAS THIRTEEN YEARS OLD AT THE TIME, AND WAS ABSOLUTELY MAD ABOUT CINEMA. SHE'D JUST GOT OUT OF THE BATH AND WAS DOING HER MAKE-UP, BRUSHING HER LONG HAIR THAT SHE WAS SO PROUD OF IN A MIRROR."

"THEY'RE LOOKING FOR A TREATMENT FOR AN EXCITING FILM LIKE JAWS. WHAT DO YOU THINK?" I ASKED HER. SHE SAID, "IF MY REFLECTION IN THE MIRROR COULD JUMP OUT AND EAT ME, THAT'D BE SCARY.'"

— DIRECTOR NOBUHIKO OBAYASHI

SERIOUSLY, HOW DOES ONE EVEN CATEGORISE THIS MIND-MELTER? HORROR? FANTASY? COMEDY? PSYCHEDELIA? IT PROVES THE ADAGE THAT THE MOST ENDURING AND IMPORTANT ART IS THE KIND THAT CANT BE EASILY DEFINED AND PIGEONHOLED. WHATEVER IT IS, ITS THE CINEMATIC REDISCOVERY OF THE YEAR, AND TELLS THE DECEPTIVELY SIMPLE TALE OF SEVEN GIRLS WHO TAKE A TRIP TO THE COUNTRYSIDE TO SPEND THEIR SUMMER VACATION AT AN OLD HOUSE BELONGING TO ONE OF THEIR AUNTS. EACH GIRL'S NAME SUITS THEIR PERSONALITY/OBSESSION: MAC (THE OVER EATER), KUNG-FU (KICKS ASS), MELODY (THE PIANO PLAYER), AND SO ON -- BUT IT IS NOT THE CHARACTERS OR PLOT THAT MAKE THIS, IT IS THE WAY IN WHICH THEY ARE AESTHETICALLY PRESENTED: WARPED AND TWISTED LIKE A GODDAMN PRETZEL.

NOBUHIKO OBAYASHI (WHO WAS A 40-YEAR-OLD FIRST-TIMER WHEN HE GOT THIS OUT IN 1977) MADE HIS 13 YEAR OLD DAUGHTER A CREDITED COLLABORATOR, AND FESTOONED HER CONCEPTS WITH NIGHTMARISH GOOF JUICE, ROCKETING THE AUDIENCE THROUGH A CRAZY CUT-AND-PASTE FUNHOUSE TOUR. AT SEVERAL POINTS I LITERALLY FELT AS IF I WAS HIGH DESPITE BEING STONE COLD SOBER. I GIGGLED LIKE A FIEND WHILE WITNESSING CLASSIC CREEPY GHOST FX, A MIRROR THAT MAKES YOUR FACE EXPLODE INTO FLAMES, A PIANO THAT EATS GIRLS, A MYSTICAL WITCH CAT, A BANANA-MAN, BENNY HILL-STYLE SPED UP ACTION, SCHOOLGIRL MARTIAL ARTS PUMMELLING, DANCING SKELETONS, DISEMBODIED HEADS, AND SO ON AND SO FORTH. AMAZING. ASTONISHED TOHO STUDIO REPRESENTATIVE ISAO MATSUOKA REPORTEDLY TOLD OBAYASHI "I'VE NEVER SEEN SUCH AN INCOMPREHENSIBLE SCRIPT," AND MEANT IT AS A COMPLIMENT. IF THAT ISNT RECOMMENDATION ENOUGH, LET ME SAY THIS: HAUSU IS LIFE-ALTERING, ENTHRALLING, AND UTTERLY REQUIRED VIEWING.

— BOUGIE
2010

メロディー

ファンタ

ガリ

スウィート

クンフー

マック

オシャレ

ILLUSTRATION BY ADAM WILSON:
HTTP://ADUBYA.LIVEJOURNAL.COM

THE STORY OF PRUNELLA

I'VE SLUNG A LOT OF INK ABOUT THE FILMS OF TIMES SQUARE XXX PRODUCTION HOUSE AVON PICTURES IN THE PAGES OF CINEMA SEWER OVER THE YEARS, BUT IT MAY WELL BE THAT I'VE SAVED THE BEST FOR LAST WITH 1982'S THE STORY OF PRUNELLA.

THE BLEAK FETISHISTIC PLOT IS RIGHT OUT OF A DIRTY BOOK STORE PAPERBACK: ON THE WAY TO A BRIDAL SHOWER PRUNELLA, (THE CLASSY AMBROSIA FOX) AND HER MOTHER ARE KIDNAPPED BY THREE PRISON ESCAPEES (GEORGE PAYNE AND CO.) WHO HAVE A PET PROSTITUTE (CHERI CHAMPAGNE) AS PART OF THEIR GANG. THE ENTIRE GROUP OF BOTH KIDNAPPERS AND KIDNAPPEES THEN STORMS INTO THE INNOCENT BRIDAL SHOWER AND THE SCENE DEVOLVES FROM CELEBRATORY INTO A SADIST'S WETDREAM. SWEATY DEGRADATION, RAPE, AND SEXUAL TORMENT BREAKS OUT LIKE WILDFIRE IN EVERY CORNER OF THE ROOM.

THE FILM IS DIRECTED BY PHIL PRINCE, NEW YORK'S GRINDHOUSE KING OF THE EARLY '80S ROUGHIE. REGARDLESS OF HIS ACTUAL INTENT, PHIL MADE SOME OF THE MOST UNIQUE ADULT FILMS IN AMERICAN MOVIE HISTORY, WITH HIS WORK ACTUALLY TRANSCENDING THE ROUGHIE GENRE AND MELTING EFFORTLESSLY INTO HORROR AND EXPLOITATION PUDDLES. AS 42ND STREET PETE ONCE WROTE: "WHERE MOST OF YOUR 1980S ADULT FILM DIRECTORS STROKED YOUR LIBIDO WITH A VELVET GLOVE, PHIL PRINCE STOKED IT WITH A FIST WRAPPED IN BARBED WIRE AND DIPPED IN CRISCO. ANYONE WANDERING INTO THE AVON 7 THEATER BACK IN THE DAY, THINKING THIS WAS YOUR TYPICAL 'SIT DOWN AND ENJOY IT' KIND OF A FILM, QUICKLY HAD THEIR LIBIDO FLATLINED."

ONLY AVAILABLE IN LOW QUALITY BOOTLEG VERSIONS FOR DECADES, THE DVD RELEASE TO HUNT DOWN IS AFTER HOURS'S SPECIAL EDITION WHICH FEATURES THE AMAZING "PRINCE OF PORN" DOCUMENTARY, AND A COMMENTARY TRACK BY EDITOR BRIAN O'HARA, WHO REVEALS ALL KINDS OF JUICY BEHIND-THE-SCENES TRIVIA ABOUT THE CONTEMPTIBLE, OVER-THE-TOP PROCEEDINGS. THE 4 MINUTES OF OUTTAKES ALSO INCLUDED ARE JUST AS RIVETING AND EYE-OPENING. AS A LONG-TIME FAN OF GEORGE PAYNE IT WAS FASCINATING WATCHING HIM TRANSFORM FROM A NORMAL SHMUCK TO A SCREAMING, SPITTING PSYCHO IN THE BLINK OF AN EYE. WHO SAYS PORN STARS DON'T HAVE ANY ACTING SKILLS?

HISTORICALLY SPEAKING, THE MOVIE (ALONG WITH AVON'S THE TAMING OF REBECCA) IS NOTEWORTHY FOR BEING SINGLED OUT BY THE CONSERVATIVE REAGAN-ERA MEESE COMMISSION AS ONE OF THE "MOST VILE AND VIOLENT EXAMPLES OF MOB-CONTROLLED PORNOGRAPHY" IN AMERICA.

THE STORY OF PRUNELLA WAS NOT ONLY ONE OF THE BEST DISCS OF 2009, IT STANDS AS ONE OF THE BEST XXX DVD RELEASES OF ALL TIME.

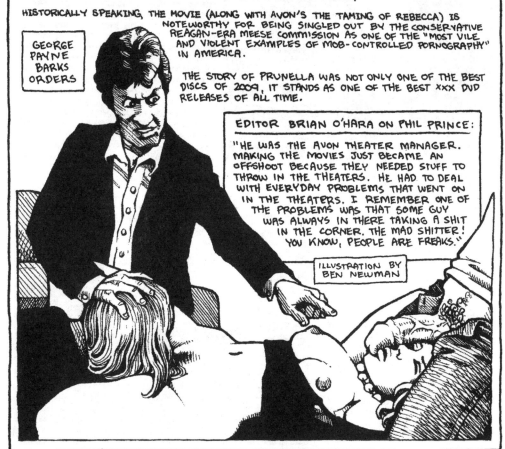

GEORGE PAYNE BARKS ORDERS

EDITOR BRIAN O'HARA ON PHIL PRINCE:

"HE WAS THE AVON THEATER MANAGER. MAKING THE MOVIES JUST BECAME AN OFFSHOOT BECAUSE THEY NEEDED STUFF TO THROW IN THE THEATERS. HE HAD TO DEAL WITH EVERYDAY PROBLEMS THAT WENT ON IN THE THEATERS. I REMEMBER ONE OF THE PROBLEMS WAS THAT SOME GUY WAS ALWAYS IN THERE TAKING A SHIT IN THE CORNER. THE MAD SHITTER! YOU KNOW, PEOPLE ARE FREAKS."

ILLUSTRATION BY BEN NEWMAN

Stingray

"WE WON'T BE SLOWING DOWN BECAUSE WE'RE DRIVING THESE WHEELS INTO THE GROUND" SINGS JERRY RIOPELLE THROUGHOUT AN EXTENDED CHASE SCENE IN STINGRAY, A PECULIAR MIXTURE OF COMEDY AND BALL BUSTING ACTION. THE ALWAYS CARDBOARD (AND YET SOMEHOW ALWAYS ENTERTAINING) CHRIS MITCHUM AND HIS PAL LES LANNOM PLAY A COUPLE OF UNASSUMING YOUNG GENTS WHO BUY A USED 1964 CORVETTE THAT TURNS OUT TO BE A STOLEN CAR JAM-PACKED WITH MOBSTER MONEY AND DRUGS. SHERRY JACKSON (AS ABIGAIL BRATOWSKI) IS A SEXY BITCHTATOR WHO DRESSES LIKE A NUN, STEALS EVERY SCENE SHE'S IN, AND SENDS HER GOONS AFTER THE BOYS. RICHARD TAYLOR WROTE, EDITED AND DIRECTED THIS GENUINELY EXCITING DRIVE-IN CLASSIC IN ST. LOUIS BACK IN 1978, BUT COULDN'T MANAGE TO PARLAY THE EFFORT INTO ANYTHING ASIDE FROM A LITTLE TURD CALLED STAKE OUT ON 10TH STREET (2005) HE MADE THIRTY YEARS LATER. THIS IS PRETTY MUCH GONNA BE REQUIRED VIEWING IF YOU'RE A SHERRY JACKSON OR CHRISTOPHER MITCHUM FAN.

YEEE-HAWW!

Get wrecked! Get chased! Get smashed! Get it on! The big red hot one is in town!

Written and Directed by
RICHARD TAYLOR

dans le ⚡⚡ lager 5 des experiences monstrueuses c'est

L'ENFER DES FEMMES

UN FILM DE
GARRONE SERGIO · avec MARCHA CARVEN · PAOLA CORAZZI

SS EXPERIMENT LOVE CAMP (1976) AKA "SS EXPERIMENT"

SERGIO GARRONE HAS GOT TO BE THE KING OF THE LOW-BUDGET NAZISPLOITATION CHUNKBLOWERS. AT LEAST, IF YOU'RE HANDING OUT PROPS FOR WHOEVER MANAGED TO CHURN OUT THE MOST. IN THIS ONE, A HERD OF FEMALE PRISONERS GET SHIPPED TO A NAZI TORTURE CAMP WHERE GROTESQUE GOOSESTEPPERS PERFORM SICKENING EXPERIMENTS ON THEIR TENDER YOUNG FLESH. ARE YOU DOWN FOR QUIVERING JEWESSES PISSING THEMSELVES AS THEY'RE ELECTROCUTED, FROZEN SOLID AND BURNED ALIVE? YOU ALSO SEE OVARIES GETTING TUGGED OUT, LAB COAT WEARING LESBO FRAULINES THAT SOUND LIKE WILMA FLINTSTONE, AN ANGRY SCROTUMLESS DUDE, AND UNDERWATER FUCKING. A PERFECT DATE MOVIE IF THERE EVER WAS ONE.

– BOUGIE

THE SUGARLAND EXPRESS (1974)

YOU YOUNGER READERS MAY THINK I'M JUST JOSHING AROUND, BUT I'M SERIOUS WHEN I SAY THAT THERE WAS ONCE A TIME WHEN STEVEN SPIELBERG DIDN'T SUCK. THERE WAS EVEN ONCE A TIME WHEN SPIELBERG WAS ONE OF THE MOST INTERESTING AND INNOVATIVE YOUNG DIRECTORS IN HOLLYWOOD! LOOK AT HIS FIRST 3 MOVIES, FOR INSTANCE: DUEL (1971), THE SUGARLAND EXPRESS (1974), AND JAWS (1975). FLIPPIN' INCREDIBLE MOVIES, ALL THREE. SUGARLAND EXPRESS IS PROBABLY THE LEAST KNOWN, BUT IT'S WELL-LOVED BY THOSE OF US WHO APPRECIATE A GOOD DRIVE-IN HICKSPLOITATION ROAD MOVIE. CHECK THIS ONE OUT.

IT'S NOT EVERY DAY YOU TAKE A RIDE LIKE THIS!

A ZANUCK / BROWN PRODUCTION **GOLDIE HAWN**
in **THE SUGARLAND EXPRESS**

co-starring
BEN JOHNSON MICHAEL SACKS · WILLIAM ATHERTON
Music by JOHN WILLIAMS · Screenplay by HAL BARWOOD
& MATTHEW ROBBINS · Story by STEVEN SPIELBERG and HAL BARWOOD &
MATTHEW ROBBINS · Directed by STEVEN SPIELBERG · Produced by RICHARD D. ZANUCK

22

NOT SHOWING UP ON NEARLY AS MANY CRITICS' "TOP SPAGHETTI WESTERN" LISTS AS THE USUAL SUSPECTS FROM THE BRILLIANT FILMOGRAPHIES OF LEONE OR CORBUCCI THE TONINO VALERII CLASSIC DAY OF ANGER (1967) NONETHELESS DESERVES THE SAME ACCOLADES, AND WILL FIND SOME ON THIS PAGE. I'M GONNA ACCOLADE A BOOT UP ITS ASS, BUT FIRST LET US MOSEY ON THROUGH A SYNOPSIS.

SCOTT (GIULIANO GEMMA) IS A YOUNG GUY WORKING FOR PENNIES AS A SHIT SWEEPER/GARBAGE COLLECTOR IN A SMALL WESTERN TOWN CALLED CLIFTON. AN ORPHANED "BASTARD CHILD OF A WHORE" WITH NO SELF-RESPECT, SCOTT IS TREATED LIKE THE TOWN TARD BY THE LOCALS, WHO MOCK AND BULLY HIM ONLY BECAUSE THEY CAN DO SO WITH IMPUNITY. BUT WHEN A GUNFIGHTER NAMED FRANK TALBY (LEE VAN CLEEF) STRIDES INTO TOWN, HE WORKS INTO A CASUAL FRIENDSHIP WITH SCOTT, AND BLOWS AWAY ONE OF THE JERKS WHO ABUSES HIM.

DREAMING OF ADVENTURE AND AN ESCAPE FROM THE CRUEL DIPSHIT TOWNSFOLK, SCOTT PUPPYDOGS AFTER TALBY, WHO ENDS UP ADOPTING THE YOUNG MAN AS HIS APPRENTICE. JUNIOR HAS NO FLIPPIN' CLUE WHAT HE'S GETTING INTO, BUT HE'LL GET PLENTY OF CHANCES TO PROVE HIS WORTH AS A GUNFIGHTER-IN-TRAINING. YOU SEE, TALBY IS ON THE HUNT FOR A MAN NAMED WILD JACK (AL MULOCK), A GANG LEADER WHO OWES TALBY $50,000 BONES -- WHICH ADJUSTED FOR INFLATION WOULD BE, LIKE, $134 MILLION DOLLARS. MAJOR CASH.

Lee Van Cleef
has been dirty, "ugly"
and downright mean...
now watch him
get violent.

National General Pictures Presents
LEE VAN CLEEF in
"DAY OF ANGER"

GIULIANO GEMMA
AND
LEE VAN CLEEF

THERE ARE MANY EXCELLENTLY TOLD PLOT POINTS TO FOLLOW (ONE OF WHICH IS THEIR RETURN TO CLIFTON, WHERE SCOTT GETS TO VISIT SOME OF THE DICKDORKS WHO TREATED HIM LIKE POOP) BUT I WON'T GO INTO SPOILERY DETAIL. I WILL POINT OUT, HOWEVER, THAT THIS FILM IS A MUST SEE, AND THAT IT'S ONE OF THE FEW ITALIAN WESTERNS TO BE BASED ON A NOVEL. ("DER TOD RITT DIENSTAGS", BY RON BARKER). THE ACTION (AND THERE'S A DECENT DOUSE OF IT) COMES QUICK AND FURIOUS, AND IS STAGED QUITE EXPERTLY. VALERII WAS A PROTEGE OF LEONE, AND ACTUALLY HAS JUST AS MANY TRICKS UP HIS SLEEVE AS THE OLD MASTER DID.

SQUINTY-EYED LEE VAN CLEEF APPEARED IN THIS AFTER COMING OFF OF LEONE'S DOLLARS TRILOGY, AND FINDING HIMSELF A MEGASTAR IN EUROPE. HE FIRST APPEARS TO BE THE TYPICAL OLD WEST ANTI-HERO SO FAMILIAR TO GENRE FANS, BUT BLINK AND YOU'LL MISS WHAT IS REALLY GOING ON AS VAN CLEEF USES HIS EXPRESSIONS TO SILENTLY EMPLOY SUBTLE CHARACTER ELEMENTS. I ESPECIALLY LIKED HOW HE COULD BE DECENT AND RUTHLESS IN EQUAL PROPORTIONS, AT ONE MOMENT A CONFIDENT FATHER FIGURE -- AND A POWER-HUNGRY VILLAIN THE NEXT. IT IS AN ASTONISHING PERFORMANCE, AND THE VIEWER IS KEPT GUESSING AS TO WHAT SIDE HIS SPINNING COIN WILL EVENTUALLY FALL ON. GREAT STUFF.

-BOUGIE. 2011.

FOR VICTORY

THE STORY OF A HISTORIC TIMES SQUARE LANDMARK

☆☆☆ BY ROBIN BOUGIE ☆☆☆
· 2015 ·

41 MINUTES INTO THE 1969 OSCAR-WINNING FILM MIDNIGHT COWBOY, JON VOIGHT GOES TO A FILM IN A TIMES SQUARE THEATER, THEN LEAVES WALKING PAST A MARQUEE AT THE VICTORY THEATER FOR THE OBSCURE SEXPLOITATION CLASSIC THE TWISTED SEX (1966). THAT ADDRESS IS 209 WEST 42ND STREET AND IT WAS BUILT AS THE THEATRE REPUBLIC IN 1900 -- ONLY THE THIRD THEATER BUILT ON 42ND STREET AT THAT TIME. IT WAS A GLORIOUS VENUE; A GIANT OVAL PAINTED CEILING AND 2 TIERS OF BALCONIES ABOVE THE MAIN FLOOR — EVERY ONE OF THE 499 SEATS WITH AN AMAZING VIEW. MEDIUM SIZED, BUT A FUCKING EPIC THEATER NONETHELESS, AND IT WOULD BECOME ONE OF THE MOST LEGENDARY AND EVER-PRESENT THEATERS FOR GENERATIONS OF NEW YORKERS.

IN 1930 IT WAS CONVERTED INTO A GORGEOUS BURLESQUE VENUE NAMED MINSKY'S BURLESQUE, AND OLD MR. MINSKY SMARTLY HAD A DOUBLE RUNWAY INSTALLED DOWN THE MIDDLE OF THE AUDITORIUM FOR HIS LOVELY STRIPPERS, THE MOST INFAMOUS OF WHOM WAS THE AMAZING GYPSY ROSE LEE. THE LAVISH AUDITORIUM LASTED IN THIS INCARNATION FOR 10 YEARS WHEN THEN MAYOR FIORELLO LAGUARDIA SHUT IT DOWN DURING HIS HIGHLY PUBLICIZED 1937 CRACKDOWN ON VICE IN THE CITY. CHECK OUT THE 1968 WILLIAM FRIEDKIN MOVIE THE NIGHT THEY RAIDED MINSKY'S FOR MORE ON THAT-- BUT TAKE NOTE THAT FRIEDKIN'S MOVIE WASN'T ACTUALLY FILMED IN THE OLD VICTORY. THEY SHOT THAT ONE AT THE 1,200-SEAT VILLAGE EAST THEATER OVER AT 181 2ND AVENUE.

THANKS TO THE GREAT DEPRESSION THE BRANDT THEATER CHAIN WAS ABLE TO TAKE ADVANTAGE OF MANY OF THE BUILDING OWNERS ON 42ND STREET BEING FORECLOSED UPON, AND BOUGHT UP SEVEN (THE APOLLO, THE LIBERTY, THE LYRIC, THE SELWYN, THE TIMES SQUARE, THE EMPIRE AND THE VICTORY) OF THE FIFTEEN THEATERS THERE IN ONE FELL SWOOP — AND ON THE CHEAP NO LESS. AND SO IT WAS IN 1942 THAT THE VENUE BECAME THE VICTORY AND BECAME INFAMOUS FOR PLAYING MOSTLY ACTION AND ADVENTURE PICTURES IN THE FIFTIES -- MOVIES YOU COULD TAKE THE WHOLE FAMILY TO. BY THE MID 1960S, HOWEVER, IT WAS ADULTS ONLY. NO MORE KIDS STUFF. THE VICTORY WAS NOW PLAYING NUDIES AND SEXPLOITATION FILMS, AND A FEW YEARS AFTER MIDNIGHT COWBOY THEY BEGAN SHOWING HARDCORE PORNO FEATURES — THE FIRST ON 42ND STREET TO DO SO. THE ONLY ADULT THEATER IN THE BRANDT CHAIN, THE OWNERS CLEARLY DIDN'T THINK MUCH OF IT, AND THE BUILDING BEGAN TO FALL INTO DISREPAIR, EVEN AS IT CONTINUED TO SERVE A MULTITUDE OF VIEWERS UNABATED.

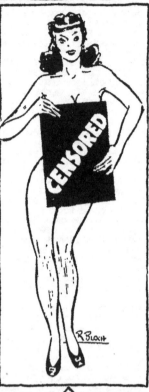

R.BLOIT

ILLUSTRATION THAT RAN IN THE 'TOLEDO BLADE' WHEN MINSKY'S WAS RAIDED...

"THE SECOND BALCONY, LABELED 'THE THIRD TIER' WAS A COMMON RENDEZVOUS POINT FOR PROSTITUTE AND PATRON", ROB CRAIG WROTE IN HIS 2012 BOOK, GUTTER AUTEUR. "THIS TRADITION WAS CARRIED INTACT ALL THE WAY THROUGH THE PORNOGRAPHY INVASION OF THE 1970S AND EARLY 1980S, WHEN SCORES OF DRUG-ADDLED PROSTITUTES OF BOTH GENDERS PROWLED THE AISLES, DESPERATELY SEEKING 'JOHNS!'"

"BACK IN 1971 THE VICTORY WAS SHOWING HARDCORE FILMS WITH THE SEX SCENES EDITED OUT", 42ND STREET PETE (AKA PETE CHIARELLA) TOLD ME VIA E-MAIL IN 2015. "ADMISSION WAS $1 AND THAT PRICE ATTRACTED 'SLEEPERS'. THAT IS, HOMELESS GUYS, AKA WINOS, BUMS, AND HOBOS LOOKING FOR A PLACE TO CRASH. YOU HAVE TO REMEMBER THAT PORN WAS STILL A GRAY AREA, LEGALLY, AND THEATERS WERE GETTING BUSTED AT THAT TIME. THEY WENT TO LOW QUALITY SOFTCORE FEATURES AROUND 1972-73, THAT WERE ADVERTISED AND BALLYHOOED AS HARDCORE TO SUCK IN TOURISTS OR THE UNWARY."

"SOMEWHERE AROUND 1974-75 THEY MADE THE SWITCH TO 3 CONTINUOUS HARDCORE FEATURES FOR THE $2 ADMISSION", PETE CONTINUED. "AFTER 6PM, THE PRICE WENT TO $2.50. THE FILMS HAD ALREADY MADE THE ROUNDS OF THE TIMES SQUARE PORN THEATERS, SO THE PROGRAMMING WAS NOTHING SPECIAL. MOST WERE THE 45 TO 65-MINUTE-LONG STORE FRONT FEATURES THAT MYSELF, SOMETHING WEIRD VIDEO AND OTHER COMPANIES PUT OUT DOWN THE ROAD. THE SAME 3 FEATURE PROGRAM KEPT UP INTO THE EARLY 80S. I DIDN'T REALLY FREQUENT THE VICTORY MAINLY BECAUSE OF ITS BAD REPUTATION FOR FALSELY ADVERTISING FILMS AND THAT IT WAS A SINK HOLE. THERE WERE CLEANER AND SAFER THEATERS WITH SIMILAR BARGAIN BASEMENT PROGRAMMING."

ONE SPECIFIC FILM TO SCREEN AT THE VICTORY DURING THIS TIME WAS 1976'S KINKORAMA. DIRECTED BY ITALIAN PORNMEISTER, LASSE BRAUN, KINKORAMA IS A FLAGRANTLY DIRTY MOVIE. NOT "DIRTY" AS IN

"LOOK AT THOSE NAUGHTY PEOPLE HAVING SEX" (ALTHOUGH IT IS THAT AS WELL), BUT RATHER "DIRTY" AS IN THE CONCEPT IN WHICH NO AMOUNT OF SCRUBBING CAN WASH AWAY. THE MOVIE IS A LOOP CARRIER (MEANING A FEATURE FILM THAT USED BLOWN UP 8MM PEEPSHOW BOOTH LOOPS AS A WAY TO PAD OUT THE RUN TIME) AND THOSE CLIPS ARE FADED, SCUM-COATED IMAGES OF HAIRY PUSSIES PISSING, COCKS POUNDING INTO WOMEN FROM EVERY WHICH WAY, AND EVEN ACCIDENTALLY-CAPTURED FOOTAGE OF A BIG HOUSE FLY WHICH LANDS ON A PROSTHETIC HOOK (WHICH BELONGS TO A HORRIBLE, HAIRY TOOTHLESS MAN WITH TWO BLACK EYES) GETTING SHOVED INTO CLAUDINE BECCARIE'S SWEATY GRUNT-HOLE. ALL OF THIS FILM ALMOST SEEMS AS IF IT WERE SCRAPED ALONG A GRAVEL ROAD AND LEFT OUT IN THE SUN FOR YEARS. SURE, A LOT OF THAT IS DUE TO THE FADED, AGED PRINT THEY USED TO MAKE THE DVD, BUT AN EQUAL AMOUNT IS NOT AT ALL. IT'S SIMPLY FILTHY, THROUGH AND THROUGH. THERE'S NO OTHER WAY TO PUT IT.

THE IRONY OF HOW SCUMMY THE PRESENTATION SEEMS QUANTIFIED WHEN THE FILM ITSELF IS TRYING TO EDUCATE US THAT FILTHY SEX IS NOT ABNORMAL OR SHAMEFUL AT ALL. THE LATE, GREAT ADVOCATOR OF PORNOGRAPHY, GLORIA LEONARD PLAYS A SHORT-HAIRED THERAPIST WITH BIG TINTED SOPHIA LOREN EYEGLASSES THAT COUNCILS YOUNG COUPLES WITH "KINK ISSUES" ON WHAT HEALTHY SEX IS. SHE DOES THIS BY SITTING THEM DOWN IN HER OFFICE AND SHOWING THEM A BUNCH OF LASSE BRAUN'S EURO-KINK PORN LOOPS THAT "RELATE TO VARIOUS SEXUAL FANTASIES AND ABERRATIONS THAT PROVE THAT YOUR DESIRES ARE FAR MORE NORMAL THAT MOST PEOPLE WOULD EXPECT." OF COURSE, AS PART OF THEIR TREATMENT SHE TAKES OFF HER PROFESSIONAL BUSINESS SUIT AND SHOWS THEM PRECISELY HOW IT'S DONE RIGHT THERE ON HER DESK. THEY TAKE TO HER CUNT LIKE DUCKS TO WATER.

"IT ALWAYS WORKS OUT THIS WAY!" SHE SAYS RIGHT INTO THE CAMERA WITH A SMILE AS THE ENTHUSIASTIC 'CURED' COUPLE CROWD AROUND HER AND SUCK AT HER PENDULOUS BREASTS LIKE FEEDING INFANTS. "NOW IF ONLY SOMEONE WOULD EXPLAIN ALL THIS TO *MY* HUSBAND. HE'S SUCH A SQUAAAARE!!"

CROWDS WERE GETTING VERY SPARSE BY THE 1980S AND THE THEATER COULD BE RENTED FOR NEXT TO NOTHING, WHICH OF COURSE MADE IT A PERFECT LOCATION FOR FILM DIRECTORS ON A BUDGET. ONE SUCH MOVIE TO UTILIZE THE SPACE WAS 1985'S THE LAST DRAGON, WHICH USED THE INTERIOR OF THE VICTORY FOR THE MOVIE'S INFAMOUS SCENE WHERE THE CHARACTERS WATCH BRUCE LEE'S ENTER THE DRAGON. RON VAN CLIEF CHOREOGRAPHED THE FIGHT THAT TAKES PLACE AND HAMMY ACTOR JULIUS J. CARRY III (AS "SHO NUFF") PERFORMED HIS OWN STUNTS. IT'S A GREAT FUCKING SCENE, AND ANY MEGA-FAN OF EIGHTIES CULT FILMS WILL TELL YOU LIKEWISE, AND WILL PROBABLY ELABORATE ON THE MANY REASONS WHY.

"AT THE TIME IT WAS ONE OF THE SEEDIEST TIMES SQUARE THEATERS," PRODUCTION ASSISTANT JOSPEH PIERSON TOLD FAST-REWIND.COM IN 2009. "IT WAS A VILE LOCATION, ESPECIALLY BECAUSE OF THE TOM CATS THAT ROAMED FREELY WHILE WE FILMED."

"IN THE 1980S, I WAS CURIOUS TO SEE WHAT ONE OF THE 42ND ST GRINDHOUSES LOOKED LIKE INSIDE, SO I WENT TO THE VICTORY," A USER OF CINEMATREASURES.ORG NAMED RIVOLI157 NOTED. "(IT WAS) DARK, DIRTY, SMELLY, AND IN AWFUL CONDITION. OH, AND THERE WERE MANY MEN ROAMING AROUND IN THE SHADOWS."

IN 1990 THE CITY OF NEW YORK TOOK OVER POSSESSION BUT JUST PRIOR TO THAT IN THE MIDDLE OF 1989, WHILE NENEH CHERRY'S "BUFFALO STANCE" AND YOUNG MC'S "BUST A MOVE" BLARED OUT OF EVERY CAR RADIO IN THE NEIGHBOURHOOD, SOME UNNAMED INDIVIDUAL GOT ACCESS TO THE GIANT THREE SIDED MARQUEE OVERHANGING ON THE SIDEWALK OF 42ND STREET. THEY'D FOUND THE BOX OF OLD LETTERS THAT USED TO MAKE UP THE STREET-LEVEL LISTING FOR SEX FILMS LIKE DIRTY LILY, INSATIABLE, AND WET RAINBOW, AND USED THEM TO POTENTIALLY GIVE PAUSE TO ANYONE WALKING OR DRIVING BY. THE THREE 12 FOOT HIGH MARQUEES NOW READ: "CATEGORIZING FEAR IS CALMING", "DRAMA OFTEN OBSCURES THE REAL ISSUES", AND "BOREDOM MAKES YOU DO CRAZY THINGS." WITH THE BUILDING EMPTY AND NO FILMS TO ANNOUNCE, IT WAS A SUCCESSFUL BID TO "MAKE ART OUT OF LIFE", AS RAYMOND CARVER USED TO SAY. OR AS PORN LEGEND ANNIE SPRINKLE PUT IT WHEN I ASKED HER ABOUT THE VICTORY: "THEY HAD THE BEST MARQUEES."

OTHER ARTISTS WERE REPURPOSING THE SPACE AS WELL. IT WAS DURING THESE YEARS THAT AMERICAN THEATRE DIRECTOR, WRITER AND ACTOR ANDRE GREGORY (WHO PLAYED HIMSELF IN LOUIS MALLE'S 1981 FILM MY DINNER WITH ANDRE) BROUGHT A GROUP OF LOCAL NEW YORK ACTORS TOGETHER ON A

VOLUNTARY BASIS TO DO PERFORMANCE WORKSHOPS IN THE OLD DILAPIDATED VICTORY. ONLY CLOSE FRIENDS AND SPECIAL INVITEES WERE EVER PRESENT AS AN AUDIENCE, WITH GREGORY PUTTING THE EXERCISE TOGETHER FOR HIS FELLOW ACTORS SIMPLY AS A WAY TO BETTER UNDERSTAND THE WORK OF CHEKHOV, THE RUSSIAN AUTHOR AND PLAYWRIGHT.

SCREENWRITER DAVID MAMET GOT INVOLVED, AND WHEN LOUIS MALLE DID AS WELL IT WAS DECIDED TO FILM THE MOSTLY UNSEEN PLAY AS THEY HAD DEVELOPED IT. AND THAT IS EXACTLY WHAT THEY DID AFTER MOVING THE PRODUCTION OVER TO THE ALSO ABANDONED NEW AMSTERDAM THEATER ACROSS THE STREET. THE CRITICALLY ACCLAIMED FILM WAS CALLED VANYA ON 42ND STREET (1994), AND IT LAUNCHED THE CAREER OF ACTRESS JULIANNE MOORE. IT'S WORTH NOTING THAT CHEKHOV'S ORIGINAL 1897 STORY, ENTITLED UNCLE VANYA, WAS WRITTEN A MERE THREE YEARS BEFORE THE VICTORY WAS BUILT.

THE CITY OF NEW YORK MADE THE BUILDING THE FIRST TIMES SQUARE THEATER TO BE RESTORED AND REMODELLED, UNDERGOING AN $11.4 MILLION RENOVATION. TODAY THE BUILDING EXISTS AS THE NEW VICTORY, AND HAS A FOCUS TOWARDS PERFORMANCE ART FOR KIDS AND THEIR UPWARDLY MOBILE FAMILIES. UPON ITS REOPENING ON DECEMBER 11TH, 1995, IT CONTINUED ITS TRADITION AS THE OLDEST OPERATING THEATER IN NYC. IT ONCE AGAIN HAS A VERY DISTINCTIVE STAIRCASE IN FRONT OF THE BUILDING, WHICH WAS COPIED FROM THE ORIGINAL, WHICH HAD TO BE REMOVED IN 1910 TO CONFORM WITH THE CITY'S WIDENING OF 42ND STREET.

WITH ITS DECADES OF EXISTENCE AS A DEGENERATE SEX FILM AUDITORIUM WHERE THE AUDIENCE WERE OFTEN EMULATING THE DEBAUCHED ACTS HAPPENING UPON THE SCREEN, ONE IS LEFT TO WONDER HOW MANY PARENTS OF THE NEW VICTORY'S CURRENT PATRONS WERE CONCEIVED IN THOSE SAME SEATS.

> "I'd rather be politically incorrect and even offensive than to be beholden to a moralizing and missionary set of speech restrictions, or to unspoken taboos that certain subjects are off limits."
>
> -- Tekno 2600, Jan 11th 2015, dailykos.com

THE LEGEND OF THE ORGASM BIKE
AKA "ACME BICYCLE EJACULATION!" (SOD. 2008. DIR: HAJIME YARIGASAKI

IF YOU'RE A GAL AND YOU'VE EVER DEMANDED TO KNOW WHY YOU CAN'T COMBINE BICYCLE-RIDING AND MASTURBATION, YOU'LL NO DOUBT BE THRILLED TO NOTE THAT THE BRILLIANT JAPANESE SENSORY TECHNICIANS AT SOD (SOFT ON DEMAND) HAVE BEEN BURNING THE MIDNIGHT OIL DESIGNING WAYS FOR BIKES TO GET YOU OFF WHILE YOU PEDAL THEM.

VARIOUS ADORABLE PORN IDOLS ARE GIVEN SPECIAL CRUISER BIKES THAT HAVE BEEN OUTFITTED WITH NOT ONLY PUSS-CRUSHING CHAIN-MOUNTED DILDOS AND VIBRATORS, BUT ALSO HALF A DOZEN TINY PRIVACY-SHATTERING CAMERAS WHICH FILM THE ACTION FROM NEARLY EVERY POSSIBLE ANGLE. SAID FEMALES THEN RIDE THE BIKES AROUND PUBLIC STREETS AND PARKS IN TOKYO, AND TRY THEIR BEST NOT TO WIPE OUT AS THEY SQUIRM THEIR WAY TO WET, ROLLING ECSTASY.

AND WHEN I SAY WET, I MEAN **REALLY WET.** MANY OF THESE LADIES (MOE OISHI, AKIRA ICHINOSE, MINAMI TSUKASA, ANRI HIRAMATSU, YUKA OSAWA) WERE CAST BECAUSE THEY ARE BIG-TIME JAV SQUIRTERS, AND THEY HAPPILY DRIBBLE PLENTIFUL PUDDLES OF GIRL GOO AS THEY ROCK AND ROLL. THE BIKE SEATS ARE MOSTLY MADE OF CLEAR PLASTIC, SO THERE ISN'T MUCH LEFT TO THE IMAGINATION AS THE FEMALE EJACULATE STARTS FLOWING.

I CAN'T UNDERSTAND A DAMN THING ANYONE IS SAYING SINCE I DON'T SPEAK THE LANGUAGE (AND THIS DOESN'T HAVE ENGLISH SUBTITLES) BUT MOST OF THEM SEEM LEGITIMATELY AMAZED AND BEMUSED THAT THE SELF-PROPELLED SEX MACHINES ARE AS SUCCESSFUL AS THEY ARE AT BRINGING THEM OFF.

THE FASTER THESE BITCHES PEDDLE, THE HARDER AND QUICKER THEY ARE PENETRATED/VIBRATED, BUT MOST OF THESE WHIMPERING YOUNG GUSHERS ARE EVENTUALLY FORCED TO A MERE CRAWL AS THEIR EYES ROLL BACK IN THEIR SKULLS AS THEY STRUGGLE TO REGAIN NOT ONLY THEIR COMPOSURE, BUT THE BASIC MOTOR CONTROL SKILLS NEEDED TO NAVIGATE PEDESTRIAN TRAFFIC.

OTHER HIGHLIGHTS: SOD'S BEHIND-THE-SCENES RESEARCH AND DEVELOPMENT, RIO HAMASAKI SQUEALING DOWN A BIG HILL, FOUR OF THE GIRLS HAVING A PLEASURE-PACKED RACE THROUGH THE PARK, BYSTANDERS CLEARLY BEFUDDLED BY THE AMOUNT OF HIGH PITCHED MOANING AND WHIMPERING COMING FROM FEMALE CYCLISTS, INNOCENT-LOOKING TSUBOMI IN PIGTAILS AND HER GYM OUTFIT, AN ORGASM BIKE BUILT FOR TWO, YUKI MIZUHO'S WHINY GRIMACE-FILLED RIDE, AND MEGURU KOSAKA (WITH HER SHORT BLACK PIXIE HAIR AND LARGE BREASTS) WIDELY GRINNING LIKE SHE HAS THE MOST WONDERFUL AND HILARIOUS PRIVATE SECRET.

DESPITE VERY LITTLE ACTUAL NUDITY, THIS IS ONE OF THE MOST ENDEARING JAPANESE HARDCORE VIDEOS I HAVE SEEN IN AGES, AND A MUST TO LOAN TO YOUR PALS THAT THINK THIS STUFF IS SOLEY COMPRISED OF SUBWAY GROPING AND PIXELATED RAPE SCENES.

REVIEW BY **ROBIN BOUGIE** : CINEMASEWER.COM
ART BY **BEN NEWMAN**: BENNEWMANART.BLOGSPOT.COM

HE WAS "STICKS", THE DRUMMER FOR RICHIE CUNNINGHAM'S BAND ON HAPPY DAYS, HE WAS "BUBBLES" IN SUN-RA'S SPACE IS THE PLACE, HE WAS "C.C." ON ABC'S SATURDAY MORNING LIVE ACTION SERIES THE KROFFT SUPERSHOW, AND HE WAS ALSO THE GUY IN NEW WAVE HOOKERS THAT GETS HIS COCK SUCKED BY KRISTARA BARRINGTON. HE WAS BORN JOHN ANTHONY BAILEY, BUT HE'S BETTER KNOWN AS JACK BAKER, AND I PERSONALLY CONSIDER HIM TO BE ONE OF THE TEN BEST ACTORS TO EVER WORK IN XXX.

CULT FILM EXPERT CHRIS POGGALI ONCE APTLY WROTE THAT WONDERBUG WAS "A DIME STORE CROSS BETWEEN DISNEY'S THE LOVE BUG AND HANNA-BARBERA'S SPEED BUGGY THAT MANAGED TO MAKE THOSE TRASHY SUPERBUG MOVIES FROM WEST GERMANY LOOK LIKE DAVID LEAN PRODUCTIONS BY COMPARISON," THE SHOW WOWED KIDS FOR TWO SEASONS IN THE 1970S, AND STARRED A SELF-AWARE DUNE BUGGY WITH THE VERY JEWISH-SOUNDING NAME OF "SCHLEP CAR". HE WAS A VERY LUCKY VEHICLE, HAVING BEEN SAVED FROM THE SCRAP HEAP BY THREE BELL-BOTTOMED TEENS (ONE OF WHICH WAS JACK) WHO USE A MYSTICAL HORN TO TRANSFORM THE JUNKY LEMON INTO A SLEEK FLYING CRIME-FIGHTING MACHINE. THE CAR HAD ARTICULATED EYEBALL HEADLIGHTS, AND A CUSTOM BUMPER THAT RESEMBLED A MOUTH. SOMETIMES DIFFERENT BUMPERS WERE UTILIZED TO GIVE WONDERBUG DIFFERENT FACIAL EXPRESSIONS.

"I HUNG WITH JACK IN THE EARLY 1990S. I THINK I FIRST MET HIM IN '88", BILL BAKER (NO RELATION) TOLD ME VIA E-MAIL IN 2014. "WE MET AT THE CES SHOW. SOMEHOW WE HIT IT OFF. WE JUST STARTED TALKING ABOUT MUSIC AND STUFF. HE LIKED THAT I REPAIRED GUITARS AND WAS INTO HENDRIX AND KISS. I HAVE A PIC OF HIM WEARING MY KISS SHIRT, WHICH I STILL HAVE. WE HUNG OUT OVER THE WEEKEND AND HE GAVE ME A PHONE NUMBER, WHICH WAS A FRIEND'S BECAUSE HE WAS KIND OF HOMELESS. I GUESS I WAS THE ONLY ONE THAT WOULD PUT HIM UP. HE HAD NO MONEY. I EVEN BOUGHT HIM A PAIR OF SHOES ONE YEAR BECAUSE HE HAD ELECTRICAL TAPE ON THEM. HONESTLY, IT DIDN'T SEEM LIKE HE HAD TOO MANY FRIENDS."

CINEMA SEWER PRESENTS:

JACK BAKER

PORN'S LORD OF LAUGHS

"HE HAD TOLD ME HE HAD BEEN BLACKLISTED FROM NORMAL TELEVISION. HE'D DONE MASH, HAPPY DAYS, GOOD TIMES, AND WONDERBUG (I HAVE THE LUNCH BOX), AND ALL OF A SUDDEN NO ONE WOULD HIRE HIM OR TALK TO HIM. PEOPLE TURNED THEIR BACKS ON HIM."

"I GUESS I WAS A LITTLE TOO VISIBLE" JACK SAID IN AN INTERVIEW WITH BLACK TAIL MAGAZINE IN JULY 1993. IT WAS 1980, AND AN ACTORS STRIKE HAD HIT HOLLYWOOD. "ED ASNER EVEN TOLD ME THAT EVERY TIME HE TURNED AROUND HE SAW ME WALKING ON THE PICKET LINE... I GOT A FEELING THE PRODUCERS WERE A LITTLE MIFFED, AND I GOT KINDA BLACK-BALLED. IN 1982, SOME FRIENDS OF MINE IN THE X BUSINESS TOLD ME THEY WERE REALLY GOING TO START NEEDING ACTORS, AND THAT I SHOULD GIVE IT A GO."

JACK KNEW DAMN WELL THAT GOING INTO PORN MEANT THAT HIS MAINSTREAM CAREER WAS CERTAINLY AS GOOD AS OVER, BUT THE FRUSTRATION OF NOT GETTING ANY ACTING WORK WEIGHED HEAVILY. NOT BEING ABLE TO PUT ANY FOOD IN THE FRIDGE WAS A SCARY THOUGHT, AND THE RENT NEEDED TO BE PAID. A CONSUMMATE PROFESSIONAL, JACK GAMELY PUT ON ONE OF HIS TRADEMARK TOOTHY SMILES AND TOOK OUT HIS DICK. HE NEVER ACTED LIKE HE WAS BETTER THAN HIS CO-STARS BECAUSE OF HIS LEGIT ACTING BACKGROUND. HE NEVER LOOKED DOWN ON ANYONE.

"ALTHOUGH HIS DICK REALLY DIDN'T WORK, HE WAS A GENUINELY TALENTED AND ALMOST ALWAYS GOOD-NATURED FELLOW", PORN INDUSTRY LEGEND BILL MARGOLD TOLD ME IN FEB OF 2014. MARGOLD WAS THE FIRST ONE TO CAST JACK IN HIS GIRLFRIEND DREA'S SHOT-ON-VIDEO 1984 PRODUCTION, HOT CHOCOLATE. MARGOLD WROTE THE SCRIPT.

"HE WAS, FOR AWHILE, PART OF THE HOLE IN THE WALL GANG THAT WAS WRANGLED UP BY SAM MENNING ON THE SECOND FLOOR OF 6912 HOLLYWOOD BLVD", MARGOLD REMEMBERED. "THERE WAS A MOMENT WHEN DREA WANTED ME TO STUNT-COCK FOR HIM BY SHOOTING IN VERY LOW LIGHT, FOR A BLOW JOB SCENE IN HOT CHOCOLATE. I OPTED OUT THOUGH, BECAUSE I WAS LISTENING TO A LIONS GAME."

"AT FIRST, THE LEGENDARY PHOTOGRAPHER SAM MENNING ONLY HAD THE OFFICE AND STUDIO BELOW ME, BUT AS HE NEEDED MORE SPACE, HE SIMPLY BEGAN TO KNOCK DOWN THE WALLS BETWEEN THE NEXT COUPLE OF SPACES UNTIL HE DOMINATED THE ENTIRE SECOND FLOOR. MANY PEOPLE, INCLUDING MISTY DAWN, CHRISTINE DE SHAFFER, A PHOTOGRAPHER NAMED JACK GREEN AND THE AFOREMENTIONED BAKER WERE THERE. PLUS GUYS NAMED JAY, TINY, GARY AND MARK, ALONG WITH A NOAH'S ARK OF ANIMALS, POPULATED THE PLACE, AND THEY WOULD ALL RUN WILD THROUGHOUT THE BUILDING. MY BELOVED FELINE 'HARDCORE', CAME FROM SAM'S MENAGERIE AT 6912 HOLLYWOOD BLVD."

"YEAH, SAM'S DOGS AND CATS HAD FREE RUN OF THE MAIN SUITE AND THE UN-PICKED UP SHIT (AND THE HORRIBLE SMELL) WERE WHAT EVERYONE REMEMBERS." HART WILLIAMS, FORMER PORN SCREENWRITER AND FORMER RESIDENT

OF THAT SECOND FLOOR, TOLD ME IN AUGUST 2014. "I REMEMBER 'HARDCORE. BLACK AND WHITE CAT.'"

SAM MENNING WAS AN OLD SCHOOL PORNOGRAPHER. HE WAS THE HOUSE PHOTOGRAPHER FOR GARGOYLE DISTRIBUTION IN THE 1950S, AND WAS THE GENT WHO TOOK THE LAST PIN-UP PICTURES OF BETTIE PAGE BEFORE SHE RETIRED. HE EVEN DATED HER FOR A WHILE. MENNING REINVENTED HIMSELF IN THE 1980S AS A CHARACTER ACTOR, AND PORTRAYED A STEREOTYPICAL HOMELESS GUY IN DOZENS OF TV SERIES AND MOVIES OVER THE YEARS. SAM PASSED AWAY AT THE AGE OF 85 IN 2010.

KROFFT SUPERSHOW Presents

Wonderbug

DAVID LEVY, CAROL ANNE SEFLINGER AND JACK RIP AROUND IN THE OL' SCHLEPCAR.

"A SHITLOAD OF PORN STARS WERE PHOTOGRAPHED ON MENNING'S SECOND FLOOR OF THE CINEMART BUILDING," HART WILLIAMS NOTED. "MANY CRASHED THERE, TOO -- INCLUDING JAMIE GILLIS AND JOHN HOLMES. SAM HAD BEEN IN THE MERCHANT MARINE IN WWII, AND FIXED A POT OF BEANS EVERY NIGHT SO THAT THE KIDS COULD GET SOMETHING IN THEIR STOMACHS. THE CINEMART WAS RIGHT ACROSS THE STREET FROM THE GRAUMAN'S CHINESE THEATER. I USED TO SLEEP ON THE HIDE-A-BED WITH THE CLICHE NEON LIGHTS FLASHING THROUGH THE BLINDS, EXCEPT THAT IT WAS THE CHINESE THEATER THAT WAS CASTING THE CHEESY NOIR LIGHTING. THE ALPHA AND OMEGA OF TINSELTOWN, YOU MIGHT SAY."

"I LIVED THERE WITH JACK IN THE SUMMER OF 1984," WILLIAMS REMINISCED. "THE PENTHOUSE ISSUE WITH VANESSA WILLIAMS AND THE TRACI LORDS CENTERFOLD HAD JUST COME OUT AND WAS THERE ON THE TABLE IN THE KITCHEN. OUR OTHER ROOMMATES AT THE TIME WERE DINO ALEXANDER, MARK WALLICE, AND A STARLET WHOSE NAME I FORGET. JACK LIVED THERE A LOT LONGER THAN I DID."

"THE BUILDING WAS OWNED BY EDDIE NASH", MARGOLD EXPLAINED. "I MANAGED IT FOR OVER EIGHT YEARS IN CONJUNCTION WITH MY RUNNING SUNSET INTERNATIONAL. EDDIE NASH OWNED MANY BUILDINGS IN HOLLYWOOD, INCLUDING THE SEVEN SEAS, WHICH WAS THE ENTIRE BOTTOM FLOOR OF THE BUILDING."

"THE SEVEN SEAS WAS, AT ONE TIME, HOLLYWOOD'S PREMIER TIKI RESTAURANT," HART WILLIAMS EXPLAINED. "YOU CAN FIND THEIR OLD POSTCARDS ONLINE.. BY THE EIGHTIES, NASH OWNED IT, AND IT BECAME A HANGOUT FOR HARDCORE PUNKS. STILL HAD THE TIKI DECOR, BUT IT HAD BECOME A DUMP. WE AVOIDED IT, BECAUSE BAD SHIT HAPPENED THERE."

FOR THOSE OF YOU WHO MIGHT NOT KNOW THE NAME "EDDIE NASH", HE WAS A NOTORIOUS LA CLUB OWNER WHOSE ESTABLISHMENTS WERE SIMPLY FRONTS FOR HIS DRUG EMPIRE. HE WAS HEAVY USER HIMSELF, FREEBASING 3 OUNCES OF COCAINE A DAY, BUT HE ALSO SOMETIMES MIXED CRACK WITH HEROIN. HE WAS PLAYED VERY CONVINCINGLY BY ERIC BOGOSIAN IN THE MOVIE WONDERLAND FROM 2003. THAT'S RIGHT, JACK BAKER'S LANDLORD WAS THE WEALTHY CRIME BOSS THAT WAS ROBBED BY JOHN HOLMES' HEROIN JUNKIE FRIENDS, AND THEN BRUTALLY MURDERED THEM IN RETALIATION BY SMASHING THEIR HEADS APART ON JULY 1ST 1981. I MENTION THIS BECAUSE IT WAS WHILE JACK WAS STAYING AT MENNING'S PORNO CLUBHOUSE OWNED BY EDDIE NASH THAT A HORRIFIC INCIDENT WITH A BASEBALL BAT TOOK PLACE.

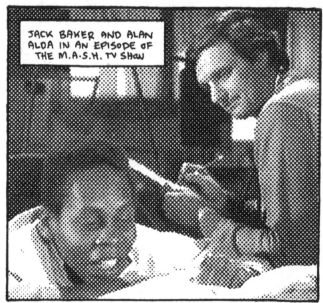

JACK BAKER AND ALAN ALDA IN AN EPISODE OF THE M.A.S.H. TV SHOW

"THE ALLEY BEHIND THE SEVEN SEAS WAS THE SCENE OF SOME BAD SHIT, AND THAT'S WHAT JACK WANDERED INTO. SOME THUG, OR THUGS, GOT HIM", WILLIAMS NOTED. "AND IT'S A SHAME, BECAUSE HE DIDN'T ACTUALLY HAVE ANYTHING WORTH STEALING."

JACK WAS BEATEN SO BADLY THAT HE SUFFERED EPILEPTIC SEIZURES FOR THE REST OF HIS LIFE. COULD EDDIE NASH HAVE HAD ANYTHING TO DO WITH JACK GETTING NAILED IN THE HEAD WITH A BAT? HE WAS OUT OF PRISON ALREADY FOR HIS INVOLVEMENT IN THE THE WONDERLAND MURDERS DESPITE GETTING SENTENCED TO 8 YEARS. HE'D ALREADY BRIBED A JUROR IN THE TRIAL FOR $50,000, AND AS THE NEW TIMES LOS ANGELES REPORTED IN SEPTEMBER 2001, HE WAS NOW FREE FAR EARLIER THAN EXPECTED BECAUSE "AN ASSOCIATE OF NASH'S LATER ADMITTED THAT THEY HAD BRIBED THE JUDGE WITH ABOUT $100,000".

IT WAS PROBABLY AN UNRELATED MUGGING OUTSIDE NASH'S CLUB, BUT JACK WASN'T FOND OF SPEAKING ABOUT

JACK AND SUZE RANDALL, HAMMING IT UP ONSTAGE, AT THE 1987 XRCO AWARDS

THE DETAILS OF HIS BRUTAL BEATING. I DO KNOW THAT THE PALESTINE-BORN NASH (AKA ADEL GHARIB NASRALLAH) WAS THE ONLY GUY THAT THE WORLD-WEARY JOHN HOLMES CONSIDERED TO BE "EVIL", AND I HAVEN'T READ OR HEARD AN ANECDOTE FROM ANYONE WHO PERSONALLY KNEW HIM THAT DIDN'T TAKE NOTE OF HOW SCARY AND REPREHENSIBLE HE WAS. ACCORDING TO JOHN'S SECOND WIFE LAURIE (KNOWN AS "MISTY DAWN" IN THE PORN INDUSTRY) SPEAKING IN A 1989 PLAYBOY MAGAZINE INTERVIEW, NASH WOULD "LEAVE THE BATHROOM WITHOUT USING TOILET PAPER, THEN OFFER THE YOUNG WOMEN COCAINE IF THEY'D LICK HIS ASS CLEAN."

IT'S RATHER INTERESTING TO NOTE THAT DESPITE MULTIPLE STAYS IN PRISON, AND THE FACT THAT HIS CRIME EMPIRE WAS BROUGHT TO ITS KNEES -- EDDIE NASH IS STILL ALIVE AND IS, AS OF THIS WRITING, A FREE MAN. HE SOLD THE DECREPIT AND LARGELY UNOCCUPIED SEVEN SEAS (AKA THE CINEMART) BUILDING IN 2007 TO HOLLYWOOD DEVELOPERS KNOWN AS THE CIM GROUP, FOR A COOL $42 MILLION. ABC TELEVISION'S JIMMY KIMMEL LIVE! BEGAN BROADCASTING IN THE BUILDING NEXT DOOR, AND IN 2013 THE PROPERTY, WITH THE STARS IN THE PAVEMENT ON THE HOLLYWOOD WALK OF FAME IN FRONT OF IT, WAS VALUED AT $35 MILLION.

JACK BROUGHT A LITTLE OF THAT HOLLYWOOD MAGIC WITH HIM TO THE WORLD OF X. HE REALLY EXCELLED AT THE ACTING AND COMEDY ASPECTS OF ADULT MOVIES. NOT SO MUCH THE FUCKING, BUT WITH JACK CAST IN A PORN PRODUCTION, YOU KNEW THAT IT WAS GOING TO BE ENTERTAINING AND UNPREDICTABLE, ESPECIALLY IF IT WAS A DARK BROS FILM. GREGORY DARK KNEW, BETTER THAN ANYONE, HOW TO USE JACK'S TALENTS. ONE SUCH SHOT-ON-VIDEO MOVIE THEY RELEASED WAS THE WILDLY ENTERTAINING 1985 TAPE, BLACK BUN BUSTERS. IN THIS ONE HE'S A BEARDED AND BESPECTACLED SEX THERAPIST NAMED "I.B. BROWN"

-- AN ELDERLY INTELLECTUAL WHO HOLDS A GROUP THERAPY SESSION, LOOKING TO HELP A GROUP OF BLACK EIGHTIES PORNO LUMINARIES SUCH AS F.M. BRADLEY, SAHARA, LADY STEPHANIE, AND STEVE HARPER GET BETTER ACQUAINTED WITH SWEET CHOCOLATE BUMS.

"DOCTOR I.B. BROWN IS MY SPIRITUAL LEADER", PORN FAN SHAWN PORTER TOLD ME IN 2014. "HE'S KIND OF LIKE THE UNCLE REMUS OF ANAL. THERE TO EDUCATE US, ENTERTAIN US AND TO ULTIMATELY BE MISUNDERSTOOD. ACTUALLY, HE'S MORE LIKE THE UNCLE REAM-US, NOW THAT I THINK ABOUT IT."

SOME SAY THAT BOBBY ASTYR WAS THE "CLOWN PRINCE OF PORN", BUT IT WAS WITH KNEE-SLAPPING PERFORMANCES LIKE THIS THAT BAKER TOOK THAT CROWN IN MY OPINION. HIS CONSTANT USE OF THE PHRASE "RECTAL INTIMACIES" IS FUNNY ENOUGH, BUT THEN YOU HAVE HIM GETTING UP IN FRONT OF EVERYONE AND DOING A FREESTYLE RAP. "WIGGLE IT! JIGGLE IT! SQUEEZE IT! GET DOWN PEOPLE, GOT TO GET INTO IT!" HE SINGS WHILE STRUTTING AROUND. "YOU CAN PUT IT IN A TIGHT BIKINI, AND YOU CAN PUT IT IN YO FAAACE!!"

SAM MENNING

"BOBBY ASTYR WAS JUST SOME NY WANNABE", HART WILLIAMS SAID. "JACK WAS A REAL FUCKING ACTOR; A TALENTED GUY IN AN INDUSTRY THAT DESPISED TALENT. HE WAS ALSO INTELLIGENT, FUNNY, REASONABLY WELL READ AND WE COULD TALK. DOWN TO EARTH. NO PARTICULAR AIRS. SOLID GUY."

"HIS WORK IN THE EARLY FILMS OF THE DARK BROTHERS WAS REALLY IMPRESSIVE TO ME", TRASH JOURNALIST GLENN SALTER WROTE IN HIS DEC 2013 ZINE GRUNTS N' GROANS. "THIS IS THE WORK THAT BEST SUITS JACK'S PARTICULAR TALENTS, THE SHUCKIN' AND JIVIN' THAT HE'S HONED TO PERFECTION. AND THESE FILMS GAVE HIM HIS BEST DIALOGUE AND CHARACTERS...(IT'S) SOME OF JACK'S VERY BEST WORK AS AN ACTOR, PERIOD. AND HE HIMSELF HAD OFTEN FELT VINDICATED BY THE ACCOLADES GIVEN HIM FOR THIS VERY WORK.

"AS FAR AS I'M CONCERNED, I WON MY OSCAR ALREADY WHEN THE X-RATED CRITICS ASSOCIATION GAVE ME THE AWARD FOR BEST ACTOR IN A NON-SEX ROLE FOR THE DEVIL IN MISS JONES 3 AND 4", BAKER SAID.

GREGORY DARK'S FATHER WAS AN OCCULTIST AND GREG BECAME KNOWN FOR TRANSGRESSIVE AND POLARIZING SMUT. FILMS THAT WERE EDGY AT THE TIME, BUT PROBABLY WOULDN'T REGISTER AS ANYTHING PARTICULARLY OUTLANDISH IN TODAY'S INDUSTRY. "(DARK) WAS INTERESTED NOT ONLY IN TURNING PEOPLE ON BUT IN MAKING THEM FEEL UNCOMFORTABLE ABOUT IT", WROTE TOM JUNOD IN ESQUIRE MAGAZINE IN 2001. "JUST AS HE WAS INTERESTED IN INDICTING HIS

EDDIE NASH

30

PERFORMERS FOR THE ACT OF PERFORMING, FOR THE SIN OF PRIDE. HIS OEUVRE IS, FROM TOP TO BOTTOM, ABSOLUTELY FREAKING FILTHY, DEDICATED TO THE TASK OF MAKING HUMAN SEXUAL CONGRESS LOOK INHERENTLY UNWHOLESOME AND UNNATURAL."

"MOVIES LIKE NEW WAVE HOOKERS AND PORNOGRAPHERS LIKE THE DARK BROTHERS RESCUED THE DISCONTENTED RAINCOATERS OF THE MID 1980S," WROTE NATALIE PURCELL IN HER 2012 BOOK, VIOLENCE AND THE PORNOGRAPHIC IMAGERY. THIS 260-PAGE TEXT EXISTS AS AN ACADEMIC RANT ABOUT THE VILE MACHINATIONS OF "FILTHY" PORN, AND PURCELL SAVES SOME OF HER BEST FINGER-WAGGING FOR THE DARK BROTHERS AND THEIR AUDIENCE. "MANY BIG-TIME CINEMATIC PORN MOVIES -- ESPECIALLY CROSSOVERS AND COUPLES FEATURES -- WERE NO LONGER MADE PRIMARILY FOR THEM. COUPLES FARE DID NOT HAVE THE FEEL OF TRANSGRESSION AND TABOO VIOLATION THAT MIGHT COME FROM WATCHING EDGIER, MORE MISOGYNISTIC, MORE OPENLY 'FILTHY' PORN THAT DIDN'T CONCERN ITSELF WITH THE PRESUMED FEELINGS AND PREFERENCES OF WOMEN, OR OTHERS WHO MIGHT TAKE OFFENCE TO

SEXISM, RACISM, AND EVEN ROUGH PHYSICALITY."

AFTER GREG GOT OUT OF DIRECTING SMUT HE BECAME A MUSIC VIDEO
DIRECTOR. HE DID HUNDREDS OF THEM, MANY FOR VANILLA-WHITE
VIRGINS LIKE A YOUNG BRITNEY SPEARS, AN UNTOUCHED MANDY MOORE
AND NICK CARTER'S LITTLE SISTER -- LESLIE. IT MIGHT SEEM LIKE A
TOTALLY DIFFERENT LINE OF WORK, BUT THE SEXUALIZATION AND
AESTHETIC FETISHIZATION OF YOUNG WOMEN IN THE MUSIC INDUSTRY
ISN'T FAR OFF FROM WHAT DARK MADE HIS LIVING DOING IN THE 1980S
AND 1990S. IN FACT, IT'S VERY CLOSELY RELATED.

ONE OF THE BEST MOVIES THAT DARK AND BAKER MADE TOGETHER WAS
THE DEVIL IN MISS JONES 3: A NEW BEGINNING (1987). IT WAS MADE
FOR $200,000 AND FILMED IN JANUARY 1986 OVER 7 DAYS -- ABOUT 5
OR 6 DAYS LONGER THAN WHAT MOST PORNOGRAPHERS WERE SPENDING
AT THE TIME. LOIS AYERS PLAYS A GIRL ON THE REBOUND WHO BOUNCES
RIGHT INTO THE ARMS OF A PIMP (BAKER) WHO ATTEMPTS TO LURE
HER INTO THE LIFESTYLE OF STREETWALKING WHORE. WHEN SHE'S KILLED
AND HER SOUL DEPARTS TO HELL, BAKER IS HER GUIDE AND THEIR
TERRIFIC BANTER BACK AND FORTH IS SOME OF THE BEST FILMED IN
PORN IN THE 1980S. BAKER AND AYRES REHEARSED FOR SEVERAL WEEKS
PRIOR TO SHOOTING TO REALLY GET A FEEL FOR THEIR CHARACTERS.

A MATCHBOOK COVER FOR THE
SEVEN SEAS, CIRCA 1940S

AND IT PAID OFF. THE MOVIE WAS A BIG SUCCESS FINANCIALLY AND WON NUMEROUS AWARDS, INCLUDING JACK'S
AFOREMENTIONED XRCO TROPHY.

"HE WAS A GOOD PERSON AND YOU LIKED BEING ON SET WITH HIM", JAMIE GILLIS TOLD ME IN 2006 WHEN I ASKED
ABOUT HIS ROLE WITH BAKER IN NEW WAVE HOOKERS. "WE WORKED WELL TOGETHER. WE GOT ALONG QUITE GOOD,
AND WE BOTH TOOK THE ACTING PART OF THE JOB SERIOUSLY. I APPRECIATED THAT ABOUT HIM."

"HE WAS A WILD AND CRAZY GUY", PORN PERFORMER JON MARTIN TOLD ME OF JACK ON FACEBOOK IN 2012. "YOU
NEVER KNEW EXACTLY WHAT HE WOULD DO IN A SCENE WITH YOU. KEPT YOU ON YOUR TOES!"

"I ONLY EVER DID THE ONE SCENE WITH HIM IN NEW WAVE HOOKERS", SEX GODDESS GINGER LYNN MENTIONED WHEN
I ASKED HER ABOUT JACK IN 2014. "I REMEMBER BEING SORT OF INTIMIDATED BY HIM BECAUSE I THOUGHT HE WAS
JUST SO COOL."

HE WAS INDEED. NOT MANY ACTORS EVER DID A SCENE WITH THE FONZ ON HAPPY DAYS AND HELD THEIR OWN IN THE
"COOL" DEPARTMENT. 'STICKS' DID, AND MADE IT LOOK ALL-TOO EASY, EVEN IN THE FACE OF BIGOTRY. "WHY DO I
GET THE FEELIN' I WAS JUST HUMILIATED?" BAKER (AS STICKS) REMARKS TO RICHIE CUNNINGHAM, AS TWO WHITE
TEENAGE GIRLS BACK OUT OF THE ROOM, UTTERLY HORRIFIED AT THE IDEA THAT RICHIE MIGHT BE TRYING TO SET
THEM UP WITH A BLACK BOY -- EVEN ONE INTRODUCED AS "A FRIEND OF THE FONZ."

THE XXX INDUSTRY WAS JUST FINALLY COMING OUT OF A BIGOTED ERA IN THE MID 1980S WHEN BAKER WAS MAKING
HIS DEBUT. SOME WOULD ARGUE THAT IT NEVER REALLY SHED THAT SKIN, BUT MOST WOULD AGREE THAT IS WHEN
CHANGE BEGAN. GINGER LYNN (AS WELL AS DOZENS OF OTHER WHITE STARS) HAD PREVIOUSLY SAID THEY WOULDN'T
WORK WITH AFRICAN-AMERICANS, BUT FROM 1985 TO 1987, INTERRACIAL SCENES SLOWLY BECAME FAR MORE
PREVALENT. I DON'T NECESSARILY THINK IT WAS BECAUSE THEY WERE ALL RACISTS, THOUGH. JUST COWARDLY. BEING
SEEN PENETRATED BY BLACK COCK WAS PUBLICLY CONSIDERED CAREER SUICIDE BY VARIOUS WHITE WOMEN IN THE
INDUSTRY, MAINLY BECAUSE IT WAS PRESUMED THAT A DECENT PERCENTAGE OF THE INDUSTRY'S PROFITS WERE
GENERATED IN THE AMERICAN SOUTH.

"BLACKS DON'T GO OVER IN THE SOUTH," AN ANONYMOUS PORN PRODUCER TOLD ADAM FILM WORLD MAGAZINE IN THEIR
JUNE 1983 ISSUE. "THAT'S A BIG PIECE OF THE MARKET. BLACK GIRLS, YES, AS LONG AS THEY AREN'T DOMINANT, JUST
WOMEN WHO ARE FUCKED."

ACCORDING TO VARIOUS SOURCES, AGENTS AND PRODUCERS WERE CONSTANTLY IN THE STARS' EARS ABOUT IT, TELLING
THEM THAT DOING AN INTERRACIAL SCENE COULD DEEPLY HURT THEIR CAREER. OF COURSE, WE ALL KNOW NOW THAT

JACK AS THE
ESTEEMED
DR. I.B. BROWN,
HERE TO MAKE
YOU FEEL GOOD
ABOUT BUTT LOVE.

ALL RIGHT,
LET'S DISCUSS
RECTAL
INTIMACIES!

TURNED OUT TO BE TOTALLY
UNTRUE, BUT FOR A WHILE THAT
SHAMEFUL THEORY WAS A TANGIBLE
PART OF THE WAY THE INDUSTRY
DID BUSINESS. THAT SAID, EVEN IN
THE MID TO LATE 1980S, WHEN
BLACKS DID FINALLY START SHOWING
UP IN MAINSTREAM PORN, THE
TITLE OF THE VIDEO WOULD ALWAYS
ANNOUNCE THAT FACT. ALMOST LIKE
A WARNING.

"THE PORN INDUSTRY REGARDS THE
USE OF BLACKS AS A TAX ON THEIR
OPERATIONS RATHER THAN AS THE
PEOPLE THEY WANT TO EMPLOY",
PAT RILEY FUMED ON RAME.COM IN
FEBRUARY 1997. "ONLY AN ENDEMIC
ATTITUDE BY THE INDUSTRY, ITS
CUSTOMERS OR THE
INTERMEDIARIES IS A REASONABLE
EXPLANATION FOR THIS RACISM. I'M
HAPPY TO BELIEVE IT'S THE
CUSTOMERS, AND NOT NECESSARILY
IN THE SOUTH, WHO ARE BEING
PANDERED TO BY A GENERALLY
SPINELESS INDUSTRY."

"I KEEP HEARING A LOT ABOUT 'THE POWERS THAT BE' THAT TELL WHITE WOMEN THAT IT'S NOT IN THEIR INTEREST TO WORK WITH BLACKS," SHELDON RANZ REPLIED IN THAT SAME RAME.COM THREAD. "WHEN BARBARA DARE AND HYAPATIA LEE CONFESSED THEIR REFUSAL TO WORK WITH BLACK PERFORMERS, THEY AT LEAST DID NOT INSULT OUR INTELLIGENCE BY CLAIMING THAT THEY WERE "TOLD" BY MYSTERIOUS, UNNAMED PARTIES NOT TO INTERRACIALLY INDULGE, NOR DID THEY OFFER PARTICULAR COMPLAINTS ABOUT BLACK PERFORMERS OR CLAIM THAT THEY FOUND BLACK MEN UNATTRACTIVE. STACY MITNICK (DARE) IS AN OPEN RACIST, WHILE VICKI LYNCH (LEE) CLAIMS SHE WAS RAPED BY BLACK MEN PRIOR TO DOING PORN. EVER WONDER IF SHE WOULD HAVE SWORN OFF WHITE MEN IF SOME OF THEM HAD RAPED HER? WHEN NINA HARTLEY'S HUSBAND, DAVE, POSED THIS QUESTION TO THE LEES YEARS AGO, THE RESULT WAS A SHOUTING MATCH."

BAKER, FOR HIS PART, NEVER WEIGHED IN ON THE DEBATE ABOUT RACISM IN THE INDUSTRY, AT LEAST NOT IN ANY INTERVIEWS I'VE FOUND. HE JUST WORKED STEADILY, AND IN THAT RESPECT MANAGED TO MAKE A BUNCH OF DECENT (ALTHOUGH VERY LOW BUDGET) XXX RELEASES THAT DIDN'T HAVE ANYTHING TO DO WITH THE DARK BROS. ONE THAT I LIKE IS 1985'S HILL STREET BLACKS. IT'S INCREDIBLY CHEAP LOOKING AND HONESTLY PRETTY DUMB, BUT JACK MAKES IT SO FUN TO WATCH. ONE OF THE VERY FIRST SHOT-ON-VIDEO PICTURES IN THE TEN-YEAR DIRECTORIAL CAREER OF SCOTTY FOX, THIS SPOOF OF THE GRITTY COP TV SERIES HILL STREET BLUES FEATURES BAKER AS THE GRUMPY PRECINCT SERGEANT WHO DOES EVERYTHING BY THE BOOK. HIS CO-STAR, WHO WORKED CLOSELY WITH HIM IN DOZENS OF FILMS, IS F. M. BRADLEY. THE TWO OF THEM WERE A DEPENDABLE COMBO, WITH BAKER PROVIDING THE FUNNY AND BRADLEY BEING THE STRAIGHT MAN WITH THE BIG ERECT COCK.

SERGEANT JACK BAKER CAN'T ABIDE THE CONSTANT RUTTING BY HIS FELLOW OFFICERS IN 1985'S HILL STREET BLACKS.

THE PLOT IS PRETTY SIMPLE. THE ALL AFRICAN-AMERICAN PRECINCT BOOKS FIVE WHITE AND ASIAN PROSTITUTES, AND THE ARRESTING OFFICERS TAKE THEM IN THE BACK ROOM ONE BY ONE AND "PUMP THEM FOR INFORMATION". BAKER IS THE FLY IN THE OINTMENT, TRYING TO CLEAN UP THE PLACE AND CATCH HIS DEPUTIES IN THE ACT SO HE CAN GET THEM FIRED. LADY STEPHANIE (A GORGEOUS SMALL-BREASTED BLACK PORN STAR FROM THE 1980S WHO DOESN'T GET NEARLY ENOUGH PROPS FROM XXX HISTORIANS) IS GREAT AS A FIRM OFFICER WHO PROVES IT ISN'T JUST MALE OFFICERS OF THE LAW WHO ABUSE THEIR POSITIONS OF POWER. SHE SITS ON ONE OF THE WHORE'S FACES AND GRINDS OUT AN ORGASM FOR HERSELF.

"ALL I TRY TO DO IS RUN THIS STATION RIGHT, AND THEY TRY TO TURN IT INTO SHIT!" BAKER STOMPS AND FUMES AS HE REALIZES THE MOVIE IS SOON TO COME TO A CLOSE, AND HE HASN'T BUSTED EVEN ONE OF THE HORNY AND CONSISTENTLY UNPROFESSIONAL COPS THAT WORK FOR HIM. "THEY TURN EVERYTHING INTO SHIT! MY LIFE IS SHIT!" WHEN SLUTTY KATIE THOMAS DROPS TO HER KNEES AND TRIES TO CHEER HIM UP BY SUCKING HIS COCK AND USING HER SHAPELY TITS TO CATCH HIS SQUIRTING CUM, HE GOES FOR IT BECAUSE F.M. BRADLEY TRICKS HIM INTO THINKING SHE IS AN UNDERCOVER OFFICER FROM ANOTHER PRECINCT. OF COURSE, SHE TURNS OUT TO BE A REAL HOOKER.

"BAKER LIVED HIS LIFE LIKE HIS MANY COLOURFUL CHARACTERS, ON THE EDGE AND SOMETIMES WAY WAY OVER THE EDGE", PORN DIRECTOR TOBY DAMMIT WROTE IN AN ISSUE OF SMUTZINE, "HE ALWAYS HAD SOMETHING BREWING AND WAS HUSTLING THIS AND SCHEMING THAT... BAKER CRAMMED ABOUT 30 LIFETIMES INTO HIS SHORT-LIVED ONE."

"JACK WAS AS FUCKED UP AS THEY COME," REMEMBERED TOBY. "I NEVER MET HIM WHEN HE DIDN'T ASK ME FOR A COUPLE OF BUCKS... I MISS HIM. HE WAS A UNIQUE SPIRIT AND TOTALLY INSANE. NOW WE CAN GIVE HIM THE RESPECT THAT HE DESERVES, 'CAUSE HE'S UP THERE WITH A BOTTLE OF JACK IN ONE HAND AND HIS PECKER IN THE OTHER, LAUGHING AT US ALL DOWN HERE".

TOBY (REAL NAME TONY BINER) PASSED AWAY FAIRLY RECENTLY, HIMSELF. I'D BEEN CHATTING WITH HIM ON FACEBOOK A FEW DAYS EARLIER ABOUT SETTING UP AN INTERVIEW WITH HIS FRIEND, 1970S PORN DIRECTOR ED DEPRIEST, BUT IT NEVER PANNED OUT. DESPITE ONLINE RUMOURS OF A TRYST WITH A HOOKER GONE WRONG, TOBY DIED OF A

GREG AND WALTER DARK, THE BAD BOYS OF THE LATE 1980s PORNO SCENE.

Dark Bros
PURVEYORS OF FINE FILTH

PULMONARY EMBOLISM IN HIS HOME IN VAN NUYS, CALIFORNIA ON JANUARY 1ST, 2014.

"JACK BAKER WAS DIAGNOSED WITH CANCER OF THE BLADDER TOO LATE", JACK'S FORMER ROOMMATE, HART WILLIAMS, SAID WHEN HE BROKE THE NEWS OF JACK'S DEATH ON THE ALT.SEX.MOVIES NEWSGROUP. "THE DOCTORS COULD DO NOTHING FOR HIM, BUT HE TOOK 2 YEARS IN DYING, AND WASTED AWAY TO NOTHING. HIS BLADDER WAS REMOVED, AND HE WAS FORCED TO WEAR A BAG (THE URINARY EQUIVALENT OF A COLOSTOMY BAG). THE CANCER CONTINUED TO SPREAD. HE WAS TESTED AND PRODDED AND POKED TO EXCESS."

LEGENDARY PORN MAGAZINE PHOTOGRAPHER AND UNDERGROUND CULT FILM ACTOR/DIRECTOR TITUS MOEDE WAS JACK'S BEST FRIEND AND BUSINESS PARTNER. AFTER THINGS WENT SOUR AT MENNING'S CINEMART, TITUS LET JACK MOVE IN SO HE'D HAVE A PLACE TO STAY AND WOULDN'T BE OUT ON THE STREET. DESPITE THEIR AGE DIFFERENCE (TITUS WAS QUITE A BIT OLDER) THE TWO OF THEM LOOKED OUT FOR ONE ANOTHER, AND HAD BIG PLANS TO MAKE MORE ADULT MOVIES TOGETHER. TITUS STATED THAT JACK TOOK PRETTY GOOD CARE

OF HIMSELF, COMPARED TO MANY OF HIS CO-STARS IN THE ADULT INDUSTRY. "HE ATE WELL, DIDN'T DO DRUGS, SMOKED THE OCCASIONAL CIGARETTE AND WOULD DRINK BEER, BUT TWO BEERS WOULD GIVE HIM A BUZZ." TITUS SWORE UP AND DOWN THAT JACK WASN'T A DRUG ADDICT OR A BOOZER AS SOME HAD SUSPECTED, AND THAT EVERY MINOR AND INSIGNIFICANT VICE HE HAD WAS ENJOYED IN MODERATION. JACK APPARENTLY DIDN'T PARTY ALL THAT HARDY.

DURING THE LONG, EXCRUCIATING TWO YEARS THAT IT TOOK JACK TO DIE OF CANCER, HE STAYED AT OLIVE VIEW HOSPITAL IN SYLMAR, THEN A CONVALESCENT HOSPITAL IN BURBANK. JUST BEFORE THE END OF HIS LIFE IN 1994, JACK WAS ESSENTIALLY PARALYZED. THE CANCER WAS SPREADING TO HIS BRAIN. IT WAS THEN THAT TITUS GOT THE BAD NEWS THAT JACK HAD BEEN SHIPPED OFF TO LOS ANGELES COUNTY HOSPITAL, AND INSTANTLY KNEW IT WOULDN'T BE LONG. HE'D GET TO SEE HIS FRIEND JUST ONE LAST TIME.

"ABOUT 25 MEDICAL PERSONNEL WERE IN THE ROOM, HART WILLIAMS WROTE OF JACK'S LAST HOURS. "AND JACK, HANDS FOLDED ACROSS HIS CHEST, GAVE ONE LAST

BAKER REVEALS THE INS AND OUTS OF A "BITCH'S ASS" IN 1985's BETWEEN THE CHEEKS.

SPEECH. HE IDENTIFIED TITUS AS HIS PARTNER, AND TOLD ABOUT THE FILMS THEY WERE GOING TO DO WHEN HE GOT BETTER. HE EXPLAINED THAT HE MADE PORN FILMS, AND ANSWERED QUESTIONS. HE WAS IN GOOD SPIRITS THROUGHOUT. HE HAD BEEN IN GOOD SPIRITS FOR THE ENTIRE TWO HELLISH YEARS. HE ASKED, WHEN IT WAS OVER, IF HE COULD HAVE A CIGARETTE AND A DRINK. IT WOULD BE HIS LAST REQUEST. IT WAS DENIED.

TITUS AND SHARON MITCHELL PLANNED TO VISIT JACK ON SUNDAY, NOVEMBER THE 13TH. "THE MORGUE CALLED ME AT 6 AM," TITUS SAID. HE CALLED SHARON, AND WHEN SHE PICKED UP, HE QUIETLY SAID: "WE'RE NOT GOING TO BE VISITING JACK TODAY." JACK BAKER WAS DEAD. HE WAS 47 YEARS OLD.

WATCHIN' MOVIES IN MAH UNDIES

THAT'S WHAT I DO!

NEARLY EVERY FILM I WATCH AT HOME IS VIEWED IN NUTTIN' BUT THESE TIGHTY WHITIES!

THE ONLY REASON I DO THIS IS FOR MY OWN SAFETY.

IT'S TRUE.

IF I WEAR PANTS AND WATCH, I MIGHT EXPLODE OR SOMETHING.

COULD HAPPEN

34

REMEMBERING THE CAPRI

THE CAPRI WAS PART OF A TRIO OF TIMES SQUARE'S MOST INFAMOUS PORNO-DENS, WHICH ALL LINED UP RIGHT NEXT TO EACH OTHER AT 738 8TH AVENUE (ON THE CORNER OF 46TH STREET) IN NEW YORK. THE OTHER TWO WERE THE EROS (WHICH SPECIALIZED IN GAY FILMS AND MALE STRIPPERS), AND THE VENUS (FORMERLY THE EROS 2).

THE BUILDING WAS A PLAIN-JANE 4 STORY MULTIPLE-FAMILY DWELLING BUILT IN THE 1920S, AND IN 1957 THE FIRST AND SECOND STORY WERE CONVERTED INTO A RESTAURANT. IN SEPTEMBER OF 1969 A THEATER WITH A SEAT CAPACITY OF 171 ON THE 1ST FLOOR AND 66 BALCONY SEATS ON THE SECOND FLOOR (WHICH ALSO HOUSED THE PROJECTION

BOOTH) WAS BUILT. THE UPSTAIRS TENANTS WERE KICKED OUT, AND A "CARETAKER'S DUPLEX APARTMENT" WAS INSTALLED ON THE 3RD AND 4TH FLOORS.

"IN THE EARLY 1990S, WHILE THE THEATER WAS STILL IN FULL OPERATION, I HAD OCCASION, IN A WORK CAPACITY, TO VISIT THE UPSTAIRS CARETAKER'S DUPLEX APARTMENT. IT WAS ACCESSED THROUGH A VERY NARROW, HIDDEN-PANEL TYPE DOOR BEHIND THE BOX OFFICE, WHICH LED TO FLIGHTS OF STAIRS. THERE I ENCOUNTERED AN OFFICE-LIKE APARTMENT WITH A VERY INTEGRATED AND COOL 1960S DESIGN, WITH A NUMBER OF OLD-STYLE 5-LINE TELEPHONES VISIBLE ON END TABLES. IT WAS OCCUPIED BY A PLEASANT, GRANDMOTHERLY WOMAN. SOMEONE THERE SAID IT WAS THE APARTMENT OF THE OWNER OF THE THREE THEATERS ON THE BLOCK. I ASKED WHETHER THE ELDERLY WOMAN WAS THE OWNER'S MOTHER, AND WAS TOLD, 'NO, STUPID, SHE IS THE OWNER.'"   – "MDCHANIC," CINEMATREASURES.ORG

"THE CAPRI CINEMA WAS OPENED BY CHELLY WILSON IN 1969", SAID LEGENDARY ADULT FILM DIRECTOR SHAUN COSTELLO. "SHE OPERATED THIS VENUE FOR ONLY A YEAR BEFORE SELLING IT TO ANOTHER GREEK IMMIGRANT, TEDDY KARIOFILIS, WHO, WITH MINOR PARTNER TOM GIOULOS, OPERATED THE THEATER UNTIL THE EARLY EIGHTIES. WITH HIS POCKETS FILLED WITH PORNOCASH, TEDDY KARIOFILIS LEFT THE THEATER IN GIOULOS'S HANDS AND RETURNED TO GREECE TO HIS FAMILY'S SHEEP FARM. GIOULOS CONTINUED TO OPERATE THE CAPRI, WHICH HAD BECOME A CRACK HOUSE, UNTIL IT WAS FINALLY PUT OUT OF ITS MISERY, AND BLESSEDLY CLOSED. I MADE MANY OF THE FILMS SHOWN AT THE CAPRI FROM 1974 UNTIL 1978, AND KNEW BOTH TEDDY AND TOM QUITE WELL. THE THEATER WAS A SERIOUS CASH COW, AND PLAYED CONTINUOUS PORN TO FULL HOUSES, WITH LITTLE ADVERTISING."

THE FIRST TIME HE MET TOM AND TEDDY IN 1973, COSTELLO TOOK THE OL' SUBWAY TO TIMES SQUARE AND ARRIVED AT THE CAPRI FIRST THING IN THE MORNING AS THE THEATER WAS OPENING. THERE TO SEE IF HE COULD GET THE TWO BUSINESSMEN TO INVEST IN HIS NEXT PORNO, SHAUN WAS HAPPY TO SEE

THE THEATER AS IT APPEARED IN THE QUIRKY 1971 DOCUMENTARY **AMERICAN SEXUAL REVOLUTION** (DIR: J.W. ABBOTT)

THAT THE NAME OF ONE OF HIS PREVIOUS FILMS, **SEXUAL FREEDOM IN THE OZARKS**, WAS UP ON THE MARQUEE. "IT WASN'T YET 10AM AND PEOPLE WERE ALREADY PAYING TO GET IN," HE WROTE ON HIS BLOG ABOUT THE EXPERIENCE.

"THE BOX OFFICE ATTENDANT WAS PRETTY GRUFF AND KEPT REPEATING 'FOUR DOLLARS, FOUR DOLLARS', UNTIL I FINALLY GOT HIS ATTENTION BY TELLING HIM I WAS THERE TO SEE TOM. AFTER MAKING A CALL HE WAVED ME THROUGH THE TURNSTILE, POINTING UP AND SHOUTING, 'UPSTAIRS, UPSTAIRS'. THERE WAS A NARROW STAIRWAY TO THE BALCONY, WHICH WAS PRETTY CROWDED EVEN AT THIS EARLY HOUR, AND AS I CLIMBED UP TOWARD THE PROJECTION BOOTH I HEARD A FAMILIAR VOICE, MY OWN. I TURNED, AND UP THERE ON THE SCREEN WAS A PORN ACTRESS NAMED ANDREA TRUE, BENT OVER A FEW BALES OF HAY, AND STANDING BEHIND HER WAS ME, NAKED EXCEPT FOR COWBOY BOOTS, AND FUCKING MS. TRUE FOR ALL THE WORLD TO SEE. I LAUGHED OUT LOUD, WHICH SEEMED TO DISTURB SOME MEMBERS OF THE AUDIENCE WHOSE CONCENTRATION HAD BEEN BROKEN BY MY CARELESS LEVITY."

"A CRACK OF LIGHT APPEARED IN THE BACK OF THE BALCONY AS THE DOOR TO THE NEXT LEVEL OPENED. MY EYES HAD NOT YET FULLY ADJUSTED TO THE DARKNESS SO I SLOWLY CLIMBED THROUGH, AND AS THE DOOR CLOSED BEHIND ME A GLAD HAND GRABBED MINE. 'SHAUN, HOW YA DOIN. GREAT TO MEETCHA. C'MON UP, TEDDY'S DYIN' TO SEE YA'. THIS WAS TOM, WHO HAD CALLED ME A FEW DAYS

EARLIER. HE LED ME UP THE STAIRS AND INTO THEIR OFFICES ABOVE THE THEATER, WHERE WE WALKED THROUGH A PRIVATE PROJECTION ROOM AND INTO A LARGE, WOOD PANELLED OFFICE THAT FACED EAST. BEHIND A DESK THAT SEEMED MUCH TOO LARGE FOR ITS OCCUPANT SAT A LITTLE ROUND MAN WITH AN ENORMOUS BALDING HEAD, WHO JUMPED UP WHEN I ENTERED THE ROOM AND APPROACHED ME WITH BOTH ARMS OUTSTRETCHED. 'OH SHUN, SHUN, YOU MAKE ME SO HAPPY. YOU COME TO SEE TEDDY HUH? OH, SHUN, SHUN'."

"HIS HEAD WAS LOW AND COCKED TO ONE SIDE, AND THE MUSCULATURE IN HIS FACE WAS TIGHT. 'OH, SHUN, SHUN. I GOT NO MONEY'. I WONDERED IF HE WAS GOING TO ASK ME FOR A LOAN. ANYTHING WAS POSSIBLE UNDER THESE PREPOSTEROUS CIRCUMSTANCES. SO I CONTINUED TO LISTEN. 'OH, SHUN, SHUN, WHAT CAN I DO UH? WHAT CAN TEDDY DO? SHUN, I GOT NO MONEY'. I'M STILL LISTENING. 'OH SHUN, YOU HELP TEDDY UH? YOU WORK CHEAP FOR TEDDY UH. I GOT NO MONEY'."

"I SUGGEST THAT HIS THEATER, EVEN AT TEN O CLOCK IN THE MORNING, WAS PACKED WITH PAYING CUSTOMERS, AND HIS FACE CHANGED SHAPE AGAIN. HE LOOKED AWAY FOR MOMENT, THEN THOUGHTFULLY TURNED HIS SLIGHTLY COCKED HEAD BACK TO ME, AND NEARLY IN TEARS REPLIED, 'OH, SHUN, SHUN, IT'S SO COLD OUTSIDE. I LET THE PEOPLE IN FOR FREE TO KEEP THEM WARM. THEY GOT NO MONEY, BUT I KEEP THEM WARM FOR FREE, UH? TEDDY KEEPS THEM WARM'. AT THIS POINT I REMINDED HIM THAT I WAS DOWNSTAIRS AND WATCHED THE CUSTOMERS PAYING FOUR DOLLARS EACH FOR HIS WARMTH, AND HIS FACE CHANGED AGAIN. HE APPEARED CONCERNED, BUT BEHIND HIS CONCERN AN INVISIBLE GRIN WAS REVEALING ITSELF AS HE SAID, 'OH SHUN, HEAT COSTS MONEY UH?' AND SLOWLY ALL OF HIS FEATURES TURNED UPWARD, HE THREW HIS HEAD BACK, AND ROARED WITH LAUGHTER. TOM SLAPPED ME ON THE BACK, AND TEDDY SEEMED BESIDE HIMSELF. 'OH, SHUN, SHUN, IT NEVER HURTS TO BARGAIN A LITTLE UH? WE MAKE MOVIES, YOU AND ME. WE MAKE MOVIES'. TEDDY COULD TAKE THIS ROUTINE TO THE CATSKILLS AND MAKE A LIVING AS A COMEDIAN."

"DURING THE EIGHT MONTHS THAT FOLLOWED, AND UNDER THE NAME OSCAR TRIPE, I WOULD DELIVER THREE FEATURES TO TEDDY AND TOM. THE FIRST WAS **COME FLY WITH US**, A STEWARDESS BUDDY MOVIE THAT DID BIG BOX OFFICE AT THE CAPRI, AND MADE TEDDY KARIOFILIS A VERY HAPPY GREEK. THE SECOND WAS **LADY ON THE COUCH** A LOST IDENTITY "PSYCHOANALYTICAL PORNODRAMA" STARRING ANDREA TRUE. IT DID HEALTHY, IF NOT GANGBUSTER BOX OFFICE, KEEPING TEDDY SMILING. AND THE THIRD WAS **THE LOVE BUS**, A CHEAPLY MADE, SILLY SEX FARCE THAT PLAYED TO STANDING ROOM ONLY AUDIENCES AT THE CAPRI CINEMA."

COSTELLO'S **TEENAGE NURSES** PLAYED AT THE CAPRI FOR A SOLD-OUT 9 WEEKS, FROM 14 MAY - 15 JULY 1974. ASIDE FROM LUIS ANTONERO'S **TEMPTATIONS** (1976), THIS WOULD BE THE LONGEST RUN IN THE HISTORY OF THE CINEMA, WHICH SAYS A LOT ABOUT THE AUDIENCE AT THE CAPRI, CONSIDERING HOW CONFUSING, DISJOINTED AND ODD THIS TRIPPY FUCKING THING IS. ORIGINALLY SHOT BY DIRECTOR DOUG COLLINS IN 1971 UNDER THE TITLE **AN AMERICAN IN BETHESDA**, TEENAGE NURSES WAS INTENDED AS A PORNO-MUSICAL. NOT SURPRISINGLY, THE IDEA WAS A TOUGH SELL, AND COLLINS WAS FORCED TO SELL OFF HIS UNMARKETABLE WAD OF WEIRDNESS TO COSTELLO, WHO SHOT A BUNCH OF UNAPPEALING XXX FOOTAGE AND ADDED A LAUGH TRACK. "VIETNAM VETS, VAUDEVILLE AND VIVACIOUSNESS", READ THE ADVERTISING FOR THE MOVIE.

"AS A SEX FILM IT WAS JUST GOD-AWFUL", COSTELLO ADMITTED. "IT WAS VERY SELF-INDULGENT BEHAVIOUR ON MY PART, IN KEEPING WITH MY BEHAVIOUR IN GENERAL BACK THEN. TALKING TEDDY KARIOFILIS INTO PUTTING HIS MONEY INTO SOMETHING RIDICULOUS WAS ONE OF MY FAVOURITE ENDEAVOURS... TEENAGE NURSES IS LIKE A CINEMATIC THALIDOMIDE BABY."

IN LATE 1976, TEDDY AND TOM STOPPED RUNNING ADS FOR THEIR FILMS IN THE VILLAGE VOICE AND OTHER LOCAL PAPERS, DEEMING IT A NEEDLESS EXTRAVAGANCE WHEN THEY WERE REGULARLY FILLING THE PLACE ANYHOW. UNFORTUNATELY THIS PENNY-PINCHING ATTITUDE PLAYED A INTEGRAL PART IN DETRIMENTALLY CHANGING THE OVERALL MAKE UP OF THE CAPRI'S AUDIENCE. FILM FANS AND ADULT FILM ENTHUSIASTS FROM OTHER HOODS BEGAN TO STAY AWAY, AND THEY WERE REPLACED BY SMELLY STREET SCUM. AS THE '70S CAME TO A CLOSE, THE AREA AROUND THE CAPRI GOT ROUGHER AND ROUGHER, WITH CRIME AND PROSTITUTION RUNNING RAMPANT.

"BETWEEN PIMPS, DRUGS AND THE CLIENTELE, PROSTITUTES GET USED UP IN A HURRY IN TIMES SQUARE," WROTE FRANK FORTUNATO ABOUT THE PISS-STAINED SIDEWALK IN FRONT OF THE CAPRI, EROS, AND VENUS IN THE OCT. 1979 ISSUE OF SWANK MAGAZINE. "WHEN A GIRL IS NO LONGER FIT TO COMPETE NORTH OF 42ND STREET, HER PIMP WILL MOVE HER ONE NOTCH DOWN THE LADDER, WHICH TRANSLATES TO SOUTH OF 42ND. HOOKERS WORKING HERE GENERALLY TRICK FOR A FEW BUCKS LESS THAN THEIR SISTER SLUTS WORKING NORTH OF THE 42ND STREET DEMARCATION LINE. THEY ARE MORE LARCENOUS, HOWEVER, AND THIS AREA IS VERY MUCH A CRIME ZONE. BE FOREWARNED."

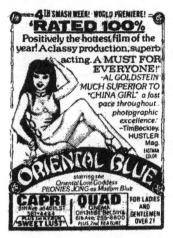
"PIMPING IS A GROWTH INDUSTRY ON 8TH AVENUE", FORTUNATO CONTINUED. "THE NATIONAL MEDIA (MOST RECENTLY 60 MINUTES) HAS INTRODUCED THIS STREET ACROSS AMERICA AS THE STREET WHERE PIMPS RECRUIT GIRLS FROM AS FAR AWAY AS THE MIDWEST. THE RECRUITING IS DONE TWO BLOCKS SOUTH OF 42ND STREET AT THE PORT AUTHORITY BUS TERMINAL. AROUND THE CLOCK THE PREDATORS CRUISE THE BUS STATION PLAYING THE SPIDER AND FLY GAME WITH RUNAWAYS FRESH OFF THE BUSES. THE PIMPS USE THE SAME TACTICS -- LIES, HEROIN, AND PHYSICAL INTIMIDATION -- TO TURN OUT THEIR VICTIMS INTO SEXUAL MONEYMAKING MACHINES. HORROR STORIES START AT THE PORT AUTHORITY, AND NEITHER SEX IS IMMUNE. THE GIRLS WIND UP SOLICITING ON 8TH AVE, WHILE THE BOYS WORK AROUND THE CORNER ON 42ND STREET."

"IN THE MID-'80S TIMES SQUARE WAS NOT YET THE STERILE LITTLE TOKYO IT IS NOW," WROTE MICHELLE CLIFFORD IN THE

FIRST ISSUE OF HER ZINE, METASEX. "(THOSE THEATERS) ON 8TH AVENUE BETWEEN 45TH AND 46TH STREETS WERE THE APOTHEOSIS OF THE ALL-NIGHTER. A MIASMA OF SOCIETAL OUTCASTS WOULD DRIFT THROUGH AFTER MIDNIGHT. HOMELESS GUYS LOOKING FOR A WARM PLACE TO CRASH, FLASHERS, SHIT QUEENS, JUNKIES, CRACKHEADS, PICKPOCKETS, THE OCCASIONAL BEWILDERED, FLABBERGASTED OUT-OF-TOWNERS WHO'D DRIFT UP FROM THE PORT AUTHORITY BUS TERMINAL, AND QUITE A FEW REAL FREAKOS WHO DEFY CLASSIFICATION."

CLIFFORD REVEALED THAT BY 1985, THE CAPRI, EROS, AND THE VENUS HAD THEIR 16MM SMUT PRINTS SUPPLIED BY A SMALL NYC COMPANY CALLED VARIETY FILMS. "THROUGHOUT THE YEARS THE FILMS HAD BEEN RE-SPLICED BY PROJECTIONISTS AND PADDED OUT

TO THE POINT THAT THEY'RE MUTATIONS OF THEMSELVES", SHE WROTE. "FOOTAGE FROM THREE DIFFERENT MOVIES WOULD BE STITCHED TOGETHER TO FILL OUT AN HOUR LONG FEATURE. ONE OF THESE WAS RAPE ME DADDY WITH A GIRL IN AN INSANE ASYLUM. A CHEAPLY SURREALISTIC SCENE OF A GUY IN A GORILLA COSTUME IS CUT IN...ANOTHER IS WITCHCRAFT, WITH ITS TACKED-ON OPENING OF TWO DOMINATRIXES FORCING THEIR MALE SLAVE TO SUCK A DILDO."

BY THE LATE 1980S, THE PISS AND SEMEN-CAKED THEATER HAD DELVED TO ITS LOWEST AND MOST DISREPUTABLE POINT, OPERATING AS A CRACK DEN. POLICE MADE 11 ARRESTS IN 7 MONTHS IN 1989, ALL FOR SALES OF CRACK. FINALLY IN AUGUST 1989, 15 POLICE OFFICERS SWARMED THE PLACE AND SHUT IT DOWN FOR FEW MONTHS. IN OCTOBER 1995, NEWLY APPOINTED MAYOR RUDY GIULIANI AND HIS COUNCIL PASSED A ZONING ORDINANCE THAT WAS DESIGNED TO CLEAN UP TIMES SQUARE. IT FORBADE "X-RATED BUSINESSES" FROM OPERATING WITHIN

500 FEET OF RESIDENTIAL HOMES, SCHOOLS, HOUSES OF WORSHIP, OR EACH OTHER. UNDER THIS ORDINANCE, ONLY 28 OF THE 177 MANHATTAN COMMERCIAL SEX ESTABLISHMENTS WOULD SURVIVE.

THIS NEW LAW WOULD HAVE BEEN THE DEATH OF THE CAPRI HAD IT NOT ALREADY BEEN TARGETED A FEW MONTHS EARLIER FOR "VIOLATING 10 NYCRR SUBPART 24-2, AND NYC ADMIN. CODE -- 7-703(E)". THIS WAS A COURT ORDER PUSHED THROUGH THAT WAS DESIGNED TO HALT THE SPREAD OF THE HIV VIRUS BY CLOSING DOWN ANY BUSINESS WHERE PEOPLE WERE HAVING SEX IN PUBLIC.

ON MARCH 3, 1995, DR. BENJAMIN A. MOJICA, THE ACTING COMMISSIONER OF THE NEW YORK CITY HEALTH DEPARTMENT (NYC HEALTH DEPARTMENT), WROTE TO THE OWNERS OF THE CAPRI, STATING:

WORLD PREMIERE — 2½ Hr. Show

hot rods

PLUS EXTRA FEATURE

ALL MALE CAST — ADULTS ONLY

1st Run — EROS 1 — 732 8th AVE, 45th & 46th ST, 581-4594 — CONT 9 AM TILL MIDNIGHT

AN EXAMPLE OF THE GAY PORN FARE THAT WOULD PLAY AT THE CAPRI'S BROTHER THEATER, THE EROS 1.

"YOU ARE HEREBY NOTIFIED THAT THIS DEPARTMENT HAS REASON TO BELIEVE THAT YOUR ESTABLISHMENT HAS FACILITATED THE OCCURRENCE OF LEGALLY PROHIBITED SEXUAL ACTIVITIES ON THE PREMISES. SPECIFICALLY, ACTS OF FELLATIO HAVE BEEN OBSERVED IN VARIOUS PARTS OF YOUR ESTABLISHMENT."

THE CAPRI HAD A GOOD, FILTHY 27-YEAR RUN, STARTING WITH THE VERY FIRST HARDCORE EROTICA AND FOLLOWING THAT UP WITH A QUARTER CENTURY OF PROVIDING NEW YORKERS WITH NO-NONSENSE XXX FUCK FOOTAGE. TOWARDS ITS END, THE THEATER AVERAGED APPROXIMATELY 1200 PATRONS A WEEK, WHO CAME IN FROM THE COLD FROM 9AM UNTIL 6AM THE NEXT DAY. ALL FOR A MERE $5 ADMISSION PRICE.

IN 1996, PERMITS WERE ISSUED TO DEMOLISH AND RENOVATE THE 1ST FLOOR, TEAR OUT THE MEZZANINE AND REMOVE THE STOREFRONT AND MARQUEE. TODAY, NEARLY 20 YEARS AFTER BEING GUTTED, AN EMPTY GRAVEL LOT SURROUNDED BY CHAINLINK FENCES MAKES UP THE FORMER ADDRESS OF THE CAPRI CINEMA. IT REMAINS, AS OF THIS WRITING, ONE OF THE FEW UNDEVELOPED PARCELS OF LAND IN THE AREA.

HERE'S TO THE CAPRI! REST IN PEACE

GREAT HOLLYWOOD SPOOF SMUT THAT NEVER REALLY HAPPENED (BUT SHOULD HAVE)

THE STORY BEHIND THE LOGO FONT:

CINEMA SEWER

BY ISSUE 9 I REALIZED THAT IT WAS TIME TO WORRY ABOUT BRANDING AND MAKING IT EASIER FOR RETURN READERS TO RECOGNIZE CINEMA SEWER WHEN THEY SAW IT ON THE SHELF. ONE NIGHT I WAS THUMBING THROUGH A BEAT UP OLD ITALIAN LANGUAGE FILM MAGAZINE FROM 1973 CALLED CINESEX, AND ALL THROUGH IT THEY USED THIS REALLY COOL FONT TO HEADLINE EACH MOVIE THEY WERE REVIEWING. I RECOGNIZED IT AS A FONT THAT WAS USED OFTEN FOR VINTAGE EXPLOITATION, WOMEN IN PRISON, AND NAZISPLOITATION FILM POSTERS, AND ITS COLD, HARD LINES PUT ME IN MIND OF OLD SLEAZY MEN'S MAGAZINES. I CAREFULLY CLIPPED OUT EACH LETTER I'D NEED AND ASSEMBLED A LOGO WITH A GLUESTICK. THE ONLY PROBLEM WAS THAT THERE WASN'T A 'W' ANYWHERE IN THAT OLD ISSUE OF CINESEX, SO I JUST INVERTED A LETTER M. LATER, AFTER I BOUGHT A CATALOG FROM THE 1970S, I DISCOVERED THAT THIS NEGLECTED OLD FONT IS CALLED FUTURA DISPLAY, AND WAS DESIGNED BY A GERMAN NAMED PAUL RENNER IN 1932. RENNER SPOKE AGAINST THE NAZIS, AND WAS ARRESTED BY THEM FOR IT IN 1933.

THE SKYJACKER
(who almost became a spaghetti western star)

ON OCTOBER 31, 1969, A-19-YEAR OLD MARINE FROM SEATTLE (WHO EARNED THE PURPLE HEART WHILE ON DUTY DURING THE VIETNAM WAR) HIJACKED A TWA PASSENGER JET AND ORDERED THE PILOT TO FLY TO ROME, ITALY. IT WOULD BECOME THE LONGEST HIJACKING IN HISTORY, SPANNING 6,900 MILES AND 14 HOURS, AND WHEN IT WAS ALL OVER THE YOUNG HIJACKER WOULD BE OFFERED A MOVIE CONTRACT TO STAR IN A SPAGHETTI WESTERN.

RAFFAELE MINICHIELLO'S STORY IS A UNIQUE ONE. HE WAS BORN IN THE ITALIAN PROVINCE OF AVELLINO IN 1950, AND AT THE AGE OF 12, AN EARTHQUAKE DEMOLISHED THE FAMILY HOME. LEFT TO REBUILD AND START OVER, HIS MOTHER AND FATHER PACKED UP AND MOVED TO SEATTLE, WASHINGTON. THEN, 5 YEARS LATER IN 1967, RAFFAELE DROPPED OUT OF HIGH SCHOOL AND RAN OFF TO JOIN THE MARINES. HE WANTED TO SERVE HIS COUNTRY IN VIETNAM.

BY ALL ACCOUNTS, MINICHIELLO WAS AN EXCELLENT SOLDIER WHILE DOING A VERY TAXING TOUR OF DUTY, EVEN EARNING THE PURPLE HEART FOR HIS COURAGE IN BATTLE. BUT AS WITH SO MANY SOLDIERS, WAR BROKE HIS BRAIN A LITTLE BIT. HE WAS SHELLSHOCKED, AND THEN BEFORE YOU KNEW IT HE'D GONE OFF THE DEEP END. HE HIJACKED A TWA BOEING 707, AND DEMANDED THAT IT BE FLOWN TO ROME. IT WOULD BE THE FIRST TRANSATLANTIC HIJACKING IN HISTORY.

WHY RAFFAELE WANTED SO DESPERATELY TO GET BACK TO ITALY VARIES DEPENDING ON WHO TELLS THE STORY. IN ONE VERSION, RAFFAELE LEARNED THAT HIS BELOVED FATHER GOT CANCER WHILE HE WAS AWAY AT WAR, AND THE OLD MAN RETURNED TO HIS ROOTS TO COMMUNE WITH FAMILY IN THE OLD COUNTRY BEFORE HE PASSED AWAY. I.E. HE WANTED TO SEE HIS POPS ONE LAST TIME. IN ANOTHER, RAFFAELE BURGLARIZED A SUPPLY STORE AT MILITARY BASE CAMP PENDLETON, AND THE DAY HE WAS TO APPEAR AT HIS COURT MARTIAL IS THE DAY HE DECIDED TO BOARD THAT PLANE. IN ANOTHER ACCOUNT, AN ITALIAN NEWSPAPER, IL MESSAGGERO, REPORTED THAT THE REAL REASON BEHIND THE YOUNG SOLDIER'S AIR PIRACY WAS TO RECONNECT WITH AN OLD GIRLFRIEND NAMED ROSALIA, FROM NAPLES.

ALL THREE WERE TRUE TO SOME EXTENT, BUT THE REASON THAT WAS MOST PARAMOUNT IN HIS MIND -- THE THING THAT MADE HIM MOST FRUSTRATED AND VOLATILE -- WAS THAT THE US MILITARY HAD REFUSED SOME $200 THAT HE CLAIMED HAD BEEN PROMISED HIM. AND WHEN HE ASKED WHY THE CHEQUE HADN'T COME, HE WAS "TREATED WITHOUT THE PROPER RESPECT". WITH THAT INSULT ON HIS MIND, HE HELD UP THE CAMP PENDLETON SUPPLY STORE AS A WAY TO ENACT REVENGE.

$15.50 WAS ALL IT COST FOR A TICKET FROM LOS ANGELES TO SAN FRANCISCO AT THE TIME, SO RAFFAELE BOUGHT ONE AND BOARDED THE AIRCRAFT WITH A BAG FULL OF WEAPONS. HE HAD AN M-1 CARBINE RIFLE, 250 ROUNDS OF EXTRA AMMO, DYNAMITE BLASTING CAPS, AND A KNIFE. (KEEP IN MIND THAT AIRPORT SECURITY WAS VERY LAX IN 1969) THEN, WHILE THE PLANE WAS OVER FRESNO, CALIFORNIA, THE YOUNG SOLDIER STORMED THE COCKPIT AND ORDERED THE GROUP OF FOUR MEN IN IT TO FLY TO ITALY BY WAY OF NEW YORK. THE PILOT DID AS HE WAS TOLD, AND FOLLOWED THE ORDERS WITHOUT INCIDENT.

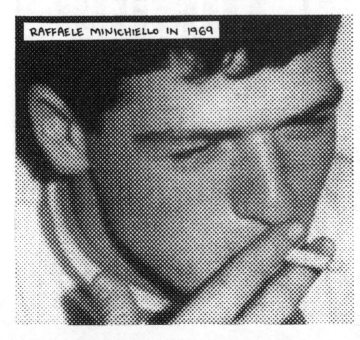

RAFFAELE MINICHIELLO IN 1969

WHILE STOPPED IN DENVER TO REFUEL, MINICHIELLO ALLOWED ALL 39 PASSENGERS AND TWO FLIGHT ATTENDANTS TO LEAVE, ALTHOUGH TWO OTHER FLIGHT ATTENDANTS AND ALL FOUR PILOTS STAYED ON. THE PLANE THEN MADE ANOTHER STOP IN NEW YORK CITY, WHERE THE FBI FRANTICALLY TRIED TO BRING THE HIJACKING TO AN END WHILE THE PLANE WAS ON THE TARMAC AT JOHN F. KENNEDY INTERNATIONAL AIRPORT. RESPLENDENT IN BULLETPROOF VESTS, A SWAT TEAM SURROUNDED THE AIRCRAFT, AND THEN QUICKLY BEAT A HASTY RETREAT WHEN MINICHIELLO RESPONDED BY FIRING A ROUND INTO THE CEILING OF THE CABIN. THE PARTY WAS JUST GETTING STARTED.

"I NEVER USED FORCE DURING THE HIJACKING", MINICHIELLO SAID IN A 2013 INTERVIEW WITH THE ITALIAN WEBSITE, 2DUERIGHE.COM. "THE ATMOSPHERE WAS RELAXED. I NEVER POINTED THE GUN AT ANYONE. I NEVER ABUSED THOSE

THE BOEING 707 ON THE GROUND IN DENVER.

PEOPLE. DURING THE CROSSING OF THE ATLANTIC, THE TWO HOSTESSES WERE ASLEEP AND I WAS SPEAKING ABOUT THIS AND THAT WITH THE FIRST CLASS CAPTAIN. I REMEMBER AT ONE POINT I WENT TO THE BATHROOM AND FORGOT TO TAKE THE GUN WITH ME, AND WHEN I RETURNED FROM THE BATHROOM THE GUN WAS STILL THERE ON THE GROUND... AND I'LL TELL YOU ANOTHER THING; WITH ONE OF THE AIRLINE HOSTESSES I DID A LITTLE FLIRTING. WE SHARED A PLATONIC LOVE FOR SOME TIME."

MORE STOPS WOULD BE MADE (BANGOR, MAINE AND SHANNON, IRELAND) BEFORE FINALLY ARRIVING IN ROME. THERE, MINICHIELLO HELD AN ITALIAN COP AT GUNPOINT WHILE HIJACKING HIS CAR. AFTER DRIVING TO A SMALL RURAL CHURCH 10 MILES SOUTH OF THE AIRPORT, THE OFFICER WAS RESCUED WHEN POLICE (AND A SMALL ARMY OF REPORTERS) FINALLY TRACKED THEM DOWN 5 HOURS LATER. IT WAS NOVEMBER 1ST, 1969 -- RAFFAELE'S 20TH BIRTHDAY.

LAUDED AS AN INNOCENT VICTIM OF THE IMPERIALIST AMERICAN WAR MACHINE, THE ITALIANS SAW HIM AS A FOLK HERO, A SEX SYMBOL, AND AN INSTANT CELEBRITY. MARRIAGE PROPOSALS POURED IN BY THE BOX-LOAD, AND TEENAGE GIRLS TOTALLY LOST THEIR SHIT. THEY SWOONED OVER RAFFAELE'S HUNKY LOOKS, AND OFFERED SUGGESTIONS FOR HIS NEXT ACT: A SINGER, AN ACTOR, A MODEL, OR AN ATHLETE. ANYTHING WHERE THEY COULD MOISTEN THEIR PANTIES OVER GETTING TO SEE HIS HANDSOME FRAME.

"ITALIAN TEENAGERS WOULD TALK ABOUT HOW MUCH THEY WANTED TO MARRY HIM AND HOW MORE BEAUTIFUL HE WAS THAN MOST MATINEE IDOLS IN THAT COUNTRY", AUTHOR BRENDAN KOERNER TOLD NPR RADIO IN 2014. HE WROTE A BOOK (THE SKIES BELONG TO US) ABOUT THE HISTORY OF PLANE HIJACKINGS. "IN DOING THE RESEARCH AND SEEING THE KIND OF FLIPPANT ATTITUDE PEOPLE HAD ABOUT HIJACKINGS, (I FOUND THAT) A LOT OF PEOPLE SAW THEM AS AN ADVENTURE."

"HE'S EVEN BETTER THAN GIULIANO GEMMA," ONE 17-YEAR-OLD GIRL SQUEALED WHEN ASKED BY AN ITALIAN STREET REPORTER ABOUT MINICHIELLO IN 1971. "I WOULD LIKE TO MARRY HIM!"

A FEW DAYS LATER IN NORWOOD OHIO, A 14-YEAR-OLD KID NAMED DAVID BOOTH SAW THE SUCCESSFUL RESULTS OF RAFFAELE'S HOSTAGE CRISIS ON THE NIGHTLY NEWS, AND CUT CLASS THE NEXT DAY. ARMED

THE M-1 CARBINE RIFLE USED IN THE HIJACKING.

WITH A NICE BIG HUNTING KNIFE, HE CAUGHT A BUS TO THE AIRPORT IN CINCINNATI WHERE HE GRABBED AN 18-YEAR-OLD BALLERINA WAITING IN THE TERMINAL. THROUGH TEARS SHE HEARD HIM SAY THAT THE TWO OF THEM WERE GOING TO STOLKHOLM, SWEDEN, AND THE NEXT THING SHE KNEW SHE WAS BEING HUSTLED ONTO A DELTA DC-9. UNFORTUNATELY FOR BOOTH, DC-9'S ARE UNABLE TO CROSS THE ATLANTIC AND HE WAS EVENTUALLY CONVINCED TO LET THE GIRL GO AND SURRENDER PEACEFULLY. ZERO PANTIES WERE MOISTENED AND BOOTH DISAPPEARED FROM THE PUBLIC'S RADAR.

THE ITALIAN GOVERNMENT REFUSED TO EXTRADITE MINICHIELLO TO AMERICA (ITALIAN LAW DID NOT PERMIT EXTRADITION FOR ANY OFFENCE THAT CARRIED THE DEATH PENALTY), AND INSTEAD TRIED AND CONVICTED HIM IN AN ITALIAN COURT FOR FAR LESSER OFFENCES SUCH AS WEAPONS POSSESSION. AT HIS TRIAL, THE DEFENCE LAWYER STATED THAT HIS CLIENT WAS AN "UNCULTURED PEASANT" WHOSE MIND HAD BEEN UNFAIRLY SWAYED BY "A CIVILIZATION OF AIRCRAFT AND WAR VIOLENCE." MINICHIELLO WAS SENTENCED TO SEVEN AND A HALF YEARS IN PRISON, WHICH WAS THEN REDUCED TO 3 YEARS BY AN APPEALS COURT, BEFORE ITALIAN PRESIDENT GIUSEPPE SARAGAT DECLARED A GENERAL AMNESTY -- KNOCKING TWO YEARS OFF OF ALL SENTENCES IN THE COUNTRY. RELEASED AFTER SERVING ONLY 18 MONTHS, THE YOUNG HIJACKER RETURNED TO CIVILIAN LIFE WITH A HERO'S WELCOME.

FILM PRODUCER CARLO PONTI (THE LONG-TIME HUSBAND OF SOPHIA LOREN AND THE MAN BEHIND BLOW UP, DOCTOR ZHIVAGO, ZABRISKIE POINT, FLESH FOR FRANKENSTEIN, AND DIRTY WEEKEND) TOOK NOTICE OF ALL THE ATTENTION, AND LOOKED TO MAKE A MOVIE ABOUT EUROPE'S NEWEST HEART-THROB. THE PROJECT WAS GREEN-LIT AND PONTI TOLD THE MEDIA THAT HE'D BE FILMING THAT MONTH IN SEATTLE, NEW YORK, LOS ANGELES AND ROME. THE AWKWARD WORKING TITLE OF THE MOVIE WAS REPORTED TO BE "THEY STOLE $200 FROM ME, AND I TOOK IT BACK". IT NEVER PANNED OUT, THOUGH. MAYBE THE CRUDDY TITLE HAD SOMETHING TO DO WITH IT BEING SHIT-CANNED.

ANOTHER PRODUCER ACTUALLY SIGNED THE HIJACKER TO A FILM CONTRACT TO STAR IN A SPAGHETTI WESTERN, BUT THAT PROJECT ALSO NEVER SAW THE LIGHT OF DAY -- OBVIOUSLY MAKING IT A VERY HARD THING TO RESEARCH FOR THIS ARTICLE. AUTHOR ELIZABETH RICH WROTE ABOUT THIS NEAR MISS IN HER 1972 BOOK, FLYING SCARED, ALTHOUGH SHE NEGLECTED TO MENTION WHO THIS MYSTERIOUS FILMMAKER WAS. SHE DID INTERVIEW MINICHIELLO HIMSELF THOUGH, AND HE SPOKE EMPHATICALLY ABOUT WHY THE WHOLE HORSEBACK GUNSLINGER THING NEVER ACTUALLY TRANSPIRED.

"HE SAID THAT HE DIDN'T LIKE 'THOSE FANCY PLACES'," RICH REVEALED IN HER BOOK. "HE DIDN'T KNOW WHAT PEOPLE WANTED FROM HIM. HAVING SIGNED THE CONTRACT TO STAR IN A WESTERN, HE WAS ALREADY DISENCHANTED WITH THE FILM INDUSTRY. 'I DON'T LIKE THESE PEOPLE AND I HAVE ASKED MY LAWYER TO GET ME OUT OF THE CONTRACT. I CAN'T WORK WITH PEOPLE LIKE THAT, THEY ARE ALL KINDS LIKE HOMOSEXUALS AND BAD PEOPLE.' HE SHUDDERED AT THE THOUGHT OF THEM. 'AND THIS GIRL, I GO OUT WITH HER,' HE CONTINUED. 'I THINK SHE LIKE ME AND THEN SHE TELL ME THAT SHE IS LESBIAN AND ONLY WANTS TO GO OUT WITH ME BECAUSE I AM FAMOUS AND IT WOULD BE GOOD FOR HER CAREER IF SHE BE SEEN WITH ME'."

HE WOULDN'T HAVE BEEN THE ONLY NON-ACTOR TO MAKE THE TRANSITION TO SPAGHETTI WESTERN PERFORMER. BEATLES DRUMMER, RINGO STARR HAD SOME ACTING EXPERIENCE IN MOVIES LIKE A HARD DAY'S NIGHT (1964) AND HELP! (1965), BUT NEITHER CALLED UPON HIM TO ACTUALLY BE A THESPIAN THE WAY HE WAS 1971'S BLINDMAN, WHICH WAS A REALLY TERRIFIC WESTERN BY DIRECTOR FERDINANDO BALDI.

DESPITE HIS DISTASTE FOR THE FILM INDUSTRY AND ALL OF THE GAYS AND LESBIANS THAT WERE INVOLVED IN IT, MINICHIELLO SOAKED UP THE ATTENTION FROM THE MEDIA, WHOM HE INFORMED THAT HE INTENDED TO GO TO COLLEGE. THAT DIDN'T HAPPEN. IN ACTUALITY HE FLOUNDERED AROUND FOR A WHILE, EVEN POSING IN THE NUDE A COUPLE TIMES FOR A PIN-UP MAGAZINES. TWO YEARS LATER HE LANDED A MORE SECURE POSITION, A BARTENDING JOB, AND MET A LOVELY 16-YEAR OLD-GIRL NAMED CINZIA, WHOM HE MARRIED AND HAD A CHILD WITH. THE TWO OF THEM WERE VERY HAPPY TOGETHER DESPITE THE TEEN BEING SIX YEARS HIS JUNIOR. HE WENT ON TO OPEN A GAS STATION, AN ICE CREAM PARLOUR, AND EVEN A SHORT-LIVED PIZZERIA WITH THE UTTERLY TASTELESS NAME OF "HIJACKING". BUT THEN 12 YEARS LATER, IN 1985, TRAGEDY STRUCK. AFTER GETTING PREGNANT YET AGAIN, CINZIA AND THEIR BABY BOTH DIED DURING CHILDBIRTH.

MINICHIELLO: FROM CRIMINAL, TO THE BELLE OF THE BALL, AND BACK TO BEING A NOBODY AGAIN.

RAFFAELE WAS COMMITTED TO THE IDEA THAT HIS WIFE AND CHILD WERE KILLED DUE TO THE GROSS NEGLIGENCE OF THE HOSPITAL STAFF. GRIEF-STRICKEN AND ENRAGED, MINICHIELLO DREW UP PLANS TO SHINE A SPOTLIGHT ON ISSUES OF MALPRACTICE IN THE ITALIAN HEALTH SYSTEM BY COMMITTING A SHOCKING ATTACK UPON DOCTORS ATTENDING A MEDICAL CONVENTION HELD IN THE ITALIAN CITY OF FIUGGI. HE AND HIS KIDNAPPING VICTIMS HAD BEEN LUCKY ENOUGH TO GET THROUGH HIS FIRST ESCAPADE UNSCATHED, BUT THE CHANCES OF GETTING THOUGH ANOTHER ARMED HOSTAGE-TAKING WOULD REALLY HAVE REALLY BEEN PUSHING IT.

"I SUED THE HOSPITAL, SAID MINICHIELLO. "BUT I WANTED TO CONTINUE MY BATTLE. I WANTED TO CHANGE THE COURSE OF MEDICINE."

ACCORDING TO MINICHIELLO, DURING THIS PLANNING PHASE FOR HIS "ASSAULT ON FIUGGI", HE MET A YOUNG MAN WHO GOT HIM INTERESTED IN READING THE BIBLE. CHRISTIANITY ENDED UP BEING A FAR HEALTHIER WAY TO SOOTHE HIS FURY AND OVERCOME THE DEEP SORROW OF THIS PERIOD OF MOURNING, AND HE REALLY GOT INTO LOUDLY THUMPING HIS BIBLE FOR ANYONE WHO WOULD LISTEN, A PRACTICE HE CONTINUES TO THIS DAY. IN 1999 RAFFAELE HAD HIS CRIMES PARDONED BY THE UNITED STATES, RETURNED SEVERAL TIMES TO VISIT RELATIVES IN SEATTLE, AND TODAY HAS A YOUTUBE CHANNEL DEDICATED TO HIS FAVOURITE HOBBY: PLAYING THE ACCORDION.

-ROBIN BOUGIE JAN. 2ND 2015.

RANDOM ☆ TRIVIA

☆ DAVID CRONENBERG WAS ONE OF THE DIRECTORS APPROACHED AND ASKED IF HE'D LIKE TO DO 1985's WITNESS, BUT HE REFUSED, BALKING AT THE "IDEALIZED" REPRESENTATION OF THE AMISH. "TO ME THEY WERE A VERY REPRESSIVE, SORT OF CULTISH GROUP THAT I DIDN'T HAVE MUCH AFFECTION FOR", CRONENBERG STATED.

☆ BLADE RUNNER (1982) WAS LOOSLY BASED ON PHILIP K. DICK'S STORY "DO ANDROIDS DREAM OF ELECTRIC SHEEP?", BUT THE TITLE CAME FROM A TOTALLY DIFFERENT SOURCE. NAMELY, ALAN E. NOURSE'S 1974 NOVEL ABOUT A SUPPLIER OF BLACK MARKET MEDICAL SUPPLIES IN A FUTURISTIC SETTING.

DAZZLER™ THE MOVIE

BOUGIE '12

FOR DECADES, THE WAY YOU GOT COMIC BOOKS WAS AT A NEWS STAND, GROCER, TRUCK STOP, OR ANYWHERE ELSE THEY SOLD MAGAZINES IN YOUR TOWN. THE MODERN DAY MEANS (SOON TO BE TAKEN OVER BY DIGITAL MEDIA, IT SEEMS) OF ACQUIRING ANYTHING OTHER THAN AN ARCHIE COMIC BOOK IS IN A COMIC BOOK STORE, OR "DIRECT MARKET" AS IT WAS CALLED BY THE SUITS IN 1980. THAT WAS THE YEAR THE VERY FIRST COMIC FROM A MAJOR PUBLISHER DESIGNED TO BE SOLD EXCLUSIVELY IN THIS NEW DOMAIN OF NERDS APPEARED. IT SOLD 428,000 COPIES AT A TIME WHEN 150,000 TO 200,000 COPIES WAS THE USUAL. TODAY THE TOP SELLING TITLES ARE LUCKY TO HIT THE 60,000 MARK.

THAT COMIC WAS MARVEL'S **DAZZLER** #1. A SEQUIN-COVERED, JUMPSUIT WEARING, DISCO-DANCING MUTANT ON ROLLER SKATES, DAZZLER WAS A YOUNG WOMAN NAMED ALISON BLAIRE. HER CHARACTER FALLS INTO THAT CLASSIFICATION OF MIND BOGGLING EARLY 1980S MARVEL GIMMICK-CHARACTERS (LIKE THE TRUCKER COMIC **U.S.1**, AND THE EVEL KNIEVEL INSPIRED **TEAM AMERICA**) THAT WERE CREATED TO CASH IN ON A POPULAR FAD, BUT ALWAYS SEEMED TO SHOW UP A YEAR TOO LATE TO BE SUCCESSFUL. BUT THIS TIME, DAZZLER COMICS SOLD IN SPITE OF THE PREVALENT ANTI-DISCO SENTIMENT, AND THE BOOK LASTED FOR FIVE YEARS AND FORTY TWO ISSUES.

DAZZLER WAS CREATED TO MILK THE GLITTERY CAREFREE DISCO DANCE CRAZE THAT NOT ONLY FADED AWAY, BUT WITNESSED A FEROCIOUS PUBLIC BACKLASH THAT PROPELLED THE MANIC ENERGY OF HAIR METAL AND HIP-HOP TO THE TOP OF THE CHARTS. NEVER MIND THAT SHE ROLLED AROUND IN KISS MAKEUP AND UTILIZED THE COMPLETELY FUCKING USELESS MUTANT POWER OF TRANSMUTING SOUND INTO LIGHT, DAZZLER DEFIED THE ODDS, AND SOMEHOW MANAGED TO STICK AROUND.

ONE OF A KIND DAZZLER ACTION FIGURE CREATED BY SHANNON CRAVEN '12

BUT HERE'S WHAT YOU PROBABLY DIDN'T KNOW: DAZZLER WAS ACTUALLY SUPPOSED TO BE <u>A MOVIE</u>

MORE SPECIFICALLY, SHE WAS SUPPOSED TO BE A FICTIONAL COMIC BOOK CHARACTER THAT WAS TO BE LAUNCHED IN HER OWN COMIC AT THE SAME TIME AS HER THEATRICAL ANIMATED FILM WAS TO APPEAR. ON TOP OF THAT, ALISON WAS A SINGER SO A REAL LIFE DISCO MUSIC CAREER WAS PLANNED AS WELL. THEN-MARVEL EDITOR-IN-CHIEF, JIM SHOOTER, HAD IT ALL MAPPED OUT. CASABLANCA RECORDS WAS BROUGHT IN TO "SIGN" THE FICTIONAL MISS BLAIRE, AND SHOOTER GOT TO WORK ON A SCRIPT TREATMENT FOR THE DAZZLER FEATURE FILM.

SOME CONCESSIONS WOULD HAVE TO BE MADE THOUGH. SHOOTER WOULD HAVE TO KEEP NEIL BOGART OF CASABLANCA RECORDS HAPPY, AND BOGART WANTED THE STARS HE HAD UNDER CONTRACT TO BE WELL REPRESENTED, AND PROVIDING VOICES FOR THE NON-MARVEL CHARACTERS. SHOOTER WOULD HAVE TO COME UP WITH CHARACTERS TO PLAY FOR THE VARIOUS STAND UP COMEDIANS AND MUSIC ACTS ON CONTRACT AT CASABLANCA.

THE TREATMENT SHOOTER PUT TOGETHER READS LIKE A FREAKY POP CULTURE HALLUCINATION. HE'S GOT CHER AS "THE WITCH QUEEN", DONNA SUMMER AS HER RIVAL; "THE QUEEN OF FIRE", RODNEY DANGERFIELD PLAYING FOUR CHARACTERS (THREE OF WHOM ARE NEARLY IDENTICAL), ROBIN WILLIAMS AS A LOVE INTEREST, LENNY AND SQUIGGY (FROM THE **LAVERNE AND SHIRLEY** SHOW) AS COURT JESTERS, AND IF YOU CAN FUCKING FATHOM THIS: KISS FACE OFF IN A BATTLE AGAINST THE VILLAGE PEOPLE, WITH EACH MEMBER OF THE BANDS GIVEN CRAZY SUPER POWERS. WOW!

THERE IS ALSO SOME OTHER WEIRDNESS GOING ON. DESPITE THE FACT THAT THE MOVIE IS CHOCK-FULL OF ROCK AND DISCO STARS AND WAS DESIGNED TO LAUNCH DAZZLER'S REAL LIFE MUSIC CAREER, WE ONLY GET ONE MUSIC PERFORMANCE PLOTTED, WHICH TAKES PLACE AT THE BEGINNING OF THE FILM. FROM THERE, DAZZLER, SPIDER-MAN AND THE AVENGERS GET ZAPPED INTO A

DYSTOPIAN FUTURE VERSION OF THEIR FAMILIAR NEW YORK STOMPING GROUNDS, WHERE UNICORN-MOUNTED WARRIORS BATTLE LIZARD-MOUNTED WARRIORS, ALL OF WHOM DRAG AROUND BATTLE CHARIOTS MADE OUT OF "OLD DATSUN PICK UP TRUCKS".

NO SERIOUSLY, IT GETS CRAZIER. THEN, MARVEL STAFF MEMBER ALICE DONENFELD, WITH THIS WIGGIDY-WACK TREATMENT IN HAND, JETS OFF TO CANNES IN MAY OF 1980 AND MANAGES TO SMOOTH-TALK HERSELF INTO A MEETING WITH BO DEREK. THERE IS EVEN PROOF OF THIS CONVERSATION ON THE COVER OF A NATIONAL PERIODICAL: PEOPLE MAGAZINE. THE SHOT IS OF BO AND HER HUSBAND JOHN AT CANNES, AND HE'S HOLDING A STACK OF MARVEL COMICS. THE FIRST ISSUE OF SHE-HULK RESTS ON TOP.

"BO DEREK WAS FRESH FROM THE SUCCESS OF 10, WITH DUDLEY MOORE", WROTE JIM SHOOTER ON HIS BLOG IN 2011. "SHE WAS THE HOTTEST STAR IN HOLLYWOOD, TOP OF THE "A" LIST OF "BANKABLE" STARS. BANKABLE MEANS THAT THE MERE ATTACHMENT OF SUCH A STAR GUARANTEES STUDIO FINANCING, SO SUDDENLY THERE WAS A BIDDING WAR AMONG THE STUDIOS FOR THE PROJECT!"

"THEN MARVEL COMMISSIONED A SCREENPLAY BY LESLIE STEVENS. WHY NOT ME? I WAS THE HORSE WHO GOT US THERE. BUT, SUDDENLY, BECAUSE IT WAS HOLLYWOOD, FOR REAL AND BIG TIME, I WAS 'JUST A COMIC BOOK WRITER'. THEY DECIDED THEY NEEDED A SCREENWRITER. STEVENS IGNORED WHAT I HAD WRITTEN COMPLETELY AND WROTE A PIECE OF CRAP THAT DEFIES DESCRIPTION. IN THOSE DAYS, DESPITE THE REASONABLE SUCCESS OF THE FIRST SUPERMAN MOVIE, COMICS WERE STILL THOUGHT OF AS SILLY AND CAMPY, SO THAT'S WHAT STEVENS WENT FOR. IT WAS MORONIC. STEVENS ALSO DISCARDED THE LIGHT POWERS AND GAVE DAZZLER THE POWER TO MAKE PEOPLE TELL THE TRUTH."

THEN IT ALL FELL THROUGH. CASABLANCA RECORDS WAS BOUGHT OUT AND ACCOUNTING IMPROPRIETIES WERE BEING ALLEGED. DISCO MUSIC WENT INTO CARDIAC ARREST AND DIED A HIDEOUS DEATH, AND BO DEREK WAS WEIRDLY INSISTENT THAT HER HUSBAND, JOHN DEREK (INFAMOUS FOR BEING BOX OFFICE POISON) DIRECT. EVERY STUDIO BIDDER WITHDREW, AND DESPITE ANOTHER TRY WITH A PRE-SPLASH DARYL HANNAH SIGNED ON TO PLAY THE LEAD ROLE, THE PROJECT WAS DEAD IN THE WATER.

WITH DAZZLER OFF THE TABLE, JOHN DEREK WOULD INSTEAD DIRECT HIS WIFE IN **TARZAN THE APE MAN** (1981), A CRITICALLY REVILED TURD (NOMINATED FOR SIX RAZZIE AWARDS) IN WHICH BO WOULD GET HER NIPPLE SUCKED ON BY A CHIMP.

DAZZLER™ AND © MARVEL CHARACTERS INC

RAD MEMORIES

SUMMER 1985. CALGARY, ALBERTA, CANADA.

MY FRIEND LEON AND I WERE 13 YEARS OLD THAT SUMMER, AND ON THIS PARTICULAR DAY WE WERE MAKING OUR WAY TO THE FOOD COURT WHILE WALKING THROUGH WESTBROOK MALL. SUDDENLY THIS STRANGE GUY COMES UP TO US AND SAYS "HEY KIDS! WANNA BE IN A MOVIE?" NEEDLESS TO SAY WE WERE TOTALLY SKETCHED OUT BY THIS CREEPY QUESTION AND I'M SURE IT SHOWED ON OUR FACES, BUT THEN HE GOES; "NO NO! IT'S OK! IT'S A MOVIE ABOUT BMX CYCLING! WE NEED COOL KIDS TO BE IN THE CROWD".

WE CERTAINLY CONSIDERED OURSELVES AS COOL, AND SINCE WE BOTH RODE BMX BIKES EVERYWHERE, HE DIDN'T NEED TO SAY MUCH MORE TO CONVINCE US. THE FILM, AS IT HAPPENED, WAS 1986'S **RAD**, WHICH IS BASICALLY **KARATE KID** ON WHEELS, AND IS FIRMLY CONSIDERED IN GEEK CIRCLES AS THE ULTIMATE OLD SKOOL BMX MOVIE. MUCH OF THE PRODUCTION TOOK PLACE IN A LITTLE TOWN OUTSIDE OF CALGARY CALLED COCHRANE (SUCH AS THE INFAMOUS "SCHOOL DANCE ON BIKES" SCENE) BUT THE BMX RACING SEQUENCES WERE SHOT IN A SUBURB OF CALGARY CALLED BOWNESS, AND LEON AND I WERE NOW ARMED WITH CARDS ALLOWING US ON SET AS EXTRAS FOR 2 DAYS OF SHOOTING THE BIG FINAL RACE ON AN AMAZING SET CALLED "THE HELLTRACK"!

A STUNTMAN-TURNED-DIRECTOR WAS AT THE HELM FOR THE PRODUCTION, AND HAL NEEDHAM SEEMED LIKE A NICE GUY, ALTHOUGH WE EXTRAS DIDN'T INTERACT WITH HIM MUCH. WE JUST DID WHAT THE CROWD-WRANGLERS TOLD US TO DO. HAL WAS BEST KNOWN BACK THEN FOR HIGH-OCTANE, MACHISMO-PACKED 1980S COCK-ROCK CINEMA LIKE **SMOKEY AND THE BANDIT**, **CANNONBALL RUN**, **MEGAFORCE**, AND **STROKER ACE**.

"IN A SMALL COUNTRY TOWN THE TEENAGE PAPER BOY, CRU JONES, IS CUTTING LOOSE", READS THE SYNOPSIS AS IT APPEARS ON THE VHS TAPE RELEASE FOR THE MOVIE. "A WEEK AGO HE WAS CHEWING OVER SOME UP-COMING COLLEGE ENTRANCE EXAMS. NOW HE'S GOT $100,000, A RED CORVETTE AND A STUNNING BRUNETTE LINED UP. IT'S ALL HIS FOR THE TAKING -- THAT'S IF HE CAN OUTSMART THE RACE ORGANIZER WHO HAS A VESTED INTEREST IN MAKING SURE CRU DOES NOT START IN AMERICA'S RICHEST BMX RACE. HE'S ALSO GOT TO CONVINCE HIS MOTHER THAT EVERYTHING'S COOL, AND APART FROM ALL THAT HE'S GOT TO BEAT THE WORLD'S NUMBER ONE PRO RIDER! BUT HE'S GOT THE WHOLE TOWN BEHIND HIM, AND THAT'S INSPIRATION ENOUGH. THE KID IS SET FOR THE RIDE OF HIS LIFE!"

CRU (SHORT FOR 'CRUISER', FILM'S SCREENWRITER) IS OF NOTE ACTING-WISE, BUT WITH LOU DIAMOND PHILLIPS. WHEN GOING TO ACTING

ACCORDING TO SAM BILL ALLEN, WHO DIDN'T WENT ON

BERNARD, THE DO MUCH ELSE TO BE IN A BAND THE TWO MET SCHOOL TOGETHER

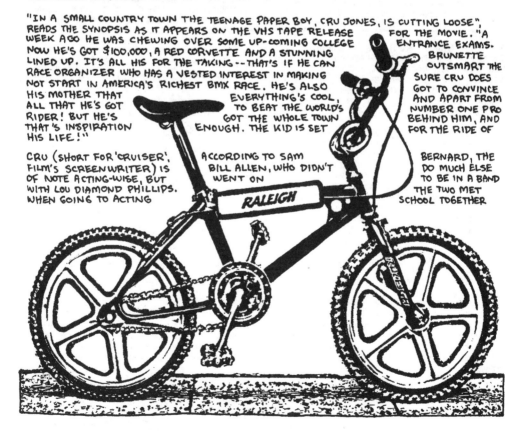

RALEIGH

IN THE EARLY '80S. ALSO STARRING AS HIS PERKY TEENAGE LOVE INTEREST IS LORI LOUGHLIN, WHO SOME MAY REMEMBER AS BECKY ON THE INSIPID TV SITCOM, **FULL HOUSE**. PERSONALLY, I WISH SHE WAS BETTER KNOWN FOR STARRING IN NOT ONLY **RAD**, BUT ALSO SEAN CUNNINGHAM'S UNDERRATED 1985 HORROR-THRILLER, **THE NEW KIDS**. UNFORTUNATELY, **FULL HOUSE** HAD A MUCH FURTHER REACH AND ITS NOSTALGIA-FACTOR REMAINS STRONG.

RAD FANS - YOU KNOW THE BACKFLIP THAT CRU DOES OUT OF THE CEREAL BOWL ON THE HELLTRACK? WELL, AT THE TIME, THE GUY WHO DID THAT WAS THIS BMX RIDER NAMED JOSE YANEZ, AND HE WAS THE FIRST AND ONLY GUY IN THE WORLD WHO COULD DO THAT TRICK AT THAT TIME. THAT'S RIGHT, A BACKFLIP. CAN YOU IMAGINE? WITH ALL THE CRAZY TECHNICAL STUNT WIZARDRY THEY CAN DO ON BIKES NOW? JOSE HAD TO DO THE BACKFLIP THREE TIMES TO PULL IT OFF, AND HE HAD A GIANT RAMP THAT WENT RIGHT UP INTO THE CROWD BLEACHERS SO HE COULD GET ENOUGH SPEED. HE WIPED OUT PRETTY GOOD THE FIRST TIME, BUT NAILED IT ON THE THIRD ATTEMPT, AND IN THE FILM IT LOOKS LIKE HE JUST RIDES UP THE SPOON IN THE CEREAL BOWL AND GOES WHOOP, AS EASY AS YOU PLEASE! HAHA!

ANYWAY, WHILE ALL THIS WAS GOING ON, THERE WERE THESE TWO GIRLS THAT LEON AND I WERE CHASING AROUND. IF THERE WAS A BREAK IN SHOOTING, WE WERE ALL OVER THEM, STONE COLD MACKIN'. THEY WERE OUR AGE, QUITE CUTE, AND WE WUZ 7TH GRADE ROMEOS. THIS ALL CAME TO A HEAD WHEN WE TOOK THEM UNDER THE BLEACHERS WITH THE INTENTION OF GETTING SOME SMOOCHES, BUT WE GOT NONE. LEON EVEN GOT KICKED IN THE BALLS FOR HIS TROUBLE, AND NEARLY THREW UP. HE WOULD TALK (WITH A VERY SERIOUS AND DISTANT LOOK IN HIS EYES) ABOUT THAT AGONIZING TESTICLE-PUMMELLING FOR YEARS AFTERWARDS. SHE ACTUALLY MANAGED TO BRUISE THEM!

ANYWAY, LONG STORY SHORT, LEON AND I DIDN'T MAKE THE FINAL CUT. MY BIG SCREEN ABSENCE COULD HAVE SOMETHING TO DO WITH THE FACT THAT I DIDN'T WEAR A HARO, MONGOOSE, REDLINE, OR A KUWAHARA T-SHIRT, AND INSTEAD DONNED WHAT I FELT WAS THE MOST STYLIN' THING IN MY CLOSET: A WHITE DON

JOHNSON JACKET WITH BIG SHOULDER PADS -- LIKE HE WORE ON **MIAMI VICE**. I WAS JUST OFF CAMERA IN 3 CROWD SCENES, AND YOU CAN SEE MY SLEEVE FOR LIKE A SECOND IN ONE OF THEM, BUT THAT HARDLY COUNTS. SIGH, LEFT ON THE CUTTING ROOM FLOOR.

RAD WAS ONLY RELEASED ON PAN-AND-SCAN VHS AND LASERDISC (AS OF THIS WRITING IT HAS YET TO GARNER A DVD OR BLU FORMAT ISSUE) BUT QUICKLY FOUND A CULT FOLLOWING AND BECAME A TOP-TEN VIDEO RENTAL FOR TWO YEARS AFTER THE FILM'S HOME FORMAT RELEASE. THE SOUNDTRACK, RELEASED ON 12" VINYL AND CASSETTE BY CURB RECORDS, IS TO THIS DAY A HIGHLY SOUGHT-AFTER COLLECTIBLE.

WHEN **RAD** FINALLY CAME OUT IN THEATERS IN 1986, I WAS IN SASKATOON AT THE TIME, AND WENT TO SEE IT WITH MY MOM A FEW DAYS AFTER IT OPENED. MY MOTHER MORTIFIED ME BY ANNOUNCING TO EVERYONE IN THE LINE FOR THE

LEON GETS LEVELED

HARD WHOMP

CONCESSION STAND THAT HER SON WAS STARRING IN THE MOVIE WE WERE ALL GOING TO BE SEEING TONIGHT. SEEING AS AT BEST I WOULD BE IN A CROWD SCENE FOR A FEW SECONDS, OR I WOULDN'T BE IN IT AT ALL (AS WAS THE CASE), IT WAS YET ANOTHER ONE OF MY MOTHER'S INFAMOUS AUDACIOUS STATEMENTS THAT NEVER FAILED TO TURN ME BEET RED. OH MOM....

AND HEY, THANKS TO BRYAN 'SHU-IZMZ' SCHUESSLER FOR DEMANDING THAT I COMPILE THESE RAD MEMORIES IN CINEMA SEWER FOR YOU ALL TO SEE. PEAS OUT!

BOUGIE · 2012 ·

TO HELGE AND BACK!!

A VOYAGE THROUGH THE FILMS OF SWEDISH DIRECTOR MATS HELGE

BY IAN JANE (WITH THANKS TO SWEDISH JOE FOR TRANSLATING) WWW.ROCKSHOCKPOP.COM

MATS HELGE OLSSON WORKED IN SWEDISH CINEMA FROM THE SEVENTIES TO THE EARLY NINETIES AND DEBUTED IN 1975 WITH THE WESTERN **I DÖD MANS SPAR** (DEAD MAN'S TRACKS). BEN WALKER (CARL GUSTAF LINDSTEDT) IS A COWBOY WHO HELPS HOOKER ISABELLA (ISABELLA KALIFF), THE DAUGHTER OF HIS RECENTLY DEAD FRIEND WHO LEFT HER A MAP TO A STASH OF GOLD. BAD GUYS ALSO WANT THIS GOLD, LEADING TO LOTS OF SHOOT-OUTS AND FISTICUFFS. AT A QUICK SEVENTY-ONE MINUTES, IT'S A DISPOSABLE MOVIE BUT WAS SHOT AT A WESTERN-THEMED AMUSEMENT PARK IN SWEDEN. THIS SWEDISH TAKE ON THE AMERICAN WESTERN GENRE FEATURES SHOTGUN TOTIN' BARTENDERS, SURLY BAD GUYS, AND A SKINNY DIPPING SCENE WHERE ISABELLA SHOWS OFF HER PLUMP SWEDISH RUMP (RIPE FOR SPANKING)!

NEXT CAME **THE FROZEN STAR**, ANOTHER WESTERN, BUT IT FLOPPED, AND ACCORDING TO DANIEL EKEROTH'S BOOK "SWEDISH SENSATIONSFILMS", IT'S NOW LOST. IN 1980 HE MADE **TVINGAD ATT LEVA** (AKA FORCED TO LIVE), AN ATMOSPHERIC BLACK AND WHITE THRILLER SET IN A HOSPITAL FEATURING NEAT NOIRISH PHOTOGRAPHY, AND LATER THAT SAME YEAR PRODUCED **SVERIGE AT SVENSKARNA** (SWEDEN FOR THE SWEDES). DIRECTOR PER OSCARSSON PLAYS KING GUSTAV, AND GRUFF BO SVENSON AND LOVELY CHRISTINA LINDBERG ALSO SHOW UP IN THIS ONE, WHICH IS TODAY CONSIDERED TO BE SWEDEN'S BIGGEST BOX OFFICE FLOP.

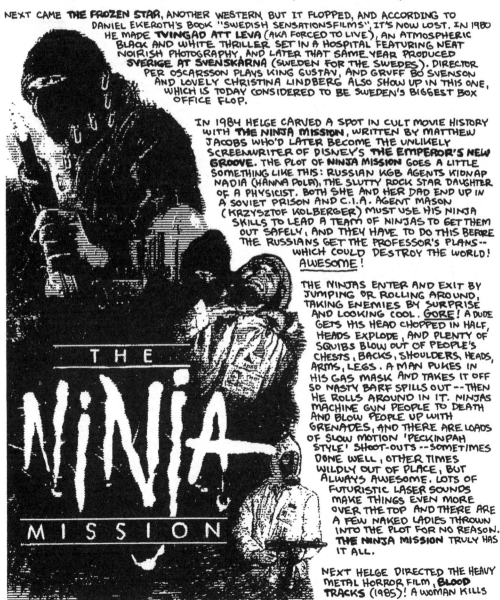

IN 1984 HELGE CARVED A SPOT IN CULT MOVIE HISTORY WITH **THE NINJA MISSION**, WRITTEN BY MATTHEW JACOBS WHO'D LATER BECOME THE UNLIKELY SCREENWRITER OF DISNEY'S **THE EMPEROR'S NEW GROOVE**. THE PLOT OF **NINJA MISSION** GOES A LITTLE SOMETHING LIKE THIS: RUSSIAN KGB AGENTS KIDNAP NADIA (HANNA POLA), THE SLUTTY ROCK STAR DAUGHTER OF A PHYSICIST. BOTH SHE AND HER DAD END UP IN A SOVIET PRISON AND C.I.A. AGENT MASON (KRZYSZTOF KOLBERGER) MUST USE HIS NINJA SKILLS TO LEAD A TEAM OF NINJAS TO GET THEM OUT SAFELY, AND THEY HAVE TO DO THIS BEFORE THE RUSSIANS GET THE PROFESSOR'S PLANS-- WHICH COULD DESTROY THE WORLD! AWESOME!

THE NINJAS ENTER AND EXIT BY JUMPING OR ROLLING AROUND, TAKING ENEMIES BY SURPRISE AND LOOKING COOL. GORE! A DUDE GETS HIS HEAD CHOPPED IN HALF, HEADS EXPLODE, AND PLENTY OF SQUIBS BLOW OUT OF PEOPLE'S CHESTS, BACKS, SHOULDERS, HEADS, ARMS, LEGS. A MAN PUKES IN HIS GAS MASK AND TAKES IT OFF SO NASTY BARF SPILLS OUT -- THEN HE ROLLS AROUND IN IT. NINJAS MACHINE GUN PEOPLE TO DEATH AND BLOW PEOPLE UP WITH GRENADES, AND THERE ARE LOADS OF SLOW MOTION 'PECKINPAH STYLE' SHOOT-OUTS -- SOMETIMES DONE WELL, OTHER TIMES WILDLY OUT OF PLACE, BUT ALWAYS AWESOME. LOTS OF FUTURISTIC LASER SOUNDS MAKE THINGS EVEN MORE OVER THE TOP AND THERE ARE A FEW NAKED LADIES THROWN INTO THE PLOT FOR NO REASON. **THE NINJA MISSION** TRULY HAS IT ALL.

NEXT HELGE DIRECTED THE HEAVY METAL HORROR FILM, **BLOOD TRACKS** (1985)! A WOMAN KILLS

HER HUSBAND AND TAKES OFF WITH HER KIDS. JUMP AHEAD TO WHERE THE BAND SOLID GOLD (REAL LIFE BAND EASY ACTION, FEATURING FUTURE MEMBERS OF EUROPE AND SHOTGUN MESSIAH) RULED. THEY'RE ON A MOUNTAIN FILMING A VIDEO WITHOUT REALIZING THAT THEY'VE BROUGHT SO MUCH FUCKING METAL THUNDER WITH THEM THAT THEY'VE CAUSED AN AVALANCHE! THE BAND AND THEIR GROUPIE SLUTS HOLE UP IN A NEARBY BUILDING WHERE THEY GET STALKED AND KILLED, AND IN BETWEEN MURDERS PEOPLE HAVE SEX AND FLAGRANTLY USE WALKIE-TALKIES. REMEMBER WALKIE-TALKIES? YEAH, CELL PHONES FUCKING RUINED THEM FOR US. **BLOOD TRACKS** IS GREAT IN ITS OWN HORRIBLE WAY IF YOU DIG GUYS DRESSED LIKE CINDERELLA (OR MAYBE WHITE LION) AND ARE INTO BOOBS.

BLOOD TRACKS IS STUPID, GORY, FREQUENTLY HILARIOUS AND BEST WATCHED UNDER THE INFLUENCE. DIG THAT SOUNDTRACK! ALSO: WATCH FOR A SCENE WHERE A GUY GETS AN AXE IN THE HEAD AND GOES CAREENING OVER A WALKWAY TO HIS DEATH BELOW. THOSE WHO GET EXCITED OVER 'DUMMY' SCENES WILL DEFINITELY DISLODGE SOME PRE-CUM OVER THIS ONE. STICK AROUND FOR THE END CREDITS, BECAUSE SMIRNOFF VODKA IS THANKED, AND AN EASY ACTION POWER BALLED CALLED 'IN THE MIDDLE OF NOWHERE' PLAYS OVER TOP OF THEM.

IN 1986 HELGE MADE **EAGLE ISLAND** (A.K.A. NINJA MISSION 2!) WHICH BEGINS WITH GUYS SCUBA DIVING, SEEMINGLY UP TO NO GOOD. THEN WE SEE GUYS FIGHT ON A CLIFF, RELAX, DRINK BEERS, AND FIND PIPES SCATTERED ON THE SWEDISH COASTLINE. A GUY NAMED SIMON GOES TO DEVIL'S ROCK AND FINDS TOM'S PIPE. WHAT? ALARMS GO OFF IN DIFFERENT SECTORS OF THE ISLAND CAUSING PEOPLE TO STRESS OUT. HUH? DOES THIS RELATE TO THE SCUBA DIVERS EARLY ON? LADIES WITH BIG HAIR ZIP AROUND IN A MOTORBOAT, HELICOPTERS SHOW UP, AND THE CHICKS FROM THE BOAT TURN OUT TO BE PHOTOGRAPHERS WHO RUN INTO TROUBLE WITH SECURITY GUYS WITH TEXAN ACCENTS. THIS MOVIE IS A MESS WITH NO NINJAS IN IT AT ALL, BUT IS KIND OF ENTERTAINING IN THAT YOU CAN WATCH IT WITH A GROUP AND EACH OF YOU WILL COME AWAY WITH YOUR OWN UNIQUE INTERPRETATION OF WHAT HAPPENED.

IN 1987 A CHILDREN'S MOVIE, **SPÖKLIGAN**, FOLLOWED BUT THERE'S NO ENGLISH TRANSLATION AVAILABLE, MAKING IT TOUGH TO REVIEW. IT'S GOT BIKERS IN IT AND ANNOYING ARYAN LOOKING KIDS BUT LET'S SKIP RIGHT TO **SILENT CHASE** MADE THAT SAME YEAR — OH WAIT, IT'S ANOTHER HELGE PICTURE THAT APPEARS TO BE LOST.

1988'S **FATAL SECRET** WAS HELGE'S FIRST COLLABORATION WITH DAVID CARRADINE, WHO PLAYS MICHAEL LEWINTER A DRUG DEALER WITH A DISC OF SECRET INFORMATION STOLEN BY A KGB GUY WHO INTENDS TO SELL IT. LEWINTER HOLDS THE DISC HOSTAGE, OFFERING TO SELL IT TO

THE CIA HIMSELF, BUT SOMEONE GETS THE DISC AND DECIDES TO PLAY MIDDLE MAN. MEMORABLE FOR A SCENE WHERE A DUDE GETS HANGED WITH A NOOSE AROUND HIS NECK AND OBLITERATED BY A GUN-HAPPY BAD GUY WHO JUST UNLOADS ON HIM — BUT OTHERWISE NOT GREAT.

HELGE AND CARRADINE DID **ANIMAL PROTECTOR** NEXT, A MOVIE ABOUT TWO POOFY-HAIRED BLONDE LADIES AND THEIR BUTCHY FRIEND WHO ARE SORT OF LIKE PETA COMMANDOS. THEY STORM A SECRET ISLAND TO FREE ANIMALS BEING USED IN EXPERIMENTS, AND THEIR STORY COINCIDES WITH ANOTHER MISSION WHERE TWO C.I.A. AGENTS — JOHN SANTINO (A.R. HELLQUIST) AND RICK LOMAX (MATS HUDDÉN) TAKE DOWN A ROGUE MILITARY TYPE NAMED COLONEL WHITLOCK (CARRADINE). LOTS OF FIST FIGHTS IN THIS ONE, MORE SLOW MOTION SEQUENCES AND PROBABLY THE MOST EXPLOSIONS OUT OF ANY OF HELGE'S PREVIOUS PICTURES. CARRADINE SLEEPWALKS AND SHOWS ZERO ENTHUSIASM, BUT THANKFULLY THERE'S ENOUGH VIOLENCE AND A BAR SHOOT OUT -- AND JUST LOOK AT ALL THOSE UZIS!

IN 1989 HELGE CO-DIRECTED **THE MAD BUNCH** WITH ARNE

MATTSON, HIS LAST COLLABORATION WITH CARRADINE. IT'S A TYPICAL 'DIRTY DOZEN' STYLE FILM WITH EXPLOSIONS, SQUIBS, BIG BLONDE HAIRDOS AND BAD DUBBING, BUT IT'S GOT A GREAT FIGHT ON A BEACH, MAN, SO MANY PEOPLE GET PUNCHED IN THIS MOVIE IT SHOULD HAVE BEEN CALLED THE FACE PUNCHING BUNCH. THEY EVEN REPLAY THE PUNCHES OVER THE END CREDITS, IN CASE YOU MISSED THEM.

HELGE ALSO CO-DIRECTED **THE HIRED GUN** WITH MATTSON, A MOVIE ABOUT SOME NEO NAZIS WHO HIRE A MERCENARY TO STEAL DOCUMENTS. NOT MUCH OF A PLOT HERE BUT MORE SHIT BLOWS UP AND PEOPLE GET PUNCHED. BY THIS POINT, HELGE USED A LOT OF THE SAME ACTORS OVER AND OVER AND THE SCRIPTS STARTED TO GET PRETTY GOSH-DARNED SIMILAR.

HELGE WENT TO DENMARK IN 1989 TO MAKE **THE RUSSIAN NINJA**, STARRING DANISH PLAYMATE HELLE MICHAELSEN. A RUSSIAN NINJA STARTS RUNNING AROUND FUCKING STUFF UP, SO A BEARDED FASHION PHOTOGRAPHER WITH FRIZZY HAIR DECIDES TO STOP HIM. THE DEADLY PHOTOGRAPHER AND HIS POSSE OF ULTRA-DANGEROUS SCANDINAVIAN MEN TAKE DOWN THE NINJA TO SAVE THE WORLD AND MAKE IT SAFE FOR THOSE WHO LOVE FREEDOM AND GLOSSY MAGAZINE SHOOTS. **THE RUSSIAN NINJA,** DESPITE ITS EXCITING TITLE, IS PRETTY BLOODLESS. THERE ARE A FEW DECENT ACTION SCENES BUT WHERE ARE THE EXCELLENT ARTERIAL SPURTS AND GORE THAT HIGHLIGHTED HELGE'S EARLIER FILMS?

IN THE ENGLISH LANGUAGE VERSION **THE RUSSIAN NINJA** IS HILARIOUSLY DUBBED AND WHENEVER HE'S ON SCREEN KICKING ASS AND TAKING NAMES THE MOVIE IS PRETTY SOLID. PROBLEMS ARISE WHEN HE'S NOT, AND WE'RE FOLLOWING THE PHOTOGRAPHER. HE DOES BUST OUT A FEW INTERESTING MOVES WHEN HE FIGHTS A BARE-CHESTED BURLY GUY IN FRONT OF A FIREPLACE, AND HE'S NOT BAD WITH A MACHINE GUN BUT HE'S WRONG FOR THE PART.

HELGE KICKED OFF THE NINETIES WITH HORROR/ACTION FILM **GROTTMORDEN** (THE FORGOTTEN WELLS) WHERE A TV CREW HEADS OUT TO MAKE A DOCUMENTARY. AS THEY SHOW UP, A GANG OF UZI TOTING THUGS HOLD EVERYONE HOSTAGE. ONE OF THE TV CREW, PETER SAVAGE (A.R. HELLQUIST AGAIN), IS A FORMER MILITARY EXPERT AND TAKES IT UPON HIMSELF TO RIP OFF HIS SHIRT AND SAVE THE DAY BY TRAIPSING AROUND CAVES WHERE A MUTANT MONSTER LIVES! LOOK FORWARD TO BAD FASHION, INSANE DIALOGUE, MEATY BEARDED SHIRTLESS GUYS WITH GUNS, AND A SEWER DWELLING MONSTER. YEAH, THIS IS WORTH FINDING.

HELGE'S CAREER ENDED WITH A WHIMPER UPON THE RELEASE OF A 1992 TV MOVIE CALLED **NORDEXPRESSEN,** A PARODY OF HIS EARLIER ACTION FILMS WHICH WAS NEITHER FUNNY NOR EXCITING. IN MORE RECENT YEARS HE'S RUN INTO TROUBLE WITH SWEDISH TAX COLLECTORS, AND IN 2001 HE PRODUCED THE LESLIE NIELSEN COMEDY **KEVIN OF THE NORTH,** BUT STILL OWES MILLIONS IN DEBT. HELGE NOW LIVES IN HIDING, NOT UNLIKE A CHARACTER FROM HIS MOVIES.

— IAN JANE'12

CINEMA SEWER'S UNDERAPPRECIATED FUCK STARS: ANELI POPPEA

ANELI IS A SOFT CORE MODEL (WHO MAY OR MAY NOT BE FRENCH OR RUSSIAN - BUT MY GUESS IS RUSSIAN-BORN AND LIVES IN FRANCE) AND SHE IS THE TITS! I MEAN, SHE IS THE NATURAL TITS! SHE'S BEEN ALL OVER THE NET POSING FOR SITES LIKE MET-ART.COM SINCE THE EARLY 2000'S, AND STOPPED MODELING IN LATE 2007. ANELI IS JUST AN ABSOLUTE GODDESS, PLAIN AND SIMPLE. I ADORE HER ABSO-FUCKING-LUTELY STUNNING CURVY BODY AND THICK THIGHS! -RB

49

Rob and Lizzy Go to Jail:
The Obscenity of Extreme Associates

☆ ARTICLE BY WESLEY BARNETT. 2014 ☆

THE WHOLE ORDEAL STARTED WITH A YOUNG, BRASH ROB BLACK (ROB ZICARI) SITTING BEHIND AN EMPTY FORMICA-STYLE DESK WITHOUT ANY TRINKETS. THERE ARE CUTS GOING ACROSS HIS FOREHEAD. THESE SEEM STRANGE AT FIRST, BUT BLACK ALSO RAN AN INDEPENDENT WRESTLING PROMOTION AT THE TIME CALLED XPW. IT WAS A REAL BLOOD AND GUTS TYPE OF WRESTLING WHERE PEOPLE WOULD JUST BEAT THE SHIT OUT OF EACH OTHER WITH LIGHT TUBES AND BASEBALL BATS WRAPPED IN BARBED WIRE. IT WOULD BE REASONABLE TO ASSUME THIS IS WHERE THE CUTS HAVE COME FROM. THERE ARE NO PICTURES ON THE WALL AND THE DESK.

HE IS GIVING AN INTERVIEW TO PBS FRONTLINE, WHICH IS A DOCUMENTARY SERIES KIND OF LIKE 60 MINUTES, EXCEPT PBS IS FUNDED BY THE PUBLIC. THE TOPIC FOR THIS PARTICULAR EPISODE IS "AMERICAN PORN". PEOPLE FROM HUSTLER ARE INTERVIEWED. A LOT OF THE RUNNING TIME IS SPENT EXPLAINING HOW PROFITABLE THE PORN INDUSTRY IS AND HOW CABLE COMPANIES ARE MAKING A MINT OFF PAY-PER-VIEW CHANNELS. FIRST AMENDMENT HERO LARRY FLYNT IS ALSO GIVEN AMPLE SCREEN TIME AS HE EXTOLS THE VIRTUES OF FREE SPEECH IN AMERICA.

AND ROB BLACK, SITTING IN HIS BARREN OFFICE, IS INTERVIEWED AS WELL. NOT JUST A WRESTLING PROMOTER, ROB ALSO RUNS A PORN COMPANY CALLED EXTREME ASSOCIATES, A COMPANY HE STARTED BY EMBEZZLING MONEY FROM HIS FATHER'S PORNOGRAPHIC BOOKSTORE WHERE HE HAD BEEN THE ACCOUNTANT.

AND BECAUSE THIS WAS PBS, THE BASTION OF JOURNALISTIC INTEGRITY, THEY NEEDED A SCAPEGOAT FOR THE EVILS OF PORNOGRAPHY. A BAD GUY. ROB BLACK AND EXTREME ASSOCIATES (A COMPANY PRODUCING LURID FLICKS LIKE ASS ALIENS AND BLONDE BUTTFUCK BITCHES) WERE THE PERFECT CANDIDATES TO SHOW HOW LITTLE REDEEMABLE VALUE THERE IS IN PORN IN THE MODERN AGE. AT ONE POINT EARLIER IN THE DOCUMENTARY, THE CAMERA CREW GOES TO THE SET OF A FILM EXTREME ASSOCIATES ARE MAKING CALLED FORCED ENTRY, WHICH IS DIRECTED BY BLACK'S WIFE LIZZY BORDEN (REAL NAME JANET ROMANO). THE CREW IS SO DISGUSTED BY A SCENE BEING SHOT IN WHICH STAR VERONICA CAINE IS DEPICTED AS BEING BRUTALLY (ALTHOUGH CONSENSUALLY) RAPED, THEY MAKE A SCENE AS THEY CUT THEIR CAMERAS AND PROCEED TO FLEE THE SET.

UNLIKE LARRY FLYNT, WHO SPEAKS RATHER ELOQUENTLY ABOUT HIS SMUT, NEITHER BLACK NOR BORDEN ARE PARTICULARLY WELL SPOKEN IN THEIR APPEARANCE IN THE PBS DOCUMENTARY. WHEN ASKED ABOUT WHETHER OR NOT SHE THINKS THE FILMS SHE DIRECTS ARE TOO MUCH, LIZZY JUST SORT OF SHRUGS HER SHOULDERS AND EXPLAINS THAT, "I DONT SHOOT THE LOVEY-DOVEY PORNO THAT YOU WATCH ALL THE TIME. THIS IS FOR PEOPLE WHO WATCH PORNO ALL THE TIME, AND THEY'RE SICK OF THE HUSBAND AND THE WIFE MAKING LOVE WITH CANDLES. THIS IS IF YOU WANT TO JERK OFF TO FUCKIN' PORNO WITH YOUR OLD LADY, AND YOU'RE WATCHING IT AND YOU'RE GETTING INTO IT, AND IT'S HOT, STEAMY SEX THAT YOU'RE, LIKE– AFTER YOU GET DONE YOU FEEL LIKE YOU JUST DID DRUGS. LIKE, YEAH!"

AFTER THE CREW STORMS OFF THE SET OF FORCED ENTRY, THEY CUT TO BLACK SITTING IN HIS OFFICE. SOMEONE OFF CAMERA ASKS HIM IF HE IS WORRIED ABOUT PRESIDENT BUSH'S RECENT STATEMENT OF WANTING TO CRACK DOWN ON OBSCENE MATERIAL. BLACK SMILES SLYLY AND SAYS, "WE'VE GOT TONS OF STUFF THEY TECHNICALLY COULD ARREST US FOR. I'M NOT OUT THERE SAYING I WANT TO BE THE TEST CASE, BUT I WILL BE THE TEST CASE. I WOULD WELCOME THAT. I WOULD WELCOME THE PUBLICITY. I WOULD WELCOME EVERYTHING TO MAKE A POINT IN, I GUESS, OUR SOCIETY."

ROB BLACK AND LIZZY BORDEN

AMERICAN PORN WAS AIRED ON FEBRUARY 7TH, 2002. THIS CHALLENGE WOULD BE THE OPENING SALVO IN A WAR BETWEEN EXTREME ASSOCIATES AND THE US GOVERNMENT THAT WOULD LAST FOR ALMOST EIGHT YEARS AND LEAVE THE COMPANY COMPLETELY DESTROYED, NOT TO MENTION SEND ROB BLACK AND LIZZY BORDEN TO FEDERAL PRISON.

MARY BETH BUCHANAN WAS A NO NONSENSE BITCH WHEN IT CAME TO OBSCENITY IN THE UNITED STATES. IN SEPTEMBER OF 2001 SHE WAS APPOINTED AS THE UNITED STATES ATTORNEY OF PENNSYLVANIA BY NONE OTHER THAN DUBYA HIMSELF. DURING HER TIME AS ATTORNEY, SHE WAS RUTHLESS IN HER ASSAULT ON OBSCENITY. IN 2007 SHE HAD NO PROBLEMS

BRINGING A 56-YEAR-OLD WOMAN NAMED KAREN FLETCHER TO TRIAL FOR POSTING HORROR STORIES ON THE INTERNET THAT INVOLVED CHILDREN. STORIES, NOT VIDEOS OR PICTURES. DOES ANYONE REMEMBER WHEN TOMMY CHONG WENT TO PRISON FOR SELLING PIPES? WELL, THAT TRIAL STARTED IN PENNSYLVANIA AND WAS HEADED UP BY MISS BUCHANAN.

"WE WANT PRODUCERS TO KNOW THAT THESE THINGS ARE NOT TOLERATED," BUCHANAN SAID IN AN IN INTERVIEW WITH THE NEW YORK TIMES IN 2007. HER BELIEF WAS THAT THE RARITY OF OBSCENITY PROSECUTIONS DURING THE EIGHT YEARS OF THE CLINTON ADMINISTRATION MEANT THAT THE PORNOGRAPHY INDUSTRY HAD COME TO BELIEVE THAT LAW ENFORCEMENT HAD TACITLY "AGREED TO AN ANYTHING-GOES APPROACH."

BUCHANAN WAS WATCHING THAT EPISODE OF FRONTLINE WHEN IT ORIGINALLY AIRED AND SHE TOOK ROB BLACK'S COMMENTS TO HEART. SHE TOLD ABC NEWS, "ZICARI'S STATEMENTS ON THE 'FRONTLINE' EDITION AND THE TRANSCRIPT OF THOSE INTERVIEWS WERE VERY HELPFUL FOR LAW ENFORCEMENT TO BE ABLE TO ASSESS WHAT ROB ZICARI'S INTENT WAS. IT HELPED US TO DETERMINE THAT THIS WAS NOT A PRODUCER WHO WAS TRYING TO COMPLY WITH THE LAW. THIS IS NOT A PRODUCER WHO WANTED TO MAKE SURE THAT HIS PRODUCTS WOULDN'T VIOLATE THE COMMUNITY STANDARDS. WHAT WE LEARNED FROM THIS INTERVIEW IS THAT ROB ZICARI INTENDED TO VIOLATE FEDERAL LAW."

TO HER, BLACK WAS DIRECTLY CHALLENGING NOT JUST THE MORALS OF AMERICAN CITIZENS, BUT THE FEDERAL GOVERNMENT ITSELF. SO SHE HATCHED A PLAN. ON SEPTEMBER 9TH, 2002, SHE HAD JOSEPH MCGOWAN, A POSTAL WORKER IN PENNSYLVANIA, JOIN THE MEMBERS SECTION OF THE EXTREME ASSOCIATES WEBSITE UNDER THE NAME KIM WALLACE. MCGOWAN HAD A THREE MONTH MEMBERSHIP TO THE SITE AND WOULD ROUTINELY VIEW VIDEOS IN THE "PISS ZONE" AREA. HE WOULD ALSO ORDER THREE TAPES FROM THE WEBSITE AND HAVE THEM SHIPPED FROM LOS ANGELES TO PENNSYLVANIA.

THIS LAST PART IS ACTUALLY IMPORTANT FOR TWO REASONS. THE FIRST IS THAT BY EXTREME ASSOCIATES SHIPPING THE VIDEOS ACROSS STATE LINES, THIS WOULD ADD ANOTHER FELONY CHARGE IF THE COMPANY WAS TO BE FOUND GUILTY OF OBSCENITY. THE SECOND REASON IS BECAUSE OF THE SEMANTICS INVOLVED IN DEFINING OBSCENE MATERIALS. ONE OF THE BIGGEST WINS IN THE PROSECUTION OF OBSCENITY HAPPENED WHEN THE SUPREME COURT DEVELOPED THE MILLER TEST AFTER THE TRIAL OF BOOKSELLER MARVIN MILLER. ONE OF THE WAYS TO DECIDE IF SOMETHING IS OBSCENE IS IF IT VIOLATES "COMMUNITY STANDARDS." IT IS A CLASSIC BATTLE OF STATE RIGHTS VERSUS FEDERAL RIGHTS, WHICH ALLOWS FOR OBSCENITY TO BE PROSECUTED ON A CASE BY CASE BASIS — FURTHER BLURRING THE LINES ON ANY OFFICIAL DEFINITION FOR SMUT PRODUCERS TO ADHERE TO. AND BECAUSE BUCHANAN THOUGHT THAT A JUDGE OR JURY IN HOLLYWOOD WOULD HAVE A DIFFERENT TAKE ON COMMUNITY STANDARDS THAN ONE IN PENNSYLVANIA, BY HAVING THE TAPES SENT THROUGH THE MAIL, SHE COULD BRING THEM TO TRIAL IN STATE.

"I DEFINITELY WILL NOT SIT HERE AND CRY A BUNCH OF TEARS. REMEMBER WHEN THE PBS FRONTLINE SPECIAL CAME OUT (WHICH A NUMBER OF THE INSPECTORS MADE REFERENCE TO WHEN CONDUCTING

AMERICAN PORN

it's a multibillion dollar business - and growing. can anything stop it?

'IT'S BIG AND SCARY, AND IT MUST BE STOPPED' IS HOW PBS WENT ABOUT MARKETING THEIR 2002 'AMERICAN PORN' EPISODE.

THE GOVERNMENT WAS WATCHING AND AGREED WHOLEHEARTEDLY.

INTERVIEWS), IT WAS I WHO CHALLENGED LAW ENFORCEMENT TO COME AFTER US FOR OBSCENITY. SO, WHILE SOME MAY CALL THIS KARMA, I WANT TO REMIND EVERYONE THAT I INVITED THIS... AND FOR THOSE OF YOU WHO HATE US (AND I KNOW THAT WOULD TAKE US ALL 10 DAYS OF THE WARRANT TO LIST), I WILL SIMPLY ACCEPT YOUR THANK YOUS QUIETLY, WITH MAYBE A PASSING WINK OR SMILE, WHEN IT IS US WHO FIGHTS THIS CASE AND WINS STANDING UP FOR THE ENTIRE BUSINESS AND ALLOWING YOU TO CONTINUE YOUR BUSINESS UNHAMPERED BY THE GOVERNMENT. IT WILL BE US THAT WILL BE LISTED IN THE BOOKS AS THE ONES WHO BEAT THE UNITED STATES GOVERNMENT. HEY, MAYBE IN ABOUT 10 YEARS I CAN GET THE HAL FREEMAN "FREEDOM ISN'T FREE" OR REUBEN STURMAN AWARD OR EVEN THAT GOOD GUY THING. AHH FUCK, I DON'T WANT ANYTHING EXCEPT FOR MAYBE A LITTLE PEACE AND QUIET (AND A MILOS FORMAN DIRECTED MOVIE ABOUT MY LIFE)" – A POST ON THE EXTREME ASSOCIATES WEBSITE BY ROB BLACK, APRIL 9TH, 2003, THE DAY AFTER HIS OFFICES WERE RAIDED.

IN AUGUST OF THAT YEAR, EXTREME ASSOCIATES WERE BROUGHT TO TRIAL IN PITTSBURGH. OF THEIR ENTIRE CATALOG, ONLY FIVE FILMS WERE DEEMED OBSCENE ENOUGH TO BE USED AGAINST THEM – EXTREME TEENS 24, COCKTAILS 2, ASSCLOWNS 3, 1001 WAYS TO EAT MY JIZZ, AND OF COURSE – THE INFAMOUS FORCED ENTRY.

ROB BLACK CONTINUED PRODUCING MOVIES IN NORTH HOLLYWOOD THE ENTIRE TIME HE AND HIS WIFE WERE ON TRIAL, AND SAW THE WHOLE FIASCO AS A WAY TO CONTINUE GARNERING PUBLICITY FOR HIS COMPANY. HE EVEN WENT SO FAR AS TO PACKAGE ALL FIVE OF THE PROSECUTED FILMS IN QUESTION IN ONE BOX SET CALLED "THE FEDERAL FIVE". SALES WENT THROUGH THE ROOF.

BLACK'S CONFIDENCE WAS FURTHER BOOSTED IN JANUARY OF 2005 WHEN HE SCORED A VICTORY IN THE CIVIL TRIAL. AFTER A RATHER TRADITIONAL BACK AND FORTH BETWEEN THE PROSECUTION AND DEFENCE WHERE THE TWO ARGUED OVER THE RHETORIC OF THE MILLER TEST AND WHETHER OR NOT ADULTS SHOULD BE ALLOWED TO VIEW HARDCORE PORNOGRAPHY IN THE PRIVACY OF THEIR OWN HOME, JUDGE GARY L. LANCASTER RULED IN FAVOUR OF EXTREME ASSOCIATES. HE FOUND THE CURRENT ANTI-OBSCENITY LAWS UN-CONSTITUTIONAL, ESPECIALLY AS FAR AS THE INTERNET WAS CONCERNED, SINCE NOTHING OBSCENE HAS TECHNICALLY TRAVELED ACROSS STATE LINES. THIS ALSO FACTORED IN THE TAPES THAT MCGOWAN HAD ORDERED, BECAUSE ANY OF THE CONTENT COULD ALREADY BE SEEN ON THE WEBSITE, WHICH ADULTS COULD VIEW IN PRIVATE.

BUT THIS VICTORY WAS SHORT LIVED. IN FEBRUARY OF 2005, GEORGE W. BUSH, IN HIS QUEST TO IMPRISON SMUT PRODUCING, CONSENTING ADULTS, CREATED THE OBSCENITY PROSECUTION TASK FORCE AND APPOINTED A DEVOUTLY CATHOLIC MAN NAMED ALBERTO GONZALEZ AS THE UNITED STATES ATTORNEY GENERAL. LIKE BUCHANAN BEFORE HIM, HE LOOKED AT ROB BLACK AND EXTREME ASSOCIATES AS THE ABSOLUTE SCUM OF THE EARTH AND DECIDED TO APPEAL THE RULING.

GONZALEZ TOLD ABC NEWS THAT HE INTENDED "TO MAKE THE INVESTIGATION AND PROSECUTION OF OBSCENITY ONE OF MY HIGHEST CRIMINAL ENFORCEMENT PRIORITIES." DURING HIS CONFIRMATION HEARINGS, GONZALES SAID THAT "OBSCENITY IS SOMETHING ELSE THAT VERY MUCH CONCERNS ME. I'VE GOT TWO YOUNG SONS, AND IT REALLY BOTHERS ME ABOUT HOW EASY IT IS TO HAVE ACCESS TO PORNOGRAPHY."

MARY BETH BUCHANAN -- THE ATTORNEY THAT SPEARHEADED THE FIRST PORN OBSCENITY CONVICTION IN THE USA IN OVER TWENTY YEARS.

ACCORDING TO MR. GONZALEZ, LANCASTER'S RULING SPAT IN THE FACE OF MANY YEARS OF THE SUPREME COURT UPHOLDING ANTI-OBSCENITY LAWS. ALBERTO FELT THAT PEOPLE WHO POST ONLINE CONTENT, REGARDLESS OF WHETHER OR NOT PHYSICAL MEDIA EXISTS, SHOULD STILL BE HELD ACCOUNTABLE FOR WHAT THEY PUT OUT INTO THE WORLD, AND THE COURT OF APPEALS SIDED WITH HIM. IN A DESPERATE BID TO AVOID GOING TO TRIAL ONCE AGAIN IN PITTSBURGH, BLACK AND BORDEN PETITIONED THE SUPREME COURT TO HEAR THE CASE, BUT THEY WERE FLATLY DENIED AND ON DECEMBER 8TH OF 2005 THEY WERE ONCE AGAIN BROUGHT BEFORE JUDGE GARY L. LANCASTER.

THE PROFITS FROM THE SALES OF "THE FEDERAL FIVE" BOX SET WERE A DROP IN THE BUCKET OF WHAT BLACK AND HIS WIFE WOULD NEED TO BATTLE THE STATE. BETWEEN THE STRESS AND HIGH LEGAL FEES OF THE LONG WAITING PERIOD IN THE RE-TRIAL, EXTREME ASSOCIATES WAS SLOWLY HEMORRHAGING MONEY. PRODUCTION ON NEW MATERIAL SLOWED TO A CRAWL AND EXTREME ASSOCIATES STARTED LOOKING FOR NEW ONLINE DISTRIBUTION MODELS FOR THEIR OLDER CONTENT. IN 2007, THEY STOPPED PRODUCING DVDS ENTIRELY, EFFECTIVELY CUTTING OUT RETAILERS, ALLOWING EXTREME ASSOCIATES TO RETAIN ALL PROFITS. BLACK EXPLAINED THE ECONOMIC BREAKDOWN OF THE DECISION—: "TURNING A PROFIT FROM SELLING PIECES THESE DAYS IS A LUDICROUS PROPOSITION. WITH TODAY'S SALES, EVEN IF I SELL 1,000 UNITS AT $10 A POP WHOLESALE, THAT'S ONLY $10,000. I WOULD LOSE MY ASS! I KNOW GONZO MOVIES ARE CHEAP THESE DAYS, BUT NOT THAT CHEAP."

BY LATE 2008, THE COUPLE AND THEIR ATTORNEY, H. LOUIS SIRKIN, WERE READY TO THROW IN THE TOWEL. BECAUSE THE FEDERAL GOVERNMENT WAS NERVOUS ABOUT LANCASTER JUDGING IN FAVOUR OF BLACK AND BORDEN AGAIN, THE PROSECUTORS OFFERED THEM A PLEA BARGAIN WHICH WOULD REDUCE THEIR SENTENCES. AS OPPOSED TO INTERSTATE TRANSPORTATION OF OBSCENE MATERIALS, THE TWO WOULD BE CONVICTED OF CONSPIRACY TO DISTRIBUTE OBSCENE MATERIALS. THIS WOULD KEEP THEM FROM HAVING TO REGISTER AS SEX OFFENDERS.

SIRKIN EXPLAINED THEIR DECISION TO TAKE THE BARGAIN BY TELLING REPORTERS, "WHEN YOU'RE DEALING WITH PEOPLE WHO BELIEVE IN THE PROTECTIONS OF THE FIRST AMENDMENT, THESE CASES ARE VERY DIFFICULT. HAVING SOMETHING OVER YOUR HEAD FOR SIX AND A HALF YEARS IS A NIGHTMARE." ON MARCH 11TH, 2009, THE COUPLE PLED GUILTY, AND IN JULY OF THAT YEAR WERE SENTENCED TO FEDERAL PRISON FOR ONE YEAR AND A DAY. THIS WOULD BE THE FIRST TIME IN TWENTY YEARS THAT A PORNOGRAPHER IN AMERICA WAS CONVICTED ON OBSCENITY CHARGES.

THINGS WOULD START OUT BAD. INSTEAD OF REPORTING TO THE INTENDED MINIMUM-SECURITY SATELLITE FACILITY, BLACK MISTAKENLY REPORTED TO A TEXAS PRISON'S PRIMARY FACILITY, WHERE OFFICIALS PLACED HIM IN SOLITARY CONFINEMENT FOR NEARLY A MONTH BECAUSE IT (ACCORDING TO HIS ATTORNEY) "WAS THE ONLY SPACE THEY HAD AVAILABLE". BORDEN WAS SHIPPED TO THE OTHER SIDE OF THE COUNTRY -- WASECA, MINNESOTA.

AS SAN FRANCISCO JOURNALIST GREG BEATO NOTED, "THE RAPES AND MURDERS THEY STAGED WERE NO LESS IMAGINARY THAN THE RAPES AND MURDERS HOLLYWOOD STAGES... (BUT) THEY HAD THE AUDACITY TO MIX GENRES OF ENTERTAINMENT THAT, WHILE PERMISSIBLE ON THEIR OWN, ARE APPARENTLY NOT ALLOWED TO BE COMBINED. THEY MANAGED TO ACHIEVE WHAT NOT EVEN JOHN WATERS EVER ACCOMPLISHED: THEY WERE SENT TO PRISON FOR HAVING BAD TASTE."

IT ALL GOES BACK TO THE AMERICAN PORN EPISODE OF FRONTLINE ON PBS. THERE IS A SEGMENT WHERE THE NARRATOR MAKES A POINT TO EXPLAIN THAT THERE IS NO REAL RELATIONSHIP BETWEEN THE DIFFERENT PORN COMPANIES, AND THAT FOR THE PRODUCERS OF THE MORE EXTREME CONTENT, THERE WILL BE A DAY OF RECKONING. AFTER SERVING THEIR SENTENCES IN SEPARATE FACILITIES, BLACK AND BORDEN ARE STILL MARRIED AND HAVE RETURNED TO THE INDUSTRY AND HAVE DIRECTED A NUMBER OF FILMS FOR DIFFERENT COMPANIES WHILE ALSO STARTING ROB BLACK PRODUCTIONS. THIS NEW COMPANY HAS EVEN BEEN RE-RELEASING A BUNCH OF OLDER EXTREME ASSOCIATES VIDEOS THAT HAD BEEN THOUGHT LOST.

WHEN ASKED AFTER HE WAS RELEASED FROM PRISON IN 2010 ABOUT WHETHER OR NOT HE REGRETTED WHAT HE HAD SAID IN THE FRONTLINE EPISODE, ROB BLACK TOLD AVN NEWS, "SURE, IN HINDSIGHT, I'D TAKE WHAT I SAID BACK. BUT, YOU KNOW, EVERYTHING HAPPENS FOR A REASON. I DON'T QUITE KNOW THAT REASON RIGHT NOW, BUT I NEED TO SEE WHERE LIFE TAKES ME. AND EVERYTHING THAT'S GOING ON IN MY LIFE TODAY POSSIBLY WOULDN'T HAVE HAPPENED IF THIS SEVEN-YEAR SAGA DIDN'T HAPPEN. IT WAS A CHAIN OF EVENTS THAT LED ME TO THIS PLACE."

☆ WORDS: WESLEY BARNETT • ART: ROBIN BOUGIE

La Traque (aka The Track. 1975. France. Dir: Serge Leroy)

THIS IS NOT ONLY ONE OF THE MOST UNDERRATED GENRE FILMS TO COME OUT OF FRANCE IN THE 1970S, IT'S ALSO ONE OF MY TOP FIVE FAVOURITE FRENCH MOVIES OF ALL TIME. LA TRAGUE IS EQUALLY BREATHTAKING AND HEARTBREAKING. THAT IT HAS -- AS OF THIS WRITING -- NEVER BEEN RELEASED ON DVD IN FRANCE, NEVER MIND NORTH AMERICA, WILL EXPLAIN WHY IT IS RELATIVELY UNKNOWN, BUT IT DOESN'T MAKE IT ANY LESS GALLING THAT NO ONE I TALK TO HAS EVER HEARD OF IT. SHIT, IT'S LIKE FINDING OUT THAT ALL OF YOUR FRIENDS HAVE NEVER TASTED ICE CREAM.

RUN A CLIP COLLECTION OF **STRAW DOGS** (1971) AND **DEATH WEEKEND** (1976) THROUGH YOUR MOVIE-ADDLED BRAIN, AND YOU'RE IN THE RIGHT FRAME OF MIND TO FIGURE OUT THE VIBE AND CATEGORY FOR THIS ONE. IT'S A RAPE/REVENGE MOVIE AT FIRST GLANCE, BUT WITH ENOUGH TWISTS ON THE GENRE CLICHES THAT IT FEELS UNLIKE ANY OTHER EXAMPLE, AND ULTIMATELY DOESN'T REALLY FIT THAT GENRE AT ALL. BUT BEFORE I HYPE IT UP TOO MUCH (READING OVER WHAT I'VE WRITTEN, IT'S CLEARLY ALREADY TOO LATE FOR THAT) HERE'S A GUICK AND SIMPLE SYNOPSIS WITHOUT TOO MANY SPOILERS.

MIMSY FARMER PLAYS A LOVELY YOUNG ENGLISH TEACHER WHO GETS OUT OF THE CITY, AND STAYS BY HERSELF AT A HOME OUT IN THE WILDERNESS. IN THOSE SAME WOODS, A GROUP OF MEN MEET TO HUNT WILD BOAR. BUT WHEN THE TWO MEET, ONE OF THE LESS RESPECTABLE GUYS IN THIS MACHO GROUP

BRUTALLY RAPES THE YOUNG WOMAN, AND WHEN HIS FRIENDS FIND OUT, THEY COME TO AN IMPASSE. WITH MIMSY STANDING RIGHT THERE WATCHING THEM RUTHLESSLY PONDER HER FATE, THEY DECIDE WHAT TO DO WITH HER.

THE ACTING FROM EVERYONE IN THIS CHARACTER STUDY IS FLAWLESS, AND MIMSY'S PERFORMANCE IN PARTICULAR IS RESOLUTELY SYMPATHETIC. SHE'S THE VICTIM IN CONCEPT ONLY, WITH HER CHARACTER EASILY COMING OFF AS THE STRONGEST OF ANYONE EVEN THOUGH SHE'S THE ONLY ONE WHO IS UNARMED. YOU CAN'T BELIEVE THIS IS HAPPENING TO HER, BUT JUST BY THE ANGRY AND HURT LOOK ON HER FACE, YOU FEEL THAT IF ANYONE HAS A CHANCE OF LIVING THROUGH THIS INSANE AND TORTUROUS EXPERIENCE, IT'S HER. MAYBE THAT'S WHY MIMSY FARMER HERSELF POINTS TO THIS WHEN ASKED WHAT SHE THINKS WAS THE SINGLE BEST MOVIE OF HER LONG CAREER.

MAKE NO MISTAKE, THIS TIGHTLY WOUND, SUSPENSEFUL THRILLER IS A SEARING, ANGRY SPOTLIGHT ON THE INEQUALITY OF THE FEMALE EXPERIENCE IN OUR CULTURE, BUT EVEN MORE THAN THAT, IT'S A MEDITATION ON CLASS WARFARE. THE WAY IN WHICH NORMAL MEMBERS OF THE RULING CLASS, WITH SO MUCH TO LOSE IN TERMS OF THE DAMAGE A DARK SECRET CAN HAVE ON SOCIAL STANDING AND SELF-IMPORTANCE, WILL STOOP TO BRUTALITY. THE WAY IN WHICH KEEPING THE POWER AND THE LIFESTYLE TO WHICH ONE HAS BECOME SO VERY DEPENDANT UPON, CAN SEND A NORMAL PERSON TO IGNORE MORALITY AND FREELY RELINGUISH THEIR VERY HUMANITY ITSELF. AND YET IT DOESN'T FEEL AT ALL LIKE THE MESSAGE IS "RICH PEOPLE ARE MONSTERS". IT ACTUALLY DOESN'T FEEL LIKE THERE IS A MESSAGE AT ALL, BUT RATHER A QUESTION: "WHAT WOULD YOU DO? WHAT DO YOU THINK YOUR FRIENDS WOULD DO?" THE TRACK ADEPTLY DISPLAYS THE VERY PLAUSIBLE STEPS THESE FRIGHTENED AND NERVOUS MEN TAKE AS THEY HOPELESSLY LOSE SIGHT OF THE FOREST DURING THEIR HUNT, AND END UP ONLY SEEING EACH INDIVIDUAL TREE.

THERE HAVE BEEN A LOT OF TV AND FILM INCARNATIONS OF 1932'S **THE MOST DANGEROUS GAME** -- INCLUDING A HORRIFYING REAL LIFE SERIAL KILLER NAMED ROBERT HANSEN WHO KIDNAPPED NEARLY 20 WOMEN AND INDIVIDUALLY FLEW THEM OUT INTO THE ALASKAN WILDERNESS TO HUNT THEM -- BUT THIS 1975 CINEMATIC MASTERWORK WRITTEN AND DIRECTED BY SERGE LEROY MAY INDEED BE THE MOST HARROWING OF ALL. TRACK THIS ONE DOWN FOR YOURSELF, IF YOU CAN.

— BOUGIE '14

REVENGE OF THE CHEERLEADERS (USA. 1976.)

1973'S **THE CHEERLEADERS** WAS THE FIRST CHEERLEADER EXPLOITATION FILM. IT WOULD DIRECTLY INSPIRE A XXX PORN VERSION (THE FAMOUS **DEBBIE DOES DALLAS** STARRING BAMBI WOODS) AND ALSO SPAWNED A LEGITIMATE QUASI-SEQUEL -- 1976'S **REVENGE OF THE CHEERLEADERS**. RICHARD LERNER (DIRECTOR OF PHOTOGRAPHY ON THE FIRST FILM) WAS PUT IN CHARGE OF REVISITING THE FRANCHISE, AND DID IT PROUD WITH A WHOLE OTHER LEVEL OF CARTOONISH SLAPSTICK ZANINESS (AN R-RATED **SCOOBY DOO** BEING A COMPARISON MORE THAN ONE FILM HISTORIAN HAS MADE), A FAR MORE DIRECT EMPHASIS ON DRUG CULTURE, A 40-FOOT BRONTOSAURUS, AND THE SAME OL' CAN'T-MISS NAKED CHEERLEADER FORMULA.

THIS CAMPY CULT CLASSIC OBJECTIFIES THE BOYS JUST AS MUCH AS THE GIRLS, TOUTS YET ANOTHER WAFER-THIN PLOT, AND FEATURES A WELCOME TURN FROM THE LEGENDARY (R.I.P.) CHERYL "RAINBEAUX" SMITH, WHO STEALS HER SHARE OF THE SHOW WHILE QUITE PREGNANT WITH THE BABY OF THE GUY WHO DID THE SCORE, JOHN STERLING.

"I WORKED UP UNTIL MY 9TH MONTH WITH AN EXCELLENT GROUP OF GALS", SAID SMITH ABOUT THE EXPERIENCE OF FILMING. "HERE ARE THESE BEAUTIFUL GIRLS WITH ALL THIS ENERGY AND ME WADDLIN' 'ROUND LIKE A FAT DUCK."

"WE CAST HER AND DIDN'T REALIZE SHE WAS PREGNANT", RICHARD LERNER TOLD REVENGE OF THE CHEERLEADERS MEGA-FAN, MARSHALL CHRIST. "THEN WE SAID, 'THE HELL WITH IT. WE'LL USE IT.' WE DEFINITELY WANTED HER. SHE HAD AN ANGELIC FACE. WE REALLY WANTED TO COMPLIMENT THE LOOK OF THE FIVE -- INITIALLY SIX -- WOMEN, WE HAD ONE BLACK ONE, ONE ASIAN, AND TWO BLONDES -- ALMOST LIKE A LITTLE UNITED NATIONS."

PART OF THE MULTINATIONAL COALITION ON DISPLAY IS STUNNING PENTHOUSE PET HELEN LANG (WHO WAS A DANCER AND ONLY APPEARED IN THREE FILMS DURING HER ALL-TOO-SHORT ACTING CAREER) AND SASSY SOUL SISTER JERII WOODS, WHO ALSO APPEARED IN JACK HILL'S BRILLIANT **SWITCHBLADE SISTERS** FROM 1975.

ALSO OF NOTE IS DAVID HASSELHOFF, WHO MAKES HIS NOTABLE FILM DEBUT AS "BONER". DAVEY GETS HOOKED ON A FEELING AND SEEMS QUITE COMFY PLAYING THE STAR BASKETBALL PLAYER WHO DELIRIOUSLY CUTS RUGS, ENGAGES IN SLOPPY SEX, AND PROVES TO BE READILY REVIVED FROM AN ETHER-INDUCED TORPOR BY THE MERE WHIFF OF A PAIR OF USED PANTIES. HEY -- DON'T HASSLE THE HOFF, BUT DO RUB YOUR FRAGRANT SCUM-CATCHERS ON HIS KISSER!

YEAH, THIS TIME OUT THE GIRLS REALLY RUN SHIT, AND AREN'T CONTENT WITH JUST BEING LIBIDO INSPIRATION FOR A GROUP OF DROOLING JOCKS. HERE AT ALOHA HIGH, CHIPPER FUCKPUMPS RULE THE ROOST WITH THEIR OWN LOCKER ROOM, AND OPENLY SMOKE REEFER WITH THEIR BOOBS HANGING OUT WHILE THEY WATCH THE BASKETBALL TEAM PRACTICE. STEPPING IN TIME WITH THE FANTASY ASPECT OF THE FIRST INSTALMENT, OUR GIRLS DON'T APPEAR TO HAVE PARENTS, CAN'T BE BOTHERED TO ATTEND CLASS, LOVE DISHING OUT A GOOD GIRL-ON-GUY RIM-JOB (!!!), AND AREN'T SHY ABOUT REPEATEDLY STOPPING WHAT THEY'RE DOING AND LEADING EVERYONE IN A FUNKY MADCAP DANCE NUMBER. THIS HEDONISTIC EXISTENCE, WITH ALL ITS TENDER EXPOSED FLESH AND EASY-GOING ORGIASTIC SEX PARLAYS INTO ONE OF THE MOST ENTERTAINING TEENAGE SEX COMEDIES OF ALL TIME.

CRITICAL RESPONSE TO BOTH CHEERLEADER FILMS AT THE TIME OF THEIR RELEASE WAS DISMISSIVE AT BEST, BUT IT IS THE SAVAGING OF R.O.T.C. FROM FILMFACTS MAGAZINE (VOL. 20, 1977) THAT REALLY TICKLED ME:

"REVENGE OF THE CHEERLEADERS IS A

ALL NEW!

revenge
of the
cheerleaders
RAH

Allan Shackleton presents
A CHEERFUL FILM

Starring Jerri Woods Rainbeaux Smith Helen Lang
Patrice Rohmer and Susie Elene

Produced by   Directed by
Richard Lerner and Nathaniel Dorsky   Richard Lerner

IN COLOR · A MONARCH RELEASE   **R**

·CONTINUED FROM PREVIOUS PAGE.

RANCID MOVIE...A DECADE FROM NOW SOME PSEUDO-INTELLECTUAL FILM CLIQUE WILL DECLARE REVENGE OF THE CHEERLEADERS TO BE A NOTEWORTHY AND LAUDABLE EXAMPLE OF COUNTER-CINEMATIC EXPRESSIONISM OF THE '70S."

INDEED THEY DID, AND INDEED IT IS. CONGRATS, NOSTRADAMUS!

—BOUGIE '12

FOR ADULTS ONLY

IMMORAL MR TEAS AND THE ADVENTURES OF LUCKY PIERRE (NUDIE CUTIES THAT PITTED BUMBLING PROTAGONISTS AGAINST BUXOM DISTRACTIONS), MANY NUDIST FILMS OPTED FOR A DOCUMENTARY STRUCTURE IN WHICH A NARRATOR EXTOLS THE HEALTH BENEFITS OF A CLOTHES-FREE LIFESTYLE WHILE TOPLESS MODELS AND DANCERS STRIKE COY CHEESECAKE POSES. AS THE BOUNDARIES OF ON-SCREEN SEX WERE DEMOLISHED BY MORE DARING FEATURES IN THE 1960S AND EARLY '70S HOWEVER, THE CHEERY TONE AND LOOK-BUT-DON'T-TOUCH PHOTOGRAPHY THAT LARGELY CHARACTERIZED NUDIST FILMS CAST THEM AS NAIVE AND CAMPY RELICS OF A MORE RESTRICTIVE TIME.

THE SHORT LIFESPAN OF THE NUDIST CAMP FILM BOOM MAY EXPLAIN WHY CANADA'S MOVIEMAKERS NEVER REALLY GOT IN ON THE ACT, OR MAYBE IT'S JUST TOO COLD TO BARE ALL FOR VERY LONG IN THE CHILLY NORTH. CANADA'S ONLY CONTRIBUTION TO THE TREND WAS 1963'S HAVE FIGURE WILL TRAVEL, A BREEZY TRAVELOGUE BY CBC VETERAN LEO ORENSTEIN THAT SAW A TRIO OF TORONTO GIRLS INNOCENTLY TOURING NUDIST COLONIES SOUTH OF THE BORDER. COMING MORE THAN 15 YEARS LATER, ANTHONY TUDHOPE'S MONDO NUDE IS A FAR MORE

MONDO NUDE
REVIEW BY PAUL CORUPE
WWW.CANUXPLOITATION.COM

A DOCUMENTARY ON THE 1978 MISS NUDE WORLD PAGEANT, MONDO NUDE IS ONE OF THE MORE INTERESTING TAX SHELTER FILMS OUT OF CANADA. THE FIRST INSTALMENT OF A TRILOGY OF EXPOSED-FLESH EXPOSES PRODUCED BY ANTHONY KRAMREITHER, IT'S A SURPRISINGLY COMPELLING DOCUMENTARY FOR DIFFERENT REASONS THAN VIEWERS MIGHT EXPECT.

UNDER THE GUISE OF A RESPECTFUL PORTRAYAL OF THE NATURALIST PHILOSOPHY THAT HAS STEADILY GAINED POPULARITY SINCE THE 1920S, "ADULTS ONLY" NUDIST FILMS WEREN'T EXACTLY SUBTLE ABOUT THEIR REAL INTENT, NAMELY: SEXUALIZED DEPICTIONS OF THE FEMALE BODY. WHILE SIMILAR TO 1960S FARE LIKE THE

A TRULY REVEALING FILM

MONDO NUDE

ACCOMPLISHED WORK, A BEHIND-THE-SCENES PEEK AT THE MISS NUDE WORLD COMPETITION, WHERE DOZENS OF FEMALE NATURALISTS VIE FOR THE TITLE BEFORE AN OGLING AUDIENCE AT THE FOUR SEASONS FAMILY NUDIST RESORT IN FREELTON, ONT. (JUST OUTSIDE OF NIAGARA FALLS).

AFTER THE TRADITIONAL TITLE CARD THAT FRAMES THE MOVIE AS AN EDUCATIONAL EXERCISE, THE CAMERA TAKES VIEWERS ON A BRIEF TOUR OF THE FOUR SEASONS' IMPRESSIVE FACILITIES BEFORE PAUSING AT A NUDE VOLLEYBALL GAME FOR A SERIES OF LINGERING CLOSE-UPS. AFTER THIS FROTHY INTRODUCTION, THE FILM INTRODUCES THE RESORT DIRECTORS AS THEY PREPARE FOR THE ANNUAL CONTEST INTENDED TO PROMOTE NATURALISM TO A WIDER AUDIENCE. ON THEIR ARRIVAL, THE YOUNG, FRESH-FACED CONTESTANTS, MOST OF WHOM WERE RAISED IN NUDIST FAMILIES, PLAN THEIR ROUTINES ON A HUGE OUTDOOR WOODEN STAGE BUILT ESPECIALLY FOR THE EVENT. THIS CANDIDLY SHOT PRODUCTION THEN FOLLOWS SEVERAL OF THE GIRLS AS THEY PROMOTE THE EVENT TO THE MEDIA AND BY GREETING PASSERSBY ON THE STREETS OF

TORONTO AND NIAGRA FALLS. THE TONE IS ALL VERY LIGHT
UNTIL THE PAGEANT DRESS REHEARSAL (OR SHOULD THAT
BE NON-DRESS REHEARSAL?) WHERE IT IS REVEALED
THAT THE SLEAZY RESORT OWNER HAS CHARGED A
GROUP OF "AMATEUR PHOTOGRAPHERS" $15 APIECE
FOR RINGSIDE SEATS TO SNAP PICS OF THE GIRLS
PRACTICING THEIR STAGE STRUTS.

WHAT'S INTRIGUING ABOUT THIS DEVELOPMENT IS THAT IT
PORTRAYS THE OWNER AS A BUSINESSMAN MORE
INTERESTED IN EXPLOITING THE GIRLS' BODIES, THAN
A TRUE BELIEVER PROMOTING NUDISM. IRONICALLY,
THIS IS THE SAME CRITICISM LEVELLED AT THE
NUDIST MOVIE DIRECTORS OF THE '60s (AND, BY
EXTENTION, THIS FILM TOO). RATHER THAN SWEEP ASIDE
THE OBVIOUS ISSUE OF THE THORNY RELATIONSHIP BETWEEN
NATURALISM AND SEX, TUDHOPE INTERVIEWS ONE OF THE
YOUNG LADIES, WHO EXPRESSES REAL CONCERNS ABOUT
THE DIRECTION OF THE CONTEST AND THE INTENTIONS
OF FOUR SEASONS. SHE WAS RIGHT TO BE CONCERNED
AS THE DAY OF FESTIVITIES GETS UNDERWAY, AND
THE EVENT'S SIZABLE AUDIENCE IS REVEALED TO BE
PRIMARILY MADE UP OF WHISTLING, CAT-CALLING MALE
GAWKERS, WITH A FEW LESS-INTERESTED NUDISTS IN
LAWN CHAIRS OFF TO THE SIDE. AND THEN THERE'S ONE
GIRL WHO EXPLAINS TO THE JUDGES THAT SHE ONLY
"OFFICIALLY" BECAME A NUDIST A FEW DAYS PRIOR,
OBVIOUSLY ONLY TO SATISFY PAGEANT RULES.

WHEN THE ONSTAGE COMPETITIONS FINALLY BEGIN,
TUDHOPE ESCHEWS EXPECTATIONS AND IGNORES
THE SUSPENSE OVER WHO WILL WIN TO FOCUS ON
THE MINUTIAE OF RUNNING THE EVENT. FROM
THIS POINT ON, THE FILM FOLLOWS GIRLS BEING
FERRIED TO AND FROM A NEARBY MOTEL,
ENGAGING IN NERVOUS BACKSTAGE BANTER
AND BRUSHING OFF HARASSMENT FROM THE
SWEATY AUTOGRAPH SEEKERS. THROUGH IT ALL,
TUDHOPE MAINTAINS A DISTINCT DIRECT
CINEMA STYLE, USING HANDHELD CAMERAS

TO ACHIEVE AN UNOBTRUSIVE, NATURALISTIC
FEEL PIONEERED BY MICHEL BRAULT'S NATIONAL
FILM BOARD DOCUMENTARIES OF THE 1950s AND
1960s. WHILE OTHER EXPLOITATION-FOCUSED
DOCS OF THE 1980s ALSO APE THESE SMOOTH
TECHNIQUES, FEW ARE AS HEAVILY INDEBTED TO
THE NFB'S DOCUMENTARY MOVEMENT AS MONDO
NUDE, WHICH INSTILLS THE FILM WITH A
DISARMING HONESTY THAT SEEMS TOTALLY
AT ODDS WITH THE INTENTIONALLY
TITILLATING SUBJECT MATTER.

ONE CAN'T HELP WONDER IF TUDHOPE
WAS REMOVED FROM THE PICTURE ONCE
PRODUCER KRAMREITHER SAW THAT
THE FILM ROSE ABOVE ITS MORE
SALACIOUS PURPOSE. IT'S POSSIBLE,
SINCE THE LEERING VOLLEYBALL
GAME AT THE BEGINNING DOESN'T
REALLY MATCH THE MORE RESPECTFUL
COVERAGE OF THE PAGEANT ITSELF,
AND KRAMREITHER SLIPPED INTO
THE DIRECTOR'S CHAIR FOR TWO
FOLLOW-UPS, **MONDO STRIP** (1980)
AND **MONDO MACHO** (1983), MORE
SEXUALIZED DOCUMENTARIES THAT
COVERED THE EXOTIC DANCING PROFESSION
FROM BOTH GENDERS. IT'S ALSO TELLING THAT
TUDHOPE NEVER DIRECTED AGAIN (HIS PLANNED
DRAMATIC FEATURE **ANNE AND JOEY** WAS AN
APPARENT CASUALTY OF THE TAX SHELTER COLLAPSE.

THAT'S A SHAME, BECAUSE **MONDO NUDE** IS AN
OFTEN ACCOMPLISHED WORK, A DISTINCTIVE
CANADIAN CURIO, AND AN ENGAGING (IF UNEXPECTED)
EXAMPLE OF DIRECT CINEMA THAT REVEALS THE
NAKED TRUTH IN MORE WAYS THAN ONE.

GOOD GIRL, BAD GIRL (1984. DIR: RON DORFMAN)

CLAD ONLY IN A SWEAT-STAINED WIFEBEATER AND A HEADBAND, JERRY BUTLER LOOKS COKED OUT OF HIS GODDAMN GOURD AS HE PLANTS HIS HAIRY LOVE SPUDS INTO THE MOUND OF A RICH ACTRESS NAMED VELVA (COLLEEN BRENNAN), ALL THE WHILE HOLLERING SWEARS AND INSULTS AT HER. MOMENTS LATER HE'S SHOT A CUP OF TADPOLE TEA ALL OVER HER BACK, AND THEN STARTS RUDELY ROOTING THROUGH HER OTHER JEWEL BOX, HOPING TO SCAM SOME VALUABLE PEARLS. VELVA CONFRONTS THE CROOK, PULLS OUT A GUN, SHOTS ARE FIRED, AND WHEN THE SMOKE CLEARS, BRENNAN'S CHARACTER LAYS DEAD ON THE FLOOR, AND BUTLER HAS MADE HIS GETAWAY.

JOEY SILVERA IS A HARD-NOSED, OBSESSIVE GUMSHOE ASSIGNED TO SOLVE THE CASE IN THIS LITTLE-KNOWN SHOT-ON-FILM PORN-NOIR CLASSIC THAT IS DIRECTLY BASED ON 1944'S **LAURA**. OUR INTRODUCTION TO HIM IS OUR INTRODUCTION TO THE ENTIRE CAST, AS HE SITS EACH ONE DOWN AND INTERROGATES THEM. I LOVE THE WAY EACH ACTOR AND ACTRESS'S REAL NAME APPEARS AS THEY DRIFT THROUGH THE SCENE, MARKING ONE OF THE MOST ORIGINAL OPENING CREDIT SEQUENCES I'VE EVER SEEN FOR AN ADULT MOVIE.

TURNS OUT COLLEEN'S VELVA CHARACTER WAS THE STAR OF A SLEAZY PLAY THAT DOUBLED AS A SIMULATED SEX SHOW, AND SCRUMPTIOUS TAIJA RAE IS NEXT IN LINE TO TAKE OVER THE ROLE. COULD SHE BE INVOLVED SOMEHOW? THIS IS A REALLY EARLY APPEARANCE FOR TAIJA, WHO WOULD GO ON TO BE ONE OF THE BIGGEST ADULT STARS OF THE LATE '80S, AND BE TOUTED BY HUSTLER MAGAZINE AS ONE OF "PORN'S BIG FOUR" -- A TINY GROUP OF ELITE MEGASTARS WHO COMMANDED MORE THAN $1000 A DAY AT THE TIME.

THERE ARE A NUMBER OF GOOD XXX COUPLINGS IN THIS, ONE OF WHICH IS A FLASHBACK TO HOW VELVA GOT THE SEX SHOW GIG FROM A LOUD-MOUTHED SHITBAG DIRECTOR NAMED ARTIE ZOLTAN, WHO IS PLAYED BY THE ALWAYS ENTERTAINING GEORGE PAYNE. A NOTORIOUS TIMES SQUARE HUSTLER AND JUNKIE, GEORGE THROWS ENTHUSIASTIC FUCKS INTO SHARON MITCHELL AND COLLEEN BRENNAN WHILE JOINED BY HIS ROOMMATE AND PORNO PROTEGE, BOBBY SPECTOR -- BETTER KNOWN TO CULT FILM FANS AS SLEAZOID EXPRESS AUTHOR BILL LANDIS.

"GEORGE BEGAN TROTTING ME AROUND TO VARIOUS PORN DIRECTORS AS 'THE NEW KID'," LANDIS WOULD WRITE OF THIS TIME IN A PIECE FOR THE VILLAGE VOICE. "I GAVE UP CASUAL HUSTLING, BUT I DID HAVE A MORBID CURIOSITY ABOUT TRADING ON MY NEW PERSONA FOR CASH AS AN ESCORT. THIS WAS A SCENE GEORGE KNEW TOO WELL. WHEN I INQUIRED, THE INSCRUTABLE MR. PAYNE LOOKED ME UP AND DOWN AND SAID MATTER-OF-FACTLY, 'THEY'LL EAT YOU ALIVE, LIKE PIRANHAS.'"

THE TWO WOULD DO MASSIVE AMOUNTS OF COCAINE, VALIUM AND PERCODAN, A DRUG THAT LANDIS WOULD DESCRIBE AS GIVING "A SUDDEN MANIC SURGE OF EUPHORIA AND A SENSE OF SEXUAL EXCITEMENT, PRODUCING AN INVOLUNTARY ERECTION IN SOME MEN. PERCODANS CAN GIVE YOU THE COURAGE OF A LION, BUT YOUR TOLERANCE RISES VERY QUICKLY AND THE CRASH IS EMOTIONALLY DEVASTATING."

"WE WOULD START EACH DAY WITH A MANIC JOLT, SHARING AN ENTIRE ENTENMANN'S CHOCOLATE MARSHMALLOW CREAM CAKE FOR BREAKFAST AND PLAYING ON THE TELEPHONE LIKE CHILDREN, PRANKING ENEMIES IN THE SEX BUSINESS. THEN WE'D MAKE AN EXHAUSTIVE RUN HITTING UP DIRECTORS FOR WORK."

APPARENTLY RON DORFMAN WAS ONE OF THE MANHATTAN PORN DIRECTORS THAT SAID YES TO THE TWO OF THEM, ALTHOUGH AS PER USUAL, SPECTOR ISN'T REALLY MUCH OF A WOODSMAN, AND ONLY GETS A HARD-ON LONG ENOUGH TO SQUIRT A MEAGRE DRIBBLE FOR BRENNAN TO LAP AT. A BETTER SCENE IS WHEN SILVERA SETS UP A WIRE TAP TO SPY ON SHARON'S CHARACTER AND LEAVES TWO COPS STAKED OUT IN A VAN. IN TRUE PORN FASHION, IT ALL GOES AWRY WHEN THE TWO UNDERCOVER AGENTS

TAIJA RAE

GET TURNED ON BY WHAT THEY'RE HEARING, AND CAN'T KEEP FROM FUCKING ONE ANOTHER.

AS USUAL, GEORGE PAYNE IS STELLAR AND STEALS NEARLY EVERY SCENE HE'S IN. I LOVE HIM WHEN HE'S FRANTICALLY SHOWING THE PERFORMERS IN HIS PLAY HOW TO DO ON-STAGE SIMULATED SCREWING, OR SCREAMING AT A SNOOTY BRITISH THEATER CRITIC PLAYED BY PAULA MEADOWS. HE ALSO FUCKS SILVER STARR IN THE ASS, ALL WHILE GIGGLING AND SNEERING "OH, DOES IT HURT? DOES IT HURT? HEE HEE HEE!" WHAT A SLIMEBALL!

AS IN ALL MURDER MYSTERIES, PORNO OR OTHERWISE, EVERYTHING IS NOT AS IT APPEARS, BUT I'M NOT GONNA GIVE AWAY THE BIG (AND QUITE SURPRISING) TWIST ENDING IN THIS ONE. SHAME ABOUT THE TOTALLY GENERIC TITLE THAT IS PROBABLY THE REASON THIS HAS GONE UNDER SO MANY VINTAGE PORN FAN'S RADARS, BUT Y'ALL SHOULD CHECK IT OUT YOURSELVES IF YOU CAN TRACK IT DOWN.

—BOUGIE '12

RANDOM TRIVIA ☆

☆ IN 2007 A BRITISH TEENAGER SUED HOUSTON TEXAS COMPANY TVX FILMS (WHO ARE KNOWN FOR REISSUING CRAPPY VERSIONS OF CLASSIC XXX MOVIES ON DVD) FOR USING A PHOTO OF HER (AGED 14) ON THE COVER OF THEIR DVD RELEASE OF 1982's **BODY MAGIC**. HER INITIAL REQUEST FOR COMPENSATION WAS MET WITH THIS E-MAIL REPLY FROM TVX: "NICE TRY, TOOTS". THE IMAGE, STOLEN FROM THE WEBSITE OF THE YOUNG GIRL, ENDED UP COSTING TVX ALMOST $130,000 WHEN THEY LOST THE CASE IN 2010. UNDERLINE EXCELLENT WORK, TOOTS.

☆ **INEVITABLE LOVE** (1985) WAS THE FIRST GAY PORN MOVIE TO HAVE PERFORMERS WEARING CONDOMS.

☆ THE GRAPHIC XXX BLOWJOB SCENE IN **THE BROWN BUNNY** WAS FILMED USING REMOTE CAMERAS. ONLY VINCENT GALLO (THE SUCKEE) AND CHLOE SEVIGNY (THE SUCKER) WERE IN THE ROOM AT THE TIME. I WISH _I_ WERE IN THE ROOM AT THE TIME.

THE ARK OF THE SUN GOD (1984. ITALY)

ONE OF THE THINGS TO WATCH FOR WHEN YOU NOTICE THAT A MOVIE IS DIRECTED BY ANTONIO MARGHERITI ARE THE CRASHING AND EXPLODING MODEL TOY CARS, PLANES AND TRAINS THAT SUBSTITUTE FOR THE REAL THING IN ORDER TO BRING MASSIVE ACTION SCENES TO HIS CHEAP-ASS FILMS. REVIEWERS OFTEN MAKE FUN OF THE FX WHEN YOU LOOK UP HIS MOVIES ONLINE, BUT IF YOU ASK ME THE PROFESSIONALISM WITH WHICH THEY ARE EXECUTED MAKES THESE SO-CALLED "CHEESY" EFFECTS FAR MORE FUN TO WATCH THAN SO MANY OF THE MULTI-MILLION DOLLAR COMPUTER EFFECTS IN MODERN HOLLYWOOD GENRE FILMS. SERIOUSLY.

I MEAN, AT THE RISK OF SOUNDING LIKE AN OLD 'GET-OFF-MY-LAWN' TYPE GROUCH, IT'S AT TIMES LIKE THESE THAT I WONDER IF I JUST HAVE A TOTALLY DIFFERENT IDEA OF WHAT LOOKS "COOL" THAN A WHOLE GENERATION OF YOUNGER FILMGOERS. AND IF YOU'RE WONDERING IF YOU'RE IN THAT GROUP, ALL YOU HAVE TO ASK YOURSELF TO FIND OUT IS: WOULD I RATHER SEE A GUY IN A GODZILLA SUIT ROCK THE SHIT OUT OF AN INTRICATELY BUILT SCALE-SIZED MODEL REPLICA OF TOKYO, OR WITNESS THE SAME THING TOTALLY RENDERED ON COMPUTERS, WITH THE "CAMERA" CONSTANTLY WHIPPING AROUND 360 DEGREES TO CATCH ALL THE ACTION?

ARK OF THE SUN GOD FEATURES THE LATE DAVID WARBECK AS A RUGGED SAFECRACKER WHO IS EMPLOYED BY AN ERUDITE WHEELCHAIR-BOUND DOUCHEBAG NAMED LORD DEAN (JOHN STEINER) TO GO TO ISTANBUL AND FIND A SACRED AND MASSIVELY POWERFUL SCEPTER THAT ONCE BELONGED TO THE FREAKY GOD GILGAMESH. THE THING IS THAT A BUNCH OF OTHER SWARTHY SCUMBAGS ALSO WANT TO GET THEIR NASTY MITTS ON THE ANCIENT ORNAMENTAL ROD, AND SO NOW THE FUCKIN' RACE IS ON! GO, WARBECK, GO! CRACK SOME SAFES _AND_ SOME HEADS!

YEAH, AS YOU PROBABLY GUESSED, THE "ARK" IN THE TITLE IS JUST A PREDICTABLE AND CRASS CASH-IN ON THE WILDLY POPULAR **RAIDERS OF THE LOST ARK** (1981) WITH QUITE A BIT OF JAMES BOND REFERENCE ADDED AS WELL. IT'S NO **LAST HUNTER** (1980) BUT IN MARGHERITI'S DEFENCE, THIS IS ONE OF THE MORE WATCHABLE INDY CLONES, AND IT HAS A GREAT THEME SONG. LOOK FORWARD TO TRANS-AM MUSCLE CARS RACING IN THE DESERT, PLANE CRASHES, FREAKY TARANTULAS, KILLER RATS, SNAKE PITS, VILE COCKFIGHTING, BLACK MAGIC, POISONOUS DARTS, AND A MOUNTAIN RANGE SHAPED LIKE A DAMN SWASTIKA!

—BOUGIE.

THE ARK OF THE SUN GOD

EAT SHIT, TRACI LORDS

AS AUTHOR ROBERT ROSEN SAID IN HIS 2012 BOOK BEAVER ST.: "SHE HAD ENOUGH TALENT TO PORTRAY A TWENTY-ONE-YEAR-OLD NYMPHOMANIAC SO CONVINCINGLY, HER PERFORMANCES SET THE GOLD STANDARD BY WHICH ALL YOUNG PORN NYMPHOS WILL FOREVERMORE BE MEASURED."

TOO BAD SHE WAS ONLY 16 AT THE TIME. YES, WHEN A VERY ADULT-LOOKING YOUNG WOMAN NAMED TRACI LORDS FORGED A BIRTH CERTIFICATE AND OTHER ID IN 1984 AND ROSE TO THE TOP OF THE SKIN-BIZ DURING HER UNDERAGE PORN CAREER BEFORE THROWING THE INDUSTRY UNDER THE BUS A FEW MONTHS AFTER TURNING 18, SHE SENT MULTIPLE INNOCENT PEOPLE TO JAIL FOR DISTRIBUTING UNDERAGE PORN, AND THEN NEVER SPOKE ABOUT IT AGAIN.

NOW THIS WOMAN (WHO LAUGHABLY PAINTS HERSELF AS VICTIMIZED) THINKS IT'S ANNOYING THAT, EVEN 30 YEARS LATER, INTERVIEWERS STILL WANT HER TO TALK ABOUT HER PORN CAREER. IF SHE HAD ACTUALLY ANSWERED ANY OF OUR QUESTIONS IN THE 65 PAGES OF HER AUTOBIOGRAPHY (WHERE SHE PLAYS AT EXPLAINING THE YEARS OF HER PORN CAREER) INSTEAD OF TOTALLY GLOSSING OVER EVERYTHING AND PRETENDING MOST OF IT NEVER HAPPENED -- MAYBE PEOPLE WOULD FINALLY STOP ASKING.

LORDS'S MEMOIR AND EVERY INTERVIEW SHE'S EVER DONE SHEDS NOT ONE BIT OF LIGHT ON ANYTHING. SHE'S DONE EVERYTHING IN HER POWER TO OBSCURE THE TRUTH -- SAYING SHE WAS FAR TOO DRUNK AND STONED FOR THOSE THREE YEARS TO REMEMBER A SINGLE THING THAT HAPPENED, DESPITE HER MANY CO-STARS POINTING OUT THAT SHE ALWAYS APPEARED TOTALLY SOBER. SHE NOT ONLY LEAVES OUT ALL EROTIC DETAIL IN HER BOOK ("IT WAS A BLUR OF ARMS AND LEGS" IS ABOUT AS GRAPHIC AS IT GETS), BUT SHE ALSO PROVIDES TOTAL FABRICATIONS ("I ONLY DID 21 FILMS"), AND UTTERLY LUDICROUS EXPLANATIONS FOR HER BEHAVIOUR THAT DON'T MAKE A LICK OF SENSE. ONE OF HER CO-STARS, CHRISTY CANYON, HAS GONE SO FAR AS TO SAY ABOUT LORDS'S AUTOBIOGRAPHY: "SHE WAS LYING THROUGHOUT THE WHOLE THING."

IT'S A REAL SHAME THAT SHE WAS NEVER CHARGED FOR HER CRIME. EAT SHIT, TRACI LORDS.

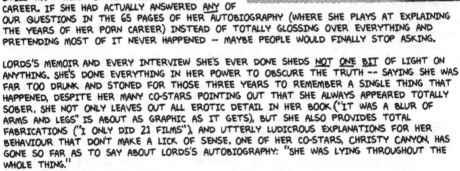

DEMONLOVER

WRITTEN AND DIRECTED BY OLIVIER ASSAYAS, 2002.

WHY BE LARA CROFT WHEN YOU CAN TORTURE LARA CROFT? THIS IS ONE OF MANY QUESTIONS RAISED BY THE BIZARRE POST-MODERN NERD TABLEAUX OF DEMONLOVER. SHARING AN AESTHETIC WITH THE NEW FRENCH EXTREMITY, DIRECTOR ASSAYAS HAS MADE A FILM THAT SEEMS TO PREDICT THE LAST CYCLE OF WILLIAM GIBSON'S POST-SF NOVELS, AS IF ADAPTED BY GASPAR NOÉ. DEALING WITH VARIOUS CORPORATE INTERESTS VYING FOR CONTROL OF TRANSGRESSIVE HENTAI AND INTERACTIVE TORTURE PORN, IT'S OF LITTLE SURPRISE THIS FILM FAILED TO CAPTURE A LARGE AUDIENCE. GUYS IN POKÉMON T-SHIRTS USUALLY AREN'T TOO KEEN ON HAVING THE NERD WORLD'S DIRTY LITTLE SECRET OF MISOGYNY INDICTED BY THE ART HOUSE CROWD. DEMONLOVER PRESAGES THE CONTINUED BLURRING OF NERD AND MAINSTREAM CULTURE, AND THEREFORE POINTS A FINGER AT OUR ENTIRE BRAVE NEW WORLD MEDIA-SCAPE. REFERENCES TO THE X-MEN'S STORM ASIDE, THIS FILM INDICTS FAR MORE THAN THE COSPLAY SET. AS THE FILM'S (ANTI) HERO, CONNIE NIELSON, FINDS HERSELF ON THE SET OF A FANTASY INTERNET TORTURE SITE, SHE LOOKS AT US THROUGH THE CAMERA, HER EYES SEEMING TO PLEAD, 'WHY?'

DEMONLOVER IS A CULT FILM WITHOUT AN AUDIENCE. WHAT FOLLOWING IT DOES HAVE IS MORE THROUGH THE INDIE MUSIC SCENE, DUE TO THE AMBIENT NOISE SCORE BY SONIC YOUTH. THOUGH DEMONLOVER IS TRULY FLAWED AND MUDDLED IN PLACES, IT REMAINS A SLICK EXAMINATION OF CONTEMPORARY EXPLOITATION AND VOYEURISM. "WE'LL SLIDE DOWN THE SURFACE OF THINGS," WROTE BRET EASTON ELLIS IN GLAMORAMA. THIS FILM DOES MORE THAN SLIDE - IT PUNCTURES. ►A. LANGE

TORSO (AKA "CARNAL VIOLENCE")
1973 ITALY. DIR: SERGIO MARTINO.

DIRECTOR SERGIO MARTINO'S NAME SEEMS TO BE FOREVER LINKED TO THE GIALLO GENRE, EVEN THOUGH HE TRAVERSED HIS WAY THROUGH VARIOUS MOVIE GENRES DEPENDING ON THE PREVAILING CINEMATIC TRENDS OF THE DAY. MARTINO MADE DOCUMENTARIES, SCI-FI, SPAGHETTI WESTERNS, SEX COMEDIES, AND VARIOUS OTHER THRILLERS BEFORE HE CAME UP WITH THE CONCEPT FOR TORSO, AND PITCHED THE IDEA TO PRODUCER CARLO PONTI. THEY HIRED GIANCARLO FERRANDO TO BE THE CINEMATOGRAPHER (WHO ALSO SHOT MOUNTAIN OF THE CANNIBAL GOD) AND WHEN THEY FINISHED, THEY'D CRAFTED A HIGHLY INFLUENTIAL PICTURE TODAY CONSIDERED TO BE ONE OF THE FORERUNNERS OF THE MODERN SLASHER GENRE.

PONTI WAS FOND OF THE STORY IDEA THAT MARTINO SENT OVER TO HIM, BUT SUGGESTED SOME CHANGES WHEN HE CALLED HIM THE NEXT DAY. CARLO'S KEY CHANGES WERE PUT IN PLACE TO MAKE SURE THE MOVIE WOULD BE EASILY MARKETABLE IN OTHER COUNTRIES LIKE THE US, THE UK, AND FRANCE. WITH THAT IN MIND, MARTINO CAST BRITISH ACTRESS SUZY KENDALL (WHO HE HAD SEEN AND LOVED IN ARGENTO'S BIRD WITH THE CRYSTAL PLUMAGE), AND FRENCH ACTRESS TINA AUMONT (THE DAUGHTER OF FAMOUS 1940S ACTRESS MARIA MONTEZ). THEN HE CAME UP WITH THE GREAT IDEA TO SHOOT THE MOVIE IN A GORGEOUS LOCATION KNOWN AS PERUGIA.

"PERUGIA IS A SMALL TOWN IN UMBRIA, IN CENTRAL ITALY", MARTINO TOLD INTERVIEWER ART ETTINGER. "THERE IS A UNIVERSITY THERE, AND THAT WAY GIRLS OF DIFFERENT NATIONALITIES COULD TAKE PART IN THE FILM."

"IT'S THE KIND OF MOVIE THAT KEEPS THE INTEREST OF AUDIENCES ALL OVER THE WORLD", MARTINO CONTINUED. "EVEN AFTER 30 YEARS. I THINK THAT'S ONE OF THE MOST IMPORTANT THINGS ABOUT THIS MOVIE -- THAT WE CAN STILL WATCH IT 30 YEARS LATER AND THINK IT'S A GOOD MOVIE."

THE FILM'S MAIN STAR, THE LOVELY SUZY KENDALL (WHO ALWAYS LOOKS LIKE A YOUNG, BLONDE JANE SEYMOUR TO ME) HAD FLOWN TO ITALY TO MAKE THE MOVIE JUST AFTER DIVORCING HER HUSBAND, FAMOUS BRITISH ACTOR DUDLEY MOORE. THEIR 4-YEAR MARRIAGE HAD COME TO AN AMICABLE CLOSE, MOSTLY BECAUSE MOORE HAD FOUND WORLDWIDE SUCCESS AND HE DIDN'T THINK THE TIME WAS RIGHT FOR RAISING CHILDREN THE WAY SHE'D WANTED TO. A DAUGHTER, ELODIE HARPER, WOULD COME LATER WITH ANOTHER HUSBAND, AND SHE WORKS TODAY AS A JOURNALIST WITH THE BRITISH TV COMPANY ITV.

TORSO IS A MOVIE THAT DEPICTS EXTREME ACTS OF VIOLENCE CARRIED OUT BY A HOODED MISOGYNIST PSYCHO. THIS KILLER DESPISES WOMEN, BUT UNFORTUNATELY THE MOVIE GIVES US ONLY A BRIEF WINDOW INTO WHY THAT MAY BE. EVEN SO, THE BRUTAL REALITY OF SEXUAL VIOLENCE AND EVEN THE FAR MORE HABITUAL EVERYDAY REALITY OF THE MALE GAZE IS SOMETHING IT REFUSES TO SHY AWAY FROM. SWEATY, HORNY MEN OGLE AND LUST OVER DELIRIOUSLY PRETTY WOMEN IN TORSO. EVERY MAN IS A POTENTIAL RAPIST, AND THUSLY A SUSPECT FOR US, THE AUDIENCE. EVERY WOMAN IS FUCKING GORGEOUS AND PARANOID (JUSTLY, IT TURNS OUT) THAT A MAN IS GOING TO MURDER THEM FOR THE SIMPLE "CRIME" OF HAVING A PUSSY, TITS, AND THE ABILITY TO WOO.

MAKE NO MISTAKE, THIS MOVIE IS SLEAZY AS HELL. THE FEMALE CAST ARE AS OFTEN NAKED AS THEY ARE CLOTHED, AND THEY OCCASIONALLY WRITHE AGAINST ONE ANOTHER (THE LESBIAN SUB PLOT IS VERY APPEALING) PRIOR TO THE HIGHLY SEXUALIZED AND BRUTAL ATTACKS MET UPON THEM. DESPITE ALL OF THAT, AND THE AFOREMENTIONED FACT THAT THE KILLER IS A MISOGYNIST FREAK, IT'S COOL THAT THE FILM ITSELF ISN'T. THESE LADIES MAY BE SEXUAL, BUT THEY AREN'T USELESS AND SHRILL LIKE THEY ARE IN SO MANY AMERICAN SLASHERS AND ITALIAN GIALLOS. WE ARE MEANT TO EMPATHIZE WITH THE HEROINES, AND FEEL THE WHITE HOT TENSION AS THEY CONTEMPLATE HOW TO ESCAPE -- NOT CHEER FOR THEIR MESSY DEMISE AT THE HANDS

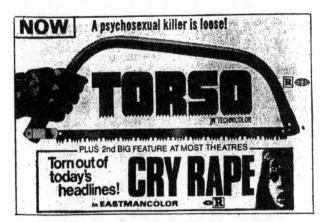
OF THE BLACK-GLOVED KILLER.

WHEN YOUR FRIENDS ARE GETTING GORILY GAKKED, I GUESS THE THING TO DO IS ROUND UP YOUR BEST GAL-PALS AND GET THE FUCK OUT OF THE CITY IN A BID TO CLEAR YOUR HEAD AND GET AWAY FROM IT ALL. THAT'S WHAT THE FEATURED PLAYERS OF TORSO DO WHEN THE GOING GETS ROUGH. ASSUMING THE COPS WILL BE EXPEDIENT ABOUT SOLVING THE CASE, THE FOUR GIRLS SHACK UP IN A VILLA ON THE TOP OF A CLIFF OVERLOOKING PERUGIA, AND START DRINKING LOTS OF J+B, PLAYING THE PIANO, LAUGHING, SUNBATHING NUDE, AND HAVING LESBIAN SEX. UNFORTUNATELY FOR THEM, THE KILLER HAS FOLLOWED ALONG.

"IT'S SUCH A FANTASTIC ITALIAN SLASHER FILM", DIRECTOR ELI ROTH TOLD AVCLUB.COM IN 2007. "BUT IT'S ALSO ONE OF THE MOVIES WHERE THE FIRST 45 MINUTES ARE KIND OF INCOMPREHENSIBLE. AS TARANTINO ONCE PUT IT, 'THE MOVIE ALMOST DARES YOU TO KEEP WATCHING IT.' BUT THE LAST 15 MINUTES – ONCE THEY GET TO THIS HOUSE, THE MOVIE JUST TAKES OFF. THE WHOLE THING IS ABOUT THE HOUSE. SO EVEN IF YOU DON'T KNOW WHAT'S GOING ON, OR IT JUST SEEMS WEIRD, OR YOU'RE CONFUSED BY WHO'S WHO, DON'T WORRY ABOUT IT. KEEP WATCHING UNTIL YOU GET TO THE HOUSE. ONCE YOU'RE AT THE HOUSE, IT'S ON. IT'S JUST UNBELIEVABLE. THE LAST 15 MINUTES OF TORSO ARE JUST SOME OF THE BEST FILMMAKING I'VE EVER SEEN."

I THINK ELI MEANT THE LAST 30 MINUTES, NOT THE LAST 15. TODAY I TOOK A CLOSE LOOK AT THE RUNTIME AND IT'S REALLY THE LAST 28 MINUTES OF THIS MOVIE WHERE EVERYTHING KICKS INTO OVERDRIVE IN TERMS OF SUSPENSE AND CHILLING THRILLS. THAT WHOLE LAST ACT IS AS MUCH EDGE-OF-YOUR-SEAT TENSION AS THE BEST 1970S THRILLERS. TORSO IS MASSIVELY UNDERRATED, AND SHOULD BE ADDED TO EVERYONE'S "MUST SEE" LIST POST-HASTE. GET ON IT!

THEY KIDNAPPED CHAPLIN'S CORPSE

FAMOUS SILENT FILM STAR CHARLES CHAPLIN ENDED UP LIVING IN SWITZERLAND IN 1952 AFTER BEING ACCUSED OF BEING A COMMUNIST SYMPATHIZER IN AMERICA. THERE HE LIVED OUT THE LAST 25 YEARS OF HIS LIFE AND DIED AT THE RIPE OLD AGE OF 88 IN DECEMBER OF 1977.

ONLY A FEW MONTHS LATER, ON MARCH 2ND, 1978, HIS COFFIN AND CORPSE WERE DUG OUT OF THE GROUND, STOLEN, AND HELD FOR RANSOM. HIS WIDOW AND 4TH WIFE, OONA, REFUSED TO PAY THE OUTRAGEOUS RANSOM REQUEST, SAYING THAT HER HUSBAND WOULD HAVE THOUGHT THE DEMAND "RIDICULOUS." THE BODY WAS EVENTUALLY RECOVERED BY SWISS POLICE ON 17 MAY, 1978, AND TWO POLITICAL REFUGEES WITH FINANCIAL DIFFICULTIES (ROMAN WARDAS, OF POLAND, AND GANTSCHO GANEV, OF BULGARIA) CONFESSED, DESCRIBING HOW THEY NABBED THE LITTLE TRAMP'S OAK COFFIN FROM THE VILLAGE CEMETERY AT CORSIER-SUR-VEVEY AND BURIED IT IN A SHALLOW HOLE IN A CORNFIELD LOCATED IN THE HILLS ABOVE LAKE GENEVA, NEAR LAUSANNE, SWITZERLAND.

HERE'S PART OF A MAY 1978 NEWSPAPER REPORT THAT APPEARED IN THE WASHINGTON POST:

"ALTHOUGH (CHAPLIN'S) FAMILY HAD RECEIVED MANY FALSE CALLS ASKING FOR EXORBITANT SUMS. THIS TIME THE DEMAND WAS BACKED UP WITH A PHOTOGRAPH (TAKEN OF) THE ALLEGED COFFIN JUST BEFORE ITS REBURIAL IN THE CORNPATCH. CHAPLIN'S WIDOW, OONA, REFUSED TO CONSIDER RANSOM. BUT IN ORDER TO COOPERATE WITH POLICE, THE FAMILY, THROUGH ITS LAWYER, JEAN-FELIX PASCHOUD, BARGAINED WITH THE ALLEGED GRAVE ROBBERS OVER A TAPPED TELEPHONE. BY THE TIME THE DEMAND HAD DROPPED FROM $600,000 TO $250,000, THE POLICE HAD FIGURED OUT THAT THE RANSOM CALLS WERE COMING FROM A PUBLIC PAY TELEPHONE."

"TWO EARLIER TRAPS SET FOR THE ALLEGED GRAVE ROBBERS DID NOT SUCCEED BUT A DRAGNET OF 100 POLICEMEN KEEPING AN EYE ON ALL OF LAUSANNE'S MORE THAN 200 PAY PUBLIC TELEPHONES PROVED TOO DIFFICULT TO ELUDE FOR A 24-YEAR-OLD POLISH AUTO MECHANIC, UNTIL RECENTLY UNEMPLOYED. THE TWO ACCUSED MEN FACE SEVEN-AND-A-HALF YEARS IN PRISON FOR EXTORTION AND FOR "DISTURBING THE PEACE OF THE DEAD." CHAPLIN'S FAMILY HAS NOT DISCLOSED WHAT IT PLANS TO DO WITH HIS RECOVERED COFFIN."

— BOUGIE 2014.

Duel in the Eclipse

(aka Requiem for a Gringo. 1968. Italy/Spain)

IF YOU'VE EVER SAID TO YOURSELF "YEAH OK, SPAGHETTI WESTERNS ARE REALLY COOL, BUT WHY AREN'T THERE MORE OF THEM WHERE THE HEROIC GUNSLINGER IS ALSO AN ASTROLOGIST WHO WEARS A LEOPARD SKIN PONCHO AND RIDES ON A MULE?" THEN HOT SHIT, HAVE I GOT <u>GOOD NEWS</u> FOR YOU!

THAT NOTED HEROIC GUNSLINGER IS A WEIRD GUY NAMED LOGAN (OR 'GRINGO'- DEPENDING UPON WHICH BOOTLEG YOU TRACK DOWN), PLAYED BY LANG JEFFRIES, AND HE'S COME HOME TO HIS REMOTE RANCH HACIENDA TO SEEK VENGEANCE AGAINST AN EVIL MEXICAN NAMED CARRANZA (FERNANDO SANCHO) AND HIS FETID GANG OF BANDITOS. NOT ONLY DID THESE SLIMEBALLS KILL LOGAN'S BELOVED BROTHER, BUT THEY'VE BEEN SADISTICALLY ABUSING THE LOCALS TOO. THEY'RE PRETTY WELL ORGANIZED AND VERY TOUGH, SO IT'S GOING TO TAKE A REALLY KEENLY THOUGHT-OUT PLAN TO PULL ONE OVER ON THEM. LUCKILY, LOGAN HAS BEEN PRACTICALLY FERMENTING IN PLANNING. I BET THIS GUY DOESN'T EVEN TAKE A DUMP WITHOUT DRAWING UP A BLUEPRINT FOR HOW IT'S GOING TO TRANSPIRE.

BEING A BRAINY ASTROLOGER, OUR BOY COMES FULLY EQUIPPED WITH STAR CHARTS, BOOKS ON ALCHEMY, AND A BUNCH OF OTHER DOO-DADS AND THINGAMABOBS THAT HE KEEPS IN HIS NIFTY ROOFTOP OBSERVATORY WHERE

HE CHECKS HIS MAPS AND NOTES, AND WORKS OUT HIS REVENGE DEPENDENT ON THE ALIGNMENT OF THE STARS. ONLY WHEN APRIL 17, 1867 ROLLS AROUND (WHEN A FREAKY SOLAR ECLIPSE TAKES PLACE) DOES LOGAN DON HIS LEOPARD SKIN PULLOVER AND KICK SERIOUS ASS WHILE APPEARING TO THE SWEATY, UNEDUCATED MASSES TO HAVE THE POWERS OF A VENGEFUL GOD. DUMBASSES SHOULD READ A GODDAMN BOOK SOMETIME, AM I RIGHT?

NOTED BY KEVIN GRANT IN HIS BOOK, 'ANY GUN CAN PLAY' (THE BEST BOOK EVER PUBLISHED ON THE SPAGHETTI WESTERN GENRE, IN MY OPINION) AS A KEY "HYBRID WESTERN", DUEL IN THE ECLIPSE INTERWEAVES 1960S PSYCHEDELIA AND ELEMENTS OF GOTHIC HORROR INTO THE TYPICAL AND WELL-WORN EUROWESTERN TROPES AND CLICHES, MAKING IT QUITE MEMORABLE. SEEMINGLY ANTICIPATING EL TOPO (WHICH WOULD ARRIVE ON THE SCENE 2 YEARS LATER), THIS REALLY COOL LOOKING MOVIE TAKES ADVANTAGE OF DELIRIOUSLY ODD CAMERA TRICKS SUCH AS SPASTIC ZIP PANS AND ZOOM-INS, MOST NOTABLY IN THE FINAL ACT WHEN THE EPIC STAND-OFF WITH CARRANZA TAKES PLACE.

THERE ARE SOME COOL NONLINEAR ELEMENTS TOO, NOT TO MENTION SOME BLATANT EROTICISM (MARISA PAREDES HAS A LARGE ROLE IN THE FILM, AND GETS FREAKY IN THE BATHTUB) SOME LOW-LEVEL HOMOEROTICA (CARLO GADDI ROCKS A BLACK LEATHER OUTFIT AND SEEMS TO GET OFF ON BONDAGE) AND SOME SERIOUSLY EERIE ATMOSPHERE AND A HAUNTING SCORE BY ANGELO FRANCESCO LAVAGNINO.

ALL OF THAT SAID, IT'S NOT A PERFECT MOVIE AND IN SOME WAYS READS FAR BETTER ON PAPER THAN IT DOES AS A VIEWING EXPERIENCE. I STILL TOTALLY RECOMMEND SEEING IT BECAUSE I WANT YOU TO CHECK IT OUT AND SEE IF YOU DON'T AGREE THAT THIS WOULD ACTUALLY BE A GOOD MOVIE TO REMAKE. HONESTLY, THEY ALWAYS SEEM TO REMAKE MOVIES THAT ARE PRACTICALLY PERFECT ALREADY, WHICH IS ANNOYING TO ME, ESPECIALLY WHEN THERE ARE MOVIES LIKE THIS WHICH ARE FULL OF GREAT IDEAS AND REALLY INTERESTING IN CONCEPT (AND EVEN IN EXECUTION IN KEY SCENES), BUT DUE TO PACING AND SCRIPTING ISSUES WOULD ALSO BENEFIT FROM BEING RE-IMAGINED BY A SKILLED FILMMAKER.

CONSIDER THAT A CHALLENGE, MOVIE MAKING PEOPLES! SEE WHAT YOU CAN BRING TO THIS!

GINGER SNATCH

A CHILDHOOD SPENT SMITTEN WITH MISS LYNN

☆☆☆ · BY ROBIN BOUGIE · 2009 · ☆☆☆

IN 1987, WHEN I WAS 14 -- AND BEFORE I'D EVEN EVER SEEN A PORN MOVIE -- I KNEW WHO GINGER LYNN WAS. HER, ERICA BOYER, AND TRACI LORDS WERE THE FIRST THREE WOMEN I WAS AWARE OF BY NAME THAT TOOK PART IN THIS STRANGE AND EXOTIC VOCATION WHERE PEOPLE WOULD GET SEXED UP IN FRONT OF A CAMERA IN RETURN FOR A PAYCHECK AND NOTORIETY.

WE WOULD TALK AMONGST OURSELVES WHEN WE THOUGHT NO ONE WAS LOOKING, US YOUNG BOYS JUST GETTING AQUAINTED WITH THE SEXUAL COMPLEXITIES OF THE ADULT WORLD. SOME OF US HAD MAGAZINES THAT THEY HAD STOLEN FROM CONVENIENCE STORES, FOUND IN THE WOODS, OR BORROWED FROM OLDER BROTHERS AND LIBERAL STEP-DADS.

WE BABBLED TENUOUS INFORMATION ABOUT FAMOUS SEX STARS LIKE GINGER, AS IF THE STORIES THEMSELVES WERE VALUABLE CURRENCY. SHE AND TRACI WERE MYTHICAL IN OUR CIRCLE BECAUSE WE HAD NO EASY ACCESS TO ANYTHING ABOUT THESE GODDESSES. LIKE UNDERSIZED MINSTRELS WE WOULD SHARE WHAT LITTLE WE KNEW AMONGST OURSELVES, INFORMATION THAT WAS OFTEN FALSE.

"MY FRIEND SAW A VIDEO WITH HER HAVING SEX WITH A DOG. SHE WAS PUTTING ITS DICK IN HER MOUTH." RANDY BUSH TOLD ME AS I GASPED IN AMAZEMENT -- AN ANECDOTE WHICH TURNED OUT TO BE BOGUS. WHO WAS THIS LADY? WHERE DID SHE LIVE? (WE DIDN'T EVEN KNOW THAT THE PORN INDUSTRY WAS SITUATED IN SOUTHERN CALIFORNIA, OR MUCH OF ANYTHING ABOUT THAT WORLD REALLY.) MOST OF THE

BYLINES AND "TURN-ONS AND TURN-OFFS" NEXT TO THE PHOTOS IN PORN MAGAZINES WERE TOTALLY FABRICATED, BUT WE TOOK THAT OBSCENE PULPY VERNACULAR AS IF IT WERE GOSPEL WRITTEN ON STONE TABLETS. SHIT, WE DIDN'T EVEN KNOW THAT BY 1987 GINGER LYNN HAD ALREADY DROPPED OUT OF XXX TO TRY AND PARLAY HER REPUTATION AS A CUMGOBBLING FUCKMONKEY INTO RENOWN IN THE WORLD OF LEGITIMATE ACTING.

THE FIRST TIME I SAW HER IN A VIDEO FOR MYSELF, IT WAS ONE THAT I FOUND AMONGST ONE OF MY BROTHER'S PRIVATE THINGS. I SNUCK A VIEWING OF IT WHEN NO ONE WAS AROUND, AND HAVE NO IDEA TO THIS DAY WHAT THE TAPE WAS CALLED, BUT IT WAS A COLLECTION OF CLIPS OF VARIOUS NOTEWORTHY CUM-DUMPSTERS MASTURBATING FOR A VIDEO CAMERA. I GOT THE IDEA YEARS LATER THAT IT MUST HAVE BEEN SOME PORN DIRECTOR'S PERSONAL COLLECTION, AS MOST OF THE LOCATIONS WERE VERY PEDESTRIAN CONSIDERING THE LEVEL OF TALENT ON DISPLAY, AND CLEARLY

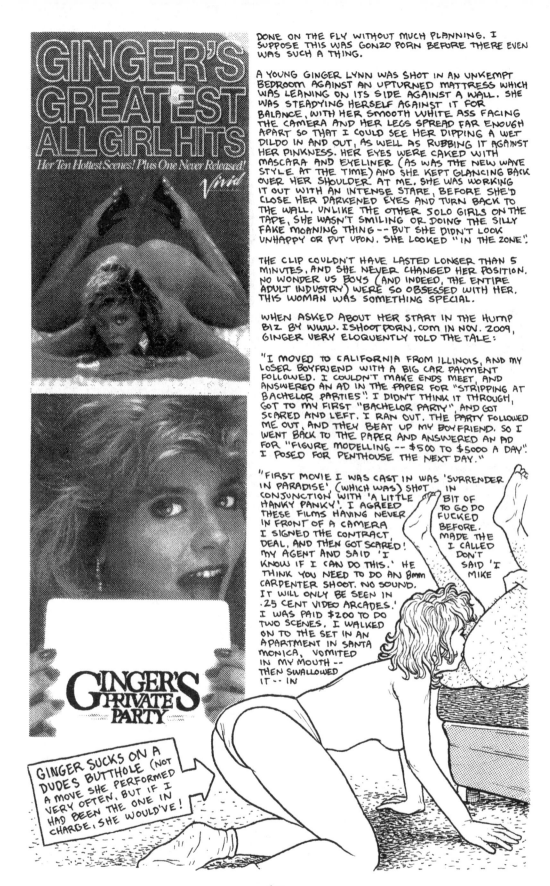

DONE ON THE FLY WITHOUT MUCH PLANNING. I SUPPOSE THIS WAS GONZO PORN BEFORE THERE EVEN WAS SUCH A THING.

A YOUNG GINGER LYNN WAS SHOT IN AN UNKEMPT BEDROOM AGAINST AN UPTURNED MATTRESS WHICH WAS LEANING ON ITS SIDE AGAINST A WALL. SHE WAS STEADYING HERSELF AGAINST IT FOR BALANCE, WITH HER SMOOTH WHITE ASS FACING THE CAMERA AND HER LEGS SPREAD FAR ENOUGH APART SO THAT I COULD SEE HER DIPPING A WET DILDO IN AND OUT, AS WELL AS RUBBING IT AGAINST HER PINKNESS. HER EYES WERE CAKED WITH MASCARA AND EYELINER (AS WAS THE NEW WAVE STYLE AT THE TIME) AND SHE KEPT GLANCING BACK OVER HER SHOULDER AT ME. SHE WAS WORKING IT OUT WITH AN INTENSE STARE, BEFORE SHE'D CLOSE HER DARKENED EYES AND TURN BACK TO THE WALL. UNLIKE THE OTHER SOLO GIRLS ON THE TAPE, SHE WASN'T SMILING OR DOING THE SILLY FAKE MOANING THING -- BUT SHE DIDN'T LOOK UNHAPPY OR PUT UPON. SHE LOOKED "IN THE ZONE".

THE CLIP COULDN'T HAVE LASTED LONGER THAN 5 MINUTES, AND SHE NEVER CHANGED HER POSITION. NO WONDER US BOYS (AND INDEED, THE ENTIRE ADULT INDUSTRY) WERE SO OBSESSED WITH HER. THIS WOMAN WAS SOMETHING SPECIAL.

WHEN ASKED ABOUT HER START IN THE HUMP BIZ BY WWW.ISHOOTPORN.COM IN NOV. 2009, GINGER VERY ELOQUENTLY TOLD THE TALE:

"I MOVED TO CALIFORNIA FROM ILLINOIS, AND MY LOSER BOYFRIEND WITH A BIG CAR PAYMENT FOLLOWED. I COULDN'T MAKE ENDS MEET, AND ANSWERED AN AD IN THE PAPER FOR "STRIPPING AT BACHELOR PARTIES". I DIDN'T THINK IT THROUGH, GOT TO MY FIRST "BACHELOR PARTY", AND GOT SCARED AND LEFT. I RAN OUT. THE PARTY FOLLOWED ME OUT, AND THEY BEAT UP MY BOYFRIEND. SO I WENT BACK TO THE PAPER AND ANSWERED AN AD FOR "FIGURE MODELLING -- $500 TO $5000 A DAY". I POSED FOR PENTHOUSE THE NEXT DAY."

"FIRST MOVIE I WAS CAST IN WAS 'SURRENDER IN PARADISE' (WHICH WAS) SHOT IN CONJUNCTION WITH 'A LITTLE HANKY PANKY'. I AGREED TO DO THESE FILMS HAVING NEVER FUCKED IN FRONT OF A CAMERA BEFORE. I SIGNED THE CONTRACT, MADE THE DEAL, AND THEN GOT SCARED! I CALLED MY AGENT AND SAID 'I DON'T KNOW IF I CAN DO THIS.' HE SAID 'I THINK YOU NEED TO DO AN 8mm MIKE CARPENTER SHOOT. NO SOUND. IT WILL ONLY BE SEEN IN .25 CENT VIDEO ARCADES.' I WAS PAID $200 TO DO TWO SCENES. I WALKED ON TO THE SET IN AN APARTMENT IN SANTA MONICA, VOMITED IN MY MOUTH -- THEN SWALLOWED IT -- IN

GINGER SUCKS ON A DUDES BUTTHOLE (NOT A MOVE SHE PERFORMED VERY OFTEN, BUT IF I HAD BEEN THE ONE IN CHARGE, SHE WOULD'VE!

ORDER TO MAINTAIN SOME SORT OF PROFESSIONALISM,
BUT THEN I REALIZED IF I COULD FUCK THIS FAT,
SMELLY, HAIRY, OLD DISGUSTING MAN -- I COULD
FUCK ANYBODY. FORTUNATELY FOR ME MY FIRST
POSITION WAS DOGGY, AND LUCKILY RON JEREMY'S
DICK WAS BIG ENOUGH TO SATISFY ME... AS LONG AS
I DIDN'T HAVE TO LOOK AT HIM. I FINISHED THE
SCENE, SAW TOMMY BYRON WALK IN -- IN ALL
HIS SCRAWNY, SKINNY GLORY -- AND I KNEW I
WAS HOME."

"I THEN FLEW TO KAUAI, HAWAII, DID MY FIRST
'OFFICIAL' SCENE ON FILM WITH JERRY BUTLER
WHILE WEARING MY RED PROM DRESS. I HAVE
PICTURES OF ME AT MY SENIOR PROM IN THE
DRESS... AND THEN LATER, IN THAT SAME DRESS,
HAVING MY FIRST ORGASM ON CAMERA."

"OBVIOUSLY FUCKING ON FILM WASN'T A PROBLEM.
IT WAS A PLEASURE. DIALOGUE, ON THE OTHER
HAND, WAS A WHOLE DIFFERENT STORY. AFTER
COMPLETING MY FIRST OFFICIAL SEX SCENE ON
CAMERA, I WAS ASKED TO JOG ALONG A DIRT PATH
WHILE JERRY RODE ALONGSIDE ME, YELLING
OBSCENITIES. I WAS SUPPOSED TO RESPOND TO
IT, AND IF LAUGHTER WAS THE CORRECT RESPONSE,

Ginger
Lynn

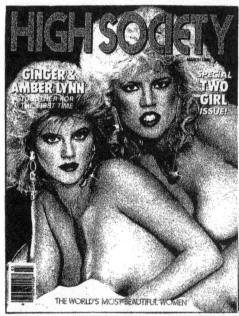

HIGH SOCIETY

GINGER &
AMBER LYNN
TOGETHER FOR
THE FIRST TIME

SPECIAL
TWO
GIRL
ISSUE!

THE WORLD'S MOST BEAUTIFUL WOMEN

I WOULD HAVE BEEN DOING MY JOB. EVERY TIME
I LOOKED AT THE GUY RUNNING ALONGSIDE ME,
I'D JUST START LAUGHING. WE DID THIS FOR FOUR
HOURS. I COULDN'T SAY MY LINE! WE FINALLY
SHUT DOWN THE SET, AND LATER THAT NIGHT
JERRY BUTLER CAME TO MY CONDO AND
ASKED ME A BUNCH OF PERSONAL QUESTIONS:
ABOUT MY FAMILY, WHAT IT WAS LIKE GROWING
UP IN ILLINOIS, THAT SORT OF THING. I
THOUGHT WE WERE   HAVING A
MOMENT UNTIL   JERRY THREW
ME ON THE BED,   BEGAN TO
RIP MY CLOTHES   OFF, AND
BEGAN TO
DISGRACE MY
FAMILY.
EVERYTHING
HE ASKED ME
HE TURNED
INTO SOMETHING
UGLY. I
FOUGHT
BACK.
HE
STOOD
UP
AND

Vivid

ONE OF THE MAGAZINES THAT CEMENTED
GINGER AS THE STUFF OF LEGEND AMONGST
THE KIDS ON MY BLOCK. AMBER LYNN (NO
RELATION) WAS NO SLOUCH, EITHER.

BACKED AWAY. JERRY THREW ME MY SCRIPT AND
SAID 'NOW DO YOUR DIALOGUE!' I NEVER HAD
A DIALOGUE PROBLEM AFTER THAT. IT WAS THE
BEST ACTING LESSON I EVER HAD."

"SO THEN AFTER THAT, JERRY AND I FALL IN
LUST. HE ASKED ME TO MARRY HIM. HE
CARVES OUR NAMES IN A TREE. HE MAKES
ME A NECKLACE OUT OF SEA SHELLS
AND FISHING WIRE. WE'RE IN
LOVE. THE NEXT DAY HE TELLS
THE MAKE-UP ARTIST (WHO HATES
ME) THAT HE WANTS TO HAVE A
THREE WAY. THE MAKE-UP
ARTIST AND I DECIDE TO GRANT
JERRY'S WISH, AND WE ALL
THREE GO BACK TO MY CONDO,
TIE JERRY TO THE BED, AND

THE MAKE-UP ARTIST AND I MAKE LOVE IN FRONT OF HIM, AND THEN LEAVE TO HAVE DINNER. WE LEFT JERRY THERE, AND NO ONE FOUND HIM TILL THE NEXT DAY. SHE AND I BECAME BEST FRIENDS, AND JERRY AND I BROKE UP."

GINGER WAS THE THE BIGGEST THING IN 1980s PORN PRETTY MUCH RIGHT OUT OF THE GATE. WITHIN A FEW MONTHS OF THE RELEASE OF THE FIRST TWO XXX FILMS MADE WITH JERRY BUTLER IN 1983 SHE WAS THE TALK OF THE INDUSTRY. MUCH OF IT HAD TO DO WITH THE FACT THAT HER LOOK WAS MODELLED DIRECTLY AFTER MADONNA (WHO WAS, AT THE TIME, REACHING THE HEIGHT OF HER SUPERSTARDOM) AND THE FACT THAT SHE WAS THE FIRST BIG-NAME PERFORMER TO NOT ONLY TAKE IT IN THE ASS, BUT TO DO DOUBLE PENETRATIONS AS WELL.

GINGER AND JERRY BUTLER PINCH NIPS ON THE SET OF 1983's 'SURRENDER IN PARADISE'.

"I WOULD SAY DOING ANAL HELPED MY CAREER," GINGER ADMITTED IN 1999.

"NONE OF THE STARS DID IT BACK THEN. I WAS THE GIRL NEXT DOOR -- I WAS NICE BUT NAUGHTY, AND THAT'S ALWAYS APPEALING".

GINGER'S OTHER BIG DRAW (ASIDE FROM HER MATERIAL GIRL LOOK AND HER VERY HUNGRY BUTT HOLE) WAS THAT HER PERFORMANCES WERE OFTEN ENHANCED BY VERY EXPLICIT AND OFTEN VERY CLEVER DIRTY TALK -- AND THE GIRL COULD ACTUALLY ACT WELL ENOUGH TO MAKE IT GENUINE. THIS TRIPLE-SLAM OF PLUSES PUT HER ON EVERY TRADE MAGAZINE COVER AND LED TO GINGER BECOMING THE FIRST VIVID ENTERTAINMENT "VIVID GIRL", BEATING OUT HER THEN UNDERAGED RIVAL, TRACI LORDS.

WHEN THE TRACI UNDERAGE BOMBSHELL DROPPED SOON THEREAFTER AND DEVASTATED THE XXX INDUSTRY, GINGER WAS CALLED TO TESTIFY ON LORDS'S BEHALF, AND AGAINST THE SMUT PRODUCERS WHO MADE THE FILMS THAT "VICTIMIZED" TRACI. BEING ONE OF THOSE PRODUCERS HERSELF (GINGER DIRECTED ONE OF TRACI'S MOVIES), GINGER FLATLY REFUSED, AND ACCORDING TO HER, WAS THEN TARGETED BY THE INTERNAL REVENUE SERVICE FOR FALSIFICATION OF A TAX RETURN. THE JUDGE, DISGUSTED BY HER PATENTLY OBSCENE LIFESTYLE, THREW THE BOOK AT HER. SHE DID ALMOST 5 MONTHS IN PRISON.

IT WOULDN'T BE THE ONLY TIME GINGER WOULD DISCOVER THAT HER PORNO FAME WOULD LAND HER SOME UNJUST TREATMENT. FROM AN INTERVIEW WITH REPORTER GENE ROSS IN 1999:

JERRY AND GINGER WERE PERFECTLY MATCHED

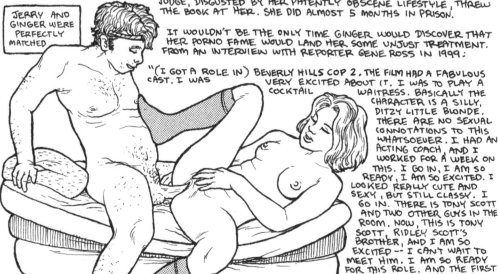

"(I GOT A ROLE IN) BEVERLY HILLS COP 2. THE FILM HAD A FABULOUS CAST. I WAS VERY EXCITED ABOUT IT. I WAS TO PLAY A COCKTAIL WAITRESS. BASICALLY THE CHARACTER IS A SILLY, DITZY LITTLE BLONDE. THERE ARE NO SEXUAL CONNOTATIONS TO THIS WHATSOEVER. I HAD AN ACTING COACH, AND I WORKED FOR A WEEK ON THIS. I GO IN, I AM SO READY, I AM SO EXCITED. I LOOKED REALLY CUTE AND SEXY, BUT STILL CLASSY. I GO IN. THERE IS TONY SCOTT AND TWO OTHER GUYS IN THE ROOM. NOW, THIS IS TONY SCOTT, RIDLEY SCOTT'S BROTHER, AND I AM SO EXCITED -- I CAN'T WAIT TO MEET HIM. I AM SO READY FOR THIS ROLE. AND THE FIRST

Bruce Seven's "The Poonies"
Starring Ginger Lynn

With
Sharon Mitchell
Amber Lynn
Bunbust Banned
Keven Lynn
Mone Welch
Paul Thomas
Bione...

THE POONIES

THE POONIES
The Poonies lead by Ginger, are a group of girls and guys who would do anything to save their house from destruction by a greedy landlord... Anything! With Sharon Mitchell, Amber Lynn, and Bionca, as "Lips".

THING OUT OF TONY SCOTT'S MOUTH IS 'CAN I GET A NUDE POLAROID?' I SAID 'I'M NOT REALLY COMFORTABLE WITH THAT'. I'M TRYING TO KEEP MY COOL. HE SAYS, 'HOW ABOUT A TOPLESS?', I SAID 'NO, I DON'T THINK SO... WHY DON'T I JUST READ FOR THE ROLE?' I'M STILL TRYING TO BE SWEET AND NICE, BUT I'M GETTING A BIT BOTHERED AT THIS POINT. I'M TALKING TO TONY, NOT THE ASSISTANT, NOT THE OTHER TWO GUYS IN THE ROOM. I READ THE PART AND HE STOPS ME A COUPLE OF SENTENCES IN. 'NO, NO, NO. YOU'RE REALLY HORNY. I WANT YOU TO DO THIS WITH A SEXUAL EDGE TO IT.' SO I REDO IT WITH A SEXUAL EDGE. HE STOPS ME IN THE MIDDLE. 'YOU WANT TO SLEEP WITH EVERY MAN THAT YOU SEE. YOU ARE A TOTAL SLUT. I WANT TO SEE THAT PART OF YOU!'"

"AND I JUST STOOD THERE. I GOT GOOSE BUMPS ON MY ARMS. I COULDN'T HOLD BACK THE TEARS. I STARTED TO CRY AND SAID 'I'M SORRY, I DON'T THINK I'M RIGHT FOR THIS ROLE'. I REALIZED AT THAT MOMENT THAT THEY HAD NO INTENTIONS. THEY WEREN'T REALLY AUDITIONING ME FOR THE ROLE. THEY JUST WANTED TO SEE GINGER LYNN NAKED. THEY WERE IN THAT WHOLE PORN-IS-TABOO THING, AND IT WASN'T COOL TO BE A PORN STAR, BUT EVERY GUY JERKED OFF TO YOUR MOVIES. IT WAS AN EYE-OPENING EXPERIENCE OF WHAT HOLLYWOOD WAS LIKE".

"I DID THIS MUSIC VIDEO FOR THE BAND METALLICA, CALLED 'TURN THE PAGE'. IT WAS SHOT LIKE A DOCUMENTARY, BUT IT WAS ALL SCRIPTED, SO IT WAS A GREAT OPPORTUNITY FOR ME TO SHOW MY ACTING SKILLS. THERE WAS A DIRECTOR WHO SAW THE VIDEO, SAW MY WORK IN IT, AND BROUGHT ME IN FOR A ROLE IN A RATHER LARGE MAINSTREAM FILM. WHEN I GOT THERE AND HE REALIZED, THE STORY CHANGED. NO LONGER WAS I A GOOD ACTRESS, I WAS A PORNO STAR. MY TALENTS HADN'T CHANGED, MY WORK IN THE VIDEO HADN'T VANISHED, IT WAS JUST HIS OPINION OF ME THAT CHANGED, AND IT PISSED ME OFF."

EMBITTERED AND FEARFUL OF SEXUALLY TRANSMITTED DISEASE IN AN INDUSTRY THAT HAD NOT YET SET UP ANY MANDATORY TESTING FOR ITS PERFORMERS, ALLEN DECIDED TO STOP MAKING ADULT FILMS IN FEB 1986, AND SWORE SHE WOULD NEVER RETURN UNTIL AIDS HAD BEEN CURED. DESPITE THAT PROMISE AND THE BIRTH OF HER SON IN 1996, SHE DID RETURN TO XXX TO MAKE THREE MOVIES. SHE THEN DROPPED OUT ONCE MORE (AFTER BEING DIAGNOSED WITH CERVICAL CANCER) AND AGAIN RETURNED TO ADULT IN 2005. SINCE THEN SHE CAN OCCASIONALLY BE SPOTTED FUCKING AND SUCKING IN MATURE-THEMED DVDS (LIKE **OLDER WOMEN, YOUNGER MEN 13** AND **SEASONED PLAYERS 4**) AND FOR KINKY FETISH SITES (LIKE THE CINEMA SEWER APPROVED ULTIMATESURRENDER.COM AND SEXANDSUBMISSION.COM) EVER SINCE.

Jamie Gillis, Cinema Sewer's favourite classic-era male porn star, on Ginger Lynn:

G-MAN
R.I.P.

"SHE WAS BRIGHT, WARM, SENSUAL, READY AND EAGER TO PLEASE, UP FOR WHATEVER. I HAVE A WARM MEMORY OF PLACING HER FACE UP UNDER A TOILET SEAT AND JERKING OFF ON IT. I DIDN'T SPEND MUCH TIME WITH HER OFF CAMERA -- IT WAS DURING HER HEYDAY THAT I WAS BUSY AT HOME WORSHIPPING AMBER LYNN'S ASS."

"HA HA! WHAT A COINCIDENCE! I HAVE A WARM MEMORY OF WATCHING YOU PLACE HER HEAD FACE UP UNDER A TOILET SEAT AND JERKING OFF ON IT! CAN'T FOR THE LIFE OF ME REMEMBER WHAT MOVIE THAT WAS FROM, BUT I DO REMEMBER IT WAS SHOT ON VIDEO, AND FOR SOME REASON I REMEMBER THAT BATHROOM FLOOR WAS CARPETED, WHICH IS FRANKLY AN ODD THING TO REMEMBER."

BOUGIEMAN

"THE ONLY OTHER THING I RECALL ABOUT THE FILM WAS THAT THE DIRECTOR WAS RON SULLIVAN, AKA HENRI PACHARD. I NEVER SAW THE SCENE -- LET ME KNOW IF YOU FIND OUT WHERE IT'S FROM."

[AFTER SOME RESEARCHING] "AH.. IT WAS **GINGER AND SPICE** FROM 1986. IT HAS NOT MADE AN APPEARANCE ON DVD AS OF YET, AND THE VHS IS A BITCH TO TRACK DOWN. I'D LOVE TO SEE THAT AGAIN. YOU TWO WERE REALLY SIZZLING!"

THIS KITTEN HAS CLAWS

AS NEW YORK TIMES FILM CRITIC MANOHLA DARGIS WROTE IN 2011, "IN MOVIE AFTER MOVIE THERE ARE NO REAL REPRESENTATIONS TO EVISCERATE, WHEN ALL OR MOST OF THE BIG ROLES ARE TAKEN BY MEN, AND THE ONLY WOMEN AROUND ARE THOSE WHOSE SOLE FUNCTION IS, ESSENTIALLY, TO REASSURE THE AUDIENCE THAT THE HERO ISN'T GAY."

THIS IS TRUE IN MAINSTREAM VANILLA HOLLYWOOD, BUT FOR GENERATIONS OF DRIVE-IN STYLE EXPLOITATION, MARTIAL ARTS, HORROR, AND ACTION MOVIES, DEPICTIONS OF PRIMAL FEMALE RAGE AND THE BONE-SNAPPING VIOLENCE IT CAUSES HAS BEEN SOMETHING THAT HAS BEEN QUITE POPULAR IN NORTH AMERICA. SOME OF THESE MOVIES DEPICT WOMEN GETTING REVENGE AGAINST ABUSIVE MEN, OR REVENGE ON OTHER WOMEN. SOMETIMES IT'S NOT EVEN REVENGE OR A SCRAPPY UNDERDOG TAKING ON THE BULLIES, BUT JUST VIOLENCE AND HANDING OUT MISERY FOR THE SAKE OF IT. THESE BLOODTHIRSTY WOMEN ARE PERHAPS A REACTION TO THE SIMILAR ACTIONS OF MALE CHARACTERS, OR PERHAPS IN SPITE OF THEM, BUT WHAT IS FOR SURE IS THAT GENRE FILM AUDIENCES ADORE VIOLENT BITCHES. WE EAT 'EM RAW LIKE SUSHI, AS A MAN NAMED RICO SUAVE USED TO SAY.

WE LIKE THEM SO MUCH, EVEN OTHER FILM INDUSTRIES BEGAN MAKING "VIOLENT CHICK" MOVIES THAT THEIR OWN DOMESTIC AUDIENCES DIDN'T PARTICULARLY WANT TO SEE, SIMPLY BECAUSE THEY KNEW THE FILM WOULD SELL WELL ABROAD. "IT WAS NEVER POPULAR IN ASIA", DIRECTOR GODFREY HO SAID IN A 2003 INTERVIEW WHEN ASKED ABOUT THE DOZENS OF GIRLS-N-GUNS MOVIES THAT CAME OUT OF CHINA IN THE 1990S. "IT ONLY SOLD WELL IN EUROPEAN MARKET AND AMERICA. THE FEMINIST CHARACTER IS NOT THAT STRONG OR ACCEPTED IN ASIA, SO IT IS NOT MADE FOR HONG KONG."

IN THE EXCELLENT (AND MOSTLY OVERLOOKED) JOE WRIGHT FILM, HANNA (2011) THE VIOLENT TEENAGE TITULAR HEROINE IS RAISED TO BE A MERCILESS KILLER IN ARCTIC ISOLATION BY HER POPS (ERIC BANA). I BRING THAT MOVIE UP, BECAUSE IT'S INTERESTING IN RECENT DECADES HOW OFTEN THE TRAINING OF YOUNG COLD-BLOODED FEMALE ASSASSINS IS OVERSEEN BY THEIR FATHERS OR A FATHER FIGURE. SCOTT GLENN IN SUCKER PUNCH (2011), NICOLAS CAGE IN KICK-ASS (2010), JEFF BRIDGES IN TRUE GRIT (2010), KENICHI ENDO IN COOL DIMENSION (2006), TERENCE STAMP IN ELEKTRA (2005), AND YOSHIO HARADA IN AZUMI (2003). CONVERSELY, NOTE THAT WHEN YOUNG MALE OR FEMALE KILLERS ARE IN TRAINING TO END OTHERS' LIVES, FILMMAKERS NEVER DEPICT THEM BEING PROMPTED TO DO SO BY THEIR MOTHERS OR A MOTHER FIGURE — AND THERE IS SOMETHING VERY TELLING ABOUT THAT. IT'S WORTH THINKING ABOUT, ESPECIALLY IN TERMS OF WHAT MODERN FILMMAKERS, AS A COLLECTIVE, ARE SAYING ABOUT FATHER/DAUGHTER RELATIONSHIPS.

WE KNOW WHAT FUELS THE FANTASY DEPICTIONS OF MALE VIOLENCE: REALITY. LET'S FACE FACTS, AN OVERWHELMING MAJORITY OF THE REAL-LIFE DEATH AND DESTRUCTION COMES AT THE HANDS OF MEN. BUT I'M CONVINCED THAT IT'S FETISHISM THAT PROVIDES THE FASCINATION, CONFUSION AND OBSESSION WITH THE SEXUAL POWER OF WOMEN AND TEENAGE GIRLS. FETISHISM, FANTASY, AND WISH FULFILLMENT.

THE LOVE BLACKMAILER

BOUGIE

AKA: ADULTEROUS AFFAIR
⭐ 84 MIN. BLACK AND WHITE ⭐
DIR: TED LEVERSUCH

A LOT OF TRASH CINEMA FANS DON'T REALIZE THAT CANADA HAS A LONG AND SLEAZY HISTORY OF SEXPLOITATION FILMS. UNTIL THE MID 2000S, DESPITE BEING A CANADIAN CITIZEN AS WELL AS '60S FILTH-FILM BOOSTER, I DIDN'T EITHER. THAT WAS WHEN I WAS CONTACTED BY MY FRIEND, SOMETHING WEIRD'S LISA PETRUCCI, AND ASKED TO WRITE THE LINER NOTES FOR A FILM PRINT SHE AND HER PARTNER MIKE VRANEY HAD DISCOVERED. BEING AS I WAS CANADIAN AND HAD WRITTEN A BUNCH OF ESSAYS TO ADORN THE BACKS OF THEIR VHS AND DVD-R RELEASES, I GUESS I SEEMED LIKE A GOOD CANDIDATE.

IT WAS FUN TRACKING DOWN INFO ABOUT THE MOVIE AND ITS DIRECTOR, TED LEVERSUCH (ALTHOUGH NOT EASY, AS HE'S BEEN ENTIRELY OVERLOOKED BY EVERY SINGLE BOOK EVER WRITTEN ABOUT CANADIAN CINEMA), SO LET ME INTRODUCE YOU NOW TO ONE OF THE MORE OBSCURE SEXPLOITATION FILMMAKERS FROM NORTH OF THE 49TH PARALLEL, AND PROVE THAT EVEN IN THE SIXTIES, CANADIANS KNEW HOW TO GET FREAKY.

THIS 1966 MOVIE INTRODUCES US TO A MALCONTENT DRIFTER, RUSS TAREN (BRUCE GRAY), WHO MAKES A MEAGRE LIVING BLACKMAILING CHEATING WIVES, BUT HE DOESN'T JUST SETTLE ON CASH FOR HIS TROUBLE -- HE WANTS THE LADIES TO PAY HIM IN NAKED SWEATY FLESH! TAREN RENTS A $10-A-WEEK ROOM FROM LOLA, A LONELY EX-STRIPPER WHO MAKES NIGHTLY VISITS TO HIS ROOM TO DRINK RYE, SMOKE CIGARETTES, AND TRY TO FINAGLE RUSS INTO THE SACK. HER GOOD-LOOKING AND SUAVE RENTER IS POLITE, ("I BET YOU LOOK LIKE A MILLION BUCKS WITH YOUR WAR PAINT ON!") BUT EVENTUALLY TIRES OF THE FORMER BURLESQUE DANCER'S CONSTANT RUTTING.

THE REAL QUARRY IS HIS LATEST VICTIM BARBARA (JEAN CHRISTOPHER), A LOVELY BUT NEGLECTED NEXT DOOR SUBURBAN TORONTO HOUSEWIFE WHO HAS SECRETLY TAKEN UP WITH A BRITISH FOP NAMED STEPHEN WHO PLIES HIS TRADE AS THE FAMILY DOCTOR. RUSS GETS HIS JOLLIES TAKING SAUCY INCRIMINATING PHOTOS OF THEM IN THE ACT (NONE OF HIS SEXY SUBJECTS EVER SEEM TO CLOSE THEIR DRAPES!), AND AFTER BARBARA AND STEPHEN RETURN FROM A CLANDESTINE NIAGARA FALLS GETAWAY, HE APPROACHES HER WITH HIS BEST B-GRADE JAMES BOND VILLAIN IMPERSONATION, AND MAKES HIS CONTEMPTIBLE DEMANDS KNOWN.

AGAINST HER BETTER JUDGEMENT, BARBARA ALLOWS HERSELF TO BE TAKEN ON AS HIS PART TIME SEX SLAVE, BUT THE LOVE BLACKMAILER ISN'T THE ONLY ONE ON THAT ASS. WITH HER HUSBAND FRANK, DR. STEPHEN, AS WELL AS RUSS ALL TAKING TURNS RIDING HER, THE FRAZZLED HOUSEWIFE BEGINS TO FEEL LIKE THE TOWN BICYCLE. WILL BARBARA CONTINUE TO ALLOW HER CONTEMPTIBLE NEXT DOOR NEIGHBOUR TO TAKE HER FOR NOT ONLY WHAT SHE'S GOT IN THE BANK, BUT IN HER PANTIES AS WELL? OR WILL SHE FIGURE OUT A WAY TO GET HER REVENGE? AND LOOK OUT GANG -- HUSBAND FRANK IS GETTING SUSPICIOUS!

THE MOVIE WAS FILMED IN TORONTO, ONTARIO, AND DESPITE NOT HAVING MUCH NUDITY ASIDE FROM SOME BARE LADY BUTTS, AND OCCASIONALLY GETTING A LITTLE TOO TALKY AND RELYING ON EXPOSITION TO MOVE THE PLOT FORWARD, IT IS A VERY WATCHABLE EXAMPLE OF TAWDRY, VOYEURISTIC (AND OCCASIONALLY VIOLENT) SLEAZE. HISTORICALLY IT'S AN INTERESTING THEATRICAL RELEASE, BECAUSE IT WAS ONE OF THE FIRST CANUCK FILMS MADE FOR AN AMERICAN AND EUROPEAN AUDIENCE THAT SPECIFICALLY TAKES PLACE NORTH OF THE BORDER. THERE AREN'T TOO MANY OUTDOOR LOCATIONS, WITH MUCH OF THE MOVIE SHOT AT NAT TAYLOR'S TORONTO INTERNATIONAL FILM STUDIOS IN KLEINBURG. THERE ARE SEVERAL NOTABLE ONTARIO LOCATIONS THAT SHOW UP, INCLUDING THE OPENING SEQUENCE DRIVING AROUND TORONTO'S NEON-LIT STREETS, RUSS PICKING UP HIS PEEPING TOM EQUIPMENT FROM A YONGE STREET PAWN SHOP, AND DR. STEPHEN AND BARBARA VISITING THE WAX MUSEUMS IN NIAGARA FALLS' CLIFTON HILL.

THE ELEGANT MISS JEAN CHRISTOPHER (WHO WAS ACTUALLY QUITE A DECENT ACTRESS) STARTED HER SCREEN CAREER AS ONE OF THE STARS OF THE INFAMOUS CBC SATIRE PROGRAM NIGHTCAP, A BAWDY LATE NIGHT HIT HOSTED BY CANUCK ENTERTAINER BILLY VAN. SHE HAD ONLY ONE OTHER STARRING ROLE IN PLAYGIRL KILLER TWO YEARS LATER. AS CANADIAN FILM HISTORIAN PAUL CORUPE POINTED OUT, "IN A CAREER MISSTEP, SHE APPARENTLY LEFT THE SHOW AT THE HEIGHT OF ITS POPULARITY TO PURSUE A FILM CAREER IN AN INDUSTRY THAT HAD NOT YET COME OF AGE". BRUCE GRAY CAN BE SEEN IN HOLLYWOOD FILMS LIKE STARSHIP TROOPERS, AND SPY HARD, BUT IS BEST KNOWN IN CANADA FOR HIS 1990S TV ROLE OF "ADAM CUNNINGHAM" ON TRADERS. BRUCE ALSO GAINED NOTORIETY IN THE GAY COMMUNITY AS THE "SHICKLE THE PICKLE" CHARACTER ON THE QUEER AS FOLK TV SERIES.

DIRECTOR TED LEVERSUCH ARRIVED IN CANADA IN THE EARLY 1960S FROM THE UK, AND ONCE OUT OF HIGH SCHOOL QUICKLY BECAME ONE OF THE MOST DARING CHARACTERS IN OUR STILL-FLEDGLING FILM INDUSTRY. HIS FIRST MOVE WAS TO PEN THE 1963 NUDIST FLICK HAVE FIGURE WILL TRAVEL FOR FUTURE STARLOST DIRECTOR LEO ORENSTEIN, AND TWO YEARS LATER, DIRECTING THE NUDIE CUTIE FRENCH

WITHOUT DRESSING. THIS WAS FOLLOWED BY A STRING OF SLIGHTLY NASTIER "ADULTS ONLY" MELODRAMAS HE AND HIS WRITING PARTNER MARGOT STEVENS WOULD TEAM UP ON, STARTING WITH THE LOVE BLACKMAILER, TAKE HER BY SURPRISE (AS PRODUCER), THE PERFECT ARRANGEMENT AND SEX AND THE LONELY WOMAN EACH FILM PROGRESSIVELY MORE KINKY THAN THE LAST. LIKE SO MANY SNOW BIRDS, IN HIS LATER YEARS, TED RETIRED TO FLORIDA, AND PASSED AWAY THERE ON MARCH 19TH, 1985, IN A TOWN CALLED HALLENDALE. HE WAS 74 YEARS OLD. I MY MIND, HE DID CANADA PROUD.

HIGH KICKS (1993. USA)

THIS SHOT-ON-VIDEO RAPE REVENGE MOVIE SHOULDN'T HAVE BEEN AS ENTERTAINING AS IT WAS, ESPECIALLY CONSIDERING THAT IT HAS A BARE-BONES PLOT, WAS SHOT WITH A CAMCORDER, AND HAS GOBS OF INSANELY BAD MARTIAL ARTS AND TERRIBLE ACTING BY ALL BUT THE LEAD ACTRESS (TARA LEE-ANNE ROTH). BUT REBECCA AND I SAT DOWN AND DILIGENTLY WATCHED IT FROM FRONT TO BACK, AND DIDN'T HATE IT ALL THAT MUCH. ACTUALLY, IT WAS KIND OF AWESOME. EVERY SINGLE LOW-RES FRAME OF THIS EFFORT LOOKS LIKE ASS, BUT AT THE SAME TIME YOU'RE COMPELLED TO SEE WHAT HAPPENS NEXT. IT ENTERTAINS.

SERIOUSLY, IT LOOKS LIKE **HIGH KICKS** TOOK A WEEKEND TO MAKE. OUR HERO, A BUBBLY BLONDE HIMBO NAMED SAM, LIVES ON HIS SAILBOAT, HAS LONG LUXURIOUS LOCKS, AND ROLLS INTO SAN DIEGO LOOKING FOR A JOB. HE ENDS UP AT THE LITTLE "HIGH KICKS" AEROBICS STUDIO OWNED BY SANDY, AND GETS A JOB AS "A HANDYMAN" -- CLEARLY SOMETHING A SMALL AEROBICS CLASS NEEDS.

BUT WHAT IS THIS? <u>DRAMA</u>. WHILE HE'S OUT A VICIOUS GANG OF HILARIOUSLY MULTICULTURAL THUGS BUST INTO THE PLACE AND RAPE SANDY. THEY ARE LED BY THE ONLY ACTOR THAT WOULD GO ON TO DO ANYTHING AT ALL AFTER **HIGH KICKS** WRAPPED, CHARACTER ACTOR LOUIS LOMBARDI (**USUAL SUSPECTS, ED WOOD, SUICIDE KINGS, WONDERLAND**). SAM DOESN'T SEEM TOO UPSET ABOUT HER ORDEAL WHATSOEVER, BUT OPERATES AS A LOVE INTEREST/KUNG FU TEACHER AFTER THE INCIDENT REGARDLESS. TOGETHER THEY HAVE ALL KINDS OF FUN, AND EVEN FIND TIME TO HUNT DOWN EACH MEMBER OF THE GANG AND DO MEAN THINGS, LIKE PUNCH THEM AND THEN CAREFULLY PLACE CIGARETTES IN THEIR EARS AND NOSES AFTER THEY'VE BEEN KNOCKED OUT. (??)

IT'S NOT "YOU VIOLATED ME, NOW DIE!!!"-STYLE REVENGE. IT'S MORE LIKE "YOU GUYS ARE TOTALLY LAME, AND WE'RE GONNA GO HAVE HAMBURGERS WITHOUT YOU."-STYLE REVENGE. VERY ODD.

THIS 82 MIN MOVIE IS FRANKLY PRETTY STUPID-FRESH. PILES OF HILARIOUS FASHIONS AND HAIRCUTS, AND BEING SHOT WITH A CAMCORDER IT LOOKS <u>EXACTLY</u> LIKE A PORN MOVIE, AND YET IT DOESN'T HAVE NUDITY. NO ONE MILKS A PEARL SACK WITH THEIR GLISTENING OTTER'S POCKET, NO ONE CHOWS DOWN ON A FLAPPY MEAL, AND THERE ISN'T A SINGLE OUNCE OF HORSEY SAUCE ON DISPLAY. DESPITE ALL OF THAT, **HIGH KICKS** STILL FEELS OUTWARDLY SLEAZY WITH ALL OF ITS LEERING CLOSEUPS OF GLORIOUS CLEAVAGE AND TONED ASS CHEEKS STRAINING AS THEY BOUNCE BACK AND FORTH IN THEIR LEOTARDS AS THEY WORK OUT. **HIGH KICKS** JUST HAS THE STINK OF 1993 ALL OVER IT. IT'S LIKE A GODDAMN TIME PORTAL.

ONE OF THINGS I FOUND INTERESTING ABOUT IT IS THAT IT FEATURES A WOMAN WHO GETS RAPED, AND DOESN'T HATE HERSELF OR BECOME NEUROTIC OR INSANE, AS IS THE CASE IN ALL OTHER EXPLOITATION FILMS OF THIS KIND. ALSO, HER MULLETED MALE CO-STAR REVEALS HE WAS ALSO RAPED BY A GANG OF MEN, AND THAT IS WHY HE GOT INTO MARTIAL ARTS! I CAN'T REALLY STRESS ENOUGH HOW UNUSUAL AND TOTALLY UNIQUE FOR A MOVIE OF THIS SORT THAT THIS REVELATION IS. I CAN ONLY ASSUME THESE AMAZING DIFFERENCES ARE HERE BECAUSE THIS

MOVIE WAS WRITTEN, PRODUCED, AND DIRECTED BY A WOMAN: RUTA K. ARAS. RUTA WAS A LINE PRODUCER ON OTHER SETS, AND WOULD NOT GO ON TO DO MUCH OF ANYTHING ELSE BEFORE HER TIME IN FILM ENDED TWO YEARS LATER.

HUH HUH

REVIEW BY ROBIN BOUGIE 2013
ART BY BEN JACQUES. 2013

HOW HAL FREEMAN FILMED SOME GIRLS GETTING FUCKED IN THE ASS, AND MANAGED TO LEGALIZE PORNOGRAPHY WHILE DOING IT   BY ROBIN BOUGIE

ANAL-THEMED PORN IS NEARLY MORE POPULAR THAN ITS VAGINAL COUSIN IN NORTH AMERICA THESE DAYS, BUT ONCE UPON A TIME -- IN THE EARLY '80S -- THE GENRE ENJOYED ONE OF ITS VERY FIRST PUCKERED ENTRIES WITH A SPHINCTERIFFIC SERIES CALLED **CAUGHT FROM BEHIND.**

VIEWING CAUGHT FROM BEHIND WAS THE FIRST TIME I EVER SAW A PENIS GO INTO AN ASSHOLE, WHICH ENDED UP BEING ONE OF MY FAVOURITE TYPES OF PORN. IT SEEMED ASTONISHINGLY KINKY TO ME AT THE TIME, BUT KEEP IN MIND IT WAS ONLY THE 5TH OR 6TH XXX MOVIE I'D SEEN, AND I WAS ONLY 16 YEARS OLD. PART ONE WAS THE DEBUT OF JESSIE BLU, FEATURED THE MARILYN MONROE-ESQUE ANGEL CASH, AND CULMINATED IN A STICKY MUD MUSCLE DOUBLE PENETRATION (ALMOST UNHEARD OF IN THOSE DAYS). IN PART TWO, "PETER PROCTOR" SPECIALISES IN "ANAL ANALYSIS", AND PLOWS HIS PATIENTS INTO A BETTER SENSUAL FAMILIARITY WITH THEIR POOPING HOLES.

THERE WERE 26 MOVIES IN THIS TRUNK-SLAMMING SERIES (THE ONLY ONES I EVER SAW WERE PARTS ONE AND TWO) WHICH HAVE BEEN MOSTLY FORGOTTEN. AND WHY WOULDN'T THEY BE? THERE IS MOUNTAINS OF FOOTAGE OF LUBED UP DONGS PISTONING IN AND OUT OF WOMEN'S ASSHOLES ON THE INTERNET, NOT TO MENTION THE HUNDREDS OF THOUSANDS OF ANAL MOVIES THAT HAVE BEEN RELEASED IN THE WAKE OF CAUGHT FROM BEHIND. THERE'S LITTLE REASON FOR IT TO STAND OUT TODAY.

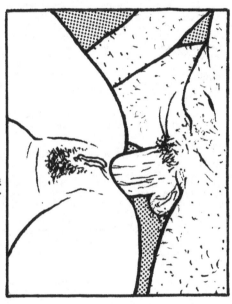

BUT WHAT MOST PEOPLE (EVEN XXX FANS) DON'T KNOW IS THAT THE PIONEER WHO MADE THE THEN-ODDBALL KINK OF ANAL PENETRATION INTO A MAINSTREAM PRACTICE AMONG HETEROSEXUALS IS ALSO ONE OF THE ULTIMATE UNKNOWN AND UNSUNG HEROES OF NOT ONLY THE PORN WORLD, BUT ANYONE WHO CARES ABOUT LIBERTY AND ARTISTIC FREEDOM.

PAUL FISHBEIN (THE FOUNDER OF ADULT VIDEO NEWS) DESCRIBED HAL FREEMAN THUSLY: "FREEMAN WAS A BIG GUY, HEAVYSET, SORT OF BALDING, HAD A BIG ARMY TATTOO ON HIS FOREARM. HAL WAS A BIG PRESENCE, WITH A BELLOWING VOICE; HE COMMANDED A LOT OF ATTENTION WHEN HE WALKED INTO A ROOM. HE WAS ONE OF THOSE GUYS WITH A LOT OF BRAVADO, BUT ACTUALLY HAD A BIG HEART, YOU KNOW?"

HAL STARTED OUT AS AN ENTREPRENEUR, BUILDING PEEP SHOW BOOTHS AND RUBBER DILDOS, AND USED THE CONNECTIONS HE MADE WITHIN THE INDUSTRY TO PARLAY HIMSELF INTO PORNO PRODUCTION JOBS IN LOS ANGELES. IN 1980, AT THE AGE OF 44, HE HIRED '60S AND '70S CULT ICON RAY DENNIS STECKLER (AKA CASH FLAGG) AS HIS CINEMATOGRAPHER, AND SHOT INTERLUDE OF LUST. BUT THIS NEW CAREER WAS RISKY, NOT BECAUSE THE PEOPLE HE WORKED WITH WERE BAD NEWS, BUT BECAUSE THE LAW WAS SNIFFING AROUND CONSTANTLY.

CALIFORNIA'S ANTI-PIMPING LAW WAS ALTERED IN 1982 TO MANDATE AN AUTOMATIC THREE-YEAR SENTENCE IF A DEFENDANT WERE TO BE FOUND GUILTY OF "PANDERING," (ALSO KNOWN AS PIMPING). SPONSORED BY DEMOCRATIC STATE SENATOR DAVID A. ROBERTI, THE LAW WAS SPECIFICALLY CREATED TO REDUCE THE STREET PROSTITUTION OVERFLOW HOLLYWOOD WAS DROWNING IN AT THE TIME.

BUT SEE, HERE IS WHERE IT GETS INTERESTING. RONALD REAGAN AND HIS MEESE COMMISSION (DESIGNED TO ERADICATE SMUT) WERE PUTTING PRESSURE ON THE SUITS IN CALIFORNIA TO CLAMP DOWN ON THE CINEMATIC SKIN TRADE . DESPERATE TO APPEASE A FORMER CALIFORNIA GOVERNOR, THE LA COUNTY DA'S OFFICE PUT ON THEIR THINKING CAPS AND GOT THE BRILLIANT IDEA THAT THE NEW PIMP MANDATE COULD ALSO BE USED TO BRING AN END TO PORN PRODUCTION IN THE STATE.

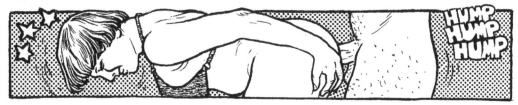

ALL THEY NEEDED WAS A GUINEA PIG.

SO IN SEPTEMBER OF 1983, THEY CHARGED HAL FREEMAN
WITH FIVE COUNTS OF PANDERING AFTER HE WAS
BUSTED FOR SHOOTING *CAUGHT FROM BEHIND, PART II*
IN RANCHO PALOS VERDES, A SUBURB JUST SOUTH OF
LOS ANGELES.

NOW KEEP IN MIND THAT GETTING BUSTED FOR FILMING
SEX OR BEING FILMED HAVING SEX WAS A VERY
COMMON PROBLEM AT THE TIME, AND MANY PORN STARS
OF THE ERA WILL TELL YOU THAT THEY WERE TAKING
PART IN A REBELLIOUS UNDERGROUND INDUSTRY THAT
FILMED SURREPTITIOUSLY IN MOTEL ROOMS AND OTHER
CLANDESTINE LOCATIONS. IT WAS A VOCATION THAT HAD
EVERYONE ON SET IN CONSTANT FEAR OF BEING
SHACKLED IN CUFFS ANYTIME THERE WAS A KNOCK AT
THE DOOR.

"BECAUSE THERE WAS NO SUCH THING AS A PERMIT, WE
COULDN'T SHOOT", RECALLED SHARON MITCHELL. "THEY
USED TO SCAN FOOTAGE AND RECOGNISE THE PALM
TREES AS LOS ANGELES, AND TRACK THE LOCATION. THEY
WERE VERY SERIOUS, VERY STORM-TROOPER-LIKE."

INITIALLY, THINGS WERE VERY GRIM FOR HAL. A SIX
DAY TRIAL FOUND HIM GUILTY ON ALL COUNTS, MAKING
HIM NO LONGER A FREE MAN -- BUT A JAILED MAN. THE
MANDATORY THREE YEAR SENTENCE WAS WAIVED (ON
THE GROUNDS THAT IT WOULD BE "CRUEL AND
UNUSUAL"), AND INSTEAD HE WAS IMPRISONED FOR 90
DAYS, FINED $10,000, AND PLACED ON PROBATION FOR 5
YEARS. THE CONVICTION SENT WORD OF MOUTH SHOCK
WAVES THROUGHOUT THE PORN INDUSTRY. WHO WOULD BE
NEXT TO TAKE THE FALL?

BUT THEN SOMETHING UNEXPECTED TOOK PLACE: FREEMAN
FOUGHT BACK, AND ASKED SEVERAL JUSTICES OF THE
CALIFORNIA SUPREME COURT TO TAKE IT UPON
THEMSELVES TO REVIEW HIS CASE. THEY DID, AND
NOTED THAT THE PERFORMERS TESTIFIED THAT THEY
WERE NOT HAVING SEX FOR PLEASURE, BUT FOR THE
MONEY, AND THAT HAL FREEMAN'S MOTIVES WERE THE
SAME. THIS CLASSIFICATION MEANT, BY DEFINITION, THAT
FREEMAN (OR ANY XXX PRODUCER) WAS CLEARLY NOT
GUILTY OF PANDERING, AND THE PERFORMERS INVOLVED
WERE NOT PROSTITUTES. THE SUPREME COURT FOUND
THE CASE "A SOMEWHAT TRANSPARENT ATTEMPT AT AN
'END RUN' AROUND THE FIRST AMENDMENT AND THE
STATE OBSCENITY LAWS," AND SOUNDLY THREW OUT
HAL'S CONVICTION IN 1988. THE RULING HAD BEEN
OVERTURNED.

THE PROSECUTION OF HAL FREEMAN WAS INITIALLY PLANNED AS THE FIRST IN A SERIES OF
LEGAL ATTACKS ON PORNOGRAPHERS, BUT THE TRUE IRONY OF THE CASE IS THAT THE VERY
MOVE THAT THE LAPD USED TO TRY TO CRIMINALISE HARDCORE PORN -- WAS THE ONE THAT
LEGALISED IT.

WHEN ASKED ABOUT THE PANDERING SCARE THAT HAD THE ADULT INDUSTRY ON THE VERGE OF
COLLAPSE IN THE EARLY '80S, DIRECTOR/ACTOR FRED LINCOLN ADMITTED, "EVERYBODY WAS SO
AFRAID. HAL FREEMAN WAS THE ONLY ONE WHO FOUGHT."

REGRETTABLY, THE HARROWING 6-YEAR LEGAL BATTLE HAD DRAINED THE LIFE OUT OF HAL, AND
HE DIED OF CANCER THAT SAME YEAR. HIS DAUGHTER SHERI FREEMAN WOULD FIGHT ON IN HIS
HONOUR AS A BOARD MEMBER ON THE FREE SPEECH COALITION, A GROUP FORMED BY THE ADULT
INDUSTRY.

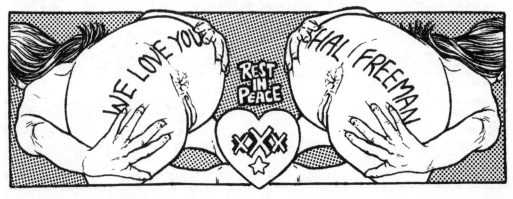

"LURID... A PILE OF PRURIENT SLEAZE...DISTASTEFULLY VOYEURISTIC..."
   - TIME OUT FILM GUIDE

"REPUGNANT... CYNICAL... GRABS US AND PLUNGES US INTO THE GARISH, ULTRA-DANGEROUS WORLD OF MANHATTAN HOOKERS."
   - THE LOS ANGELES TIMES

THE TEEN SEX TRAGEDY IS A LESSER-KNOWN EXPLOITATION SUB-GENRE THAT THRIVED FROM THE MID '70S TO THE MID '80S, AND FOUND HIGH-SCHOOL AGE SLUTS (USUALLY PLAYED BY WOMEN IN THEIR TWENTIES) TURNING TRICKS AS STREET PROSTITUTES IN FILMS SUCH AS **DAWN: PORTRAIT OF A TEENAGE RUNAWAY** (1976), **LITTLE LADIES OF THE NIGHT** (1977), **DIARY OF A TEENAGE HITCHHIKER** (1979), **OFF THE MINNESOTA STRIP** (1980), **FALLEN ANGEL** (1981), **CHRISTIANE F.** (1981), **HANNA D.** (1984), **CHILDREN OF THE NIGHT** (1985), AND THE MOST FAMOUS OF THE BUNCH, **ANGEL** (1984). I'M TICKLED TO REPORT THAT A SUBMISSION INTO THE GENRE CALLED **STREETWALKIN'** IS BETTER THAN ANY OF THEM, AND IS CRIMINALLY UNKNOWN.

"SHE DROPPED OUT OF HIGH SCHOOL THIS MORNING," SCREAMS STREETWALKIN'S POSTER TAGLINE. "TONIGHT SHE'S A TIMES SQUARE HOOKER!"

LIKE **ANGEL STREETWALKIN** (1985) IS A ROGER CORMAN PRODUCTION, AND LIKE **TERMINAL ISLAND** (1973) AND **SLUMBER PARTY MASSACRE** (1982) IT IS A TAWDRY AFFAIR DIRECTED BY A WOMAN. FUCK YES. PILES OF NUDITY, PROFANITY, SADISTIC VIOLENCE
   -- AND THIS SHIT-SCAB WAS WRITTEN AND DIRECTED BY A WOMAN? AS THE LOS ANGELES TIMES REPORTED IN 1985: "STREETWALKIN' PROVES THAT A WOMAN CAN EXPLOIT EXTREME VIOLENCE AGAINST BOTH WOMEN AND MEN JUST AS SURELY AS A MAN CAN".

SHE DROPPED OUT OF HIGH SCHOOL THIS MORNING...

STREETWALKIN'

TONIGHT SHE'S A TIMES SQUARE HOOKER

ACADEMY AWARD NOMINEE MELISSA LEO PLAYS "COOKIE", THE ALLEY WHORE.

I CAN SEE FROM JOAN FREEMAN'S IMDB.COM PAGE THAT SHE ONLY DIRECTED ONE OTHER MOVIE (THE GIRL BAND FILM **SATISFACTION** WITH JUSTINE BATEMAN AND JULIA ROBERTS IN 1988), AND SCRIPTED A NEAR REMAKE OF STREETWALKIN' IN 1991 CALLED **UNCAGED**. A NEW YORK TIMES REVIEW OF HER FILM ALSO MAKES NOTE OF HER HARVARD SCHOOLING AND NEWBIE INDUSTRY GIGS WORKING ON PBS DOCUMENTARIES IN THE EARLY '80S, BUT JOAN DOESN'T APPEAR TO HAVE BEEN INVOLVED IN ANYTHING FILM-WISE IN THE LAST 20 YEARS, AND I REMAIN QUITE CURIOUS WHAT BECAME OF HER.

MUCH LIKE 1982'S **VICE SQUAD** (ONE OF MY ALL-TIME FAVES), MOST OF THIS MOVIE TAKES PLACE IN ONE NEON-SOAKED NIGHT AS A DISREPUTABLE PSYCHOPATH PIMP NAMED DUKE (DALE MIDKIFF -- THE DAD FROM PET SEMATARY) GOES BUCKWILD WHILE TRYING TO TRACK AND KILL ONE OF HIS CYNDI-LAUPER-LOOKIN STREET-SIDE CUM-SLURPERS. THE POOR GIRL GOES BY THE NAME OF COOKIE, AND DUKE DONE TURNED HER OUT AFTER PICKING UP THE SOBBING REDHEAD RUNAWAY IN THE TRAIN STATION -- WITH HER LITTLE BROTHER IN TOW.

COOKIE (MELISSA LEO FROM **HOMICIDE: LIFE ON THE STREET**, WHO WAS BORN AND RAISED IN MANHATTAN, THIS WAS HER FIRST STARRING ROLE) REALLY SHINES AS THE AFOREMENTIONED VOCATIONAL POLE-SMOKER UNDER EXTREME DURESS, AND HER CO-STARS ARE FANTASTIC AS WELL. NOT ONLY IS ANTONIO FARGAS (HUGGY BEAR!) ON DISPLAY AS A JIVE-TALKIN PIMP, BUT WE GET TO FREAK AS CATWOMAN HERSELF, JULIE NEWMAR (AS QUEEN BEE) HUSTLES THE STROLL IN HOT RED "FUCK

ME" LINGERIE RIGHT OUTSIDE THE LEGENDARY VARIETY PHOTOPLAYS THEATER (TORN DOWN IN 2005) AND A DIVE BAR KNOWN AS THE DUGOUT. THIS WAS A LEGITIMATELY DANGEROUS SECTION OF NEW YORK AT THE TIME!

ANYWAY... THIS GLORIOUS STREET-LEVEL TURDBALL DESERVES A CULT FOLLOWING. SOMEONE PUT THIS SWEET RIGHTEOUSNESS OUT ON DVD, ASAP! WITH A MELISSA LEO/JOAN FREEMAN COMMENTARY TRACK, PLEASE! (EDIT: (2015) I GUESS THEY WERE LISTENING BECAUSE A YEAR AFTER THIS SAW PRINT ORIGINALLY, SHOUT FACTORY DVD DID EXACTLY THAT! THE COMMENTARY IS GREAT!) —BOUGIE

HOT LUNCH (1978)

THE URBAN DICTIONARY CLASSIFIES A "HOT LUNCH" AS "THE ACT OF SHITTING IN SOME CLINGFILM STRETCHED OVER SOMEONE'S OPEN MOUTH, THEN FUCKING THAT MOUTH AND AT THE POINT OF EJACULATION — BURSTING THROUGH THE CLINGFILM AND GIVING THE RECIPIENT A MIXED MOUTHFUL OF SHIT AND SPUNK".

NOW, I'M GOING TO ASSUME THAT A 'HOT LUNCH' MEANT SOMETHING ELSE IN 1978 WHEN JOHN HAYES (UNDER THE NOM DE PORN "HAROLD PERKINS") DIRECTED THIS HARDCORE MOVIE WHICH FEATURED THE SEXY MISS DESIREE COUSTEAU, BECAUSE OTHERWISE THIS FAILS TO DELIVER. MY EDUCATED GUESS IS THAT IT MEANT A MOUTHFUL OF JIT, ESPECIALLY SINCE THAT IS WHAT GETS PISTON-PUMPED INTO THE OPEN YAPPERS OF CAST MEMBERS BONNIE HOLIDAY, DOROTHY SMIGHT, AND BRIGIT OLSEN.

I LIKED THIS ONE. OVER AND ABOVE THE TYPICAL SWEATY ORAL, VAGINAL, AND ANAL PENETRATING, WE'VE GOT SOME GREEDY GIRL-ON-GIRL SALAD TOSSING, A NAKED DUDE WHO SCREWS A CHICK WHILE WEARING A GUITAR, LESBIAN 69ING ON THE FLOOR OF A RESTAURANT KITCHEN, AND LOTS AND LOTS OF RED SHAG CARPETING. MY FAVOURITE LINE? THE STRAIGHT-FACED DEADPAN DELIVERY OF "I WANT YOUR BALLS".

TRIVIA: DIRECTOR JOHN HAYES DATED GOLDEN GIRL RUE MCCLANAHAN FOR FOUR YEARS WAY BACK WHEN SHE WAS IN HER 20s. HE PASSED AWAY IN AUGUST OF 2000, AND RUE SHUFFLED OFF THIS MORTAL COIL IN JUNE OF 2010. WE ARE WORSE OFF WITH THEM GONE.

—BOUGIE
·2010·

TINTO BRASS
MOLESTED MY ASS
BOUGIE · 2014 ·

SOME OF HIS BEST MOVIES ARE **THE HOWL** (1970), **SALON KITTY** (1975), AND **CALIGULA** (1979), BUT SINCE THOSE GLORY DAYS CAME AND WENT TINTO BRASS HAS BECOME MORE GLOBALLY FAMOUS FOR BEING THE KING OF THE ITALIAN SEX COMEDY. IN AMERICA, HOWEVER, HE'S BECOME NEARLY TOTALLY IGNORED IN THAT SAME TIME PERIOD, DESPITE A ROBUST DIRECTORIAL CAREER. FRANKLY, HE'S A FAT, OLD, DROOPY-FACED PERVERT, AND LIKE ME, HE'S REALLY INTO THE FEMALE ASS. I REALLY APPRECIATE THAT ABOUT HIM, I MUST SAY. US BUTT-GUYS STICK TOGETHER -- CHEEK TO CHEEK.

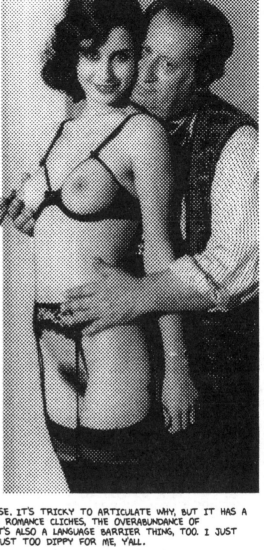

"A FACE CAN LIE, A DERRIERE CANNOT", HE TOLD INTERVIEWERS DON MANFREDO & DON TOMASO IN 2008. "A FACE CAN BE PAINTED OVER WITH MAKE-UP, CONCEAL ITS AGE OR IMPURITIES; A MOUTH CAN SPEW CRUEL LIES. A BUTT IS DEFINITELY MORE HONEST THAN THAT... WITH WOMEN, FIRST, I CHECK OUT THE BUTT. EVEN IF IT CAN'T SPEAK -- A ROUND BEHIND SPEAKS TO ME."

"HE WAS AN EXTRAORDINARY CHARACTER," FRENCH ACTOR JACQUES HERLIN TOLD EUROPEAN FILM REVIEW. "VERY SYMPATHETIC AND INTELLIGENT, CULTURED AND TOTALLY OBSESSED WITH SEX! WE WERE FRIENDS AND WOULD DINE OUT TOGETHER. I REMEMBER HIM SAYING: 'WHEN I SEND A SCREENPLAY TO A PRODUCER I ALWAYS INCLUDE MANY PICTURES OF NAKED GIRLS. IT MEANS THEY'RE SURE TO READ AT LEAST 2 OR 3 PAGES. THE PRODUCERS RECEIVE SO MANY SCREENPLAYS THEY DON'T PAY ANY ATTENTION, BUT THIS WAY...' NO, REALLY, HE WAS VERY CLEVER."

I DON'T OFTEN PRAISE TINTO'S 1980S AND 1990S FILMS IN THESE PAGES, SIMPLY BECAUSE I'M NOT INTO ITALIAN SEX COMEDIES... EVEN WELL MADE ONES LIKE THESE, STARRING INCREDIBLY GORGEOUS EUROPEAN WOMEN. I DON'T BEGRUDGE ANYONE WHO DIGS THEM (AND THEY CERTAINLY HAVE FANS), IT'S JUST THAT THERE IS SOMETHING ABOUT THE GENRE THAT MAKES ME WISH I WAS WATCHING SOMETHING ELSE. IT'S TRICKY TO ARTICULATE WHY, BUT IT HAS A LOT TO DO WITH THE HAMMY ACTING, THE DUMB ROMANCE CLICHES, THE OVERABUNDANCE OF SAXOPHONE ON THE SOUNDTRACK, AND I THINK IT'S ALSO A LANGUAGE BARRIER THING, TOO. I JUST NEVER FIND THE HUMOUR FUNNY. THIS SHIT IS JUST TOO DIPPY FOR ME, Y'ALL.

THAT SAID, I CAN'T IGNORE THE STEADFAST SKILLS BRASS HAS A FILMMAKER, NOT TO MENTION HIS REMARKABLE VISUAL SENSE, AND THE FACT THAT THESE MOVIES AREN'T CHEAP-LOOKING -- LIKE THE AMERICAN SKIN-E-MAX STUFF MADE AT THE SAME TIME IS. TINTO KNOWS WHAT HE'S DOING, AND HE DOESN'T NEED CRITICS OR JOURNALISTS LIKE ME TO PROP HIM UP. THE WORK SPEAKS FOR ITSELF.

PUTTING ASIDE HIS 1970S CLASSICS, HIS EROTICA ERA STARTS WITH **THE KEY** (1983), AND CONTINUES ALONG WITH **MIRANDA** (1985), **CAPRICCIO** (1987), **SNACK BAR BUDAPEST** (1988), **PAPRIKA** (1991), **ALL LADIES DO IT** (1992), **THE VOYEUR** (1994), **PO BOX TINTO BRASS** (1995), **MONELLA** (1998), **CHEEKY** (2000), **BLACK ANGEL** (2002) AND **DO IT!** (2003).

I ACTUALLY ENJOY THE BEHIND-THE-SCENES PROMOTIONAL PHOTOS FOR TINTO BRASS'S LATER ERA EROTICA MORE THAN I DO THE ACTUAL FILMS THEMSELVES, ODDLY ENOUGH. I'VE GOT AN ADMITTEDLY WEIRD FETISH FOR PORN FEATURING TOTALLY DISGUSTING GERIATRIC OLD MEN AND RAVISHINGLY GORGEOUS YOUNG WOMEN, AND THIS GREASY OLD CLOWN PLAYS RIGHT INTO THAT. I HAVE YET TO SEE A PROMO FOR ONE OF HIS MOVIES, OR AN INTERVIEW, OR A PUBLIC

APPEARANCE WHERE THIS FAT, CIGAR SMOKING OLD TURD-WITH-HAIR ISN'T RUBBING HIS LEATHERY HANDS ALL OVER ONE OF HIS NAKED YOUNG STARS, STROKING THEIR TITS AND ASS CHEEKS, RUBBING THEIR NIPPLES, AND SMILING HIS ITALIAN FART-SNIFFING SMILE AT THE CAMERAS WHILE HE DOES IT. THE EUROPEAN MEDIA MUST THINK THAT KIND OF THING IS CUTE OR FUN OR SOMETHING. IF A DIRECTOR HERE PULLED THAT INCREDIBLY UNPROFESSIONAL SHIT, NO ONE WOULD EVEN KNOW WHAT TO DO. WHERE WOULD THE PHOTOS EVEN RUN? PEOPLE? US MAGAZINE? NO, WE'RE WAY MORE PURITANICAL IN NORTH AMERICA, DESPITE THE COMPLAINTS I SEE ABOUT SEXUALITY RUNNING RAMPANT IN HOLLYWOOD.

WITH THAT IN MIND, YOU WOULD THINK HIS FEMALE PERFORMERS WOULD BE LINING UP TO TALK SMACK ABOUT HOW GROSS IT WAS TO GET PAWED AT BY A DIRTY OLD SPAGHETTI-SLURPER FOR WEEKS ON END WHILE ON SET. NOTHING COULD BE FURTHER FROM THE TRUTH. HE'S ADORED BY WOMEN. "TO WORK WITH TINTO WAS A DREAM COME TRUE FOR ME", SAID ACTRESS CINZIA ROCCAFORTE, WHOSE FIRST STARRING ROLE WAS IN PO BOX TINTO BRASS IN 1995. "HE'S ONE OF MY FAVOURITE DIRECTORS AND A REALLY COOL GUY."

I SHOULD PROBABLY SPEAK ABOUT THE OLD ASS-GRABBER'S CAREER IN THE PAST TENSE THOUGH, I SUPPOSE. TINTO WAS FORCED TO WRAP THINGS UP AT THE AGE OF 77 IN 2010, WHEN HE UNFORTUNATELY SUFFERED AN INTRACRANIAL HEMORRHAGE. SINCE THEN THE TITLES ADDED TO HIS FILMOGRAPHY HAVE (UNDERSTANDABLY) COME TO AN ABRUPT STOP, AND HE HASN'T MADE MANY PUBLIC APPEARANCES. GETTING OLD SUCKS.

STUPID CRITICISMS

"THAT MOVIE IS SO DATED"

"DATED" AS A CRITICISM HAS SEEMED REALLY STUPID TO ME FOR A LONG, LONG TIME NOW. THINK ABOUT WHAT IT REALLY MEANS AS A PUT DOWN: THAT SOMETHING IS BAD BECAUSE IT ISN'T WHAT IS POPULAR RIGHT AT THIS MOMENT IN TIME. WHAT? C'MON, HOW ULTIMATELY POINTLESS IS THAT? AS IF THAT HAS ANYTHING TO DO WITH ANYTHING IN THE GRAND SCHEME OF HISTORY. ONE OF THE KEY THINGS WE LOVE MOST ABOUT ARTIFACTS FROM THE PAST IS THAT THEY EACH PROVIDE A GLIMPSE INTO THAT TIME.

"HE'S ONE OF THE MOST HATED DIRECTORS"

TO BE ONE OF THE MOST HATED OR CONTENTIOUS, YOU NEED TO HAVE MADE MOVIES THAT ARE GOOD ENOUGH TO BE KNOWN BY MILLIONS OF PEOPLE. BY VIRTUE OF THAT FACT ALONE, NO DIRECTOR THAT IS THE MOST HATED WILL EVER BE TRULY DESERVING OF IT. SO MANY OF THE MUCH LESSER KNOWN DIRECTORS -- WHO ARE INSIGNIFICANT DUE TO A LACK OF TALENT, CREATIVITY, OR RESOURCES -- WILL NEVER EVEN FACTOR INTO THE DISCUSSION. THEY LITERALLY AREN'T GOOD ENOUGH TO BE HATED BY ENOUGH PEOPLE TO RANK.

SCHOOLGIRL REPORT: EVERY GIRL STARTS SOMETIME
(AKA: SMARTIE PANTS) 1976. GERMANY.
REVIEW BY IAN JANE

in throbbing color

She's got her education behind her...
What an education!!

Smartie PANTS

Starring
Gayle Sommer
Melissa Greene

THIS TENTH ENTRY IN THE SEEMINGLY ENDLESS PARADE OF SCHOOLGIRL REPORT FILMS IS ONCE AGAIN DIRECTED BY WALTER BOOS. AS IS THE NORM WITH THE SERIES, WE START OFF WITH A FRAMING DEVICE THAT ALLOWS THE MOVIE TO SEGUE INTO THE DIFFERENT STORIES THAT MAKE UP THE RUNNING TIME. THIS TIME AROUND, WE'RE SITTING IN ON A CLASSROOM FULL OF HIGH SCHOOL GIRLS (ALL OF WHOM LOOK OLDER THAN THEY'RE SUPPOSED TO BE) AS THEY DISCUSS MORALITY AND POLITICS AS THEY APPLY TO HUMAN SEXUALITY. THIS, OF COURSE, LEADS TO CONFESSIONS OF SORTS AND WE SEE JUST WHAT EXACTLY A FEW OF THESE NAUGHTY LASSES HAVE BEEN UP TO IN THEIR SPARE TIME.

THE FIRST STORY BEGINS WHEN A MALE HIGH SCHOOL TEACHER IS BROUGHT INTO THE ADMINISTRATION OFFICE AND ACCUSED OF MOLESTING A STUDENT NAMED SUSANNE (BARBEL MARKUS -- SHE LOOKS A BIT LIKE CAROLE KING, WHICH IS KIND OF ODD) AFTER PLYING HER WITH RUM DURING A PRIVATE TUTORING SESSION AT HIS HOUSE. FIRST WE HEAR SUSANNE'S SIDE OF THE STORY, IN WHICH HE MOLESTS HER, THEN WE HEAR HIS SIDE OF THE STORY WHERE HE COMES INTO THE ROOM AND SHE'S NUDE AND TRYING TO SEDUCE HIM. THE TRUTH COMES OUT FROM A THIRD PARTY, A BOY WHO HAS BEEN CRUSHING ON FRISKY SUSANNE AND TRYING TO BANG HER. THANKFULLY HIS VOYEURISTIC WAYS WILL SEE THAT JUSTICE PREVAILS!

THE SECOND STORY FOLLOWS FOXY BLONDE INGA (MARIANNE DUPONT), A SHY GIRL WHO CLAMS UP WHEN IT COMES TO THE SUBJECT OF CARNALITY. WHEN SHE'S BEHIND CLOSED DOORS THOUGH? SHE'S REALLY INTO DIDDLING HERSELF, OR AT LEAST TUGGING AT HER PUBES AND WRITHING ABOUT NUDE IN THE BED. AS SHE BECOMES MORE IN TUNE WITH HER OWN NEEDS, SHE GETS PICKED UP BY A GUY AT A BAR WHO TAKES HER BACK TO HIS PLACE. THERE HE HAS HIS WAY WITH HER AND INVITES A FEW OF HIS PALS IN. THEY FONDLE HER AND THEN LEAVE. AS SHE WANDERS AWAY, IT SEEMS HE LIVES IN A MASSIVE PALATIAL ESTATE, BUT HIS INTERIOR DECORATING SKILLS MAKE HIS PAD LOOK MORE LIKE A FLOPHOUSE. WEIRD.

MOVING RIGHT ALONG, WE SEE THE SORDID DETAILS OF AN ENCOUNTER THAT OCCURS WHEN A BOY IS DARED TO MAKE A MOVE ON HIS GIRLFRIEND'S STEPMOTHER. HE DOES, AND OFF THEY GO, BUT THE GIRLFRIEND? SHE DOESN'T THINK THIS IS COOL AT ALL. THIS FLOOZY IS CHEATING ON DEAR OLD DAD, SO SHE GRABS HER INSTAMATIC AND SETS ABOUT TO SNOOPING SO THAT SHE CAN PRESENT HER DAD WITH SOME PICTURES, THE KIND THAT TELL THE WHOLE STORY.

THE HIGHLIGHT OF THE MOVIE, AND POSSIBLY THE ENTIRE DAMN SERIES, IS THE FOURTH VIGNETTE IN WHICH WE MEET A BLONDE AND HER BOYFRIEND WHO DESPERATELY WANT TO GET IT ON BUT ARE UNABLE TO BECAUSE OF HER FAMILY'S NOSEY WAYS. AFTER HE READS A COPY OF DER EXORCIST HE DECIDES THAT THERE'S A WAY AROUND THIS -- SHE'LL CONVINCE HER PARENTS SHE'S POSSESSED BY RUNNING AROUND THE HOUSE, GRUNTING, FLASHING HER COOCH AND PEEING ON THE FLOOR, AND HE'LL DRESS UP AS RASPUTIN AND WAIT AT THE BAR FOR HER DAD TO SHOW UP. WHEN HE DOES, HE CONVINCES DAD THAT HE'S AN EXORCIST AND THAT HE CAN CLEANSE HIS DAUGHTER OF THE DEMON THAT POSSESSES HER. HE AGREES, AND THEY LOCK HIM IN THE ROOM WITH HER WHERE HE BANGS THE EVIL RIGHT OUT OF THAT GIRL. LOTS MORE GRUNTING AND JUMPING AROUND OCCURS IN A STORY THAT CAN ONLY BE DESCRIBED AS WACKY.

IN THE FINAL STORY, WE SEE WHAT HAPPENS WHEN A DARLING YOUNG WOMAN AGREES TO BOFF AN OLDER GENTLEMAN ON THE SIDE, UNBEKNOWNST TO HIS BETTER HALF. THEIR AFFAIR IS FINE AT FIRST BUT ONCE HIS CRANKY WIFE FINDS OUT, HE LEARNS THAT HELL HATH NO FURY LIKE A WOMAN SCORNED.

THIS IS A PRETTY ENJOYABLE ADDITION TO THE LINE. THE GIRLS GENERALLY LOOK GOOD AND YOU GET ALL THE SOFTCORE BUMPING AND GRINDING THAT THE SERIES IS KNOWN FOR IN EACH OF THE FIVE STORIES. THERE ARE A FEW FAMILIAR FACES HERE AND THERE (ASTRID BONER POPS UP -- HA! -- AND GINA JANSSEN AND MARIANNE DUPONT TOO) AND THE PACING IS SOLID. THE EXORCIST KNOCK OFF IS OBVIOUSLY THE BIG STAND OUT HERE -- IT'S JUST COMPLETELY INSANE AND PRETTY HILARIOUS TO WATCH. THE ACTRESSES' FACIAL EXPRESSIONS ARE SO OVER THE TOP THAT YOU CAN'T HELP BUT LAUGH AT IT ALL. IT'S NOT PARTICULARLY TITILLATING BUT IT IS PRETTY DAMN FUNNY.

ONE TIME WHEN I WAS WORKING AT THE OLD VIDEOMATICA RENTALS ON WEST 4th AVE HERE IN VANCOUVER, AN OLD GUY CAME IN AND RENTED ONE OF THESE OL' "SCHOOLGIRL REPORT" DVDS. WHEN I ASKED HIM IF THAT WAS ALL HE WANTED, HE PAUSED AND LOOKED AT ME, AND GOES "THE GIRLS BETTER BE **YOUNG** IN THIS." GUHHHH -- FUCKING CREEEEPY.

TOKYO DECADENCE

THE ACTRESS IS A WHORE

BY ROBIN BOUGIE · 2011 ·

DESPITE THE SEXUAL REVOLUTION IN THE '60S AND THE MAINSTREAMING OF PORN IN THE '90S, PROSTITUTES REMAIN -- IN THE EYES OF THE MASSES -- OUTCASTS, CRIMINALS, DISEASE CARRIERS, SEXUAL MERCENARIES, AND SOCIALLY STIGMATISED INDIVIDUALS FREE OF MORALS AND UNDESERVING OF LOVE.

SHEDDING THE SOCIAL TABOOS OF THE ACT, PROSTITUTION IS TOTALLY INNOCUOUS; TWO (OR MORE) CONSENTING ADULTS TAKE PART IN AN EXCHANGE OF MONEY FOR SERVICES. NEITHER PARTY IS INHERENTLY WRONGED BY THE TRANSACTION, AND YET IT REMAINS WHAT IT IS: VICE. WE ARE TITILLATED BY THE PRURIENT NATURE OF SEX-FOR-MONEY, BUT ALSO FLATLY REGARD IT AS DEEPLY DEGRADING FOR BOTH PARTIES INVOLVED. THE JOHNS ARE LESSER MEN BECAUSE THEY MUST PAY A WOMAN TO SLEEP WITH THEM, AND THE WHORES ARE, WELL, WHORES. THE VERY WORD ITSELF IS CONSIDERED ONE OF THE MOST HURTFUL INSULTS ONE CAN USE TO BELITTLE A FEMALE.

DESPITE THE RANCID INTERNALISATION OF THAT SCORN, MANY ESCORTS FIGHT AGAINST IT AND WORK TO VIEW THEMSELVES AS SEX THERAPISTS, SOCIAL WORKERS, AND NO DIFFERENT THAN ANYONE ELSE WHO MAKES A LIVING CHARGING FOR THEIR TIME AND SKILLS. EVERY PROSTITUTE I'VE EVER GOTTEN TO KNOW HAS TOLD ME THE SAME THING ABOUT THEIR JOB WHEN WE SPEAK ABOUT THE INTIMATE ACTS INVOLVED IN A SESSION: THAT THEY GO INTO A CHARACTER THAT THEY RELY UPON TO MAKE THEIR WAY THROUGH THEIR JOB SAFELY AND HAPPILY. THAT THIS CHARACTER CAN DO AND SAY THINGS THEY WOULD NORMALLY NOT SAY AND DO.

IN THIS RESPECT, WHORING IS ACTING, AND ACTING IS WHORING.

ACTRESS MIHO NIKAIDO TAKES UP THE REINS OF THE WORLD'S OLDEST PROFESSION IN RYU MURAKAMI'S 1992 ODE TO SUBDUED KINK, **TOKYO DECADENCE**. SHE SHOWED UP ON SET, GOT INTO HER WHORE COSTUME AND HER WHORE MAKEUP, AND CHARGED MONEY FOR HER TIME AND HER SKILLS AS AN ACTRESS. SHE SAID AND DID THINGS SHE WOULD NOT NORMALLY SAY AND DO.

NIKAIDO'S CHARACTER IS NAMED AI (THE JAPANESE WORD FOR LOVE), AND SHE IS IN NEARLY EVERY SCENE OF THE MOVIE. IT IS A VERY CONVINCING AND INTRIGUING PORTRAYAL THAT OFFERS AUDIENCES A HEARTBREAKING CHARACTER WHO IS SHY, SAD, SUBMISSIVE, AND SEEMS DESPERATE FOR HAPPINESS AND FULFILMENT OF ANY KIND. SHE IS LONELY, AND WORKS DILIGENTLY TO SATISFY THE DESIRES OF EVERYONE SHE COMES INTO CONTACT WITH, AS IF TO FIND PURPOSE BY BEING OF SOME USE TO OTHERS. AI IS A PLAYTHING, AND IS TORTURED, TIED UP, DRUGGED AND DISRESPECTED THROUGHOUT THE FILM.

MIHO NIKAIDO DIDNT EARN MUCH CRITICAL RESPECT FOR WHAT SHOULD HAVE BEEN REGARDED AS A STANDOUT, AWARD-WINNING TURN. THE SUBTLETIES OF HER PERFORMANCE ARE HAUNTING, AS SHE WORDLESSLY PARLAYS FRAGILE EMOTIONS ON-SCREEN JUST ENOUGH SO THAT WE WITNESS THEM, BUT HER CLIENTS DONT. MUCH LIKE THE CALL GIRL SHE PORTRAYS, THE FACT THAT NIKAIDO DID THIS JOB WHILE NAKED AND (DEPICTED AS) PENETRATED AND PRIED OPEN, FOUND HER SKILLS AS AN ACTRESS DEVALUED IN THE EYES OF SOCIETY. JUST AS PROSTITUTES DONT GET TO ENJOY ACCEPTANCE FOR THE JOB THEY DO, EROTIC CINEMA PERFORMERS DONT WIN ACADEMY AWARDS.

AIS CLIENTS ARE WELL-TO-DO SALARYMEN AND YAKUZA (ENTIRELY INDISTINGUISHABLE FROM EACH OTHER) WHO, FOR THE MOST PART, GET OFF ON HER HUMILIATION. THE STANDOUT SCENE DEPICTING THIS FINDS AI FORCED TO REPETITIVELY PERFORM A GYRATING ASSCHEEK-BARING STRIPTEASE FOR A MATTER OF HOURS IN

"COLD, GREY URBAN FETISHISM, VOYEURISTIC AND DEVOID OF JOY"

FRONT OF A WALL-SIZED HOTEL WINDOW OVERLOOKING ALL OF TOKYO. THIS IS COLD, GREY URBAN FETISHISM, VOYEURISTIC AND DEVOID OF JOY. THE STERN ORDER TO REPEAT THE EXHAUSTING ACTION OVER AND OVER AGAIN (WHEN IT ISNT DONE PRECISELY TO THE CLIENT'S EXACT SPECIFICATIONS) IS BOTH HARROWING, POTENTLY SEXY, AND THE SOURCE FOR MOST OF THE PROMOTIONAL IMAGERY SURROUNDING THE MOVIE.

COATED IN A LAYER OF SWEAT BY THE TIME SHE IS FINISHED, THE ACT OF BEING FORCED TO CONTINUALLY EXPOSE HERSELF AND HER PRIMAL SEXUALITY TO NOT ONLY HIM, BUT ALSO THE VERY CITY SHE RESIDES IN SPEAKS TO THE DARKER SIDE OF HUMAN DESIRE AND THE DECADENCE ALLUDED TO IN THE TITLE. ONE ALSO BEGINS TO REALISE THAT THESE SLEAZY SESSIONS ARE NOT JUST SEX, THEY ARE SOCIAL ALLEGORIES AND REPRESENTATIONS OF JAPANESE ECONOMICS OF THE TIME, AND THE DIRECT EFFECT THEY HAD.

THESE ELEMENTS (EXPERTLY EXPLAINED IN NICHOLAS RUCKA'S 1992 ESSAY, "COLOR ME TOPAZ: DECADENCE IN POST BUBBLE TOKYO") PERTAINED DIRECTLY TO THE PERIOD OF 1986 TO 1990, A TIME OF SKYROCKETING LAND AND STOCK PRICES IN THE AREA. THIS MASSIVE AND EXPEDIENT ECONOMIC BOOM WAS PARLAYED BY A JAPANESE WORKFORCE THAT WAS UNIFIED BY A GOAL OF GLOBAL FINANCIAL DOMINANCE. WAGE-EARNING WAS VERY HIGH EVEN FOR PART-TIME WORKERS, AND VOLUMINOUS AMOUNTS OF DISPOSABLE INCOME WAS SPLURGED ON EXTRAVAGANCES SUCH AS DESIGNER GOODS, LUXURY JEWELLERY AND CARS, RITZY HOTEL STAYS, AND HIGH END HOOKERS. WHEN THE BUBBLE BURST, NO ONE WAS READY.

"WHEN TOKYO DECADENCE WAS MADE", WROTE RUCKA, "THE JAPANESE SOCIETY WAS IN SOCIAL AND ECONOMIC CHAOS; IT WAS A TIME WHEN JAPAN FIRST DISCOVERED

THAT IT WAS ILL-EQUIPPED TO DEAL WITH THE SOCIAL REALITY OF A COUNTRY WITHOUT A UNIQUE IDENTITY THAT WASN'T TIED TO GROUPTHINK AND FINANCIAL SPECULATION. RYU MURAKAMI SAYS THAT THERE IS NO RETURNING TO THE PAST, THERE'S ONLY FORWARD MOVEMENT AND THAT CHANGE NEEDS TO COME FROM WITHIN."

INDEED, MURAKAMI IS RECOGNISED IN HIS HOME COUNTRY AS ONE OF THE MOST IMPORTANT AND INFLUENTIAL FIGURES OF MODERN LITERATURE. ALSO THE AUTHOR OF TAKASHI MIIKE'S CULT HORROR CLASSIC FROM 1999, AUDITION, MURAKAMI HAS WON THE YOMIURI LITERATURE PRIZE, THE AKUTAGAWA PRIZE (THE MOST AUTHORITATIVE LITERARY PRIZE IN JAPAN) AND HAS PRODUCED MULTIPLE BEST-SELLERS INCLUDING "ALMOST TRANSPARENT BLUE", "69", AND "PIERCING".

IN 1996 MURAKAMI PENNED "TOPAZ II" A SEQUEL TO TOKYO DECADENCE CONCERNED WITH A TEENAGE GIRL IN HIGH SCHOOL GETTING PAID FOR "ENJO KOSAI", AKA "COMPENSATED DATING" A PRACTICE WHEREBY OLDER DUDES PAY TEENAGE GIRLS TO SPEND TIME WITH THEM. THE BOOK WAS ALSO ADAPTED AS A LIVE ACTION MOVIE (FILMED ALMOST ENTIRELY ON HAND-HELD DIGITAL CAMERAS) CALLED LOVE AND POP (1998) BY ANIME DIRECTOR HIDEAKI ANNO.

AN UNOFFICIAL SEQUEL TO TOKYO DECADENCE CALLED NEW TOKYO DECADENCE: THE SLAVE (2007) WAS MADE BY OSAMU SATO, AND DEPICTS A SECRETARY WHO IS LED INTO THE WORLD OF PROSTITUTION AND BDSM. THE FILM IS ONE OF THE BETTER RECENT EXAMPLES OF SINCERELY SEXY JAPANESE PINK CINEMA, AND IS BASED ON LEAD ACTRESS RINAKO HIRASAWA'S PERSONAL EXPERIENCES. SHE WAS AWARDED WITH THE BEST ACTRESS AWARD AT THE PINK GRAND PRIX IN 2007 FOR HER PERFORMANCE.

MIHO NIKAIDO TODAY WORKS AS A CLOTHING DESIGNER (HER LINE "MIHO MIHO" HAS SHOWN UP IN RUNWAY FASHION SHOWS DURING NEW YORK FASHION WEEK), AND FOLLOWED UP TOKYO DECADENCE WITH SEVERAL OTHER SMUTTY PINK FILM ROLES BEFORE BECOMING THE BRIDE OF CELEBRATED AMERICAN FILMMAKER HAL HARTLEY. SHE CURRENTLY CONTINUES TO ACT IN SUPPORTING ROLES IN HER HUSBANDS FILMS.

END

SISSY'S HOT SUMMER (1979. DIR: ALAN COLBERG)

IF YOU REMEMBER THE 1970S SITCOM THREE'S COMPANY, YOU'LL RECALL THAT IT FEATURED TWO GIRLS AND A GUY WHO LIVED TOGETHER AS ROOMMATES, AND CONSISTENTLY GOT INTO HARE-BRAINED HIGH JINKS. WELL, THIS IS THE PORN VERSION, AND IT EVEN GOES SO FAR AS TO BORROW THE CHARACTER'S NAMES: JANET, SISSY (INSTEAD OF CHRISSY) AND JACK, AS THEY OFTEN WERE ON THE MASSIVELY POPULAR TV SHOW. THE TRIO ARE ON THE VERGE OF GETTING KICKED OUT OF THEIR APARTMENT BY A GROUCHY LANDLORD (MR. GROPER), AND WITH THE FEAR OF EVICTION SENDING THEM INTO A PANIC, THEY DECIDE TO SPEND ONE EVENING MAKING A FAT WAD OF CASH WORKING AS PROSTITUTES.

BEFORE THAT THOUGH, SISSY (JENNIFER WALKER) AND JACK (TONY BOND) USE A PAIR OF SOCKS TO TIE EACH OTHER UP AND PARTAKE IN A LITTLE BONDAGE-THEMED FUCKING. THEIR BACK AND FORTH CONVERSATION THROUGHOUT THIS IS VERY CASUAL AND IMPROVISATIONAL, WHICH IS A NICE CHANGE OF PACE ESPECIALLY WITH THE THESPIAN SKILLS OF THIS CAST BEING AS WEAK AS THEY ARE. YOU CAN'T REALLY BLAME THE ACTORS FOR HOW LACKLUSTRE THIS TAME, UNMOVING PORN FILM IS

THOUGH. THEY'RE ALL DECENT LOOKING, AND DO THEIR BEST WITH A WEAK SCRIPT AND SOME UNINSPIRED CINEMATOGRAPHY -- EVERY BORING HUMP SCENE IS SHOT FROM A SINGLE UNMOVING CAMERA. IT DOESN'T TAKE MUCH EFFORT FOR JOHN HOLMES TO STEAL THIS SHOW IN HIS SHORT SCENE WHERE HE PLAYS A LOINCLOTH CLAD FREAK WHO THINKS HE'S TARZAN. QUITE A DISAPPOINTMENT.

-BOUGIE

THE FLINTSTONES MADE ME AN ALCOHOLIC !!
ARTICLE BY MIKE SULLIVAN ☆ 2009 ☆

I HAVE NEVER LIKED THE FLINTSTONES. I'M SORRY IF I'VE OFFENDED ANYONE BUT IT NEEDED TO BE SAID. IT WASN'T BECAUSE THE SHOW WAS BORING OR UNFUNNY OR STIFFLY ANIMATED (ALTHOUGH THOSE WERE CONTRIBUTING FACTORS) BUT BECAUSE OF HANNA-BARBERA'S PRETENCE THAT IT WAS INTENDED FOR ADULT AUDIENCES. IT WOULD BE ONE THING IF THE FLINTSTONES WAS A POIGNANT BUT DRYLY COMIC EXAMINATION INTO THE LIVES OF LOWER MIDDLE CLASS CAVEMEN, BUT IT WASN'T. IT WAS A SHITTY CARTOON ABOUT TWO GUYS IN MAN-DRESSES AND THEIR DAILY INTERACTIONS WITH SARCASTIC KITCHEN APPLIANCES. BUT EVERYONE ACCEPTED THE LIE, MOST NOTABLY ANHEUSER-BUSCH WHO IN 1967 DECIDED THAT A CHARACTER WHO TURNED INTO AN APE AND OCCASIONALLY TRAVELLED THROUGH TIME WITH THE HELP OF A FEY GREEN ALIEN WOULD BE THE BEST PERSON TO SELL BEER TO GROWN UPS.

BETTER KNOWN BY ITS DAZZLING PROMOTIONAL TITLE 'BUSCH ADVERTISING 1967' AND FUNCTIONING AS A SORT OF PRIMITIVE INFOMERCIAL, BUSCH ADVERTISING 1967 WAS DESIGNED SPECIFICALLY TO INFORM BUSCH BEER DISTRIBUTORS ABOUT THE TELEVISION AND RADIO ADS THEY COULD EXPECT TO SEE IN THE UPCOMING YEAR. IT WAS NEVER INTENDED FOR GENERAL AUDIENCES OR TO BRING LAUGHTER OR JOY.

AS BA 1967 OPENS, FRED AND BARNEY'S IGNORANCE OF PROPER DINOSAUR OPERATION HAS GOTTEN THEM IN TROUBLE WITH THEIR BOSS MR. SLATE YET AGAIN. BUT JUST AS SLATE IS ABOUT TO FIRE THEM, FRED INDIGNANTLY ANNOUNCES THAT HE QUITS. THE DUO THEN HEAD OVER TO A LOCAL BAR (WHICH IN TYPICALLY UNFUNNY HANNA-BARBERA FASHION IS CALLED 'TAVERN-TYPE INN BAR GRILL LOUNGE SALOON') WHERE THEY GO FIGURE OUT WHAT TO DO NEXT. AFTER A FEW SIPS OF COLD, FROSTY BUSCH BEERS (REMEMBER FRED FLINTSTONE SAYS, "WHEN YOU'RE DUE FOR A BEER, BUSCH DOES IT!") A SPARKLING DISEMBODIED HAND APPEARS ABOVE FRED, PATS HIM ON THE HEAD, CALLS HIM TIGER AND SEXILY COOS THAT EVERYTHING WILL BE OK. ALMOST IMMEDIATELY FRED GETS THE BRILLIANT AND IN NO WAY DRUNKEN IDEA TO GO HOME, LIE TO THEIR WIVES AND FIND NEW JOBS IN THE MORNING. BARNEY THEN ANNOUNCES HE IS GOING TO KILL HIMSELF. THEY BOTH LAUGH HEARTILY AT THIS OBVIOUS CRY FOR HELP.

BARNEY, YOU ARE A..A..B-BEAUTIFUL MmmAAAN. HA HA HA HA HA I...I CAN'T FEEL MY FACE...

WOBBLE WOBBLE

DRUNNNNK!!

AFTER A DEPRESSING NIGHT THAT FINDS THE TWO FRIENDS GETTING EVEN DRUNKER ON REFRESHINGLY SMOOTH BUSCH BEER ("YOU CAN'T SAY BEER BETTER!") IN FRED'S KITCHEN THEY DRIVE TO THE UNEMPLOYMENT OFFICE AND FIND THAT THE ONLY JOBS THEY'RE SUITABLE FOR ARE THE JOBS THEY JUST QUIT. DEPRESSED, FRED AND BARNEY HEAD BACK TO THEIR LOCAL BAR. IN A SITCOM-Y TURN OF EVENTS THE BARTENDER HAS TO LEAVE EARLY TO GO TO STONE CITY (STONE CITY? ARE YOU FUCKING KIDDING ME? WHAT? WERE THEY SAVING ALL OF THEIR A MATERIAL FOR THE JETSONS MEET THE FLINTSTONES?) SO INSTEAD OF SIMPLY CLOSING THE BAR EARLY HE DECIDES TO LEAVE IT IN THE HANDS OF TWO HALF-IN-THE-BAG NEANDER-TARDS WHO COULDN'T DIG HOLES IN A GRAVEL PIT WITHOUT NEARLY KILLING THEMSELVES AND OTHERS.

WITH THE BARTENDER GONE, FRED TURNS ON THE TELEVISION AND IS GENTLY ASSAULTED BY A SPECIAL ADVANCED CLOSED CIRCUIT PROGRAM FOR ANHEUSER-BUSCH WHOLESALERS. SURPRISINGLY, FRED AND BARNEY COULDN'T BE HAPPIER TO SEE THIS. THEY REACT AS IF THE HAND OF GOD REACHED DOWN FROM HEAVEN AND JERKED THEM OFF. AND WHO WOULDN'T? WHEN I THINK OF ENTERTAINMENT I THINK OF INDUSTRIAL FILMS FROM THE LATE '60S THAT TALK ABOUT THEIR CUSTOMER BASE IN THE MOST CONDESCENDING WAY POSSIBLE. IN THE EYES OF ANHEUSER-BUSCH, THE PEOPLE WHO DRINK THEIR BEER ARE DESTITUTE MORONS WHOSE LIVES ARE SO GODDAMNED MISERABLE THAT A TALL GLASS OF BUSCH BEER ("COLD AS A MOUNTAIN STREAM!") IS THE ONLY THING KEEPING THEM FROM MURDERING A DOZEN STUDENT NURSES. YET, THE ONLY PEOPLE ANHEUSER-BUSCH HATES MORE THAN ITS LOATHSOME, SHIT-UGLY CUSTOMERS ARE WOMEN WHO ARE DEPICTED IN THE VARIOUS COMMERCIALS AS EMASCULATING HARPIES WHOSE ONLY PURPOSE IN LIFE IS TO HIT YOUR CAR, YELL AT YOU, AND BURN YOU WITH TOASTERS. YOU ARE A GLITTERING RAINBOW OF HATE, ANHEUSER-BUSCH.

AS THE CLOSED CIRCUIT PROGRAM IS FINISHING UP, THE AFTER WORK RUSH HAS ALREADY BEGUN. FRED AND BARNEY ARE NOW FORCED TO SERVE SPARKLING, NON-LETHAL BUSCH BEER ("LIKE A MINTY FINGER CRAMMED DOWN YOUR FACE HOLE") TO ACTUAL CUSTOMERS. TO MAKE MATTERS MORE STRESSFUL, MR. SLATE HAS JUST WANDERED INTO THE BAR CAUSING THE TWO CAVEMEN TO DON MAKESHIFT DISGUISES (FRED PUTS A MOP ON HIS HEAD WHILE BARNEY WEARS A TURBAN). WHY THE DISGUISES? AFTER ALL, THEY BOTH QUIT THEIR JOBS AND BARTENDING PROBABLY PAYS BETTER THAN WHATEVER IT WAS THEY DID IN THAT GRAVEL PIT. I GUESS THEY DIDN'T WANT SLATE TO RECOGNISE THEM WHEN THEY RUB THEIR GRIMY CAVE-BALLS ALL OVER HIS BUFFALO WINGS OR WOOLY MAMMOTH WINGS, OR WHATEVER. MR. SLATE ORDERS A BEER AND BEMOANS THE FACT THAT WORK HASN'T BEEN THE SAME SINCE FRED AND BARNEY LEFT, BUT IS AFRAID HE'LL LOSE FACE IF HE HIRES THEM BACK. THANKFULLY, A GARDEN-FRESH GLASS OF BUSCH BEER ("IT MAY LOOK LIKE PISS BUT IT DOESN'T SMELL LIKE PISS") HELPS TO MAKE THIS DIFFICULT DECISION FOR HIM. SLATE NOT ONLY HIRES THEM BACK BUT THEY GET RAISES AS WELL! AH, THE CURATIVE POWERS OF TERRIBLE WATERY BEER.
AT THIS POINT, THE ASSHOLE OF A TINY BIRD TELLS US THAT IT IS THE END.

ACCORDING TO FILM THREAT'S PHIL HALL, BA 1967 WAS THE LAST PROMOTIONAL FILM HANNA-BARBERA EVER MADE. THAT IS NOT REALLY SURPRISING BECAUSE BA 1967 HAS TO BE THE MOST INEFFECTUAL AND DEPRESSING INDUSTRIAL FILM EVER PATCHED TOGETHER. EVERY ONE OF THE CHARACTERS IS A SELF-DESTRUCTIVE IDIOT WHO CAN ONLY MAKE DECISIONS WHILE DRUNK. WHY ANYONE THOUGHT THIS WOULD INSTIL CONFIDENCE IN BUSCH'S PROMOTIONAL CAMPAIGN IS A COMPLETE MYSTERY. STILL, BA 1967 IS SO ILL-CONCEIVED AND MISGUIDED THAT IT MUST BE WITNESSED, TREASURED AND PASSED DOWN TO FUTURE GENERATIONS.

BOYS! I AM NOT IMPRESSED WITH THESE ANTICS!

HHEAAHH.... YOU GONNA MAKE US SUM MUNNY, BITCH.

HOOKERS, HUSTLERS, PIMPS AND THEIR JOHNS (1993, UK)

A YEAR BEFORE SHE STARTED WORK ON **TO WONG FOO THANKS FOR EVERYTHING, JULIE NEWMAR**, BRIT DIRECTOR BEEBAN KIDRON MADE A SORDID PILGRIMAGE TO THE MEAN STREETS OF THE SOUTH BRONX TO PEER INTO THE FILTHY ORIFICE OF NEW YORK'S THRIVING PROSTITUTION INDUSTRY. HER DOCUMENTARY, RARELY SEEN OUTSIDE OF A FEW TV AIRINGS IN THE UK (AS WELL AS A BOOTLEGGED DVD-R THAT HAS BEEN CIRCULATING AMONGST PERVS LIKE MYSELF) PROVIDES A VERY DIVERSE, 1993-ERA VIEW OF THE BIG APPLE'S AMAZING SEXUAL MARKETPLACE.

THANKFULLY, KIDRON'S MOVIE IS FAR LESS JUDGMENTAL THAN THE MAJORITY OF DOCUMENTARIES ABOUT WHORES. HER GRITTY, CANDID FILM INTIMATELY COVERS NOT ONLY THE HARROWING JUNKIE LIFESTYLE OF THE STREET LEVEL HUSTLER/PROSTITUTE, BUT ALSO THE STRIPER, THE HIGH-PRICED CALL GIRL, THE CROSS-DRESSER, THE DOMINATRIX (THE SCENE WITH THE CHEESE GRATER IS NOTE-WORTHY), AND ALSO THE JOHNS THAT PAY FOR ALL THESE GENITAL-THEMED SERVICES.

INTERVIEWS ARE UTILISED, BUT SO TOO ARE CONCEALED CAMERAS AND NIGHT-TIME FILMING, WHICH ALLOW THE RATS OF THE SEX INDUSTRY TO SCURRY, SLEAZE AND SUCK AS THEY WOULD NORMALLY, LAYING BARE THE SEXUAL POLITICS OF THE URBAN CASH-FOR-GASH TRANSACTION.
—BOUGIE

LA FEMME OBJET

AKA "PROGRAMED FOR PLEASURE" (1980)
FRANCE. DIRECTED BY CLAUDE MULOT

BOUGIE
·2011·

CLAUDE MULOT (ALSO KNOWN UNDER THE PSEUDONYM OF FREDERIC LANSAC) FASHIONED A CAREER AS ONE OF THE GREATEST ADULT FILM AUTEURS DURING AN OUTSTANDING PERIOD OF QUALITY TRIPLE-X MOVIE MAKING IN FRANCE THAT TOOK PLACE BETWEEN 1975 AND 1981. KNOWN FOR HIS INVENTIVE SCRIPTS (USUALLY MELDING REAL-LIFE AND SCIENCE FICTION ELEMENTS), REMARKABLE CINEMATOGRAPHY, AND SUBVERSIVE LEFT-LEANING POLITICS, MULOT WAS BORN IN PARIS IN AUGUST OF 1942, AND DROWNED IN SAINT-TROPEZ ON OCTOBER 13TH, 1986 IN A SWIMMING ACCIDENT.

IN BETWEEN THEN MULOT CREATED A RESPECTABLE FILMOGRAPHY OF SOFTCORE AND HARDCORE SEX FEATURES. MOVIES SUCH AS 1975'S **PUSSY TALK**, 1976'S **A CHANGE OF PARTNERS**, 1977'S **LA GRANDE BAISE**, 1980'S **THE IMMORAL ONE**, AND 1980'S **LA FEMME OBJET**.

THE LATTER IS A QUIRKY LITTLE MORALITY TALE OF A SEX-ADDICTED SCI-FI AUTHOR NAMED NICOLAS, AN EMOTIONALLY STILTED PLAYBOY WHO IS COMPLETELY ADDICTED TO FORNICATION -- TO THE POINT WHERE HE IS DISPIRITEDLY DRILLING HIS DONG INTO EVERY AVAILABLE FEMALE NO MATTER WHAT ELSE SHE HAPPENS TO BE OCCUPIED WITH AT THE TIME. NEEDLESS TO SAY, A LONG LINE OF FUMING GIRLFRIENDS, SECRETARIES AND FEMALE CO-WORKERS TIRE OF THE CONSTANT HUMPAGE, AND TELL HIM WHERE HE CAN SHOVE HIS PERMANENT ERECTION.

IT'S A SAD REALISATION TO MAKE, COMING TO THE DIRE CONCLUSION THAT NO LIVING WOMAN ON EARTH CAN SATISFY YOU -- AND IN RESPONSE TO THAT, OUR BEARDED PROTAGONIST BUILDS A SECLUDED LABORATORY WHERE HE RESOLUTELY FASHIONS A REMOTE-CONTROLLED ANDROID REAL-DOLL NAMED KIM. KIM IS MUTE, AND IS PLAYED BY THE ASTONISHINGLY GORGEOUS MARILYN JESS. TOTALLY UNINHIBITED AND DESIGNED TO SATISFY, HER STACKED BOD HAS ABSOLUTELY NO TUSSLE KEEPING UP WITH THE AMOUNT OF TIMES PER DAY THAT NICOLAS NEEDS TO DRAIN HIS NUTSACK. IT TOTALLY SEEMS LIKE A PERFECT MATCH FOR BOTH NICOLAS AND THE MASTURBATING AUDIENCE WATCHING HIM -- BUT NOT SO FAST.

THE EXPERIMENT GOES WILDLY AWRY WHEN THE NUBILE BLONDE ROBOT DEVELOPS HER HER OWN PERSONALITY AND SEXUAL INTERESTS, AND DECIDES NOT TO OBEY THE FRANTIC COMMANDS OF HER CREATOR. NICOLAS SIMPLY CAN'T BRING HIMSELF TO KILL (UNPLUG?) KIM, BUT HIS LIBIDO CAN'T DEAL WITH THE LACK OF AVAILABLE HAIRDIE IN HIS MODERN PARISIAN CRIB, EITHER. TO THAT END, HE BUILDS ANOTHER SERVILE "FEMALE OBJECT" (A LOVELY BLACK ONE, WITH THE HOPE THAT IT WILL BE MORE SLAVE-LIKE) AS A REPLACEMENT.

> tsk!

BUT SLY KIM HAS PLANS OF HER OWN, AND NICOLAS HAS NO FLIPPIN' IDEA HOW POORLY HE HAS MISCALCULATED HER CONVICTION AND NEWFOUND POWER.

IT IS FASCINATING HOW SUCCESSFULLY MULOT LAYERS THE SUBJECT OF WOMEN'S LIBERATION INTO A PORN FILM GEARED TOWARDS MEN, AND THEN UNDERTONES

ILLUSTRATIONS BY BEN NEWMAN © 2011

IT WITH ELEMENTS OF COMPLICATED S+M MASTER/SERVANT DYNAMICS, RACE-RELATIONS, AND THE JOYLESS ROBOTIC NATURE THAT IS SEX DEVOID OF LOVE OR EVEN PASSION. THESE ARE SUBJECTS THAT MOST PORNOGRAPHERS WOULD BE SIMPLY AGHAST TO TACKLE FOR FEAR OF GETTING TOO LOFTY OR TURNING AN AUDIENCE OFF, BUT MULOT GLEEFULLY GRAPPLES WITH THEM BETWEEN CUMSHOTS. I ALSO LOVE HOW HE INCORPORATES A REMOTE-CONTROLLED R2D2 INTO SEVERAL FUCK SEQUENCES AS A WAY TO PLAYFULLY SPOTLIGHT THE ONGOING SEX-TOY THEME.

BELGIAN CINEMA SEWER CONTRIBUTOR DRIES VERMEULEN HAD A VERY INTERESTING TAKE ON THIS UNUSUAL AND MOSTLY FORGOTTEN EURO ADULT CLASSIC THAT I'D LOVE FOR YOU TO SEE, SO I'M GOING TO PASS YOU OFF TO HIM NOW TO FINISH THIS REVIEW. TAKE IT AWAY, DRIES:

★★★★★★★☆

"ORIGINATING FROM AN INTELLIGENT AND LITERATE SCRIPT THAT PROVES A PARTICULARLY CRUEL SPIN ON THE PYGMALION MYTH WITH A DASH OF FRANKENSTEIN, LA FEMME OBJET OFFERS AN INCISIVE CRITIQUE ON THE PORNOGRAPHIC REPRESENTATION OF MEN (AS VIRILE AND IRRESISTIBLE) AND WOMEN (AS AVAILABLE AND ACCOMMODATING) BY EXPANDING UPON THESE STEREOTYPES AND TAKING THEM TO GROTESQUE EXTREMES. FRUSTRATED BY THE GENRE'S LIMITATIONS, MULOT PROCEEDED TO GIVE ADULT AUDIENCES 'EXACTLY WHAT THEY WANTED'."

"STAYING TRUE TO THE FUCK FILM FORM, ALBEIT WITH OFTEN INTENTIONALLY JOYLESS ENCOUNTERS, MULOT'S EXPLICIT TESTAMENT FALLS INTO THAT SMALL NICHE OF PORNOGRAPHIC PICTURES THAT USE THE TOOLS OF THEIR TRADE TO QUESTION THEIR OWN NATURE, MOVIES THAT IN RETROSPECT HAVE ME WONDER JUST HOW THE AVERAGE ADULT AUDIENCE RESPONDED TO THEM AT THE TIME OF THEIR FIRST RELEASE. BY THEIR ABERRANT IDEOLOGY, MOST OF THESE FILMS ULTIMATELY ACQUIRE CULT STATUS. STEPHEN SAYADIAN'S EQUALLY UNIQUE CAFE FLESH WOULD BE ANOTHER GOOD EXAMPLE OF SUCH IDIOSYNCRASY. BOTH MOVIES SHARE A STARK BLACK AND WHITE CONTRAST BETWEEN UNSATISFYING "ENFORCED" SEXUAL PERFORMANCE AND THE FULFILMENT OF ITS LOVING "HUMANE COUNTERPART.""

"WITHOUT DIALOG FOR BENEFIT, MARILYN JESS ACHIEVES AMAZING ELOQUENCE IN THE EVOLUTION OF BLANK-EYED "LOVE DOLL" TO EROTICALLY AUTONOMOUS LIBERATED WOMAN, A "MONSTER" TO THE MANIPULATIVE NICOLAS. CONTRARY TO CAFE FLESH, SEVERAL SEX SCENES HERE ARE INDEED PLAYED FOR POWERFUL EROTIC EFFECT (FURTHER ENHANCED BY VETERAN CAMERAMAN FRANCOIS ABOUT'S EXQUISITELY COLORFUL, BRIGHTLY LIT CINEMATOGRAPHY) AS WOMEN TAKE CHARGE, A MOVE MULOT PERHAPS FELT WAS NECESSARY IF PORN WAS TO SURVIVE AS A GENRE AND AN ART FORM."

BOUGIE + VERMEULEN © 2011 ☆

NICOLAS CREATES (AND THEN GROPES) NEW LIFE

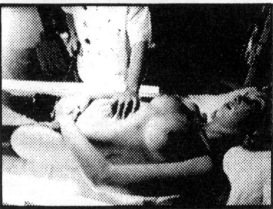

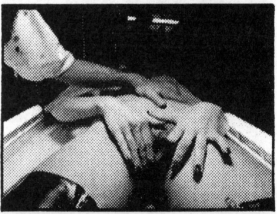

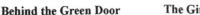

Behind the Green Door
1 part midori melon liquor
1 part amaretto almond liquor
1 part 7-up
shake, strain into glass

Debbie Does Drambuie
1 part drambuie
1 part blue kool-aid
a splash of southern comfort
a splash of soda water
shake, strain into glass
garnish with two cherries

The Bob Chinn
2 parts pineapple juice
1 part malibu
1 part tonic water
a splash of agave syrup
shake and pour over ice
garnish with a twist of lemon

The Ginger Lynn
2 parts ginger ale
1 part white rum
a splash of southern comfort
a drizzle of honey
1 stick of fresh ginger for garnish

The Crannie Sprinkle
2 parts cranberry juice
1 part cointreau
a splash of apple juice
whipped cream on top
garnish with rainbow sprinkles

The Vanessa Del Rio
1 part blue curacao
1 tsp kirschwasser cherry brandy
1 part dr pepper
3 oz crushed passion fruit pulp
crushed ice

The Long Jeanne Silver
1 part silver patrón tequilla
a splash of lemon juice
a lemon twist
follow with an "absolut screw" as a chaser
(a screwdriver made with absolut brand vodka)

The Tabooze
1 part twinings earl grey tea
1 part triple sec
1 part tequila
1 part gin
1 part vodka
1 part coca-cola
serve on ice
share with a sibling

The Waterpower
2 parts canfield's chocolate soda
1 part vodka
splash of grenadine
serve on ice with a straw
make a toast to the enema bandit
before consuming

The Carter Stevens
1 part wild turkey 101
1 part tequila
1 part bacardi 151 rum
make sure the parts are layered
Set on fire, blow it out, serve

The Jamie Gillis
1 part dry vermouth
1 part gin
1 part sailor jerry's spiced rum
a splash of Angostura bitters
a liberal squeeze of an orange
shake, serve in a martini glass
serve with a stick of beef jerky
and two jalapeno stuffed olives

Special thanks to Jeanne Silver and her 17 years of experience
tending bar. The suggestions were really helpful.

CINEMA SEWER'S 7 FAVOURITE HELICOPTER CRASHES

THE OTHER DAY I WAS WORKING IN VIDEOMATICA, THE DVD STORE I WORK IN THAT SPECIALIZES IN CULT/FOREIGN/ARTHOUSE/AWESOME MOVIES, AND MY BOSS BRIAN ASKED WHY EVERY TIME HE CAME IN, WAS I PLAYING A FILM THAT HAD HELICOPTERS CRASHING. I DIDN'T REALIZED THAT I HAD, BUT IT GOT ME THINKING ABOUT HOW NOTHING SAYS "KICK ASS ACTION SCENES" LIKE A GOOD HELICOPTER CRASH. THERE IS SOMETHING ABOUT THOSE SPINNING BLADES THAT JUST SCREAMS "OH SHIT, THIS IS DANGEROUS!", AND GETS PULSES POUNDING. SO SPIN YOUR ROTORS AND PULL UP YOUR SOCKS, BECAUSE HERE'S MY PICKS FOR THE MOST ENTERTAINING HELICOPTER CRASHES IN FILM HISTORY.

BEFORE WE STRAP OURSELVES IN AND BEGIN THOUGH, A NOTE: SURE, THERE ARE A GREAT MANY MODERN HELICOPTER CRASH SCENES THAT HAVE BIGGER FIREBALLS AND WILDER NAUSEA-INDUCING CAMERA ANGLES, BUT THEY'RE ALSO MOSTLY DONE (AND OBVIOUSLY SO) ENTIRELY IN CGI, AND THEREFORE AREN'T NEARLY AS INTERESTING OR EXCITING IN MY OPINION. IN-CAMERA EFFECTS AND EXCELLENT WORK DONE WITH MINIATURES WERE GIVEN BIG BONUS POINTS IN MY RANKING OF THESE SCENES.

7. ATTACK OF THE KILLER TOMATOES (1978)
IT'S A SCENE THAT PROVIDES A FINE AND TELLING EXAMPLE OF THE INGENUITY OF LOW-BUDGET FILM-MAKERS BACK IN THE 1970S. IF SOMETHING UNFORESEEN HAPPENS, YOU KNOW -- LIKE A HELICOPTER CRASHING RIGHT INTO A FIELD ON-CAMERA WHILE YOU'RE FILMING -- HEY, JUST WRITE IT INTO THE SCENE AND HAVE THE ACTORS REACT TO IT! <u>LOVE IT</u>. THE ACCIDENTAL CRASH OF A RENTED HELICOPTER VALUED AT OVER $60,000 USED UP MORE OF THE BUDGET THAN EVERY OTHER ASPECT OF THE FILM COMBINED, AND THE PILOT AND ACTORS IN THE SCENE LUCKILY ESCAPED WITH ONLY MINOR INJURIES. THIS WAS, OF COURSE, VERY UNLIKE THE RESULT OF A SIMILAR ACCIDENT THAT TOOK PLACE DURING THE FILMING OF TWILIGHT ZONE: THE MOVIE BY JOHN LANDIS FIVE YEARS LATER. THAT ON-SET STUNT, WHICH WAS RECKLESSLY PLANNED AND NEEDLESSLY DANGEROUS FOR CAST AND CREW, WOULD SADLY CLAIM THREE ACTORS' LIVES.

6. BROKEN ARROW (1996)
I'M REALLY NOT A BIG FAN OF THIS MOVIE FOR THE MOST PART, AS I THINK JOHN WOO WAS SORT OF WASTED AFTER LEAVING HONG KONG DURING HIS CHOW YUN FAT FILLED HEYDAY. OF THESE AMERICAN-MADE ACTION MOVIES, HARD TARGET AND FACE-OFF ARE FAR MORE SATISFYING (AND BROKEN ARROW IS MOSTLY JUST ANNOYING) BUT EVEN WOO'S LESSER FILMS ALWAYS HAVE SOMETHING WORTH GETTING TICKLED ABOUT. IN THIS CASE, IT'S TOTALLY THAT PART WHERE JOHN TRAVOLTA'S CHARACTER SETS OFF A MASSIVE BOMB THAT THEN TAKES A HELICOPTER RIGHT OUT OF THE SKY, SENDING IT TO THE RUMBLING DESERT FLOOR IN A CRAZY BLAZE OF DESTRUCTION. I THINK IT'S THE WAY IT UNCEREMONIOUSLY SLAMS DOWN NOSE-FIRST THAT I LOVE SO MUCH. TRAVOLTA'S CHARACTER'S REACTION OF "GAWD-DAUY-UM! WHOTTA RUSH! WOO!" PRETTY MUCH SUMS UP MY FEELINGS AS WELL.

5. BLUE THUNDER (1983)
OF COURSE A MOVIE THAT IS ENTIRELY ABOUT THE MOST BADASS FLYING GUNSHIP KNOWN TO MAN IS GOING TO HAVE A KICK-ASS HELICOPTER EXPLOSION SCENE. IT HAD TO, RIGHT? AND NOT ONLY THAT, BUT BLUE THUNDER HAS ONE THE BEST HELICOPTER CHASE SCENES AS TWO COPTERS ZOOM (MOSTLY IN REALLY COOL POV ARIEL SHOTS) AROUND THE STREETS OF LOS ANGELES, NAILING SKY SCRAPERS WITH HEAT-SEEKING MISSILES UNTIL BLUE THUNDER DOES A TOTALLY IMPOSSIBLE LOOP-DE-LOOP MANOEUVRE TO GET THE MUCH NEEDED UPPER HAND. THIS ALLOWS PILOT ROY SCHEIDER TO BLOW THE PUPPYFUCK OUT OF THE SPEEDY LITTLE COPTER ON HIS BUTT. BURNING WRECKAGE RAINS ALL OVER THE CITY OF ANGELS LIKE 40 POUND BLACK AND ORANGE SLOWFLAKES OF DEATH, AND THAT IS WHEN I ALWAYS MUTTER SOMETHING LIKE "NOW THAT'S HOW YOU FUCKIN' DO IT" BEFORE QUIETLY LAUGHING TO MYSELF. THE MOVIE HAD REAL HELICOPTERS, AND ALSO UTILIZED AMAZINGLY REALISTIC RADIO-CONTROLLED FLYING MODELS BUILT BY FAMED MODEL BUILDER, GREGORY JEIN, WHO PREVIOUSLY TO THIS WORKED ON THE ORIGINAL STAR TREK MOVIE AND CLOSE ENCOUNTERS OF THE THIRD KIND.

4. SKYFALL (2012)
USING AN EXPLODING ENGLISH CASTLE TO TAKE OUT AN IMPOSING HELICOPTER GUNSHIP IS PRETTY BALLS-OUT COOL, AND THE EXECUTION ON THE EFFECT IS REALLY SOMETHING SPECIAL IN THIS RECENT JAMES BOND FEATURE. THE EXPLOSION THAT RESULTS FROM THE MATING OF THESE TWO UNLIKELY LOVERS IS SO HUGE AND DEEPLY FELT RIGHT DOWN UNDER ONE'S LABIAS/SCROTUM (ESPECIALLY WHEN THEY HAVE THAT DOLBY STEREO SOUND TURNED UP), THAT I CAN'T REMEMBER FEELING A MORE IMPRESSIVE KA-BOOM IN ANY OF MY RECENT THEATER GOING EXPERIENCES. WHAT A GREAT WAY TO END THE BEST BOND FILM IN NEARLY 30 YEARS. TOTALLY GOOD SHIT!

CLIFFHANGER (1993)

3. STONE COLD (1991)
FOOTBALL STAR TURNED ACTION HERO BRIAN BOSWORTH SOMEHOW FIGURED OUT HOW TO BE TOTALLY RAD IN THIS MOVIE DIRECTED BY TALENTED STUNTMAN, CRAIG R. BAXLEY. DEEP UNDERCOVER TO INFILTRATE A BIKER GANG RUN BY A SCENE-STEALING LANCE HENRIKSEN, 'THE BOS' (WITH HIS TRADEMARK MULLET IN FULL RESPLENDENCE) EVENTUALLY SQUARES OFF AGAINST THE INSANE CRIMINAL IN THE HALLWAYS AND ATRIUM OF THE LOCAL COURTHOUSE. HERE ONE OF LANCE'S GOONS GUNS IT ON HIS HARLEY, ONLY TO BE SHOT RIGHT OUT OF THE SADDLE BY BRIAN, WHICH SENDS THE MOTORBIKE RIGHT OUT THE WIDOW AT THE END OF THE HALLWAY, LIKE A RIDERLESS MISSILE DESIGNED TO TAKE OUT NEARBY CHOPPERS. WHICH IT DOES, IN A TOTALLY JAW-DROPPING SCENE WHICH ONLY ENDS WHEN THE FLAMING WRECKAGE NONE-TOO-DELICATELY COVERS THE CARS IN THE COURTHOUSE PARKING LOT BELOW.

2. RAMBO III (1988)
THIS IS SUCH AN ODD MOVIE BECAUSE IT WAS MADE AS AMERICAN CONFLICT PROPAGANDA AT A TIME WHEN THE U.S. CONSIDERED THE MUJAHIDEEN IN AFGHANISTAN AS "NOBLE FREEDOM FIGHTERS" BECAUSE THEY WERE GOING AT IT WITH THOSE MEAN OL' RUSKIES. IT'S TOTALLY WORTH A WATCH IF YOU WANNA SEE RAMBO BEING SUPER-PALS AND FIGHTING ELBOW-TO-ELBOW WITH VIOLENT RELIGIOUS EXTREMISTS WHO ONLY A FEW YEARS LATER STARTED CALLING THEMSELVES THE TALIBAN. DEDICATING A PATRIOTIC AMERICAN ACTION FILM TO SAID TERRORISTS AND DEPICTING THEM AS BEING ALL ABOUT HONOUR, FREEDOM, AND RESPECT FOR WOMEN AND CHILDREN (IT'S LIKE IF THE TALIBAN EXISTED IN A BIZARRE NORMAN ROCKWELL PAINTING) IS WONKY ENOUGH, BUT THE PART OF THE MOVIE THAT MADE ME LAUGH THE HARDEST WAS WHEN JOHN RAMBO HOPS IN A TANK AND PLAYS CHICKEN WITH... A RUSSIAN HELICOPTER!? THAT'S RIGHT, A THING THAT CAN GO UP AND DOWN AND ALL AROUND IN THE SKY. INSTEAD OF DOING ANY OF THAT IT FLIES RIGHT AT HIM IN HIS TANK, 5 FEET OFF THE GROUND AND PREDICTABLY DOESN'T FARE WELL IN THE HEAD-ON HIGH-SPEED COLLISION. WTF!? PURE CHEST-PUMPING PATHETICALLY PATRIOTIC AWESOMENESS.

1. CLIFFHANGER (1993)
SLY STALLONE TAKES UP THE TOP TWO SPOTS, BUT I DEFY YOU TO ARGUE HIS CINEMATIC HELICOPTER-DESTRUCTION DOMINANCE! IN THIS EXAMPLE, HE'S NOT LUCKY ENOUGH TO BE IN A TANK, SO HE JUST SAYS FUCK IT AND BRINGS DOWN A HELICOPTER BY CLIPPING ITS TOW CABLE TO THE SIDE OF A CLIFF, AND THEN JUMPING ABOARD SO THAT HE CAN BEAT THE BAD GUY (JOHN LITHGOW) SENSELESS. HE DOES ALL THAT BEFORE DIVING BACK ONTO THE CLIFF AND SENDING THE HELICOPTER TO LAND IN THE VALLEY BELOW WITH A MIGHTY KA-FOOFLE, NOT UNLIKE A LIVE ACTION ROADRUNNER CARTOON. THE WAY THIS INSANE STUNT IS FILMED, WITH LIFE-SIZED STUFF MESHING SEAMLESSLY WITH AMAZING "BIGGATURE" MODELS THAT ARE FILMED IN SLOW MOTION WITH ONE OF THOSE HIGH SPEED SUPER CAMERAS, IS SIMPLY A <u>DELIGHT</u>.

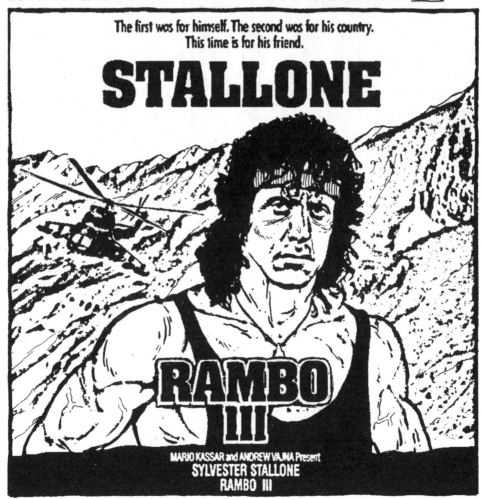

RAISING A PET GIRL (2009. JAPAN V & R PRODUCTS)

AS THIS JAPANESE PORN RELEASE OPENS, THE CAMERA PANS ACROSS A SERIES OF CAGES IN WHICH NAKED GIRLS LAY. THEY STARE BLANKLY, BITE AT THE BARS, PLAY WITH THE PAPER LINER, AND GET STUPIDLY EXCITED WHEN A COUPLE OF CLOTHED GUYS ENTER THE ROOM AND DISCUSS A TRANSACTION WHICH WILL END WITH ONE OF THE YOUNG LADIES BEING TAKEN TO A NEW HOME.

THIS ISN'T YOUR TYPICAL "CAGED WOMEN" BONDAGE S AND M MOVIE. IN FACT, THERE IS NOTHING TYPICAL ABOUT THIS THING WHATSOEVER. I EVEN HESITATE TO CALL IT PORN, SINCE IT IS WORDLESS, AND DOESN'T SEEM BOTHERED WHATSOEVER WITH TURNING THE AUDIENCE ON. THESE PERFORMERS ARE MAXING OUT THEIR ACTING SKILLS AS THEY -- WITHOUT A HINT OF CONCERN WITH LOOKING UNFEMININE OR SILLY -- PRETEND TO HAVE MENTAL LEVELS NO MORE ADVANCED THAN A DOG, CAT OR HAMSTER. THEY NEVER SMIRK, SPEAK, OR BREAK CHARACTER. THEY GIVE 100% OF THEMSELVES TO THE PART AS THEY OCCASIONALLY NIP, SEEM SAD AND LONELY WHEN LEFT ALONE, GET EASILY DISTRACTED AND ACT GOOFY IN THAT WAY THAT PLAYFUL ANIMALS DO.

AFTER PICKING OUT A VERY CUTE YOUNG WOMAN AND TAKING HER HOME, WE'RE INTRODUCED TO AN ELABORATE CAGE SET UP. IT'S PINK AND WHITE AND HAS AN 8 FOOT HIGH CEILING, A HUMAN SIZED LITTER TRAY, A BLANKET, PLASTIC BOWLS WITH FOOD AND WATER IN THEM, A RUBBER BALL, AND A STUFFED TOY.

NOW, IF THIS WERE A NORTH AMERICAN-MADE XXX DVD, THE GIRL'S OWNER WOULD IMMEDIATELY EXERT HIS CONTROL, AND HE'D FUCK HER. THE CONCEPT AND PRETENCE ESTABLISHED WOULD BE UNCEREMONIOUSLY TOSSED OUT THE WINDOW, AND WE'D JACK/JILL OFF. BUT NOT HERE, WHERE THE JAPANESE PRODUCERS AT V & R PRODUCTS MILK THIS ONE BUT GOOD. HE TREATS HER EXACTLY HOW A LOVING PET OWNER WOULD TREAT A SHOW ANIMAL; HE COMBS HER HAIR, REMOVES HER EYE-BOOGERS, MAKES SURE HER COLLAR ISN'T TOO TIGHT, CHECKS HER TEETH AND FINGERNAILS, PETS HER, AND CLINICALLY EXAMINES HER (DIGITALLY CENSORED) GENITALS. ALL OF THIS IS PORTRAYED WITH A DECIDEDLY UNEROTIC BENT, WITH TOTAL CHARACTER IMMERSION BEING THE ENDGAME. THAT REALISM IS FURTHER DEMONSTRATED WHEN WE WITNESS THE USE OF THE LITTER BOX, A ROUSING GAME OF "BITE THE STUFFED TOY", SLEEPING, EATING, AND A BANANA ON A STRING DROPPED FROM THE CEILING OF THE CAGE.

THAT SAID, EVENTUALLY (40 MIN. IN!) THE DIRECTOR GIVES US A SLIGHT BREAK, AND ALLOWS HIS CHARACTERS TO DO IT. YES, THE OWNER OF THE PET GIRL GETS THE IDEA IN THE MIDDLE OF THE NIGHT THAT IF HE STICKS HIS COCK THROUGH THE BARS OF HER CAGE, THE GIRL WILL HUNGRILY SUCK HIM OFF AS HE FUCKS HER FACE. HOWEVER, WITH THE AMOUNT OF CHARACTER BUILDING THAT HAS GONE ON, WHAT WOULD NORMALLY BE A TYPICAL PORN FILM BLOW JOB HAS NOW BECOME SOMETHING UTTERLY PERVERSE. AND WHEN THE MAN FINALLY SHOOTS OFF IN HER MOUTH, HE QUICKLY SHOVES HIS FINGERS IN AND UNROMANTICALLY SCOOPS THE GUNK OUT, AS ONE WOULD WHEN THEIR DOG HAS EATEN SOMETHING IT WASN'T SUPPOSED TO. AS THE SEMEN AND SPIT DRIP DOWN HER DUMB FACE, SHE LOOKS UTTERLY BAFFLED.

ANOTHER EQUALLY COMPELLING SEQUENCE IN THIS STRANGE ADULT MOVIE IS WHEN A

MALE "PET" IS INTRODUCED IN A BID TO MATE THE FEMALE. IT'S ACTUALLY A LITTLE SCARY. THIS EXUBERANT MALE IS FAR MORE AGGRESSIVE (NOT TO MENTION MORE MESSY) THAN SHE IS, AND GENERALLY ASSERTS HIS DOMINANCE OVER HER AFTER THE TWO ARE LOCKED IN THE CAGE TOGETHER. CONTINUE TO KEEP IN MIND THAT THIS IS NOT ANYTHING RELATED TO A HUMAN SEXUAL-STYLE DOMINANCE, HOWEVER. WE'RE RIGHT BACK INTO EXTREME PET REALISM MODE AGAIN, A FACT MANIFESTED WHEN WE WITNESS HIM EAT ALL HER FOOD AND THEN TAKE A SHIT (I MEAN _ACTUALLY_ SHIT) IN HER LITTER BOX. WHEN SHE GINGERLY GOES OVER AND SNIFFS THE PILE OF CRAP AFTER HE'S GONE TO SLEEP, I KNEW WE WERE IN SOME WEIRD AND PREVIOUSLY UNSEEN TERRITORY, HERE. I REALIZED THAT THERE WAS SOMETHING BEING SAID IN THIS FILM WITH NO WORDS.

THANK YOU ONCE AGAIN, JAPAN! THANK YOU FOR SHOWING US THAT NOT EVERYTHING HAS BEEN DONE TO DEATH! THANK YOU FOR RAISING A PET GIRL!

WORDS: R. BOUGIE
ART: BEN NEWMAN

DOMME DELUISE MEETS LONG DONG DELUISE.

SLUT.

hee hee

WAX

FROM THE TALENTED PEN OF BRANDON GRAHAM GO TO: ROYALBOILER.WORDPRESS.COM

HEAT OF THE MOMENT (1983)

OH YEAH, SOCK IT TO ME, SUGAR!

GIGGLING MARIA TORTUGA AND JENNIFER WEST STEAL A CUTE YELLOW CONVERTIBLE JEEP (LIKE THE ONE DAISY DUKE DROVE ON THE DUKES OF HAZZARD) FROM JOHN HOLMES, AND BOOT AROUND SUNNY SOUTHERN CALIFORNIA BACK ROADS WHILE TOPLESS AND RUBBING THEIR GLISTENING LABIAL FOLDS. BEFORE LONG THEY PICK UP A HUNKY DOUCHE (MARC WALLICE) WHOSE 10 SPEED HAS GIVEN OUT ON HIM. THE FUN-LOVIN' GALS GET HIM TO SUCK THEIR TWATS IN RETURN FOR A LIFT INTO TOWN, AND MARC EVEN GETS A VIGOROUS TONGUE MASSAGE ON HIS NUTS AND TAINT BEFORE PLOWING HIS ENGORGED EIGHT INCH DONG-MEAT INTO SPLAYED GULLY. NOT A BAD TRADE, EXCEPT AFTER HE BUSTS A NUT THEY CHUCK HIM OUT ON HIS ASS AND TAKE OFF WITH HIS PANTS.

OTHER HIGHLIGHTS: JOHN HOLMES FUCKING A GIRL WITH HIS BIG TOE (??), AN AMAZING SUNBURST-DESIGN RUG IN THE MIDDLE OF A GREEN CARPETED ROOM, A HOT HONEY WITH A SWEET HEADBAND, AND HOLMES PUMPING A FORTY-SOMETHING PAT MANNING FROM BEHIND WITH HIS FAT CROTCH ROCKET, WHILE FILLING HER PANTING, GASPING MOUTH FROM THE FRONT WITH HIS GRUBBY JUNKIE FINGERS.

HEAT OF THE MOMENT IS VIRTUALLY PLOTLESS, POORLY PACED, AND COATED WITH VAPID ELEVATOR MUZAK IN PLACE OF A SOUNDTRACK, AND NO, IT UNFORTUNATELY DOESN'T FEATURE THE SONG (BY BRITISH SUPERGROUP ASIA) THAT IT WAS CLEARLY NAMED FOR. IT'S ALSO ODDLY BLANK IN TERMS OF ANY FORM OF PRODUCTION OR DIRECTORIAL CREDITS, WHICH NEVER BODES WELL.

IT IS, HOWEVER A 59-MINUTE DIRTY MOVIE COMPETENTLY SHOT ON 35MM STOCK WITH LOTS OF LUSH OUTDOOR SEQUENCES. YOU ALSO GET TO SEE ANAL QUEEN MISTY DAWN A FEW YEARS BEFORE SHE MARRIED JOHN HOLMES, NOT TO MENTION SCUMBAG MARC WALLICE PERFORMS HERE YEARS BEFORE HE CONTRACTED HIV, FAKED DNA AIDS TESTS, AND INFECTED 6 FEMALE CO-STARS WITH THE VIRUS. THE UNFORTUNATE VICTIMS WERE KIMBERLY JADE, BROOKE ASHLEY, JORDAN MCKNIGHT, NENA CHERRY, TRICIA DEVEREAUX, AND FRENCH PERFORMER DELFIN.

ROLLING VENGEANCE ·1987· CANADA

REVIEW BY PAUL CORUPE www.canuxsploitation.com

EXPLOITATION FILMS HAVE ALWAYS LATCHED ON TO POP CULTURE TRENDS TO TURN A QUICK BUCK, BUT FEW WOULD HAVE GUESSED THAT THE MAINSTREAM'S BRIEF FASCINATION WITH THE MONSTER TRUCK PHENOMENON IN THE MID-1980S WOULD WARRANT ANY SORT OF CINEMATIC RECORD. THE AUTOMOTIVE WORLD'S EQUIVALENT OF PROFESSIONAL WRESTLING, MONSTER TRUCKS ENJOYED INCREDIBLE POPULARITY AT THE TIME, WITH TOURING SHOWS OF CONVENTIONAL PICK-UP TRUCKS TRICKED OUT WITH GIGANTIC TRACTOR TIRES AND SUSPENSION SYSTEMS THAT ALLOWED THEM TO DRIVE OVERTOP OF JUNKED FAMILY SEDANS. DRAWING ON THE TIMELY POPULARITY OF THE SPORT, ROLLING VENGEANCE OFFERS THE SAME LOWBROW DELIGHTS AS THE REAL LIVE EVENTS, OFFERING VIEWERS A SIMPLISTIC REVENGE STORY THAT PRIZES TWISTED METAL ABOVE ALL ELSE.

IT'S A HIGH OCTANE MIX OF SEX, BOOZE AND VEHICULAR MAYHEM, BUT IT'S STILL STRONGLY PACED, AND HEAVY ON THE CAR-CRUNCHING CARNAGE, WHICH IS ALL ANYONE COULD ASK FOR IN A FILM THAT PROUDLY BILLS ITSELF AS COMPLETELY DESTROYING MORE THAN 65 VEHICLES DURING PRODUCTION. DIRECTOR STEVEN STERN, AN AMERICAN VETERAN OF THE TV MOVIE-OF-THE-WEEK SCHOOL NAVIGATES THE BARELY-THERE PLOT TO DELIVER A PARADE OF GRATUITOUS BUT ALWAYS FREE-SPIRITED ACTION SEQUENCES THAT ARE WHOLLY APPROPRIATE FOR THE FILM'S DECIDEDLY LOWBROW TONE. IT'S LIKE AN R-RATED EPISODE OF **THE DUKES OF HAZZARD** WHERE ROSCO GETS A LITTLE TOO FREE WITH DAISY, AND BO REPEATEDLY RUNS HIM OVER WITH A TRACTOR, BUT THERE IS STILL A FREEZE-FRAME OF EVERYONE LAUGHING AT THE END.

DON MICHAEL PAUL AND LISA HOWARD SHARE THE LIMELIGHT WITH A GIANT 4-WHEELED METAL MONSTER

OBVIOUSLY, THE ONLY REASON ANYONE WOULD WANT TO CHECK OUT ROLLING VENGEANCE IS THE VIGILANTE TRUCK ITSELF, SO STERN DOESN'T SKIMP ON LEERING SHOTS OF THE

MECHANIZED KILLER, MORE OF A SHEET METAL TANK ON ENORMOUS WHEELS THAN ANYTHING THAT ACTUALLY RESEMBLES A REAL VEHICLE, IT'S AN ADMITTEDLY IMPRESSIVE SIGHT AS IT BARRELS DOWN ON THE BACKWOODS BULLIES, OCCASIONALLY SWITCHING TO POV CAMERA WORK AS THE TRUCK SLAMS INTO CARS, BUILDINGS, AND ANYTHING ELSE THAT GETS IN ITS WAY.

THE FILM ALSO BENEFITS FROM BETTER-THAN-EXPECTED ACTING. LAWRENCE DANE LENDS A TOUCH OF CANADIAN CLASS TO THE FILM AS AN OUTRAGED TRUCKER PATRIARCH NAMED BIG JOE, WHILE FELLOW CANADIANS SUSAN HOGAN AND LISA HOWARD BRING UP THE REAR WITH SURPRISINGLY AUTHENTIC PORTRAYALS. STILL, IT'S THE LEATHER-CLAD NED BEATTY WHO REALLY STEALS THIS SHOW, OFFERING UP HIS BEST CORRUPT BOSS HOGG IMPRESSION. HE'S CLEARLY HAVING WAY TOO MUCH FUN IN THE ROLE, MAKING OBSCENE JOKES, DESPERATELY PRAYING TO GOD FOR REVENGE, AND SLINGING MASHED POTATOES AT HIS UTTERLY UNDISTINGUISHABLE BUMPKIN BROOD, ALL OF WHOM SPORT NICKNAMES LIKE FINGER, HAIR LIP AND MOON MAN.

SHOT IN 1987 (THE LAST YEAR OF THE TAX SHELTERS) ROLLING VENGEANCE FEATURES SOME FINE LOCATION WORK IN THE CORNFIELDS AND RURAL ROUTES OF ONTARIO, BUT IT MAKES LITTLE REFERENCE TO ITS CANADIAN ORIGINS. THAT'S PERFECTLY UNDERSTANDABLE, THOUGH. AFTER ALL, IF YOU WERE MAKING A FILM ON A SUBJECT AS UNASHAMEDLY AMERICAN AS MONSTER TRUCKING, WOULDN'T YOU WANT IT TO HAVE AS MUCH COMMERCIAL APPEAL FOR THE HEARTLAND AS POSSIBLE?

REGARDLESS OF ITS FAILURE AS A NATIONAL ARTIFACT OF CANADIANA, ROLLING VENGEANCE IS STILL ONE OF THE BETTER CANADIAN B-MOVIES OF THE DECADE, DELIVERING MORE THAN ITS SHARE OF METAL-CRUNCHING, WINDSHIELD-POPPING, EXHAUST-BILLOWING THRILLS.

FATHOM (1967 Dir: Leslie Martinson)

TAGLINE: "THE WORLD'S MOST UNCOVERED UNDERCOVER AGENT!"

THIS SHOULD HAVE BEEN TITLED "RAQUEL WELCH IN A TINY GREEN BIKINI", BECAUSE THAT'S HOW THEY MARKETED IT, AND IT'S THE MAIN REASON TO SIT THROUGH IT. FATHOM IS A LIGHTHEARTED 1960S SPY-SPOOF PICTURE, A TRIED AND TRUE FORMULA THAT WAS SET IN STONE BY MATT HELM LONG BEFORE AUSTIN POWERS EVER APPEARED. YUP, IT'S ALL HERE: AN ESPIONAGE-PACKED RECOVERY MISSION FOR SOME VALUABLE STOLEN THINGAMAJIG, HALF-HEARTED ATTEMPTS TO DERIVE SUSPENSE BY MAKING THE AUDIENCE WONDER WHO THE HEROES AND VILLAINS ARE (AS THEY WAX COVERT ABOUT THEIR TRUE MOTIVES), A FEW ATTEMPTS AT HUMOUR, SOME WITTY DIALOG, MEGA-SEXY FOXES WITH PERFECT HAIR AND MAKEUP, AND A SPRINKLING OF ACTION SCENES.

RAQUEL PLAYS FATHOM, A SKYDIVING DENTAL ASSISTANT ON VACATION IN SPAIN. AFTER ONE SUCH BIKINI-CLAD LEAP INTO THE ABYSS, SHE'S GIVEN A RIDE BY A DUDE WHO TAKES HER TO H.A.D.E.S. HEADQUARTERS — A TOP SECRET GROUP OF BRITS THAT WANT OUR GAL TO PARACHUTE INTO THE BAD GUYS' HIDEOUT AND ACTIVATE A TRANSMITTER DEVICE. THEY WON'T TRAIN OR PREPARE HER IN ANY WAY FOR THIS DANGEROUS MISSION, BECAUSE THE PLAN IS THAT SINCE SHE'S A HOTTIE, SHE CAN JUST PLAY DUMB AND THE SCUMBAGS WILL JUST LET HER GO INSTEAD OF RAPING HER AND FEEDING HER LOVELY CORPSE TO THEIR DOGS. NEEDLESS TO SAY, NOTHING GOES AS PLANNED.

IT'S NOT THAT FUNNY, NOR IS IT ALL THAT THRILLING, BUT I DID ENJOY FATHOM, AND THERE ARE SOME PRETTY ENTERTAINING HIGHLIGHTS IN THIS GENIAL LITTLE ROMP. RAQUEL TRAPPED IN A SPANISH BULL RING IN A RED DRESS WHILE AN ENRAGED BULL TRIES TO SNUFF HER IS ONE (THIS SCENE LOOKED GENUINELY DANGEROUS FOR THE STUNT PEOPLE), AND THE EXTENSIVE BREATHTAKING TECHNICOLOR AERIAL PHOTOGRAPHY OF THE SPANISH LOCATIONS IS ANOTHER.

20th CENTURY-FOX presents

TONY FRANCIOSA

RAQUEL WELCH AS

Fathom

CINEMASCOPE · COLOR by DELUXE

UNDERAPPRECIATED FUCK STARS:
CHLOE CAMILLA
MISS SUPERSEX

"IF I COULD TELL PEOPLE THAT I HAVE AN EXTREMELY WELL PAYING JOB THAT I LOVE, THAT CHALLENGES AND INTERESTS ME, WHERE I GET TREATED WITH RESPECT, GET TO SET MY OWN BOUNDARIES, CHOOSE MY OWN WORKING HOURS, AND HAVE SO MUCH FUN, THEY WOULD CONGRATULATE ME! BUT AS SOON AS THEY KNOW IT'S ANY FORM OF SEX FOR MONEY (BECAUSE I THINK THIS CAN BE TRUE FOR ESCORTS AND OTHER FORMS OF SEX WORKERS AS WELL AS PORN PERFORMERS), THEY FIND IT IMPOSSIBLE TO BELIEVE."

CHLOE IS ONE OF MY FAVE CURRENT SEX PERFORMERS, AND IS INFAMOUS FOR THE MOST INCREDIBLE ONSCREEN FEMALE ORGASMS THE INDUSTRY HAS **EVER** SEEN.

CINEMA SEWER READER'S POLL:
WHAT IS THE BEST AMERICAN-MADE 1990s ACTION FILM?

150 CINEMA SEWER READERS RESPONDED TO THIS QUESTION ASKED IN 2014, AND HERE ARE THE RESULTS IN ORDER:

1. STONE COLD
2. TERMINATOR 2
3. HARD TARGET
4. LONG KISS GOODNIGHT
5. STARSHIP TROOPERS
6. TRUE ROMANCE
7. CLIFFHANGER
8. THE MATRIX
9. FACE/OFF
10. THE LAST BOY SCOUT

I DON'T CONSIDER TRUE ROMANCE TO BE AN ACTION FILM, BUT IT'S A PRETTY GOOD LIST OTHERWISE. WHO COULD HAVE PREDICTED BACK IN THE 1990s THAT STONE COLD WITH BRIAN BOSWORTH WOULD END UP WITH A MORE DEVOUT CULT FOLLOWING THAN THE MATRIX OR TERMINATOR 2? THAT'S FUCKING AMAZING, MAN.
— BOUGIE

I LIKE TO STRIKE UP LITTLE CONVERSATIONS WITH THE LOCAL DIRTY BOOK STORE SHOPKEEPS. THEY'VE SEEN IT ALL. HERE IS MY FAVE LINE ANY OF THEM HAVE EVER SAID TO ME.

☆ ☆ ☆ ☆ ☆ ☆ ☆

MY FRIEND! WOULD YOU LIKE TO KNOW THE BEST THING ABOUT OWNING A PORN STORE?

THE BUSINESS COMES IN SQUIRTS!

THERE ARE NOT A LOT OF KING FRAT FANS OUT THERE, SO WHEN I GOT TWO DIFFERENT UNSOLICITED SUBMISSIONS FOR THE SAME MOVIE, I KNEW THAT THE KING FRAT GODS HAD SPOKEN AND IT WAS TIME TO GIVE THE 1979 MOVIE ITS DUE. HERE NOW, ARE TWO VIEWS ON KING FRAT, BY ACCLAIMED COMIC ARTIST SAM HENDERSON, AND POP CULTURE ENTHUSIAST ETHAN KAYE, WHO HAS WRITTEN FOR WIZARD, MTV, AND TOYFARE MAGAZINE.

King Frat
by Sam Henderson
themagicwhistle.blogspot.ca/

The late seventies and early eighties represent a generational schism in humor. It shows how blatant the difference is between "saying funny things" and "saying things funny". There were movies like AIRPLANE that worked because they were directed and performed like the disaster movies of the time, and HISTORY OF THE WORLD on the other side, which had to constantly let you know it was "funny". It was a weird time for humor where older comedians, in an attempt to be more like their younger contemporaries, (d)evolved into scatological versions of what they were already doing with limits. Richard Pryor was off-color because he said what he wanted, John Byner was because he could be.

The breakthrough hit NATIONAL LAMPOON'S ANIMAL HOUSE spawned a new kind of teen movie. The recent surge in eighties nostalgia has made them popular once again, but retrospectives always mention the same pedestrian examples. Don't get me wrong, it's not like I feel they're beneath me. Quite the opposite, I prefer the bottom of the barrel.

There were many imitations of ANIMAL HOUSE, all of which also emulated the Jack Davis school of poster art in which every cast member is caricatured and every scene from the movie is on the poster. Despite the shortcomings of most imitations, I must credit them for being more accurate in portraying the squalor associated with fraternities.

None of these imitations were lower, in production values or content, than KING FRAT (If I'm wrong, please let me know immediately!). To my knowledge, none of the people involved ever worked on anything else. The movie begins with our beloved Deltas driving around on campus mooning people. They see the dean jogging and pick him for their next target, farting in his direction and killing him! Later, a rasta brother blows pot smoke into the church vents at the dean's funeral, causing all the mourners to laugh. This is only the first few minutes.

The turning point in the film occurs when J.J. "Gross-out" Gumbroski, the Belushi stand-in, is reading a newspaper on the toilet, which has the headline "FART CONTEST ANNOUNCED!" What's assumed a throwaway sight gag ends up being the main plot to the movie. Gross-out is a shoo-in for the contest, and to ensure he wins, the Native American brother has developed a special potion for him to drink backstage. Instead, a dog drinks it by mistake, which makes it fly across the room. Gross-out gets disqualified for "drawing mud" and to add insult to

COVER ART FOR THE ITALIAN VHS RELEASE OF **KING FRAT**

95

injury, his ex-girlfriend wins.

This movie may seem overly flatocentric, but there's more to it. A rush's first lay at a whorehouse turns out to be the frigid girl he's dating. A gorilla-suited peeping tom accidentally gets "stuck" inside a co-ed. Pranks galore. The stereotypical portrayal of blacks and Indians is nonetheless good-natured and reverent, though possibly overlooked by an extremely vile and racist gag about Chinese food (no, it's not about dogs).

A Devoted King Frat Fan Speaks!
By Ethan Kaye

Every time I run into someone that's seen KING FRAT it is like discovering someone's a Freemason. "Really? You saw it too? I had no idea. Never would have guessed." It has its fans but we're a lonely, lonely bunch. Which is sad, because KING FRAT is ridiculously fun.

COVER ART FOR THE AMERICAN VHS RELEASE OF **KING FRAT**

Sure, it's a shameless rip-off of ANIMAL HOUSE. Sure, about half the jokes are about farts and the other half are about sex. Sure there's a Belushi clone in John DiSanti's Gross-Out Gumbroski. But I've always gotten the feeling that the characterization is better in KING FRAT, which makes it stand out.

All the archetypes are there, but with something extra added that adds more spice to the recipe. Kevin is the nerd…who uses his smarts to get more beer. Fred is the smooth-talking frat president…who dresses like an ape and peeps on girls. Splash is the token black guy…who steals a ceramic idol from the WASP-y frat on campus (and a double-headed dildo, which makes no sense and isn't explained). Chief is the shell-shocked Native American handyman…who's been going to school for years on the GI Bill, but is still a sophomore. Whereas ANIMAL HOUSE introduced the prototype, KING FRAT enlarged it to its logical, humorous, yet stupid, extreme.

The gag scenes aren't quick, which is why I think it works better than Belushi just smashing a guitar or pouring cheese on himself. Once a KING FRAT gag is in place, it expands on and on. For example, during the dean's funeral the frat brothers light up a brick of ganja the size of a shoe and waft it through the air vents. It would be easy to end the scene with mourners cracking up, and they do, but everything gets heightened when the new

96

dean goes psycho, cursing out the corpse and kicking the casket out the door…where the frat guys promptly steal it. The corpse of the dean then appears throughout the film, propped up in places like the toilet stall or the back of the courtroom.

From what I gathered from a now-defunct KING FRAT message board, the film was shot over a few weeks in both Miami and Coral Gables, Florida, using mostly locals paid in beer. The band playing the frat party is Natural Magic, a Florida bar band, who spent an afternoon jamming a few tunes while scenes were filmed around them. It had a very limited release to Florida drive-ins during the summer of 1979, with most runs lasting no longer than a week (or a weekend). I have one of the drive-in posters from the original run and it's just some crude scribblings of generic frat dudes with a half-clothed woman superimposed (the same generic model image, incidentally, shows up on several drive-in posters and ads from the same time).

Unlike most films in CINEMA SEWER, KING FRAT has had plenty of video and DVD releases, the most recent in 2009 from New Star Video. Scenes deleted from earlier versions (including some frat party sex hijinks and some coed-on-man-in-gorilla-suit-action) are thankfully restored. And the cast and crew aren't all no-names that faded into obscurity (although most are). Director Ken Wiederhorn went on to write and direct MEATBALLS 2 and RETURN OF THE LIVING DEAD PART 2 and Roy Sekoff, the pledge Tommy, went on to become one of the founding editors of Huffington Post. See what a good education gets you?

Beneath modern London lives a tribe of once humans. Neither men nor women ...they are the raw meat of the human race!

"Raw Meat" starring an American International release
Donald Pleasence · Norman Rossington · David Ladd
Sharon Gurney and Christopher Lee   Technicolor
screenplay by Ceri Jones based on an idea by Gary Sherman
produced by Paul Maslansky directed by Gary Sherman

RAW MEAT (1972. AKA "DEATH LINE")

LONDON'S TUBE TUNNELS AREN'T UNFAMILIAR TO HORROR FILM NERDS, WHAT WITH THE LEGENDARY SCENE FROM AN AMERICAN WEREWOLF IN LONDON (1981), AND THE SOMEWHAT UNDERRATED CREEP (2004) STARRING THE LOVELY MISS FRANKA POTENTE. THERE IS, HOWEVER A FILM THAT DOES BOTH OF THOSE ONE BETTER IN TERMS OF ITS CREEPY DEPICTION OF THE LOCATION, AND IT ISN'T NEARLY AS WELL KNOWN.

THAT MOVIE IS A DEFTLY-ACTED, EXCELLENTLY SHOT, FUNNY, POIGNANT, LOW BUDGET CLASSIC FROM THE 1970S, AND ONE OF DIRECTOR GUILLERMO DEL TORO'S ALL-TIME FAVOURITE FILMS. IT'S CALLED RAW MEAT (AKA DEATH LINE) AND IT'S THE FIRST MOVIE DIRECTED BY GARY SHERMAN, THE SAME RAD CAT RESPONSIBLE FOR DEAD AND BURIED (1981), VICE SQUAD (1982), WANTED DEAD OR ALIVE (1986) AND LISA (1990).

THE UNDERGROUND SUBWAY SYSTEM IS WHERE WE FIND A DERANGED MORLOCK BRUTE (THE DESCENDENT OF TUNNEL WORKERS WHO WERE TRAPPED IN A CAVE-IN AT THE TURN OF THE CENTURY AND ABANDONED BY THE GOVERNMENT) WHO VENTURES UP TO MESSILY MASSACRE HAPLESS VICTIMS, AND DRAG THEM BACK TO HIS DECREPIT LAIR SO HE CAN FEED HIS WOMAN. IT'S ALL VERY UNSETTLING, BUT DON'T WORRY, BECAUSE DONALD PLEASENCE IS THERE TO PROVIDE SOME RELIEF. PHEW!

SHERMAN SHOT A FEW SCENES AT ALDWYCH STATION, WHICH HAS BECOME MORE FAMOUS AS A FILM SET SINCE ITS CLOSURE IN 1994 (AND MORE PROFITABLE THAN DURING ITS LIFE AS A WORKING TUBE STATION, FOR THAT MATTER), BUT WAS UNABLE TO GET LONDON TRANSPORT TO ALLOW HIM TO TAKE UP TIME AND SPACE BY SHUTTING DOWN A SUBWAY LINE TO THE PUBLIC.

GARY SHERMAN
YOU, SIR -- ARE A GODDAMN NATIONAL TREASURE!

THERE ARE NO WINNERS IN SHERMAN'S FILM, ONLY SURVIVORS, AND DESPITE HAVING LITTLE PLOT TO SPEAK OF, THIS MOVIE IS EXCELLENT REGARDLESS. EVEN ITS FINALE MIXES SOME UNCOMPROMISING BRUTALITY WITH A WONDERFUL SENSE OF PATHOS. CHECK IT OUT!

Fly Me (1973)

SHOT IN THE PHILIPPINES, **FLY ME** FOLLOWS THREE SEXY STEWARDESSES NAMED TOBY (SAUCY PAT ANDERSON), SHERRY (LYLLAH TORENA, WHO IS CURIOUSLY UNBILLED), AND ANDREA (TV ACTRESS LENORE KASDORF), ALL OF WHOM FIND THEMSELVES IN JET-SETTING TROUBLE A LONG, LONG WAY FROM HOME.

IT'S A MOVIE THAT MIXES PILES OF BARE BREASTS, (TERRIBLE) MARTIAL ARTS, AMAZING 1970'S FASHIONS, STOCK FOOTAGE OF PLANES, COMEDY, EXOTIC LOCATIONS IN THE ORIENT, AND A 'RAPED-BY-A-CANADIAN' SCENE. YOU KNOW WHAT YOU'RE IN FOR WHEN THE MOVIE STARTS WITH A

SEE STEWARDESSES BATTLE **KUNG FU** KILLERS!

Fly Me

R

A NEW WORLD PICTURES RELEASE

STARRING PAT ANDERSON · LENORE KASDORF · LYLLAH TORENA · NAOMI STEVENS
KUNG FU SEQUENCES BY DAVID CHOW   DIRECTED BY CIRIO SANTIAGO   **METROCOLOR**

PRETTY BLONDE FLIGHT ATTENDANT CHANGING INTO HER ADORABLE LITTLE PURPLE AND GREEN UNIFORM IN THE BACK OF A CAB DRIVEN BY DICK MILLER. DISTRACTED BY HER JIGGLING SNOOPIES, HE THEN DRIVES OFF THE ROAD. HA!

YEAH, IT'S A SALTY LITTLE TURD. AS EXPLOITATION MOVIE EXPERT MARTY MCKEE ONCE WROTE "(THIS) MUST BE THE ONLY FILM TO COMBINE A WACKY COMIC-RELIEF MOTHER PROTECTING HER ADULT DAUGHTER'S VIRGINITY WITH A SLEAZY STORYLINE INVOLVING DRUGGING NUDE WOMEN AND SELLING THEM INTO SEX SLAVERY."

AS FUN AS THAT MAY SOUND, THIS GETS A LITTLE TEDIOUS IN PARTS AND ISN'T QUITE AS ENTERTAINING AS IT SHOULD HAVE BEEN. AND YET, THERE IS MORE THAN ENOUGH HERE THAT MAKES THE WHOLE THING UNIQUE AND UNUSUAL IN THE WAY THAT IT IS HAPHAZARDLY CRAMMED TOGETHER. IT'S CERTAINLY WORTH A WATCH, BUT IT WOULDN'T BE MY FIRST CHOICE, FOR SAY, A GATEWAY MOVIE LOANED TO A FRIEND TO TRY TO GET THEM INTO THESE KINDS OF TRASHY DRIVE-IN MOVIES.

DIRECTOR CIRIO SANTIAGO (1936 -- 2008) WAS RAISED IN A WEALTHY HOUSEHOLD IN THE PHILIPPINES. HIS DAD WAS A SURGEON, AND HIS MOTHER WAS A PHARMACIST, AND TOGETHER THEY OWNED AND OPERATED A SUCCESSFUL DRUGSTORE. IN 1946, CINEMATOGRAPHER RICARDO MARCELINO TALKED SANTIAGO'S FATHER INTO GETTING IN ON THE GROUND FLOOR OF THE EMERGING TAGALOG FILM INDUSTRY, AND THE FAMILY STARTED 'PREMIERE PRODUCTIONS.' THAT WAS THE FOUNDATION, BUT CIRIO DIDN'T REALLY FIND SUCCESS UNTIL HE TEAMED UP WITH AN AMERICAN NAMED ROGER CORMAN, WHO HAD JUST STARTED A FLEDGLING INDEPENDENT FILM COMPANY CALLED NEW WORLD PICTURES IN 1970.

"CORMAN GAVE ME MY FIRST BREAK - $3,000 TO MAKE **SAVAGE**, ALSO KNOWN AS BLACK VALOR." SANTIAGO TOLD INTERVIEWER ERIKA FRANKLIN IN 2009. "ROGER BELIEVED THERE WERE THREE WAYS OF MAKING A FILM, THE RIGHT WAY, THE WRONG WAY AND THE CORMAN WAY."

BY THE TIME SANTIAGO PASSED AWAY, HE'D DIRECTED ALMOST ONE HUNDRED MOVIES, OWNED ONE OF THE BIGGEST FILM PRODUCTION COMPANIES IN THE PHILIPPINES, AND WAS BEST KNOWN IN HIS NATIVE LAND FOR DIRECTING WESTERNS AND MUSICALS, DESPITE HIS LEGENDARY STATUS IN NORTH AMERICA AS THE KING OF TAGALOG EXPLOITATION, WOMEN-IN-PRISON, AND POST APOCALYPSE CINEMA. AND WHEN I SAY "THE KING", I'M NOT DICKING AROUND. MUCH OF CIRIO'S CLASSIC FARE IS STUFF YOU NEED TO SEEK OUT IF YOU'RE A FAN OF CINEMA SEWER, BECAUSE IT'LL SURELY APPEAL TO YOUR SENSIBILITIES. START WHERE CIRIO DID, WITH **SAVAGE** (1973), AND CONTINUE WITH **EBONY, IVORY AND JADE** (1976), **THE MUTHERS**, (1976), **HELL HOLE** (1978), AND GO ON FROM THERE.

SHOUT FACTORY RELEASED THIS ON DVD IN NORTH AMERICA IN 2022 IN A SET CALLED LETHAL LADIES 2. HEY, DID ANYONE ELSE NOTICE THAT THE PLOT SYNOPSIS ON THE BACK OF THE DVD IS FOR AN ENTIRELY DIFFERENT MOVIE? NOT THAT IT'S A BIG DEAL OR ANYTHING, BUT IT'S AN AWFULLY ODD ERROR. IT MADE ME LAUGH SEEING ALL THE ONLINE REVIEWERS WHO BLINDLY REPEATED IT, REVEALING THAT THEY DON'T ACTUALLY WATCH THE SCREENERS THEY GET, AND SIMPLY JUST REGURGETATE THE PRESS RELEASES. HAHA! BUUUUSTED! -BOUGLE

THIS AIRLINE SERVES THREE WILD DISHES TAKE YOUR CHOICE

METROCOLOR

Fly Me

SEE STEWARDESSES BATTLE **KUNG FU** KILLERS!

R

The Psychic (aka Seven Notes in Black) 1977 Dir: Lucio Fulci

THE CREATIVE PEAK OF FULCI'S HORROR FILM CAREER BEGAN IN 1979 AND ENDED IN 1981. IN THOSE 3 SHORT YEARS HE DIRECTED **ZOMBIE, CITY OF THE LIVING DEAD, THE BEYOND, THE BLACK CAT** AND **HOUSE BY THE CEMETERY.** THESE WERE FIVE OF THE GREATEST HORROR FILMS OF HIS FILMOGRAPHY AND SOME ONE WOULD SAY FIVE OF THE BEST ITALIAN HORROR FILMS ON TOP OF THAT. ALL OF THEM WERE THE RESULT OF FULCI'S DIRECTORIAL PROWESS WHEN ADDED TO THE LUSCIOUS CINEMATOGRAPHY SKILLS OF SERGIO SALVATI, THE CRAFTY WRITING OF DARDANO SACCHETTI, AND THE DIABOLIC ORIGINAL MUSIC OF FABIO FRIZZI. BUT WHAT MANY HORROR FANS DON'T REALIZE IS THAT THIS MOVIE, **THE PSYCHIC** – MADE TWO YEARS EARLIER – MARKED THE FIRST TIME LUCIO WORKED WITH ALL THREE MEN. ON TOP OF THAT, HE WAS AFFORDED A DECENT BUDGET, ONE OF THE BIGGEST OF HIS FILMMAKING CAREER.

ITALY, 1976. VIRGINIA DUCCI (PLAYED BY THE GORGEOUS AND SENSUAL JENNIFER O'NEILL, WHOM YOU MAY REMEMBER FROM CRONENBERG'S **SCANNERS**) BEGINS EXPERIENCING A SERIES OF CONFUSING, FRAGMENTED VISIONS WHICH CULMINATE IN SEEING A DARK HOLE CUT OUT OF A WALL. 18 YEARS EARLIER, HER MOTHER COMMITTED SUICIDE BY JUMPING OFF A CLIFF (AND SMASHING HER PRETTY FACE AGAINST NEARLY EVERY BOULDER ON THE WAY DOWN -- IN CLOSE UP SHOTS, NO LESS) AND POOR LITTLE VIRGINIA SAW THAT AS WELL. SOMETIMES IT <u>SUCKS</u> TO BE A PSYCHIC.

TURNING TO HER FRIEND DR. LUCA FATTORI (PLAYED BY MARC POREL), AN ASTUTE GENT WITH A DEEP INTEREST IN THE PARANORMAL, VIRGINIA DESCRIBES TO HIM THE CRAZY SHIT SHE'S BEEN SEEING, AND THEN PROCEEDS TO DRIVE UP TO SCOPE OUT A JUNKY OLD VILLA. IT'S A HOME OWNED BY HER HUSBAND, A PLACE THE TWO OF THEM INTEND TO CLEAN UP AND MOVE INTO. BUT BEFORE THAT CAN HAPPEN, VIRGINIA DISCOVERS THAT MUCH OF THE IMAGERY FROM HER VISIONS EXIST IN REAL LIFE IN THIS DUSTY OLD HOME, INCLUDING THE MYSTERIOUS AFOREMENTIONED WALL. GRABBING A PICK AXE AND SOBBING LIKE A LITTLE GIRL, SHE SMASHES THE SHIT OUT OF THE WALL AND FINDS NOT ONLY A NASTY SKELETAL CORPSE BURIED INSIDE IT, BUT ALSO INSPIRATIONS FOR EVEN MORE SPOOKY VISIONS. EDGAR ALLAN POE, EAT YOUR HEART OUT.

THE POLICE PROCEED TO ARREST HER HUSBAND FOR THE MURDER AND ILLEGAL DISPOSAL OF THE BODY SHE DUG OUT OF THE WALL. WITH THE HELP OF HER PARANORMAL-OBSESSED PAL, VIRGINIA WORKS LIKE THE DICKENS TO USE HER SPOOKY VISIONS TO TRY TO PUT THE PIECES TOGETHER IN A BID TO PROVE HER HUBBY'S INNOCENCE AND TRACK DOWN THE REAL KILLER IN THE PROCESS. DECIPHERING THE PSYCHIC CLUES SEEMS TO BE WORKING OUT PRETTY WELL FOR HER, THAT IS UNTIL VIRGINIA REALIZES THAT SHE'S BEEN HAVING VISIONS OF THE FUTURE AND NOT OF THE PAST. SUDDENLY NOTHING IS QUITE AS IT APPEARS.

"IT WAS ONE OF MY MOST BEAUTIFUL, AND AT THE SAME TIME, UNSUCCESSFUL FILMS", FULCI TOLD INTERVIEWER LUCA PALMERINI IN 1991 WHEN ASKED WHY THE FILM WAS A FLOP. "IT COST ME A LOT OF GRIEF FOR PERSONAL REASONS...YOU SHOULD NEVER INTERFERE WITH DESTINY. POLANSKI ONCE TOLD ME 'I TOUCHED THE DEVIL, AND YOU SHOULD NEVER MEDDLE WITH THE DEVIL, BECAUSE THEN YOU HAVE TOUCHED DESTINY.'"

"(MAKING MOVIES) IS A VERY INTENSE EXPERIENCE FOR ME", FULCI NOTED. "AFTER THAT I DON'T EVEN GO SEE THE SCREENING. I AGREE WITH MY FRIEND, MELVILLE, WHO USED TO SAY 'IF I GO AND SEE A FILM I'VE JUST FINISHED, I JUST GET ANNOYED BECAUSE I ALWAYS THINK I'VE MADE A LOT OF MISTAKES'. UNFORTUNATELY, WE

CAN'T PUT THINGS RIGHT, LIKE FELLINI OR WOODY ALLEN. THEY CAN DO TAKE AFTER TAKE; INSTEAD WHEN WE'VE FINISHED A SHOT, THAT'S WHAT IT'S GOING TO BE, AND THAT'S THE END OF IT. SO, I GIVE IT EVERYTHING I'VE GOT RIGHT UP TO THE END, AND THEN I FORGET ABOUT IT. IT'S LIKE FOR HORSES; WHEN A MARE GIVES BIRTH, IT'S AS THOUGH SHE'S GETTING RID OF A GREAT PAIN, AFTER WHICH SHE JUST LICKS THE FOAL CLEAN AND THEN LEAVES IT ALONE."

HEAVY ON ATMOSPHERE, THE PSYCHIC IS EASILY ONE OF THE MOST UNDERRATED EFFORTS OF FULCI'S FILMOGRAPHY. THE FIRST ACT IS ENGROSSING, AND EVEN THOUGH THE MIDDLE PART SAGS AND MAKES ONE A LITTLE SLEEPY, IF YOU STICK WITH IT YOU'LL BE REWARDED WITH ONE OF THE BEST ENDINGS IN EURO GENRE FILM HISTORY. GIVE THIS ONE A TRY.

BONUS FUN: IF YOU'VE BEEN TRYING TO FIGURE OUT WHERE THAT UNFORGETTABLE MELODY USED IN **KILL BILL** CAME FROM, LOOK NO FURTHER. IT'S EVEN A KEY PART OF THE END SCENE.

JENNIFER O'NEILL l'héroine de « UN ETE 42 »

un film de **LUCIO FULCI**

CINE DECOR g. ferro

L'EMMUREE VIVANTE

SELECTIONNE AU FESTIVAL DU FILM FANTASTIQUE DE PARIS

"I REGRET EVER HAVING DONE AN X-RATED FILM. BUT I'VE DONE SO MANY OF THEM, AND GOD KNOWS, BY NOW I'VE MADE MY BED. I HAD A FABULOUS HEAD START IN A LEGITIMATE CAREER. MY PRIDE IN MY LEGITIMATE WORK FAR SURPASSES MY PRIDE IN MY X-RATED WORK I'VE DONE. BUT I'VE MADE AN X-RATED CAREER FOR MYSELF. I DON'T NECESSARILY THINK IT WAS A WISE DECISION, BUT I'VE GENERALLY OPTED FOR WHAT'S EASY AND FOR WHAT'S FAST. AND BELIEVE ME, I'VE PAID THE PRICE."

"MY GOD, THE SITUATIONS THAT WE IN THE BUSINESS HAVE TO GO THROUGH! THE SPUR OF THE MOMENT STUFF... FOR US TO TURN OUT--FOR $100,000 IN 7 DAYS -- A FILM THAT IS PALATABLE AND MILDLY ENTERTAINING IS A MAJOR FEAT. IMAGINE IF WE WERE GIVEN A MILLION DOLLARS AND TWO MONTHS -- WHICH IS STILL A SMALL BUDGET FOR A LEGIT FEATURE -- YOU COULD HAVE HENRI PACHARD OR ANTHONY SPINELLI DIRECTING AND YOU COULD COMPETE WITH THE MAJOR FILM COMPANIES. WE HAVE THE TALENT... BUT I DON'T THINK WE CAN GROW FROM THE POINT WE'RE AT. I THINK WE'RE STUCK, AND THE REASON IS THAT IF WE'RE DOING A FILM FOR $100,000 WE HAVE TO HAVE A HOOK. AND OUR HOOK IS THAT IT'S HARDCORE."

"MOST OF THE WOMEN THAT COME INTO THIS BUSINESS DON'T HAVE THE INTELLIGENCE, STRENGTH OR SOPHISTICATION THAT I LOOK FOR IN A WOMAN. THEY ARE MOSTLY LOST LITTLE GIRLS. AND I WILL LET SOMEONE ELSE BABYSIT THEM."

"SWINGING AND SWAPPING JUST BECAME TOO POLYESTER... THE PEOPLE WERE NOT VERY EROTIC PEOPLE. I DON'T REALLY ENJOY SWINGING TOO MUCH ANYMORE. THE MOST IMPORTANT PART OF MY SEX LIFE IS ATTEMPTING TO FINALLY BE ALONE WITH A WOMAN THAT I LOVE. I NEED TO RECAPTURE THAT EXPERIENCE ONCE AGAIN, BECAUSE THE LUST IS ALL TOO EASILY CAPTURED. THERE IS PLENTY OF LUST OUT THERE IN PRIVATE AND IN PUBLIC, AT ANY DISCO, AT ANY BAR, ANY X-RATED FILM SET. THERE IS PLENTY OF LUST. IT IS LOVE THAT IS IN SHORT SUPPLY."

-- PAUL THOMAS, ONE OF THE PREMIERE ACTORS IN XXX FILMS IN THE '70S AND '80S, BEING INTERVIEWED BY X-RATED CINEMA IN THEIR DEC. 1984 ISSUE., THREE YEARS AFTER THIS, HE WOULD GO ON TO BECOME ONE OF THE MOST PROLIFIC DIRECTORS IN PORN INSTEAD, DIRECT NEARLY 500 FEATURE FILMS AND VIDEOS, AND STILL WORKS BEHIND THE CAMERA (EXCLUSIVELY FOR VIVID VIDEO) EVEN TODAY.

FUCK ME GENTLY WITH A CHAINSAW

WHEN "OH MY GOD" JUST DOESN'T CUT IT, THAT'S HOW ALPHA-BITCH HEATHER CHANDLER (KIM WALKER -- PLAYING PERHAPS THE SNARKIEST TEENAGE GIRL IN FILM HISTORY) ARTICULATES HER EXASPERATION WITH WANNABE 'HEATHER' VERONICA -- PLAYED BY WINONA RYDER. HEATHERS (1988) IS JUST THAT KIND OF MOVIE. A MASSIVE CULT HIT TODAY, THE FILM COST AN ESTIMATED $3 MILLION TO PUT TOGETHER BUT GROSSED A MEASLY $1.1 MILLION IN ITS INITIAL RUN IN THEATERS. AUDIENCES SIMPLY DIDN'T GET ITS DARKLY COMIC TONE.

I MEAN, IT'S A TEEN MOVIE ABOUT SUICIDE AND MURDER, AND AS DARK AS IT WAS, THE ORIGINAL SCRIPT HAD AN EVEN MORE SINISTER ENDING. IT HAD THE PARTYGOERS AT THE PROM DRINKING PUNCH SPIKED WITH DRAIN CLEANER, WINONA RYDER SHOOTING J.D. (CHRISTIAN SLATER -- DOING HIS BEST JACK NICHOLSON IMPERSONATION), THEN STRAPPING A BOMB ON AND BLOWING HERSELF UP. THE CONCLUSION OF THE MOVIE WOULD THEN HAVE TAKEN PLACE AT A PROM IN HEAVEN, THE ONE PLACE WHERE THE VARIOUS CLIQUES WOULD FINALLY SEE EYE TO EYE.

THIS IS THE TEEN MOVIE FOR PEOPLE WHO HATE TEEN MOVIES. A <u>MUST-SEE</u>.

THE SISTERHOOD

DIRECTED BY CIRIO SANTIAGO
PHILIPPINES 1988 75 MIN ☆

ARTICLE BY ROBIN BOUGIE
ART BY BEN NEWMAN '11

THE YEAR IS 2021 AD. A TRAGIC NUCLEAR HOLOCAUST HAS LEFT MUCH OF THE EARTH SCORCHED AND DEVASTATED. IN THIS VOLATILE NIGHTMARE WORLD, FEMALE SURVIVORS HAVE BEEN ENSLAVED BY A BRUTAL ARMY OF BARBARIC PATRIARCHAL MEN. THEIR ONLY HOPE FOR FREEDOM? A MYTHICAL BAND OF UNITED AND HIGHLY-SKILLED LASER-EYED NOMADIC WARRIORS: THE SISTERHOOD. WITH THE AID OF THEIR BLADES, BOWS, AND AMAZING POWERS OF WITCHCRAFT, THESE GRITTY GALS ARE RAW AND READY TO UNCHAIN THEIR FELLOW FEMALE POPULACE.

IN A SHITTY DESERT SETTLEMENT IN THIS VIOLENT NEW SOCIETY RESIDES 18-YEAR-OLD MARYA (LYNN-HOLLY JOHNSON) AND HER LITTLE BROTHER GIL (TOM McNEELEY). MARYA IS A COMELY YOUNG THANG, AND BECAUSE OF SOME MUTATIONAL AFTER-EFFECTS OF THE BOMB (THAT MANIFEST THEMSELVES AT PUBERTY) SHE HAS A PSYCHIC LINK WITH HER HAWK, LADY SHIRI.

TOO BAD FOR THE TWO OF THEM THAT MIKAL (CHUCK WAGNER) AND HIS ENGINE-REVVING GANG OF BLADE-WIELDING, LEATHER-CLAD SCALLYWAGS HAVE COME TO TOWN AND ARE LOOKING FOR SOME PUSSY TO POUND. FOR WHATEVER REASON (ALTHOUGH JUNKER CARS ARE STILL QUITE ABUNDANT IN THIS POST-NUKE WASTELAND) NO GUNS ARE KICKING AROUND -- SO ALL OF THEIR RAPING AND PILLAGING IS DONE WITH SWORDS, AXES, BOWS, AND ERECT DONGS. OH, AND A NUMBER OF ROCKET-PROPELLED GRENADE LAUNCHERS AS WELL, MOSTLY BECAUSE IT IS FUN TO SEE THINGS GO BOOM.

CHUCK WAGNER

IT'S MASS CHAOS AND THREE DOZEN CASUALTIES PILE UP FAST. UNFORTUNATELY, ONLY MARYA ESCAPES, AND DOES SO JUST BEFORE SEEING HER POOR BROTHER GET GAKKED BY MEAN OL' MIKAL. OH YEAH, IT'S FUCKIN' REVENGE TIME, IS WHAT IT IS. SEEKING RESPITE AT A NEARBY TAVERN (RUN BY AN EXPLOSIVES NUT NAMED "DYNAMITE WILLY"), MARYA BEFRIENDS TWO OTHER YOUNG WOMEN, ALEE (REBECCA HOLDEN) AND VERA (BARBARA HOOPER) WHOSE POWERS ARE TELEKENISIS AND "HEALING HANDS". TURNS OUT THESE TWO BAD ASSES ARE MEMBERS OF THE FABLED SISTERHOOD, AND THE THREE MAKE FAST FRIENDS. THESE ARE THE KIND OF TESTICLE SMASHERS THAT LAUGH IN THE FACE OF RULES DICTATING THAT WOMEN CAN'T TRAVEL WITHOUT BEING ACCOMPANIED BY THEIR OWNER, OR BEAR ARMS.

BEFORE LONG MIKAL AND HIS GOONS WILL SNATCH VERA AND TIE HER TO THE BACK OF THE SWEET TRIKE THAT MIKAL DRIVES AROUND, AND THEN GIVE HER SOME SWEATY RAPES. ALEE AND MARYA WILL DO THEIR BEST TO RETRIEVE THEIR FRIEND, AND THERE WILL BE RUN-INS WITH RADIOACTIVE PLANTS, THE HARE-LIPPED LORD BARAK (ROBERT DRYER), LORD JAK (ANTHONY EAST), A JOURNEY THROUGH THE FORBIDDEN ZONE (HOME TO A CAVERNOUS NETWORK OF TUNNELS FULL OF MUTANT WEIRDOS), AND A TRIP TO CALCARA, 'THE CITY OF ULTIMATE PLEASURE'!

THEY ENCOMPASS THE LATTER PART OF THAT LIST WHILE ROLLIN' IN A SWEET ARMOURED PERSONNEL CARRIER, MORE SPECIFICALLY THE CADILLAC-GAGE V-150 COMMANDO LIGHT ARMOURED VEHICLE ARMED WITH A POWER TURRET WITH A SINGLE M-2 .50 CALIBER

MACHINE GUN. NEVER YOU MIND THE FACT THAT IT'S BEEN SITTING AROUND UNUSED FOR OVER 40 YEARS WHEN THEY DISCOVER IT, AND NONE OF THEM SHOULD HAVE A CLUE HOW TO OPERATE THE DAMN THING. THERE IS NO TIME FOR SUCH DETAILS! THERE IS TOO MUCH ASS TO KICK!

FRIEND OF CINEMA SEWER, JACK JENSEN INTERVIEWED HENRY STRZALKOWSKI (WHO PLAYED THE SWORDSMAN IN SUNGLASSES AND FOOTBALL SHOULDER PADS) IN 2012, AND HENRY HAD THIS TO SAY:

"DURING A SWORD FIGHT REHEARSAL, (LYNN-HOLLY JOHNSON) ACCIDENTALLY STRUCK ONE OF OUR STUNTMEN. ACTUALLY, SHE LOPPED OFF THE END OF HIS INDEX FINGER. SINCE WE WERE USING DULL ALUMINUM PROP SWORDS, SHE MORE OR LESS CRUSHED IT. THE STUNTMAN WAS GREG ROCERO, I'LL NEVER FORGET SEEING HIM JUST WINCE AND STOP. WHEN HE PULLED OUT HIS HAND, WE REALIZED WHAT HAD HAPPENED. HE WENT STRAIGHT TO THE HOSPITAL AND SHOWED UP A COUPLE OF HOURS LATER WITH HIS SEVERED FINGER IN A BOTTLE. I'M NOT JOKING. I ASKED HIM WHY HE WAS BACK AND HE SIMPLY SAID, 'I GOTTA DRIVE MY TRUCK BACK'. I ASKED HIM IF IT HURT AND HE SAID 'IT JUST THROBS A BIT'. WHAT A GUY... ALL IN A DAY'S WORK. THE RISKS YOU TAKE. LYNN-HOLLY WAS DEVASTATED FOR THE REST OF THE PICTURE."

FILIPINO FILMMAKING LEGEND CIRIO H. SANTIAGO MADE THIS ENTIRELY IN HIS HOMELAND, AND HE DOES NOT DISAPPOINT. I ADORE THE POST APOCALYPTIC GENRE, BUT LET'S FACE IT, MOST OF THEM ARE JUST LOW-BUDGET RIP-OFFS OF THE ROAD WARRIOR. WHILE THE SISTERHOOD MAY NOT HAVE MUCH OF A BUDGET, IT IS QUITE RICH IN IDEAS, HEART, AND CREATIVITY.

BOUGIE .2011.

REBECCA HOLDEN AS "ALEE"

FIREWORKS WOMAN
(1975. DIR: WES CRAVEN)

WHAT DID A NIGHTMARE ON ELM STREET CREATOR WES CRAVEN DO AFTER HE DIRECTED THE LAST HOUSE ON THE LEFT? MANY HORROR MOVIE NERDS WILL FLATLY INFORM YOU THAT FIVE YEARS LATER HIS NEXT PRODUCTION WAS THE HILLS HAVE EYES, BUT WE CLASSIC PORN FANS KNOW BETTER. WE'RE QUITE AWARE OF WHAT THAT NAUGHTY BEARDED BOY WAS GETTING INTO DURING HIS FIVE YEARS AWAY FROM THE BLOOD AND GORE BIZ -- NAMELY, THE PUSSY AND DICK BIZ.

YUP, WES WAS CRAVIN' HOT SEX, BABY. IN FACT, I HAVE IT ON GOOD AUTHORITY THAT THE LAST HOUSE ON THE LEFT WAS ORIGINALLY PLANNED AS A HORROR-THEMED XXX MOVIE, BUT THAT STAR DAVID HESS BAULKED AT THE EXPLICITNESS OF THE PLANNED HUMP SCENES. HAVEN'T HORROR FANS EVER WONDERED WHY MOST OF LHOTL'S CAST MEMBERS WERE BETTER KNOWN AS PORN PERFORMERS AND SEX FILM STARS?

CRAVEN APPEARS IN NON-SEX ROLES AS AN ACTOR IN SEVERAL HARDCORE FEATURES, INCLUDING 1973'S IT HAPPENED IN HOLLYWOOD, THE FIREWORKS WOMAN, AND THE WILD TWINCEST PORNO SWEET CAKES FROM 1976. AND THOSE ARE JUST THE ONES THAT FANS HAVE SPOTTED. THERE COULD WELL BE MORE, BUT THE DIRECTOR SEEMS QUITE EMBARRASSED ABOUT HIS TENURE IN XXX, AND STAYS MUM ON THE TOPIC WHEN INTERVIEWED. AS CULT MOVIE BLOGGER HEATHER DRAIN SNIPED "WES SHOULD BE MORE ASHAMED OF DRECK LIKE "MUSIC OF THE HEART" AND PRODUCING THE INCREDIBLY SHITTY "DRACULA 2000" THEN ANYTHING BLUE HE WORKED ON."

WE ALSO KNOW THAT HE DIRECTED AT LEAST ONE OF THE SMUT FILMS HE APPEARED IN, THE AFOREMENTIONED FIREWORKS WOMAN FROM 1975. IT'S AN OBSCURE LITTLE NUGGET, BUT ONE THAT SOME (INCLUDING ME) HAVE NOTED AS SOME OF THE FINEST WORK OF CRAVEN'S CAREER. UNFORTUNATELY IT'S AN EFFORT THAT NO ONE HAS PROPERLY PEEPED SINCE ITS THEATRICAL RUN, WHICH IS BECAUSE THE UNCUT VERSION OF THE FIREWORKS WOMAN HAS BEEN LOST. A TRUNCATED 72 MIN. VERSION HAS CIRCULATED AMONGST BOOTLEGGERS AND FANS, BUT IT IS MISSING MUCH OF THE CRAZY FOOTAGE THAT THE OLD RAINCOATERS SPEAK OF. NAMELY: PISSING, FISTING, AN EXTENTION OF THE EXISTING SEASIDE RAPE SEQUENCE, AND THEN ONE OF THE RAPISTS FROM SAID SCENE USING A DEAD FISH TO FELLATE HIMSELF. OH, I'VE GOT YOUR ATTENTION NOW, DON'T I?

NOW SOMETIMES THESE WILD "LOST FOOTAGE" TALES CAN TAKE ON A LIFE OF THEIR OWN, BUT I CAN PERSONALLY BACK UP THE FISH BLOWJOB CLAIMS. A FEW SECONDS OF IT WILL PERMANENTLY BURN ITSELF UPON THE RETINAS OF ANY VIEWER WHO EYEBALLS THE RARE FIREWORKS WOMAN TRAILER THAT WAS INCLUDED BY MIKE VRANEY ON THE SWV VHS COLLECTION "BUCKY'S '70S TRIPLE XXX MOVIE HOUSE TRAILERS, VOL. 16". I NEARLY CHOKED ON A PEANUT BUTTER SANDWITCH WHEN I SAW IT.

IN THE FILM, "ANGELA" IS PORTRAYED WITH APLOMB BY JENNIFER JORDAN, WHO IS DEEP IN PANTY-SOAKED LUST WITH HER OWN BROTHER, PLAYED BY ERIC EDWARDS. NOW NORMALLY IF YOU DIDN'T WANT TO PLOW YOUR RUTTING SISTER, YOU COULD JUST POLITELY SAY NO, BUT IN THIS INSTANCE THERE IS A CATCH. ANGELA IS THE FIREWORKS WOMAN, WHICH MEANS SHE HAS THE SUPERPOWER TO MAKE ANYONE -- EVEN THE UNWILLING -- DESPERATELY WANT TO POGO THE PUDDING OUT OF HER. ASHAMED OF THE FEELINGS HE HAS FOR HIS SEXY SIBLING, HER POOR BROTHER BECOMES A PRIEST, AND WE ALL KNOW HOW WELL THE CATHOLIC CHURCH WORKS AS A RESPITE FOR THOSE WITH SOCIALLY FROWNED-UPON SEXUAL ISSUES.

NONE OF THIS IS ENOUGH TO STOP ANGELA AND HER INCEST-HUNGRY PUSS. SHE USES THE CONFESSIONAL AS A WANTON GROVELLING BOOTH -- A PLACE WHERE HER BROTHER IS A CAPTIVE PRIVATE AUDIENCE TO HER INCESSANT PLEADING FOR FUCKS. AT HIS WITS' END,

✳ CONTINUED FROM PREVIOUS PAGE ✳

HE SENDS HIS SISTER TO WORK FOR ONE MRS. WALTERS (ERICA EATON), A WEALTHY ARISTOCRATIC CONGREGATION MEMBER WHO PROMPTLY EMPLOYS ANGELA AS A SEX SLAVE, SENDING HER EVEN FURTHER INTO THE ABYSS OF INSANITY. THROUGHOUT ALL OF THIS, ANGELA IS FOLLOWED BY A MYSTERIOUS CREEP IN A TOP HAT, PLAYED BY MR. WES CRAVEN HIMSELF.

PORNO AS RELIGION-FUELED EXISTENTIAL TRAGEDY? BY GOD, THIS IS A MASTERPIECE, AND ANY ONE OF US SHOULD BE THRILLED TO SEE CRAVEN MAKE A SKIN FLICK AT THIS POINT IN HIS CAREER. CAN YOU IMAGINE IT?? THE MAN HAS BEEN REHASHING NOTHING BUT CINEMATIC PABLUM FOR DECADES, BUT I'M THINKING THAT GETTING BACK INTO HIS OWN GRIM BRAND OF ARTHOUSE-ADULT COULD ACTUALLY PUT HIM BACK ON TRACK.

COULDN'T BE ANY WORSE THAN **MUSIC OF THE HEART**, ANYWAY.

—BOUGIE · 2011 ·

HELL OF THE LIVING DEAD (1980)

HELL OF THE LIVING DEATH

SLEAZY NUDITY, OVER-THE-TOP VIOLENCE, LOTS OF UNCOMFORTABLE FOOTAGE OF WHITE PEOPLE HAPPILY KILLING BLACK ZOMBIES, A CAT JUMPING RIGHT OUT OF A WOMAN'S GORY STOMACH CAVITY, AN UNDEAD KID, AND A SHITLOAD OF TOTALLY UNINTENTIONAL LAUGHS. YES, PLEASE. HOOK IT UP TO MY VEINS, MAN. DADDY WANTS TO OVERDOSE.

THIS ATROCITY STARTS OFF IN SOME KIND OF CHEMICAL FACTORY WHERE A REALLY VIOLENT RAT SHREDS A DUDE ALIVE, AND THIS RESULTS IN A GREEN GAS GETTING RELEASED THAT TURNS EVERYONE INTO ZOMBIES. SEE? WE'RE ALREADY OFF THE MAP, HERE. I ESPECIALLY LOVE WHEN ONE OF THE SCIENTISTS, AFTER WITNESSING ALL OF THE ZOMBIE CARNAGE IN HIS WORKPLACE, SETTLES DOWN AND RECORDS SOME NOTES. "THE EXPERIMENTAL PROJECT: 'OPERATION: SWEET DEATH' HAS BEEN A COMPLETE FAILURE", HE SAYS CALMLY INTO THE MIC. WOW, MAYBE YOU NIMRODS JINXED YOURSELVES WITH THAT TITLE? (FACE PALM)

AFTER THAT WE'RE THEN LED INTO YOUR BASIC AND TRADITIONAL ZOMBIE FILM NARRATIVE ABOUT A GROUP OF COMMANDO SURVIVORS FIGHTING OFF AN UNDEAD HOARD, EXCEPT DIRECTOR BRUNO MATTEI (UNDER HIS VINCENT DAWN AKA) PLOPS THEM DOWN ON A JUNGLE ISLAND IN PAPUA NEW GUINEA. THERE HE TEAMS THEM UP WITH A JOURNALIST AND HER CAMERAMAN AND MIXES IN A BIT OF THE CANNIBAL GENRE INTO HIS ZOMBIE RECIPE. THAT SORT OF BLOOD AND MAGGOT-CAKED COMBO REALLY IS A HORROR MATCH MADE IN HELL.

I LOVE THE CORNY DIALOG SOOOO MUCH! WHEN A GROUP OF CHARACTERS STUMBLE UPON A BUILDING ONE OF THEM PLAINLY STATES THAT "BUILDINGS HAVE PEOPLE IN THEM, WE'D BETTER GO INVESTIGATE". OH REALLY? HAHA! ONE OF THE UNIFORMED SOLDIERS THAT THE MOVIE FOLLOWS, ZANTORO, IS BEYOND AMAZING. WITH HIS BEADY EYES, FLOPPY MOP OF HAIR, AND SHRILL LAUGH, HE STEALS THE SHOW. FRANCO GAROFALO'S PERFORMANCE IS LOADED WITH STUPID QUIPS, OVER-ACTING, AND ESPECIALLY HILARIOUS IS HIS GLEEFUL TAUNTING OF THE UNDEAD WITH HIS DELIVERY OF "YA BASTARDS! YOU'RE LIKE A BUNCH OF TURDS! BRAINLESS MONKEYS! HEE HEE HEE! YA CAN'T CATCH ME! GET BACK TO YOUR GRAVES!"

When the Creeping Dead devour the living flesh!

ZOMBIE CREEPING FLESH

THE RIP-OFF ASPECTS ARE TOTALLY AUDACIOUS. AWKWARD STOCK FOOTAGE OF JUNGLE ANIMALS JUMPING AROUND, THE MUSIC BEING LIFTED FROM GOBLIN'S SCORE FOR **CONTAMINATION** AND **DAWN OF THE DEAD**...OH, AND THERE IS PILES OF FOOTAGE OF NATIVES SHAMELESSLY STOLEN FROM THE 1972 BARBET SCHROEDER DOCUMENTARY, **LA VALLEE**. IT'S PADDED AND NONSENSICAL AS SHIT, THE ENDING DRAGS ON AND ON, AND THIS 101-MINUTE RELEASE COULD HAVE STOOD TO HAVE BEEN TRIMMED BY 20 MINUTES (HELL, JUST CUT ALL THE STOCK FOOTAGE OF ANIMALS, PLEASE), BUT OVERALL THIS EURO-GOREFEST IS ENTERTAINING AND QUITE WATCHABLE. IT WAS RELEASED IN THE UK AS 'ZOMBIE CREEPING FLESH' IN 1982. IT DIDN'T GET AN AMERICAN THEATRICAL RELEASE UNTIL EARLY 1984, WHEN IT HIT US GRINDHOUSES AND DRIVE-INS IN A DUBBED VERSION CALLED 'NIGHT OF THE ZOMBIES.' WHEN IT FINALLY HIT VHS IT HAD THE TITLE IT IS BEST KNOWN AS TODAY: 'HELL OF THE LIVING DEAD.'

104

THE SINFUL DWARF (1973)
AKA: ABDUCTED BRIDE

I HAVE A REAL AFFINITY FOR THIS SCABBY LITTLE DANISH/BRITISH CO-PRODUCTION (SHOT IN COPENHAGEN AND LONDON) THAT COMES IN BOTH A HARDCORE AND A SOFTCORE VERSION. IT'S A MIND-BENDING SLICE OF SADISTIC GRATUITY THAT SUCCESSFULLY HITS SOME OF THOSE PRIME CINEMA SEWER SWEET SPOTS. I MEAN, CHECK OUT THIS BRIEF SYNOPSIS AND TELL ME YOU AREN'T FLIPPIN' STOKED TO SEE IT:

OLAF (THE LATE TORBEN BILLE) IS A WEIRD LITTLE DWARF WITH BUG EYES AND A CRAZY GRIN. HE LOOKS EXACTLY LIKE A SHRUNKEN JACK BLACK (SERIOUSLY) AND LIVES IN A BOARDING HOUSE WITH HIS SCAR-FACED, CABARET-LOVING, LOUD-MOUTH DRUNK OF A MOTHER NAMED LILA (CLARA KELLER). WHEN THEY AREN'T RUNNING DRUGS (THEY HIDE THE SMACK IN TEDDY BEARS!) THE TWO OF THEM KIDNAP AND IMPRISON YOUNG WOMEN WHO THEY KEEP IN A SQUALID ATTIC, DRUGGED OUT OF THEIR MINDS. THEN, FOR A SMALL FEE, PERVERTS ARE GRANTED ACCESS TO GO UPSTAIRS AND HUMP THE CHAINED JUNKIE OF THEIR CHOICE ON A STAINED OLD MATTRESS ON THE FLOOR.

SEE? WHAT'S NOT TO LOVE? PURE NASTY-TRASH BLISS THAT WAS ACTUALLY BANNED FROM THEATRICAL DISTRIBUTION IN SWEDEN BACK IN THE 1970S. LISTEN, YOU KNOW AN EXPLOITATION FILM IS REALLY SOMETHING SPECIAL WHEN IT GETS STUCK IN YOUR BRAIN FOR A FEW DAYS AFTER YOU WATCH IT FOR THE FIRST TIME, AND MOST PEOPLE I'VE SPOKEN TO ABOUT THIS MOVIE DESCRIBE THAT SAME EXPERIENCE. IT'S LIKE A SICKNESS.

WHAT WAS THE TERRIFYING SECRET OF THE ATTIC?!

HARRY NOVAK PRESENTS

THE SINFUL DWARF

WARNING: Not Recommended for people with weak hearts!

ADMISSION RESTRICTED

Color

starring ANNE SPARROW · TONY EADES · CLARA KELLER · introducing TORBEN as THE DWARF
screenplay by WILLIAM MAYO · produced by NICOLAS POOLE · directed by VIDAL RASKI ·
A BOXOFFICE INTERNATIONAL PICTURES, INC. Release

YES, USING WINDUP TOYS AS ENTICEMENT (WHO THOUGHT OF THAT?) OLAF LURES YOUNG WOMEN TO BE FUCKED AND TORTURED. INTO THIS SORDID SET-UP ARRIVES A NEWLY MARRIED COUPLE TO STAY IN THE BOARDINGHOUSE. MARY DAVIS (PLAYED BY ANNE SPARROW) AND HER HUSBAND PETER DON'T SUSPECT WHAT IS GOING ON FOR A SECOND, BUT MARY WORKS AS A WRITER AND IT DOESN'T TAKE HER LONG TO GO INTO NANCY DREW MODE. OLAF DOESN'T APPRECIATE SNOOPS, SO IT SHOULDN'T TAKE THREE GUESSES TO FIGURE OUT WHAT HE AND MAMA HAVE IN STORE FOR HER. THIS IS ONE-OF-A-KIND DEPRAVITY.

A YOUNG BRIDE...LEFT ALONE TO THE LEWD PASSIONS OF AN EVIL DWARF

AS FUN AS THE STUMPY LUNATIC OLAF IS, LILA IS JUST ASTONISHING. AT ONE POINT SHE PUTS ON HER CARMEN MIRANDA OUTFIT SO SHE CAN PERFORM THE "CHO-CHO BAMBA", AND THEN DURING ANOTHER NUMBER THE CAMPY OL' BAT DRESSES UP LIKE MARLENE DIETRICH SO SHE CAN CROON "THE GAME OF LOVE". AND I DIDN'T EVEN MENTION THE WEIRD-AS-FUCK PERCUSSION-HEAVY ORIGINAL SOUNDTRACK BY OLE ORSTED. THE NOW-CLOSED AND DEARLY LAMENTED MONDO VIDEO IN LOS ANGELES WAS ONE OF THE EARLIEST PROMOTERS OF THIS TRASH-CLASSIC, AND EVEN HAD A SUBSECTION IN THEIR STORE BASED UPON IT, ENTITLED: "HORNY MIDGETS". HONESTLY, THIS IS THE KIND OF VINTAGE, DEBAUCHED UNDERGROUND DISCOVERY THAT IS PRECISELY THE VERY REASON I DO CINEMA SEWER. IT'S ALL FOR YOU, SINFUL DWARF. IT'S ALL FOR YOU.

PRESSBOOK IMAGES FOR THIS ARE COURTESY THE COLLECTION OF MIKE ACCOMANDO. MIKE USED TO DO AN AWESOME MOVIE ZINE CALLED DREADFUL PLEASURES -- WHICH I STILL MISS TERRIBLY. HE SELLS PILES OF COOL SHIT ON EBAY UNDER THE NAME "SEACHEESE"

HARRY NOVAK PRESENTS

ABDUCTED BRIDE

HER UNWILLING YOUNG BODY FLAMING INTO A CRAZED, UNCONTROLLABLE PASSION

A VALIANT INTERNATIONAL PICTURE in COLOR

THE CENTERFOLD GIRLS (1974)

HEY, DID YOU KNOW THAT SOME GIRLS ARE FOR LOVING AND SOME GIRLS ARE FOR KILLING? I DIDN'T EITHER, BUT THAT'S WHAT I LEARNED FROM THE ADVERTISING CAMPAIGN FOR THE CENTERFOLD GIRLS. BUT WHAT I WANT TO KNOW IS JUST HOW DOES ONE KNOW WHICH IS WHICH? IT WOULD BE REALLY QUITE UNFORTUNATE TO ACCIDENTALLY KILL A GIRL WHO WAS MADE FOR LOVING, WOULDN'T IT? THAT WOULD RUIN MY DAY, QUITE FRANKLY.

YOU KNOW WHO YOU SHOULDN'T ASK FOR ADVICE ON THAT ONE? THE MAIN CHARACTER IN THIS MOVIE PLAYED BY ANDREW PRINE. AS FAR AS HE'S CONCERNED, ALL WOMEN ARE FOR KILLING IF THEY GIVE ANY INDICATION THAT THEY ARE SEXUAL BEINGS. HE'S NOT A MENTALLY HEALTHY DUDE, THIS AWKWARD, SEXUALLY REPRESSED WEIRDO WHO WEARS REALLY TACKY LEISURE SUITS AND HORN-RIMMED GLASSES. IN FACT HE'S BETTER DESCRIBED AS A DEPRAVED RELIGIOUS FANATIC, BEING AS HE TAKES IT UPON HIMSELF TO ERADICATE ALL OF THE "IMMORAL WOMEN" WHO POSED FOR A PORN MAGAZINE HE BOUGHT. SHEESH. I GUESS EVEN UNHINGED MISOGYNIST NUT-JOBS NEED A HOBBY.

I'M PRETTY SURE THIS VERY CLEVER, MEAN-SPIRITED EXPLOITATION MOVIE WAS AN INSPIRATION FOR QUENTIN TARANTINO'S **DEATH PROOF** (2007), BECAUSE IT OPERATES IN A SIMILAR FASHION WHEN IT COMES TO ITS STRUCTURE. WE FOLLOW THE MORALISTIC EXTREMIST CREEP AS HE METHODICALLY HUNTS DOWN HIS SEXY QUARRY, AND THE MOVIE BREAKS INTO A SEPARATE SEGMENT FOR EACH HUNTED WOMAN. THIS TRANSFORMS THE PICTURE INTO SOMETHING OF AN ANTHOLOGY, WITH NOT ONLY THE SETTING ALTERING FOR EACH SCUMMY STORY, BUT THE VIBE AS

WELL, THE FIRST PART FEELS A LIKE A GIALLO (BLACK GLOVES AND A STRAIGHT RAZOR), THE NEXT A SLASHER MOVIE OR BLOODY VARIATION ON THE MURDER MYSTERY **AND THEN THERE WERE NONE** (1945), AND THE LAST VOLUME ENCAPSULATES AN EXPLOITATION-THEMED ACTION FILM, WHAT WITH ITS HARROWING CHASE SCENE.

THERE IS A LOT TO LIKE HERE, MY PEEPS. I LOVE THE TWISTS AND TURNS IN THE PLOT WHERE YOU HAVE NO IDEA WHO IS GOING TO SURVIVE. THERE ARE SHIT-LOADS OF LOWLIFE CHARACTERS (RAPISTS, DOPERS, WEIRDOS, MANSON-ESQUE HIPPIE CULTS, ETC) WHICH REALLY AMP UP THE SLEAZE FACTOR. AND THEN THERE ARE THE PROTRUDING PILES OF SUPPLE FEMALE FLESH, GRITTY BLOOD-SOAKED VIOLENCE, AND A MINIMAL SCORE TO PROVIDE BACKGROUND GRINDHOUSE THRILLS TO THE STARK CINEMATOGRAPHY AND GRAINY FILM STOCK. THE COMBINED EFFECT REALLY DOES PROVIDE A+ TRASHY FUN THAT I KNOW ALL YOU PERVY BOYS AND GIRLS USUALLY HAVE TO LOOK TO NO-BUDGET 1970S AND '80S PORNO FILMS TO FIND. ON TOP OF THAT, THE DRAMA IS KEENLY AND TENSELY PACED, DIRECTLY INVOLVING THE VIEWER IN THE HARROWING ATTEMPTS OF THE POOR VICTIMS TO SURVIVE UNTIL THE MOVIE COMES TO A SATISFYING CONCLUSION IN THE BLACKENED AND STARKLY ASHY REMAINS OF A BURNT FOREST.

IT WAS COOL SEEING TIFFANY BOLLING AS A TOUGH FLIGHT ATTENDANT WHO GOES TOE-TO-TOE WITH THE KILLER. I ALWAYS FUCKING DIG ON HER. TIFFANY'S FIRST STARRING ROLE WAS IN THE UNDERRATED ARTHUR MARKS DRIVE-IN CLASSIC **BONNIE'S KIDS** (1972). SHE WENT ON TO FEATURE PROMINENTLY IN SOME STAND-OUT GENRE FILMS OF THE ERA, SUCH AS **THE CANDY SNATCHERS** (1973), **WICKED, WICKED** (1973), AND **KINGDOM OF THE SPIDERS** (1977). YOU CAN ALSO SEE TIFFANY IN HER BIRTHDAY SUIT IF YOU MANAGE TO TRACK DOWN THE APRIL 1972 ISSUE OF PLAYBOY. I'D SAY IT'S WORTH THE HUNT FOR THAT ISSUE, AND FOR THE CENTERFOLD GIRLS AS WELL. GREAT STUFF.

WATCH MORE GAY PORN

I THINK IF YOU'RE A STRAIGHT GUY, AND WATCHING TWO GAY MEN HAVE SEX MAKES YOU WINCE AND GET ALL SQUIRELLY 'N' GROSSED OUT, A GOOD THING TO DO IS...WATCH A BUNCH OF GAY PORN.

HEAR ME OUT! I REALLY MEAN IT. I'LL LEVEL WITH YOU, NOW. IT HONESTLY USED TO WIG ME OUT WHEN I WAS IN MY TWENTIES -- LOOKING AT TWO DUDES GET FREAKY. BUT OVER THE YEARS BEING A PORN JOURNALIST MEANS I LOOK AT ALL KINDS OF PORN AS PART OF MY JOB AND HOBBY, AND THAT INCLUDES PORN THAT DOESN'T REALLY DO MUCH FOR ME. AND AFTER THAT, I HAVE TO SAY THAT I'VE GOTTEN PAST THE 'YUCK' PHASE. IT'S LIKE ANYTHING WHERE YOU GET DESENSITIZED TO IT UPON EXPERIENCING IT. HOMO PORN DOESN'T EVEN MAKE ME BLINK ANYMORE, AND I THINK THAT'S GOOD. IF GAY MEN GOTTA CONSTANTLY LOOK AT US STRAIGHTS NAKED AND RUTTING IN ALL OF THEIR MEDIA, THE VERY LEAST WE CAN DO IS MEET THEM HALFWAY.

"BUT ROBIN", YOU ARE PERHAPS THINKING AS YOU READ THIS. "LOOKING AT THE JUNK OF ALL THOSE NAKED HAIRY GUYS MAKES ME KINDA UNCOMFORTABLE." C'MON, MAKE A TINY FUCKING EFFORT HERE. JUST GET YOUR HEAD AROUND IT, THAT'S ALL. AND THAT REALLY ISN'T SO HARD WHEN YOU REMEMBER THAT YOU'VE BEEN JERKING OFF YOUR WHOLE LIFE TO SMUT WITH PILES OF NAKED GUYS IN IT.

THAT'S RIGHT, YOU HAVE -- REMEMBER? IT'S CALLED <u>STRAIGHT PORN</u>.

HERE'S A BONUS TIP FOR THE NERVOUS GAY PORN NOOBS: IT'S GONNA BE GOOD TO START OUT WITH SOME STUFF THAT HAS OTHER ASPECTS WHICH YOU WILL ENJOY. YOU KNOW, RAD FASHIONS, FUN DIALOG, COOL MUSIC, QUIRKY PLOTS, ETC -- SO I'D SUGGEST STARTING WITH THE VINTAGE MATERIAL. JUST LIKE VINTAGE STRAIGHT PORN, GOOD CLASSIC GAY SMUT HAS OTHER LEVELS ON WHICH IT CAN BE ENJOYED, OVER AND ABOVE JUST WANK-INSPIRATION. AND THAT'S GOOD NEWS FOR YOU, STRAIGHT GUY.

DO SOME RESEARCH ON PERFORMERS LIKE KIP NOLL, CASEY DONOVAN, RICK DONOVAN, PAUL BARRESI, DICK FISK, LEO FORD, AND BILL HENSON. HOW ABOUT DIRECTORS LIKE WAKEFIELD POOLE, WILLIAM HIGGINS, TIM KINCAID, MATT STERLING, AND MUSICIANS LIKE PATRICK COWLEY? MAYBE YOU'LL FEEL BETTER IF YOU'RE SEEING SOME FAMILIAR FACES FROM VINTAGE STRAIGHT PORNO, LIKE: PETER NORTH, JACK WRANGLER, GEORGE PAYNE, AND JEFF STRYKER. AND IF YOU'RE MORE INTO ART, GET YOURSELF SOME TOM OF FINLAND. YOU CERTAINLY DON'T HAVE TO BE A FAGGOT TO ADORE HIS DELICATE LINEWORK, AND THATS A GODDAMN <u>FACT</u>.

IT'S PAINFULLY CLEAR THAT TOO MUCH OF THE HOMOPHOBIA IN OUR SOCIETY IS DIRECTLY RELATED TO THE "GAYS GROSS ME OUT" FACTOR, AND 99% OF THAT OBVIOUSLY STEMS FROM DEPICTIONS OR DISPLAYS OF SEXUALITY. I'M NOT SAYING Y'ALL ARE HOMOPHOBES IF YOU DON'T LOOK AT GAY PORN, BUT I AM SAYING THAT I FEEL THAT YOU AND I WILL BE FAR LESS LIKELY TO DISCRIMINATE IF WE ARE COMFORTABLE WITH THIS STUFF ON A VISCERAL, GUT LEVEL. I'M TALKING ABOUT THAT PRIMAL, SMUTTY PLANE OF EXISTENCE THAT I REALLY DO BELIEVE ACTS AS A GREAT EQUALIZER, BECAUSE IT BRUSHES AWAY OUR DIFFERENCES. WE'RE ALL SEXUAL BEINGS, AND WE ALL JUST WANT TO BE WANTED.

US PERVERTS HAVE GOT TO STICK TOGETHER (*WET SOUND EFFECT*), BECAUSE THOSE THAT WANT TO TAKE US DOWN CERTAINLY ARE.

LOOKIT' 'EM GO!

CAMP ATROCITIES: NAZI EXPLOITATION AND DEATH CAMP HORRORS

BY: DAVID HINDS

A HEARTY "ACHTUNG!" TO ALL YOU KINKY KOMMANDANTS AND SLEAZY SHE-WOLVES OUT THERE! YOU'RE HERE FOR THE NAUSEATING SAUERKRAUT SICKNESS, YOU SAY? WELL, PUT ON YOUR LEATHER JACKBOOTS AND YOUR POINTY PICKELHAUBE HELMETS MY FRIENDS -- AND READ ON!

THE CINEMATIC NAZI EXPLOITATION CYCLE FINDS ITS PERVERSE ROOTS IN THE WOMEN IN PRISON (WIP) GENRE, CONTAINING MANY OF THE SAME INGREDIENTS AND A SIMILAR APPROACH. IT'S AN INFLAMMATORY GENRE ALMOST WHOLLY ATTRIBUTED TO ITALIAN FILM INDUSTRY OUTPUT WITH A FEW NOTABLE CONTRIBUTIONS FROM FRANCE, USA AND CANADA. THESE BAD TASTE ODDITIES ARE ESSENTIALLY COLLECTIONS OF SOFTCORE GROPING, LESBIANISM, RAPE, AND THE OCCASIONAL FLOURISH OF BLOODY VIOLENCE AND CRUEL EXPERIMENTS AS FEMALE PRISONERS OF WAR ARE ABUSED AND BRUTALISED BY NAZI GUARDS (MALE AND FEMALE), AND ARE USUALLY HOUSED IN A CONCENTRATION CAMP OR PRISON SETTING.

AS WITH THE ROUGHIES RESIDING IN NEW YORK'S GRINDHOUSES, THE SEX ON DISPLAY HERE HAS BRUTAL TENDENCIES, OFTEN IN THE FORM OF SEXUAL ABUSE, RAPE, TORTURE, DOMINATION AND DEGRADATION. SADOMASOCHISM IS A STAPLE INGREDIENT, AS VICTIMS ARE BOUND AND SHACKLED, FLAGELLATED, ALL WHILE PERVERSE POWER PLAY GAMES ARE UTILISED. PACKAGE ALL OF THIS UP AGAINST A BACKDROP OF THE HOLOCAUST AND YOU'VE GOT A MORALLY BANKRUPT GENRE OF FETISHIST FILMS UNLIKE ANY OTHER.

SCRAPING THE VERY BOTTOM OF THE BARREL, THE MAJORITY OF SS CAMP OFFERINGS ARE LOW-BUDGET, WORKMANLIKE PRODUCTIONS -- WITH THE FIRST OFFICIAL ENTRY BEING THE AMERICAN PRODUCTION **LOVE CAMP 7** FROM 1968. DIRECTED BY R.L. FROST (ALSO RESPONSIBLE FOR THE HARDCORE A CLIMAX OF BLUE POWER). THIS SCABBY T'N'A FLICK ESTABLISHED THE TEMPLATE FOR THE SUB-GENRE FOR THE NEXT DECADE, IT IS ONE THAT WOULD BARELY CHANGE OR EVOLVE.

IN 1974 EXPLOITATION LEGEND DAVE FRIEDMAN GAVE THE WORLD THE WORLD THE INFAMOUS CULT SLEAZE-FEST **ILSA, SHE WOLF OF THE SS**. DESPITE ITS YANK BRAVADO AND CAMP ATTITUDE, ILSA REMAINS (IN MY OPINION) THE MOST ENTERTAINING NAZISPLOITATION

MOVIE, AND ALSO ONE OF THE MOST DISTURBING (SECOND ONLY TO THE SICKENING **WOMEN'S CAMP 119**).

THE ITALIAN FILM INDUSTRY WAS QUICK TO RESPOND TO THE BOX OFFICE SUCCESS OF MOVIES LIKE CANADIAN DIRECTOR DON EDMONDS'S **ILSA, SHE WOLF OF THE SS** (1974) LILIANA CAVANI'S **THE NIGHT PORTER** (1974), PASOLINI'S **SALO** (1975), AND **SALON KITTY** (1976), WHICH SPAWNED FORTH FROM THE FETID IMAGINATION OF TINTO BRASS. UNABLE TO IGNORE THE HEALTHY BOX OFFICE NUMBERS, THE ITALIANS RUBBER-STAMPED THE VILE NAZISPLOITATION TEMPLATE WITH INFAMOUS COPYCAT TITLES SUCH AS **SS EXPERIMENT CAMP, SS CAMP 5: WOMENS HELL,** AND **SS GIRLS**. INDEED, BETWEEN 1976 AND 1977, ITALY'S SCUMMIEST FILMMAKERS CONTRIBUTED A DOZEN OF THESE MOVIES, RANGING IN QUALITY AND EXTREMITY.

DELIBERATELY OFFENSIVE, THE NAZI EXPLOITATION GENRE ESSENTIALLY DIED JUST PRIOR TO THE REAGAN ERA, AND STANDS TODAY AS A BIZARRE FOOTNOTE IN CULT FILM HISTORY. BELOW IS AN EXHAUSTIVE (BUT NOT DEFINITIVE) RUNDOWN IN ALPHABETIC ORDER FOR YOU, BUT AS STEPHEN THROWER SO VERY ELOQUENTLY PUT IT IN THE EYEBALL COMPENDIUM (FAB PRESS), "NAZI EXPLOITATION FILMS ARE LIKE COCKROACHES — JUST WHEN YOU THINK YOU'VE GOT RID OF THE LAST ONE, ANOTHER SCUTTLES INTO VIEW."

ILSA SHE-WOLF OF THE SS

ACHTUNG! THE DESERT TIGERS
(1977, ITALY, DIR. LUIGI BATZELLA)
THE DESERT TIGERS DELIVERS STANDARD WHIPPINGS, BRUTALISED WOMEN, A CASTRATION SCENE AND PLENTY OF NUDITY. THERE ARE SOME BELOW AVERAGE COMBAT SCENES AND DIRECTOR BATZELLA SEEMS TO BE UNEASY ON WHICH DIRECTION TO GO. IT FAILS AS BOTH A Z-GRADE MILITARY ACTION FLICK AND AS A SLEAZY NAZI WIP SEXPLOITATION. QUITE HARD TO FIND, BUT THERE ARE BOOTLEGS AVAILABLE IF YOU LOOK HARD ENOUGH. ONLY FOR COMPLETISTS OF SS THEMED SLEAZE.

THE BEAST IN HEAT
AKA SS HELL CAMP
(1977, ITALY, DIR. LUIGI BATZELLA)
IN A REMOTE NAZI OCCUPIED VILLAGE A BEAUTIFUL BUT SADISTIC NAZI DOCTOR, FRAULEIN KRATSCH, INDULGES IN THE SADISTIC DEGRADATION OF YOUNG WOMEN TO SATISFY HER PERVERSE DESIRES AND TO OBTAIN INFORMATION ABOUT THE LOCAL RESISTANCE. THROUGH BIOLOGICAL EXPERIMENTATION

DEPORTED WOMEN OF THE SS SPECIAL SECTION (1976, ITALY)

THE MAD DOCTOR HAS CREATED A VERY
HORNY HALF MAN-HALF BEAST WHO SHE
KEEPS LOCKED IN A LARGE CAGE AND
SATISFIES ITS SEXUAL URGES BY
ALLOWING IT TO LITERALLY RAPE HER
FEMALE PRISONERS TO DEATH. THE
PROLONGED RAPE SCENES BETWEEN THE
BEAST AND ITS SCREAMING NAKED
VICTIMS ARE MORE FUNNY THAN
DISTURBING, BUT THE FILM DOES
DELIVER SEVERAL TRULY OUTRAGEOUS
SCENES, THE MOST FAMOUS BEING THE
BEAST RIPPING OFF AND THEN EATING
A WOMAN'S PUBIC HAIR LEAVING BLOODY
LUMPS AROUND HER MAULED GENITALIA.
NOW THAT IS HOW TO EAT PUSSY, FOLKS!
IN ANOTHER SCENE GERMAN TROOPS
ATTACK A SMALL VILLAGE AND RAPE A
YOUNG WOMAN, BEFORE A SOLDIER
THROWS A BABY INTO THE AIR AND
SHOOTS IT DEAD! BATZELLA ALSO SERVES
US A PROLONGED TORTURE SCENE IN
WHICH ONE NAKED WOMAN HAS HER
FINGERNAILS TORN OUT WITH PLIERS AS
SHE CASUALLY EXCLAIMS "IT HURTS, IT
HURTS". GUINEA PIGS ARE PLACED
INSIDE A STEEL BUCKET OVER A WOMAN'S
BELLY AND A FLAME IS LIT ABOVE THEM
SO THEY TUNNEL INTO HER BOWELS. THIS
INSANE CHUNK OF EURO TRASHOLA WAS
BANNED IN THE UK AS A VIDEO NASTY,
AND THE BANNED VHS TAPE ON THE JVI
LABEL UNBELIEVABLY SOLD FOR PRICES
AS HIGH AS $1,000 AT COLLECTORS
CONVENTIONS AND ON EBAY! ESSENTIAL
VIEWING.

**DEPORTED WOMEN OF THE SS SPECIAL
SECTION**
(1976, ITALY, DIR RINO DI SILVESTRO)
THIS DARK AND DEPRESSING SLICE OF

↯↯ CAMP 5 (ITALY 1977) ➡

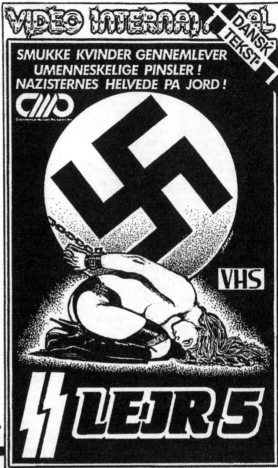

VIDEO INTERNATIONAL · DANSK TEKST·

SMUKKE KVINDER GENNEMLEVER
UMENNESKELIGE PINSLER !
NAZISTERNES HELVEDE PA JORD !

CMD
Continental Motion Pictures Inc.

VHS

⚡⚡ LEJR 5

⬅ THE BEAST IN HEAT (ITALY 1977)

LA BÊTE EN CHALLOR
(LES MONSTRES NAZIS)

MACHA MAGALL
JOHN BRAUN
XIROS PAPAS

LES FILMS DU VERSEAU
Eastmancolor

HET BEEST OP DRIFT
(DE MONSTERS VAN HET NAZI-REGIME)

EURO-SLEAZE HAS GOOD PRODUCTION
VALUES AND IS TECHNICALLY VERY
COMPETENT. WHEREAS MORE INFAMOUS
TITLES SUCH AS SS EXPERIMENT CAMP AND
SS GIRLS WERE EITHER SILLY OR
DERANGED EXERCISES IN SLEAZE AND
TORTURE, DWOTSSSS IS A FAR MORE
REALISTIC AND UNPLEASANT AFFAIR. THE
ACCOMPLISHED AND FLUID PHOTOGRAPHY
IS, FOR MOST OF ITS RUNNING TIME,
IMMERSED WITHIN BLEAK GREY WALLS, AND
GROTTY CLAUSTROPHOBIC ROOMS. THIS IS
A PLACE WERE HOPE DOES NOT EXIST.
HEADS AND GROINS ARE SHAVED, LESBIAN
GUARDS OBSERVE AND PROBE PUSSIES
WITH TRUNCHEONS, AND THE MOST
BEAUTIFUL OF THE INMATES ARE FORCED
TO WORK AS FIELD WHORES FOR THE SS.
THE DEGRADATION CONTINUES WITH
SCENES OF FORCED LESBIANISM, SUICIDE
AND A CRAZY SCENE IN WHICH THE CAMP
COMMANDANT SODOMISES HIS MALE
ASSISTANT AFTER A FIRESIDE MASSAGE!
WHEN THE MANDATORY PRISON REVOLT
TAKES PLACE, NAZIS ARE STABBED,
STRANGLED AND SUFFOCATED, AND THE
LEAD HEROINE WANDERS THE CAMP
GROUNDS COMPLETELY NAKED WITH A
MACHINE GUN, PEPPERING TROOPS WITH
BULLETS UNTIL SHE IS BLOWN AWAY
HERSELF. FAR MORE SERIOUS THAN MOST
OTHER ENTRIES IN THE SUB-GENRE,

DEPORTED WOMEN IS VERY UNPLEASANT
VIEWING AND HARD TO FIND UNCUT.

ELSA, FRAULEIN SS
(1977, FRANCE, DIR. PATRICE RHOMM)
SET IN 1943, THIS WEAK FRENCH
NAZISPLOITATION EFFORT DEPICTS A
LOVE TRAIN FOR GERMAN OFFICERS IN
WHICH THEY CAN INDULGE IN THE
PLEASURES OF THE FLESH. LED BY ELSA,
THE GIRLS WEED OUT ANY UNPATRIOTIC
OFFICERS AND HAVE THEM SHOT. THE
RESISTANCE HAVE ALSO SMUGGLED AN
UNDERCOVER AGENT ON BOARD, AND THE
FINALE SEES THE RESISTANCE ATTACK THE
TRAIN IN TYPICAL LOW-BUDGET FASHION.
PIGGYBACKING ON THE SUCCESS OF ILSA,
SHE WOLF OF THE SS AND SALON KITTY,
THIS IS VIRTUALLY IDENTICAL TO SPECIAL
TRAIN FOR HITLER -- AND ALTHOUGH SHE
DOES LOOK THE PART ELSA IS
CERTAINLY NO ILSA. THE VIOLENCE IS
DULL, AND ODDLY ENOUGH FOR THIS
GENRE THE SADISTIC ELSA DOESN'T GET
HER COMEUPPANCE IN THE FINALE. FRENCH
XXX PORN STAR CLAUDINE BECCARIE IS
AMONGST THE SEXY FEMALE CAST.

FRAULEINS IN UNIFORM (AKA FRAULEIN WITHOUT UNIFORM)
(1973, GERMANY, DIR. ERWIN C. DIETRICH)
THE ONLY GERMAN NAZISPLOITATION
MOVIE! THIS IS A HANDSOMELY PRODUCED
SOFTCORE SEX AFFAIR FROM JESS
FRANCO COLLABORATOR DIETRICH. DR. KUHN
IS A KINDLY GERMAN DOCTOR WHO IS
GIVEN THE TASK OF EXAMINING AND
ENLISTING HOT YOUNG FEMALES INTO

THE THIRD REICH TO FIGHT ALONGSIDE THE MALE
TROOPS. THE DOC HAS TWO DAUGHTERS OF HIS OWN,
AND UNDERSTANDS THAT THE WOMEN ARE LIKELY TO BE
ABUSED WHILST SERVING ON THE FRONT LINES, SO HE
SENDS MOST OF THEM BACK HOME. THE GESTAPO DO
NOT LOOK FONDLY UPON THIS ACTION, AND PUNISH HIM
BY FORCING HIM TO SERVE ON THE RUSSIAN FRONT.
UNBEKNOWNST TO HIM, BOTH OF HIS DAUGHTERS HAVE
BEEN FORCED TO ENLIST AND ONE OF THEM IS BEING
HELD PRISONER IN A VILLAGE HE IS ABOUT TO ATTACK
WITH HIS TROOPS. DIETRICH ENSURES THE SCREEN IS
AWASH IN NAKED FEMALE FLESH FROM BEGINNING TO
END, AND THE JAW-DROPPING FINALE IN WHICH NAKED
GERMAN WOMEN RUN AROUND A BATTLEFIELD WITH
BOMBS AND BULLETS GOING OFF AROUND THEM IS
WORTH THE ADMISSION PRICE ALONE. QUITE HARD TO
TRACK DOWN, BUT REWARDING ENOUGH FOR LOVERS OF
SOFTCORE EUROSPLOITATION.

LES GARDIENNES DU PENITENCIER
(1979, FRANCE, DIR. ALAIN DERUELLE CREDITED AS
ALLAN W. STEEVE)
QUITE POSSIBLY THE CHEAPEST ENTRY IN THE NAZI
EXPLOITATION GENRE. THIS DREADFUL HACK JOB
BARELY QUALIFIES AS NAZISPLOITATION, AND IS
COMPRISED OF FOOTAGE CULLED FROM SEVERAL OTHER
FILMS, AND SPLICED TOGETHER WITH A COUPLE OF NEW
SCENES. THERE'S A HEAVY DOSE OF BARBED WIRE
DOLLS TO SET THE SCENE, A SPRINKLE OF SPECIAL
TRAIN FOR HITLER AND A PINCH OF ELSA, FRAULEIN SS
FOR GOOD MEASURE. EVEN THE SCORE BY DANIEL
WHITE IS STOLEN FROM OTHER FILMS. THIS MOVIE
PISSED ME OFF, AND IS A COMPLETE WASTE OF TIME.
DON'T BOTHER.

GESTAPO'S LAST ORGY
(AKA CALIGULA REINCARNATED AS HITLER)
(1977, ITALY, DIR. CESARE CANEVARI)
PACKED WITH SUFFERING, CRUELTY, SADOMASOCHISM
AND GOOD OLD FASHIONED BAD TASTE. A NAZI
COMMANDANT BECOMES OBSESSED WITH A JEWISH
PRISONER CALLED LISE, AND SETS ABOUT MAKING HER
HIS PERSONAL SEX SLAVE. THE BULK OF THE FILM IS
TOLD IN FLASHBACK AND IN THE PRESENT LISE AND
THE COMMANDANT (CLEARED OF WAR CRIMES) REUNITE
IN THE DECREPIT CAMP IN WHICH THEIR RELATIONSHIP
BEGAN. THE FREQUENT SOFT FOCUS NUDITY AND RAPE

ENSUE IN TYPICAL FASHION. ON THE GORE FRONT THERE IS LITTLE TO SPEAK OF ASIDE FROM TWO SCENES THAT CERTAINLY STAIN THE BRAIN. THE FIRST INVOLVES A COLLECTION OF DEFORMED, OVERWEIGHT OLD NAKED LADIES AND PREGNANT WOMEN WHO ARE LED INTO A TUNNEL TO BE INCINERATED, AND THE SECOND DEPICTS A NAZI DINNER PARTY IN WHICH A JEWISH BABY IS THE MAIN COURSE, FOLLOWED BY A CANNIBALISTIC FEAST OF A BURNED BODY IN A CASKET. SOME SCENES ARE SURPRISINGLY EXPLICIT, AND THEMES OF FORCED INCEST AND SCATOLOGY ARE ALSO REFERENCED. ON THE TORTURE FRONT LISE IS SUSPENDED UPSIDE DOWN AND NAKED ABOVE A TANK OF RATS, WHO ARE PLAYED BY HARMLESS GERBIL THESPIANS DOING RATHER INAUTHENTIC RAT IMPERSONATIONS. GENERALLY CONSIDERED ONE OF THE NASTIEST NAZI SLEAZEFESTS, BUT BEWARE THE UNRATED US DVD VERSION ON THE ALTERNATIVE CINEMA LABEL RELEASED AS **CALIGULA REINCARNATED AS HITLER** -- IT IS HEAVILY CUT. THE DANISH VHS RELEASE AVAILABLE ON THE DVD-R BOOTLEG CIRCUIT IS THE MOST COMPLETE VERSION.

HELGA, SHE WOLF OF SPILBERG
(1977, FRANCE, DIR. PATRICE RHOMM)
THIS FRENCH EUROCINE PRODUCTION IS A COMPANION PIECE TO **NATHALIE: ESCAPE FROM HELL**, WHICH WAS MADE BACK TO BACK AT THE SAME TIME, AND FEATURES MANY OF THE SAME ACTORS, CREW, LOCATIONS AND SETS. THIS IS THE MORE WELL KNOWN OF THE TWO, DELIBERATELY RIFFING ON THE TITLE OF THE FAR MORE SUCCESSFUL **ILSA, SHE WOLF OF THE SS**. SADLY, THIS IS WHERE THE SIMILARITIES END AS HELGA (MALISA LONGO) IS MORE OF A SHE-PUPPY THAN A SHE-WOLF. LIKE NATHALIE, THIS IS AN OVERLONG AND TEDIOUS AFFAIR WHICH SKIMPS ON THE NASTINESS AND SLEAZE. THE OFFICERS AND SOLDIERS IN THIS EFFORT ARE NOT ACTUALLY CHARACTERISED AS GERMAN AND THE SWASTIKA IS REPLACED WITH A SIMILAR SYMBOL OF RED, WHITE AND BLACK. SOME LOW-BUDGET POLITICAL SHENANIGANS DRESSED UP IN WWII STYLE TRAPPINGS FRAME A FLIMSY PLOT IN WHICH CRUEL WARDRESS HELGA DOES HER BEST TO BED AS MANY WOMEN AS POSSIBLE. THE SEX IS BRIEF AND SOFT, AND THE RAPE SCENES ARE TAME ENOUGH TO PLAY ON TV. A STRUGGLE TO SIT THROUGH.

HOLOCAUST 2: THE MEMORIES, DELIRIUM AND THE VENDETTA PART 2
(1978 - RELEASED IN 1980, ITALY, DIR. ANGELO PANNACCIO)
THIS IS A TERRIBLE CAR WRECK OF A MOVIE. IT TAKES PLACE IN THE PRESENT DAY (LATE 1970S) AS A GROUP OF JEWISH ACTIVISTS TRACK DOWN THE NAZIS RESPONSIBLE FOR KILLING THEIR RELATIVES. THIS INTRIGUING IDEA IS WASTED IN THIS RAMBLING, INSANE MOVIE THAT SEEMS TO HAVE BEEN MADE BY MANIACS! THE MESSY EDITING IS WITHOUT RHYME OR REASON AND CHARACTERS ARE INTRODUCED IN SUCH A HAPHAZARD WAY THAT THE WHOLE THING BECOMES NEEDLESSLY CONFUSING. IN ONE SCENE, A KIDNAPPED MAN IS TIED TO A TABLE AND A GOAT LICKS HIS FEET UNTIL HE DIES OF TICKLE TORTURE. I AM SERIOUS. THIS MOVIE IS NUTS! THERE ARE SEVERAL INTERESTING MOMENTS: NOTABLY THE BRUTAL FLASHBACKS DEPICTING WOMEN BEING GUNNED DOWN AND ABUSED BY GERMAN SOLDIERS ACCOMPANIED BY A CHOIR OF CHILDREN. ONE

FEMALE PRISONER GOES INTO A FRENZY AND ENDS UP VOLUNTARILY GIVING ONE OF THE SOLDIERS A BLOW JOB IN FRONT OF EVERYONE BEFORE HE BLOWS HER GUTS OUT WITH HIS RIFLE. FOR THE RECORD, THERE IS NO HOLOCAUST PART ONE.

ILSA, SHE WOLF OF THE SS
(1974, CANADA, DIR: DON EDMONDS)
THE MOST INFAMOUS AND EXTREME OF ALL THE NAZI EXPLOITATION FILMS, ILSA RIDES AN OCEAN OF NASTINESS WITH KINKY SEX, RAPE, NUDITY, FETISHISM, VIOLENCE AND HORRIFIC GORY EXPERIMENTS. THIS IS A GENUINE GUILTY PLEASURE AND A THOROUGHLY ENTERTAINING SLICE OF UNREPENTANT GARBAGE. THE MATERIAL IS PRESENTED IN A DELIBERATELY OFFENSIVE MANNER AND PACKAGED IN SCHUTZSTAFFEL TRAPPINGS. DYANNE THORNE IS OUTSTANDING AS THE NYMPHOMANIAC TITULAR CHARACTER, PREYING AROUND THE CAMP LIKE A HUNGRY TARANTULA WITH HER TWO BLACK WIDOWS (TWO SEXY BISEXUAL BLONDE ASSISTANTS) IN TOW. SHE COLDLY USES THE MALE PRISONERS FOR SEX, AND

IF THEY FAIL TO SATISFY HER, SHE HAS THEM CASTRATED. MEANWHILE, SICK MEDICAL EXPERIMENTS ARE CONDUCTED BY NONE OTHER THAN JOHN CARPENTER REGULAR GEORGE "BUCK" FLOWER, WHO DELIVERS ONE OF THE CAMPIEST GERMAN ACCENTS TO EVER GRACE THE SCREEN. ILSA'S GOAL IS TO PROVE TO HER HIGH RANKING GERMAN SUPERIORS THAT WOMEN HAVE A STRONGER PAIN THRESHOLD THAN MEN AND SHOULD THEREFORE BE ALLOWED TO SERVE ON THE FRONT LINES, AND TO VALIDATE HER ARGUMENT ONE WOMAN HAS SYPHILIS-INFECTED MAGGOTS POURED INTO A GROTESQUE OPEN WOUND ON HER LEG. BIG BREASTED USCHI DIGARD IS PLACED IN A PRESSURE CHAMBER AND BLOOD POURS FROM HER MOUTH AND STREAMS OVER HER AMPLE BOSOM. A STRONG WILLED WOMAN BECOMES ILSA'S GUINEA PIG AND IS SICKENINGLY BOILED, HER SKIN A RED, BLISTERING, PEELING MASS HANGING FROM HER ENTIRE BODY. DURING A NAZI DINNER PARTY A NAKED JEWISH GIRL IS SUSPENDED BY A NOOSE AS SHE STANDS ON A MELTING BLOCK OF ICE FOR THEIR SICK AMUSEMENT. PRODUCED BY GRINDHOUSE LEGEND DAVID F. FRIEDMAN, ILSA BECAME A BOX OFFICE SMASH IN EUROPE AND HAD A LEGENDARY RUN ON 42ND STREET. ACTRESS DYANNE THORNE FOUND IT CHALLENGING TO GET WORK IN THE WAKE OF THE FILM, BUT WOULD REPRISE HER ROLE IN ILSA, HAREM KEEPER OF THE OIL SHEIKS, ILSA, THE TIGRESS OF SIBERIA AND JESS FRANCO'S ILSA, THE WICKED WARDEN.

LOVE CAMP 7
(1968, USA, DIR: R.L. FROST)
T 'N' A SLEAZE DRESSED UP IN NAZI REGALIA, AND SPIT FORTH FROM THE TWISTED MIND OF SLEAZE MERCHANT R.L.

You will not forget in your lifetime the horrors you will witness...

LOVE CAMP 7

The story of LOVE CAMP SEVEN is based on fact. Two young American W.A.C. Officers volunteer to throw themselves into the unspeakable indignities and horrifying humiliation of a Nazi Love Camp. These camps were used entirely to service the pleasures and perversions of the Nazi Front Line Officers. Then at 03.00 hours on the fifth day the area French Resistance was scheduled to break them free...

Filmed in Eastman Colour.

FROST (ZERO IN AND SCREAM, A CLIMAX OF BLUE POWER). THIS WAS THE FIRST GENUINE THEATRICAL NAZI EXPLOITATION FILM AND IT DELIVERS PLENTY OF WRITHING BODIES AND SWEATY SOFTCORE SEX DURING ITS RUNNING TIME. TWO UNDERCOVER AMERICAN OFFICERS ENTER A GERMAN PRISON CAMP TO OBTAIN SOME SECRET INFORMATION FROM A SCIENTIST WHO IS HELD CAPTIVE THERE. THE WOMEN AT THIS NAZI WAR CAMP ARE MAULED AND RAPED BY THE GUARDS AS WELL AS BEING TORTURED, AND THESE TORTURES ARE MOSTLY HILARIOUS. IN ONE SUCH SCENE, A WOMAN IS MASTURBATED IN AN ATTEMPT TO EXTRACT SOME INFORMATION, AND IN ANOTHER A GROUP OF WOMEN ARE FORCED TO WALK AROUND WITH BUCKETS OF WATER. DESPITE THESE SILLY SCENARIOS DIRECTOR FROST DELIVERS SOME PAINFULLY GRAPHIC AND GENUINELY REAL FLAGELLATION - WE LITERALLY SEE WELTS AND RED SORES APPEARING ON THE ACTRESSES' BODIES, AND THE CAMERA DOES NOT CUT AWAY. THESE PUNISHMENTS ARE ADMINISTERED BY INFAMOUS GRINDHOUSE PRODUCER BOB CRESSE, WHO COLLECTED SS REGALIA, AND ALSO ENJOYED WHIPPING PRETTY WOMEN IN HIS PRIVATE LIFE. THIS IS QUITE EVIDENT, GIVEN HOW CLEARLY INTO THIS ROLE BOB APPEARS.

The incredible voyage of a train-load of lovely young girls...

HITLER'S LUST TRAIN SS

COLOR

⇐ ALL ABOARRRD THE LUST TRAIN!

NATHALIE: ESCAPE FROM HELL
(1977, FRANCE, DIR. ALAIN PAYET)
NATHALIE IS A RUSSIAN DOCTOR
WORKING IN A FRENCH RURAL VILLAGE.
ON ONE FATEFUL DAY WHILST MAKING
HER HOUSE CALLS TO THE ILL AND
INFIRM, SHE SAVES NAZI OFFICER
MULLER'S LIFE (EUROCINE REGULAR
JACK TAYLOR) WHEN HIS SQUADRON IS
SHOT TO PIECES BY THE FRENCH
RESISTANCE. NONETHELESS, NATHALIE IS
ARRESTED AND TAKEN TO A CHATEAU
IN SPILBERG -- ONE RUN BY THE
PERPETUALLY DRUNK COLONEL GUNTHER,
WHOSE SECOND IN COMMAND IS A CRUEL
AND SADISTIC MISTRESS NAMED HELGA.
AS A RELATIONSHIP BLOSSOMS BETWEEN
NATHALIE AND MULLER, THE COUPLE
EXCHANGE A LONG MEANINGFUL LOOK
BEFORE MULLER DRY HUMPS HER
THROUGH THE BED SHEETS. THIS VERY
CHEAP EUROCINE PRODUCTION IS
POORLY EDITED, SLOW PACED, SADLY
LACKING IN SORDID DETAILS, AND HAS
LITTLE TO OFFER EXPLOITATION
HOUNDS. DESERVEDLY ONE OF THE MOST
OBSCURE ENTRIES ON THIS LIST.

NAZI LOVE CAMP 27
AKA. LIVING NIGHTMARE
(1977, ITALY, DIR. MARIO CAIANO)
A YOUNG GERMAN COUPLE ARE FORCED
APART DURING WORLD WAR II. THE
GIRL (SIRPA LANE) IS JEWISH AND
SENT TO CAMP 27 WHERE SHE'S
FORCED TO WORK AS A SEX SLAVE. HER
LOVER IS FORCED TO SIGN UP AND
FIGHT ALONGSIDE THE NAZIS. LANE
REFUSES TO ADHERE TO THE RULES OF
THE PROSTITUTION CAMP AND IS ABOUT
TO BE PUNISHED BY THE CRUEL
WARDRESS WHEN THE CAMP COMMANDANT
TAKES A FANCY TO HER. MOVING HER
INTO HIS LUXURIOUS QUARTERS, THE
TWO BEGIN AN AFFAIR -- BUT THIS
COMMANDANT IS AN ODD CROSS-
DRESSING SADIST WHO TRIES TO GET
LANE TO HAVE SEX WITH HIS PRIZE
ALSATIAN. WAR IS CLEARLY HELL, AND
AS IT RAGES ON LANE'S HATRED FOR
HER CAPTORS GROWS, CULMINATING IN A
VIOLENT REVOLT OF FURY AT A
BURLESQUE BORDELLO PARTY. CAIANO'S
EFFORT PLAYS MORE LIKE A SERIOUS
DRAMA THAN MANY OTHER FILMS OF ITS
ILK, AND SIRPA LANE IS VERY GOOD IN
THE LEAD. LIKE **THE GESTAPO'S LAST
ORGY**, THE FILM IS NOTABLE FOR
MAKING EXPLICIT REFERENCE TO THE
ENSLAVED WOMEN AS BEING JEWISH,
SOMETHING MOST FILMS IN THE GENRE
SURPRISINGLY SHY AWAY FROM.

THE NIGHT PORTER
(1974, ITALY, DIR. LILIANA CAVANI)
A BLEAK AND DEPRESSING FILM
STARRING DIRK BOGARDE AS MAX,
A NAZI WAR CRIMINAL HIDING OUT IN POST WAR VIENNA WHERE HE WORKS AS A NIGHT
PORTER IN A PRESTIGIOUS HOTEL. WHEN MAX CHECKS IN A BEAUTIFUL YOUNG WOMAN NAMED
LUCIA (CHARLOTTE RAMPLING) THEY IMMEDIATELY RECOGNISE ONE ANOTHER. TURNS OUT LUCIA
WAS MAX'S PERSONAL JEWISH SEX SLAVE WHOM HE DOMINATED IN A CONCENTRATION CAMP
DURING THE WAR. SMALL WORLD, HUH? THEY QUICKLY REKINDLE THEIR ODDBALL
SADOMASOCHISTIC LOVE AFFAIR BUT MAX IS SOON HARASSED BY A SECRET ORDER OF NAZIS.
THE NIGHT PORTER HAS AN EXCITING CONCEPT BUT SADLY DOES LITTLE WITH IT. ALTHOUGH
CINEMATIC AND EXQUISITELY ACTED, IT IS A SLOW-MOVING ARTHOUSE AFFAIR. NIGHT PORTER
IS EASILY THE MOST CRITICALLY RESPECTED FILM ON THIS LIST -- EVEN GARNERING A SPOT
IN THE CELEBRATED CRITERION DVD CATALOGUE.

THE RED NIGHTS OF THE GESTAPO
(1977, ITALY, DIR. FABIO DE AGOSTINI)
A NAZI OFFICER, WERNER VON UHLAND, HAS THE DIFFICULT TASK OF PREVENTING A
CONSPIRACY TO MURDER HITLER. HE BEGINS RECRUITING NYMPHOMANIACS INTO THE ARMY, WHICH
IS OBVIOUSLY AS GOOD A PLACE AS ANY TO BEGIN SUCH A MISSION. THE VIOLENT HIGHLIGHT IN
THIS ONE IS A SCENE WHERE A WOMAN IS RAPED WITH A GUN BEFORE HAVING HER NIPPLE

The RED NIGHTS of the
Gestapo
A blood drenched journey into the most depraved
society the world has ever known...
BOUGIE · 2012 ·

DEPRAVED
DECADENT
DAMNED

NAZI GERMANY 1939

SEX IS NOT ONLY AN ART
BUT A WEAPON WITH **X**

Madam Kitty

X
NO ONE UNDER 17 ADMITTED
(Age and may vary
in certain areas)

A Trans-American Release

HELMUT BERGER · INGRID THULIN in "MADAM KITTY"
with TERESA ANN SAVOY and with JOHN STEINER
SARA SPERATI · JOHN IRELAND · TINA AUMONT
with the participation of STEFANO SATTA FLORES and BEKIM FEHMIU
Production Designer KEN ADAM · Music by FIORENZO CARPI
Written and Directed by TINTO BRASS · Color prints by DELUXE®
READ THE BALLANTINE PAPERBACK.

BITTEN OFF. DESPITE THAT VILE DISPLAY, THIS IS A SOMEWHAT ROUTINE ENTRY THAT FOCUSES ON SEX AND NUDITY INSTEAD OF GRIM EXPERIMENTS AND JACKBOOT BRUTALITY. ALTHOUGH SLICKLY PRODUCED AND SHOT IN CINEMASCOPE, RED NIGHTS WILL PROBABLY SEEM RATHER DULL TO EXPERIENCED EXPLOITATION FANS.

SALON KITTY

AKA MADAM KITTY
(1976, ITALY, DIR. TINTO BRASS)
EPIC NAZISPLOITATION WITH LAVISH PRODUCTION VALUES FROM THE DIRECTOR OF **CALIGULA** BLENDS ART HOUSE AESTHETICS AND EXPLOITATION INTO A FASCINATING SPECTACLE. SET IN BERLIN IN 1939, THE FILM DETAILS THE GOINGS-ON WITHIN MADAME KITTY'S BURLESQUE BORDELLO, A PERVERSE BROTHEL WHERE GERMAN OFFICERS COME TO INDULGE IN THEIR WILDEST WARTIME FANTASIES. THE BEAUTIFUL MARGHERITA (TERESA ANN SAVOY) BEGINS WORKING AS A PROSTITUTE AT THE BORDELLO BUT IS ACTUALLY A SPY FOR POWER HUNGRY SS OFFICER WALLENBERG (HELMUT BERGER) WHO WISHES TO BLACKMAIL AND OVERTHROW HITLER BY LEARNING INSIDER SECRETS FROM OTHER HIGH RANKING OFFICERS WHO ATTEND THE BROTHEL. DECADENT AND LACED WITH DARK HUMOUR, SALON KITTY MANAGES PLENTY OF SALACIOUS SEXPLOITATION AND FETISHISM. IN ONE SCENE, A GERMAN OFFICER HAS A WHORE LAY ON A BED WHILST HE PROJECTS IMAGES OF HITLER OVER HER SEMI-NUDE BODY. INSTRUCTING HER TO HOLD A PHALLIC LOAF OF BREAD BETWEEN HER LEGS, HE BEGINS SUCKING AND CHEWING ON IT. KITTY'S REPULSIVE HIGHLIGHT, HOWEVER, DEPICTS A DECEASED NUDE WOMAN ON AN OPERATING TABLE WITH HER DEAD BABY HANGING FROM HER GUTS AFTER AN ATTEMPTED ABORTION. ESSENTIAL EPIC VIEWING, AND THE DIRECTOR'S CUT RUNS 133 MINS!

SS BORDELLO

(1978, FRANCE, DIR. JOSE BENAZERAF, AKA **BORDEL SS**)
A XXX BRIGITTE LAHAIE PORNO, DIRECTED BY FRENCH AUTEUR JOSE BENAZERAF ALL DECORATED IN KINKY NAZI REGALIA? SOUNDS LIKE A TWISTED TREAT! SADLY, THIS WAS A MAJOR LETDOWN. MOST OF THE "ACTION" TAKES PLACE IN THE BORDELLO OF THE TITLE. VERY LITTLE ACTUALLY HAPPENS, AND THE HARDCORE SEXUAL ENCOUNTERS ARE SO BRIEF AND ANTI-CLIMACTIC, (LITERALLY) THEY BARELY QUALIFY AS PORNO. EXTREMELY DIFFICULT TO FIND, THIS RARITY SEEMS TO HAVE SURVIVED THROUGH VHS BOOTLEGS AND A FEW FOREIGN DVD RELEASES.

SS EXPERIMENT CAMP

(1976, ITALY, DIR. SERGIO GARRONE)
ONE OF THE MOST NOTORIOUS NAZI SLEAZE FILMS OF ALL TIME THANKS TO ITS INSANE DIALOGUE, THIS ENTRY IS A WONDERFUL SLICE OF EURO-SLEAZE THAT HAS TO BE SEEN TO BE BELIEVED. THERE IS NO ATTEMPT AT REALISM AND THE FILM

IS BASICALLY A SERIES OF BIZARRE SEXUAL EXPERIMENTS, SUCH AS PLACING LOVEMAKING COUPLES IN VATS OF WATER AND THEN FREEZING THEM MID-SEX! THINGS START OFF WELL WITH AN OPENING SCENE SHOWING NAZIS TORTURING A NAKED WOMAN IN AN ELECTRIC CHAIR CAUSING HER TO PISS HERSELF, AND THE MAIN SUBPLOT CONCERNS THE COMMANDANT'S QUEST FOR A NEW PAIR OF TESTICLES, WHICH HE ACQUIRES FROM AN UNKNOWING (!?) GERMAN OFFICER. THIS GUY DOESN'T EVEN REALISE HE'S GOT NO BALLS UNTIL HE ATTEMPTS TO BED ONE OF THE PRISONERS, INCLUDES THE HILARIOUS LINE OF DIALOGUE "YOU BASTARD! WHAT HAVE YOU DONE WITH MY BALLS?!" THE MOST PECULIAR ELEMENT ABOUT THE MOVIE IS GARRONE'S WILD REPRESENTATION OF THE GAS OVENS IN WHICH THE DEAD PRISONERS ARE DISPOSED OF: THE BODIES ARE DUMPED INTO THE FLAMES AND THEY BEGIN TO DANCE AND TWITCH SPASTICALLY. VERY ODD.

SS CAMP 5: WOMEN'S HELL
(1977, ITALY, DIR. SERGIO GARRONE)
A GROUP OF WOMEN ARRIVE AT CAMP 5 TO SERVE AS SEX SLAVES AND TEST SUBJECTS IN A VARIETY OF HORRIBLE EXPERIMENTS. THE CRUEL DOCTORS ARE WORKING TO FIND A CURE FOR BURNS SO YOU'VE GOT A GOOD IDEA WHAT KIND OF SICK EXPERIMENTS THIS ONE CONTAINS. IN ONE SCENE A SCREAMING WOMAN HAS OIL POURED OVER HER LEG AND IS THEN SET ON FIRE. THIS NO-HOLDS BARRED CRAP IS VERY JOLTING — WHEN HER LEG IS SET ABLAZE, THE CAMERA

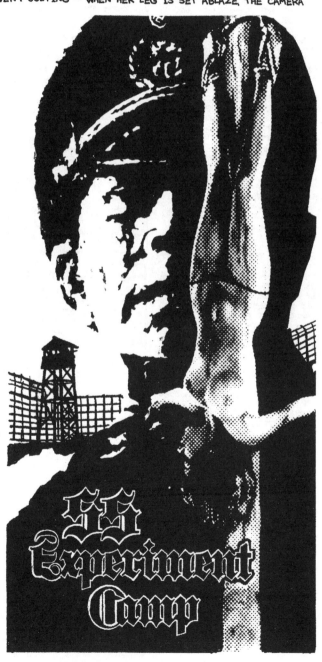

DOESN'T CUT AWAY AND THE EFFECT IS HORRIFIC. GARRONE REPEATS THE SAME EFFECT LATER WITH SIMILAR AGONISING RESULTS. LATER A GROUP OF ESCAPEES ARE BURNED ALIVE IN A GAS OVEN AND WE SEE SUPERIMPOSED FLAMES SET THEM ABLAZE. IN A TORTURE DUNGEON THE SADISTIC CAMP COMMANDANT TORTURES SEVERAL GIRLS. ONE HAS HER TONGUE TORN OUT WITH PINCERS, AND ANOTHER UNLUCKY VICTIM HAS FLAMING BAMBOO STICKS FORCED UNDER HER FINGERNAILS. WE SEE ONE WOMAN'S HEAD SICKENINGLY CRUSHED IN A VICE, AND YET ANOTHER IS PUNCHED REPEATEDLY IN THE GUTS WITH A SPIKED KNUCKLE-DUSTER. ADD TO THIS SOME UNSAVOURY SHOWER SCENES AND A ROUGH RAPE, AND YOU'VE GOT A DISREPUTABLE NAZI SLEAZE CHUNKBLOWER. SS CAMP 5 WAS SHOT BACK TO BACK WITH **SS EXPERIMENT CAMP** UTILISING THE SAME SETS AND ACTORS. ABSOLUTELY ESSENTIAL TRASHOLA.

SS GIRLS
(1977, ITALY, DIR. BRUNO MATTEI)
MAD GERMAN SS OFFICER HANS SCHELLENBERG IS INSTRUCTED BY HITLER TO WEED OUT ANY TRAITORS AMONGST THE THIRD REICH, AND HE DOES THIS BY CREATING A CRACK TROOP OF HIGH CLASS WHORES WHO SEDUCE INDIVIDUALS INTO REVEALING THEIR TRUE FEELINGS ABOUT DER FÜHRER. THE WHORES ARE TAUGHT HOW TO FIGHT AND HOW TO PLEASURE A VARIETY OF CLIENTS, INCLUDING DISABLED AND OBESE MEN, AND A DOG IN A SIMULATED BESTIALITY SCENE. THEY ARE ALSO TAUGHT BALLET AND FENCING! THE SEX SCENES COME AND GO UNTIL THE DEATH-FILLED FINALE. SS GIRLS DELIVERS PLENTY OF FULL FRONTAL FEMALE NUDITY BUT LACKS THE AGGRESSION AND UNCOMPROMISING ABUSE THESE FILMS ARE KNOWN FOR.

STALAG 69
(1982, USA, DIR. SELRAHC DETREVREP)
STAR TREK'S ANGELIQUE PETTYJOHN STARS AS A NASTY NAZI WHO DELIVERS SOME ROUGH PUNISHMENT AND PLEASURE TO

ADD A LITTLE HARROWING ACTION TO THE S/M THEMED PROCEEDINGS. ALTHOUGH QUITE SILLY, THIS IS HOT STUFF AND THE SEXY UNIFORMS ADD SOME KINK TO THE STANDARD SUCKING AND FUCKING. BASED ON "A TRUE STORY" YEAH RIGHT, WE BELIEVE YOU.

WOMEN'S CAMP 119
(1977, ITALY, DIR. BRUNO MATTEI)
COMPARED WITH BRUNO MATTEI'S EXTREMELY DAFT **SS GIRLS**, THIS IS A FAR MORE SERIOUS AND DISTURBING AFFAIR THAT COMMENDABLY PLAYS IT STRAIGHT. IMBUED WITH AN ATMOSPHERE OF GRIME AND DECAY FROM THE OFFSET THIS MOVIE IS REPULSIVE IN THE EXTREME. THE SETTING IS MEDICAL CAMP ROSENHAUSEN, WHERE WOMEN ARE ROUTINELY SEXUALLY MOLESTED, CUT UP, AND BRUTALISED BY SADISTIC WARDENS AND OFFICERS -- SOUND FAMILIAR? MATTEI GOES OUT OF HIS WAY TO OFFEND, DELIVERING A MULTITUDE OF REPUGNANT IMAGES, WITH THE FIRST SHOT WITHIN THE CAMP DEPICTING VARIOUS BLOODIED LIMBS AND BODY PARTS SCATTERED OVER SEVERAL OPERATING TABLES. THREE FEMALE PRISONERS ARE STRIPPED NAKED AND THEN EXCESSIVELY BEATEN WITH BATONS AS THE NEW INMATES LOOK ON IN HORROR. THEN A GROUP OF WOMEN ARE GASSED TO DEATH WITH ZYKLON B, A SCENE THAT IS INTER-CUT WITH THE CAMP OFFICERS HAVING THEIR DINNER BEFORE SHOWING US THE DEAD VICTIMS COVERED IN THEIR OWN EXCREMENT! WE SEE THE RESULTS OF A UTERUS TRANSPLANT AS A DEAD WOMAN LIES ON AN OPERATING TABLE WITH HER LEGS SUSPENDED IN STIRRUPS, AND A RETARDED MADMAN NAMED CRAZY KURT IS CAJOLED INTO RAPING TERRIFIED PRISONERS. AS IF ALL OF THIS WASN'T GROSS ENOUGH MATTEI ALSO INCLUDES SOME GENUINE DOCUMENTARY FOOTAGE OF CONCENTRATION CAMP VICTIMS, A DISTASTEFUL INCLUSION THAT PROPELS THIS TRASH INTO A WHOLE FURTHER STRATOSPHERE OF BAD TASTE. BLEAK AND UGLY, THIS IS UNDOUBTEDLY AMONGST THE NASTIEST AND MOST OVERTLY DISTURBING OF THE CLASSIC NAZISPLOITATION FILMS. YOU HAVE BEEN WARNED!

AUTHOR DAVID HINDS ALSO WORKS UNDER THE PSEUDONYM OF NICK NIHILIST FOR THE MUSIC PROJECT DEATHTRIPPING --RECYCLED MUSIC FROM THE GUTTERS OF THE MIND. WWW.DEATHTRIPPING.COM

CINEMA SEWER MAILBAG

DEAR ROBIN,
"I FEEL LIKE CINEMA SEWER REALLY UNDERSTANDS ME. IT IS THE VERY FIRST MAGAZINE I'VE EVER READ WHERE I GET THAT FEELING. THE BOOK COLLECTIONS YOU DO ARE THE BEST. HOW MANY ARE YOU PLANNING ON PUBLISHING IN TOTAL? ALL OF MY GIRLFRIENDS DON'T GET IT. THEY DON'T UNDERSTAND WHY I WOULD EVER WANT TO WATCH THESE KINDS OF MOVIES, AND THEY JOKE ABOUT WHAT CHEESY TASTE I HAVE. MEANWHILE ALL THEY WANT TO WATCH ARE FUCKING ROMANTIC COMEDIES, HUNGER GAMES OR STUFF LIKE HARRY POTTER. PLEASE LET YOUR READERS KNOW THAT NOT ALL CHICKS ARE LIKE THAT, AND THAT A LOT OF US LIKE COOL SHIT. I LOVE THE SMUT YOU DO, BOTH YOUR COMICS AND YOUR WRITING, AND ESPECIALLY LOVE THE FACT THAT YOUR WORK DOESN'T HAVE MANY (ANY?) BOUNDARIES. WHAT YOU DO IS INSPIRING TO MY BRAIN, AND IF I'M BEING HONEST, TO MY COOCHIE TOO. PLEASE KEEP GOING."

—BETH, NEW YORK

LADIES OF THE 80s (1985. DIR: MARK RICHARDS)
MY FRIEND TODD SENT ME THIS BECAUSE HE THOUGHT IT WAS PROBABLY A COMPILATION OF TASTY 1980s PORN STAR SCENES. IT ISN'T. IT'S A PORN MOVIE ABOUT AN OLDER WOMAN (KAY PARKER) WHO HOSTS A RETREAT FOR YUPPIE BITCHES WHO ARE UNHAPPY WITH THEIR LIVES AND WANT ADVICE. WHO THE HELL WANTS TO TRY TO JERK OFF TO WOMEN COMPLAINING ABOUT THEIR PROBLEMS?! HAHAHA! I MEAN, IT REALLY SEEMED LIKE AN ADULT FILM WRITTEN BY A COMMITTEE: "LISTEN, WE NEED TO CASH IN ON THIS NEW YUPPIE THING. LETS MAKE AN EROTIC FILM THAT MAKES WOMEN FEEL LIKE THEIR LIFE AND RELATIONSHIP CONCERNS ARE BEING HEARD!". THIS SUCKED IN A TOTALLY FASCINATING WAY, I MUST SAY. IT WAS UNLIKE ANY OTHER XXX MOVIE I'VE SEEN. —BOUGIE

Rosario 1930: The vintage porno journalism of Curt Moreck

CURT MORECK WAS A GERMAN WRITER ACTIVE IN THE 1920S AND '30S WHO DEVOTED MUCH OF HIS WORK TO DOCUMENTING THE VARIOUS SEXUAL SUBCULTURES OF HIS DAY (TRY TO TRACK DOWN A COPY OF HIS 1931 FÜHRER DURCH DAS "LASTERHAFTE" BERLIN, OR GUIDE TO "DEPRAVED" BERLIN). HIS GREAT GIFT TO PORN SCHOLARS ARE A PAIR OF ARTICLES DETAILING HIS VISITS TO SOME EARLY SCREENINGS OF SOME STAG FILMS IN ARGENTINA, THE TWO OLDEST SUCH ACCOUNTS THAT I KNOW OF. ONE IS FROM HIS 1926 BOOK SITTENGESCHICHTE DES KINOS (OR A MORAL HISTORY OF THE CINEMA) AND IS QUOTED EXTENSIVELY IN JACK STEVENSON'S 2000 BOOK, FLESHPOT.

THE OTHER, REPRODUCED BELOW, IS "ROSARIO, THE PORT OF THE STEPPES," FROM 1930. I RAN ACROSS THIS ONE IN A LARGER ANTHOLOGY OF GERMAN WRITING ABOUT HUMAN SEXUALITY THROUGHOUT THE WORLD (SITTENGESCHICHTE DER KULTURWELT UND IHRER ENTWICKLUNG IN EINZELDARSTELLUNGEN VOL. VIII, EDITED BY LEO SCHIDROWITZ), AND THOUGHT IT WAS TOO GOOD TO STAY BURIED IN AN OUT-OF-PRINT AND ALL-BUT-FORGOTTEN VOLUME. THIS HAS ENOUGH OF THE HALLMARKS OF THE "TRIP TO SEE A DIRTY MOVIE ON THE WRONG SIDE OF TOWN" GENRE THAT IT

COULD HAVE COME FROM SLEAZOID EXPRESS, AND HAS VERY DETAILED DESCRIPTION OF THE ACTION IN THE FILM. ADDITIONALLY, IF ANY OF YOU AFICIONADOS OF OLD-TIMEY PORN OUT THERE CAN FIGURE OUT WHAT MOVIE HE'S TALKING ABOUT, GET IN TOUCH!

TRANSLATION BY ME, DAN ERDMAN, AND ILLUSTRATIONS BY NOAH VAN SCIVER. ENJOY!

THE PARANÁ RIVER RUSHES BY, YELLOW AND DIRTY, IN A FLYING CURRENT FROM THE HEART OF THE ARGENTINE STEPPE AND INTO THE MOUTH OF THE RIVER PLATE. UNDER AN OPPRESSIVE SUN, A STEAMER TRAVELS UP FROM BUENOS AIRES TO ROSARIO, A PORT CITY IN THE INTERIOR OF ARGENTINA. ONLY A FEW SHIPS GO ON FROM HERE; THERE IS ONLY ENDLESS STEPPE, THROUGH WHICH THE STEAMER WILL TRAVEL FOR MANY DAYS. ON EACH SIDE OF THE RIVER, AS FAR AS THE EYES CAN SEE, THERE IS FLAT LAND COVERED WITH SHORT GRASS, LOW HUTS IN THE REEDS, SHOUTING NEGROES ON THE BANKS AND ON THE TIGHT, TENSE BLUE OF THE HORIZON SHINES ROSARIO.

ENGLISH COAL-BARGES, DIRTY STEAMERS FROM THE COLONIES MANNED BY NEGROES, STINKING CHINESE JUNKS, CARGO BOATS FROM SWEDEN, SHIPS RECENTLY ARRIVED FROM MOROCCO: ALL ARE HERE TO PICK UP OR UNLOAD CARGO. BEFORE THE PIERS RISES A STEEP, SANDY DUNE; THOSE WHO DWELL THERE EARN THE MONEY NECESSARY FOR LIFE WITH A FEW ESSENTIAL FISHING SKILLS. THE SUN SHINES THROUGH THE PATCHY RAGS THEY WEAR, ILLUMINATING THEIR TERRIBLE, POCK-MARKED CARCASSES. LIFTING THEIR SKIRTS, THE OLD, WRINKLED, ALMOST DECAYED WOMEN GO DAILY BEFORE THE EYES OF THE TEAMS LOUNGING ON THE PIERS, WHO HURL OBSCENITIES IN ALL LANGUAGES.

THE CITY OF ROSARIO REMINDS ONE SOMEWHAT OF THE GOLD RUSH IN ALASKA. IT IS WILD AND ROUGH, AND FILLED WITH FRIGHTS WHICH LAST THROUGH THE BLOODY EVENING HOURS. THESE HOURS ARE MARKED BY THE FAR-OFF BANG OF THE BROWNING PISTOL AND HISSES OF THE KNIFE; THE STRUGGLE RAGES IN ALL SALOONS, WITH ONLY VICTORY OR DEATH ENDING THE FIERCE BRAWLS OVER WOMEN OR PESOS. BETWEEN THE INDIANS AND GAUCHOS, MULATTOS AND NEGROES, YELLOW AND WHITE, THERE IS NO SIGN OF CULTURE ANYWHERE. HORSES LAY DEAD AND DECAYING ON THE RAILROAD TRACKS — NOBODY CARES. A MAN TAKES A WHORE FROM A HOUSE, HAVING PUSHED A SHARP, SHORT SOUTH AMERICAN KNIFE INTO A PIMP'S HEART — NO ONE'S TEMPERATURE RISES OVER THIS. CIVILIZATION AND VICE LIVE SIDE BY SIDE, AND NOTHING SURPRISES ANYONE.

THE STREETS ARE FULL OF MEN WHO COME FROM THE PAMPAS. THEIR MONEY, EARNED FROM THE TRADE OF CORN, IS BLOWN HERE IN CELEBRATION OF A SUCCESSFUL SALE. THE STREETS SWARM WITH THE COLORFUL UNIFORMS OF ALL KINDS OF SAILORS. THE SCENE IS THE SAME EVERYWHERE. MEN CLOSE THEIR BUSINESS AND THEN USE THE WOMEN OF THE STREETS, OR ELSE MAKE AN ARRANGEMENT WITH THE BROWN DAUGHTERS OF THE LAND. IN THIS WAY, THESE EVENTS PLAY THEMSELVES OUT HERE EXACTLY AS IN ALL OTHER PORTS. BUT ROSARIO DOES HAVE ITS OWN PECULIARITIES.

IN THE EVENINGS, WHEN IT BECOMES DARK AROUND 10 O'CLOCK, MEN CAN BE OBSERVED REGULARLY IN THIN STREAMS COMING FROM ALL DIRECTIONS, ARRIVING FINALLY AT ONE STREET, CALLE FLORIDA, IN UNISON. FROM HERE THEY APPROACH A HOUSE WHICH FROM THE OUTSIDE LOOKS AS TRIVIAL AND

BORING AS A RED BRICK BUILDING CAN. AT THIS INCONSPICUOUS FACADE, ONE WILL PERHAPS BE SURPRISED TO FIND AN OLD WOMAN SITTING AT THE DOOR COLLECTING A STEEP ENTRANCE-FEE, BUT PERHAPS THIS MAY BE THE ENTRANCE TO A CLUB? ONE ENTERS (HAVING PAID HIS FIVE MARKS) AND PASSES THROUGH A DARK FOYER INTO A LARGE HALL WHICH HOLDS PERHAPS FOUR HUNDRED PERSONS, PACKED WITH ASCENDING ROWS OF WOODEN FOLDING CHAIRS. THE MOOD ALL AROUND IS LANGUOROUS, AS MUCH IN THE FACE OF THE CHINESE COOK AS IN THE STARING GRIMACE OF THE NIGGER ATTENDANT, IN THE LEATHERY, DULL FACE OF THE ARGENTINE GAUCHOS AS IN THE WIDE FEATURES OF THE AMERICAN SAILORS: EVERYWHERE THE SAME NERVOUS GREED, THE SAME LUST, THE SAME FLICKERING GLANCES. A MAN WALKS ABOUT OFFERING BRANDY AND WINE ON A LARGE TRAY. AND THEY ALL DRINK, POURING THE BOOZE DOWN THEIR DRY THROATS LIKE A SPEEDING TRAIN, AND EVEN BEFORE THE DRAMA BEGINS THE PEOPLE HAVE DRUNK THE HEAVY LIQUID AND BECOME SILENT, AND OBSCENITY ITSELF IS IN THE OPPRESSIVE SILENCE. THE HALL IS FILLED WITH THE PORNOGRAPHIC LANGUAGES OF ALL NATIONS, OF THE HORNY VISIONS OF INTOXICATED, DRIVEN MEN.

AND THEN THE LIGHT GOES OUT AND THE MUSIC BEGINS. ONE HEARS ONLY THE SLURPING OF THE DRINKS; ON THE SCREEN THE FILM BEGINS.

ALTHOUGH THESE FILMS ARE KNOWN ALSO IN TOKYO AND HAVANA, THEY ARE REGARDED AS A SOUTH AMERICAN SPECIALTY. THEIR PLACE OF MANUFACTURE IS NEAR PARIS OR EVEN BUENOS AIRES. THE FILMS ARE MOSTLY VERY CRAFTILY MADE AND THE HUMAN MATERIAL IS, ESPECIALLY IN THE FILMS OF SOUTH AMERICAN ORIGIN, OFTEN VERY BEAUTIFUL - NEVERTHELESS, NEVERTHELESS, IT REMAINS A NAUSEATING, LOW-BROW FILTHINESS. BUT THERE IS HARDLY ANOTHER PORNOGRAPHIC BUSINESS WHICH, OPERATING IN "OFFICIAL SECRECY," YIELDS MORE MATERIAL REWARDS THAN THIS "FILM INDUSTRY." IN ORDER TO ILLUSTRATE THE LOW MORAL LEVEL AND SQUALOR OF ITS CREATORS (SUCH AS THE ACTORS), AS WELL AS OF THE PSYCHE OF THE SPECTATOR IN THIS PORT CITY, A SUMMARY OF A FILM WILL BE GIVEN.

FIRST ACT.
IN A LANDSCAPE ONE SEES TWO PALACES. CLOSE-UP OF THE FIRST. ON ITS ENTRANCE ARE THE WORDS: CASA-PENSION DI HIJAS. IN GERMAN: BOARDING SCHOOL FOR GIRLS. NEW SHOT. ONE SEES A LARGE HALL WITH WHITE FURNITURE, IN WHICH ARE TWENTY WHITE BEDS. IN EACH OF THESE BEDS LAY A SLEEPING YOUNG WOMAN. OVER THE DOOR ONE SEES A BELL CHIMING. THE TWENTY YOUNG WOMEN ARE SHOWN IN NEGLIGEES, ALTERNATELY TEASING AND POSING. THEN, DURING THE COMMON BATHS, TWO YOUNG GIRLS, IN A CLOSE-UP, PERFORM VARIOUS SEXUAL VIOLATIONS ON EACH OTHER. AT THE END OF THESE ACTS, WHICH

LAST SOMETHING LIKE TEN MINUTES, THE GIRLS FORM IN A ROW: TENDER HALF-CASTES, FULL-FIGURED EUROPEANS AND TWO SPLENDIDLY-BUILT NEGRESSES IN SHORT-CUT DRESSES, UTTERLY "NATURAL."

SECOND ACT.
IT SHOWS THE SECOND HOUSE, IT IS A YOUNG MENS' SCHOOL. THE SAME PICTURE— THE WHITE HALL, THE TWENTY MALE-BODIES, AGAIN MIXED AND WHITE, ALSO TWO NIGGERS, ALL SLIM AND JUST WASHED, EVEN IF THEIR BODIES ARE MOSTLY SLACK AND THEIR FACES APPEAR GREY AND PALE. THE SAME PICTURE: TWO YOUNG MEN IN MUTUAL GRATIFICATION AND EMBRACE.

THIRD AND LAST ACT.
THE MEETING OF THE TWENTY YOUNG MEN AND WOMEN. OBVIOUSLY THESE ALLEGED BOARDING SCHOOLS ARE WITHOUT SUPERVISION (OR THE FILM'S DIRECTOR WANTS TO SAVE A FEE); IN ANY CASE, THE THIRD ACT FINDS IN THE MIDST OF THE WOMEN'S DORMITORY A LONG TABLE ON WHICH THE CULINARY AND ALCOHOLIC PLEASURES OF THE FOUR CONTINENTS CAN BE FOUND. IN THIS SETTING, AS IN SO MANY OTHER DETAILS OF THE DIRECTION, WE SEE THE PRODUCERS' TALENTS AND GIFTS. SAD, THEN, THAT THESE SKILLS ARE SQUANDERED ON SUCH UNWORTHY MATERIAL. ALSO SKILLFUL ARE THE INTERWOVEN SCENES OF ABSOLUTE HARMLESSNESS AND CONVENTION. THE ACTORS GREET EACH OTHER WITH CEREMONY AND CHIVALRY AND, TAKING A PLACE IN MIXED ROW AT THE TABLE, BEGIN TO EAT AND DRINK. BUT EVEN HERE THE SEXUAL SEASONING IS NOT WANTING, AND MAY BE SEEN IN SLOW CLOSE-UPS OF THE YOUNG LADIES' LEGS AND THIGHS, LINGERIE AND UNDERWEAR.

IN THE THEATER A SULTRY, OPPRESSIVE ATMOSPHERE PREVAILS. IT IS QUIET ENOUGH TO HEAR A PIN DROP, ONLY THE PANTING, FLYING BREATH OF THE SPECTATORS CAN BE HEARD; THE MAN SELLING DRINKS CREEPS BACK AND FORTH THROUGH THE DARK ROOM AND ONE HEARS, WITHOUT SEEING, BOOZE POURED DOWN THE THROATS. THEN FROM THE WHEEZING COMES FORTH A SLOW GROAN, AND ONE NOTICES AMONG THE BENCHES A REGULAR UNMISTAKABLE SOUND WHICH DEMONSTRATES THE DISASTROUS EFFECT OF THIS FILM, COUPLED WITH THE DEVIL ALCOHOL, ON THE MIND OF THE SPECTATOR.

ON THE SCREEN, THE MOOD OF THE STUDENTS LIVENS. THE LADIES BEGIN TO UNDRESS AND DANCE ON THE TABLE. THE LADS DO THE SAME. AND THEN, SLOWLY, SLOWLY, AFTER MANY INTERLUDES THE GREAT ORGY BEGINS. TWENTY CLOSE-UPS OF TWENTY PAIRINGS SHOW ALL THE DIFFERENT POSSIBILITIES OF BODILY UNION. AND — ONCE AGAIN, A TESTAMENT TO THE COMMERCIAL REFINEMENT OF THE BUSINESSMAN — ALL THE PAIRS FULFILL THEIR ASSIGNED TASKS NOT ONLY APPARENTLY, BUT ACTUALLY AND MOST RECOGNIZABLY. THIS IS VISIBLE IN

Noah Van Sciver

121

CERTAIN DETAILS, WHOSE DESCRIPTION WOULD DISGUST OR FRIGHTEN THE READER; IT LEAVES NO MYSTERY TO THE SEXUAL GRATIFICATION BETWEEN MAN AND WOMAN. WITH THE EXHAUSTION OF ALL THE ACTORS, THE FILM ENDS.

THE LIGHTS FLICKER ON IN THE THEATER. THE MEN, STILL SEATED, HAVE COMPLETELY CHANGED, NOW FINDING SWEAT SOAKING THEIR FOREHEADS AND FACES AND BREATHING HEAVILY, HAVING BEEN FLOGGED BY EXCESS OR EXHAUSTED TO THE POINT OF APATHY. SOME RUN OUT OF THE THEATER TO THE BORDELLOS OF THE SECLUDED STREETS, WHILE OTHERS STAY SEATED. AGAIN COMES THE MAN BEARING SCHNAPPS, COLLECTING THE ADMISSION CHARGE; THE MUSIC PLAYS AND THE FILM ROLLS ITSELF OUT AGAIN. AND THE MEN SIT HERE UNTIL THE MORNING, AS LONG AS THE HOUSE IS OPEN; UNDER THE LASH OF THEIR OWN APPETITES, PERPETUALLY DRUNK AT THE SWAMPY BOTTOM OF AN INFERNAL WORLD.

TO REFLECT THE MORAL SCENE AT ROSARIO'S HARBOR, ONE MUST NOT FORGET TO TELL OF THE HOUSES OF ILL REPUTE, WHICH – ABSURD AS IT MAY SOUND – SURPASS CONSIDERABLY THE ROMANCE AND POETRY, THE CHARM AND BEAUTY OF EVEN THE YOSHIWARA DISTRICT OF JAPAN. THERE ARE NOT MANY HOUSES OF THAT KIND AROUND: MOST ARE SIMPLY VULGAR IN THE FACE OF THE FAMOUSLY DEMANDING SAILORS OF THE WORLD. BUT THESE OTHERS LAY IN A FLOURISHING, BLOSSOMING, RICHLY COLORFUL GARDEN, AND HERE CAN BE FOUND WOMEN WHOSE BODIES HAVE THE SMELL OF THE EARTH, THE GLOSS OF THE SUN AND THE LUSTS OF A PHANTASMAGORIA. IF ONE WANDERS THE STREETS IN WHICH THEY LIVE, ONE HEARS FROM THE DEPTHS OF A SAFFRON-RED SHRUB A WHISPERED WORD, A COOLLY TEMPTING CRY WHICH ONE CAN HARDLY RESIST. STEPPING INTO THE OPEN-AIR GARDEN, ONE IS GREETED BY A WOMAN - ALTHOUGH IT IS IMPOSSIBLE TO TELL HER RACIAL ORIGIN, OR EVEN WHICH CONTINENT SHE HAILS FROM, SHE IS DEFINITELY BEAUTIFUL.

OFTEN SHE IS FROM THE DEEP INTERIOR OF THE COUNTRY, DISCOVERED BY A TRAVELING AGENT OF THE BROTHEL, BUT ONE FINDS ALSO PERFECT BEAUTIES FROM EGYPT OR HONOLULU. IN THIS GARDEN ONE SPENDS THE NIGHT UNDER THE STARS AND THE MOON AND A SHINING HEAVEN. THE WOMEN COLLECT NO MONEY, DON'T NAG THE CUSTOMER, AND THEY ARE NOT PUSHY OR GREEDY – AS THOUGH THEY ARE NOT PROSTITUTES, BUT SWEETHEARTS. SWEETHEARTS TO MANY MEN, TO ANY MAN, BUT STILL THE PERFECT SWEETHEART FOR A NIGHT. THUS ONE FORGETS THAT THE MINIMUM COST OF THESE NIGHTLY JOYS IS 200 MARKS. EVEN THIS IS CHEAP, AS THE LORDS OF THE STEPPE, BARONS OF THE MEAT AND GRAIN TRADE, LEAVE BEHIND THOUSANDS UPON THOUSANDS OF PESOS FOR A SINGLE NIGHT OF LOVE...

IN A FEW YEARS, A WOMAN WILL HAVE EARNED ENOUGH TO TRAVEL AS THE "GRAND COQUETTE" AMONG THE WORLD'S GREAT CITIES, BUT WILL MOST LIKELY FIND HER WAY TO HAVANA, THE QUEEN OF THE WEST...

FULFILLING YOUNG CUPS

Reviewed by Ian Jane (rockshockpop.com)

IN THE OPENING SCENE OF THIS NEEDLESSLY CONVOLUTED DOG-THEMED 1979 'JASON TARONE' ADULT MOVIE WE SEE CANNIBAL HOLOCAUST STAR ROBERT KERMAN PLAYING A MAN NAMED DELANEY. HE'S GETTING HEAD FROM KITTY (SERENA) WHILE SOME WEIRD COUNTRY MUSIC PLAYS, AND KITTY'S NARRATION TELLS US SHE'S INTO IT AS HE POKES HER AND CHOWS DOWN. FROM THERE WE CUT TO MRS. FEINBERG (MARLENE WILLOUGHBY) AND DELANEY AT A DESK. SHE WANTS TO ADOPT A DOG SO HE TAKES HER INTO A KENNEL AND SHOWS HER SOME. THEY FILL OUT PAPERWORK -- DONE. SHE'S GOT A DOG, AND HE TELLS HER SHE NEEDS TO PAY $25 TO HAVE IT FIXED. SHE DOESN'T WANT THAT TO HAPPEN AND BRIBES HIM OUT OF IT AND HEADS TO THE CAR WITH HER MASSIVE MASTIFF. JUST THEN: OH NO! CAR TROUBLE! SHE TAKES SOME TRANQUILIZERS TO COPE (???) WHILE DELANEY TRIES TO GET THE CAR STARTED UNAWARE THAT SOMEONE'S STEALING A DIFFERENT DOG RIGHT BEHIND HIS BACK.

DELANEY DRIVES HER HOME THEN BANGS FEINBERG WHILE SERENA WINDS UP GETTING IT ON WITH AN OFFICER SMITH (JAMIE GILLIS), A DIRTY COP ON THE SCENE. HE COERCES HER INTO BONING HIM, CALLS HER A "FUCKING HORNY BITCH" AND ACCUSES HER OF SUCKING OFF THE DOGS. SHE FIGHTS BACK A BIT BUT YOU CAN'T FIGHT GILLIS. IF HE WANTS TO RAPE YOU, HE'S GOING TO RAPE YOU. A BAND THAT SOUNDS LIKE KISS (BUT ISN'T) PLAYS IN THE BACKGROUND AS HE GETS ROUGH WITH POOR OLD SERENA. NEARBY RITA (VANESSA DEL RIO) TREATS A GUY BITTEN BY A DOG BY BLOWING HIM AND LETTING HIM GO TO TOWN ON

HER WITH HIS WANG. MORE OBSCURE SEVENTIES ROCK POLLUTES THE SOUNDTRACK, AND THEN WE CUT TO DELANEY HAVING PHONE SEX WITH KITTY. SHE TELLS HIM "PEOPLE ARE JUST RUNNING AROUND FUCKING AND FUCKING AND COMING ALL OVER EACH OTHER!", AND MASTURBATES IN FRONT OF SOME KENNELS WHILE THE DOGS SORT OF STARE AT HER AND LOOK CONFUSED. IT TURNS OUT A LESBIAN THREW KITTY IN A VAN AND SUCKED HER PUSSY REAL GOOD -- DELANEY SHOULD GO THERE AND FOLLOW THEM. A MYSTERY GUY WAS LISTENING IN ON THIS CALL.

MEANWHILE, RITA DROPS OFF A DOG TO OFFICER SMITH, WHO IS ENJOYING MILLER HIGH LIFE ON HIS FRONT STEP. THEY TALK BUT THERE'S NO AUDIBLE DIALOGUE, SO THEY GO TO A VAN WHERE THE COP STICKS HIS WILLY UP HER BUM-HOLE. THIS IS ACTUALLY A PRETTY HOT SCENE AS VANESSA GETS INTO GILLIS'S 'TAKE CHARGE' APPROACH TO BUTT BANGING AND STARTS GETTING ALL TOUCHY-FEELY WITH HER HOOTERS. BACK AT THE KENNEL, KITTY IS INTRIGUED BY BUCK (MARC VALENTINE), WHO SHOWS UP TO TALK ABOUT DOG TRAINING. A WOMAN NAMED ELVIRA ARRIVES WITH HER DOG AND BUCK ASKS IF THAT DOG HAS EVER BEEN FUCKED. WHILE THIS IS GOING ON, MYSTERY GUY WATCHES RITA IN THE BATHROOM WASHING A DOG WHICH SOMEHOW LEADS TO HER FUCKING GILLIS IN A BUBBLE BATH WHILE DOGS BARK IN THE BACKGROUND. BUCK AND ELVIRA HAVE SEX IN FRONT OF KITTY, APPARENTLY TURNED ON BY WATCHING THEIR DOGS FUCK (THIS PART IS EDITED IN A VERY CHOPPY MANNER IMPLYING THAT MAYBE THERE WAS SOME DOG SEX IN THE ORIGINAL VERSION OF THIS?). RITA SHOWS UP AT THE KENNEL AND WE CUT TO DOGS DRINKING WATER BEFORE WATCHING RITA AND KITTY HAVE SEX, WHICH THEN TURNS INTO AN ORGY WITH THE OTHER COUPLE. THERE'S SOME REALLY DISTURBING SLURPING SOUNDS OVERDUBBED HERE, AND THE SOUNDTRACK MUSIC IS SOME WEIRD ADULT CONTEMPORARY GARBAGE WITH ANNOYING FEMALE VOCALS OVERTOP.

KITTY SNEAKS INTO THE KENNEL AND FINDS SAL THE KENNEL BOY (OUR MYSTERY MAN) JERKING OFF. THEY SCREW AND HE SLAPS HER IN THE FACE WITH HIS SCHLONG AND HE TELLS HER THAT ON THE 4TH OF JULY BUCK IS GOING TO THROW A BIG BBQ! KITTY SAYS SHE'LL BE THERE AND SHE KEEPS HER PROMISE. PEOPLE GRILL SOME BURGERS AND ENJOY SOME BREWS AND THEN MRS. FEINBERG FINDS KITTY HANGING WITH RITA AND DECIDES TO THROW HER INTO A CAGE. SEE, FEINBERG IS THE HEAD OF AN ANIMAL RIGHTS GROUP DETERMINED TO MAKE SERENA'S CHARACTER PAY FOR HELPING FIX DOGS AT THE KENNEL, AND PUTTING HER IN A CAGE SOMEHOW SEEMS LIKE A RATIONAL PUNISHMENT. DUDES SHOW UP AND START STICKING THEIR DICKS INTO THE CAGE SO KITTY CAN BLOW THEM, AND THEN RITA SCREWS OTHER GUYS WHILE BAD MUSIC AND THE LOOPED SOUND OF A BARKING DOG ON THE SOUNDTRACK.

AS THE MOVIE COMES TO A CLOSE, KITTY COMPLAINS ABOUT NOT BEING ALLOWED TO COME AND FEINBERG MAKES HER SWEAR SHE'LL STOP CASTRATING DOGS. THE LAST SHOT SHOWS US A DIARY THAT KITTY HAS BEEN WRITING IN AND JUST AS A SONG THAT SOME GUY ANNOUNCES HE'S WRITTEN FOR KITTY IS ABOUT TO PLAY, THE MOVIE JUST ABRUPTLY ENDS.

ROBIN BYRD AND A TROPHY. NEITHER SHOW UP IN THIS FILM.

FULFILLING
YOUNG
CUPS

...THEY LOVED EVERY DROP

FULFILLING YOUNG CUPS DOESN'T MAKE A WHOLE LOT OF SENSE BUT IT'S VERY OBVIOUS ON THE VERSION RELEASED BY ALPHA BLUE ARCHIVES THAT SOME MATERIAL IS MISSING -- THE ENDING IS GONE AT THE VERY LEAST. THE MOVIE IS A QUICK ONE (LESS THAN AN HOUR IN LENGTH) AND THIS COMES AT THE COST OF A DECENT STORY. THERE'S PLENTY OF BUMPING AND GRINDING ON HAND TO OGGLE BUT THE NARRATIVE IS QUITE CHOPPY AND NONSENSICAL. IT'S WORTH SEEING FOR THE A-LIST CAST AND THE FACT THAT SERENA AND DEL RIO ARE LOOKING QUITE GOOD HERE, BUT DON'T GO INTO THIS ODD LITTLE 1979 OBSCURITY EXPECTING IT TO BE YOUR NEW FAVOURITE ADULT MOVIE. IT'S NOT VERY GOOD, BUT IT IS DEFINITELY WEIRD, AND MALE LEADS (KERMAN AND GILLIS) ARE GOOD IN THEIR RESPECTIVE ROLES.

-END-

JOE BIKINI
King of the blackjack

THERE IS A FAIRLY OBSCURE EUROPEAN-MADE MOVIE SHOT IN NEW YORK CALLED PLEASURE SHOP ON 7TH AVE (1979 AKA THE "PORN SHOP ON 7TH AVE") AND IT IS KNOWN AMONGST GENRE FANS AS A TERROR FILM. TERROR FILMS WERE A SMALL CYCLE OF (USUALLY ITALIAN) HORROR-EXPLOITATION WITH A HOME-INVASION THEME DIRECTLY INSPIRED BY WES CRAVEN'S 1972 CLASSIC THE LAST HOUSE ON THE LEFT. THIS PARTICULAR ONE WAS DIRECTED BY ONE OF THE MOST LOVED EUROSLEAZERS, JOE D'AMATO. WHILE D'AMATO (BORN: ARISTIDE MASSACCESI) TOOK PART IN MANY GENRES (SPAGHETTI WESTERNS, HORROR, CANNIBAL, WAR, PEPLUM, FANTASY) BEFORE HE DIED IN ROME IN 1999, HE WAS MOST PROLIFIC IN THE GENRE OF LURID SOFTCORE (AND ALSO HARDCORE) GRINDHOUSE MOVIES.

IT'S A FAIRLY EXCELLENT KIDNAPPER-THEMED ROUGHIE SHOCKER, AND IT'S MOSTLY OF NOTE TO CINEMA SEWER READERS BECAUSE IT HAS PILES OF MANHATTAN STREET FOOTAGE IN ITS FIRST REEL. MARQUEES CAN BE SEEN WITH BRING ME THE HEAD OF ALFREDO GARCIA (1974), TINTORERA (1977), BOB CHINN'S LOVE SLAVES (1976), VIRGIN DREAMS (1977), AND 7 INTO SNOWY (1977). ALL OF THIS STUFF IS SUCH A TREAT FOR GRINDHOUSE AND HARDCORE PORN HISTORY BUFFS. 42ND STREET AT ITS GRIMIEST HERE, ITS FETID AIR SEEMINGLY SMELLABLE IN EVERY SHOT OF THIS ITALIAN-MADE SCUM-SUCKER. RUGGERO DEODATO'S HOUSE ON THE EDGE OF THE PARK MAY BE THE BEST ITALIAN TERROR FILM, BUT WITH HARDCORE SEX MIXED IN WITH THE KIDNAPPING AND VIOLENCE, THIS RAUNCHY RARITY IS HIGHLY WORTHY OF BEING REDISCOVERED.

A VERY DECENT PORTION OF THE FIRST ACT OF THE MOVIE TAKES PLACE IN THE TITULAR PLEASURE SHOP ON 7TH AVENUE, AND THIS LOCATION WAS AT 210 WEST 42ND STREET (AND 7TH AVE). I'M TALKING ABOUT THE INFAMOUS BLACK JACK BOOKS (WHICH ALSO HOUSED THE FRISCO S&M THEATER), WHICH WAS LOCATED DOWNSTAIRS FROM THE NEW YORK CHESS AND CHECKER CLUB. THIS NASTY LITTLE FLEA-PIT WAS LEGENDARY FOR HAVING ONE OF THE BEST PORN SELECTIONS IN THE CITY, WITH 8MM FILMS, STROKE MAGAZINES, HARDCORE SLICKS, DILDOS, BLOWUP DOLLS, AND PEEPSHOW BOOTHS BEING THE MAIN ATTRACTIONS.

IT WAS A FAVOURITE DESTINATION FOR STREET LEVEL NEW YORK MASTURBATORS OF THE ERA, SUCH AS PETE CHIARELLA...THE MAN KNOWN AS 42ND STREET PETE. WHEN I ASKED HIM ABOUT HIS VISITS TO THE STORE IN 2014, HE HAD THIS TO SAY:

YEP.

42ND STREET PETE IN HIS NATURAL HABITAT.

NO READI

"BLACK JACK BOOKS WAS ONE OF THE MORE SQUALID OF THE SCUMATORIUMS. IT HAD WOODEN FLOORS AND SAWDUST SPRINKLED ON THEM. I CAN NEVER REMEMBER THE PLACE BEING CLOSED. IT WAS A BOOK STORE, PEEPSHOW, AND HAD A LIVE S&M SHOW UPSTAIRS. MALE HUSTLERS USED TO HANG OUT IN FRONT AND TURN TRICKS IN THE BOOTHS. I REMEMBER DRIVING A FRIEND IN TO CATCH A 5AM BUS, AND THERE IT WAS, OPEN AT 4AM. THERE WAS A PASSED OUT TRANNY SLEEPING ON ONE OF THE COUNTERS, AND A WINO WAS SLEEPING IN ONE OF THE OPEN PEEP BOOTHS. A COUPLE OF SCUZZY STREET WALKERS WERE TRYING TO PICK GUYS UP UNTIL THIS EMPLOYEE, AT LEAST I THINK HE WAS, CHASED THEM OUT WITH A BASEBALL BAT. AND REMEMBER, THIS WAS ALL AT 4AM."

"THE LOOPS THE BLACK JACK HAD REALLY RAN THE GAMUT. IT WENT FROM STRAIGHT SEX, TO GAY, TO THE OUTRIGHT BIZARRE AND NAUSEATING. THE OLD COLOR CLIMAX LOOPS, GERMAN SCAT, PISS AND FIST FUCKING LOOPS, HARDCORE S&M AND TORTURE, THE FAKE SNUFF LOOPS, AND THE PERENNIAL LINDA LOVELACE DOG FUCKING LOOPS. AT ONE POINT THE S&M SHOW BECAME A LIVE, WINDOWLESS PEEP SHOW WHERE 'DANCERS' WOULD LET PATRONS LICK THEIR TITS AND PUSSY FOR A BUCK. DURING THE DAY, THE PLACE WAS PACKED, BUT BROWSING WAS LOUDLY DISCOURAGED AS IMPATIENT EMPLOYEES WOULD SCREAM AT PATRONS TO PICK UP THE BOOKS WITH BOTH HANDS!"

"I HONESTLY DON'T REMEMBER WHEN BLACK JACK OPENED. IT SEEMED IT WAS ALWAYS THERE. WHILE OTHER 'EMPORIUMS' LIKE SHOW WORLD AND LES GALS WERE STATE OF THE ART AND CLEAN, BLACK JACK SEEMED STUCK IN TIME, RETAINING THAT TIMES SQUARE SQUALOR RIGHT UP UNTIL IT CLOSED. BROKEN PEEP BOOTHS, UNKEMPT, MAGAZINE RACKS, AND AGGRESSIVE GAY MEN CRUISING FOR SEX WAS ITS LEGACY. IN THE EARLY 1980S I WENT FROM BEING A SMUT CONSUMER TO A SMUT PEDDLER AS I SAW THE $$$ IN THE NEW HOME VIDEO MARKET. SO IN THE LATER 1980S I REALLY DIDN'T FREQUENT THESE PLACES."

"WE BROWSED AT THE BLACK JACK BOOKSTORE," WROTE AN UNCREDITED WRITER IN THE AUGUST 8TH, 1974 ISSUE OF THE VILLAGE VOICE. "(IT) STOCKS HIGH-PRICED QUALITY PORN, A SEPARATE SECTION FOR GAYS, SPECIALITY ITEMS, AND A DIVERSITY OF LURID PEEP SHOWS. A SIGN AMONG THE PEEP SHOW BOOTHS GUARANTEED THAT 'ANYONE CAUGHT PISSING IN THE BOOTHS WILL GET THEIR LEGS BROKEN. TRY IT AND SEE.' A SCOWLING BLACK DUDE (BLACK JACK HIMSELF??) FONDLING A LENGTH OF CHAIN APPEARED READY TO REDEEM THAT PROMISE. I TIGHTENED MY BLADDER AND MOVED ON."

THE ACTUAL OWNER OF THIS NOTORIOUSLY SLEAZY SMUT SHOP WAS JOE BROCCHINI, A "MADE MAN" IN THE TRAMUNTI CRIME FAMILY (ONE OF THE 5 MAJOR CRIME FAMILIES IN NYC) WHO HAD A CRIMINAL BACKGROUND IN LOAN SHARKING AND EXTORTION. HE WENT BY THE NICKNAME "JOE BIKINI", AND WAS THE PROUD OWNER OF THREE ADULT BOOKSTORES, A MAGAZINE AND 8MM FILM DISTRIBUTOR, AND OWNED A USED CAR DEALERSHIP ON TOP OF THAT.

BEFORE JOE BIKINI CAME ALONG, MARTY HODAS (THE ORIGINATOR OF THE PEEP BOOTH MACHINE) OPENED AND OWNED NOT ONLY THE BLACK JACK, BUT HAD A MONOPOLY ON ALL OF THE LUCRATIVE PEEP SHOW ACTION IN TIMES SQUARE. BY 1970 HE HAD 400 PEEP SLOT MACHINES SHOWING 8MM FILMS, AND THEY WERE SCATTERED AROUND NEW YORK; IN THE BASEMENTS OF THEATERS, THE BACK ROOMS OF PORN SHOPS, AND IN VENUES DESIGNED SPECIFICALLY FOR THEIR USE. THE ORGANIZED CRIME CONTROL BEAUREAU ESTIMATED THAT NUMBER HAD JUMPED TO MORE THAN A THOUSAND BY 1972. HODAS WAS TAKING IN MORE THAN 20 GRAND A WEEK BEFORE HE WAS JAILED FOR TAX EVASION IN 1974.

SENSING AN OPPORTUNITY, A 38-YEAR-OLD JOE STEPPED UP AND TOOK A BITE OUT OF THE PEEPSHOW RACKET. "HODAS HAD BEEN PAYING THE BOB $5,000 A WEEK IN PROTECTION MONEY", JAY GERTZMAN REPORTED IN HIS EFANZINES.COM ARTICLE ENTITLED 'TIMES SQUARE WISE GUY'. "AFTER THE 1971 SHOOTING OF JOE COLOMBO WEAKENED HODAS' CHANCES OF PROTECTION FROM THE COLOMBO CRIME FAMILY, BROCCHINI STEPPED IN AND REPLACED HODAS' PEEP SHOW BOOTHS WITH HIS OWN."

LIVE PEEP SHOWS WERE ALSO SOMETHING YOU COULD TAKE IN AT BLACK JACK, AND THERE WAS NO WINDOW KEEPING THE CUSTOMER AND THE GIRL APART LIKE THERE WERE IN THE UPSCALE PEEP PALACES LIKE SHOW WORLD. "THE LIVE PEEPS WERE THE STRAIGHT MAN'S CLOSEST EQUIVALENT TO THE UNDERSIDE OF GAY NIGHTLIFE", JOSH ALAN FRIEDMAN WROTE IN HIS EXCELLENT 1986 BOOK, TALES OF TIMES SQUARE. "(YOU) WANDERED INTO A DARK BOOTH TO MOUTH THE SLIMY GENITALS OF STRANGE WOMEN, WHOSE BREASTS WERE COVERED IN THE SLOBBER OF FIFTY PREVIOUS TIT-BITERS AND WHOSE SUCKED-OUT CUNTS GLISTENED AT PREMIUM RATES."

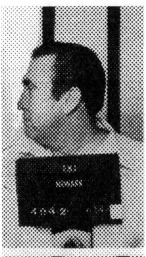

IN MAY 1976 JOE BIKINI SEALED HIS FATE BY UNWISELY PUNCHING NOTORIOUS GAMBINO CRIME FAMILY CONTRACT KILLER, ROY DEMEO, RIGHT IN THE KISSER. THEY HAD BEEN ARGUING OVER JOE'S EXTENSIVE PROFITS PERTAINING TO HIS VENTURES IN THE PORNOGRAPHY BUSINESS, AND AN INFURIATED DEMEO FOUND HIMSELF WITH A BLACK EYE BY THE END OF THE HEATED ARGUMENT. EXPERIENCED WITH KILLING AT LEAST 90 PEOPLE (ALTHOUGH MORE THAN A FEW CRIMINOLOGISTS HAVE PUT THE NUMBER AS HIGH AS 200), ROY ENACTED HIS BLOODY REVENGE A WEEK LATER, SENDING OVER A COUPLE OF HIS GOONS TO PUT 5 BULLETS IN THE BACK OF JOE'S HEAD WHILE THE SMUT PEDDLER SAT IN THE OFFICE OF HIS USED CAR DEALERSHIP -- PARLIAMENT AUTO SALES, AT 69-11 ROOSEVELT AVE IN QUEENS.

THE GANGSTERS THEN RANSACKED THE BUILDING TO MAKE IT LOOK LIKE AN ARMED ROBBERY GONE WRONG. AS YOU MAY REMEMBER IF YOU EVER SAW GOODFELLAS, KILLING A MADE MAN WITHOUT PERMISSION WAS A SERIOUS VIOLATION OF MAFIA CODE, AND IT WOULD HAVE MEANT CERTAIN DEATH FOR DEMEO AND HIS CREW IF IT WERE EVER TRACED BACK TO HIM. NOT SURPRISINGLY ROY DEMEO HIMSELF WOULD BE SHOT AND KILLED AND LEFT IN A CAR TRUNK IN 1983. IT WAS A MURDER THAT TOOK PLACE UNDER ORDERS OF JOHN GOTTI, A MEMBER OF DEMEO'S OWN CRIME FAMILY. THE TRIGGER-HAPPY GOOMBAH HAD SIMPLY ATTRACTED FAR TOO MUCH ATTENTION FROM THE FBI, AND THEY WERE WORRIED HE WAS GOING TO BRING DOWN THE ENTIRE GAMBINO MAFIA EMPIRE.

ONLY A FEW DAYS AFTER HIS MURDER, BROCCHINI'S BROTHER-IN-LAW (ALFRED SCOTTI), HIS BROTHER JAMES, AND TWO BEST FRIENDS (RALPH AND VINCENT BORELLO) DIVIDED UP BROCCHINI'S HOLDINGS AMONGST THEMSELVES OVER DRINKS IN A LOCAL BAR. WHAT THEY WEREN'T AWARE OF, ACCORDING TO R. THOMAS COLLINS (A NEW YORK JOURNALIST OF THE ERA) IS THAT A POLICE INFORMANT WAS SEATED NEARBY. COLLINS WOULD CALL THE BLACK JACK "THE MOST SUCCESSFUL DIRTY BOOK STORE ON WEST 42ND" IN HIS ARTICLE ABOUT THE INCIDENT IN THE NEW YORK DAILY NEWS. THE PAGE FOUR HEADLINE READ: "THE KING IS DEAD; LONG LIVE THE SMUT EMPIRE"!

IN SEPTEMBER 1991 BLACK JACK BOOKS SHUTTERED ITS WINDOWS AND CLOSED FOREVER. FOR A FEW YEARS AFTERWARDS A PORN VIDEO STORE USED THE SPACE, BUT TODAY IT IS A SUBWAY SANDWICH SHOP TUCKED AMONGST HIGH END TOURIST GIFT STORES AND EXPENSIVE THEATER PERFORMANCE VENUES.

"I'M PRETTY SURE BLACK JACK MIGHT HAVE BEEN CLOSED WHEN AIDS REARED IT'S UGLY HEAD", PETE CHIARELLA NOTED. "THE CITY WAS SHUTTING DOWN 'HIGH RISK' PLACES LIKE GAY BATH HOUSES AND THEATERS. BEING THAT BLACK JACK HAD A CRUISING SCENE, I WOULD SAY THAT MIGHT HAVE LED TO ITS DEMISE."

"LIKE EVERYTHING ELSE, IT WAS FUN WHILE IT LASTED", PETE SAID WITH A SIGH. "NOW ALL THAT REMAINS ARE FOGGY MEMORIES..."

ROY DEMEO'S MUGSHOT. THIS GAMBINO FAMILY CONTRACT KILLER WAS NAMED THE 3RD MOST DEADLY MAFIA HITMAN IN HISTORY BY ALIZUL BLOG IN '12.

BURNING QUESTION: "DID ANNETTE HAVEN EVER HAVE ANAL SEX OR DO FACIALS IN HER MOVIES? WOULD BE GOOD TO KNOW." -GREG B. RED HILL, ALABAMA.

NO CUM ALLOWED

POPULAR 1970S AND 1980S PORN FILM STARLET ANNETTE HAVEN WAS A NOTORIOUS CUM-DODGER. SHE RARELY PARTOOK IN TADPOLE TEA (SOFT PLACES AND SEXSATIONS ARE THE ONLY FILMS I CAN THINK OF, AND MANY FANS BELIEVE THE CUM-INGESTING SHE DID IN THESE SCENES WAS FAKED WITH CAMERA TRICKERY AND EDITING), NEVER DID A FACIAL, AND NEVER DID AN ANAL SCENE TO THE BEST OF MY KNOWLEDGE.

I'VE HAD A SHAMPOO BOTTLE IN MY ASS SO I CAN UNDERSTAND THAT ANAL SEX ISN'T FOR EVERYONE. I GET THAT. BUT I DON'T GET THE AVERSION TO CUM, THOUGH. WHAT SORT OF SAD-SACK LOVER WOULD A MAN BE IF HE ANNOUNCED "I WON'T EAT WOMEN OUT BECAUSE I DON'T LIKE PUSSY JUICE"? IT GOES THE SAME FOR WOMEN. IF YOU THINK THE PHYSICAL MANIFESTATION OF MEN'S ORGASMS IS DISGUSTING, YOU REALLY SHOULDN'T BE DOING PORN. YOU'RE A LIGHTWEIGHT. SHIT OR GET OFF THE POT. OR AS THE OTHER ANNETTE (ANNETTE HEINZ) FROM THE GOLDEN AGE OF ADULT FILMS IS QUITE FOND OF SAYING: "WHO WANTS A 'LADY' IN THE BEDROOM?"

DAD MADE DIRTY MOVIES

DAD MADE DIRTY MOVIES IS A LITTLE-SEEN 2011 DOCUMENTARY THAT TELLS THE AMAZING TRUE STORY OF STEPHEN C. APOSTOLOF (AKA A. C. STEPHEN) THE BULGARIAN-BORN AMERICAN PRODUCER, SCREENWRITER AND DIRECTOR THAT ESCAPED A COMMUNIST DICTATORSHIP IN EASTERN EUROPE TO TRAVEL TO THE US AND MAKE HIS AMERICAN DREAM A REALITY. TOGETHER WITH HIS CLOSE PAL, ECCENTRIC CROSS-DRESSER ED WOOD, STEPHEN MADE SEVENTEEN LOW-BUDGET EROTIC FEATURE FILMS IN THE 1960S AND '70S, AND BECAME ONE OF THE EARLIEST PURVEYORS OF SEXPLOITATION CINEMA.

HIS MOST SUCCESSFUL EFFORT WAS **ORGY OF THE DEAD** (1965), WHICH MAINLY JUST OPERATES AS A WAY TO FEATURE TOPLESS GIRLS DOING LETHARGIC INTERPRETIVE STRIP-TEASE DANCES WITH THE MUMMY AND THE WOLFMAN. NOT SURPRISINGLY, TODAY THE MOVIE HAS A DEVOTED CULT FOLLOWING. APOSTOLOF DEVELOPED SEVERAL FILM IDEAS THAT HE WASN'T ABLE TO FINISH BEFORE HE DIED IN AUGUST OF 2005, THE MOST NOTABLE BEING A SEQUEL TO **ORGY OF THE DEAD** CALLED **THE NEW GENERATION.**

I REALLY ENJOYED THIS DOCUMENTARY, AND LOVED THE IDEA THAT DIRECTOR JORDAN TODOROV (A FILMMAKER AND JOURNALIST LIVING IN SOFIA, BULGARIA) WOULD CHOOSE SUCH AN OBSCURE AND FASCINATING CHARACTER ON WHICH TO BASE A MOVIE. ED WOOD HAS BEEN COVERED AD NAUSEAM BY JOURNALISTS AND FILMMAKERS, BUT TO DATE THIS IS THE FIRST TIME ANYONE HAS EVER SHONE A PROPER LIGHT ON THE CAREER OF GOOD OL' A.C.

TODOROV GRADUATED WITH AN MA IN FILM STUDIES FROM THE NATIONAL ACADEMY OF THEATRE AND FILM ARTS IN SOFIA, BULGARIA, AND HAD BEEN WORKING AS FULL TIME EDITOR FOR THE BULGARIAN EDITION OF ROLLING STONE UP UNTIL AUGUST, 2011. HE TOOK TIME TO CHAT WITH ME IN AUGUST OF 2012.

JORDAN, WHAT MADE YOU DECIDE TO MAKE A MOVIE ABOUT A.C. STEPHEN?

This is the second documentary that I wrote and directed. My desire was to find who this person was, and it took me more than five years to finish it, but it was worth it. I wanted to explore Stephen Apostolof's life and unique career, but also I wanted to explore his relationship with Ed Wood, who is one of the greatest American counter-culture heroes.

HOW DID YOU FIND OUT ABOUT APOSTOLOF?

I stumbled upon his story by chance in 2005. A friend of mine one day just told me, 'Why don't you

ASTRA FILMS PRESENTS

ORGY OF THE DEAD

Come...Let Me Take You In My GOLDEN ARMS..!

IN GORGEOUS **ASTRAVISION** and SHOCKING **SEXICOLOR**

look up on the internet who directed the erotic screenplays of Ed Wood?' I checked the name and I was fascinated. I found Stephen C. Apostolof's life and career to be incredibly inspiring.

First, I started researching the subject because I wanted to write an article for the newspaper I was working for at the time. But the editor in chief said the story was not interesting enough (laughs) so I decided to make a documentary out of it. I got in touch with Martichka Bozhilova, probably one of the finest European documentary producers, and we started developing the project. She loved the story. We thought it would be easy to get financing because of the tits and ass, but then it turned out that no television want to show T and A in primetime! Luckily we got co-producers from Germany and ARTE/ZDF television on board.

GETTING READY TO FUCK IN MOTEL CONFIDENTIAL (1967)

Then it became an obsession. The figure of A.C. Stephen was so obscure and what little information about him out there was so confusing that I had the strange feeling that I was looking for a nonexistent person. Was he in the French foreign legion in the 1940s or not? Did he study at the Sorbonne or not? Did he exist at all? At one point I thought 'I'm going mad'. I thought that Stephen Apostolof was born out of my own imagination. It was downright scary! Later on, this mystery kind of determined the overall style and structure of the film, and I chose to tell the story through a chorus of voices that contradict each other.

YEAH, I LIKED THAT ASPECT OF THE MOVIE. THIS DIRECTOR DOESN'T SEEM ON THE SURFACE LIKE THERE WOULD BE VERY MUCH TO SAY ABOUT HIM BUT YOU UNCOVERED A LOT.

Once we started developing the project I realized what a huge task I had taken on. The scale of this kind of film is huge. The challenge was to cover a life of almost 80 years. I quit my day job as staff writer for the biggest weekly newspaper in Bulgaria in order to work on that film. This was five years ago and I have been working on this film more or less every day since then.

HOW DID YOU GET IN CONTACT WITH HIS FAMILY?

I found the phone number of someone named "Steve Apostolof". I called and it turned out that he was the oldest son of the elder Stephen Apostolof. From there it was easy. I managed to gain their trust through the years and they accepted me as a member of their extended family. They revealed many family secrets that otherwise they would not have told. They even started calling me "our Bulgarian cousin".

Through the years I developed a special relationship with Stephen Apostolof, even though I've never met

SCENES FROM **DROP-OUT WIFE** (1972)

him. It's a strange feeling – to be so close to someone you didn't know personally. I have dreams about him often. The last time I asked him about his opinion on the title of my documentary – Dad Made Dirty Movies. He said he couldn't think of a better title of a biopic on his life and work. The title actually came from one of the daughters – she told me a story of her as a teenager in the Sixties when she was bragging to her schoolmates, saying - "My dad makes dirty movies!" It's one of the funniest moments in the film.

YOU DID A LOT OF TRAVELLING FOR THIS MOVIE, RIGHT?

We shot the family in Arizona and California primarily in 2009 and 2010. We shot in four states and eight cities in total. I stumbled upon a strange world of porn stars, Communist spies, producers of porn films with insects, FBI agents turned actors, ex go-go dancers and producers of low-budget horror movies. It was a wild journey.

APOSTOLOF NEVER DID HARDCORE, INSTEAD DOING SEXPLOITATION MOVIES UNTIL THE GENRE SLOWLY DIED OUT. IT SEEMS TO ME THOUGH THAT HIS MOVIES GOT PROGRESSIVELY DIRTIER UP UNTIL DROP-OUT WIFE – WHICH GETS FAIRLY RAUNCHY. I IMAGINE HE WAS FEELING SOME PRESSURE TO SHOW PENETRATION FROM DEEP THROAT COMING OUT JUST PRIOR TO THAT. I THOUGHT IT WAS COOL THAT YOU COVERED THAT ELEMENT OF ADULT FILM HISTORY, AND ALSO REVEALED WHAT PART APOSTOLOF'S WIFE HAD TO PLAY IN HIS CHOICE NOT TO SHOOT HARDCORE FUCKING.

Yes, Apostolof never did hardcore even though he was pretty close to it with Drop-Out Wife in 1972. Yes, he felt pressure to show penetration on the screen but he managed to withstand that pressure and instead tried to enter the mainstream market with Hot Ice. He refused to go into much more profitable porn films because of his Christian values and his standards of a family man. His wife told him that they would end up in divorce court if he tried to make porn.

Ed Wood died in 1978. The same year Apostolof made his last film Hot Ice - a James Bond flick with less nudity and more action. The film bombed at the box-office and Apostolof got broke. He lost his home, got forced out of the film business and started moving around the country with his third wife. His traces got lost. Many people thought he was dead. Others – that he had never existed. Some even proposed the wild theory that he and Ed Wood actually were one and the same person. Apostolof took these speculations very seriously. Later on, in 1994, when Tim Burton's film with Johnny Depp came out, Stephen Apostolof was kind of jealous of Ed's newly found fame. But that's life.

VERY TRUE. I'M A BIG RENE BOND FAN, AND WAS HOPING TO SEE HER STORY COVERED A LITTLE MORE IN YOUR FILM, ALTHOUGH YOU MANAGED TO GET HER IN THERE A LITTLE.

I also like Rene Bond a lot, but I think she deserves a documentary of her own.

AGREED!

I covered only part of Rene's story because she was one of the several stars Apostolof worked with in the '60s and '70s, the other being Marsha Jordan, Rick Lutze and Harvey Shane. Rene is the archetypal "girl next door", I love her. It's a shame that she died so young. Speaking of sexploitation stars, I managed to find the whereabouts of Marsha Jordan. She lives in a small city in California and I talked to her husband, but he said she is not interested in doing any documentaries. She was a dear, dear friend of Apostolof. They were almost like brother and sister. I suppose Marsha (who must be in her '80s by now) is happily married and does not want to remember the old times.

AWW. THAT'S A SHAME. WELL, THAT'S COOL THAT YOU FOUND HER AND SHE'S STILL KICKING AROUND.

Another actress that I can't name threatened to sue me if I continue calling her. Oh, and I recently managed to find Fawn Silver – she played the Black Ghoul in Orgy of the Dead. But most of all, I'm very curious about Pat Barrington, she kind of disappeared in the late 1960s.

YOU GET PRETTY IN-DEPTH INTO A LOT OF INTERESTING MOVIES. CLASS REUNION, THE SNOW BUNNIES, MOTEL CONFIDENTIAL, SUBURBIA CONFIDENTIAL. THERE ARE A LOT OF FUN AND WILD SEXPLOITATION FILMS IN THE STEPHEN FILMOGRAPHY, BUT MY PERSONAL FAVE A.C. STEPHEN MOVIE, 5 LOOSE WOMEN (AKA FUGITIVE GIRLS) STARRING RENE BOND WASN'T COVERED. WHY DID YOU LEAVE THAT ONE OUT?

I chose to leave this film out intentionally. Even though it's one of the best known films of Stephen Apostolof, I needed to create a sense of rapid transition from the '60s through '70s to '80s because I wanted to underline the decline of Apostolof's career in late '70s. Fugitive girls is a very successful film but I didn't feel it was that important to the story.

SOPHIE'S CHOICE: WHICH IS YOUR PERSONAL FAVOURITE FILM WHEN IT COMES TO THE A.C. STEPHEN FILMOGRAPHY?

I would say I love all of his films – every one of them has something to it. I graduated from the National Academy for Theatre and Film

Stephen C. Apostolof presents
HOT ICE
THE ZANIEST CAPER OF THE JET SET

Arts in Sofia as a film critic where I was taught to like the films of Fellini, Tarkovski, Bergman and other masters of cinema. I never knew such a thing as sexploitation existed, much less that one day I would become a fan of it. And yet, if I have to pick one, I would say Orgy of the Dead. It's very naive and charming in a way! It has a very strange surreal quality. Of course, saying all that, I must add that most of the attacks on Stephen Apostolof's films are simply vile and unjustified. Yes, his movies are not masterpieces but they weren't worse than the standard sexploitation fare at the time. We should give respect where respect is due. The man tried his best and lived life full of courage and optimism. But most important of all, he got the bug of being a filmmaker. I could relate on a personal basis to that.

SOLDIER BLUE (1970. DIR: RALPH NELSON)

IN 1864, COLONEL JOHN M. CHIVINGTON USED A LOCAL MILITIA TO CARRY OUT ONE OF THE MOST VILE MASSACRES IN AMERICAN HISTORY, THE VIOLENT RAPE AND OBLITERATION OF A DEFENCELESS VILLAGE OF PEACEFUL CHEYENNE AND ARAPAHO ON THE COLORADO EASTERN PLAINS. A YEAR LATER, IN 1865, THE JOINT COMMITTEE ON THE CONDUCT OF WAR REVIEWED THE DAMNING DETAILS OF THE INCIDENT, AND DECLARED:

"(CHIVINGTON) DELIBERATELY PLANNED AND EXECUTED A FOUL AND DASTARDLY MASSACRE WHICH WOULD HAVE DISGRACED THE VERIST SAVAGE AMONG THOSE WHO WERE THE VICTIMS OF HIS CRUELTY. HAVING FULL KNOWLEDGE OF THEIR FRIENDLY CHARACTER, HAVING HIMSELF BEEN INSTRUMENTAL TO SOME EXTENT IN PLACING THEM IN THEIR POSITION OF FANCIED SECURITY, HE TOOK ADVANTAGE OF THEIR IN-APPREHENSION AND DEFENCELESS CONDITION TO GRATIFY THE WORST PASSIONS THAT EVER CURSED THE HEART OF MAN... HE SURPRISED AND MURDERED, IN COLD BLOOD, THE UNSUSPECTING MEN, WOMEN, AND CHILDREN ON SAND CREEK, WHO HAD EVERY REASON TO BELIEVE THEY WERE UNDER THE PROTECTION OF THE UNITED STATES AUTHORITIES."

IN 1970, WITH THE VIETNAM WAR IN FULL SWING, AMERICAN DIRECTOR RALPH NELSON MADE AN EMOTIONALLY DEVASTATING MOVIE ABOUT THE SAND CREEK MASSACRE, CRAFTING A CLEVER ALLEGORY OF THE MY LAI MASSACRE THAT HAD STOKED THE FLAMES OF THE ANTI-VIETNAM WAR MOVEMENT. RALPH CAST A YOUNG (AND VERY SEXY) CANDICE BERGEN AND PETER STRAUSS AS FICTIONAL CHARACTERS TO BEAR WITNESS TO THE ATROCITY, ONE THAT MOST AMERICANS AT THE TIME HAD LITTLE KNOWLEDGE OF. THEY PROVIDE SOME DRAMA AND ROMANCE LEADING UP TO THE OVERTLY BLOODY FINALE IN THIS THOUGHT-PROVOKING PICTURE, WITH MUCH OF THE DECIMATED TRIBE PLAYED BY AMPUTEES. REALISTIC PROSTHETIC LIMBS WERE PLACED ON THEIR STUMPS, AND THEN MERCILESSLY HACKED OFF, AND THEN THERE WERE THE GRAPHIC CHILD KILLINGS DEPICTED IN A STYLE THAT FEW FILMMAKERS HAVE DARED TO EMULATE SINCE. WITH PERHAPS ONLY THE GORY AND VIOLENT DEATHS OF BONNIE AND CLYDE IN ARTHUR PENN'S 1967 FILM OF THE SAME NAME, AUDIENCES HADN'T SEEN ANYTHING QUITE LIKE IT UP TO THAT POINT. IT WAS, AS THE TAGLINE READ, "THE MOST SAVAGE FILM IN HISTORY", AND IT PUT A SPOTLIGHT ON THE RACISM AND GENOCIDE THAT THE MORE POPULAR AMERICAN WESTERNS WHITEWASHED. SOLDIER BLUE IS STILL WAITING TO BE DISCOVERED IN THE US — EVEN NOW, OVER 45 YEARS LATER.

AUTHOR OF THE 2008 BOOK, 'THE MOST SAVAGE FILM,' P.B. HURST IS THE SOLDIER BLUE EXPERT, SO I'LL DEFER TO HIM TO SUM THIS UP: "A MASSIVE HIT IN GREAT BRITAIN AND MUCH OF THE REST OF THE WORLD, SOLDIER BLUE WAS, IN THE WORDS OF ITS MAVERICK DIRECTOR, RALPH NELSON, 'NOT A POPULAR SUCCESS' IN THE UNITED STATES. THIS PROBABLY HAD LESS TO DO WITH THE PICTURE'S GROUNDBREAKING VIOLENCE, AND MORE TO DO WITH THE FACT THAT IT WAS THE U.S. CAVALRY WHO WERE BREAKING NEW GROUND. FOR NELSON'S PORTRAYAL OF THE BOYS IN BLUE AS BLOOD-CRAZED MANIACS, WHO BLOW CHILDREN'S BRAINS OUT AND BEHEAD WOMEN, SHATTERED FOR EVER ONE OF AMERICA'S MOST ENDURING MOVIE MYTHS -- THAT OF THE CAVALRY AS GOOD GUYS RIDING TO THE RESCUE -- AND RENDERED SOLDIER BLUE ONE OF THE MOST RADICAL FILMS IN THE HISTORY OF AMERICAN CINEMA."

THE MOST SAVAGE FILM IN HISTORY!

THE ORDER WAS MASSACRE, AND GOOD SOLDIERS FOLLOW ORDERS. THESE SOLDIERS WERE THE BEST.

SOLDIER BLUE
CANDICE BERGEN
PETER STRAUSS
DONALD PLEASENCE

Directed by RALPH NELSON

"DON'T MAKE ME HURT YOU, BITCH"

THE TOP 20 ROUGHIES

ANOTHER TURD BY ROBIN BOUGIE

WHAT A "ROUGHIE" IS ALWAYS SEEMS TO NEED TO BE DEFINED BEFORE ONE CAN TALK ABOUT THEM, I FIND. DEPENDING ON WHO YOU ASK, SOME GENRE FANS WILL TELL YOU THAT ANY SORT OF PORN WITH BONDAGE, FORCED SEX THEMES OR DEGRADATION IS A ROUGHIE, BUT I SPECIFICALLY LABEL THEM AS:

NARRATIVE BASED SEX FILMS WHICH HAVE A SPECIFIC FOCUS ON FORCED SEX AND/OR SEXUALIZED DEGRADATION. IN A ROUGHIE, HUMAN RELATIONSHIPS ARE BASE, PRIMAL, AND CHARACTERIZED BY EXPLOITATION.

THE "NARRATIVE" PART IS IMPORTANT, BECAUSE WITHOUT THE STORYLINE, YOU'RE JUST TALKING ABOUT GONZO STYLE PORNO, WHICH IS A TOTALLY DIFFERENT ANIMAL. ALSO, FOR THE PURPOSES OF NARROWING THE SCOPE, I'M GOING TO STICK TO AMERICAN-MADE FILMS FOR THIS PIECE. IF YOU WANT TO TALK ABOUT VINTAGE BRAZILIAN, EUROPEAN, SWEDISH, OR JAPANESE CINEMA WITH FORCED SEX THEMES, THAT WILL BE A DIFFERENT DISCUSSION, BECAUSE THEY HAVE A TOTALLY DIFFERENT FEEL, AESTHETIC AND HISTORY. THERE ARE SOME REALLY GOOD VINTAGE GAY ROUGHIES AS WELL, BUT THEY SHOULD PROBABLY BE WEIGHED ON THEIR MERITS SEPARATELY. (I'M FRANKLY RATHER EMBARRASSED BY MY LACK OF KNOWLEDGE ABOUT THEIR HISTORY, BUT MY HETERO ADULT MOVIE-WATCHING HABITS HAVE RATHER PREDICTABLY SHAPED THE SCOPE OF MY EXPERIENCE).

ROUGHIES, BY MY DEFINITION, STARTED IN 1964 WITH JOSEPH MAWRA'S WHITE SLAVES OF CHINATOWN, AND WERE QUICKLY FOLLOWED UP BY FILMS LIKE JOHN AMERO AND MICHAEL FINDLAY'S BODY OF A FEMALE, AND LEE FROST'S THE DEFILERS. BUT OF COURSE THE FOUNDATIONS OF THE GENRE ARE ENTRENCHED DEEPER THAN THAT. I THINK THAT FILMMAKERS SINCE THE VERY BEGINNING OF THE FILM MEDIUM ITSELF, WITH THEIR TROPE OF THE CACKLING SCOUNDREL TYING THE WHIMPERING, SCANTILY-CLAD MAIDEN TO THE TRAIN TRACKS, HAVE KNOWN WHAT SELLS TICKETS. THEY TAPPED INTO THE UNDENIABLE FACT THAT SEXUALITY COMBINED WITH VIOLENCE IS INTOXICATING FOR AN AUDIENCE, REGARDLESS IF THEY ARE TITILLATED OR OFFENDED. IN BOTH INSTANCES, THE HEART RACES.

BEFORE WE GET ON WITH IT, THOUGH, OF SOME MINOR CONCERN TO ME IS HOW A HANDFUL OF ONLINE REVIEWERS IN RECENT YEARS HAVE BEGUN USING THE TERM "ROUGHIE" AS A SUBSTITUTE FOR THE WORD "SEXPLOITATION". IT'S SLOPPY, AND IN DOING THIS, THEY TOTALLY IGNORE THE WIDELY ACCEPTED DEFINITION ABOVE AND CONFUSINGLY USE THE TERM TO DESCRIBE MANY 1960S SEX MOVIES THAT ARE UTTERLY PASSIVE, COY, AND HAVE NOTHING ROUGH HAPPENING IN THEM WHATSOEVER. I'M HOPING THIS BULLSHIT IS JUST A PASSING PHASE SOON TO BE IGNORED, BECAUSE IF IT CATCHES ON, IT MAKES IT AWFULLY HARD TO COMMUNICATE WHICH SUBGENRES OF SEXPLOITATION FILMS YOU'RE TALKING ABOUT.

THERE ARE ALSO A LOT OF GREAT MOVIES NOT ON MY LIST BECAUSE THEY ONLY HAVE ONE SCENE THAT REALLY CAN BE CORRECTLY CITED AS PERTAINING TO THE "ROUGHIE" GENRE, AND THE REST OF THE FILM DOESN'T FIT. MOVIES LIKE RUSS MEYER'S LORNA (1964), A SMELL OF HONEY, A SWALLOW OF BRINE (1966), SMOKE AND FLESH (1968), AND EASY (1978). QUITE FRANKLY, EVERY OTHER ADULT MOVIE FROM THE LATE '60S TO EARLY '80S HAS A RAPE SCENE, SO I'VE HAD TO BE A BIT MORE SPECIFIC HERE.

I LOVE MAKING LISTS, AND FOR THIS ONE I'LL BE DIVIDING BETWEEN 1960S SOFTCORE, AND THE HARDCORE ROUGHIES MADE FROM THE EARLY 1970S AND BEYOND. THEY'RE FAR DIFFERENT VIEWING EXPERIENCES, SO IT WAS WORTH SEPARATING THEM FOR THIS EXERCISE. TO RANK THE PICTURES THAT MADE MY LISTS, I WEIGHED THEM ON THE USUAL TYPES OF THINGS FILM REVIEWERS WOULD DEEM IMPORTANT (ACTING, PLOT, CINEMATOGRAPHY, DIRECTION, EDITING), BUT ALSO TOOK INTO ACCOUNT HOW KINKY AND ROUGH THE SEX GOT, HOW FILTHY THE DIRTY TALK WAS, AND HOW DERANGED THE FIENDISH PSYCHOS WERE. YOU KNOW, THE SHIT THAT MAKES THOSE NASTY OL' ROUGHIES MEMORABLE!

STAN BORDEN Presents

OLGA'S GIRLS

DIRECTED BY JOSEPH P. MAWRA

I am watching you through a telescope you must do anything and everything I say or I will kill your son...

HE MADE HER AN ANIMAL... NOW ALL HE NEEDED WAS A LEASH

THE ANIMAL

there could be nothing lower

BOTH THE 1960S SOFTCORE FILMS AND THE 70S HARDCORE ONES WERE AS BRUTAL AND AS CONFRONTATIONAL AS CINEMA GOT AT THE TIME, BUT IN RETROSPECT THESE MUCH MALIGNED EFFORTS WORK ON VARIOUS LEVELS ASIDE FROM JUST MEAN-SPIRITED TITILLATION. THEY CAN BE RUDIMENTARY IN THEIR PLOT STRUCTURE, BUT THERE'S MORE GOING ON WITHIN THESE FILMS THAN MOST PEOPLE ARE WILLING TO ADMIT. IN THE PROVOCATIVE 1960S ROUGHIES, THE AUDIENCE GETS TRANSPORTED BACK IN TIME TO SLAP PAVEMENT ON TIMES SQUARE STREETCORNERS, TO BEAR WITNESS TO THE STRANGE TIME CAPSULE DETAILS OF MIDDLE-CLASS APARTMENTS USED AS CHEAP LOCATIONS, AND THEN THERE ARE THE SATURATED COLOURS AND TEXTURES OF LOS ANGELES MOTEL ROOMS AND POOLS. WITHOUT FAIL, THE INSTRUMENTAL MUSIC SCORES ARE ALWAYS JAZZY AND WAY-OUT, AND THE MOD DRESSES, GO-GO BOOTS, BLACK LACE UNDERGARMENTS, AND FEATHERY NEGLIGEES ENRAPTURE, EVEN AS THEY ARE RIPPED OFF THEIR SQUEALING VICTIMS.

THE 1970S ROUGHIES ARE INDICATIVE OF THEIR TIME AS WELL. THE DEVASTATION OF THE VIETNAM WAR WAS RINGING IN AMERICANS' HEADS, ALTAMONT HAD CRIPPLED THE HIPPIES, AND BIRTH CONTROL, PORNO CHIC, AND THE EMERGENCE OF KINK CULTURE HAD SEXUAL EXPLORATION LOOKING NOT NEARLY AS UNDERGROUND AND VERBOTEN. THE TRADITIONAL RELATIONSHIP BETWEEN MEN AND WOMEN FELT ON THE CUSP OF CHANGE AS WELL, WHICH SEEMED TO BOTH INVIGORATE AND ALTERNATELY HORRIFY DEPENDING ON WHO YOU WERE.

I DON'T WANT TO SAY THAT MANY OF THE DIRECTORS OF THESE SCUMMY OLD MOVIES HAD LOFTY ARTISTIC GOALS OR SOCIAL MESSAGES TO RELAY, BUT IF YOU'RE PAYING ATTENTION EVEN THE MOST DISREPUTABLE ENTERTAINMENT WILL TELL YOU A LOT ABOUT A CULTURE. ROUGHIES, DEVOID OF PRETENSION, ARE A FUNHOUSE MIRROR ON THE ALL TOO PREVALENT REPRESSIVE SEXUAL MORES THAT SHAME SEX, AND SIMPLY WRITING THEM OFF AS "WRONG" OR "MISOGYNIST" FAILS TO TACKLE THE COMPLEX NATURE OF SEXUAL VIOLENCE AND THE POWER DYNAMIC BETWEEN MEN AND WOMEN AT PLAY IN OUR SOCIETY. (AND IN THE CASE OF THE GAY SEX ROUGHIES, THE POWER DYNAMIC BETWEEN MEN AND MEN, AND WOMEN AND WOMEN).

NOTE: **HARDCORE** (1974) AND **THE DEVIL INSIDE HER** (1976) ARE NOT MISSING FROM THE HARDCORE LIST BECAUSE OF ANY NOTED FAILING ON THEIR PARTS (THEY'RE BOTH VERY ENTERTAINING MOVIES), BUT SIMPLY BECAUSE THEY FIT IN THE "HORROR PORN" GENRE MORE COMFORTABLY THAN THEY DO THE ROUGHIE GENRE.

Lock your doors tonight, Miss. Don't go out tonight, Miss.

THE PSYCHO LOVER is loose!

ISLEY BROTHERS and MEDFORD FILM CORPORATION present "THE PSYCHO LOVER" Starring LAWRENCE MONTAIGNE · JOANNE MEREDITH · ELIZABETH PLUMB · FRANK CUVA as "Marco"

BAD GIRLS GO TO HELL

THE TOP 20 1960S SEXPLOITATION ROUGHIES

1. THE ANIMAL (1968 DIR: LEE FROST)
2. THE PSYCHO LOVER (1970 DIR: ROBERT VINCENT O'NEILL)
3. THE DEFILERS (1965 DIR: LEE FROST)
4. AROUSED (1966 DIR: ANTON HOLDEN)
5. THE KISS OF HER FLESH (1968 DIR: MICHAEL FINDLAY)
6. THE ULTIMATE DEGENERATE (1969 DIR: MICHAEL FINDLAY)
7. THE PICK-UP (1968 DIR: LEE FROST)
8. A THOUSAND PLEASURES (1968 DIR: MICHAEL FINDLAY)
9. THE RAVAGER (1970 DIR: CHARLES NIZET)
10. THE DEBAUCHERS (1970 DIR: SIDNEY KNIGHT)
11. THE BIG SNATCH (1970 DIR: BYRON MABE AND DAN MARTIN)
12. THE GIRL GRABBERS (1968 DIR: SIMON NUCHTERN)

> "More Shocking than 'PSYCHO,' the best acting ever seen in a porno film. The ending will blow your mind."
> Nelson Knight/MANS WORLD MAG.

> "C.J. Laing never looked better."
> Schneiderman/PLEASURE MAG.

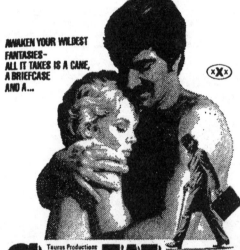

13. INVITATION TO RUIN (1968 DIR: KURT RICHTER)
14. OLGA'S GIRLS (1964 DIR: JOSEPH MAWRA)
15. THE TOUCH OF HER FLESH (1967 DIR: MICHAEL FINDLAY)
16. BAD GIRLS GO TO HELL (1965 DIR: DORIS WISHMAN)
17. BODY OF A FEMALE (1964 DIR: JOHN AMERO AND MICHAEL FINDLAY)
18. TORTURED FEMALES (1965 DIR: ARCH HUDSON)
19. WHITE SLAVES OF CHINATOWN (1964 DIR: JOSEPH MAWRA)
20. HOT SPUR (1968 DIR: LEE FROST)

THE TOP 20 XXX HARDCORE ROUGHIES:

1. THE TAMING OF REBECCA (1982 DIR: PHIL PRINCE)
2. A CLIMAX OF BLUE POWER (1975 DIR: LEE FROST)
3. THE STORY OF PRUNELLA (1982 DIR: PHIL PRINCE)
4. SEX WISH (1976 DIR: VICTOR MILT)
5. HOT SUMMER IN THE CITY (1976 DIR: HARRY MAHONEY)
6. FORCED ENTRY (1973 DIR: SHAUN COSTELLO)
7. DR BIZARRO (1983 DIR: PHIL PRINCE)
8. WATERPOWER (1977 DIR: SHAUN COSTELLO)
9. THE DEFIANCE OF GOOD (1975 DIR: ARMAND WESTON)
10. FEMMES DE SADE (1976 DIR: ALEX DE RENZY)
11. THE TAKING OF CHRISTINA (1976 DIR: ARMAND WESTON)
12. THE STORY OF JOANNA (1975 DIR: GERARD DAMIANO)
13. TALES OF THE BIZARRE (1982 DIR: PHIL PRINCE)
14. WINTER HEAT (1976 DIR: CLAUDE GODDARD)
15. KNEEL BEFORE ME (1983 DIR: PHIL PRINCE)
16. INTRUSIONS (AKA THE INTRUSION) (1975 DIR: AUTHUR NOUVEAU)
17. THE ABDUCTION OF LORELEI (1977 DIR: RICHARD RANK)
18. SECRET DESIRE (1975 DIR: JOE SERKES)
19. UNWILLING LOVERS (1977 DIR: ZEBEDY COLT)
20. THE LOVE SLAVES (1975 DIR: BOB CHINN)

☆☆☆☆☆☆☆☆☆☆

〈INSERT SOME CRAZY PSYCHO TALK ABOUT WHORES, SLUTS AND HOW SCARY DICKS ARE IN THIS SPACE HERE〉

EEEP!

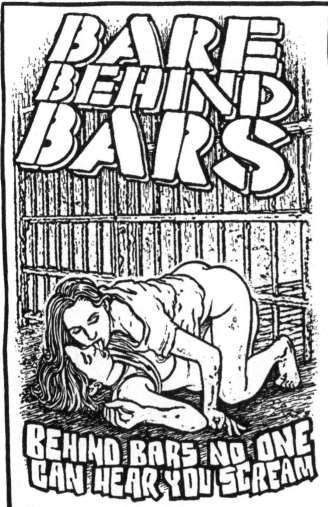

BARE BEHIND BARS

BEHIND BARS NO ONE CAN HEAR YOU SCREAM

ARTICLE BY: BOUGIE '11
AND ART BY:
BOUGIE AND NEWMAN

THE WOMEN-IN-PRISON GENRE MAY WELL BE MOSTLY FORGOTTEN BY THE FILMIC MAINSTREAM NOW, BUT THERE WAS A TIME WHEN THE GENRE WAS SO POPULAR AND EVER-PRESENT THAT EVERY SINGLE COUNTRY WITH A FILM INDUSTRY HAD AT LEAST ONE ENTRY IN IT. MOST OF THEM ORIGINATED FROM THE SAME PLACES THAT CULT FILM HAS ALWAYS BEEN FOSTERED AND EXPERTLY MANAGED: AMERICA, ITALY, AND ASIAN COUNTRIES SUCH AS JAPAN AND THE PHILIPPINES -- BUT SOUTH AMERICAN COUNTRIES SUCH AS BRAZIL ALSO CAME CORRECT WITH THEIR FAIR SHARE OF CHICKS-IN-CHAINS.

BRAZIL'S "PORNOCHANCHADA" EXPLOITATION GENRE SAW ITS HEYDAY BETWEEN 1977 AND 1985. LOW-BUDGET "CHADA MOVIES" (A NICKNAME ADMINISTERED BY THEIR ADORING FANS) ARE A SIBLING OF THE PINK FILMS OF JAPAN, THE ITALIAN SEX-COMEDY, AND THE ROUGHIES OF THE 1960S AMERICAN SEXPLOITATION FILM INDUSTRY. IT IS A VULGAR GENRE THAT SOLELY EXISTED TO SHOCK, TITILLATE, AND BUST THE CHERRY OF CULTURAL TABOOS SUCH AS RAPE, MISOGYNY, BESTIALITY, NECROPHILIA, AND OTHER FORMS OF KINKY SEX. IF YOU'RE A NEWBIE TO LATSPLOITATION (AND THE MAJORITY OF US ARE SIMPLY BECAUSE SO FEW OF THESE MOVIES HAVE EVER BEEN PROPERLY TRANSLATED INTO ENGLISH), YOU'RE IN FOR A TREAT.

REGARDLESS OF THE STRICT CENSORSHIP AND DOMINANT CATHOLIC DOCTRINE THAT BRAZIL FACED IN THE ERA IN QUESTION, STATE-RUN FILM COMPANIES WERE EAGER TO SUPPORT PORNOCHANCHADAS FOR TWO SIMPLE REASONS:

1.THEY WERE PROVEN MONEY MAKERS, AND 2. DESPITE THEIR MANY EXPLOITIVE TENDENCIES, THE MOVIES WERE NOT AT ALL CRITICAL OF THE CURRENT REGIME THAT WAS IN GOVERNMENT.

IN FACT, MORE AND MORE PRODUCTION COMPANIES BECAME DEPENDENT ON THE LOWLY CHADA MOVIES TO HELP THEM COMPETE WITH THE JUGGERNAUT THAT WAS THE AMERICAN FILM INDUSTRY; AN OUTSIDE FORCE THAT WAS SLOWLY TAKING OVER THE BRAZILIAN THEATRICAL MARKET.

WITH A SCUMMY FILMOGRAPHY ANY EXPLOITATION FILMMAKER COULD BE PROUD OF, (INSATIABLE FUGITIVES, BRUCE LEE VS GAY POWER, AMAZON JAIL, BACCHANALS ON THE ISLE OF THE NYMPHETS) CINEMATOGRAPHER OSWALDO DE OLIVEIRA COULD WELL HAVE BEEN CONSIDERED THE JOE D'AMATO OF SAO PAULO'S GRINDHOUSE DISTRICT. BUT IT WAS WITH HIS 1980 FILM A PRISÃO (BETTER KNOWN THROUGHOUT THE WORLD AS BARE BEHIND BARS) THAT HE CREATED HIS MASTERPIECE OF SLEAZE.

DARKER AND MORE CYNICAL THAN YOUR AVERAGE LIGHT-HEARTED PORNOCHANCHADA, OLIVEIRA'S MOVIE STILL INVOKED COMEDY AND TONGUE-IN-CHEEK MADNESS, IF ONLY TO HELP OFFSET THE CARNAL DEBAUCHERY TAKING UP THE MAJORITY OF ITS RUNTIME. INDEED, BARE BEHIND BARS COULD WELL BE THE FILTHIEST AND MOST PORNOGRAPHIC WOMEN'S PRISON MOVIE EVER MADE OUTSIDE OF THE XXX CLASSIFICATION. IT IS LURID AS HELL.

KEEP IN MIND THAT THE EXPLOITATION GENRE HAS A RIPE AND STORIED HISTORY OF MISREPRESENTING FILMS WITH WILDLY INAPPROPRIATE COVER ART AND DECEPTIVE TITLES

THAT ARE DESIGNED TO DRAW YOU IN AND TAKE YOUR MONEY. IT'S WHAT THE GENRE WAS BUILT ON AND THIS CARNIVAL BARKER HISTORY OF HUCKSTERISM AND SLEIGHT OF HAND IS WHAT MAKES AN OTHERWISE CHEAP AND TAWDRY EFFORT LIKE BARE BEHIND BARS SUCH A BREATH OF FRESH AIR. THE MOVIE DOESN'T DARE TAKE ITSELF SERIOUSLY FOR AN INSTANT, AND YOU'RE GETTING EXACTLY WHAT YOU'RE BEING SOLD: NAKED WOMEN IN PRISON. IN FACT, THERE AREN'T MANY SCENES IN THIS DISREPUTABLE CLASSIC WHERE FULLY CLOTHED PEOPLE EVEN TAKE UP SCREEN SPACE. IT'S ALL FURRY BEAVER SHOTS, NATURAL JUGS, 69-ING, MASTURBATING, AND THE COLD GREY STEEL OF PRISON IRON. <u>AWESOME</u>.

ITS EXECUTION MAY BE A LESSON IN TRANSGRESSIVE LATSPLOITATION, BUT THE PLOT IS PRETTY STANDARD WIP FARE. WE HAVE A PSYCHOPATHIC SADOMASOCHIST WARDEN WHO TAKES PERVERSE PLEASURE IN THE AGONY OF HER DETAINEES (WHOM SHE LOOKS TO SELL OFF ON THE WHITE SLAVE TRADE MARKET) A GUARD WHO HAS CONCERNS ABOUT THE EXCESSIVE ABUSE AND NEFARIOUS TREATMENT OF THE GALS, OVERSEXED INMATES PLANNING A PRISON BREAK, AND ALL KINDS OF QUIVERING YOUNG LATINA FLESH, NOT THE LEAST OF WHICH BELONGS TO WHAT FANS OF THE GENRE CALL "THE NEW FISH" -- THE ROOKIE GIRL ON THE CELL BLOCK. WE VIEW THIS WORLD THROUGH HER EYES.

PRISON IS NEVER SUPPOSED TO BE A VERY NICE PLACE TO STAY, BUT THIS DIRTY, UNREGULATED SHIT-PIT HOUSES MULTIPLE FEMALE CRIMINALS CRAMMED INTO SQUALID CONDITIONS WHERE ONLY RATS PROVIDE A SYMPATHETIC FURRY EAR. THESE SOUTH AMERICAN LOVELIES ARE RESOLVED TO THEIR FATE IN THIS WRETCHED INSTITUTION, WHERE DIRE SADISM AND FORCED SEX ARE PROUDLY PRESENTED IN PLACE OF PALLIATIVE JUSTICE. INDEED, IF THESE SWEATY, SPLAYED LOVELIES ARE LUCKY ENOUGH TO AVOID THE TORTURE CHAMBER IT WILL ONLY BE BECAUSE THEY'VE BRAVELY BARTERED THEIR BEAUTIFUL BODS OR SUBMITTED TO THE WANTON DESIRES OF THE PRISON'S DIZZY MARILYN MONROE-ESQUE NURSE.

IT'S NOT ALWAYS CRUDDY IN THE HOOSEGOW, THOUGH. DON'T FORGET THAT FEMALE PRISONERS GET TO SHOWER TOGETHER AS A MEANS OF BONDING. HERE, A MULTITUDE OF THEM REGULARLY GET LATHERED UP AGAINST EACH OTHER WHILE SQUEALING, GIGGLING AND WIGGLING A WHOLE LOT. FAR FROM A SAUSAGE PARTY, OSWALDO SAW TO IT THAT FEW NUDE DUDES WOULD APPEAR IN FRONT OF HIS CAMERA IN THIS ONEROUS ODE TO FEMALE SLAVERY.

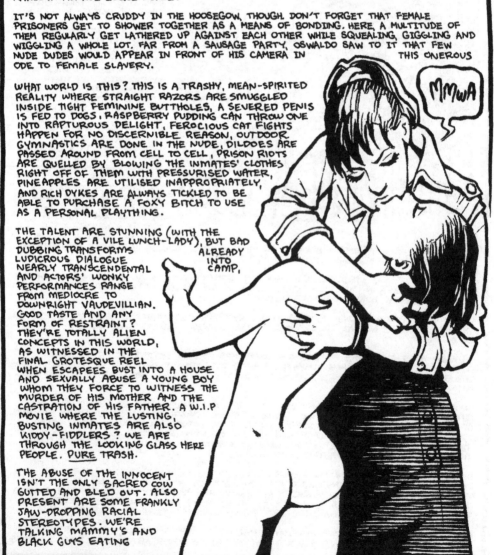

WHAT WORLD IS THIS? THIS IS A TRASHY, MEAN-SPIRITED REALITY WHERE STRAIGHT RAZORS ARE SMUGGLED INSIDE TIGHT FEMININE BUTTHOLES, A SEVERED PENIS IS FED TO DOGS, RASPBERRY PUDDING CAN THROW ONE INTO RAPTUROUS DELIGHT, FEROCIOUS CAT FIGHTS HAPPEN FOR NO DISCERNIBLE REASON, OUTDOOR GYMNASTICS ARE DONE IN THE NUDE, DILDOES ARE PASSED AROUND FROM CELL TO CELL, PRISON RIOTS ARE QUELLED BY BLOWING THE INMATES' CLOTHES RIGHT OFF OF THEM WITH PRESSURISED WATER, PINEAPPLES ARE UTILISED INAPPROPRIATELY, AND RICH DYKES ARE ALWAYS TICKLED TO BE ABLE TO PURCHASE A FOXY BITCH TO USE AS A PERSONAL PLAYTHING.

THE TALENT ARE STUNNING (WITH THE EXCEPTION OF A VILE LUNCH-LADY), BUT BAD DUBBING TRANSFORMS LUDICROUS DIALOGUE ALREADY INTO CAMP. NEARLY TRANSCENDENTAL AND ACTORS' WONKY PERFORMANCES RANGE FROM MEDIOCRE TO DOWNRIGHT VAUDEVILLIAN. GOOD TASTE AND ANY FORM OF RESTRAINT? THEY'RE TOTALLY ALIEN CONCEPTS IN THIS WORLD, AS WITNESSED IN THE FINAL GROTESQUE REEL WHEN ESCAPEES BUST INTO A HOUSE AND SEXUALLY ABUSE A YOUNG BOY WHOM THEY FORCE TO WITNESS THE MURDER OF HIS MOTHER AND THE CASTRATION OF HIS FATHER. A W.I.P MOVIE WHERE THE LUSTING, BUSTING INMATES ARE ALSO KIDDY-FIDDLERS? WE ARE THROUGH THE LOOKING GLASS HERE PEOPLE. <u>PURE TRASH</u>.

THE ABUSE OF THE INNOCENT ISN'T THE ONLY SACRED COW GUTTED AND BLED OUT. ALSO PRESENT ARE SOME FRANKLY JAW-DROPPING RACIAL STEREOTYPES. WE'RE TALKING MAMMY'S AND BLACK GUYS EATING

WATERMELONS LEVEL HERE. IS THERE ANY WONDER THIS MOVIE WAS BANNED FOR DECADES IN THE UK AND GIVEN AN X-RATING IN THE U.S.?

WITH THE END OF THE MILITARY REGIME AND THE INTRODUCTION OF HARDCORE PORNO, BY THE MID 1980s THE PORNOCHANCHADA MARKET HAD BEEN DEALT A SEVERE DEATH BLOW. IT WAS AN ALL-TOO-FAMILIAR DECLINE TO FANS OF THE AMERICAN SEXPLOITATION GENRE, WHICH SUFFERED SIMILARLY IN THE EARLY '70s WHEN TRIPLE-X FARE SUCH AS *DEEP THROAT* MADE ITS ORIFICE-PACKED PRESENCE KNOWN.

YES, THE DEGENERATE CHADA SEX MOVIE ERA HAD COME TO AN UNCEREMONIOUS CLOSE, BUT TO THE MAJORITY OF ENGLISH-ONLY SPEAKERS WORLD-WIDE, BRAZILIAN SOFTCORE SEX CINEMA IS ONLY IN RECENT YEARS BEING PRESENTED, HUNGRILY UNWRAPPED, AND GOBBLED UP BY A WHOLE NEW GENERATION OF CULT FILM FANS.

MONKEY HUSTLE (1976)

"MONKEY HUSTLE: A SITUATION IN WHICH THE PEOPLE INVOLVED YANK YOUR CHAIN TO CREATE THE ILLUSION THAT PROGRESS IS HAPPENING EVEN THOUGH IT ISN'T."
-- URBANDICTIONARY.COM

SIMILAR TO ANOTHER BLAXPLOITATION ENSEMBLE EFFORT OF THE SEVENTIES CALLED *CAR WASH*, DIRECTOR ARTHUR MARKS GOES ABOUT INTRODUCING VIEWERS TO SOME LIKEABLE BLACK GHETTO INHABITANTS TRYING TO STOP WHITEY FROM BUILDING A HIGHWAY THROUGH THEIR SOUTH SIDE CHICAGO HOOD. THE GANG ENLISTED TO PUT THIS PLAN INTO ACTION (A PLAN WE'RE NEVER MADE PRIVY TO, BY THE WAY) ARE A SMALL TIME FLIMFLAM MAN NAMED DADDY FOXX (YAPHET KOTTO), HIS HORNY 14-YEAR-OLD PROTEGE (KIRK CALLOWAY), AND A FLAMBOYANT GLITTERIN' GOLDIE PLAYED BY RUDY RAY MOORE. THE CIVIC ACTIVISM IS ACTUALLY ONLY A FOIL, AND SERVES SIMPLY AS A TENUOUS LINK FOR SEVERAL UNRELATED MISADVENTURES FOR THE MAIN CHARACTERS.

YOU DON'T WATCH A MOVIE LIKE MONKEY HUSTLE FOR THE PLOT, WHICH IS A GOOD THING BECAUSE THIS ONE WAS FILMED MISSING A FEW KEY NARRATIVE ELEMENTS THAT WOULD ALLOW IT TO MAKE ANY KIND OF SENSE. THE REAL DRAW HERE ARE THE COLOURFUL CHARACTERS, THE GROOVY FASHIONS (I CAN'T GET ENOUGH OF SWEET LYNN HARRIS IN HER "SWEET POTATO" BABY-T), THE DATED EBONIC STREET SLANG, AND THE GROANER "COMEDY". RINKY-DINK HUSTLES GET RUN, SCAMS ARE SCOOTED, AND AFROED HOMIES TALK JIVE AND SLAP FIVE!

IT'S CERTAINLY WORTH A VIEWING OR FOUR (ESPECIALLY IF YOU'RE A CHICAGO NATIVE), BUT THIS IS NOT TO SAY THAT MONKEY HUSTLE IS A GENRE STAND OUT. IT'S SADLY BEREFT OF NUDITY, VIOLENCE, A FUNKY-ASS SCORE, AND MOST INFURIATING -- IT FEATURES A PG-RATED RUDY RAY MOORE. NOT ALLOWING RUDY TO SWEAR IS LIKE GETTING JIMI HENDRIX TO PLAY CLARINET IN YOUR BAND.

ISN'T IT FUNNY HOW INTERESTED SO MANY WHITE FOLK ARE IN '70s BLACK MOVIES/MUSIC? I WONDER HOW MANY CAUCASIONS GAVE A FUCK ABOUT IT AT THE TIME...

BOUGIE

COCKSUCKER BLUES

THE 10 BEST DRAMAS TO TAKE PLACE IN THE PORN INDUSTRY

WHEN THE BIOPIC LOVELACE CAME OUT IN 2013, I HAD ALL KINDS OF PEOPLE ASKING ME FOR MY OPINION ON IT. MOST OF THE TIME I DIDN'T WANT TO GET INTO IT. I JUST MUMBLED "YOU'RE BETTER OFF WATCHING THE DOCUMENTARY INSIDE DEEP THROAT". I DIDN'T JUST SAY THAT BECAUSE I WAS BEING A DISMISSIVE COCK-HOLE, I SAID IT BECAUSE INSIDE DEEP THROAT WAS NOT ONLY A FAR SUPERIOR MOVIE WATCHING EXPERIENCE, BUT IT ALSO TOOK GREAT PAINS TO TELL LINDA LOVELACE'S ACTUAL STORY, AND THAT OF THE INFAMOUS MOVIE SHE DEEP-THROATED DONGS IN.

AS GERARD DAMIANO JR, THE SON OF THE MAN WHO DIRECTED DEEP THROAT WROTE, "LINDA WAS IN AN ABUSIVE RELATIONSHIP WITH CHUCK TRAYNOR. SHE HAD A PARTICULAR TALENT FOR SUCKING COCK. AS THE STAR OF THE ADULT FILM 'DEEP THROAT', SHE EXPERIENCED A LEVEL OF UNPRECEDENTED FAME AND CELEBRITY. THESE ARE FACTS. THE REST OF THE FILM LOVELACE IS FICTION, RANGING FROM THE PLAUSIBLE TO THE ABSURD."

NOT ONLY IS MOST OF LOVELACE FICTION, THEY ALSO DON'T BOTHER TO INCLUDE THE 'DOGFUCK AT GUNPOINT' OR THE 'SAMMY DAVIS JR DEEP THROATING CHUCK TRAYNOR'S COCK' SCENES, WHICH WERE NOT SURPRISINGLY THE MOST TALKED-ABOUT PARTS OF LINDA'S ORDEAL BOOK. I'M NOT A MORON — I KNOW WHY THE CREATORS OF LOVELACE LEFT OUT EVEN PG-RATED DEPICTIONS OF THEM (BECAUSE IT MAKES HER STORY SOUND IMPLAUSIBLE, AND THE FILMMAKERS WERE WORKING TO LEGITIMIZE HER) BUT DOING AN ADAPTATION OF ORDEAL AND LEAVING THOSE PARTS OUT IS SORT OF LIKE DOING AN ADAPTATION OF PIERRE BOULLE'S THE BRIDGE OVER THE RIVER KWAI AND NOT BOTHERING TO SHOW THE BRIDGE.

AMANDA SEYFRIED   PETER SARSGAARD

LOVELACE

FACT: YOU CAN'T GET INTO HEAVEN IF YOU DON'T REPENT AND SAY YOU WERE FORCED TO DO EVERYTHING SINFUL YOU DID IN YOUR YOUTH. LINDA WAS THE CONSUMMATE VICTIM HER ENTIRE LIFE. I'VE READ ALL HER BOOKS, AND MOST OF THE INTERVIEWS SHE EVER GAVE, AND SHE WAS NEVER ONCE RESPONSIBLE FOR ANYTHING THAT HAPPENED IN HER PORN CAREER. I'VE ALSO READ THE INTERVIEWS AND SPOKEN PERSONALLY TO MANY OF THE PEOPLE WHO WERE THERE, AND EVERY SINGLE ONE OF THEM CONFIRMS THAT LINDA'S LACK OF ENTHUSIASM ABOUT BEING IN PORN ONLY CAME ABOUT YEARS LATER. LINDA ONCE STATED THAT SHE'D ONLY SPENT 17 DAYS IN THE PORN INDUSTRY, AS IF TO SAY THAT MEANT IT DIDN'T REALLY COUNT. SHE DIDN'T WANT US TO JUDGE HER FOR IT, BUT MORE IMPORTANTLY SHE DIDN'T WANT TO JUDGE HERSELF. LISTEN, I KNOW THEY MADE THEM QUICK BACK IN THE DAY, BUT ONE THEATRICAL FEATURE AND 6 LOOPS (CHECK OUT THE AMAZING ONE WHERE SHE GETS FUCKED WITH A FOOT IF YOU GET THE CHANCE) IN 17 DAYS IS QUITE A FEAT.

ONE THING THAT NO ONE WILL DEBATE IS THAT LINDA WAS IN AN ABUSIVE RELATIONSHIP WITH CHUCK TRAYNOR. THAT IS A FACT THAT EVEN CHUCK ADMITTED TO. WHAT IS UP FOR DEBATE IS WHAT THE HECK THAT HAS TO DO WITH PORN. IF LINDA WAS A SHOE SALESMAN, IT WOULDN'T HAVE BEEN THE SHOE INDUSTRY'S FAULT THAT SHE MARRIED A GUY THAT KICKED HER AND PUNCHED HER EVERY NIGHT. BUT SOCIETY DOESN'T THINK THAT WAY WHEN IT INVOLVES THE ADULT INDUSTRY. WE DON'T GIVE PORN

THAT SAME CONCESSION, BECAUSE WE AS A SOCIETY BELIEVE THAT SEX IS DIRTY, AND THAT PORN IS SOMETHING WOMEN WOULD NEVER DO UNLESS THEY WERE FORCED AND COERCED.

LINDA LIVED AT A TIME WHEN THERE WASN'T A HEALTHY AND DEVELOPED PUBLIC DIALOGUE ABOUT DOMESTIC ABUSE OR ABOUT WOMEN'S SEXUALITY, AND HER POST-PORN BOOKS WERE SORT OF A FUMBLED RESPONSE TO THAT. WAS SHE SUBJECTED TO LONG-TERM EMOTIONAL AND PHYSICAL ABUSE? IT SEEMS CERTAIN SHE WAS. I ALSO BELIEVE SHE WAS A SUBMISSIVE, SOMETHING THAT -- ALONG WITH HER STRICT RELIGIOUS UPBRINGING -- MADE HER SITUATION A HUNDRED TIMES MORE EMOTIONALLY COMPLICATED, ESPECIALLY WHEN LOOKED AT IN HINDSIGHT AS A MIDDLE-AGED WOMAN TRYING TO FIT IN WITH HER CHURCH GROUP. REGRET IS A WEIRD EMOTION. IT CAN CAUSE PEOPLE TO QUESTION THEIR OWN SENSE OF REALITY AND EVERYONE ELSE'S, BUT THAT SHOULDN'T EXCUSE HER FOR POINTING FINGERS RECKLESSLY AT HER CO-STARS AND PORNOGRAPHY PEERS. ACCUSATIONS OF RAPE ARE A VERY SERIOUS BUSINESS, AND I WILL ALWAYS RESPECT PEOPLE WHO TAKE RESPONSIBILITY FOR THEIR OWN ACTIONS, AND ACTIVELY DISRESPECT THOSE WHO DON'T.

LOVELACE THE FILM REALLY WAS SHITTY AND THAT'S NOTEWORTHY BECAUSE IT HAD TALENTED ACTORS, A REALLY NICE VISUAL STYLE, GREAT PRODUCTION VALUES, AND DECENT MUSIC. AND YET, THE MOST IMPORTANT PART, THE STORY... WHAT A WASHOUT. IF YOU'RE GOING TO MAKE A MOVIE ALMOST PURE FICTION, AT LEAST HAVE THE COMMON SENSE NOT TO BASE IT ON A REAL PERSON. OF COURSE ANY BIOPIC IS GOING TO HAVE ELEMENTS THAT ARE CHANGED FOR THE SAKE OF A NARRATIVE, BUT YOU CAN'T CHANGE THAT MUCH. I MEAN WTF — THE PART WHERE THE MOB ARE THE ONES THAT RESCUE LINDA FROM TRAYNOR? HAHAHAHA! TALK ABOUT REWRITING THE STORY.

I'D BE OK WITH THE CREATORS OF LOVELACE TAKING CREATIVE LIBERTIES IF THE ONES THEY TOOK ACTUALLY MADE ANY SENSE (THE SHOCKING TRUE STORY THEY DIDN'T TELL IS FAR MORE INTERESTING AND ENTERTAINING THAN THE BLAND FICTIONAL ONE THEY DECIDED TO PUT ON THE SCREEN) OR IF THEY CHANGED HER NAME -- AS P.T. ANDERSON DID WITH JOHN HOLMES IN BOOGIE NIGHTS. THE FACT IS, ONCE ANDERSON HAD TRANSFORMED HOLMES INTO DIRK DIGGLER, HE CAN GO HOG WILD WITH THE CHARACTER AND THE WORLD HE LIVED IN. HE'S NO LONGER BOUND BY HISTORY AND THE AUDIENCE IS INSTANTLY NO LONGER GOING TO EXPECT A DIRECTOR TO TELL THE TRUE FACTS ABOUT JOHN'S LIFE. THAT IS INCREDIBLY FREEING AND BENEFICIAL TO A STORYTELLER AND IT KEEPS THE HISTORIANS AND THE NERDS (LIKE ME) HAPPY.

THANKFULLY THERE HAVE BEEN GREAT MOVIES MADE WHERE THE SCREENWRITERS DIDN'T CHANGE THE NAME OF THE PLAYERS, AND THERE HAVE ALSO BEEN SOME GREAT ONES THAT WERE TOTALLY FICTIONAL. HERE ARE MY 12 FAVOURITE DRAMAS THAT TAKE PLACE IN THE PORN INDUSTRY, WITH DOCUMENTARIES EXCLUDED. THEY'LL GET THEIR OWN LIST AT A LATER DATE.

BOOGIE NIGHTS

1. BOOGIE NIGHTS (1997 USA)
THERE'S NOT TOO MUCH I NEED TO SAY TO DESCRIBE THIS MOVIE, AS THE MAJORITY OF YOU WILL HAVE SEEN IT OR WILL KNOW ABOUT IT AT THE VERY LEAST. I WILL SAY THIS, HOWEVER: I KNEW A LITTLE ABOUT 1970S AND 1980S PORN, BUT IT WASN'T UNTIL I SAW BOOGIE NIGHTS IN THE THEATER THAT A FIRE WAS LIT UNDER MY ASS AND I REALLY BECAME INTERESTED IN EXHAUSTIVELY RESEARCHING ITS COLOURFUL HISTORY. SAY WHAT YOU WILL ABOUT THE CREATIVE LIBERTIES IT TAKES AND CRITICIZE THE WAY IT LINKS PORNOGRAPHY WITH VIOLENCE IF YOU ARE SO INCLINED, BUT IT'S A DAMN GOOD BET THAT CINEMA SEWER WOULD NEVER HAVE BECOME THE MAGAZINE AND BOOK SERIES THAT IT IS WITHOUT THE RELEASE OF P.T. ANDERSON'S FILM. LITTLE KNOWN FACT: THE SKINNY BLONDE GIRL THAT SHOWS UP AT THE PARTY AS THE COLONEL'S DATE AND THEN PROCEEDS TO OVERDOSE IS ACTUALLY LIL' CINDERELLA (AKA AMBER HUNTER AKA FAYE HUNTER), WHO IS BETTER KNOWN TO PERVERTS AS SOMEONE WHO HAS SWALLOWED A FAIR AMOUNT OF MAX HARDCORE'S PISS. IN FACT SHE'S WEARING THOSE SAME SUNGLASSES IN ONE OF HER XXX APPEARANCES WITH MAX.

2. WONDERLAND (2003 USA)
PRIOR TO WONDERLAND'S RELEASE I REMEMBER BEING RATHER BUMMED THAT VAL KILMER HAD BEEN CAST TO PLAY JOHN HOLMES, SINCE HE REALLY DOESN'T LOOK MUCH LIKE HIM. THAT ALL CHANGED WHEN I SAW HIM ON SCREEN, THOUGH. AS HE PROVED IN PLAYING JIM MORRISON IN OLIVER STONE'S THE DOORS, VAL IS A GODDAMN CHAMELEON. HE GOT ALL OF THE LITTLE MANNERISMS DOWN PAT, MAN. THE REST OF THE CAST, PLOT, MUSIC, EDITING, AND DIRECTOR ARE ALSO ALL A+ IN THIS 2003 PICTURE, AND I'M CONSTANTLY SHOCKED THAT THIS DOESN'T GET MORE LOVE FROM FILM FANS. IT'S REALLY FUCKING GREAT.

STAR 80

3. STAR 80 (1983 USA)
WHEN STAR 80 FIRST CAME OUT IT GOT A PRETTY GOOD DEAL OF CRITICAL ACCLAIM INCLUDING A GOLDEN GLOBE NOMINATION. AND YET AS THE YEARS HAVE GONE BY, IT'S SOMEHOW FALLEN THROUGH THE CRACKS. THE FILM HASN'T AGED BADLY, SO I DON'T GET IT. THIS IS BOB FOSSE'S BIOPIC ABOUT THE HEARTBREAKING DEMISE OF PLAYBOY PLAYMATE DOROTHY STRATTEN, WHO WAS FROM MY HOMETOWN OF VANCOUVER. GREAT MOVIE, INCREDIBLE PERFORMANCES BY MARIEL HEMINGWAY AND ERIC ROBERTS, AND MUCH OF IT WAS FILMED IN THE ACTUAL HOME WHERE STRATTEN WAS MURDERED, MAKING IT EXTRA CHILLING TO WATCH THOSE SCENES.

PERHAPS IF THE MOVIE HAD GOTTEN MORE IN THE WAY OF THE INDUSTRY ACCOLADES THAT IT DESERVED, IT WOULD BE REMEMBERED BETTER TODAY. ROGER EBERT TOOK NOTE OF THIS SEVERAL YEARS LATER IN 1986, DUBBING THE OSCAR SNUBBING OF A LIKE-MINDED MOVIE AS "STAR 80 SYNDROME". EBERT WAS ADAMANT THAT ERIC ROBERTS "SHOULD HAVE BEEN (OSCAR) NOMINATED", AND COMPARED THE ACADEMY'S LACK OF FORESIGHT TO THE WAY IT IGNORED GARY OLDMAN'S BRILLIANT PORTRAYAL OF SID VICIOUS IN SID AND NANCY (1986). "HOLLYWOOD WILL NOT NOMINATE AN ACTOR FOR PORTRAYING A CREEP, NO MATTER HOW GOOD THE PERFORMANCE IS", EBERT SAID.

4. HARDCORE (1979 USA)
I'VE SPOKEN WITH ADULT FILM STARS WHO AREN'T FANS OF THIS MOVIE BECAUSE IT PAINTS A VERY UNREALISTIC PORTRAIT OF THE INDUSTRY. WHILE THIS IS VERY TRUE, I'D COUNTER THAT MOST MOVIES PAINT A VERY UNREALISTIC VIEW OF SOCIETY, AND THAT AT LEAST THIS MOVIE IS GODDAMN ENTERTAINING. IT DOESN'T CLAIM TO TELL A TRUE STORY OR PURPORT TO DEPICT AN ACTUAL INDIVIDUAL'S LIFE, SO I'M MORE THAN WILLING TO ALLOW IT TO TAKE WHATEVER CREATIVE LIBERTIES IT WISHES.

GEORGE C. SCOTT PLAYS A CONSERVATIVE (SPECIFICALLY CALVINIST) FATHER WHO SEARCHES THROUGH THE SCUMMY LOS ANGELES AND SAN FRANCISCO UNDERGROUND FOR HIS DAUGHTER, WHO HAS VANISHED BUT LEADS HIM TO HER WHEREABOUTS VIA AN APPEARANCE IN AN 8MM XXX MOVIE. CAN GEORGE FIND HIS DAUGHTER BEFORE SHE IS CAST IN A SNUFF MOVIE, OR IS SHE ALREADY THE VICTIM OF ONE? THE PLOT OF THE MOVIE WAS REUSED FOR THE NICHOLAS CAGE MOVIE 8MM IN 1999, WHICH DIDN'T MAKE THIS LIST BECAUSE IT ISN'T HALF AS GOOD AS HARDCORE, AND I ONLY HAVE ROOM FOR ONE OF THEM.

5. THE PEOPLE VS LARRY FLYNT (1996 USA)
WHILE NOT A PERFECT MOVIE (IT'S A BIT HAM-FISTED, IDEALIZED, AND EVEN MAUDLIN IN PARTS), I STILL REALLY APPRECIATE WHAT WAS ACCOMPLISHED BY MILOS FORMAN IN THIS BIOPIC OF CONTROVERSIAL HUSTLER MAGAZINE PUBLISHER LARRY FLYNT. THE MOVIE SPANS 35 YEARS OF HIS LIFE, AND SOMEHOW TRANSFORMED A MAN PREVIOUSLY SEEN AS SCUMMY AND REPREHENSIBLE BY THE MAINSTREAM INTO SOMETHING OF A FIRST AMENDMENT RIGHTS HERO. I MEAN, US FELLOW DEGENERATE PERVERTS HAVE ALWAYS RESPECTED LARRY'S ABILITY AND WILLINGNESS TO FIGHT FOR EVERYONE'S RIGHT TO FREE SPEECH, BUT THIS MOVIE MADE THE REST OF THE WORLD BELIEVE IN HIM AS WELL. THAT'S NO MEAN FEAT, RIGHT THERE.

INTERESTINGLY, WHEN I ASK PEOPLE ABOUT THIS MOVIE TODAY, THEY USUALLY DON'T REMEMBER THE OSCAR NOMINATIONS FOR WOODY HARRELSON AND MILOS FORMAN, BUT DO REMEMBER IT BEING A BOX OFFICE SUCCESS — WHILE IT ACTUALLY ONLY MADE BACK ABOUT TWO THIRDS OF ITS 35 MILLION DOLLAR BUDGET.

6. ZOOM UP: THE BEAVER BOOK GIRL (1981 JAPAN)
DIRECTOR TAKASHI KANNO SERVES UP A TOP-TIER NIKKATSU PINK FILM SET IN THE WORLD OF WATER-SPORTS AND SCHOOLGIRL-PANTY PHOTOGRAPHY IN THE JAPANESE PORN INDUSTRY OF THE LATE 1970S. THERE IS MILD BONDAGE, RAPE (AND REVENGE), SUSPENSE, SATIRE, AND ALL MANNER OF PEE-PORN.

BASED ON A MANGA SERIES BY TAKASHI ISHII, THIS BRISK 65-MINUTE FEATURE FOCUSES ON A FREELANCE PHOTOGRAPHER WHOSE NICKNAME IS MAESTRO, AS WELL AS HIS ASSISTANT KOUICHI. THEY MOSTLY SPECIALIZE IN SCHOOLGIRL PANTY LAYOUTS FOR DIRTY MAGAZINES, AND THEIR MAIN MODEL IS A GIRL NAMED MAKO

(KUMIKO HAYANO) WHO LIKES TO WEAR A JAWS SWEATSHIRT AND EAT SPAGHETTI. LIFE SEEMS PRETTY SIMPLE FOR THE THREE OF THEM, BUT ALL OF THAT CHANGES, HOWEVER, WHEN A MYSTERIOUS OLDER SEXPOT NAMED NAMI (JUNKO MABUKI) WITH A FETISH FOR PISSING SHOWS UP AND WANTS TO MAKE SOME MONEY MODELLING FOR MAESTRO. HER SECRET AGENDA IS REVEALED IN THE FINALE OF THE MOVIE, WHICH TAKES PLACE IN A PIT INSIDE AN ABANDONED WAREHOUSE. THIS IS GREAT STUFF IF YOU LIKE JAPANESE PINK FILMS.

A SERBIAN FILM

7. A SERBIAN FILM (2010 SERBIA)
SRDJAN SPASOJEVIC'S FIRST FEATURE FILM IS ONE OF THE BEST AND MOST MOVING DEBUTS I'VE SEEN IN YEARS. I PERSONALLY THINK IT GOT REALLY OVERHYPED (AND OVER-REACTED TO) WHEN IT FIRST CAME OUT, BUT IT'S STILL CERTAINLY GOOD ENOUGH TO MAKE THIS LIST AND INTERESTING ENOUGH TO LEAVE ME WONDERING WHAT SRDJAN WILL DO FOR AN ENCORE. I MIGHT EVEN RANK IT HIGHER DEPENDING ON MY MOOD, BUT FOR TODAY IT'LL REST HERE IN THE NUMBER 7 SPOT.

I'D HAPPILY GO INTO THE GORY DETAILS, BUT I HONESTLY BELIEVE THAT A SERBIAN FILM IS BETTER SEEN KNOWING AS LITTLE AS POSSIBLE ABOUT IT. IN SHORT, THE PLOT RELATES THE STORY OF A SERBIAN PORN THESPIAN WHO HAS FALLEN ON RATHER HARD TIMES AND AGREES TO DO AN "ART FILM" ONLY TO HORRIFICALLY DISCOVER THAT HE'S BEEN ROPED INTO STARRING IN SOMETHING FAR MORE SINISTER AND VILE. AS A TESTAMENT TO ITS VARIOUS GRAPHIC DEPICTIONS OF SEX MIXED WITH BRUTAL VIOLENCE, THE FILM IS CURRENTLY BANNED IN SPAIN, FINLAND, FRANCE, AUSTRALIA, NEW ZEALAND, MALAYSIA, SINGAPORE, AND NORWAY, AND ONLY AVAILABLE IN A CENSORED VERSION IN VARIOUS OTHER COUNTRIES. NOTE: THE UNCUT VERSION IS 104 MINUTES.

8. DRYING UP THE STREETS (1978 CANADA)
THE CANADIAN PRECURSOR TO 1979'S HARDCORE. THIS IS THE LEAST-KNOWN MOVIE ON THIS LIST, GETTING ONLY A VERY LIMITED RELEASE EVEN IN CANADA. WHERE IT DIFFERS FROM HARDCORE IS THAT IT ISN'T SO MUCH ABOUT A "GOOD" MAN TRYING TO LOCATE A DAUGHTER WHO HAS GONE "BAD", BUT RATHER A MAN HAS SEEN AND DONE A LOT OF SHIT HIMSELF, AND WANTS TO SAVE HIS DAUGHTER FROM SOME OF THE SAME MISTAKES. THAT THE FILMMAKERS MANAGE TO DEPICT THAT WITHOUT BEING PREACHY IS PRETTY IMPRESSIVE.

IT'S A VERY SEEDY, GRITTY MOVIE THAT TAKES PLACE ON THE SIN-SOAKED STREETS OF TORONTO WHERE THE SEX TRADE PREYS ON AND EXPLOITS THE UNWARY AND UNWANTED. HERE, A FORMER STREET-LEVEL RADICAL NAMED PETE (DON FRANCKS) GETS PRESSURED INTO HELPING THE COPS BRING DOWN A PORN AND PROSTITUTION RING, WHICH HE AGREES TO DO ONCE HE'S MADE AWARE THAT HIS OWN DAUGHTER MAY BE INVOLVED. SMUT, DRUG USE, OVERDOSES, VIOLENCE, STRIP CLUBS, WHORING, UNDERAGE RUNAWAYS, AND A GREAT PERFORMANCE BY AUGUST SCHELLENBERG AS A MEAN, NASTY UNDERWORLD ENFORCER.

9. SHATTERED INNOCENCE (1988 USA)
THEY CHANGE SHAUNA GRANT'S (AKA COLLEEN APPLEGATE) NAME TO PAULEEN ANDERSON (APTLY PLAYED BY JONNA LEE), BUT MAKE NO MISTAKE, THIS IS A DRAMATIZATION ABOUT HER TRAGIC LIFE AND DEATH, AND A PRETTY WELL-MADE ONE CONSIDERING THAT IT IS A LOW-BUDGET TV MOVIE. I'VE SEEN MORE THAN ONE PERSON COMMENT ONLINE THAT THIS IS ONE OF THE BEST TV MOVIES EVER MADE, AND I'M INCLINED TO AGREE. PAULEEN IS NOT MUCH OF A SYMPATHETIC CHARACTER, BUT THAT DOESN'T MATTER BECAUSE WATCHING HER HURTLING TOWARDS HER EARLY DEMISE PLAYS OUT IN SUCH AN ENTERTAINING (AND DARE I SAY, SHOCKING) WAY. THE STORY PLACES HER AS THE HOME-SPUN 17-YEAR-OLD SMALL TOWN GIRL ACHING TO START HER LIFE AND GET OUT ON HER OWN. LEAVING HOME IN A HUFF AND GOING TO THE BIG CITY WITHOUT ANY SKILLS TO SPEAK OF, SHE QUICKLY BECOMES A NUDE MODEL TO MAKE ENDS MEET, AND THEN A HARDCORE PORN STAR, THEN A DRUG ADDICT, AND THEN ULTIMATELY WORM FOOD WHEN SHE CAN'T KEEP HER SHIT TOGETHER AND FIZZLES OUT.

IT'S PRETTY OBVIOUS THAT THE PRODUCERS AND WRITERS OF SHATTERED INNOCENCE SET OUT TO PAINT A PICTURE OF THE EVILS OF THE PORN INDUSTRY AND WHY IT IS SOLELY TO BLAME FOR THE DESTRUCTION OF INNOCENCE AND YOUNG LIVES, BUT THEY DIDN'T MANAGE TO GET THERE IN A CONVINCING WAY. IN FACT, IT ALMOST SEEMS AS IF THEY ACCIDENTALLY ENDED UP WITH SOMETHING FAR MORE HONEST IN SPITE OF THEMSELVES -- WHICH IS THAT THIS GIRL WAS ACTUALLY TO BLAME FOR HER OWN IMPATIENCE AND "HAVE IT ALL NOW" ATTITUDE. IT'S A GREAT LESSON ON THE DANGERS OF IMPULSIVITY AND QUICK-FIXING, RESULTING IN A CHARACTER SIGNING FIGURATIVE CHECKS SHE SIMPLY COULDN'T CASH. A FUNNY IDEA, CULPABILITY AND PERSONAL RESPONSIBILITY! I WISH MORE MOVIE-OF-THE-WEEK MORALITY TALES LIKE THIS FOUND SOME WAY TO WORK WITH THAT CONCEPT.

10. FALLEN ANGEL (1981 USA)
I'M TORN ON THIS ONE. I FEEL LIKE MAYBE I SHOULDN'T HAVE INCLUDED FALLEN ANGEL SINCE IT IS ACTUALLY ABOUT THE CHILD PORNOGRAPHY INDUSTRY AND NOT THE PORN INDUSTRY. BEING AS I FIND IT FRUSTRATING HOW OFTEN ANTI-PORN CRUSADERS ACT AS IF THE TWO ARE ONE AND THE SAME, I'M SENSITIVE TO READERS DRAWING THAT SAME PARALLEL. I THINK, THOUGH, THAT WE'RE ALL GROWN UP ENOUGH HERE TO KNOW THAT ISN'T THE COURSE I'M TAKING OR THE POINT I'M TRYING TO MAKE. FALLEN ANGEL IS THE VERY POIGNANT STORY OF A 12-YEAR-OLD GIRL PLAYED BY A VERY UNDER-DEVELOPED BUT RASPY-VOICED 16-YEAR-OLD DANA

HILL (WHO LOOKED 12 EVEN IN HER EARLY 20S) WHO GETS TAKEN ADVANTAGE OF BY A WEIRDO COACH
WHO TAKES PHOTOS OF HER AND TRIES TO SELL HER INTO A KIDDIE PORN RING. IT'S QUITE WELL
DONE. A GOOD LITTLE MOVIE.

"I CONSIDER IT MY FAVOURITE OF THE FILMS I'VE BEEN INVOLVED WITH", DANA SAID WHILE BEING
INTERVIEWED IN 1985 ON THE SET OF EUROPEAN VACATION. "BECAUSE IT WAS REALLY THE FIRST FILM
THAT BROKE GROUND ABOUT SOCIAL ISSUES PERTAINING TO SEXUAL MATTERS WITH CHILDREN." SHE'S
QUITE RIGHT TO BE PROUD OF THIS 1981 TV MOVIE, AS HER PERFORMANCE IS VERY POWERFUL. SADLY,
DANA SUFFERED FROM DIABETES ALL THROUGH HER LIFE AND WOULD DIE AFTER SUFFERING A PARALYTIC
STROKE IN JULY OF 1996. SHE WAS 32. REST IN PEACE, SISTER. YOU AREN'T FORGOTTEN.
— BOUGIE

FOREST SHITAKER
AND OTHER HOLLYWOOD POOPFORMERS

ON AUGUST 29TH, 2014 I ASKED FRIENDS AND FANS OF CINEMA SEWER TO JOIN ME IN THE VERY MATURE AND
NOBLE PURSUIT OF CREATING "POOP VERSIONS" OF MOVIE ACTORS' NAMES. I STARTED THE BALL ROLLING WITH
AN EXAMPLE: FOREST SHITAKER, AND THEN LET THE GANG TAKE IT FROM THERE. HERE ARE SOME OF MY
FAVOURITES OF THE NEARLY 400 NAMES THAT WERE SUBMITTED:

Al Poocino
Anal Alda
Barbara Hershey-squirts
Brad Shit
Cacampbell Scott
Colon Firth
Daniel Bidet Lewis
Dave Shatppelle
DefeKate Winslett
Deuce Willis
Diarrhea Pearlman
Dumphrey Bogart
Elizabeth Swirley
Emma Squatson
Faye Dungaway

Gabe Kraplan
George Went
George C. Scatt
Griffin Dung
Helena Bonham Farter
James Caanstipated
Jennifer Anustown
Joaquin Feces
Kate Blanshitt
Keanu Relieves
Kirsten Dumps
Lauren Fee-cal
Lavatory Spelling
Mary Steamturdin
Meat Loaf

Michael Dingleberryman
Nicole Skidman
Peter O'Stool
Reb Brown
Richard Skidmark
Ron Howturd
Scatman Crothers
Scheisse Minnelli
SphincTor Johnson
Shelly Winturds
Sofia Crapola
Spray Liotta
Ted Nugget
W.C. Fields
William Scatner

ACTION!

FRANKLY MY REAR, I DON'T GIVE A DAMN!

NOW THATS ENTERSTRAIN MENT!

142

ACTION SLASHERS
THE RISE AND FALL OF A GENRE

☆ BY: STEPHEN LAMBRECHTS · 2014

WE LOVE OUR SLASHER FILMS AROUND THESE PARTS AND THE LATE '70S AND EARLY '80S HAD SOME OF THE VERY BEST. SURE, THEY'RE MOSTLY INTERCHANGEABLE, WITH ALMOST IDENTICAL STORY LINES AND VILLAINS, AND AFTER A WHILE IT BECAME EASIER TO TELL THESE FILMS APART BY NUDITY RATHER THAN CHARACTER, BUT THEY'RE STILL FUN AS HELL.

THE SLASHER IS ONE OF THE NASTIEST AND MOST EXPLOITATIVE SUB-GENRES IN HORROR. GREAT WRITING AND FLESHED-OUT CHARACTER-WORK IS USUALLY TOSSED ASIDE IN FAVOUR OF HIGH BODY COUNTS WHERE VICTIMS ARE VIOLENTLY HACKED, STABBED, DRILLED, CHOPPED, IMPALED, SAWED OR STRANGLED TO DEATH BY A TERRIFYING STALKER WITH A MOTIVE. THE KILLER CUTS HIS VICTIMS DOWN ONE BY ONE UNTIL A FINAL GIRL OR BOY MANAGES TO OVERCOME THEIR TORMENTOR AND MAKE IT OUT ALIVE. BONUS POINTS FOR SHOWING TITS.

CRITICS LOATHED SLASHERS, BUT AUDIENCES LOVED THEM, SOMETHING THAT STUDIO EXECS KNEW ALL TOO WELL. FIGURING THAT INTRODUCING THESE THRILLING SLASHER ELEMENTS INTO MORE MARKETABLE GENRES COULD MAKE TRUCKLOADS OF MONEY, AMERICAN FILM STUDIOS STARTED TAKING BIG ACTION STARS AND MAKING FILMS WITH THEM THAT HAD AN UNMISTAKABLE SLASHER EDGE. THUSLY, THE ACTION SLASHER GENRE WAS BORN.

WHILE THE TERMINATOR FRANCHISE WOULD EVENTUALLY BECOME A BOX-OFFICE JUGGERNAUT AND ACTION EXTRAVAGANZA, MANY FORGET ITS HUMBLE BEGINNINGS IN 1984 AS A LEAN, MEAN, SLASHER-INFLUENCED SCI-FI THRILLER. ARNOLD SCHWARZENEGGER'S ORIGINAL TERMINATOR WASN'T MAKING FRIENDS WITH LITTLE KIDS ~ IT WAS A SCARY, COLD MACHINE THAT KILLED WITH ABSOLUTELY NO REMORSE. TWO YEARS BEFORE THAT FILM, COLUMBIA PICTURES RELEASED THE CHUCK NORRIS STARRING FILM SILENT RAGE (1982), A MARTIAL ARTS-SLASHER HYBRID IN WHICH CHUCK PLAYED A TEXAS SHERIFF WHO MUST STOP A FRANKENSTEIN-LIKE PSYCHOPATH WHO CAN'T BE KILLED. "SCIENCE CREATED HIM. NOW CHUCK NORRIS MUST DESTROY HIM," READ THE TAGLINE FOR THE FILM, MAKING IT ABSOLUTELY IRRESISTIBLE TO ACTION FANS.

WHEN CRAZY BASTARD JOHN KIRBY (BRIAN LIBBY) FLIPS OUT AND MURDERS SOME PEOPLE IN THE HOUSE HE'S STAYING AT, CHUCK NORRIS APPEARS (AS HE TENDS TO DO, LIKE A LOOMING SPECTRE OF RIGHTEOUS DEATH) AND BEATS THAT MOTHERFUCKER DOWN. ALAS, THE AXE-

A TYPICAL KILLER FROM THE GENRE. THEY WERE USUALLY ONE PART JASON, ONE PART TED BUNDY, AND ONE PART BODYBUILDER.

-MURDERER DOES NOT DIE (PRESUMABLY BECAUSE CHUCK SKIPPED BREAKFAST THAT MORNING) AND AFTER ATTEMPTING TO ESCAPE AND BEING SHOT DOWN BY SEVERAL DEPUTIES, KIRBY IS TAKEN TO AN INSTITUTE WHERE A MAD DOCTOR AND GENETIC ENGINEER (STEVEN KEATS) APPLIES AN EXPERIMENTAL FORMULA TO THE PSYCHO IN AN ATTEMPT TO SAVE HIS LIFE. UNFORTUNATELY, THIS MAKES KIRBY AN INVULNERABLE DEATH MACHINE; ONE THAT ONLY CHUCK NORRIS CAN STOP.

WHILE NOT THE MOST VIOLENT SLASHER AROUND, THE UNSTOPPABLE KILLER PROVIDES THE FILM WITH A REAL SENSE OF MENACE, NOT UNLIKE THAT OF THE ORIGINAL TERMINATOR FILM THAT WOULD COME TWO YEARS LATER. EVENTUALLY, KIRBY PROVES NO MATCH FOR CHUCK'S SLOW-AS-MOLASSES ROUNDHOUSE KICKS, AND IS KNOCKED DOWN TO THE BOTTOM OF A WELL. WITH KIRBY PRESUMED DEAD, CHUCK LEAVES, AND IN A MOMENT THAT FREAKED THE SHIT OUT OF ME AS A CHILD, KIRBY'S HEAD EMERGES OUT OF THE WATER AGAIN RIGHT BEFORE THE CREDITS ROLL.

CHUCK NORRIS in SILENT RAGE

WHICH BRINGS ME TO MY PERSONAL FAVOURITE OF THE SUB-GENRE -- 10 TO MIDNIGHT (1983) FROM CANNON FILMS, STARRING CHARLES BRONSON. HERE, THE SLASHER FILM GETS THE DEATH WISH TREATMENT, WITH CHARLES BRONSON PLAYING AN LAPD COP WHO MUST BREAK THE RULES (AND THE LAW) TO STOP PATRICK BATEMAN-ESQUE KILLER WARREN STACY (GENE DAVIS), A MAN WHO LIKES TO STALK AND KILL WOMEN WHO REJECT HIS SEXUAL ADVANCES. DID I MENTION HE LIKES TO KILL THEM WHILE BUCK-ASS NAKED?

SHIT GETS PERSONAL WHEN BRONSON (NO CHARACTER NAME NECESSARY, WE ALL KNOW HE'S PLAYING HIMSELF) REALIZES THAT THE KILLER'S LATEST VICTIM IS HIS DAUGHTER'S CHILDHOOD FRIEND. WHILE WARREN IS CAUGHT PRETTY QUICKLY, THE SLIMY PRICK MANAGES TO CREATE A ROCK SOLID ALIBI FOR HIMSELF AND IS SET FREE. THIS FORCES BRONSON TO PLANT EVIDENCE IN ORDER TO TRY TO MAKE THE ARREST STICK, BUT WHEN HIS TAMPERING IS REVEALED IN COURT AND HIS CAREER RUINED, HE MUST PICK UP A GUN AND TAKE THE LAW INTO HIS OWN HANDS, BEFORE THE KILLER GETS TO HIS DAUGHTER, LAURIE (LISA EILBACHER).

THE FILM IS FILLED WITH COPIOUS AMOUNTS OF VIOLENCE AND TITS, WITH AN INCREDIBLE (AND LUDICROUS) FINALE THAT HAS SEVERAL DORM-ROOM GIRLS GETTING THEMSELVES KILLED IN ORDER TO PROTECT LAURIE FROM WARREN. THE FILM IS NASTY, MEAN-SPIRITED AND GRATUITOUS; EXACTLY WHAT EVERY SLASHER SHOULD AIM TO BE! NEED MORE OF AN ENDORSEMENT? ROGER EBERT FAMOUSLY GAVE THE FILM ZERO STARS IN HIS REVIEW, SAYING, "THIS IS A SCUMMY LITTLE SEWER OF A MOVIE, A CESSPOOL THAT LINGERS SADISTICALLY ON SHOTS OF A KILLER TERRIFYING AND KILLING HELPLESS WOMEN, AND THEN IS SHAMELESS ENOUGH TO END WITH AN APPEAL TO LAW AND ORDER." SERIOUSLY, HOW COULD YOU POSSIBLY PASS THAT UP?

EVEN CLINT EASTWOOD GOT IN ON THE ACTION, RETURNING TO THE SERIAL KILLER THEME HE'D EXPLORED IN DIRTY HARRY (1971) AND TAKING IT UP A NOTCH IN THE WARNER BROS. FILM TIGHTROPE (1984), BETTER KNOWN AS "THAT CLINT EASTWOOD MOVIE THAT USES THE BLADE RUNNER FONT." IN THIS FEATURE, CLINT PLAYS WES BLOCK, A (YOU GUESSED IT) COP ON THE EDGE. THERE'S A MASKED KILLER ON THE LOOSE, RAPING AND STRANGLING PROSTITUTES, EXCEPT THIS KILLER STARTS MAKING THINGS PERSONAL BY KILLING SOME HOOKERS THAT BLOCK HAD BEEN INTERVIEWING (AND SLEEPING WITH) AS PART OF HIS INVESTIGATION. ASIDE FROM THE PROSTITUTES, HE HAS ALSO BEEN WORKING WITH BERYL THIBODEAUX (GENEVIEVE BUJOLD), A WOMAN THAT RUNS A RAPE PREVENTION PROGRAM.

EVENTUALLY THE VICIOUS KILLER BREAKS INTO BLOCK'S HOUSE, KILLING HIS PETS AND NANNY, AS WELL AS THREATENING HIS FAMILY. OF COURSE THAT SHIT DON'T FLY IN CLINT'S HOUSE, AND NOW HE'S PISSED. EASTWOOD EVENTUALLY FIGURES OUT THE KILLER'S IDENTITY, TRACKING HIM DOWN RIGHT IN THE MIDDLE OF A BERYL-CHOKING SESSION. LIKE ANY GOOD SLASHER, THE FILM IS FILLED WITH SEXUALIZED VIOLENCE, A MASKED MANIAC AND MANY CREEPY STALKING AND KILLING SCENES.

ABEL FERRARA'S FEAR CITY (1984) IS A FANTASTIC PIECE OF SLEAZY SLASHER GOODNESS SET IN THE GRIMY HEYDAY OF '80S TIMES SQUARE. A MARTIAL ARTIST KILLER (STRANGELY NOT CREDITED, THOUGH THOUGHT TO BE A GUY CALLED JOHN FOSTER) IS RUNNING AROUND MANHATTAN, SLASHING UP STRIPPERS, AND IT'S UP TO EX-BOXER TURNED STRIP-CLUB TALENT PROVIDER MATT ROSSI (TOM BERENGER) AND COP AL WHEELER (BILLY DEE WILLIAMS) TO STOP HIM. NO ONE CAPTURES THAT DARK, GRITTY UNDERBELLY OF NEW YORK QUITE LIKE ABEL FERRARA. HERE, HIS CAMERA PROWLS THE CREEPY ALLEYWAYS, SUBWAY STATIONS AND STRIP BARS IN EXTREME VOYEURISTIC DETAIL. THE NAKED DANCERS INCLUDE RAE DAWN CHONG, MARIA CONCHITA ALONSO, OLA RAY AND A YOUNG MELANIE GRIFFITH, THE ONE STRIPPER THAT ROSSI FALLS FOR AND MUST PROTECT BEFORE THE KILLER GETS TO HER — AND YOU KNOW HE WILL.

THERE'S AN IMMENSE LEVEL OF TENSION THAT BUILDS UP, WHERE ROSSI MUST DECIDE WHETHER HE'S GOING TO TAKE THE GUY DOWN ONCE AND FOR ALL. ADD TO THAT THE MOUNTING PILE OF WOMEN GETTING STABBED, AND THE LOOMING THREAT ON HIS MAIN SQUEEZE, IT ALL CULMINATES IN AN AMAZING CLIMAX WHERE ROSSI MUST USE HIS BOXING SKILLS AGAINST THE KILLER'S KARATE SKILLS IN AN ALLEYWAY FIGHT FOR THE AGES. THIS IS AN UNMISSABLE ACTION SLASHER.

SYLVESTER STALLONE WOULD EVENTUALLY COME UP WITH HIS OWN VERSION OF THE DIRTY HARRY / TIGHTROPE FORMULA IN COBRA (1986), A DARK AND MENACING FILM IN WHICH SLY MUST TAKE ON A SERIAL KILLER. RIGHT OFF THE BAT, THE FILM FEELS DRENCHED IN DEATH, WITH SLY'S VOICEOVER INFORMING US ABOUT HOW MANY RAPES AND MURDERS OCCUR ON A DAILY BASIS IN THE UNITED STATES. THE IDEA IS TO PLACE THE AUDIENCE INTO A MINDSET OF FEAR AND DREAD, WITH MARION "COBRA" COBRETTI BEING THE ONLY GUY CAPABLE OF KILLING THE SHIT OUT OF ANYTHING THAT IS WILLING TO HARM US.

BRIDGITTE NIELSEN PLAYS A MODEL WHO IS ATTACKED BY A KNIFE-WIELDING MANIAC CALLED THE NIGHT SLASHER (BRIAN THOMPSON). TURNS OUT, HE IS PART OF A GREATER SCHEME — A MURDEROUS CULT CALLED THE NEW ORDER, AND COBRA MUST RID THIS VERMIN BY KILLING ALL 41 OF ITS MEMBERS (YES, THAT'S THE FILM'S KILL COUNT). HE SAVES THE BEST KILL FOR LAST HOWEVER, WHICH I WON'T SPOIL FOR THOSE WHO

BRONSON

...is in town.

10 to Midnight

HAVEN'T SEEN THE FILM (SERIOUSLY THOUGH, GO
WATCH IT NOW).

COBRA IS EASILY ONE OF STALLONE'S DARKER
FILMS, WITH AN OPPRESSIVE, VIOLENT
ATMOSPHERE COVERING THE ENTIRE FILM. THE
NIGHT SLASHER LOOKS CREEPY AS HELL, AND THE
WAY THAT HE STALKS HIS VICTIMS IS TEXTBOOK
SLASHER-STYLE. WHILE THE FILM EVENTUALLY
GIVES OVER TO STALLONE'S ACTION SIDE, WITH
CAR CHASES AND SHOOTOUTS GALORE, THAT NASTY
VIBE REMAINS RIGHT UNTIL THE VERY END.

FAR LESSER KNOWN THAN COBRA IS ANOTHER
ACTION-SLASHER FROM THE SAME YEAR, THE NIGHT
STALKER (1986). THIS ONE STARRED GRAVEL-
THROATED CHARLES NAPIER AND ROBERT VIHARO
AS STREET-WISE COPS TRYING TO TRACK DOWN
A HUGE SERIAL KILLER WITH A PENCHANT FOR
SNAPPING HOOKERS' NECKS AND PAINTING THEIR
FACES LIKE JAPANESE KABUKI PERFORMERS. THE
COMICALLY WEIRD-LOOKING ROBERT Z'DAR PLAYS
THE KILLER WHO ALWAYS SEEMS ONE STEP AHEAD
OF THE GUMSHOES, AND EVEN WHEN THEY DO
FINALLY CATCH UP TO HIM THEIR BULLETS SEEM
TO BOUNCE RIGHT OFF. NAPIER'S CHARACTER CAN'T
STOP BOOZING, THE CALL-GIRLS OF HOLLYWOOD
CAN'T SEEM TO STAY SAFE (AND ARE PICKED OFF
IN ONE UNSETTLING AND FEROCIOUS ATTACK
AFTER ANOTHER), THERE'S A JIVE-TALKING PIMP
NAMED JULIUS THAT CAN'T SEEM TO SHUT UP, AND
THE FINALE HAS A NOTABLY HIGH COP BODY
COUNT -- IF YOU'RE THE TYPE WHO LIKES TO
WITNESS SUCH THINGS.

THE HITCHER IS A NOTABLE ENTRY IN THE SUB-
GENRE THAT SEES AN UNHINGED RUTGER HAUER
TERRORIZE A YOUNG C. THOMAS HOWELL AFTER
BEING GIVEN A RIDE ON A DESERT HIGHWAY.
LIKE ANY GOOD SLASHER, THERE'S A RELENTLESS

CLINT EASTWOOD
TIGHTROPE

A cop on the edge...

PURSUIT BY AN OTHERWORLDLY PSYCHOPATH, A MOUNTING BODY COUNT LEFT BEHIND IN HIS WAKE,
AND A TENSION SO THICK, YOU CAN SLASH IT WITH A KNIFE. WHAT MAKES THE HITCHER SPECIAL,
ASIDE FROM THE PERFORMANCES, IS THAT IT'S BEAUTIFULLY SHOT WITH THE PANACHE OF AN ACTION
THRILLER BY DIRECTOR ROBERT HARMON, WHO WOULD LATER GO ON TO DIRECT THE VAN DAMME ACTION
VEHICLE, NOWHERE TO RUN. ONCE AGAIN, ROGER EBERT WOULD BRING DOWN HIS WRATH ON ANOTHER
ACTION SLASHER, CALLING THE HITCHER "DISEASED AND CORRUPT" IN HIS NO-STAR REVIEW.

THE GREAT BILL LUSTIG WOULD EVENTUALLY ENTER THE SUB-GENRE WITH A BANG, COMBINING THE
GENRES OF HIS TWO PRIOR (NON PORN) MOVIES, MANIAC AND VIGILANTE, TO CREATE AN ACTION

Some ladies of the night
will not live to see
the light of day.

THE NIGHT STALKER

© 1986 Almi Pictures, Inc. All Rights Reserved.

R   AN ALMI PICTURES, INC® RELEASE

SLASHER HYBRID IN MANIAC COP (1988). JAWSOME B-ACTOR
EXTRAORDINAIRE ROBERT Z'DAR AGAIN PLAYS THE MURDEROUS
TITULAR CHARACTER, ALONGSIDE GENRE FAVOURITES TOM ATKINS
AND BRUCE CAMPBELL. HERE, A GUY IN A POLICE UNIFORM IS
OUT ON THE STREETS OF L.A. KILLING INNOCENT PEOPLE AT
RANDOM, CAUSING PANIC IN THE CITY. WHEN PEOPLE SEE A COP
COMING, THEY CROSS THE STREET TO BE SAFE!

BRUCE CAMPBELL PLAYS THE CHIEF SUSPECT, AND WHILE HIS CHIN
AND JAW ARE CERTAINLY IMPRESSIVE, WILL THEY BE ABLE TO
MATCH Z'DAR'S MAGNIFICENT MANDIBLE? YOU'LL HAVE TO WAIT
UNTIL THE WONDERFUL CLIMACTIC CHASE SCENE INVOLVING A
POLICE TRUCK AND A PIER TO FIND OUT. LUSTIG WOULD DIRECT
TWO MORE ENTRIES IN THE SERIES — MANIAC COP 2 (1990),
WHICH MANY BELIEVE TO BE SUPERIOR TO THE ORIGINAL, AND
MANIAC COP 3: BADGE OF SILENCE (1993). CAMPBELL AND Z'DAR
WOULD RETURN FOR BOTH, WITH ROBERT DAVI TAKING OVER
THE DETECTIVE SPOT FROM ATKINS. LIKE JASON VOORHEES
BEFORE HIM, THE MANIAC COP IS AN UNDEAD KILLING MACHINE
THAT CAN'T BE STOPPED!

LUSTIG WOULD GO ON TO MAKE ANOTHER ACTION SLASHER IN
THE YEAR FOLLOWING THE FIRST MANIAC COP. RELENTLESS (1989)
SEES JUDD NELSON PLAY A DERANGED KILLER WHO PICKS HIS
VICTIMS AT RANDOM OUT OF THE PHONE BOOK. A COUPLE OF
DETECTIVES, PLAYED BY LEO ROSSI AND ROBERT LOGGIA, ARE
HOT ON HIS TRAIL, BUT SINCE THE KILLER WAS ONCE TRAINED
AS A COP AND KNOWS HOW TO COVER HIS TRACKS, THEY KEEP
COMING UP SHORT IN CATCHING HIM. ONCE AGAIN LUSTIG OPTS
FOR A NICE CAR CHASE SEQUENCE AND SEVERAL SHOOTOUTS TO
GO ALONG WITH THE MORE TRADITIONAL SLASHER STALKING
SCENES, INCLUDING ONE WHERE NELSON FORCES A WOMAN TO
STRANGLE HERSELF!

THE FRANCHISE WOULD CONTINUE WITHOUT THE INVOLVEMENT OF
LUSTIG OR NELSON WITH THREE MORE DIRECT-TO-VIDEO ENTRIES

STARRING LEO ROSSI. DEAD ON: RELENTLESS II (1992) SEES THE DETECTIVE CHASE A CRAZY MARTIAL ARTIST PATRIOT SERIAL KILLER PLAYED BY MILES O'KEEFE, WHILE RELENTLESS 3 (1993) SEES ROSSI CHASING YET ANOTHER SERIAL KILLER, THIS TIME PLAYED BY WILLIAM FORSYTHE. THIS SICK FUCKER LIKES TO MAIL PIECES OF HIS VICTIMS TO THE COPS. RELENTLESS IV: ASHES TO ASHES (1994) IS A FORGETTABLE FINAL ENTRY, NOTABLE MOSTLY FOR STARRING FAMKE JANSSEN BEFORE SHE WAS FAMOUS, AND FOR HAVING A DECENT AMOUNT OF SEX AND NUDITY. WITH EACH INSTALMENT, THE RELENTLESS SERIES WOULD DISTANCE ITSELF MORE AND MORE FROM ITS ACTION SLASHER ELEMENTS AND SETTLE INTO GENERIC THRILLER TERRITORY.

DEATH WARRANT (1990) HAS THE DISTINCTION OF BEING ONE OF CANNON FILMS' LAST PICTURES, THE STUDIO HAVING GONE TITS-UP RIGHT BEFORE THE FILM WAS FINISHED. THE DEBUT SCRIPT FROM DAVID S. GOYER (OF BLADE AND DARK KNIGHT FAME), DEATH WARRANT SEES JEAN-CLAUDE VAN DAMME AS A CANADIAN COP WHO MUST GO UNDERCOVER IN A PRISON TO INVESTIGATE SEVERAL MURDERS OF PRISONERS, DESPITE BEING WAY TOO PRETTY FOR THAT KIND OF THING. WHILE THE FILM DISPLAYS MANY TYPICAL PRISON MOVIE TROPES, IT HAS SLASHER ELEMENTS ALL OVER IT, ESPECIALLY IN SCENES WHERE VAN DAMME AND HIS HIGH KICKS MUST FACE OFF AGAINST A SERIAL KILLER KNOWN AS "THE SANDMAN" WHO SEEMINGLY CAN'T BE KILLED.

YA LIKE WHAT YA SEE?

HUH?

1980's HOOKERS WERE THE BEST HOOKERS!

IF ACTION SLASHER FILMS TAUGHT US ANYTHING, IT IS CERTAINLY THAT!

BOOGIE

BODIES KEEP PILING UP IN THE PRISON, LEADING TO THE DISCOVERY OF A GRISLY ORGAN HARVESTING OPERATION.

LIKE THE SLASHER GENRE ITSELF, THE ACTION SLASHER SUB-GENRE WOULD PRETTY MUCH DIE OFF ENTIRELY, WITH ONE LAST GASP EARLY IN THE NEW MILLENNIUM, HOPING TO PIGGYBACK ON THE SUCCESS OF BOX-OFFICE HITS LIKE SCREAM AND URBAN LEGEND. THAT FILM WAS D-TOX (A.K.A. EYE SEE YOU), AND IN IT SLY STALLONE PLAYS JAKE MALLOY, A COP WHO GOES DOWN THE TUBES WHEN HIS FRIEND AND FIANCE ARE MURDERED BY THE SERIAL KILLER HE'S BEEN TAILING FOR YEARS. AFTER SOME HEAVY ALCOHOL ABUSE AND AN ATTEMPTED SUICIDE, MALLOY IS CHECKED INTO A REHAB FACILITY FOR COPS. UNFORTUNATELY FOR ALL OF THE PATIENTS AT THE FACILITY, A BLIZZARD COMES ALONG AND TRAPS THEM IN THE PLACE, MAKING ALL OF THEM PERFECT TARGETS FOR A KILLER WHO STILL HAS A SCORE TO SETTLE. THE CAST (FEATURING CHARLES S. DUTTON, STEPHEN LANG, KRIS KRISTOFFERSON, TOM BERENGER, ROBERT PATRICK AND POLLY WALKER) IS EXCELLENT, AND WHILE I CAN'T REMEMBER TOO MUCH ABOUT THE MOVIE, IT MIGHT BE ONE WORTH REVISITING NOW THAT SOME TIME HAS PASSED.

SADLY IT SEEMS THAT THE DAYS OF THE ACTION SLASHER ARE LONG BEHIND US, THOUGH IT WOULD BE FUN TO DREAM-CAST SOME NEW FILMS WITH TODAY'S BIG ACTION STARS. IMAGINE THE ROCK OR JASON STATHAM TAKING ON A HATCHET-WIELDING KILLER? GET HOLLYWOOD ON THE PHONE, WE NEED TO MAKE THIS HAPPEN!

END

THE GREAT HOLLYWOOD RAPE SLAUGHTER

REVIEWED BY
MIKE SULLIVAN

"FAKE BILLY JACK AND HIS DEAD, CRUCIFIED EX GIRLFRIEND SCOOT AROUND ON A MOTORCYCLE."

I'VE BEEN A FAN OF B-MOVIES FOR SO LONG THAT I CAN NO LONGER FEEL DISAPPOINTMENT. MY DISSATISFACTION FOR THE GENRE HAS BECOME SO FAMILIAR THAT IT NOW FEELS COMFORTABLE. I'VE SEEN ENOUGH TO KNOW THAT I SHOULDN'T EXPECT MUCH FROM THESE MOVIES ANYMORE EVEN THOUGH MY EXPECTATIONS WEREN'T HIGH TO BEGIN WITH. OVER THE YEARS I'VE LEARNED THERE'S ONLY ONE SWITCHBLADE SISTERS. NOT EVERYTHING IS THE CANDY SNATCHERS. I DRINK YOUR BLOODS DO NOT GROW ON TREES. I FEEL NEITHER HIGHS NOR LOWS YET IT DOESN'T SEEM TO BOTHER ME. I'M JADED. JUST SO OVER IT.

EVERY SO OFTEN, HOWEVER, A MOVIE COMES ALONG THAT SHAKES ME OUT OF MY SELF-IMPORTANT STUPOR AND FIRMLY BUT GENTLY REMINDS ME WHAT DISAPPOINTMENT FEELS LIKE. THE GREAT HOLLYWOOD RAPE SLAUGHTER IS THAT MOVIE. I HAVEN'T FELT DISAPPOINTMENT LIKE THIS IN YEARS. THE DISAPPOINTMENT I EXPERIENCED FROM THIS FILM WAS SO RICH, SO FULL-BODIED, IT TRANSPORTED ME BACK TO A TIME WHEN I JUST STARTED GETTING INTO B-MOVIES AND WAS SPENDING UP TO $25 ON 7TH GENERATION VHS DUPES OF MOVIES-- LIKE FUNNYMAN OR THE "UNCUT" VERSION OF THE DENTIST-- THAT WERE INTERRUPTED BY A BLOCK OF GREEN ACRES EPISODES HALFWAY THROUGH THEIR RUNTIME. I CAN'T REMEMBER THE LAST TIME I SAID, "THIS REALLY WASN'T THE MOVIE I WAS EXPECTING" AND I MISSED THAT GNAWING SENSE OF BEING RIPPED OFF, PROFOUNDLY. THANK YOU, THE GREAT HOLLYWOOD RAPE SLAUGHTER FOR ENSURING THAT THE LITTLE BLACK RAIN CLOUD THAT'S ALWAYS HANGING ABOVE MY HEAD RAINED JUST A LITTLE HARDER THAN USUAL.

OF COURSE, A LOT OF MY DISAPPOINTMENT IS BASED ON THE FACT THAT THE TRAILER FOR THE GREAT HOLLYWOOD RAPE SLAUGHTER LOOKED US IN THE EYES, IN FRONT OF GOD AND OUR FAMILIES, AND LIED TO US. LINDA RONSTADT IS NOT IN THIS MOVIE. AND, IF YOU'VE GOT BALLS BIG ENOUGH TO TELL ME THAT THE FORMER STONE PONEYS FRONT-LADY IS STARRING IN A MOVIE CALLED THE GREAT HOLLYWOOD RAPE SLAUGHTER SHE BETTER BE SINGING A HEARTFELT BALLAD ABOUT GREAT, HOLLYWOOD RAPE-SLAUGHTER OR AT THE VERY LEAST ATTEMPTING TO SLAUGHTER-RAPE (HOLLYWOOD-STYLE) SANDY DENNY AND SOME OF THE OTHER MEMBERS OF THE FAIRPORT CONVENTION. OTHERWISE, YOU'VE JUST BAIT AND SWITCHED THE ENTIRE UNIVERSE AND YOUR CAMERA AND BADGE NEED TO BE PLACED ON THE FILM COMMISSIONER'S DESK BY MONDAY MORNING. GRANTED, I'M NOT ONE OF HER FANS BUT, EVEN STILL, THE PROMISE OF RONSTADT, HOLLYWOOD RAPE AND GREAT SLAUGHTER IS JUST TOO MUCH TO BEAR.

ADDITIONALLY, THE GREAT HOLLYWOOD RAPE SLAUGHTER ISN'T EVEN A MOVIE. THIS IS JUST RANDOM SELECTIONS OF SECOND UNIT FOOTAGE THAT WAS SWEPT OFF THE FLOOR OF AN EDITING SUITE, PLACED IN A LAUNDRY BASKET AND GIVEN TO A DISTRIBUTOR SIMPLY BECAUSE THE FILMMAKERS COULDN'T BRING THEMSELVES TO THROW IT AWAY. SCENES BEGIN AND END IN MID-SENTENCE, ADR IS DESPERATELY USED AND ABUSED, THE ENDING IS CLEARLY CANNIBALIZED FROM ANOTHER UNFINISHED MOVIE (MORE ON THAT LATER) AND EVERYBODY IS COVERED IN THE KIND OF BLACK, COARSE '70S BODY HAIR THAT RESEMBLES THAT OTHERWORLDLY FUNGUS THAT CONSUMES STEPHEN KING IN CREEPSHOW. IT'S A DVD EXTRA THAT SOMEHOW EARNED A ONE-SHEET.

THE GREAT HOLLYWOOD RAPE SLAUGHTER (ALTERNATELY KNOWN AS SUPER BALL) FOLLOWS THE EXPLOITS OF STEVE (ASSOCIATE PRODUCER AND CO-WRITER MICHAEL PLAMONDON) A DEEPLY UNLIKEABLE FILM SCHOOL GRAD WHO SITS IN SMUG JUDGMENT OF EVERYBODY AND HAS THE EERIE LIFELESS QUALITY OF A MUPPET WITHOUT ITS PUPPETEER. HE'S JUST THIS INFLEXIBLE PILE OF FELT WITH DEAD, LIFELESS EYES THAT PERFORMS ITS SCENES AS IF IT WAS UNEASILY PROPPED AGAINST THE WALL WHILE ITS OPERATOR TOOK A SMOKE BREAK. PLAMONDON IS THE PUREST KIND OF TERRIBLE. AT ANY RATE, STEVE SEEMS TO THINK THAT HIS EXPERIMENTAL FILM (WHICH IS BASICALLY JUST STOCK FOOTAGE OF A GUNFIGHT SUPERIMPOSED

OVER STOCK FOOTAGE OF RENE BOND
SEXIN' IT UP, DOWN AND ALL AROUND) WILL
TAKE HOLLYWOOD BY STORM AND SOON
HE'LL BE DIRECTING RESPECTABLE FILMS
FOR THE MAJOR STUDIOS. BUT IT DOESN'T
WORK OUT THAT WAY AS A NEWLY HUMBLED
STEVE TAKES A JOB DIRECTING PORNO
MOVIES SOLELY OUT OF DESPERATION. AT
THIS POINT I SHOULD NOTE THAT THE
GREAT HOLLYWOOD RAPE SLAUGHTER REALLY
WANTS TO STICK IT TO THE PORNO
INDUSTRY, BUT TOO OFTEN THE FILM'S
CRITIQUES ARE INSANE AND REMINDED ME
OF THE THINGS LINDA LOVELACE USED TO
SAY AFTER SHE BECAME ANDREA DWORKIN'S
PERSONAL PORNCHURIAN CANDIDATE. THEN
AGAIN, MAYBE IT'S JUST ME. DO PORN
PRODUCERS ABDUCT TEENAGE RUNAWAYS,
PRETEND TO RAPE THEM AND THEN REWARD
THEM WITH AN ORANGE JULIUS IF THEIR
SCREAMS ARE CONVINCING ENOUGH? ARE
PORNO MOVIES ROUTINELY SHOT IN THE
SCUMMIEST, ABANDONED BASEMENTS THAT
CROATIA HAS TO OFFER? ARE PORNO
ACTORS LITERALLY HOUSED WITHIN CASTING
OFFICES MUCH IN THE SAME WAY THAT
FIREFIGHTERS ARE HOUSED WITHIN A FIRE
STATION? I REALLY CAN'T SAY BECAUSE I'M
NOT IN THE BUSINESS, I JUST MASTURBATE
TO IT (AND BY THAT, I LITERALLY MEAN
THE BUSINESS SIDE OF THE INDUSTRY. NOT
THE ACTUAL-FACTUAL FUCKING).

SEE HOW SUPER SEXY CINEMA REALLY STARTED

SUPER BALL

TODAY AT
6:30 8:05 9:40

X

SUPER BALL
TELLS IT ALL!!!

FROM THERE THE GREAT HOLLYWOOD RAPE SLAUGHTER BREAKS DOWN INTO A SERIES OF BARELY CONNECTED
EVENTS AS IT MORPHS INTO BOOGIE NIGHTS AS RECOUNTED BY SOMEBODY WHO JUST SUFFERED SEVERE
HEAD TRAUMA. PASTY UNCOMFORTABLE BODIES LISTLESSLY GRIND AGAINST EACH OTHER IN A GRIM
APPROXIMATION OF SEX. A MAN DECLARES HIMSELF THE "HORSE-DICK PRICK OF WEST VIRGINIA" SHORTLY
BEFORE HE'S APPLAUDED FOR REMOVING HIS WIG. ANOTHER MAN BLOWS SMOKE RINGS AND SAYS, "FEH" A
LOT. ALL OF THESE EROTICALLY CHARGED EVENTS CAUSES STEVE TO GET HIS PENIS IN SUCH AN UPROAR, HE
FEARS HE'LL VENTURE DOWN A DARK ALLEY AND GET ADDICTED TO CHEST MOUNTED DILDOS AND TOP HATS
WITH THE WORD SUPERBALL SHARPIE-D ACROSS IT. PORNOGRAPHY IS EATING STEVE ALIVE AND AFTER HE
HALFHEARTEDLY DIRECTS A SCENE IN WHICH AN ANNOYED COUPLE JOSTLE EACH OTHER IN A SEX-LIKE MANNER,
HE BOLDLY FISTFIGHTS HIS WAY OUT OF HIS CONTRACT AND SOMEHOW MANAGES TO GET HIS DREAM
PROJECT BANKROLLED. AND WHAT IS STEVE'S DREAM PROJECT, EXACTLY? WELL, IT'S AN UNLICENSED BILLY
JACK FAN-FILM THAT FINDS A PASSABLE TOM LAUGHLIN STAND-IN FORCING HIS EX-GIRLFRIEND TO FUCK A
CORPSE AT GUNPOINT AS OTHER CORPSES (ONE OF WHICH I'M PRETTY SURE IS A YOUNG JOHN
RATZENBERGER) LOOK ON. AS THE TEMPLE OF SCHLOCK HAS NOTED, THIS SEQUENCE SEEMS TO BE EDITED IN
FROM ANOTHER POSSIBLY UNFINISHED MOVIE. PLAMONDON CLEARLY DOESN'T PLAY FAKE BILLY JACK, NOR IS
HE THE CAMERAMAN WHO CAPTURES THE SCENE WHERE FAKE BILLY JACK AND HIS DEAD, CRUCIFIED EX-
GIRLFRIEND SCOOT AROUND ON A MOTORCYCLE. WHAT THIS SCENE IS FROM AND HOW IT CAME TO BE A
PART OF THE GREAT HOLLYWOOD RAPE SLAUGHTER ARE JUST SOME OF THE MANY FASCINATING MYSTERIES
BEHIND THE MAKING OF THIS VAGUELY MOVIE-LIKE THING.

IT'S HARD TO BELIEVE THAT A MOVIE WITH A TITLE LIKE THE GREAT HOLLYWOOD RAPE SLAUGHTER COULD
BE SO UNDERWHELMING. IT'S EVEN HARDER TO BELIEVE THAT I INITIALLY FELT THAT IT WAS SO HARD TO
BELIEVE A MOVIE WITH A TITLE LIKE THE GREAT HOLLYWOOD RAPE SLAUGHTER COULD BE SO UNDERWHELMING
BUT I'VE GROWN OVER THE COURSE OF A SENTENCE. IT'S EXPLOITIVE, SURE, BUT IT DOESN'T EXACTLY
ROLL OFF THE TONGUE AND IT READS LIKE SOMETHING YOU'D FIND ON ONE OF THE SUBJECT LINES IN YOUR
SPAM FOLDER (RE: HELLO. HAVING A GREAT HOLLYWOOD? RAPESLAUGHTER IN PERFORMANCE COMFORT). BUT
STILL, IT'S FITTING THAT THE TITLE IS JUST A RANDOM SELECTION OF WORDS BECAUSE THE FILM ITSELF
IS JUST A RANDOM COLLECTION OF SCENES. IT'S RARE TRUTH IN ADVERTISING. THE GREAT HOLLYWOOD RAPE
SLAUGHTER IS JUST TOO FRAGMENTARY AND DISJOINTED TO QUALIFY AS ANYTHING MORE THAN AN OVERLONG
TRAILER. AS I NOTED EARLIER, THIS FILM IS DISAPPOINTING, BUT IT'S NOT THE TRITE, SECOND-TIER
DISAPPOINTMENT OF DROPPING YOUR FLUFFERNUTTER SANDWICH ON THE RUG. NO, THIS IS THE FULL-BODIED,
WELL-AGED, ALMOST SHATTERING DISAPPOINTMENT OF HAVING SOMEBODY YOU ADMIRE POLITELY ADMIT THAT
THEY FIND YOU BORING, UGLY AND UNTALENTED. THE GREAT HOLLYWOOD RAPE SLAUGHTER OPENS UP OLD
WOUNDS AND SPITS HALF-EATEN JALAPENO POPPERS ALL OVER THEM. IT'S NOT FUN.

HAMBURGER BUN PUSSY!

ONE OF THE COOL THINGS ABOUT PORN AND THE
WAY THAT IT FETISHIZES THE HUMAN BODY, IS
THAT I'M CONSTANTLY REALIZING THAT I'M
TURNED ON BY THINGS THAT I HAD NO IDEA
EVEN TURNED ME ON. A PERFECT IS EXAMPLE
IS THE HAMBURGER BUN PUSSY. YOU KNOW,
WHERE A WOMAN PRESSES HER THIGHS
TOGETHER, AND FROM THE BACK IT MAKES HER
VULVA COMPRESS INTO THE SHAPE OF TWO
SMALL HAMBURGER BUNS, AND I'M NOT ALONE...
I'VE BROUGHT THIS UP AMONGST A FEW OF MY
MALE AND LESBIAN FRIENDS WHEN TALKING
ABOUT PORN WE LIKE, AND THEIR FACES LIGHT UP!

Baby Doll (1956)

EVER WONDER HOW THE BABYDOLL NIGHTGOWN GOT ITS NAME? IT WAS DERIVED FROM THE COSTUME WORN BY CARROLL BAKER'S CHARACTER IN THIS 1956 RELEASE, A RELATIVELY STEAMY FILM ABOUT A MIDDLE AGED COTTON GIN OWNER (KARL MALDEN), HIS 19-YEAR-OLD VIRGIN BRIDE (SOMETIMES NOTED AS 17 IN THE FILM'S ADVERTISING) PLAYED BY CARROLL BAKER, AND A RIVAL (ELI WALLACH) INTENT ON SEDUCING THE OVERTLY FLIRTY YOUNG WOMAN. THE SETTING? A DILAPIDATED PLANTATION HOUSE IN MISSISSIPPI.

TWO WEEKS BEFORE ITS RELEASE, A GIANT BILLBOARD DISPLAY WAS BUILT IN NEW YORK, DEPICTING THE NOW-ICONIC IMAGE OF A SCANTILY CLAD BAKER, LAYING IN A CRIB AND SUCKING HER THUMB. THE CONTROVERSY WAS IMMEDIATE, AND BY THE TIME THE MOVIE WAS RELEASED A LARGELY SUCCESSFUL EFFORT TO BAN IT WAS PUT IN PLACE BY THE ROMAN CATHOLIC LEGION OF DECENCY. THE GROUP GAVE THE PICTURE A "C" (FOR CONDEMNED) AND NOTED THAT IT WAS "GRIEVOUSLY OFFENSIVE TO CHRISTIAN AND TRADITIONAL STANDARDS OF MORALITY AND DECENCY." 77% OF AMERICAN THEATERS WOULD WITHDRAW THE FILM FROM CIRCULATION, EVEN THOUGH IT LATER RECEIVED MULTIPLE AWARD NOMINATIONS, INCLUDING 4 OSCAR NODS. EVEN TIME MAGAZINE WOULD REMARK THAT THEY FELT IT WAS THE "DIRTIEST AMERICAN-MADE MOTION PICTURE THAT HAD EVER BEEN LEGALLY EXHIBITED", EVEN THOUGH THERE WAS NO NUDITY AND NO SWEARING. TO PUT IT IN A MODERN CONTEXT, IT IS A MOVIE THAT IS SHOWN TODAY, UNEDITED, ON BASIC TELEVISION.

ON THE 2006 DVD RELEASE OF THE MOVIE, ACTRESS CARROLL BAKER WAS QUOTED IN A FEATURETTE SAYING THAT SHE AND EVERYONE ELSE INVOLVED HAD "NO IDEA" THAT THE MATERIAL WOULD BE CONTROVERSIAL. AS AN ASIDE, CARROLL WROTE AN AUTOBIOGRAPHY IN 1983 CALLED BABY DOLL, WHICH WAS REVIEWED BY PEOPLE MAGAZINE THUSLY: "IN THE FIRST TWO CHAPTERS OF HER NEW AUTOBIOGRAPHY THE ACTRESS GRAPHICALLY DESCRIBES HER BED-WETTING, HER FIRST PERIOD, HER ATTEMPT TO KILL HER SISTER, HER HATRED OF THE STEPMOTHER SHE CALLS 'OLD TITLESS,' HER TWO NERVOUS BREAKDOWNS AND HER FATHER'S BIZARRE SEXUAL HABITS. WAIT TILL YOU GET TO THE RAPE SCENE IN CHAPTER FOUR." LEFT OUT OF THE AUTOBIOGRAPHY WAS THE STORY ABOUT HER SHOOTING ON LOCATION IN AFRICA FOR THE 1965 MOVIE MISTER MOSES, WHERE A MAASAI CHIEF OFFERED 150 COWS, 200 GOATS, SHEEP, AND $750 FOR HER HAND IN MARRIAGE.

FOR HIS PART, STAR ELI WALLACH TOLD ENTERTAINMENT WEEKLY IN 2006 THAT HE FELT THE FILM WAS "ONE OF THE MOST EXCITING, DARING MOVIES EVER MADE", WHILE ADDING: "PEOPLE SEE IT TODAY AND SAY, 'WHAT THE HELL WAS ALL THE FUSS ABOUT?'"

The Stone Killer (1973. USA. Directed by Michael Winner)

IN A SHORT THREE-YEAR JUNCTION IN THE EARLY 1970S DIRECTOR MICHAEL WINNER DIRECTED THREE VIOLENT CHARLES BRONSON FILMS: THE MECHANIC (1972), THE STONE KILLER (1973) AND DEATH WISH (1974).

TWO OF THE MOVIES WENT ON TO SPAWN REMAKES, SEGUELS, AND A HOST OF CLONES AND IMITATORS. THE OTHER -- THIS FILM -- WAS BARELY NOTICED.

FRANKLY, IT'S KINDA HARD TO KNOW HOW TO REACT TO THE STONE KILLER. IT'S A MOVIE THAT GOT ALMOST NO ATTENTION FOR DECADES (ASIDE FROM ROGER EBERT SAYING IN 1973 THAT THIS WAS "PROBABLY THE BEST VIOLENT BIG-CITY POLICE MOVIE SINCE DIRTY HARRY") AND THEN IN RECENT YEARS IT'S BEEN SOMEWHAT OVERHYPED SINCE BEING REDISCOVERED ON DVD. DESPITE A FEW RESERVATIONS I WILL SAY THIS: STONE KILLER CERTAINLY ISN'T BORING. IN FACT, IT'S BLESSED WITH ONE OF THE SINGLE BEST CAR CHASE SCENES IN FILM HISTORY, AND ALSO A GREAT DUMMY-FALLING-OUT-OF-THE-WINDOW SCENE AS WELL. THE CAMERA DOESN'T EVEN CUT AWAY WHEN IT HITS THE PAVEMENT! MAYBE THE ULTIMATE LESSON HERE IS THAT IT'S BEST TO NOT LISTEN TO ANYONE TELL YOU HOW GOOD OR BAD STONE KILLER IS. JUST EXPERIENCE IT.

SUNSET STRIP
REVIEW AND ILLUSTRATIONS BY MR. ROBERT DAYTON ·2011·

THE CREATORS OF THIS 1993 STRAIGHT-TO-DOLLAR-STORE PRODUCTION ARE VERY CLEVER BECAUSE THEIR MOVIE'S TITLE HAS TWO MEANINGS: 1) THE SETTING IS LA'S SUNSET STRIP AND 2) MUCH OF THE MOVIE TAKES PLACE IN A STRIP CLUB AFTER SUNSET!

PRESENTED BY PM ENTERTAINMENT (WHO TRULY DO THEIR BEST WORK AFTER NOON AND BEFORE MIDNIGHT) SUNSET STRIP IS DIRECTED BY PETER G. VOLK AND FEATURES 48 MINUTES OF TRAILERS (THEY SAY 48 MINUTES BUT I DIDN'T TIME IT) AFTER THE FEATURE PRESENTATION. THIS SELECTION OF PREVIEWS REVEAL THAT PM ENTERTAINMENT SPECIALISE IN ACTION-EROTIC FILMS, EROTIC-COMEDY FILMS (SUCH AS BIKINI SUMMER 1 WHICH IMPLIES THAT THERE WAS TO BE A BIKINI SUMMER 2 -- AND INDEED THERE WAS! THEY PUT THEIR NOSES TO THE GRINDSTONE, SHOWED INITIATIVE AND DETERMINATION AND GOT ALL THE WAY UP TO A PART 3 AS WELL!) ACTION PICTURES, SCI-FI-ACTION, AND JUST PLAIN EROTIC.

JEFF

SUNSET STRIP IS ABOUT A SERIOUS DANCER NAMED HEATHER WHO WANTS TO IMPROVE HER CRAFT. THE ELDERLY MENTOR OF THE DANCE STUDIO SCHOOL HEATHER STUDIES AT SHOWS HER SOME OLD PHOTOS OF WHEN SHE DID BURLESQUE AND HOW IT ADDED SEXINESS TO HER CRAFT WITH NO DAMAGE TO HER REPUTATION. FEELING VALIDATED, HEATHER SHOWS UP FOR AMATEUR NIGHT AT A STRIP CLUB RUN BY JEFF CONAWAY, WHO YOU'LL REMEMBER FROM PLAYING THE STRUGGLING ACTOR ON TAXI. NOTHING HAS CHANGED, THE CRAFT OF ACTING CAN BE A LIFE LONG STRUGGLE.

THEY FALL FOR EACH OTHER AND SHE STARTS STRIPPING. THERE IS LOTS OF NUDITY AND LENGTHY STRIPPING SEQUENCES, AND IT'S HARD TO TELL WHICH DANCER IS WHICH FROM ALL THE SILICONE, BUT THEY ALL EVENTUALLY BECOME ONE BIG SURROGATE FAMILY! THEY EVEN HAVE TIME TO HELP A ROCK BAND MAKE A MUSIC VIDEO TO GET ON MTV, COMPLETELY OBLIVIOUS THAT GRATUITOUS NUDITY WON'T HELP THE BAND GET AIRPLAY -- BUT SINCE NOBODY SAID ANYTHING IT MUST'VE BEEN OKAY!

THERE'S SOME DRAMA TOO! EVIL DRUG DEALERS CAUSE A DANCER TO O.D. LUCKILY, THESE VILLAINS GET THEIR COMEUPPANCE. IN MEMORIAM THE STRIPPERS EAT THEIR FALLEN COMRADE'S FAVE FOOD: PIZZA WITH LOTS OF PINEAPPLE. THE DELIVERY BOY EVEN GIVES IT TO THEM FOR FREE AS HE MISSES HER TOO.

HEATHER'S NEW 'FAMILY' SHOWS UP AT HER BIG SCHOOL DANCE RECITAL TO LITERALLY CHEER HER ON. ALL OF THE DANCERS AT THE SCHOOL LOOK COMPLETELY INTERCHANGEABLE FROM THE STRIPPERS RIGHT DOWN TO TECHNIQUE AND SILICONE, AND HEATHER WINS! THE GUY WITH JEANS AND GLASSES FROM EARLIER IN THE PICTURE THAT HAD A BAD UNREQUITED CRUSH ON HEATHER EVEN MEETS ONE OF THE STRIPPERS AND THEY HIT IT OFF! EVERYBODY WINS! YAY! YOU KNOW WHO ELSE WINS?

WE, THE VIEWERS DO! WE WHO ARE TRULY ALIVE (R.I.P. JEFF CONAWAY)! THANKS PM ENTERTAINMENT!

DID YOU KNOW?

* JEFF CONAWAY WAS MARRIED THREE TIMES. HIS FIRST WAS TO A DANCER WHEN HE WAS 21. HIS SECOND WAS TO RONA NEWTON-JOHN, ELDER SISTER OF OLIVIA NEWTON-JOHN, AND THE THIRD WAS TO SOME OTHER LADY.

* JEFF CONAWAY ATTEMPTED SUICIDE 21 TIMES, BUT DIED OF AN ACCIDENTAL PAIN MEDICATION OVERDOSE IN MAY OF 2011.

R.I.P. JEFF CONAWAY STAR OF SUNSET STRIP (OH, AND TAXI AND GREASE)

THE GEEKS INHERITED THE EARTH

HERE'S A MEMORY: I VIVIDLY REMEMBER THE DAY I SPOTTED A TV SHOW CALLED "COMICS!" IN THE TV GUIDE WHEN I WAS 19, AND YOU CAN'T EVEN IMAGINE HOW EXCITING IT WAS. SERIOUSLY, I PRACTICALLY SET UP A VIEWING PARTY. I WAS OVER THE MOON THAT THE OBSCURE HOBBY THAT I LOVED AND OBSESSED ABOUT FOR MY ENTIRE CHILDHOOD HAD BEEN FINALLY GIVEN ITS OWN TV SHOW! HOW LEGITIMIZING! I FANTASIZED WHAT THE SHOW MIGHT BE LIKE AS I PATIENTLY WAITED FOR 9:00PM ROLL AROUND. WOULD IT INTERVIEW THE WRITERS AND ARTISTS LIKE A TALK SHOW? WOULD IT EXAMINE A DIFFERENT COMIC SERIES EVERY WEEK IN A DOCUMENTARY STYLE? WOULD INDEPENDENT PUBLISHERS BE COVERED, OR JUST THE BIGGER COMPANIES? DUDE, THERE IS NO MAP! THEY COULD DO PRETTY MUCH ANYTHING! OH GOD! 8:56... SO CLOSE! THIS IS IIIIIIT! A SHOW ABOUT COMICS!!! AAAAAAND...

IT'S A STAND UP COMEDY THING. COMICS = COMEDIANS, YOU DUMBASS. LE <u>SIGH</u>.

TODAY I WAS READING THE LOCAL NEWSPAPER AND THERE WAS AN ARTICLE ABOUT SOME NOT PARTICULARLY EARTH SHATTERING PLOT DEVELOPMENTS IN THE NEW ISSUE OF IRON MAN. NOW...NOT IN AN IRON MAN MOVIE OR A TV SHOW, MIND YOU, BUT IN THE COMIC BOOK. THINK ABOUT THAT FOR A SECOND. THINK ABOUT HOW DIFFERENT THAT IS. I DID.

I'M NOT ANGRY OR BITTER ABOUT IT, IT'S JUST THAT IT'S SO DAMN STRANGE. ALMOST NONE OF MY FRIENDS READ COMICS WHEN I WAS IN JUNIOR HIGH, AND I WAS A COMIC BOOK FANATIC. I ALSO ADORED SPENDING PRETTY MUCH ALL OF MY FREE TIME IN VIDEO ARCADES. EVEN IF I DIDN'T HAVE MONEY TO PLAY THE GAMES, I'D JUST WATCH OTHER PEOPLE PLAY THEM. FRANKLY, ALL I CARED ABOUT WAS SUPERHEROES AND VIDEOGAMES AND I HONESTLY FELT SORT OF LIKE A FREAK BECAUSE OF IT.

FLASH FORWARD TO NOW, AND EVEN THOUGH THE 15-YEAR-OLD VERSION OF ME WAS BEYOND EXCITED THAT PLOT DEVELOPMENTS IN A COMIC BOOK ARE MAINSTREAM NEWS, THE 40-YEAR-OLD ROBIN COULD GIVE A FUCK. I REALLY DON'T CARE ABOUT SUPERHEROES OR VIDEOGAMES, EXCEPT NOW IT SEEMS LIKE EVERYONE ELSE DOES INSTEAD. IT'S HARD TO REALLY DESCRIBE HOW ODD IT IS, BUT HERE GOES MY BEST ATTEMPT AT IT:

IT'S LIKE BEING 15 AND BEING OBSESSED WITH BASKET-WEAVING, AND ALL YOU CAN THINK ABOUT IS WHERE TO GET WICKER, AND ALL THE AMAZING BASKETS YOU CAN MAKE. NEEDLESS TO SAY, EVERYONE MAKES FUN OF YOU FOR IT. YOU CAN'T POSSIBLY GET LAID AND EVERYONE ELSE WHO HAS A HEALTHY SOCIAL LIFE THINKS YOU'RE PATHETIC. YOU MANAGE TO MAKE IT TO 23 WITHOUT KILLING YOURSELF, AND THEN BEFORE YOU KNOW IT, YOU'RE 40, AND CAN'T REMEMBER THE LAST TIME YOU WOVE A BASKET OR CARED TO. BUT NOW YOU LOOK AROUND AND THE BIGGEST CONVENTION ON THE PLANET IS BASKETCON, THE BIGGEST BOXOFFICE GROSSING FILM OF ALL TIME IS 'WEAVERMAN,' AND THERE ARE PEOPLE DRESSED IN BASKETS CAMPING OUTSIDE WALMART FOR 48 HOURS PRIOR TO THE HIGHLY ANTICIPATED HARDCOVER RELEASE OF "99 AMAZING BASKETWEAVE PATTERNS TO DELIGHT YOUR FRIENDS".

I LOOK AT THE SAME CHARACTERS FROM MY CHILDHOOD, RECYCLED CONTINUOUSLY IN THE COMICS AND VIDEO GAMES OF TODAY, AND IT FEELS NOT LIKE SEEING OLD FRIENDS, BUT LIKE BEING FORCIBLY BUTTFUCKED BY AN OLD FRIEND. LIKE THEY SHOWED UP AT YOUR DOOR, AND TOLD YOU TO DROP YOUR SHORTS.

THEY'LL TURN ON YOU

THE TOP TWENTY MOST UNDERRATED AMERICAN FILMS OF THE EIGHTIES

BEFORE YOU MAKE A LIST LIKE THIS, YOU HAVE TO DEFINE YOUR TERMS. IN THIS CASE, 'UNDERRATED' MEANS "I DON'T EVER SEE/HEAR FILM FANS GIVING THIS MOVIE LOVE OR RESPECT". SO IT'S PURELY SUBJECTIVE TO MY EXPERIENCE, BUT PERHAPS YOU'LL FIND YOURSELF IN AGREEMENT/DISAGREEMENT WITH AT LEAST SOME OF MY PICKS AND GET SOME ENTERTAINMENT OUT OF IT THAT WAY. AT THE VERY LEAST, IT MIGHT GIVE YOU SOME MOVIES TO LOOK INTO.

"WHERE IS THE HORROR?" YOU MAY ASK, AND THAT IS A GREAT QUESTION. TO TELL YOU THE TRUTH, IT'S PRETTY NEAR IMPOSSIBLE TO FIND A 1980S HORROR FILM THAT IS UNDERRATED BY FILM NERDS. WHY IS THAT? WELL, SIMPLY BECAUSE HORROR FANS ARE SO INCREDIBLY PLENTIFUL, ORGANIZED (WHEN WAS THE LAST TIME YOU SAW A BIOPIC MOVIE CONVENTION FOR INSTANCE?) AND OUTSPOKEN ABOUT LOVING EVERY SINGLE THING EVER MADE IN THE GENRE. I SWEAR TO GAWD, EVEN THE WORST AMERICAN HORROR FILMS HAVE FAN CLUBS. SO I'M NOT LEAVING OUT THE HORROR MOVIES TO BE A MEANIE, IT'S JUST THAT THE LESSER CELEBRATED GENRES HAVE SO MUCH MORE TO OFFER A LIST DEVOTED TO THE UNDERRATED.

I ALSO DIDN'T COUNT A FILM AS "UNDERRATED" IF IT HAD BEEN GIVEN THE SPECIAL EDITION DVD TREATMENT BEFORE THIS ARTICLE WAS WRITTEN IN NOVEMBER 2013. CLEARLY THERE IS AN APPRECIATIVE AUDIENCE FOR A MOVIE OR THESE COMPANIES WOULDN'T GIVE THEM DELUXE 2 DISC RELEASES WITH EXTRA FEATURES AND SUCH. I ALSO DISCOUNTED ANYTHING IF I'VE EVER SEEN ANYONE WALKING AROUND IN A T-SHIRT BASED ON IT. SORRY, THAT SHIT AIN'T UNDERRATED. LASTLY, I DIDN'T INCLUDE PORN OR DOCUMENTARIES, BECAUSE OTHERWISE THIS LIST WOULD HAVE SIMPLY BEEN 90% DOCUMENTARIES AND ADULT FILMS. I KNOW I HAVE SAID THIS BEFORE BUT BOTH OF THOSE GENRES JUST GET NO RESPECT FROM THE AVERAGE CINEPHILE, ALTHOUGH I'M DOING WHAT I CAN TO CHANGE THAT.

IN ALPHABETICAL ORDER, HERE ARE MY PICKS:

52 PICK-UP (1986)
AS I MENTIONED IN MY ARTICLE ABOUT CANNON FILMS BACK IN CINEMA SEWER BOOK 3, THIS PICTURE ADAPTED FROM A NOVEL BY ELMORE LEONARD IS ONE OF MY FAVE MOVIES OF THE 1980S, AND I DON'T HEAR MANY (ANY?) PEOPLE ECHO THAT SENTIMENT. ALTHOUGH I DO FEEL LIKE IF MORE PEOPLE ONLY SAW THIS STYLISH THRILLER, THEY WOULD COMPLETELY AGREE. BRIEFLY PUT: IT'S ABOUT KIDNAPPING, EXTORTION, AND FEATURES SCARY BAD GUYS WHO RUN A STRIP CLUB. WATCH IT OR WATCH YOUR BACK, BECAUSE I'M SERIOUSLY GOING TO KICK YOUR BUTTHOLE IF I FIND OUT YOU READ THIS AND STILL HAVEN'T BOTHERED TO SEE IT.

ACTION U.S.A. (1989)
I'VE WRITTEN PLENTY ABOUT THIS ONE IN THESE PAGES BEFORE, BUT IT CAN'T BE LEFT OFF THIS LIST. SIMPLY PUT, THE MOVIE IS AN ACTION FAN'S DREAM IF YOU'RE INTO STUNTS AND CAR CRASHES. IGNORE THE LAME SOUNDING DOLLAR-STORE TITLE, THIS FUCKING MOVIE DELIVERS. LOW ON BUDGET AND HIGH ON ENTERTAINMENT -- JUST AS YOU WOULD EXPECT FROM A MOVIE MADE BY A STUNTMAN.

AMERICAN POP (1981)
THE ONLY ANIMATED MOVIE ON THIS LIST. RALPH BAKSHI HAS EARNED HIS STREET CRED FOR FRITZ THE CAT, LORD OF THE RINGS, AND EVEN WIZARDS TO A LESSER EXTENT, AND YET HIS BEST MOVIE HASN'T BEEN HONOURED WITH THE SAME FAN-FUELED ENTHUSIASTIC CULT FOLLOWING. WELL, I AIM TO DO MY BIT TO TRY AND CHANGE THAT. THIS GORGEOUS ROTOSCOPED ANIMATED FEATURE RELATES THE STORY OF FOUR GENERATIONS OF AN IMMIGRANT FAMILY IN AMERICA, AS THEIR CAREERS AND LIFE TRAJECTORIES PARALLEL THE HISTORY OF POPULAR MUSIC ITSELF. THIS SHIT IS BRILLIANT AND VISUALLY HYPNOTIC.

BEHIND ENEMY LINES (1986)
DAVID CARRADINE, MAKO, AND STEVE JAMES. WHAT ELSE DO YOU NEED TO KNOW? I DIDN'T SEE THIS TILL 2011, AND COULDN'T BELIEVE IT HADN'T BEEN PART OF MY LIFE FOR SO LONG. PURE BALLS OUT UNADULTERATED VIETNAM WAR RAMBO-WANNABE TRASH BRILLIANCE. IT'S PUT TOGETHER REALLY WELL, AND ALL IT'S MISSING IS SOME REB BROWN AND MORE GRATUITOUS NUDITY. IT NEEDS MORE LOVE ALL THE SAME. FIND IT AND PARTAKE IN IT.

THE BLOOD OF HEROES (AKA THE SALUTE OF THE JUGGER. 1989)
ONE OF OUR MOST-WATCHED FILMS THROUGHOUT THE 1990S. MY WIFE AND I JUST LIVED AND BREATHED THIS POST APOCALYPSE MOVIE ABOUT A VIOLENT FICTIONAL CO-ED SPORT PLAYED WITH A DOG SKULL.

WE COULDN'T GET ENOUGH OF IT, BUT THEN LOOKED AROUND ONCE WE GOT INTO OUR LATE TWENTIES AND REALIZED MOST PEOPLE DIDN'T QUOTE OR THINK HIGHLY OF IT LIKE WE DID. THIS MOVIE SLOWLY SEEMS TO BE GAINING SOME PROPS HERE AND THERE AS THE DECADES GO BY, BUT STILL SEEMS TO BE OFF OF A LOT OF PEOPLE'S RADAR. JOAN CHEN AND RUTGER HAUER STAR ALONG WITH VINCENT D'ONOFRIO.

BLUE STEEL (1989)
JAMIE LEE CURTIS IS BETTER REMEMBERED AS THE ORIGINAL SCREAM QUEEN, BUT HER BEST ACTING ROLE FOR MY MONEY WAS THIS 1989 POLICE FILM DIRECTED BY KATHRYN BIGELOW. THERE IS A REAL SENSE OF DREAD AND SEXUALIZED TENSION AS JAMIE KICKS BUTTOCKS AS THE FEMALE ROOKIE COP WHO GOES TOE TO TOE WITH A PISTOL WIELDING PSYCHOPATH WHO IS OBSESSED WITH HER. RON SILVER IS DOWNRIGHT INCREDIBLE AS THE BAD GUY. SCRIPT BY ERIC RED, WHO WROTE THE HITCHER, COHEN AND TATE, AND OTHER TENSION-FILLED '80S CLASSICS.

COHEN AND TATE (1988)
DID SOMEONE SAY "COHEN AND TATE"?? WELL, HERE IT IS, RIGHT ON CUE. DON'T ASK, JUST GET. THE LESS YOU KNOW ABOUT THIS ONE GOING IN, THE MORE YOU'RE GONNA LIKE THE WAY IT COLDLY SMACKS YOU AROUND, AND THEN DOESN'T EVEN GIVE YOU A PHONE CALL THE NEXT DAY TO APOLOGIZE.

COP (1988)
THERE WERE ABOUT A HALF A DOZEN JAMES WOODS MOVIES FROM THE 1980S THAT COULD HAVE MADE THIS LIST, BUT I CHOSE THIS ONE SIMPLY BECAUSE IT'S THE BEST FILM HE MADE FROM THAT TIME THAT NEVER SEEMS TO GET GUSHED ABOUT. YET ANOTHER ONE THAT WAS BASED ON A BOOK BY JAMES ELLROY, THE PLOT IS PRETTY STANDARD LAW ENFORCEMENT AND KILLERS STUFF, BUT COP REALLY BLOWS YOU AWAY WITH THE WORLD-WEARY, RUGGED AND VIOLENT PERFORMANCE JAMES WOODS DROPS SO EFFORTLESSLY.

PAM GRIER SHOOTS FROM POINT BLANK RANGE IN FORT APACHE THE BRONX.

FORT APACHE, THE BRONX (1981)
ANOTHER GRITTY NEW YORK CRIME DRAMA, BUT GODDAMN IF THEY DIDN'T KNOW EXACTLY HOW TO DO THESE IN THE LATE 1970S AND EARLY '80S. LET'S FACE IT: THE BIG APPLE WAS ROTTEN TO THE CORE AND THAT FACT GAVE FILMMAKERS A PILE OF INTERESTING MATERIAL TO WORK WITH. THIS IS THE STORY OF THE ROUGHEST AND MOST DILAPIDATED PRECINCT IN THE CITY'S ENTIRE DEPARTMENT, ONE STAFFED BY UNWANTED OR CORRUPT OFFICERS. PAUL NEWMAN, ED ASNER, PAM GRIER, DANNY AIELLO, RACHEL TICOTIN, TITO GOYA AND KEN WAHL MAKE UP THE AMAZING CAST, ALL OF WHOM WERE AT THE PEAK OF THEIR ACTING SUPERPOWERS.

THE HIDDEN (1987)
FULLY DESERVES TO BE NOTED AS ONE OF THE GREATEST SCI-FI ACTION FILMS OF ITS ERA ALONGSIDE TERMINATOR, PREDATOR AND ROBOCOP, AND YET FOR SOME REASON IT NEVER SEEMS TO HAPPEN. HOW MANY DECADES DOES THIS AWESOME, FAST-PACED MOVIE NEED TO WAIT FOR ITS AUDIENCE TO FINALLY SHOW UP? YOU CAN ONLY STAND THIS MOVIE UP FOR SO LONG, PEOPLE. PRETTY SOON IT'S GOING TO SIGH AND JUST SADLY GO HOME. THE PLOT IN A CAPSULE SENTENCE IS: AN ALIEN IN LOS ANGELES IS ON THE RUN AND KILLS EVERYONE (USING THEIR BODIES TO HOST ITSELF INSIDE) WHILE BEING CHASED BY THE UNLIKELY TEAM UP OF AN ALIEN AND A COP.

LITTLE DARLINGS (1980)
TWO 15-YEAR-OLD GIRLS (A RICH BITCH AND A TOMBOY FROM THE WRONG SIDE OF THE TRACKS) COMPETE AGAINST ONE ANOTHER TO SEE WHO CAN RACE TO LOSE THEIR VIRGINITY FIRST WHILE AT SUMMER CAMP. NO, I AM NOT A PERVY OLD MAN. THIS MOVIE RULES. OK, I'M A LITTLE BIT PERVY. OK, A LOT. (SHUT UP) TATUM O'NEAL AND KRISTY MCNICHOL STAR, AND MATT DILLON HAS A SUPPORTING ROLE. TRIVIA: MCNICHOL TOOK UP SMOKING AS PART OF PREPARING FOR HER LONER TOUGH GIRL ROLE (AND GOT TIPS FROM TATUM ON HOW TO DO IT) BUT THEN COULDN'T MANAGE TO QUIT AFTERWARDS. THAT'S DEDICATION TO YOUR CRAFT, RIGHT THERE. I HOPE BEING IN THIS MOVIE DOESN'T END UP KILLING HER.

MIRACLE MILE (1988)
THERE IS A TINY LITTLE LIST OF MOVIES THAT TAKE PLACE IN REAL TIME, AND AN EVEN SMALLER LIST OF THEM THAT ARE WORTH WATCHING TWICE. HERE IS ONE OF THEM, AND IT STARS ANTHONY EDWARDS AND MARE WINNINGHAM AS A YOUNG COUPLE MEETING AND FALLING IN LOVE ON THE DAY THAT THE WORLD ENDS. A BUMMER? YEAH, BUT STRESSING ABOUT NUCLEAR WAR WAS SOMETHING THAT REALLY COLOURED HOLLYWOOD PRODUCT IN THE MID TO LATE 1980S, AND THIS IS A PRETTY AWESOME EXAMPLE OF HOW TO DO IT RIGHT FOR THE BIG SCREEN.

NIGHT OF THE JUGGLER (1980)
BEEN SINGING THE PRAISES OF THIS UNDERAGE KIDNAPPING RACE-AGAINST-TIME EXPLOITATION MOVIE SHOT ON THE STREETS OF NEW YORK FOR YEARS, BUT IT SEEMS LIKE NO ONE BUT MY NEAREST AND DEAREST ARE LISTENING. CONSIDER THIS YET ANOTHER VOTE OF CONFIDENCE, AND YET ANOTHER REQUEST FOR A DVD/BLU RELEASE. I'LL KEEP YAPPING ABOUT IT UNTIL SOMEONE STARTS LISTENING. AGAIN, THE LESS YOU

KNOW GOING IN, THE MORE YOU'LL LOVE IT. FIND THE VHS OR A BOOTLEG OF IT, ASAP.

SONNY BOY (1989)
HOLY PUDDING, THIS IS AN ODD ONE. IT ALSO MIGHT BE THE MOST UNFORGETTABLE MOVIE ON THIS LIST. IT JUST CURLS UP ON YOUR CHEST, AND TAKES A NAP THERE — ALL HEAVY, AND LINGERING. DAVID CARRADINE IS BALLSY AS FUCK IN THIS. YOU KNOW HOW SOMETIMES YOU JUST CAN'T BELIEVE HOW BRAVE AN ACTOR IS IN A ROLE, TO THE POINT WHERE IT ALMOST STOPS BEING BRAVERY AND COMES OFF AS STUPIDITY? THAT'S WHAT'S GOING ON HERE. THERE IS NOTHING OUT THERE QUITE LIKE SONNY BOY, A MOVIE LEONARD MALTIN SAID WAS "A REPULSIVE, SOCIALLY IRREDEEMABLE WASTE OF CELLULOID .... FILMED FOR NO APPARENT REASON OTHER TO OFFEND AND APPALL." YES, PLEASE!

STREET SMART (1987)
BY RIGHTS THIS MOVIE SHOULD HAVE A CRITERION EDITION RELEASE, BE A STAPLE AT REP THEATERS, AND BE ONE OF THOSE MOVIES THAT PEOPLE ALWAYS HAVE TO RE-BUY BECAUSE THEY KEEP LOANING OUT THEIR COPY. BUT NOPE, NUTTIN'. VERY FEW CRITICAL ACCOLADES. SURE, THIS JERRY SCHATZBERG MOVIE THAT INTRODUCED MORGAN FREEMAN TO MOVIEGOERS AS A BRUTAL GUTTER-PIMP GOT A FEW NODS FROM CRITICS AT THE TIME, BUT THEN IT WAS PROMPTLY FORGOTTEN. DOWNTOWN MONTREAL SUBSTITUTES AS 42ND STREET IN NEW YORK, BUT THE EDITING IS SO SKILFUL, YOU WOULD NEVER HAVE KNOWN IF I HADN'T TOLD YOU.

STREETS OF FIRE (1984)
EVERYONE REMEMBERS AND LOVES THE WARRIORS AND 48 HRS, BUT FOR SOME REASON THIS EQUALLY AS ENTERTAINING FILM FROM AROUND THE SAME TIME, AND FROM THE SAME DIRECTOR (WALTER HILL) GETS CRUELLY PASSED BY WHEN THE FANS ARE GUSHING. IT'S A BROADLY SYMBOLIC MASH UP OF 1950S AND 1980S AESTHETICS (AS WAS POPULAR AT THE TIME — THE 'STRAY CATS' ANYONE?), AND FEATURES THE BEST SET DESIGN OF ANY FILM ON THIS LIST. DIANE LANE AND WILLEM DAFOE FANS WILL ESPECIALLY ADORE IT, AS THEY ARE BOTH AT THEIR BEST HERE. THANK YOU TO KIER-LA FOR SHOWING IT TO ME.

A SAVAGE HUNGER (AKA THE OASIS. 1984)
A PLANE CRASH IN THE MEXICAN DESERT PITS A GROUP OF HUNGRY, THIRSTY SURVIVORS AGAINST EACH OTHER IN A MORAL SPIRAL AND A DESPERATE BID FOR SURVIVAL. THIS DELIBERATELY SLOW-PACED SPARKY GREENE MOVIE IS THE EPITOME OF UNDERRATED. IN FACT, I DON'T THINK I'VE EVER MET ANYONE WHO HAS EVEN HEARD OF IT, MUCH LESS SEEN IT. OVERALL IT'S SORT OF LIKE THAT 1993 DISNEY MOVIE, ALIVE, IF IT WAS 10X MORE VIOLENT, DISTURBING, DOWNBEAT, AND UNREPENTANT ABOUT TOSSING PRETTY MUCH EVERY IMAGINABLE SOCIAL TABOO INTO THE MIX.

16-YEAR-OLD ROBIN JOHNSON STARS IN 1980'S TIMES SQUARE.

TEACHERS (1984)
MOST OF THE 1980S TEEN HIGH SCHOOL MOVIES AREN'T UNDERRATED WHATSOEVER. THE BREAKFAST CLUB AND HEATHERS, AND VARIOUS OTHER ENTRIES TO THE GENRE HAVE A LOYAL CULT FOLLOWING, BUT TEACHERS IS A DRAMEDY THAT GOT LEFT BEHIND SOMEHOW DESPITE BEING A SOLID RENTER IN THE OLD VIDEO STORE DAYS OF THE LATE 1980S. HOPEFULLY THIS ACTS AS A REMINDER FOR YOU TO SEARCH IT OUT, ESPECIALLY IF YOU SAW IT BACK THEN AND HAD FORGOTTEN HOW GOOD IT WAS. NICK NOLTE IS PERFECTLY CAST AS THE BURNT OUT TEACHER, AND A YOUNG LAURA DERN TURNS IN ONE OF HER BEST PERFORMANCES AS THE SCHOOL SLUT.

TIMES SQUARE (1980)
RIGHT FROM THAT BRILLIANT OPENING SCENE WITH ROXY MUSIC'S "SAME OLD SCENE" PROVIDING THE SCORE, YOU KNOW THIS ISN'T YOUR USUAL FILM. THIS STREET-LEVEL SHOT-ON-LOCATION NEW WAVE ROCK FANTASY FEATURES TWO RUNAWAY TEEN GIRLS, A LATE NIGHT DISC JOCKEY (TIM CURRY) AND THE SLEAZY UNDERBELLY OF 1990S TIMES SQUARE. ROGER EBERT CALLED IT A "BAD MOVIE" AND A "MISSED OPPORTUNITY", SO YOU KNOW IT'S WORTH CHECKING OUT. FOR QUITE A WHILE THE SOUNDTRACK LP FOR THIS WAS THE ONLY AVAILABLE RECORDING OF THE RAMONES' "I WANNA BE SEDATED".

WANTED: DEAD OR ALIVE (1986)
HEY, ANOTHER RUTGER HAUER ENTRY FOR THIS TOP 20 LIST! ONE TOO MANY, MAYBE? HELL NO, MOTHERFUCKERS! BITE YOUR TONGUES! IN FACT, OL' RUTGER ALMOST HAD ANOTHER ONE WITH 1981'S NIGHTHAWKS, WHICH WAS THE RUNNER-UP TITLE THAT NEARLY MADE IT. W.D.O.A IS PURE GRINDHOUSE BRILLIANCE, THOUGH. IF YOU'VE EVER WANTED TO STUFF A GRENADE IN GENE SIMMONS'S MOUTH AND THEN PULL THE PIN (FUCK, WHO HASN'T?), THEN THIS IS YOUR MOVIE.

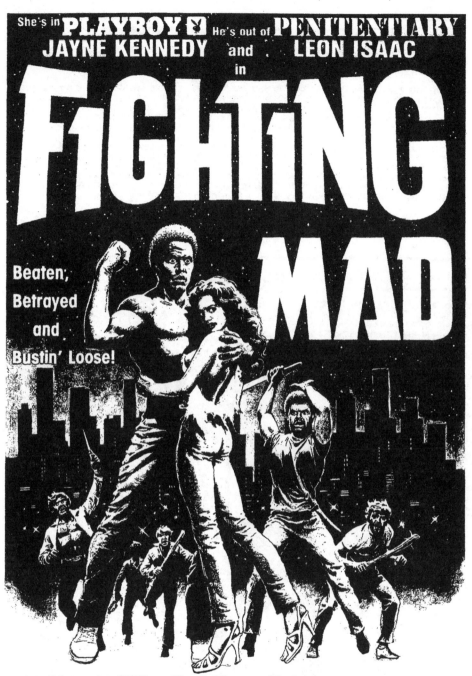

She's in **PLAYBOY** He's out of **PENITENTIARY**

JAYNE KENNEDY and **LEON ISAAC**

in

F1GHTiNG MAD

Beaten,
Betrayed
and
Bustin' Loose!

IN AN EPISODE OF DIFF'RENT STROKES FROM THE 1983 SEASON, ARNOLD HAD A CRUSH ON HIS SMOKING HOT TEACHER AND DISCOVERED SHE WAS MOONLIGHTING AS A PLAYBOY BUNNY-ESQUE WAITRESS IN A SCUMMY TITTY BAR. THAT TEACHER WAS PLAYED BY A LOVELY LADY WHO WAS CONSIDERED AT THE TIME, ONE OF THE MOST BEAUTIFUL WOMEN IN THE WORLD -- JAYNE KENNEDY.

JAYNE WAS A MODEL WHO HAD HER FACE INSURED FOR ONE MILLION DOLLARS, WAS THE FIRST BLACK WOMAN TO APPEAR ON THE COVER OF PLAYBOY, NEARLY BECAME ONE OF CHARLIE'S ANGELS, AND IN 1980 HAD THE DUBIOUS HONOUR OF BEING THE FIRST CELEBRITY TO ENDURE A HOME SEX VIDEO SCANDAL. AT THAT POINT VCRS WERE NOT YET A HOUSEHOLD ITEM AND CIRCULATION OF THE FUCK FOOTAGE WAS RESTRICTED TO A SMALL AUDIENCE OF PERVS, BUT IT IS CLEAR THAT CRAFTY DIFF'RENT STROKES SCREENWRITER JACK GROSS JR. WAS DIRECTLY REFERENCING JAYNE'S SCANDAL BY HAVING ARNOLD DISCOVER HER SHOCKING DIRTY SECRET.

UNLIKE THE REACTION TO PARIS HILTON AND PAMELA ANDERSON'S XXX VIDEOS, JAYNE'S USHERED A MASSIVE FALL FROM GRACE THAT EVENTUALLY KILLED HER PROMISING CAREER. A COUPLE OF YEARS EARLIER KENNEDY CO-STARRED WITH HER SEX-FOOTAGE CO-STAR AND

HUSBAND OF THE TIME, LEON ISAAC IN CIRIO SANTIAGO'S *FIGHTING MAD* (AKA *DEATH FORCE*). LEON WAS A PRETTY INTERESTING CAT, TOO ACTUALLY. HE CAME UP AS A POPULAR DJ (HE'D WORKED IN THREE CITIES AS A DISC JOCKEY BEFORE HE WAS EVEN SEVENTEEN) AND ENDED UP AS AN ACTION MOVIE STAR BEST KNOWN FOR HIS STARRING ROLES IN THE EXCITING *PENITENTIARY* MOVIES.

ONE OF THE MANY BLAXPLOITATION-THEMED MOVIES SET IN THE PHILIPPINES THAT CIRIO SANTIAGO MADE IN THE '70S (HE ALSO DID *THE MUTHERS* WITH JAYNE IN 1976), *FIGHTING MAD* HAD A PRETTY GODDAMN IMAGINATIVE CONCEPT. THREE SOLDIERS PLAYED BY JAMES IGLEHART, LEON ISAAC AND CARMEN ARGENZIANO RETURN FROM VIETNAM WITH A HAUL OF SMUGGLED GOLD, BUT LEON AND CARMEN GET THE IDEA TO SLIT THEIR BUDDY'S THROAT AND TOSS HIM OVERBOARD SO THEY CAN GO HOME AND FUCK HIS HOT WIFE (JAYNE) AND USE THE GOLD TO BUILD A CRIMINAL EMPIRE. NEAR DEATH, IGLEHART WASHES ASHORE A DESERTED ISLAND AND IS NURSED BACK TO HEALTH BY TWO NUTTY JAPANESE WWII SOLDIERS WHO DON'T REALISE THE WAR IS OVER. THEY TEACH JAMES HOW TO BE A RAD SAMURAI ASS-KICKER AND NEEDLESS TO SAY, HE RETURNS HOME AND CLEANS MUTHERFUCKIN HOUSE, YA'LL. I'M TALKING DECAPITATIONS WITH JUICY SQUIRTING NECK STUMPS AND TENDERIZED ASSHOLES. JUST LIKE <u>MAMA</u> USED TO MAKE.

ANYWAY, JAZZY MISS JAYNE KENNEDY, BOOTY-CRUSHING MR. LEON ISAAC, FUNKY AFROS AND FREAKY '70S FASHIONS, AND A DECENT MUSIC SCORE MAKE THIS A VERY COOL SEVENTIES REVENGE MOVIE -- AND ONE OF CIRIO SANTIAGO'S BEST EFFORTS. CHECK IT OUT!

-BOUGIE '12

MEGAFORCE (1982)

REMEMBER AMERICA IN 1982? SURE YOU DO. THE REAGAN ERA. THE GREED IS GOOD GENERATION. A TIME WHEN ENTERTAINMENT FOR YOUNG MEN MEANT ACTION-PACKED DEPICTIONS OF CLANDESTINE WISECRACKING MILITARY SHIT KICKERS USING HIGH-TECH EQUIPMENT TO CIRCUMVENT OLIVE-SKINNED FORCES OF GLOBAL TERROR. I'M TALKING ABOUT THE A-TEAM, AIRWOLF, BLUE THUNDER, FIREFOX AND <u>MEGAFORCE</u>.

MEGAFORCE WAS SUPPOSED TO BE A BLOCKBUSTER. FOR MONTHS BEFORE IT WAS RELEASED THE MOVIE WAS PROMOTED IN A MARKETING BLITZ SO OVERWHELMING, IT'S EASY TO FIND COPIOUS EVIDENCE OF IT SITTING AROUND COMIC SHOPS TO THIS DAY -- 30 YEARS LATER. THIS INCLUDED WIDESPREAD RADIO AND TV ADS, AN ATARI 2600 VIDEO GAME, MEGAFORCE HOT WHEELS VEHICLES, A FAN CLUB, AND THOSE LEGENDARY "DEEDS NOT WORDS" ADS THAT DECORATED THE BACK COVER OF ALMOST EVERY MARVEL COMIC BOOK FOR THE BETTER PART OF A SUMMER.

THIS FILM WASN'T DIRECTED, IT WAS LAUNCHED LIKE A ROASTED TURKEY OUT OF A CANNON. THE MAN RESPONSIBLE WAS STUNTMAN-TURNED -FILMMAKER HAL NEEDHAM, AN INTERESTING FELLOW BEST KNOWN FOR HELMING THE VERY FONDLY-REMEMBERED CANNONBALL RUN, SMOKEY AND THE BANDIT,

ART BY BEN NEWMAN: BENNEWMANART.BLOGSPOT.COM

BN11

156

AND **RAD: THE MOVIE**) AND FEATURED A "PHANTOM ARMY OF SUPER ELITE FIGHTING MEN WHOSE WEAPONS ARE THE MOST POWERFUL SCIENCE CAN DEVISE".

THE DEVISED WEAPONS IN QUESTION WERE TRICKED OUT COMBAT VEHICLES PAINTED BROWN, ORANGE AND TAN -- SUCH AS A FLYING JET-POWERED MOTORCYCLE CALLED THE "DELTA MK 4 MEGAFIGHTER". THE MEGAFIGHTERS FARTED BRIGHTLY COLOURED SMOKE AND WERE EQUIPPED WITH GUIDED MISSILES (ACTUALLY MODEL ROCKETS MANUFACTURED BY A COMPANY IN RAYTOWN, MISSOURI). OH, AND THEN THERE WERE DUNE BUGGIES CALLED "MEGACRUISERS" ARMED WITH LASERS THAT COULD (AND WOULD) DESTROY TANKS WITH A SINGLE BLAST. PURE RADNESS.

THE MISSION WAS LAID OUT AS "PRESERVING FREEDOM AND JUSTICE AND BATTLING THE FORCES OF TYRANNY AND EVIL IN EVERY CORNER OF THE GLOBE". TO DO THIS, THE MAYOR FROM **SPIN CITY** AND THE BALD ALIEN CHICK FROM **STAR TREK THE MOTION PICTURE** TEAM UP IN THE NEVADA DESERT WITH THE LEADER OF THE **WARRIORS**, MICHAEL BECK. THEIR ENEMY? HENRY SILVA, WHO ELSE?

THE SPIN CITY MAYOR (AKA BARRY BOSTWICK) IS NAMED ACE HUNTER AND HE PLACES HIS HANDS ON HIS HIPS A LOT WHILE SPORTING AN EMBARRASSING OUTFIT IN WHICH TO PRESERVE FREEDOM AND JUSTICE. AS JAMES ROLFE (BETTER KNOWN AS THE ANGRY VIDEOGAME NERD) WOULD SNARK: "WHAT A SCHMUCK. HE WEARS A BLUE HEADBAND AND THE MOST SKINTIGHT OUTFIT I EVER SAW. MAN, THAT OUTFIT IS TIGHTER THAN A CHIPMUNK'S ASSHOLE STRETCHED OVER A SODA CAN." WHAT ROLFE NEGLECTS TO POINT OUT IS THAT THE SKINTIGHT OUTFIT IS ALSO SKIN TONED. THIS MEANS ACE IS PARADING AROUND A STATE OF THE ART MILITARY BASE CONSTANTLY LOOKING LIKE HE'S JUST GOTTEN OUT OF THE SHOWER AND IS ABOUT TO FUCK YOU IN THE MOUTH.

THE ON-SCREEN ROMANCE BETWEEN ACE AND THE BALD ALIEN CHICK FROM STAR TREK (BETTER KNOWN AS PERSIS KHAMBATTA) DRIES UP VAGINAS AND WILTS PECKERS LIKE FEW IN FILM HISTORY. WATCH AS THEY KISS... THEIR THUMBS? THAT'S RIGHT, THEY SMOOCH THE FUCK OUT OF THOSE SEXY THUMBS OF THEIRS. THEN THEY RAISE THEM AT EACH OTHER. IF THAT WASN'T HOT AND STICKY ENOUGH, WAIT UNTIL YOU WITNESS THEIR LITERALLY UNBELIEVABLE SKYDIVING SEQUENCE FILMED IN "INTRA-VISION". AY-YI-YI.

IF THE MOVIE REMINDS YOU OF TREY PARKER AND MATT STONE'S **TEAM AMERICA: WORLD POLICE**, YOU'RE DEFTLY PICKING UP ON WHAT THEY'RE LAYING DOWN. THE **SOUTH PARK**/BOOK OF MORMON CREATORS ARE HUGE FANS, AND INTENDED FOR THEIR PUPPET-PACKED SPOOF

THE NEW MAYHEM AND MADNESS MOVIE FROM THE DIRECTOR OF SMOKEY & THE BANDIT AND CANNONBALL RUN

MEGAFORCE

OF PATRIOTISM TO SERVE AS AN ODE TO ONE OF THEIR FAVOURITE MOVIES. ORIGINALLY (AS REVEALED IN A MAY 2000 INTERVIEW IN MEAN MAGAZINE) THE PLAN WAS TO BUY THE RIGHTS TO NEEDHAM'S FILM, HIRE WEEN TO SCORE THE SOUNDTRACK, AND "DO MEGAFORCE II, LIKE 20 YEARS LATER." AT THE TIME OF MEGAFORCE'S RELEASE A SEQUEL TITLED 'DEEDS NOT WORDS' WAS ALSO PLANNED, BUT WAS QUICKLY SCRAPPED WHEN THE MOVIE TANKED.

SURE IT WAS A GIANT FLOP AND WAS NOMINATED FOR THREE RAZZIE AWARDS (WORST PICTURE, WORST DIRECTOR AND WORST SUPPORTING ACTOR: MICHAEL BECK) BUT THIS GLORIOUS WRECK IS THE CLOSEST THING TO A THEATRICAL REPRESENTATION OF THE IMPROVISED FANTASY STORYLINES PLAYING OUT IN EVERY 8-YEAR-OLD BOY'S HEAD AS HE NOODLES AROUND IN THE SAND BOX WITH HIS HOT WHEELS AND HIS ACTION FIGURES.

BOUGIE 2012

KISS MY **THUMB** IF YOU DON'T ♡ MEGA FORCE!

MEMORIES OF OCTOBER SILK

☆ BY DAVE KOSANKE ☆

BACK IN 1983, JUST AS I WAS ABOUT TO ENTER THE TEENAGE WASTELAND, A NEW PIECE OF TECHNOLOGY INFILTRATED OUR HOUSEHOLD... THE VCR. AND WITH THE ARRIVAL OF THAT MIGHTY TOP LOADING MACHINE CAME A LONE UNMARKED TAPE WHICH IMMEDIATELY PERKED MY CURIOSITY. DESPITE APPEARANCES, THE TAPE WASN'T BLANK, THOUGH. IT FEATURED FOUR MOVIES THAT WOULD BECOME MY INTRODUCTION TO THE WORLD OF PORNOGRAPY.

THE FILMS WERE (IN ORDER OF THEIR APPEARANCE) OCTOBER SILK (1980), VISTA VALLEY P.T.A (1980), AUTOBIOGRAPHY OF A FLEA (1976), AND DEBBIE DOES DALLAS (1978).

MY DAD HAD PROCURED THIS TAPE FROM A BUDDY AND HAD TRIED HARD TO HIDE IT FROM ME. I WASN'T SO EASILY FOOLED HOWEVER, AND BEFORE LONG THE SMUTTY FILMS WERE UNSPOOLING BEFORE MY UNDERAGE EYES. OCTOBER SILK WAS THE ONE I BECAME MOST OBSESSED WITH, SIMPLY BECAUSE IT WAS THE FIRST FEATURE ON THE TAPE. IT'S GOT A LOT OF MEMORABLE ELEMENTS, BUT THE SCENE THAT REALLY DID ME IN HAPPENS RIGHT AFTER THE OPENING CREDITS ROLL. A WOMAN WALKS INTO HER BEDROOM WHERE A DUDE IS SLEEPING AWAY. SHE SAYS: "C'MON LOVER, I'VE GOT TO GO TO WORK! WHAT'S HIS NAME, ANYWAY? SHIT!" SHE FINALLY GETS HIM TO RISE FROM HIS SLUMBER BY ASKING, "YOU WANT SOME HOT COFFEE?", TO WHICH HE REPLIES "NO, I WANT SOME HOT PUSSY!"

SENSING HE WON'T TAKE NO FOR AN ANSWER, SHE QUIPS "I'M NOT GOING TO GET UNDRESSED. JUST A QUICK BLOWJOB AND WE'LL BE OFF... OKAY?" FROM THAT MOMENT ON SHE BEGINS TO SUCK ON HIS SAUSAGE WHILE DUBBED-IN SOUND EFFECTS BLURT OUT (IT ALWAYS SOUNDED LIKE SOMEONE SUCKING ON A LEMON TO ME). AS THE SCENE REACHED ITS CLIMAX I BECAME AWARE OF SOMETHING: THAT I WAS GETTING READY TO REACH MY OWN CLIMAX! I KNEW WHAT WAS HAPPENING, BUT IT WAS STILL SORT OF SCARY AT THE SAME TIME. THE YOUNG DAVE KOSANKE WAS GETTING A QUICK EDUCATION ON MASTURBATION.

ANOTHER SCENE FEATURES AN OLD DUDE INSTRUCTING TWO TEENAGE GIRLS ON THE ART OF STIMULATING HIS COCK AND BALLS. OBVIOUSLY I DIDN'T HAVE A WOMAN AROUND TO PRACTICE WITH, SO I HAD TO MAKE DO WITH MYSELF -- AND BEFORE LONG IT BECAME A HABIT. THAT LONE TAPE WOULD BE IN THE MACHINE EVERY TIME MY PARENTS LEFT ME BY MYSELF FOR ANY PERIOD OF TIME, AND THE FACT THAT I HAD TO SNEAK AROUND WAS CERTAINLY PART OF THE THRILL. THIS EXPERIENCE WAS NOT JUST EXCLUSIVE TO MY HOUSE, THOUGH. NEARLY ALL OF MY BUDDIES IN THE NEIGHBORHOOD DID THE

SCANTILY CLAD

Revealing
Abigail Clayton
Candida Royalle
Lisa Deleeuw
Gloria Leonard
Samantha Fox
Arcadia Lake
Merle Michaels
Christine de Shaffer
Christie Ford
Tara Smith

SAME THING, AND BEFORE YOU KNEW IT WE WERE SOON HAVING OUR OWN PORNO PARTIES!

OCTOBER SILK (WHICH WAS WRITTEN AND DIRECTED BY LEGENDARY PORN DIRECTOR HENRI PACHARD, I FOUND OUT LATER) ALSO INTRODUCED ME TO THE CONCEPT OF THE PORNO STAR. I KNEW NOTHING ABOUT ANY OF THE PERFORMERS ON THE SCREEN BUT AFTER A FEW VIEWINGS THE TRAILERS NESTLED IN BETWEEN THE FEATURES GAVE ME A FEW CLUES THAT SOME OF THESE WOMEN WERE SUPERSTARS IN THEIR GENRE. I FOUND OUT THAT SAMANTHA FOX WAS THE GIRL FROM THE OPENING SEGMENT, THAT LISA DE LEEUW WAS THE ONE WHO LEZZES OUT WITH ARCADIA LAKE WHILE WEARING A NECK BRACE, AND I ALSO DISCOVERED THE WONDERS OF CANDIDA ROYALE. BEFORE LONG THEY BECAME MY IDOLS!

DAVE KOSANKE

HA!

DESPITE THE FACT THAT THERE WERE THREE OTHER FILMS ON THAT OLD UNMARKED TAPE, I WOULD ALWAYS RETURN TO OCTOBER SILK IN PARTICULAR. IT'S HARD TO LET GO OF THAT "FIRST TIME", IF YOU KNOW WHAT I MEAN. WHETHER OR NOT MY DAD KNEW ABOUT MY SHENANIGANS WITH HIS PORN TAPE I'LL NEVER KNOW. BEFORE LONG THE CASSETTE WAS MYSTERIOUSLY GONE BUT BY THEN I WAS BUYING MY OWN TAPES! BECOMING A PORNOHOLIC WASN'T SOMETHING THAT I PLANNED, IT JUST HAPPENED, AND THOSE FOND MEMORIES FROM 1983 WILL STAY WITH ME FOREVER.

DAVE KOSANKE IS THE CREATOR OF THE MOVIE ZINE 'LIQUID CHEESE', AND THE VINTAGE PORN ZINE KNOWN AS 'TOSS'.

Savage Streets (1984. USA)

TOM HODGE (AKA "DUDE DESIGNS") IS THE OUTRAGEOUSLY TALENTED BRITISH ILLUSTRATOR WHO DID THE HOBO WITH A SHOTGUN POSTER, AMONG OTHER CULT FILM ONE-SHEETS AND DVD RELEASES. HE ALSO DID THE COVER FOR THE 2011 UK ARROW DVD RELEASE OF THE SWEET 1984 LINDA BLAIR EXPLOITATION FILM, SAVAGE STREETS -- ONE OF MY FAVE DVD COVERS OF ALL TIME. IT'S ACTUALLY NOT THE COVER I'VE REPRODUCED HERE (WHICH IS THE VHS COVER FROM BACK

IN THE DAY) BECAUSE I DIDN'T LIKE THE WAY TOM'S COVER REPRODUCED IN BLACK AND WHITE, SO DO YOURSELF A FAVOUR AND LOOK IT UP ON YOUR OWN WHILE I ASK TOM ABOUT THE MAKING OF HIS ART:

"SAVAGE STREETS IS *THE* QUINTESSENTIAL '80S STYLE VHS VIGILANTE FILM", HODGE TOLD ME VIA E-MAIL. "IT COMES COMPLETE WITH A PUNK GANG AND SEXY GIRLS. BECAUSE OF THAT, I WANTED TO GO ALL OUT AND DO A REALLY STYLIZED VIDEO COVER. I HADN'T BROUGHT IN MUCH SEXUALITY INTO MY WORK UP TO THAT POINT, BUT THIS JOB DEMANDED IT. THE ENDING OF THE MOVIE IS BRILLIANT. LINDA BLAIR IS OFF ON THIS ANGRY VIGILANTE KILLING SPREE, BUT FIRST DOES THE MAKE UP, PUTS THE EARRINGS IN, AND GETS INTO THE BLACK JUMP SUIT. I'M NOT SURE ABOUT HER MOTIVATION BEHIND ALL THIS, BUT IT SAYS A LOT ABOUT THE FILM. I THINK YOU HAVE TO BE QUITE THEATRICAL IN YOUR DESIGN APPROACH FOR THIS KIND OF PROJECT, AND GO TOTALLY OVER THE TOP WITH ELEMENTS LIKE GUNS, BOOBS, FLAMES, AND BLOOD."

THE PERILS OF GWENDOLINE
IN THE LAND OF THE
YIK YAK
AKA: "GWENDOLINE"
· FRANCE · 1984 ·

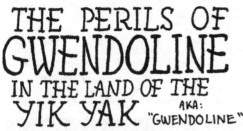

PROBABLY MORE FAMOUS FOR HER TWO SULTRY APPEARANCES IN WHITESNAKE MUSIC VIDEOS, HERE TAWNY KITAEN PLAYS THE VIRGINAL GWENDOLINE -- A YOUNG WOMAN WHO TRAVERSES THE GLOBE WITH HER MAID/VALET/CONFIDANT, BETH. BETH IS PORTRAYED BY STRIKING FRENCH MODEL/ACTRESS/DIRECTOR ZABOU BREITMAN, AND LIKE MISS KITAEN, SHE'S NEVER LOOKED MORE STUNNING THAN SHE DOES IN JUST JAECKIN'S "GWENDOLINE".

FRENCH ACTRESS ZABOU BREITMAN PLAYS BETH

IN A QUEST TO FIND GWENDOLINE'S MISSING POPS, THE TWO YOUNG WOMEN NAVIGATE DANGEROUS SHANGHAI-STYLE SEAPORT TOWNS OF A QUASI-1940s ORIENT, AND IT IS HERE THAT WE BEGIN OUR EXOTIC PULPY TALE WHEN THE TITULAR HEROINE FALLS INTO THE FILTHY HANDS OF WHITE SLAVE TRADERS. AT FIRST GLANCE THE TIMELINE AND LOCATIONS MAY SEEM DERIVATIVE OF OTHER CLIFF HANGER SERIAL-INSPIRED HIGH ADVENTURE FILMS OF THE 1980s, SUCH AS **INDIANA JONES AND THE TEMPLE OF DOOM** AND **KING SOLOMON'S MINES**, BUT THE FACT IS THAT GWENDOLINE BEAT BOTH OF THEM TO THEATERS BY A MATTER OF MONTHS.

JUST BEFORE A BOUND AND GAGGED GWENDOLINE AND BETH ARE TO BE SOLD INTO SLAVERY, AN AWESOME CINEMATIC ENTRANCE TAKES PLACE. A SWASHBUCKLING GAMBLER/SMUGGLER CHUCKS A GRAPPLING HOOK THROUGH THE BALSA WOOD BLINDS OF THE CRIME-LORD'S GAMBLING DEN AND INTO THE LEAD SCUMBAG'S SWEATY THROAT. OUR HERO

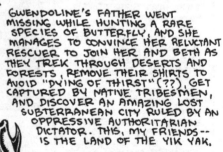

(BRENT HUFF AS "WILLARD") THEN PROCEEDS TO USE THE LINE TO SWING INTO THE ROOM, MUCH TO THE GORY DISPLEASURE OF SAID VILLAIN. BOGEY SURE AS HELL NEVER PULLED THAT MOVE IN **THE AFRICAN QUEEN**. HE ALSO NEVER GOT AROUND TO PULLING A MAN'S HEAD THROUGH A SET OF JAIL CELL BARS, LEAVING THE POOR BASTARD'S EARS BEHIND.

GWENDOLINE'S FATHER WENT MISSING WHILE HUNTING A RARE SPECIES OF BUTTERFLY, AND SHE MANAGES TO CONVINCE HER RELUCTANT RESCUER TO JOIN HER AND BETH AS THEY TREK THROUGH DESERTS AND FORESTS, REMOVE THEIR SHIRTS TO AVOID "DYING OF THIRST" (??), GET CAPTURED BY NATIVE TRIBESMEN, AND DISCOVER AN AMAZING LOST SUBTERRANEAN CITY RULED BY AN OPPRESSIVE AUTHORITARIAN DICTATOR. THIS, MY FRIENDS -- IS THE LAND OF THE YIK YAK.

THIS THIRD ACT IS WHERE THIS MOVIE REALLY SHINES, AS THE LAND OF THE YIK YAK IS REVEALED TO BE A MOSTLY NAKED FEMALE-DOMINATED ART DECO EMPIRE WHERE LEATHER-CLAD PONY GIRLS CLASH IN **BEN HUR** CHARIOT RACES! THIS WILD TURN OF EVENTS FINDS WILLARD CONFINED AS A FORCED SPERM DONOR AND GWENDOLINE AS A FETISHY GLADIATOR IN A SAVAGE BATTLE TO THE DEATH. THESE LAVISH SETS AND COSTUMES ARE FOISTED UPON THE

160

...VIEWER AS THE ADVENTURE AT HAND BECOMES MORE OUTRAGEOUS AND THE GENRE DISPLAYED BECOMES HARDER TO PIGEONHOLE. ACTION-ADVENTURE? EROTICA? COMEDY? CAMP? SHIT, IT'S ALL FOUR AND MORE!

THE MOVIE IS BASED QUITE LOOSELY ON THE UNDERGROUND COMIC BOOK "SWEET GWENDOLINE", CREATED AND ILLUSTRATED BY BONDAGE PHOTOGRAPHER JOHN WILLIE (AKA JOHN COUTTS), AND PUBLISHED BY NOTORIOUS NEW YORK FETISH PIONEER IRVING KLAW, WHO MADE BETTIE PAGE FAMOUS. THE COMIC SERIAL OF SWEET GWENDOLINE ORIGINALLY RAN IN WINK MAGAZINE FROM JUNE 1947 THROUGH FEBRUARY 1950 AND ENDED ABRUPTLY, UNFINISHED.

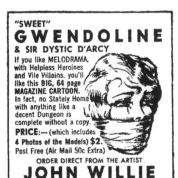

BRENT HUFF AND TAWNY KITAEN AS WILLARD AND GWENDOLINE

DESPITE BEING QUITE OBSCURE TO THOSE NOT CONCERNED WITH THE HISTORY OF PULP ART, WILLIE IS

Sweet Gwendoline.

Ah! who will save her!

JOHN WILLIE ILLUSTRATES THE FIRST APPEARANCE OF HIS CHARACTER IN THE PAGES OF BIZARRE #2, FROM JAN. 1946

CONSIDERED TODAY TO BE THE FATHER OF MODERN FETISHISM, AND WAS BORN INTO AN UPPER CLASS FAMILY IN 1902. HIS DRAWINGS AND PHOTOS WOULD CHIEFLY INSPIRE ARTISTS LIKE ERIC STANTON, DOLCETT, AND A WHOLE GENERATION OF PORNOGRAPHIC CARTOONISTS AND ILLUSTRATORS.

WILLIE MARRIED HOLLY FARAM (A MODEL AND MUSE), AND IS CITED AS THE FIRST FETISH ARTIST WHO WORKED ONLY FROM POSED SUBJECTS OR PHOTOS HE TOOK HIMSELF. UPON ENTERING HIS LOS ANGELES APARTMENT, A LARGE BLACK AND WHITE PHOTO OF A NUDE WOMAN BOUND TO A TREE WAS THE FIRST THING GUESTS WOULD SEE. "OH" WILLIE WOULD SAY WITH A SMILE, "THAT'S THE MISSUS."

ANOTHER ONE OF WILLIE'S BONDAGE MODELS WAS A LOVELY BLONDE 19-YEAR-OLD NAMED JUDY ANN DULL. SHE WAS QUITE COMFORTABLE POSING FOR WILLIE, BUT NOT SO MUCH FOR ANOTHER LOCAL BIG-EARED PERVERT NAMED HARVEY GLATMAN. HARVEY MADE HIS LIVING AS A TV REPAIRMAN, AND IN 1957 OFFERED JUDY THE HEFTY SUM OF $40 TO JOIN HIM AT HIS STUDIO AND POSE FOR SOME BOUND AND GAGGED WANK PHOTOS.

INSTEAD OF LOOSENING HER BONDS WHEN THE SHOOT WAS DONE, GLATMAN RAPED AND SODOMISED DULL, DROVE HER OUT TO THE DESERT, SHOT A FEW MORE DISTURBING CANDIDS OF THE SOBBING CO-ED CLAD ONLY IN HER PANTIES, AND THEN STRANGLED HER TO DEATH. TO FINISH, HE BURIED HER UNCEREMONIOUSLY IN A SHALLOW GRAVE.

GLATMAN QUITE ENJOYED THIS ENTIRE SICK EXPERIENCE, AND REPEATED IT WITH A BLIND DATE NAMED SHIRLEY BRIDGEFORD, A STRIPPER NAMED RUTH MERCADO, AND THEN CONTINUED TO LOOK FOR INNOCENT VICTIMS BY AVIDLY SEARCHING FOR MODEL ADS IN LOCAL NEWSPAPERS.

LORRAINE VIGIL WAS YET ANOTHER ONE OF

JOHN WILLIE'S MODELS, AND MAY WELL HAVE BEEN THE FOURTH FEMALE TO BECOME A VIOLATED CORPSE BY HARVEY GLATMAN'S HAND HAD SHE NOT BEEN SUCH A FUCKING BAD ASS.

THIS TIME GLATMAN CHANGED THINGS UP BY SHOOTING HIS VICTIM WITH A GUN TO GET THE BALL ROLLING ON HIS PLANNED EVENING OF DEMENTED PREDATORY ACTION, BUT HE ONLY SUCCEEDED IN WOUNDING LORRAINE'S LEG. NOW SHE WAS PISSED OFF. VIGIL FURIOUSLY SNATCHED THE GUN OUT OF GLATMAN'S HAND, AND HELD HIM CAPTIVE UNTIL A COP CAR HAPPENED BY. L.A. TIMES REPORTERS WOULD MARVEL AT HER RESOLUTE GRACE UNDER PRESSURE.

GLATMAN WAS EXECUTED A YEAR LATER IN THE GAS CHAMBER IN SAN QUENTIN, AND JOHN WILLIE WAS RELIEVED AS ANYONE THAT THE BOYS IN BLUE FINALLY NABBED THE MADMAN. IN THE YEAR THAT GLATMAN HAD BEEN HAPPILY RAPING AND MURDERING ROPED-UP MAIDENS, WILLIE HAD BEEN UNDER SCRUTINY AS ONE OF THE FOREMOST SUSPECTS IN THE CASE. THAT THE KILLER HAD HORRIFICALLY OFFED ONE OF HIS FAVOURITE MODELS SENT HIM INTO A DEEP DARK ALCOHOLIC DEPRESSION, AND IT IS SAID THAT JOHN FELT DIRECTLY RESPONSIBLE FOR INSPIRING THE L.A. FETISH COMMUNITY KILLING SPREE WITH HIS LURID COMICS AND MAGAZINES.

JOHN WILLIE SUBSEQUENTLY LOST ALL INTEREST IN HIS ART FORM, THREW HIS ART IN THE GARBAGE, CLOSED UP HIS SUCCESSFUL MAIL ORDER BUSINESS, AND PASSED AWAY DUE TO A BRAIN TUMOUR IN 1962. HE DIED ALONE AND PENNILESS.

Times Telephone Numbers
• MAdison 6-2345 for subscriber service calls and all other calls except those concerning classified advertising.
• MAdison 5-6611 for all classified advertising calls.

Los Angeles Times

EQUAL RIGHTS
LIBERTY UNDER THE LAW   TRUE INDUSTRIAL FREEDOM

9 A.M. FINAL

VOL. LXXVII   IN FOUR PARTS   FRIDAY MORNING, OCTOBER 31, 1958   92 PAGES   DAILY 10c

MAN ADMITS SLAYINGS OF THREE L.A. MODELS

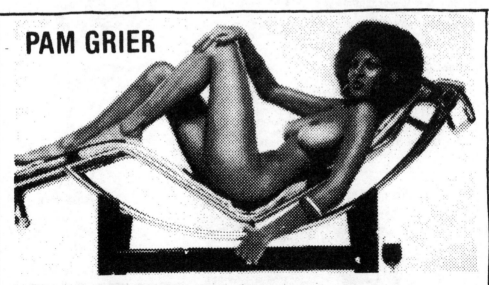

PAM GRIER

IN PAM GRIER'S MEMOIR FOXY: MY LIFE IN THREE ACTS, SHE RECOUNTS HOW A CONVERSATION WITH HER DOCTOR LED TO HER BREAKUP WITH RICHARD PRYOR. THE DOC NOTICED THAT SHE HAD A COCAINE ENCRUSTED PUSSY, AND TOLD HER HOW DANGEROUS AND UNHEALTHY THAT WAS FOR A WOMAN'S COOTER. SINCE SHE WASN'T DOING DRUGS HERSELF, SHE KNEW PRYOR, A NOTORIOUS YAY-YO FIEND, WAS TO BLAME.
—BOUGIE

IS SHE NEVER GOING TO **MOLEST ME?!**

Nocturna

NOCTURNA (1979)

DRACULA (A GERIATRIC JOHN CARRADINE) HAS A SKANK-ASS GRANDDAUGHTER NAMED NOCTURNA (NAI BONET) WHO FALLS IN LUST WITH A MORTAL LUNKHEAD MUSICIAN AFTER THE TWO MEET IN OL' DRAC'S TRANSYLVANIAN CASTLE NIGHTCLUB. FOLLOWING HIM LIKE A LOVESICK PUPPY, SHE ENDS UP IN MANHATTAN WHERE SHE AND HER BOYTOY BOOGIE THE NIGHTS AWAY AT NEW YORK'S STARSHIP DISCO, MUCH TO HER FAMILY'S CHAGRIN.

YES, THIS IS AN EXAMPLE OF ONE OF THE LESSER KNOWN CULT FILM GENRES, THE VAMPIRE DISCO SEX COMEDY. YOU WON'T WANNA MISS UNDEAD TRANSFORMATIONS VIA STUPID LOW BUDGET ANIMATION, RADICAL PERMIT-FREE 42ND STREET FOOTAGE SHOT FROM A MOVING CAR, JOHN CARRADINE'S FANG DENTURES, A BSA (BLOOD SUCKERS ASSOCIATION) MEETING TO COMPLAIN ABOUT RAMPANT DRUG USE COMPROMISING THE QUALITY OF THE CRIMSON STUFF IN QUESTION, AND MORE FUNKY-ASS DISCO THAN YOU CAN SHAKE A POLYESTER BELLBOTTOM AT.

THIS IS A ONE WOMAN SHOW. STAR, WRITER, AND EXECUTIVE PRODUCER NAI BONET RAISED $350,000 TO PRODUCE THIS NARCISSISTIC PET PROJECT, AND RAN "NAI BONET PRODUCTIONS, LTD." FROM HER APARTMENT LIVING ROOM. IF ONLINE SOURCES ARE TO BE TRUSTED, SHE GOT MOST OF THE CASH FROM WILLIAM CALLAHAN, A FORMER CHILD ACTOR/CONSTRUCTION BUSINESSMAN WHOSE TIES TO THE MOB GOT HIM AND HIS YOUNG WIFE SHOT IN THE HEAD IN 1981.

BONET BLEW $100,000 OF CALLAHAN'S COIN ON THE SCORE FOR HER FILM, WHICH FEATURES GLORIA GAYNOR SINGING NOCTURNA'S THEME SONG, "LOVE IS JUST A HEARTBEAT AWAY", WHICH MISS GAYNOR LATER ADMITTED THAT SHE REGRETTED BEING A PART OF. NAI CREATED THE SEXY

NOCTURNA ART BY AWESOME MISTER ADAM WILSON -2010

lead role for herself because she was frustrated with the lack of film work for an ethnic woman in her late 30s. Nai was a Vietnamese belly dancer who showed up in a smattering of 1970s B movies, recorded a novelty track called "Jelly Belly" for Karate Records, appeared on various belly dancing themed LP cover art, and posed naked for the April 1979 issue of Gallery magazine.

"Bonet obviously has a very high opinion of her sexual attractiveness," wrote film critic Dann Gire of Nocturna in 1979 "Hence there are plenty of scenes in which she parades around in the buff or washes every portion of her anatomy in the bathtub".

Nai can't act her way out of a soggy paper bag, but in supporting roles are some very interesting characters. First off is Yvonne De Carlo as the vampy Miss 'Jugulia Vein,' whom Nai looked after with limousine service before casting the 56-year-old Vancouverite out on the mean streets of N.Y.

"One night on 42nd street there were two, then four, then six, then ten policemen protecting me!", Yvonne told the Daily Intelligencer in September of 1978. "The police had to rescue me!"

Then you've got one of my all time faves, Brother Theodore, hamming it up as Nocturna's creepy white-haired underling. It's pretty clear that he wrote or improvised his spittle-inflected dialogue, because it's not unlike the weirdly brilliant monologues he was famous for verbally vomiting at Letterman on the late show in the mid '80s. Just try to contain a smile as Theodore riles himself up, furrowing his brow and bugging his eyes as he yowls, "Am I never going to be her little yum-yum!? Her shnootzy pootzie, her shanpsy-wappsy!?? Is she never going to molest me?!!"

After Nocturna bombed and Nai lost her shirt, she moved to the Bosnian city of Medjugorje and became a religious goods store shopkeep. The movie remains quite rare, which can be explained by the fact that when Code Red acquired the DVD rights, Nai refused to give them the go-ahead to release her film until they had edited all the nudity out. They refused.

— Bougie '11

YOR

BY MIKE SULLIVAN 2012. ART BY BEN NEWMAN

I'M NOT THE TYPE TO GET MISTY-EYED AND NOSTALGIC OVER THE '80S BECAUSE I LIVED THROUGH THAT DECADE AND I REMEMBER HOW BAD IT WAS. MANY OF YOU WILL DISAGREE AND CALL ME MISINFORMED OR CYNICAL BUT TO THOSE PEOPLE, LET ME SAY THIS, "PUT THE GAVEL AWAY AND STOP JUDGING ME". DEEP DOWN YOU REMEMBER HOW IT REALLY WAS.

ALL OF YOU REMEMBER THAT DIG DUG WAS TOO HARD, BANGS WERE AT THEIR CRISPIEST, AND EVERYBODY HAD A.I.D.S ALL OVER THEIR LIPS. I MEAN ALL OVER. IT WAS NUTS. THE ONE POSITIVE THING THAT COULD BE SAID ABOUT THE '80S IS THAT IRONY HAD NOT YET INFECTED THE POP-CULTURAL LANDSCAPE THE WAY IT HAD IN THE MID '90s. IF THERE WAS SOMETHING THAT WAS BAD, IT WAS BAD IN A PURE WAY. IT WASN'T SELF-AWARE. IT DIDN'T WINK AT YOU AND IT DIDN'T TRY TO CONVINCE YOU IT WAS IN ON THE JOKE. IT WAS TERRIBLE, BUT TOO OBLIVIOUS TO REALIZE JUST HOW TERRIBLE IT WAS.

THAT PURENESS, THAT INNOCENCE IS WHAT'S MISSING FROM BAD POP-CULTURE NOWADAYS, AND IT'S WHY WE'LL NEVER SEE ANOTHER MOVIE LIKE YOR, THE HUNTER FROM THE FUTURE EVER AGAIN. YOR THE HUNTER FROM THE FUTURE WAS THE PRODUCT OF A SIMPLER MORE HORRIBLE TIME WHEN THE CLINICALLY INSANE (AND THEIR FREQUENT COLLABORATORS, THE BAD, BAD GHOSTS THAT LIVE IN THEIR BRAIN AND NEVER, EVER STOP SHRIEKING) HAD THE CREATIVE FREEDOM TO PRODUCE SOMETHING RARE. IF YOU CHAIN A MILLION MONKEYS TO A MILLION TYPEWRITERS, THE SCRIPT FOR YOR, THE HUNTER FROM THE FUTURE IS WHAT THEY REPEATEDLY CHURN OUT UNTIL THEY ACCIDENTALLY CRAFT THE COMPLETE WORKS OF SHAKESPEARE. BUT YOU KNOW WHAT? FUCK THAT FAKER SHAKESPEARE, FUCK HIS BUTT-BUDDY FRANCIS BACON, AND FUCK JAMES FENIMORE COOPER (FOR UNRELATED REASONS). THIS IS YOR'S TIME TO SHINE.

YOR THE HUNTER FROM THE FUTURE OPENS WITH A SEQUENCE THAT PERFECTLY SETS THE TONE. IT DEPICTS AN OILY BARBARIAN/QUASI-CAVEMAN IN NOTHING BUT A LOINCLOTH AND A FUN N' FLIRTY DORIS DAY WIG AWKWARDLY TROTTING DOWN THE SIDE OF A HILL, IN SPITE OF THE FACT THAT THIS LUMBERING PORK-MOUND COULD FALL AT ANY MOMENT, HE'S WEARING THE STUPIDLY SMUG EXPRESSION OF SOMEONE WHO JUST SHIT THEIR PANTS BUT FEELS EMPOWERED BY IT. THIS MAGNIFICENTLY BRONZED MEAT LUMP IS YOR AND AS HE CONTINUES TO RE-ENACT THE CLOSING CREDITS TO LITTLE HOUSE ON THE PRAIRIE, A POWER BALLAD THAT COULD'VE BEEN WRITTEN BY SURVIVOR - IF SURVIVOR WAS FROM EASTERN EUROPE AND THEIR SONGS WERE JUST A COLLECTION OF RANDOM ENGLISH WORDS THEY DIDN'T UNDERSTAND - BLARES AWAY IN THE BACKGROUND.

AFTER THE TITLE TUNE INFORMS US THAT YOR IS, "LOST IN THE WORLD OF PAST/IN THE ECHO OF ANCIENT BLAST", "HE NEVER SEES THE SUN" AND "HE'S GOT THE FIRE BURNING/IT'S THERE IN HIS MIND", WE'RE INTRODUCED TO FELLOW CAVE-PEOPLE, PAG AND KA-LAA WHO ARE BEING ATTACKED BY A TRICERATOPS THAT APPARENTLY HIT ITS HEAD ON THE CURB AND COMPLETELY FORGOT IT WAS A HERBIVORE. FORTUNATELY, YOR ARRIVES JUST IN TIME TO SCREAM UNINTELLIGIBLY AND BLUDGEON THE CONFUSED DINOSAUR'S PAPER-MACHE HEAD UNTIL IT FESTIVELY EXPLODES LIKE A MASSIVE PIÑATA FILLED WITH SMUCKER'S JELLY AND VASELINE.

SECURE IN THE KNOWLEDGE THAT THE PLANT EATER IS DEAD AND CAN'T HURT THEIR PERENNIALS ANYMORE, PAG AND KA-LAA'S TRIBE HONOUR YOR WITH A CELEBRATORY FEAST. BUT,

SADLY, THE FEAST IS RUINED BY A TRIBE OF SHAMBLING PILES OF SPIRIT GUM AND DOG HAIR THAT BURN THE CAVE-PEOPLE'S VILLAGE TO THE GROUND AND ABDUCT ALL THE WOMEN OF THE TRIBE. WITH EVERYBODY EITHER DEAD OR KIDNAPPED, AND ALL OF THE FOOD GONE, YOR KIND OF JUST SHRUGS HIS SHOULDERS AND QUICKLY DECIDES TO EMBARK ON A MYSTICAL QUEST BECAUSE WHATEVER, DUDE, THIS PARTY BLOWS.

UNFORTUNATELY, KA-LAA IS ABDUCTED BY THE SPIRIT GUM TRIBE MERE MOMENTS INTO YOR'S INCREDIBLE JOURNEY. IT IS AT THIS POINT THAT WE LEARN THAT YOR ISN'T JUST A HALF DOZEN RUMP ROASTS BARELY HELD TOGETHER BY THE CONTENTS OF A HALF DOZEN CANS OF SPRAY TANNER. ANY THIRD-RATE CONAN KNOCK-OFF COULD'VE QUIETLY SLIPPED INTO THE TRIBE'S RAPE GROTTO AND RESCUED KA-LAA. BUT THAT'S NOT WHO YOR IS. YOR IS THE TYPE OF HERO WHO WOULD SHOOT AN ARROW AT A "BEAST OF THE NIGHT" (OR AS IT'S MORE COMMONLY KNOWN: "A LARGE WOBBLY BAT MADE OF PLYWOOD"), GRAB ONTO ITS HAUNCHES, USE IT AS A HANG GLIDER TO FLOAT INTO THE CAVE, AND THEN PROMPTLY KICK THE FACE OFF OF ANYONE WHO MIGHT BE WATCHING THIS INSANE SPECTACLE (E.G. EVERYBODY).

BUT YOR DOESN'T STOP THERE. ONCE HE RESCUES KA-LAA, HE ALSO LEVELS A DAM THAT FLOODS THE CAVE AND KILLS EVERYBODY. AND I MEAN EVERYBODY: THE EVIL CAVEMEN, THEIR SHITTY LITTLE KIDS, THE INNOCENT WOMEN THAT WERE ABDUCTED FROM PAG AND KA-LAA'S VILLAGE, AND THEIR SHITTY LITTLE KIDS. NO ONE IS SPARED. NOW, KEEP IN MIND, YOR WASN'T EVEN ANGRY. HE OPENED THE FLOODGATES MERELY BECAUSE THEY HAPPENED TO BE THERE AS HE WAS LEAVING. FOR YOR GENOCIDE IS KIND OF AN IMPULSE THING.

FOR THE NEXT TWENTY MINUTES, ALL STORYLINES ARE BRIEFLY SUSPENDED SO THAT TWO SPECIFIC SCENES CAN BE REPEATED OVER AND OVER AGAIN:

1. YOR IMPISHLY DESTROYS AN ANCIENT CIVILIZATION.

2. YOR GETS DISTRACTED BY A PRETTY FACE AND KA-LAA BECOMES VIOLENTLY JEALOUS. OH KA-LAA, DO YOU THINK THAT YOU AND YOU ALONE CAN CONTAIN YOR'S MUSKY MAN PECS? DO YOU THINK YOU CAN OWN A MALE WHOSE DIRTY PILLOWS SECRETE A NATURAL OLIVE OIL THAT KEEPS THEM PERPETUALLY GLISTENING? YOU CAN NOT. THOSE BULBOUS, HE-BOOBS BELONG TO THE WORLD, MADAM!

EVENTUALLY THIS PATTERN IS BROKEN WHEN YOR'S EFFORTS TO DESTROY ANOTHER PREHISTORIC CULTURE ARE INTERRUPTED BY A SPACESHIP THAT HELPFULLY DESTROYS THE TRIBE FOR HIM. YES, IN WHAT COULD BE CONSIDERED AN UNEXPECTED TWIST TO THOSE WHO ARE ILLITERATE, YOR, THE HUNTER FROM THE FUTURE ACTUALLY TAKES PLACE IN THE FUTURE! HERE'S A TIP FOR ASPIRING FILMMAKERS: HOWEVER TEMPTING IT MAY BE, DON'T ANNOUNCE YOUR FILM'S BIG PLOT TWIST IN THE TITLE. THERE'S A REASON WHY **CITIZEN KANE** AND **THE SIXTH SENSE** WEREN'T CALLED "ROSEBUD: THE MAGICAL SLED" AND "BRUCE WILLIS THE FRIENDLY GHOST".

FROM THERE THINGS GROW COMPLICATED AND DIFFICULT TO EXPLAIN. YOR IS KIDNAPPED BY CHARACTER ACTOR JOHN STEINER, STRAPPED INTO A CLEAR PLASTIC MRI MACHINE AND TOLD THAT HIS SEMEN WILL POWER A NEW SUPER-RACE OF ANDROIDS IN FUTURISTIC CERVICAL COLLARS. MEANWHILE BURNT ORANGE EXISTS, KA-LAA GETS STUCK IN A HOUSE OF MIRRORS, ROBOTS THAT RESEMBLE DARK HELMET FROM SPACEBALLS TRUNDLE AROUND USELESSLY, AND AT ONE POINT SOME OF THE CAST MEMBERS ARE TURNED INTO ACTION FIGURES AND GENTLY HURLED AT A MODEL OF A NUCLEAR PYLON. EVENTUALLY A SPACESHIP HAPPENS, AND THEN IT ENDS.

NOW IF I COULD BE SERIOUS FOR JUST A MOMENT, I JUST WANT TO SAY THAT UNINTENTIONAL COMEDIES AREN'T EASY TO MAKE. THEY REQUIRE A LARGE NUMBER OF ILL-FITTING PARTS THAT HAVE TO ACCIDENTALLY FALL INTO PLACE IN JUST THE RIGHT, WRONG WAY. YET AS DIFFICULT AS IT IS TO MAKE AN UNINTENTIONAL COMEDY, AN UNCONSCIOUS PARODY MOVIE IS FAR MORE COMPLEX, IF NOT OUTRIGHT IMPOSSIBLE. AND YET, YOR, THE HUNTER FROM THE FUTURE HAS TO BE THE WORLD'S FIRST UNCONSCIOUS PARODY MOVIE.

CLEARLY MADE TO CASH-IN ON THE INFLUX OF SWORD AND SORCERY FILMS THAT WERE POPULAR THROUGHOUT THE EARLY '80S, YOR THE HUNTER FROM THE FUTURE OBEDIENTLY CONFORMS TO THE ATTENDANT CLICHÉS OF GENRE. BUT POSSIBLY BECAUSE THE FILM WAS THE PRODUCT OF AN ITALIAN/TURKISH CO-PRODUCTION, ALL OF THOSE CLICHÉS ARE JUST SLIGHTLY OFF AND MADE THAT MUCH SILLIER AS A RESULT. YOR, THE HUNTER FROM THE FUTURE INADVERTENTLY DECONSTRUCTS THE VERY SAME GENRE IT DESPERATELY WANTS TO BE A PART OF, AND IT IS TRULY A THING OF BEAUTY.

MIKE SULLIVAN - 2012

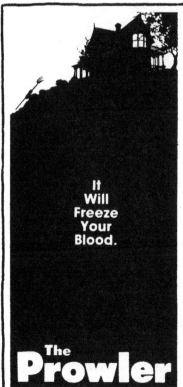

It Will Freeze Your Blood.

The Prowler

THE PROWLER (1981 USA. Dir: Joseph Zito)

A MASKED PSYCHO IN WORLD WAR II AMERICAN ARMY FATIGUES IS THE TITULAR PROWLER, AS HE RUTHLESSLY STALKS AND MURDERS THE INHABITANTS OF A SMALL NEW JERSEY TOWN. THE KILLER LURKS IN THE SHADOWS AND LOOKS TO RELIVE A 35-YEAR-OLD DOUBLE MURDER BY RETURNING ON THE ANNIVERSARY OF HIS EARLIER BLOODBATH AND CHOPPING AN INTERCHANGEABLE GROUP OF COLLEGE YOUTH TO BITS.

I THINK WHAT MOST FANS LOVE ABOUT THIS MOVIE IS NOT THAT IT HAS A GREAT STORY (IT'S DULL AND FILLED WITH LOOSE ENDS), INTERESTING CHARACTERS (CARDBOARD CUT-OUTS), OR EVEN THAT IT EXISTS AS AN ABOVE AVERAGE EXAMPLE OF ITS GENRE, THE SLASHER FILM (IT DOESN'T). WHAT MOST OF ITS FANS WILL ENTHUSIASTICALLY TELL YOU IS THE REASON THEY LIKE THE MOVIE ARE THE AESTHETICS OF ITS VIOLENT GORE EFFECTS AND KILL-SCENES. INDEED, THEY ARE TERRIFIC AND VERY MEMORABLE. THESE CINEMATIC MURDERS WERE DONE BY THE LEGENDARY TOM SAVINI, BEST KNOWN FOR HIS FX WORK ON **MANIAC**, **DAY OF THE DEAD**, AND THE **FRIDAY THE 13**TH MOVIES. TOM HAS GONE ON TO SAY IN INTERVIEWS THAT HE FEELS HE WAS AT THE VERY PINNACLE OF HIS GAME WITH HIS WORK IN THIS 1981 FILM BY JOSEPH ZITO.

SOME OF THE A+ TERRIFIC KILLS ARE: PITCHFORKED RIGHT UNDER THE TITS IN THE SHOWER (AND LIFTED), HEAD BLOWN OFF WITH A SHOTGUN, A BAYONET STABBED RIGHT THROUGH THE SKULL (EXITING THROUGH THE NECK), THROAT SLIT IN A SWIMMING POOL, A DOUBLE-BARREL SHOTGUN BLAST, AND MORE. THIS MESS IS GUARANTEED TO DISTURB AND DELIGHT EVEN THE MOST EXPERIENCED GORE-SEEKERS. IS THAT ENOUGH? FILM REVIEWER PATRICK NAUGLE DIDN'T FIND THAT IT WAS. "SAVINI BELIEVES THIS FILM FEATURES SOME OF HIS BEST EFFECTS WORK," NAUGLE COMPLAINED IN HIS 2013 REVIEW FOR DVDVERDICT. "BUT THAT'S LIKE POURING SOME OF THE BEST TASTING MARINADE ON A POUND OF ROTTEN CHICKEN."

VIDEOSTORE DIARY
ENTRY: JULY 11th, 2014.

I WAS BEHIND VIDEOMATICA JUST EMPTYING SOME CARDBOARD INTO THE BIN, AND I HEARD A VOICE BEHIND ME GOING "HELLO? HI. HI. HELLO? HELLO, SIR?". SO I TURNED AROUND.

STANDING BEHIND ME IN THE ALLEY WAS A WOMAN IN HER 60s OR MAYBE LATE 50s. I WAITED FOR HER TO SPEAK AND SUDDENLY SHE SORT OF PUSHED HER BUTT OUT A LITTLE AND **FUCKING FARTED A HUGE FART!!**

AFTER THAT SHE DIDN'T EVEN WAIT FOR MY REACTION. SHE JUST BOOKED IT DOWN THE ALLEYWAY AWAY FROM ME. HONESTLY, I WAS LOOKING AROUND FOR THE HIDDEN CAMERA, MAN. THOUGHT I MIGHT BE ON SOME PRANK SHOW, OR SOMETHING!

IT WAS A DRIVE-BY TOOTING! I WUZ ATTACKED BY THE FART BANDIT!

HONK!

END UP

RANDOM TRIVIA

☆ THE FAMOUS AND CRITICALLY BELOVED STEADYCAM TRIP THROUGH THE NIGHTCLUB KITCHEN IN **GOODFELLAS** (1990) WAS A HAPPY ACCIDENT. SCORSESE HAD BEEN DENIED PERMISSION TO USE THE FRONT OF THE BUILDING, AND HAD TO IMPROVISE.

☆ THE SCENE IN **THE EXORCIST** WHERE LINDA BLAIR PROJECTILE VOMITS ON THE FACE OF ACTOR JASON MILLER WAS AN ACCIDENT, AND HIS LOOK OF SHOCK WAS REAL. THE VOMIT WAS SUPPOSED TO HIT HIS CHEST.

☆ DURING THE "UNCLY NUTSY'S CLUBHOUSE" SCENE IN **UHF** (1989) WEIRD AL WASN'T SUPPOSED TO ACTUALLY HIT BOBBO THE CLOWN IN THE FACE, BUT DID ACCIDENTALLY, SPLITTING HIS LIP. THIS WAS THE TAKE USED IN THE MOVIE!

SISTER STREET FIGHTER (1974)

ONE OF THE BEST AND WORST THINGS ABOUT SISTER STREET FIGHTER (DEPENDING ON YOUR POINT OF VIEW) IS THAT IT FEELS VERY MUCH LIKE A MOVIE MADE BY A 10-YEAR-OLD SCREENWRITER. THERE IS MINIMAL COHERENCY, A WARPED VIEW OF THE REALITY OF DRUGS AND VIOLENCE, AND THE CHARACTERS -- DESPITE THEIR COLOURFUL, FANTASTIC COSTUMES -- ARE COMPLETELY ONE-DIMENSIONAL. BUT FOR THE INTENTS AND PURPOSES OF A MOVIE OF THIS SORT, ALL OF THAT FITS LIKE A GLOVE. IN REALITY, THE SCRIPT WAS WRITTEN BY PINKY VIOLENCE LEGEND, NORIFUMI SUZUKI.

A HIGHLY SKILLED FEMALE MARTIAL ARTIST (PLAYED BY 18-YEAR-OLD CUTIE, SUE SHIOMI) LOOKS TO RESCUE HER CAPTURED BROTHER, AN UNDERCOVER AGENT BEING HELD PRISONER BY THE DRUG SMUGGLERS HE SOUGHT TO DEFEAT.

Sonny Chiba's back... and Sue Shiomi's got 'm!

He's a one man army.
She's a one woman death squad.

Sister Street Fighter

Starring
Sonny Chiba · Sue Shiomi from NEW LINE CINEMA [R] RESTRICTED

THE HEDONISTIC KINGPIN (WHO HAS A SWEET VEGA-STYLE CLAW ON HIS HAND) IS STATIONED AT HIS SECLUDED VILLA, AND HAS COLLECTED A MENAGERIE OF THE WORLD'S MOST OUTLANDISH AND STRANGE KILLERS TO PROTECT HIMSELF AND HIS VILE INTERESTS. HIS CREW INCLUDE A GUY WHO EXPORTS HEROIN DISGUISED AS HUMAN WIGS (?), A DEFROCKED PRIEST WHO SHOOTS ARMOUR-PIERCING ARROWS OUT OF A GUN, A GANG THAT WEARS BLACK CONE-SHAPED WICKER BASKETS FOR HATS, A GROUP OF FRED-FLINTSTONE-LOOKIN' LEOPARD-PRINT-WEARING FEMALE THAI KICK BOXERS WITH HAIRY ARMPITS, AND A DART-BLOWING WEIRDO WITH AN AFRICAN SHIELD AND A THRIFT STORE CAPE. <u>RADNESS.</u>

—BOUGIE '12

168

WHILE TERMINATOR 2: JUDGMENT DAY (1991) IS A PERFECT EXAMPLE OF A MOVIE THAT GETS WEAKER AND LESS ENJOYABLE EACH TIME I SEE IT, I DO ADMIT THAT I'VE PROBABLY WATCHED IT TOO MANY TIMES, AND THAT IS MORE MY FAULT THAN ANY WRONGDOING THE MOVIE DID. LEARN SOME SELF CONTROL IF YOU DON'T WANT TO GET TIRED OF THINGS YOU LIKE. THAT SAID, JAMES CAMERON SAID A FEW INTERESTING THINGS ABOUT THE MOVIE ON THE AUDIO COMMENTARY FOR THE DVD. BEHIND-THE-SCENES THINGS THAT DON'T OFTEN GET REPEATED, AND SHOULD BECAUSE THEY'RE FUCKING INTERESTING, LIKE FOR INSTANCE...

☆ DURING THE FILMING OF THE BIKER BAR SCENE NEAR THE BEGINNING OF THE PICTURE, THEY WERE RIGHT ACROSS THE STREET FROM WHERE THE LAPD WERE BRUTALLY BEATING RODNEY KING, AND THEY WERE FILMING ON THAT VERY NIGHT, MARCH 3RD, 1991. "I ACTUALLY THINK IT HAS AN INTERESTING RESONANCE TO THIS FILM BECAUSE THE BAD GUY IS A COP IN THIS MOVIE," NOTED CAMERON.

☆ LINDA HAMILTON DID PERMANENT DAMAGE TO HER LEFT EAR DURING THE FILMING OF THE SCENE IN THE ELEVATOR WITH THE TERMINATOR FIRING A SHOTGUN. APPARENTLY BETWEEN TAKES, LINDA HAD TO PEE, AND FORGOT TO PUT HER EARPLUG BACK IN WHEN SHE RETURNED FROM THE BATHROOM. CAMERON POINTED OUT THAT THE SHOT THAT DID THE DAMAGE IS IN THE FILM.

DISK-O-TEK HOLIDAY
(1966. ENGLAND/USA. DIR: VINCE SCARZA)

SURE, THERE IS A DISPOSABLE PLOT ABOUT A WOULD-BE TEEN IDOL AND HIS CANDY APPLE SWEETIE AS THEY WANDER AROUND HARASSING REAL LIFE DISC JOCKEYS TO PLAY THEIR SHITTY SONG "EAST IS EAST," BUT THAT CAMPY CRAP REALLY ONLY EXISTS AS SAPPY GLUE TO HOLD TOGETHER OVER 20 RARE, EXCEPTIONALLY ENTERTAINING MUSIC VIDEOS. THIS WAS DECADES BEFORE MTV, SO IT WAS EITHER SCOPITONES (FOOTAGE OF BANDS PERFORMING SINGLES THAT PLAYED IN SPECIALLY MADE 16MM MOVIE JUKEBOXES) OR A MOVIE LIKE THIS IF YOU WANTED THE MUSIC VIDEO EXPERIENCE. NONE OF THE ACTS ARE WELL REMEMBERED TODAY (WHICH IS WHY THIS ENDEARING MOVIE IS SO OBSCURE AND UNKNOWN) BUT THE MAJORITY OF THEM ARE WONDERFUL.

IT'S A NICE MIX OF BOTH AMERICAN AND BRIT PERFORMERS, AND SOME OF THE HIGHLIGHTS ARE FREDDY AND THE DREAMERS DANCING LIKE IDIOTS TO "YOU WERE MADE FOR ME" AND "JUST FOR YOU", JOHNNY B. GREAT KICKING OUT "IF I HAD A HAMMER," LOUISE CORDET'S SILKY SMOOTH SQUAKBOX CROONING "IT'S SO HARD TO BE GOOD", AND JACKIE AND THE RAINDROPS PULLING A TRAIN ON "LOCOMOTION". OVER AND ABOVE THOSE, I ESPECIALLY LIKED GETTING TO SEE ONE OF MY MOST ADORED GIRL GROUPS, THE ORCHIDS, IN ONE OF THEIR FEW FILMED PERFORMANCES ("MR. SCROOGE") AND THE HIGH PITCHED BLACK PIXIE MILLIE SMALL GROOVING HER SHIT OUT ON "SUGAR DANDY". OH, AND I ALMOST FORGOT THE BIG SURF ROCK MINISKIRT FINALE OF FREDDY CANNON DOING "TALLAHASSEE LASSIE," "BUZZ BUZZ A-DIDDLE-IT", AND "BEACHWOOD CITY"! TOO COOL!

CLASSIC ENTERTAINING SHIT, AND ALONG WITH THE TAMI SHOW (1964) AND THE BIG TNT SHOW (1966), ONE OF THE THREE BEST MUSIC PERFORMANCE MOVIES OF THE SIXTIES.

YAAGHH! I LOVES IT SO MUCH!

GRAPHIC SEXUAL HORROR

DIRECTORS BARBARA BELL AND ANNA LORENTZON CREATED A
DOCUMENTARY IN 2009 THAT WAS SO FAR BEYOND THE PALE IN TERMS
OF WHAT WAS EVEN ALLOWED TO BE SEEN AND SHOWN ON
COMMERCIALLY DISTRIBUTED DVD AND IN THEATRES, THAT THE PROJECT
SEEMED DOOMED TO OBSCURITY. AS OF THIS WRITING, THEIR MOVIE HAS
FOUND A COMPANY WILLING TO RELEASE IT (SYNAPSE) AND BARBARA
AND ANNA HAVE EVEN SNUCK THEIR DEBAUCHED OPUS TO NIGHTMARISH
SEX ONTO AMAZON.COM.

THE FILM IS GRAPHIC SEXUAL HORROR, AND THEY SUM IT UP AS SUCH
IN THEIR PRESS RELEASE:

"The film takes a peek behind the terrifying facade of Insex.com, the
most notorious of bondage websites, exploring the dark mind of its
artistic creator and asking hard questions about personal responsibility.
Original Insex footage, behind-the-scenes interactions, and interviews
with its creator PD, models, members, and staff reveal deep fascinations
with bondage and sadomasochism that run parallel, and in fact become
irreversibly entwined with the lure of money."

IN EARLY 2010, I CHATTED WITH BARBARA BELL ABOUT HER
EXPERIENCES AND FEELINGS ABOUT THE MOVIE AND THE SEXUAL
POLITICS INTERTWINED WITH IT:

CINEMA SEWER: HI BARBARA! THANKS FOR TAKING THE TIME TO TALK
TO ME ABOUT GRAPHIC SEXUAL HORROR. WHAT GAVE ANNA AND YOU
THE IMPETUS TO START WORKING ON THIS FILM? HOW DID IT COME
ABOUT?

Barbara Bell: The creator of the site, PD, hired me to write a screenplay
for a mainstream project he wanted to launch. Anna and I worked
together as co-directors during the filming of that project and discovered
that we made a good team. So after Insex shut down, we got together
and talked about doing a project together. But the only thing we could
talk about was Insex. We decided we had to do a documentary on Insex
to get it out of our system before we could move on.

CS: PEOPLE WARN THAT YOU SHOULD BEWARE OF WHAT YOU PUT
ONLINE, ABOUT THE FACT THAT ONCE SOMETHING IS ON THE INTERNET,
IT IS THERE FOREVER -- BUT I HAVE FOUND THE OPPOSITE TO BE
TRUE. IT MAY AS WELL BE GONE IF IT CAN'T BE FOUND. EVENTUALLY
MOST ONLINE CONTENT (ESPECIALLY SOMETHING AS DISMISSED AS PORN)
GETS CHOPPED UP AND DILUTED INTO THE ONLINE SEA AND ALMOST
IMPOSSIBLE TO FIND AND REASSEMBLE UNLESS SOMEONE IS MAKING AN
EFFORT TO KEEP IT READILY AVAILABLE. THAT YOU THOUGHT TO MAKE
A FILM DOCUMENTING THE EXISTENCE AND HISTORY OF A SITE LIKE
INSEX IS JUST SO COOL TO ME. YOUR FILM WILL ACT AS A
PLACEMARKER. A CAPSULE OF THAT PLACE AND TIME.

BB: OOhhh. You just gave me a shiver, talking about us creating a time
capsule about Insex. . . not sure that was our intent, but YES.

CS: THE DANGER HOWEVER, AS I SEE IT, IS THAT GRAPHIC SEXUAL
HORROR ITSELF CONTAINS MUCH OF THE FULL-ON HARDCORE CONTENT
THAT GOT THIS SITE CLOSED. IT MUST BE HARD TO GET THIS MOVIE
DISTRIBUTION OUTSIDE OF A FEW FESTIVAL SCREENINGS FOR THAT
REASON -- IS IT NOT?

BB: We have had a horrific time trying to get anything in mainstream
press. And most of the so-called "edgy" festivals in the US and Europe
didn't want us. Even Austin turned us down. I have to hand it to
Slamdance, they walk the walk and talk the talk. I am a Slamdance fan
now. However, distribution is a completely different story. We made our
digital deal at Slamdance with Cinetic Rights Management. And one of
the other filmmakers at Slamdance said to me, "So many great films at
this festival, and a film about "PORN" gets distribution'. Like it was a
slam to us. And I could have said to him 'Yeah, everybody said we

should have won the best documentary award, but who's going to give it to a documentary about PORN?' So there are positives and negatives about the content. GSH will have next to NO theatrical or cable sales. but digital and DVD could be good. Like porn, it may sell when the people watching it can be rather secretive. Even though we had no interest in exploiting the porn elements, I forgot that sex sells. Duhhh.

CS: PEOPLE LOVE SEX! THE ISSUE OF CONSENT IS A REALLY INTERESTING ONE THAT YOU BRING UP IN THE MOVIE. PERSONALLY, I FEEL IN ORDER FOR FORCED-SEX FANTASIES TO REMAIN SEXY, IT IS INTEGRAL THAT THEY REMAIN FANTASIES, JUST LIKE THAT I ADORE ACTION MOVIES FILLED WITH VIOLENCE, BUT I'D BE HORRIFIED TO FIND OUT THAT THE FILMMAKERS HAD PURPOSEFULLY HACKED OFF SOMEONE'S HAND FOR REAL. MY THINKING IS THAT A MOVIE SHOULD BE AS REALISTIC AS POSSIBLE, AND YET IT MUST STILL BE USING "MOVIE MAGIC" TO ACHIEVE ITS THRILLS. THE ACTORS MUST BE CONSENTING PARTICIPANTS, OR YOU END UP WITH AN ATROCITY -- ESPECIALLY WHEN DEALING WITH VIOLENCE. I THINK THESE LINES GOT REALLY BLURRED AT INSEX.

BB: You know - I'm kind of the opposite of you. I can't stand horror films. First of all, I can't watch graphic violence. It makes me physically ill. What I wonder is if what is shown on camera is more real, then maybe we'd have different sensibilities around violence. Because real violence is much worse to watch than acted violence - in my experience.

CS: OH TOTALLY, BUT WHAT I'M GETTING AT IS THAT IN THE FILM YOU DISPLAY THE FACT, THAT AT INSEX, THERE WERE POINTS WHEN SAFEWORDS AND AGREED-UPON LIMITS WERE IGNORED -- MUCH TO THE HORROR OF THE GIRLS ON DISPLAY. AS MUCH AS I AM A FAN OF THIS SORT OF EXTREME PORN, I WAS AGHAST AT THAT. I FOUND THE VIOLATION OF TRUST BETWEEN ARTIST AND SUBJECT VERY UPSETTING.

BB: The members of Insex have a forum they still keep going. And my experience with them is that they only see PD as this really conscientious artist who knows best. They don't want to entertain the fact that it is a complex environment (like all work environments), and that PD rides the edge of consent and sometimes falls outside the bounds. They try to make up excuses because I think they don't want to think that models had ended up unhappy. The consent issue that we raised was not so much a way to show that PD was messing up, as it was a way to bring up the reality that everybody experiences these kind of things in their jobs. It just looks a lot worse when sex is involved. To me, the clip around the model that was slapped in the face is the perfect example of how just about every boss in America will cross the line with an employee and then manipulate the situation to make it look like the employee just isn't up to snuff. How many people have had the same thing happen in their job?

CS: THAT IS A GREAT POINT, AND ONE THAT ILLUSTRATES HOW SEX AND PORN ARE ALWAYS "THE OTHER" IN THIS SOCIETY. WE ALWAYS SEEM TO HAVE TO SET UP A SEPARATE SET OF RULES FOR SEX, AS IF IT IS TOTALLY ALIEN AND DIVORCED FROM ALL OTHER ASPECTS OF THE HUMAN EXPERIENCE OR SOMETHING. NOT TO SUCK YOUR LABIA TOO MUCH HERE, BUT THAT IS ANOTHER THING THAT I LOVED SO MUCH ABOUT YOUR MOVIE: THAT YOU PUT SUCH AN EFFORT INTO PUTTING A HUMAN FACE ONTO WHAT IS USUALLY A TOTALLY ANONYMOUS AND CLANDESTINE ENTERTAINMENT SOURCE. I'VE BEEN INTERESTED IN THE INSEX SITE FOR YEARS, BUT I HAD NO IDEA THAT THE GUY WHO RAN IT WAS NAMED PD, OR WHAT HIS RELATIONSHIP WITH THE GIRLS IN THE VIDEOS WERE. MAYBE SOME PERVS DON'T LIKE THEIR SMUT DEMYSTIFIED LIKE THAT, BUT I WAS LIKE A HOG IN POOP.

BB: The extremity of the climate at Insex creates the space in which it illuminates profound human dilemmas. This movie centers on Insex, but it's really about all of us - what will we do for the money? That is a crucial question in America - the land that touts capitalism more than it follows democratic principles. A country that let its leaders break national and international laws about real, actual torture (as opposed to theatrical torture scenarios like Insex created) is a country that has lost its moral compass in a big way.

CS: SPEAKING OF A MORAL COMPASS, I'M CURIOUS IF YOU'VE HAD PEOPLE COMING TO DEFEND THE HONOUR OF THE GIRLS IN YOUR

MOVIE, BECAUSE THAT SEEMS TO BE A REOCCURRING ISSUE FOR ME. SOME MALE READERS OF THIS MAGAZINE FEEL AS IF THE WOMEN IN THE PORN THAT I'M REVIEWING ARE VICTIMS THAT ARE BEING EXPLOITED, AND THAT THEY NEED TO WRITE TO ME AND STAND UP AGAINST THAT PERCEIVED SEXISM/MISOGYNY. OF COURSE NO ONE SAYS BOO IF THE PERFORMERS BEING DEGRADED ARE MEN, BECAUSE MEN ARE CONSIDERED TO BE MASTERS OF THEIR OWN DESTINY AND STRONG ENOUGH -- BOTH EMOTIONALLY AND PHYSICALLY. WHY DO YOU THINK WE STILL HAVE THAT HEAVY DISCONNECT BETWEEN MEN AND WOMEN WHEN THE SEXUAL REVOLUTION WAS 40 FUCKING YEARS AGO ALREADY?

BB: We had one guy at a screening that was about 19 and had one course in Psych and had decided that this activity was going to set up a continuum in the lives of the women and it would just get worse and worse for them - he knew EVERYTHING. If there's one thing I learned during the Bush years (beside how easy it is for politicians to lie to people - they seem to prefer to be lied to) is that it takes a VERY LONG TIME for populations to change the underlying assumptions they carry. We can do the cognitive work and change a thought in our heads, but in the end, there are just things that get lodged in people and they don't go away for a long time.

At the same time, when you see a guy that's over 6' tall in black hulking clothes standing over a naked, very tightly bound person, there is a real feeling of wanting to protect the person. I think we feel that stronger for women because we have this ingrained idea that they need more protection than men. Maybe that's true - I don't know. I think that men are more frightened of men than women are.

CS: I HAVE SEEN A COUPLE OF REVIEWS OF THIS MOVIE WHERE YOU WERE CRITICISED FOR NOT PROVIDING MORE "OUTSIDE VOICES TO DEBATE THE PSYCHOLOGICAL IMPLICATIONS OF SUCH ENTERTAINMENT". I WANT TO LET YOU KNOW HOW TICKLED I WAS THAT YOU DID NOT TAKE THAT DIRECTION -- BECAUSE IT HAS BEEN DONE TO DEATH. IT IS SUCH A PREDICTABLE AND CASUAL PATH TO TAKE WHEN SITTING DOWN TO EDIT A DOCUMENTARY DEALING WITH PORNOGRAPHY. IT'S ACTUALLY AT THE POINT NOW WHERE FILM CRITICS FEEL LIKE YOU FORGOT SOMETHING IF THEY DON'T GET EXACTLY WHAT THEY'RE EXPECTING IN TERMS OF TALKING POINTS WITH THIS SUBJECT MATTER. DID YOU AT ANY POINT CONSIDER INTERVIEWING PREACHERS OR ANTI-PORN CRUSADERS FOR THE FILM?

BB: Why interview anti-porn preachers? We already know what they are going to say. They already have their platform. People that work at places like Insex have had no public voice. We did try to put together some data on the effects of internet pornography, but there really isn't anything substantial yet. It's mostly anecdotal, though some national data is beginning to show that violence went down every year starting from the time that the internet began to take hold.

99.9% of Americans don't know what the models themselves think of this kind of material. They've never ever heard the voices of the members because people who watch this material are terrified to let anyone know what it means to them. Americans don't know who the staff are, their motivation. They know nothing about someone like PD. My main reason for doing this documentary was to show the real people and to hear their real stories. I kept telling Anna - I want to show the humanity at Insex - the reality that these aren't stereotypes. They're not cutouts that you get to draw in their features in order to hate them, or to say they've been abused or taken advantage of. They're real people. And they're interesting and thoughtful and maybe you won't like them but each one is an actual human being. That's the gold in this movie. That's the place the critics, like at Variety, forget. To me, that should be the object of a good documentary, or art for that matter - to break stereotypical thinking patterns, to bring you face to face with the reality of the "object" rather than being lost in ideas about the object. It should pull away the curtain of illusion. Real information is a very important commodity in our world.

THANKS TO BARBARA BELL FOR THE INTERVIEW. DO BE SURE TO CHECK OUT HER DOCUMENTARY, EVEN IF THIS SORT OF PORN IS NOT YOUR CUP OF EARL GREY. AS FAR AS I'M CONCERNED, IT IS REQUIRED VIEWING.
— BOUGIE

Maid In Sweden

Inga At Sixteen, Her Coming Of Age.

A CANNON RELEASE

R RESTRICTED Under 17 requires accompanying Parent or Adult Guardian

MAID IN SWEDEN (1971)

HERE IS A PERFECT EXAMPLE OF A CRAPPY, UNREMARKABLE, POORLY MADE MOVIE THAT IS STILL WORTH RECOMMENDING. THE PLOTTING, PACING, EDITING, DIRECTION, CINEMATOGRAPHY, DIALOGUE -- NONE OF IT IS WORTH A TURD. BUT IT DOES HAVE ONE SINGLE THING GOING FOR IT: IT IS THE FILM DEBUT OF DOE-EYED CHRISTINA LINDBERG. 20 YEARS OLD AT THE TIME OF FILMING, SHE'S POSSIBLY THE MOST PERFECT FEMALE SPECIMEN IN 1970S CINEMA -- AND YES, SHE GETS NAKED, MASTURBATES AND HAS YUMMY SEXYTIMES 'N' STUFF. IF YOU'VE SEEN ANY OF HER AMAZING APPEARANCES IN THE POPULAR MEN'S MAGAZINES OF THE DAY, YOU KNOW WHAT I'M SAYIN'.

HER LATER MOVIES **SEX AND FURY**, AND **THRILLER: A CRUEL PICTURE** (AKA THEY CALL HER ONE EYE) ARE MUCH RICHER CINEMATIC EXPERIENCES AND FAR BETTER FILMS OVERALL, BUT FOR THOSE SMITTEN WITH CHRISTINA (I.E. ANY STRAIGHT MAN OR GAY WOMAN WITH A PULSE) OR FOR ANY OF THE CURIOUS WHO WANT A PEEK AT WHAT MADE HER SO EYE-POPPINGLY SPECIAL, A CASUAL VIEWING OF MAID IN SWEDEN ISN'T GOING TO BE A PAINFUL EXPERIENCE WHATSOEVER.

TRIVIA: STILL IN HIGH SCHOOL, CHRISTINA HAD TO PLAY HOOKY TO TAKE PART IN FILMING. SHE LATER CALLED THE EXPERIENCE "FANTASTIC".

THE HOUSE BY THE LAKE

THE HOUSE BY THE LAKE (1976) AKA: "DEATH WEEKEND"

I LIKE TO HIGHLIGHT REALLY UNDERRATED (OR OTHERWISE FORGOTTEN) MOVIES IN THESE PAGES, AND YOU WON'T FIND A MUCH BETTER EXAMPLE FROM THE HORROR RAPE/REVENGE GENRE THAN **DEATH WEEKEND**, A CANADIAN PRODUCTION STARRING SCARY DON STROUD AND LOVELY BRENDA VACCARO. NOT JUST ANOTHER **LAST HOUSE ON THE LEFT** CLONE, DEATH WEEKEND IS A REAL WINNER BY THE TALENTED WILLIAM FRUET, WHO BY RIGHTS, SHOULD BE AS WELL KNOWN AS HIS FRIENDS AND CO-WORKERS UNDER THE 1970S CANADIAN FILMMAKING TAX-SHELTER, DAVID CRONENBERG AND IVAN REITMAN. WHAT A LOT OF EXPLOITATION FILM FANS PROBABLY DON'T REALISE IS THAT DEATH WEEKEND WAS QUITE LIKELY ONE OF THE BIGGEST INFLUENCES ON THE MOST NOTORIOUS FEMALE REVENGE FILM, **I SPIT ON YOUR GRAVE**. BASED ON A TRUE STORY, THIS CRUSTY, SUSPENSFUL RURAL NIGHTMARE ABOUT A VILE GANG OF SCUMBAGS THAT TERRORIZE AN INNOCENT VACATIONING COUPLE STILL GIVES A JOLT OR TWO AFTER ALL THESE YEARS.

MAKE SURE TO TRACK THIS ONE DOWN! I WATCH IT AT LEAST ONCE EVERY COUPLE OF YEARS OR SO.

VIVA!

RENAISSANCE WOMAN **ANNA BILLER** CRAFTS A MODERN SEXPLOITATION SENSATION WITH HER OWN TWO HANDS

☆ ROBIN BOUGIE BY: ☆ MARCUS GOODMAN

FROM THE FILM STOCK, TO THE FASHIONS, TO THE MUSIC, TO THE HAIRSTYLES, TO THE WOODEN ACTING, TO THE SEXISM, TO THE SILICONE-FREE CURVY BODIES, VIVA IS ALL ABOUT THE ATTENTION TO DETAIL IN RECREATING THE EARLY '70s SEXPLOITATION FILM, AND IT SURELY IS THE MOST SUCCESSFUL ATTEMPT I HAVE YET SEEN. ALL OTHERS UP TO NOW HAVE GONE TOO FAR WITH ATTEMPTS AT PARODY AND HUMOUR, BUT THERE WERE SEQUENCES IN VIVA WHERE I HONESTLY FORGOT I WAS WATCHING A FILM MADE IN THE LAST FEW YEARS. THE EFFECT IS THAT WELL EXECUTED, AND BY A FIRST-TIME FILMMAKER, NO LESS.

IT IS HARD NOT TO BE IMPRESSED WITH ANNA BILLER -- THE STAR, DIRECTOR, SET DESIGNER, EDITOR, ANIMATOR (OF A VERY PSYCHEDELIC ANIMATED SEQUENCE), PRODUCER, AND SEAMSTRESS FOR THIS PROJECT. THE MOVIE HAS 34 DIFFERENT SETS AND BILLER HERSELF WENT THROUGH 34 AMAZING COSTUME CHANGES IN ALL. SHE SPENT MONTHS CRAFTING THOSE COSTUMES, COLLECTING KITSCHY SET DECORATION FROM THE SALVATION ARMY, AND PAINSTAKINGLY DOING LITTLE PIECES OF MACRAME. ALL IN ALL, IT TOOK A COUPLE OF YEARS OF WEEKENDS, LABORING OVER ONE ELABORATE SCENE AT A TIME.

CLEARLY ANNA KNOWS HER POOP, AND IS KEENLY VERSED IN THE SUBJECT MATTER. HER FEMINIST ODE TO THE GENRE-WORN TALE OF A SUBURBAN HOUSEWIFE DISCOVERING HER INNER SLUT AS SHE SEXUALLY AWAKENS AND LIBERATES, GRACEFULLY ENCAPSULATES NOT ONLY THE VISUAL AESTHETIC, BUT THE CULTURAL TOMBSTONES THAT MARKED THESE MEMORABLE SKIN-FILLED MOVIES AS WELL.

WHEN ONE OF THE MALE CHARACTERS MONOLOGUES, "THERE WILL NEVER BE A BETTER TIME TO BE A MAN. ENJOY THIS TIME, FOR IT WILL SOON BE GONE, NEVER TO RETURN", IT OPENS A DOOR FOR THE AUDIENCE. THAT DOOR GRANTS US ACCESS TO A BITTERSWEET PLACE IN THE PSYCHE OF EVERY HAIRY-CHESTED SWINGER WHO SAW HIS HEYDAY COMING TO AN END WITH THE DEATH OF THE FREE-LOVE ERA AND THE ADVENT OF NOT ONLY WOMEN'S RIGHTS -- BUT HIV TOO. IT'S A DOOR THAT A LESSER STORYTELLER WOULDN'T HAVE EVEN THOUGHT TO HAVE PROVIDED.

FRIEND OF CINEMA SEWER, MARCUS GOODMAN, DID THIS INTERVIEW WITH ANNA IN MID 2010. LET'S LISTEN IN, SHALL WE?

———

HOW DID YOU CONCEPTUALISE YOUR FIRST FULL-LENGTH FEATURE, VIVA?

I wanted to do a film about a woman with a troubled sexuality, as part of my continued exploration of feminine desire. Coming across some vintage Playboy magazines, I got the idea of placing the character within the world as conceptualised through men's magazines, but from her point of view. It's a world which revolves around fantasy images of women, but that women are somehow not comfortably a part of.

174

FOR VIVA, YOU ASSUME A MULTIFACETED ROLE (DIRECTOR, ACTRESS, WRITER, ETC.). WHAT ARE SOME OF THE CHALLENGES YOU FACED AT THE HELM OF SO MUCH RESPONSIBILITY?

The most difficult part was directing and acting. I could not be in two places at once, and when I was in the makeup chair things on the set slowed down considerably. It's weird to have a set where the director simply disappears into a black hole for stretches of time. It's also very draining to act, so I required a calm set at all times. I could not let the thousands of problems of directing disturb me, or it would show on my face. So I had to switch back and forth between a furiously active thinker and a passive character with nothing at all on my face. The rest was fun - writing, editing, designing, sewing, making storyboards, etc. The only drawback is that it takes a lot of time. The art direction was 90% of the work of making the film, and the editing took fifteen months, including cutting on a flatbed and doing animation by hand.

WERE THERE ANY PRECONCEIVED NOTIONS AUDIENCES HAD ABOUT WHAT YOUR BRAND OF FEMINIST SEXPLOITATION WOULD ENTAIL?

Audiences and critics seem to have been astonished by the fetishistic attention to detail in my

BARBI/VIVA (ANNA BILLER) KISSES HER HUSBAND RICK (CHAD ENGLAND) AFTER WATCHING HIM RACE HIS CAR.

visuals, and how VIVA feels so much like a movie from 1972. So from that response I'm guessing that they thought it would be more like Hollywood movies that capture a past era via a modern style.

THERE'S A REAL VISUAL AUTHENTICITY TO VIVA THAT HARKENS BACK TO THE TECHNICOLOR SCHLOCK OF THE '70S. COULD YOU DESCRIBE THE ADVANTAGES OF SHOOTING ON 35MM FILM INSTEAD OF DIGITAL TO ACHIEVE THAT LOOK?

Film has a different quality than video all down the line, especially when it's projected. 35mm is beautiful. I also love 16mm, which has very saturated color. Video doesn't capture color and light in the same way as film. With film you get very deep blacks, white whites, and saturated reds that digital video can't handle. Film is less uniformly smooth yet softer, more grainy, has more depth, and is more forgiving than video, especially on the hot end (you can get a beautiful image on film even when overexposing by a lot). You can light film in many more ways than video. People look better on film. Technicolor was a process that died in 1975. The film stock was literally dyed. There is nothing today that can capture the beauty and vividness of Technicolor.

DO YOU SEE ANY PARALLELS BETWEEN YOU AND YOUR VIVA CHARACTER?

Only in that we are both a bit passive, and given to experimentation (which can be a bad combination when there are unethical people around). Also, we are both characters that don't quite "fit in." But she is a symbolic rather than a realistic character, a classic scapegoat.

WHAT ARE SOME OF THE UNDERLYING SUBTEXTUAL THEMES IN VIVA THAT MAY NOT BE READILY APPARENT TO VIEWERS?

There is a race theme, which really should be obvious in that my character is a mixed-race person in the middle of white suburbia, but for some reason this is hardly ever picked up on. This is one reason she doesn't "fit in" - she is exotic, other. Her friend Sheila is white and blonde and fits into suburbia perfectly. She is not harmed by the sexual revolution, because she is on the inside and feels in control. My character, Barbi, needs "love" and wants to connect with the outside world. Therefore, she is the one who is harmed. Related to this is the way Barbi is able to traverse worlds which would not seem to include her - the world of gay men, of lesbians, of bohemians and artists - but which she is part of as a family of misfits and outsiders. So, the theme of race fits into a larger sub-theme of alienation, which the sexual revolution tried also to address, and which was one of the successful things it achieved.

WHAT'S SOMETHING ABOUT YOURSELF THAT MOST READERS WOULD BE SURPRISED TO KNOW?

On the whole I'm an introspective, serious person, but my deepest love is for show business. I am someone who would have been considered really wild in the 1950s, but who probably seems strangely anachronistic today. I am shy and polite and I sing jazz standards daily.

WHAT OBSTACLES DO YOU BELIEVE WOMEN FILMMAKERS STILL FACE IN 2010?

All independent filmmakers face formidable obstacles. For women it's a little worse mostly because

MARK (JARED SANFORD) AND CHRIS (BARRY O'ROURKE) GET A SURPRISE VISIT FROM THEIR LOVELY NEIGHBOR KELLY (ANDREA LAIN).

the only recognised consciousness that's taken seriously in the culture at large is still a male consciousness. Therefore, women who feature male characters and points of view are more likely to be successful than women who direct women's stories. And then of course there are still individual men who will block your path at every step because you are female. Androgynous female directors do better in the boys' club that is the film world too, in this culture in which all things feminine are considered weak and ridiculous. One battle I constantly try to wage is to try to erase the stereotypes that equate the feminine with the weak. But we still have a long way to go.

VISIT THE ONLINE VIVA SITE AT:
WWW.LIFEOFASTAR.COM

VISIT MARCUS GOODMAN AT:
HAMSTERTRIATHLON.TUMBLR.com

FROM NERDY TO NYMPHO
THE STORY OF NANCY HOFFMAN

:COUGH: UM, HI THERE.

THE YOUNGEST OF THREE CHILDREN, NANCY HOFFMAN'S PARENTS WERE CONSERVATIVE MID WESTERN TYPES FROM OHIO, WHO MOVED TO FLORIDA WHEN NANCY WAS 9 YEARS OF AGE. AN ODDBALL ARTISTIC GEEK, HOFFMAN GREW UP WITH FEW FRIENDS AND DIDN'T FIT INTO ANY CLIQUES OR DATE MUCH IN HIGH SCHOOL. SHE DIDN'T REALLY FIT IN AT FLORIDA STATE UNIVERSITY EITHER, BUT MANAGED TO LOSE HER VIRGINITY THERE -- AT AGE 17.

"I WANTED TO BE AN ARTIST, AND COLLEGE WAS GOING TO BE MY VEHICLE TO ARTISTIC FAME AND FORTUNE. I DON'T KNOW WHY I WAS SO ENTHUSIASTIC ABOUT BECOMING AN ARTIST. MAYBE ITS BECAUSE I'VE ALWAYS BEEN AN EXHIBITIONIST."

SHE GRADUATED WITH A DOUBLE MAJOR -- BOTH IN ART AND ART HISTORY. SOON SHE BECAME RESTLESS AND UNHAPPY HOWEVER AND LIKE THE BEVERLY HILLBILLIES -- DECIDED TO MIGRATE TO CALIFORNIA.

"UNFORTUNATELY, I WRECKED MY CAR NEAR NEW ORLEANS, AND HAD TO RETURN TO TALLAHASSEE. THAT IS WHERE I WAITRESSED THROUGH THE SUMMER OF 1976. I HATED IT. I WAS BITTERLY DISAPPOINTED THAT I HADN'T MADE IT. I DETESTED THE PLACE I WORKED AT, THE PEOPLE WHO CAME IN, WHAT I WAS DOING. I DON'T THINK THERE IS ANYTHING WRONG WITH BEING A WAITRESS, BUT IN MY STATE OF MIND AT THE TIME, I WAS MISERABLE ABOUT WORKING THERE. I HAD TO DO IT THOUGH, IN ORDER TO MAKE ENOUGH MONEY SO I COULD GIVE IT ANOTHER TRY, AND SEE IF I COULD GET TO CALIFORNIA."

WIDE-EYED, 85 POUNDS SOAKING WET, AND A LITTLE SCARED, NERDY NINETEEN-YEAR-OLD NANCY FINALLY ARRIVED IN SAN FRANCISCO IN SEPTEMBER OF 1976. WITH VERY LITTLE MONEY IN HER BANK ACCOUNT, HER OPTIONS FOR DWELLINGS WERE LIMITED. A SLEAZY NORTH BEACH HOTEL SEEMED AS GOOD A PLACE AS ANY TO BED DOWN WHILE SHE BEGAN ATTENDING CLASSES AT THE SAN FRANCISCO ART INSTITUTE. IT WAS THERE AT SFAI THAT SHE BEFRIENDED A SCRUFFY JANITOR NAMED BOB. BOB'S JOB WAS TO CLEAN UP THE CLASSROOMS, BUT HE ALSO TOOK TIME TO CHAT UP THE NAIVE YOUNG ARTSY GIRLS.

"HE SEEMED REALLY NICE, AND INVITED ME TO THIS NUDE BEACH AND I FREAKED OUT. I COULDN'T HANDLE IT. HE SAID I SHOULD TAKE SOME LSD, AND I DID. AND THE WHOLE SCENE BEGAN TO TAKE ON A WHOLE DIFFERENT ASPECT. I LOVED IT. AFTERWARDS BOB TOOK ME TO HIS PLACE. I MOVED IN."

IT WAS JUST THE WILD AND ADVENTUROUS CHANGE SHE HAD ACHED FOR. SEEMINGLY OVERNIGHT THERE WAS A TRANSFORMATION. SHE WENT FROM A SHY, SOFT-SPOKEN HIPPIE ART-NERD, TO A SLUTTY POT AND LSD-FUELED SUPERCHICK. "I TOTALLY OVERHAULED MY IMAGE. WHERE BEFORE I HAD LOW SELF ESTEEM, MY CONFIDENCE BECAME BUILT UP; WHERE BEFORE I WAS STRAIGHT, I NOW BEGAN TO ENJOY THE NUANCES OF LIFE, AND BEGAN TO TAKE SOME PRIDE IN MY APPEARANCE. MY WHOLE SENSE OF

NANCY CIRCA 1976. SHY ART SCHOOL WEIRDO

NANCY CIRCA 1977. GO-TO GIRL IN L.A. PORN INDUSTRY FOR "TINY TEEN" ROLES

177

From the age of innocence... to the age of consent!

With a friend like Marla who needs Sex Education

Little Me & Marla Strangelove

A FILM BY KIRDY STEVENS

X

Starring DIANNE DALE and NANCY HOFFMAN
Directed by KIRDY STEVENS • Produced by HELENE TERRY

MY SELF CHANGED. I WAS BECOMING HAPPY. LIFE TURNED ME ON. IT WAS LIKE I WAS A NEW PERSON."

NEW FRONTIERS WERE EXPLORED AND CONQUERED. "BOB ENCOURAGED ME TO GAIN ADDITIONAL SEXUAL EXPERIENCES SINCE MY SEXUAL LIFE HAD BEEN SO LIMITED. WE WOULD GO TO BARS, AND PICK UP MEN. IT WAS A SUPERB LESSON IN ASSERTIVENESS, AND THE EXPERIENCES GAVE ME SOME NICE FEELINGS ABOUT MYSELF. ALSO, I MET A LOT OF VERY NICE MEN THAT WAY. PRETTY SOON, BOB AND I STARTED GOING TO ORGIES AND SWINGING PARTIES. THEY WERE A LOT OF FUN!"

"I FELT THAT IF I ENJOYED SEX AS MUCH AS I DID, IF THE EXPLORATIONS OF SEX WERE SO IMPORTANT, WHY NOT GET INTO THE FIELD OF SEX FOR A LIVING? SO I STARTED LOOKING AROUND, CONTACTED A FEW PEOPLE, AND GOT A PART IN A FEATURE FILM DONE IN SAN FRANCISCO BY LOS ANGELES PRODUCERS. IT WAS A LARGE PART, AND I PLAYED A TEENAGE GIRL."

THE MOVIE WAS 1977'S **TEENY BUNS**, AND NANCY STOLE THE SEXY SHOW WITH A WET COMMINGLING WITH THE ALWAYS ERECT JOHN LESLIE, THEN FOLLOWED THAT UP WITH A TERRIFIC TRYST ON THE HOOD OF A CAR WITH RAY WELLS. DIRECTOR STU SEGALL WOULD GO ON TO A DIRECTING CAREER OUTSIDE OF XXX, AND IT WAS PRETTY OBVIOUS TO ANYONE WHO HAPPENED TO PEEP **TEENY BUNS** THAT STU'S YOUNG STAR WAS GONNA BE MAKING MORE DIRTY PICTURES.

STARRING IN SHORT LOOPS TO BE PLAYED IN JERK-OFF BOOTHS AND SOLD ON 8mm REELS IN SEX SHOPS WAS ANOTHER AVENUE THAT HOFFMAN EXPLORED RIGHT OUT OF THE STARTING GATE. "I MET JERRY ABRAMS, WHO IS A MAJOR PRODUCER OF LOOPS -- AND I MET LOWELL PICKETT, WHO USED TO DO BOTH LOOPS AND FEATURE FILMS. IT'S A STRANGE, WEIRD WORLD. THE PEOPLE IN IT ARE MADCAPS, PARTICULARLY THE DIRECTORS. BUT FROM WHAT I'VE SEEN OF PORNOGRAPHIC FILMMAKING THUS FAR? I LIKE IT."

SAN FRANCISCO'S INFAMOUS AND ELEGANTLY DECORATED SUTRO BATHS ALSO LARGELY FACTORED INTO NANCY'S CHOSEN CAREER PATH. THE PLACE BEGAN AS A GAY BATHHOUSE, BUT AS THE SWINGING '70S RAMPED INTO FULL GEAR THE OWNERS DIVERSIFIED AND CATERED TO NOT ONLY THE GAY PUBLIC, BUT TO THE STRAIGHTS AS WELL. IT WAS THERE, THAT ONE EVENING WHILE RECLINING NAKED ON ONE OF THE GIANT PLUSH COUCHES THAT NANCY MET A GIRL WHO HAD RECENTLY SHOT SOME FOOTAGE WITH THE MITCHELL BROTHERS, AND WAS EXTOLLING THEIR VIRTUES. IN FACT, IT TURNED OUT THAT THE AFFABLE YOUNG VIXEN WAS SOON GOING TO BE APPEARING IN A NEW MITCHELL BROS VENTURE: THE ULTRA ROOM. NANCY WAS FASCINATED BY THESE STORIES OF SEXUAL DEBAUCHERY AND GOOD MONEY TO BE HAD, AND WENT TO SEE JIM AND ARTIE MITCHELL THE NEXT DAY. SHE WAS HIRED ON THE SPOT.

THE O'FARRELL THEATRE WAS THE MITCHELLS' HEADQUARTERS FOR THEIR CHAIN OF X-RATED MOVIE HOUSES, AND WAS WHERE THE ULTRA ROOM WAS HOUSED. THERE NANCY PLIED HER TRADE NIGHTLY IN THE LARGE DIMLY LIT ROOM COVERED IN BRASS-STUDDED BLACK VINYL. SHE WOULD DANCE NUDE AND HAVE SEX WITH OTHER FOXY WOMEN IN FRONT OF A MULTITUDE OF ONE-WAY MIRRORS (THE 30 MEN HOUSED IN THE ALWAYS-OCCUPIED BOOTHS COULD SEE HER BUT SHE COULDN'T SEE THEM) AND BY

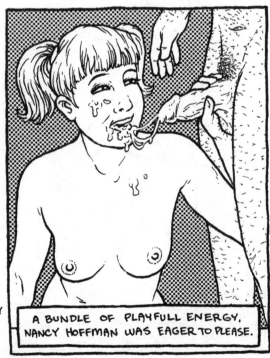

A BUNDLE OF PLAYFULL ENERGY, NANCY HOFFMAN WAS EAGER TO PLEASE.

ALL ACCOUNTS, THE EFFECT THE DIMINUTIVE NYMPHET HAD WAS STARTLING. JIM AND ARTIE WERE CONSTANTLY GETTING REPORTS BACK ABOUT HOW WELL NANCY WAS GOING OVER. THE CREEPY OLD GUYS WHO ACHED FOR THE YOUNG STUFF SEEMED PARTICULARLY TICKLED WITH HER.

"I LOVE PERFORMING IN THE ULTRA ROOM", NANCY ENTHUSIASTICALLY TOLD A REPORTER IN 1977 WHILE TOWELLING THE SWEAT FROM HER LITHE LITTLE BODY AFTER WHAT WAS A PARTICULARLY RAUCOUS PERFORMANCE.

WHEN THE INTERVIEWER SEEMED MYSTIFIED AT HOW SHE COULD POSSIBLY FEEL GOOD ABOUT AN ANONYMOUS AUDIENCE GAZING AT HER AS IF SHE WERE A PIECE OF MEAT, LITTLE NANCY VERBALLY WENT ON THE ATTACK:

"THAT IS WHAT THE ULTRA ROOM IS ABOUT," SHE BARKED. "I LOVE BEING A SEXUAL COMMODITY. IF I WERE A DOCTOR OR AN ATTORNEY, WHAT WOULD I BE SELLING? MEDICAL SKILLS OR LEGAL SKILLS. IF I WERE A SECRETARY, I'D BE SELLING MY ABILITY TO TYPE, FILE, TAKE SHORT HAND, ANSWER THE TELEPHONE. WELL, IM SELLING MY SEXUAL SKILLS, AND AT A PRICE THAT'S FAR IN EXCESS OF WHAT A SECRETARY MAKES AND AT PROBABLY WHAT MOST ATTORNEYS ARE MAKING."

NANCY WAS BECOMING -- AT A TIME WHEN IT WAS FAR MORE RARE AND FAR LESS SOCIALLY ACCEPTABLE -- A PROUD FEMALE CHAMPION OF THE PORN INDUSTRY, AND A TRUE BELIEVER IN THE VALUE AND INTEGRITY OF WHORING. SHE WAS INTELLIGENT, AND WOULDN'T BE TALKED DOWN TO OR BELITTLED.

"HAVE YOU NOTICED THAT THE WOMEN WITH ESTABLISHED NAMES AREN'T DOING PORN FILMS ANYMORE?" SHE ASKED AN INTERVIEWER IN 1977. "LINDA LOVELACE AND MARILYN CHAMBERS HAVE DROPPED OUT AND ARE SATISFIED AT BEING THIRD-RATE IN OTHER FIELDS INSTEAD OF DEVELOPING THE ART THAT GAVE THEM THEIR FAME. OTHERS, WHO MADE A SPLASH WITH ONE BIG PART, BURN OUT FOR ONE REASON OR ANOTHER. THEY THINK THEY'RE GRETA GARBO OR GLENDA JACKSON AND THEY WAIT AROUND TO BE DISCOVERED BY HOLLYWOOD, BECOME AMBIVALENT ABOUT WHAT THEY'VE DONE, OR THEY BECOME DRUG FREAKS AND DON'T CONCENTRATE ON THEIR CAREERS. I ONLY WANT TO BE A PORN STAR, TO BECOME RICH AND FAMOUS IN THE EROTIC CINEMA. AND ILL DO WHAT I HAVE TO DO TO ACCOMPLISH THIS."

HER HARD WORK AND ENERGETIC ATTITUDE WOULD SERVE HER WELL IN THE NEXT YEAR. THANKS TO A TIGHT, SMALL-BREASTED FIGURE AND FRESH-FACED PIGTAILED LOOK, NANCY SOON BECAME THE GO-TO SLUT FOR YOUNG GIRL ROLES IN COMING OF AGE PORNO SHOT IN CALIFORNIA. IF THE SCRIPT NEEDED A BEAUTIFUL YOUNG BITCH BEING INTRODUCED TO THE WORLD OF SEX FOR THE FIRST TIME, IT SEEMED LIKE NANCY WAS THE GAL WHO GOT THE PHONE CALL TO COME DOWN AND AUDITION.

TURNS AS A VIRGINAL SCHOOLGIRL, PROM QUEEN, OR OTHER SEEMINGLY BARELY LEGAL CHARACTERS MADE NANCY'S FEATURES LIKE **LITTLE ME AND MARIA STRANGELOVE**, **TAXI GIRLS**, **ONE PAGE OF LOVE** AND **THE OTHER SIDE OF JULIE** INTO PANTS-PUNCHING CLASSICS. SHE ALSO PERFORMED ONE OF PORN'S FIRSTS: THE VERY FIRST DOUBLE-FISTING! NANCY'S SMALL PAWS CAME IN VERY HANDY (HEH HEH! I COULDN'T RESIST...) FOR THE TASK, WHICH WAS DEFTLY PERFORMED UPON EILEEN WELLES IN **CANDY STRIPERS** (1978). YOU GOTTA KEEP IN MIND THAT AT THE TIME MANY PORN VIEWERS HADN'T EVEN PONDERED THE CONCEPT OF FIST-FUCKING, LET ALONE WITNESSED A DOUBLE-DOWN VAGINA/FISTS SEX-COLLISION.

ANYWAY, IT WAS A BRIGHT STAR, BUT IT SEEMS TO ME THAT IT BURNED OUT RATHER QUICKLY. NANCY SQUIRMED THROUGH ONLY 3 OR 4 STARRING ROLES IN A FILMOGRAPHY THAT REACHED NEARLY 20 FEATURES BEFORE HER EARLY RETIREMENT IN 1981. CLEARLY SHE'D NEVER GOTTEN WEALTHY FROM WORKING IN ADULT FILMS THE WAY SHE'D HOPED AND PLANNED FOR. WHEN CONTACTED BY EROTIC FILM GUIDE IN 1983, SHE LET IT BE KNOWN THAT EVEN THOUGH SHE'D SINCE DEPARTED FROM XXX, SHE HADN'T YET BEEN FORGOTTEN.

"MY FANS WON'T LET ME FORGET ABOUT MY YEARS IN FILMS. MEN STILL COME UP TO ME AND COMPLAIN THAT I'M DEPRIVING THEM OR SOMETHING, JUST BECAUSE I DON'T WANT TO DO IT IN FRONT OF A CAMERA ANYMORE."

ALTHOUGH RUMOURS HAVE HER MARRYING A RICH FOREIGN DIGNITARY JUST BEFORE DROPPING OFF THE FACE OF THE PLANET, NO ONE CAN CONFIRM THE TRUE POST CELLULOID FUCK PUMP YEARS OF MISS NANCY. CERTAINLY AN EDUCATED GUESS WOULD TAKE INTO ACCOUNT HER INDEPENDENT ADVENTURE-SEEKING NATURE AND HER PASSION FOR THE ARTS. ONCE A NERD, ALWAYS A NERD.

—BOUGIE
2010.

SKINTIGHT (1981) DIR: ED DE PRIEST

Skintight

EMOTIONALLY INTENSE AND SLIGHTLY SURREAL EARLY EIGHTIES HARDCORE IS WHERE IT IS AT, ESPECIALLY WHEN IT IS AS WELL MADE AS THIS ONE IS. THE SKINTIGHT DVD CASE SAYS IT QUITE SUCCINCTLY, I SUPPOSE:

"DIRECTOR ED DE PRIEST BRINGS YOU IN CLOSE AND TIGHT FOR PULSE-POUNDING HARDCORE ACTION! CHECK INTO DR. CHAMBER'S SEX CLINIC AND GIVE YOUR LIBIDO A THOROUGH CHECK UP. HIS TWO SEDUCTIVE THERAPISTS, MARIA AND SAMANTHA, HAVE JUST THE RIGHT PRESCRIPTION TO STIFFEN YOUR SAGGING SEX LIFE."

THIS MOVIE RULES, AND THE SOUNDTRACK IS PRETTY HARD TO BEAT. WE'VE GOT SOME EARLY B-52S, SOME SWEET-ASS OLD SKOOL VANGELIS ("PULSTAR", FROM HIS LATE '70s ALBUM "ALBEDO 0.39"), AND AS MENTIONED BY ONE MESSAGE BOARDER, THE ORIGINAL TITLE TRACK SONG WOULDN'T BE AT ALL OUT OF PLACE ON PAUL STANLEY'S 1978 SOLO EFFORT.

THE CAST IS WELL PUT TOGETHER IN TERMS OF FEMALE FLESH. ANNETTE HAVEN IS HER USUAL ALOOF ALABASTER -SKINNED SELF, CONNIE PETERSON TAKES SOME COCK UP HER BUMHOLE, ACROBATIC CHRIS CASSIDY ENJOYS A GOOEY SEMEN FACIAL, TERMINALLY PISSED OFF LEE CARROLL SLOSHES AROUND IN A HOT TUB, AND REDHEAD LISA DELEEUW WEARS AN AMAZING STUDDED COLLAR AND GOBBLES ANY DONG THAT GETS WITHIN 5 FEET OF HER YAPPER. THERE IS ALSO LOVELY MAI LIN FOR THOSE OF YOU THAT LIKE THE ASIAN STUFF, AND MARIA TORTUGA FOR THE LATINA-LOVERS.

PAUL THOMAS PLAYS A GREAT MENTALLY UNSTABLE KOOK, ALTHOUGH HE DOESN'T GO AS FAR WITH IT AS DO PORNO CRAZY MEN GEORGE PAYNE, ZEBEDY COLT OR JAMIE GILLIS -- BUT THEN AGAIN, WHO

ILLUSTRATIONS BY SCOTT FAULKNER: WWW.VINYLSAURUS.COM

DOES? PAUL DOES, HOWEVER, APTLY COMBINE HIS SEX APPEAL WITH THE OVERTLY OBSESSIVE (ONLY IN A PORN MOVIE WOULD AN S&M BONDAGE MAGAZINE DRIVE SOMEONE MAD) AND THE SINISTER. MOST OF HIS INSANITY IS DISPLAYED TO US WITHIN AN ENTERTAINING AND REOCCURRING NEW-WAVE NIGHTMARE FANTASY WHERE THE FEMALE MEMBERS OF THE CAST BECOME SEX-VIXENS DRESSED IN SKINTIGHT SLUT ATTIRE.

THESE TIGHTLY EDITED FANTASY SEQUENCES TOTALLY MAKE THE WHOLE THING WHAT IT IS, AND KEEP THE XXX CONTENT FROM BEING FORMULAIC (A MAJOR PROBLEM IN

NORTH AMERICAN SMUT). I REALLY LOVE THE GIANT CHROME AVIATOR SUNGLASSES ON THE GIRLS, THE STOCKINGS AND GARTERS, THE UNSHAVED BEAVER, AND THE PUNK/BONDAGE MUSIC VIDEO FASHION.

SIMPLY PUT, THIS IS THE XXX YOU CONFIDENTLY HAND TO YOUR YOUNG HIPSTER PALS WHO WANT SOME COOL CLASSIC SMUT, BUT AREN'T SURE WHERE TO FIND THE STUFF THAT SPEAKS DIRECTLY TO THEIR VINTAGE 1980s AESTHETICS AND MUSIC TASTES. ·2011·
-BOUGIE☆

HOOKERS ON DAVIE

ART BY BEN NEWMAN:
BENNEWMANART.BLOGSPOT.COM

ONE OF MY MOST CHERISHED DOCUMENTARIES ABOUT THE PROFESSION OF STREET SIDE SEX WORKING JUST HAPPENS TO HAVE BEEN MADE ON THE VERY PAVEMENT THAT I HOOF UPON DAILY, HERE IN MY HOME TURF OF VANCOUVER, BRITISH COLUMBIA, CANADA. IT IS A MOVIE CALLED HOOKERS ON DAVIE, AND IT DOCUMENTS A HOST OF INTERESTING PROSTITUTES IN THEIR NATURAL HABITAT.

AT THE TIME, DAVIE STREET IN VANCOUVER WAS "THE PROSTITUTION CAPITAL OF CANADA", AND JANIS COLE AND HOLLY DALE DECIDED TO RECORD THAT TIME AND PLACE WITH THEIR CAMERAS. THEY DID THEIR HOMEWORK, SPENDING EIGHT MONTHS RESEARCHING, AND TWO MONTHS FILMING THE DRIVE-IN BROTHEL THAT WAS DAVIE. THEY GAINED THE CONFIDENCE AND TRUST OF THEIR CHOSEN SUBJECTS, AND THE WORK BENEFITS.

PIMPS WERE NOT AN ISSUE FOR THESE WHORES, BECAUSE THEY WERE ORGANISED THROUGH A MUTUAL SUPPORT SYSTEM. THEY WOULD MEET UP NIGHTLY AT A NEARBY RESTAURANT CALLED THE COLUMBIAN, AND WARN EACH OTHER OF POTENTIALLY DANGEROUS CLIENTS AND DISCUSS HEALTH ISSUES. THIS ACTIVITY IS FILMED, AS IS THE SLEAZY, VIVID PROCESS OF PICKING UP JOHNS AND NEGOTIATING PRICES. ALL INVOLVED ARE CASUAL AND FORTHCOMING ABOUT WHAT IT MEANS (BOTH PERSONALLY AND SOCIALLY) TO MAKE A LIVING ON YOUR BACK.

PROSTITUTION IS LEGAL IN CANADA, BUT SOON AFTER SHOOTING FINISHED, ON JULY 4th, 1984, A SEX TRADE INJUNCTION FORCED THE LADIES OF THE NIGHT OUT OF THE WEST END OF THE 'COUV AND AWAY FROM DAVIE STREET. IT WAS AN ILL-CONCEIVED DECISION PUT IN PLACE BY HAND-WRINGING MORALISTS, AND IT HAD LETHAL CONSEQUENCES.

AT THE TIME THE CITY WAS GETTING READY TO HOST THE WORLD AT EXPO '86, AND FELT IT NEEDED MINISKIRTED WIENER SUCKERS HIDDEN AWAY FROM THE PUBLIC EYE. THE GIRLS WERE FORCED TO RELOCATE, BUT AS

SOON AS THEY BEGAN PLYING THEIR BONER-RELATED TRADE IN THE REMOTE WAREHOUSE DISTRICTS, THEY BECAME SCATTERED AND UNPROTECTED FODDER FOR VIOLENT PREDATORS. THE MOST FAMOUS OF THESE BUTCHERS WAS SERIAL KILLER/PIG FARMER ROBERT "WILLIE" PICKTON, WHO HAD A VANCOUVER HOOKER KILL COUNT OF NEARLY 50, A SCORE AMASSED WHILE VANCOUVER POLICE LOOKED THE OTHER WAY.

"THE KILLING FIELDS WERE CREATED", FORMER DAVIE ST. TRANNY PROSTITUTE JAMIE LEE HAMILTON SAYS. "THEY SENT THE MESSAGE TO WACKOS THAT IT'S OK TO COME DOWN AND HARM PROSTITUTES. 'GET RID OF THEM FOR US'."

DISPLACING THE WHORES SOLVED NOTHING, AND THE INJUNCTION INADVERTENTLY ENDED UP DESTROYING HUNDREDS OF LIVES. IT ALSO MARKED THE BEGINNING OF THE GENTRIFICATION OF THE AREA (UNPOPULAR AMONGST LOWER AND MIDDLE CLASS VANCOUVERITES), WHICH NOW FINDS THE CITY RANKED AS THE THIRD MOST EXPENSIVE PLACE TO LIVE IN NORTH AMERICA.

NEEDLESS TO SAY, THIS DOCUMENTARY IS A FASCINATING TIME CAPSULE, AND IS RELEVANT TODAY AS IT WAS IN 1984. COLE AND DALE WON "BEST DOCUMENTARY" FOR THEIR EFFORT AT THE CHICAGO INTERNATIONAL FILM FEST, ALTHOUGH HOOKERS ON DAVIE REMAINS AN ELUSIVE RARITY TO THIS DAY, WITH NO DVD RELEASE OR PLANS TO DO ONE.
— BOUGIE
. 2011.

KILLED FOR BEING TOO GOOD OF AN ACTOR?

AUUGH!

IN EARLY NOVEMBER 2010, A SECURITY GUARD SHOT AND KILLED AN ACTOR ON A MOVIE SET. POLICE IN THE PHILIPPINES, WHERE THE INCIDENT TOOK PLACE, REPORTED THAT A NIGHT WATCHMAN NAMED EDDIE CUIZON POPPED CAPS IN 32-YEAR-OLD ACTOR KIRK ABELLA THINKING THAT THE STAGED CLOSING SCENE FOR THE MOVIE **GOING SOMEWHERE**, WAS REAL LIFE. ABELLA WAS WEARING A MASK, BRANDISHING A FAKE PLASTIC GUN, AND RIDING A MOTORCYCLE WHEN HE WAS FELLED BY THE TRIGGER-HAPPY RENT-A-COP. FILIPINO NEWSPAPER DIARIO NOTED THAT BRITISH DIRECTOR ALAN LYDDIARD WAS HORRIFIED ABOUT WHAT HAD TRANSPIRED ON HIS SET, AND THAT CUIZON FACES CHARGES OF HOMICIDE AND VIOLATION OF A GUN BAN. SOME SOURCES SAY THAT CUIZON THOUGHT HE WAS KILLING ONE OF THE ARMED MEN WHO HAD BEEN LINKED TO A SERIES OF LOCAL MURDERS, AND HAD NO CLUE THAT A MOVIE WAS FILMING IN THE AREA.
— BOUGIE

THE EVIL THAT MEN DO (1984) DIR: J. LEE THOMPSON

THIS CHARLES BRONSON FILM WAS ORIGINALLY DEVELOPED BY THE CANNON GROUP, AND CERTAINLY HAS THE EXPLOITATIONAL GRINDHOUSE PUNCH OF ONE OF THEIR PRODUCTIONS -- NOT TO MENTION THE FACT THAT IT WAS DIRECTED BY J. LEE THOMPSON, A PROLIFIC CANNON HELMSMAN THROUGHOUT THE EIGHTIES.

SHOT IN MEXICO, THIS ACTION-REVENGE SHOCKER IS POLITICALLY THEMED, BUT HAS A VERY CRUEL AND SADISTIC BENT TO IT. CHARLIE PLAYS AN OUT-OF-WORK ASSASSIN WHO COMES OUT OF RETIREMENT TO TRACK A TORTURE-HAPPY DOCTOR WHO MESSILY MURDERS POLITICAL PRISONERS, AND TEACHES HIS VILE TORTURE TECHNIQUES TO HIGH PAYING SOUTH AMERICAN DICTATORS. ELECTRIFIED TESTICLES, ANYONE?

HOW BADASS IS BRONSON? ONE ANSWER TO THAT QUESTION COMES IN THE FORM OF THE "BARROOM PENIS TWISTING SCENE" (WHICH SPEAKS FOR ITSELF). ANOTHER IS WHEN HE ATTACHES A FIRE HOSE TO A MAN'S NECK, AND PUSHES HIM OFF A HIGH RISE. AND YET ANOTHER EXAMPLE IS BRONSON'S WILLINGNESS TO POSE AS A BISEXUAL SWINGER JUST TO GET CLOSE ENOUGH TO STAB A TURTLENECK-WEARING MAN IN THE NECK. I WON'T GIVE AWAY THE VIOLENT AND EXPLOSIVE ENDING, BUT I WILL SAY THAT ITS PICKAXE-THEMED FURY IS HELLA WORTH STICKING AROUND FOR. GOOD STUFF. CHECK IT OUT.
— BOUGIE

TABOO (1980) AND TABOO II (1982)

WHILE THE FIRST INSTALMENT OF THIS CLASSIC HARDCORE PORN SERIES DEVOTED TO INCESTUOUS SCENARIOS IS OFTEN MENTIONED IN THE SAME BREATH AS DEEP THROAT AS ONE OF THE BIGGEST MONEY MAKERS IN SMUT CINEMA HISTORY, IT IS ACTUALLY THE SECOND OFFERING THAT PROVIDES THE HIGHER QUALITY VIEWING EXPERIENCE. I KNOW THIS IS NOT NORMALLY THE RULE IN THIS "SEQUELS SUCK" AGE THAT WE FIND OURSELVES IN, BUT XXX IS A DIFFERENT ANIMAL THAN OTHER GENRES. WHAT IS DOWN IS UP, AND WHAT IS A GUY'S BONER INSIDE A LUBED-UP COCK GARAGE, IS ACTUALLY A GUY'S BONER INSIDE HIS SISTER.

SHOT ON FILM, TABOO II IS BLESSED WITH COMPETENT DIRECTION FROM KIRDY STEVENS, A COMPELLINGLY OFFBEAT STORY LINE WRITTEN BY HELENE TERRIE, BELIEVABLE ACTING, AND A BUTTLOAD OF STEAMY FUCK SCENES. IT CONCERNS SHERRY McBRIDE (DOROTHY LeMAY) AND HER RELATIONS WITHIN HER OWN FAMILY, AND SOME OF THIS STUFF IS PURE DYNAMITE. DOROTHY CLIMBING INTO BED WITH HER DAD -- WHILE HE LAYS NEXT TO HER SLEEPING MOM -- AND SECRETIVELY COAXING A LOAD OUT OF HIM? AMAZING PORN, MY BROTHERS AND SISTERS. LEGENDARY.

IN ITS FAVOUR, PART ONE DID TAKE THE CONCEPT FAR MORE SERIOUSLY, WHICH WILL BE MORE OF A TURN ON FOR THE TRUE INCEST FETISHISTS. UNUSUAL FOR HARDCORE, WE'RE GIVEN A REASONABLY BELIEVABLE TRIGGER FOR THE SEXUAL RELATIONSHIP TO FOLLOW BETWEEN KAY PARKER'S MIDDLE-AGED CHARACTER AND HER CONFUSED SON, PLAYED BY MIKE RANGER. KAY NOW HAS A CAREER AS A NEW AGE METAPHYSICAL COUNSELOR AND LECTURER. IN 2001, SHE PENNED AN AUTOBIOGRAPHY CALLED "TABOO: SACRED, DON'T TOUCH", AND HAS ADMITTED IN RECENT YEARS THAT THERE WAS A SERIOUS MUTUAL ATTRACTION BETWEEN HER AND RANGER, DESPITE THE 12-YEAR GAP BETWEEN THEIR AGES.

KAY WAS NOT THEN, AND IS NOT NOW -- A HOTTIE. BUT IF YOU'VE NEVER REALLY UNDERSTOOD WHAT MADE KAY WORTHY OF BONERS, YOU PROBABLY HAVEN'T SEEN THE ORIGINAL TABOO. SHE MADE HER ENTIRE FUCKING CAREER OFF THIS ONE ROLE, A PRAGMATIC PERFORMANCE THAT IS SURE TO STICK IN THE CRAWS OF MOST ANYONE WHO SAW IT, ESPECIALLY IF THEY WITNESSED IT IN THEIR FORMATIVE YEARS LIKE I DID.

BUT YOU KNOW, THERE IS SOMETHING TO SAY FOR THE LUDICROUS HEIGHTS ATTAINED HERE IN PART TWO, WITH BROTHER, SISTER, MOM AND DAD ALL GETTING IN ON THE SWEATY, LIBIDINOUS ACT. SURE, ANY PRETENCE AT REALISM IS SOUNDLY CHUCKED OUT, BUT IF YOU APPROACH TABOO II AS YOU WOULD APPROACH ROBERT CRUMB'S INFAMOUS "JOE BLOW" COMIC BOOK -- THAT IS, AS PROVOCATIVE SOCIAL SATIRE -- IT SLAYS.

— BOUGIE 2011

(IN CASE THERE IS ANY CONFUSION -- AS WHEN THE GENRE OF INCEST PORN IS DISCUSSED -- THERE SO OFTEN CAN BE -- NONE OF THE ACTORS OR CHARACTERS IN THE AFOREMENTIONED FILMS ARE UNDERAGE.)

$986,542
FIRST 11 DAYS TEXAS PREMIERE SATURATION
TINTORERA
...Tiger Shark
IS CHURNING UP A
BOX-OFFICE TIDAL WAVE!
Watch the Box-Office excitement across the U.S.A.
New Orleans/Memphis March 31
Jacksonville April 21

AS YOU CAN SEE FROM THE ABOVE AD THAT APPEARED IN VARIETY MAGAZINE, TINTORERA PLEASED THEATER OWNERS BY MAKING GOOD MONEY FOR THEM UPON ITS U.S. RELEASE IN 1978. JAWS FANS (HUNGRY FOR MORE IN THE WAKE OF SPIELBERG'S 1975 SALT-WATER FUELED BLOCKBUSTER) PACKED THEATERS, NO DOUBT EXPECTING ANOTHER TENSE BEACH BLANKET GORE-FEST. MOST OF THEM SURELY LEFT DISAPPOINTED. YOU DON'T EVEN SEE A SHARK UNTIL A HALF HOUR IN, AND THERE ARE ONLY THREE 30-SECOND LONG SHARK ATTACKS THAT SEEM TO HAVE BEEN INCLUDED AS AN AFTERTHOUGHT. OF COURSE, NONE OF THE WELL-EXECUTED, VIOLENCE-SOAKED EXPLOITATION MARKETING (POSTERS, TRAILERS, RADIO ADS) GAVE ANY CLUE OF THE LET-DOWN FACING EXCITEMENT-STARVED GENRE FANS.

NO, THE REAL MEAT AND POTATOES OF THIS MOVIE IS ROMANCE AND LAZY VACATION LIVING. SPECIFICALLY, A THREE WAY LOVE TRIANGLE BETWEEN TWO MEN (HUGO STIGLITZ, ANDRES GARCIA) AND A WOMAN (SUSAN GEORGE, WHOM YOU MAY REMEMBER FROM HER STARRING ROLE IN STRAW DOGS). THE WHOLE THING IS SHOT TRAVEL-VIDEO STYLE ON LOCATION IN BEAUTIFUL CANCUN AND PUERTO JUAREZ, MEXICO BY LEGENDARY HISPANIC SCHLOCKMEISTER RENE CARDONA JR, WHO MUST HAVE GOTTEN A DECENT KICKBACK FROM THE OWNERS OF THE EAST COAST RESORT AT WHICH MUCH OF HIS MOVIE WAS FILMED. THE RESULTING FOOTAGE FEELS LIKE A BIG LONG ADVERTISEMENT FOR A WILD AND LOVELY CANCUN THAT NOW EXISTS MERELY AS A MEMORY DUE TO THE DESTRUCTIVE EFFECTS OF COLONIZING TOURISTS AND THE AMENITIES THAT SERVICE THEM.

THAT THIS HAS ROUTINELY BEEN PUT IN THE HORROR SECTION OF VIDEOSTORES OVER THE DECADES IS PRETTY FUNNY TO ME NOW THAT I'VE SEEN IT, BECAUSE CATEGORIZING THIS AS

SWINGIN' SUN-SOAKED SEXPLOITATION CINEMA WOULD BE FAR MORE ACCURATE. SHIT, HOLMES -- IT'S MORE TINTO BRASS THAN TINTORERA. LOOK FORWARD TO SCENE AFTER SCENE OF THE CAST IN LITTLE-TO-NO CLOTHING AS THEY SWIM, DRINK COPIOUS AMOUNTS OF ALCOHOL, SMOKE, DISCUSS SEXUAL POLITICS, PARTAKE IN SOME OVERT HOMOSEXUAL SUBTEXT, DANCE TO DISCO, AND EVEN FINALLY GET AROUND TO HAVING SOME SLUTTY SEX. CARDONA JR. MADE SURE THERE WAS A FAIR BIT OF SKIN IN HIS MOVIE, WITH BOTH OF THE MALE LEADS SHOWING IT ALL, NOT TO MENTION NUDITY FROM 7 OF THE LOVELY FEMALE CAST MEMBERS. OF SPECIFIC INTEREST TO THREE'S COMPANY FANS WILL BE AN APPEARANCE BY A GIGGLY PRISCILLA BARNES, WHO IS BRIEFLY SHOWN TOPLESS. DOES ANY OF THAT SOUND TITILLATING? SORRY IF IT DID, BECAUSE AT OVER 2 HOURS THE MOVIE IS MOSTLY A YAWNER.

AND YET THERE IS SOMETHING HERE. SOMETHING JUST UNDER THE SURFACE, SNEAKING UP ON YOU JUST WHEN YOUR EYELIDS WERE GETTING HEAVY. I WAS READY TO DISMISS TINTORERA AS A CRUDDY MOVIE AND NOTHING MORE, AND I SURELY WOULD IF NOT FOR ONE OF THOSE AFOREMENTIONED 30-SECOND SHARK ATTACK SCENES. SURE, IT'S SHORT, BUT IT'S AN INCREDIBLE SEQUENCE THAT HONESTLY MAY WELL BE THE MOST REALISTIC SHARK ATTACK EVER TO BE FOUND IN A FICTIONAL FILM. BECAUSE IT IS SURROUNDED BY SUCH A LANGUID MOVIE, MOST REVIEWERS DON'T TAKE NOTE OF HOW SPECIAL THIS PART WAS IN THEIR WRITE-UPS, BUT I'M NOT THE ONLY ONE THAT WAS BEWILDERED BY WHAT RENE CARDONA JR. SURPRISINGLY SERVED UP FROM OUT OF NOWHERE. REVIEWER ELIZABETH A. KINGSLEY (WHOSE EXCELLENT FILM REVIEW WEBSITE CAN BE FOUND AT AYCYAS.COM) ALSO SAT UP AND TOOK NOTICE.

"(IT) ACHIEVES SOMETHING THAT SUCH SCENES RARELY DO", SHE WROTE OF THE SCENE IN QUESTION IN HER OTHERWISE SCATHING REVIEW OF TINTORERA. "IT CAPTURES ABSOLUTELY THE BEWILDERMENT, THE PANIC, THE HORRIFYING RANDOMNESS OF IT ALL; THE REDUCTION OF HOMO SAPIENS IN AN INSTANT TO THE PRIMAL LEVEL OF THE HERD ANIMAL, STAMPEDING IN TERROR FROM THE WATER. THERE IS SOME EXCELLENT USE OF OVERHEAD AND UNDERWATER PHOTOGRAPHY HERE, GIVING THE VIEWER A PERSPECTIVE THAT THE CHARACTERS DON'T HAVE. IT IS, FOR NO REASON IN THE WORLD, CYNTHIA WHO LOSES THE LOTTERY. SHE IS IN ESTEBAN'S ARMS, FLOATING AND BEING KISSED, WHEN THE SHARK SLIDES UP AND TAKES OFF HER LEG. THE WATER EXPLODES IN A BLOODY CLOUD. THERE IS SCREAMING, HYSTERIA. THE OTHERS FLAIL AND BLUNDER TOWARDS THE SHORE; ALL BUT ESTEBAN, WHO BRAVELY ATTEMPTS TO RESCUE THE UNCONSCIOUS CYNTHIA, CATCHING HOLD OF HER AND TRYING TO CARRY HER TO SAFETY -- ONLY TO HAVE THE SHARK CIRCLE BACK AND DRAG THE REST OF HER FROM HIS ARMS."

HOW THEY EVEN FILMED THIS BRIEF-BUT-HARROWING SEQUENCE IS BEYOND ME. IT'S CLEAR THAT THE ACTORS ARE IN THE WATER WITH A LARGE, REAL SHARK, AND IT REALLY DOES SWIM OVER AND RIP AND THRASH (WHAT REALLY DOES LOOK LIKE) CYNTHIA'S (LAURA LYONS) PRONE BODY RIGHT OUT OF ESTABAN'S (HUGO STIGLITZ) ARMS AND START TO FEED. DID THEY DRUG THE SHARK? IF SO, HOW DOES IT MOVE SO QUICK? HOW DID THEY GET THOSE SHOTS SAFELY WITHOUT PUTTING THEIR CAST IN INCREDIBLE DANGER? I KNOW LIFE IS CHEAP IN SOUTH AMERICA, BUT HOLY SHIT. AMAZING STUFF.

ASIDE FROM THAT SURPRISING AND SKILFULLY-STAGED SAVAGERY, THE ONLY TRULY MEMORABLE VIOLENCE IN THE MOVIE IS THE SENSELESS SLAUGHTERING OF ACTUAL SHARKS FOR NO GOOD REASON. IT'S EXCESSIVE, THE WAY THE MOVIE DEVOTES SUCH A SIZABLE CHUNK OF ITS RUNTIME TO MAKING US WATCH A COUPLE OF RECREATIONAL DIVING PROTAGONISTS BUTCHER (UNMOTIVATED, I SHOULD ADD) EVERY MANNER OF SMALLER SHARK AND LIVING OCEAN CREATURE SIMPLY BECAUSE THEY CAN. IT'S JUST... GROSS. SOME OF THESE SLOW MOTION SCENES LOOK LIKE STOCK FOOTAGE, BUT I'VE ALSO READ OTHER SOURCES THAT STATE THAT MANY OF THESE POOR ANIMALS WERE KILLED FOR THE SAKE OF THE MOVIE AND YOUR "ENJOYMENT". SO IF MONDO-STYLE ANIMAL DEATH BUMS YOU OUT, STEER CLEAR.

IN MEMORIAM: ANDY COPP

ON JANUARY 14th, 2013, INDEPENDENT FILMMAKER, ACTOR, ARTIST AND WRITER, ANDREW COPP, TOOK HIS OWN LIFE. HE WAS 40 YEARS OLD.

ANDY AND I HAD BEEN ONLINE FRIENDS (AND BEFORE THAT, PEN-PALS THROUGH THE MAIL) FOR OVER 12 YEARS. WE WERE INTRODUCED BY A MUTUAL FRIEND, AND WE WERE BONDED BY OUR MUTUAL LOVE OF ODD AND UNUSUAL CINEMA. WE NEVER MET IN PERSON SINCE WE LIVE IN TOTALLY DIFFERENT SECTIONS OF THE CONTINENT, BUT THE AMOUNT OF MOVIE ZINES AND FILMS WE TRADED THROUGH THE MAIL MADE ANDY COPP'S NAME A WELL-KNOWN ONE IN MY HOUSEHOLD.

BACK IN THE LATE '90S AND EARLY 2000S ANDY PUBLISHED A MOVIE ZINE CALLED NEON MADNESS. THE HIGHLIGHT OF THIS SERIES, IN MY OPINION, WAS AN EXCLUSIVE INTERVIEW THAT ANDY RAN IN

WE ALL ♡ YOU, ANDY...R.I.P.

BOUGIE '13

ITS 8TH ISSUE WITH NOW DECEASED FILMMAKER ROGER WATKINS. AS THE PUBLISHER OF CINEMA SEWER ZINE, I WAS SO JEALOUS! SPEAKING OF WHICH, ANDY WROTE THE TERRIFIC "I WISH I'D TAPED THAT: THE ORIGINAL UNDERGROUND COMPILATION VIDEOS" ARTICLE IN CINEMA SEWER #23 -- EASILY THE HIGHLIGHT OF THAT ISSUE, AND A SMART PIECE OF JOURNALISM THAT REVEALED A DEEP KNOWLEDGE AND RESPECT FOR THE MOSTLY UNKNOWN HISTORY OF VIDEO EPHEMERA. (IT WAS REPRINTED IN BOOK 4)

BUT IT WAS WITH HIS DEEPLY PERSONAL FILMMAKING THAT ANDY REALLY USED HIS CREATIVE VOICE. COPP LIVED IN DAYTON, OHIO, AND WAS AN ABSOLUTE GODFATHER OF THE UNDERGROUND LOW-BUDGET HORROR/EXPLOITATION FILM SCENE, SEEMINGLY THERE FROM THE BEGINNING WHEN IT COMES TO THIS GENERATION OF INDEPENDENT FILMMAKERS. HIS MOVIES WERE ALWAYS CHALLENGING, BLOOD-SOAKED, AND NEVER BORING. THEY DEMANDED A REACTION, AND WEREN'T EASILY FORGOTTEN, AND WITH THE AMOUNT OF UTTERLY DERIVATIVE PABLUM GENRE FANS HAVE TO WADE THROUGH TO FIND MEANINGFUL WORK, I CAN THINK OF NO BETTER COMPLIMENT TO ANDY AND HIS FILMOGRAPHY.

REST IN PEACE, MY FRIEND. YOU WERE A WONDERFUL, INTELLIGENT PERSON WHO SEEMED TO ALWAYS HAVE TIME OR WORDS OF ENCOURAGEMENT FOR OTHERS IN NEED. YOUR UNWAVERING KINDNESS WAS AND WILL ALWAYS BE FUCKING LEGENDARY, AND I SO DEEPLY WISH I COULD TALK TO YOU NOW -- BUT THIS WILL HAVE TO DO.

-- ROBIN BOUGIE, JANUARY 21ST, 2013

index

(Note: Entries in bold refer exclusively to illustrations.)

index

index

The Complete Cinema Sewer Book Collection is Published by FAB Press

CINEMA SEWER VOLUME 1
The Adults Only Guide to History's
Sickest and Sexiest Movies!

ISBN: 978-1-903254-45-5
Pages: 192
UK Price: £14.99
US Price: $19.95

"What sets Cinema Sewer apart is that even
though the coverage is of the most insane,
repellent smut around, Robin's writing never
seems to pander... it's a refreshing approach."
Neon Madness magazine

CINEMA SEWER VOLUME 2
The Adults Only Guide to History's
Sickest and Sexiest Movies!

ISBN: 978-1-903254-56-1
Pages: 192
UK Price: £14.99
US Price: $19.95

"Prepare to veer wildly between curiosity,
arousal, disgust, laughter, embarrassment,
disbelief, confusion and uncontrollable glee.
Such is the power of Cinema Sewer."
The Nerve magazine

CINEMA SEWER VOLUME 3
The Adults Only Guide to History's
Sickest and Sexiest Movies!

ISBN: 978-1-903254-64-6
Pages: 192
UK Price: £14.99
US Price: $19.95

"Overwhelmingly positive in outlook. Intelligent,
relaxed and unpretentious, the book has a DIY
aesthetic that screams punk chic while the
text offers an unrelenting renegade attitude."
Sex Gore Mutants website

CINEMA SEWER VOLUME 4
The Adults Only Guide to History's
Sickest and Sexiest Movies!

ISBN: 978-1-903254-74-5
Pages: 192
UK Price: £14.99
US Price: $19.95

"Cinema Sewer is the direct heir and foremost
survivor of decades of mayhem-trash-film
fanzines, and Bougie has proven there's still
meatballs to be pulled out of the gravy."
www.quimbys.com

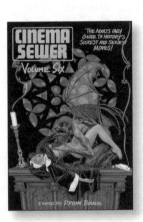

CINEMA SEWER VOLUME 6
The Adults Only Guide to History's
Sickest and Sexiest Movies!

ISBN: 978-1-903254-91-2
Pages: 192
UK Price: £14.99
US Price: $19.95

"There's no elitest attitude. These people love
movies, know their history, and like anyone
who truly loves anything, they want you to be
as stoked about is as they are."
Razorcake magazine

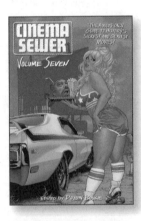

CINEMA SEWER VOLUME 7
The Adults Only Guide to History's
Sickest and Sexiest Movies!

ISBN: 978-1-913051-04-4
Pages: 192
UK Price: £14.99
US Price: $19.95

"I thought I had waded through the depth
of sleaze cinema, but Cinema Sewer
makes me realize I have only touched
the tip of the iceberg."
Kat Ellinger, thegoresplatteredcorner.com

For further information about these books and others in the acclaimed FAB Press line, visit our online store, where we
also have a fine selection of excellent cult movie magazines and other items of interest from all over the world!

www.fabpress.com